T0310733

Virtual Collaborative Writing in the Workplace:
Computer–Mediated Communication Technologies and Processes

Beth L. Hewett
University of Maryland University College, USA

Charlotte Robidoux
Hewlett–Packard Company, USA

INFORMATION SCIENCE REFERENCE

Hershey · New York

Director of Editorial Content:	Kristin Klinger
Director of Book Publications:	Julia Mosemann
Acquisitions Editor:	Lindsay Johnston
Development Editor:	Christine Bufton
Typesetter:	Myla Harty and Deanna Jo Zombro
Production Editor:	Jamie Snavely
Cover Design:	Lisa Tosheff
Printed at:	Yurchak Printing Inc.

Published in the United States of America by
Information Science Reference (an imprint of IGI Global)
701 E. Chocolate Avenue
Hershey PA 17033
Tel: 717-533-8845
Fax: 717-533-8661
E-mail: cust@igi-global.com
Web site: http://www.igi-global.com/reference

Library of Congress Cataloging-in-Publication Data

Virtual collaborative writing in the workplace : computer-mediated communication technologies and processes / Beth Hewett and Charlotte Robidoux, editors.   p. cm.
  Includes bibliographical references and index.
  Summary: "This book investigates the use of computer-mediated communication technologies and collaborative processes to facilitate effective interdependent collaboration in writing projects, especially in virtual workplace settings"--Provided by publisher.
  ISBN 978-1-60566-994-6 (hbk.) -- ISBN 978-1-60566-995-3 (ebook)
 1. Business writing. 2. Business communication. 3. Virtual work teams. 4. Telematics.
I. Hewett, Beth L. II. Robidoux, Charlotte, 1965-
  HF5718.3.V57 2010
  651.7'40285--dc22
                              2009052436
British Cataloguing in Publication Data
A Cataloguing in Publication record for this book is available from the British Library.

Dedication

Our shared vision of good writing and virtual (online) tools that enable the creation and dissemination of writing for various purposes—from expressive and therapeutic writing to the transactional and purposeful—stems from a belief that the thoughtful use of rhetoric provides a solid foundation for people to communicate. We believe that when writers collaborate, they create better, stronger pieces. Collaboration is increasingly important for communicating all kinds of thinking and information in our society, and we maintain that it is worth learning well. We hope that this book will help practitioners and academics alike—that it will help people committed to effective writing in any kind of a workplace setting.

We gratefully dedicate this book to our family and friends who have provided collaborative support, love, and patience as we undertook the effort to develop this book. Thank you all.

Table of Contents

Section 1
Intersections of Virtual Settings, Collaboration, and Writing

Chapter 1

Beth L. Hewett, University of Maryland University College, USA
Charlotte Robidoux, Hewlett-Packard Company, USA
Dirk Remley, Kent State University, USA

Chapter 2

Beth L. Hewett, University of Maryland University College, USA
Dirk Remley, Kent State University, USA
Pavel Zemliansky, James Madison University, USA
Anne DiPardo, University of Colorado, USA

Section 2
Building a Virtual Writing Team

Chapter 3

Anne DiPardo, University of Colorado, USA
Mike DiPardo, Chezelle Group, USA

Section 5
Developing Content Virtually

Section 6
Supporting Quality Writing through Virtual Collaboration

Section 7
Using New Media in Virtual Collaborative Writing

Section 8
Collaborating Virtually to Develop This Book: A Discussion

Detailed Table of Contents

Section 1
Intersections of Virtual Settings, Collaboration, and Writing

Beth L. Hewett, University of Maryland University College, USA
Charlotte Robidoux, Hewlett-Packard Company, USA
Dirk Remley, Kent State University, USA

This chapter defines collaboration in some of its many variations and settings, and then it locates collaboration in the virtual world of contemporary writers connected through digital technology. In this way, Chapter 1 offers a snapshot of the kinds of collaboration about which this book's writers write in Sections 2 – 7, while it also uses that collaboration in its own development. In other words, the understandings reflected in this chapter are the product of intense collaboration among this book's writers, who have brought to it their own expertise in this subject matter. This chapter addresses (1) the literature of collaboration and collaborative writing in general, (2) the move from traditional collaborative writing efforts into that of virtual collaborative writing, and (3) six principles inherent to virtual collaborative writing. Taken together, they help us to develop the definitions on which we have based this book's approaches to virtual collaborative writing.

Beth L. Hewett, University of Maryland University College, USA
Dirk Remley, Kent State University, USA
Pavel Zemliansky, James Madison University, USA
Anne DiPardo, University of Colorado, USA

This chapter draws on various rhetorical, media-based, social presence–based, activity-based, and systems-based frameworks for understanding virtual collaborative writing. Such theoretical understanding is helpful for bridging the gap between those who study virtual collaborative writing to develop theories of the practice and those who draw on theory to develop effective practices.

Section 2
Building a Virtual Writing Team

Chapter 3

Anne DiPardo, University of Colorado, USA
Mike DiPardo, Chezelle Group, USA

This chapter presents a case study detailing how geographically dispersed software developers employ writing in the process of creating and troubleshooting products for use in the healthcare industry. It focuses particularly on their efforts to arrive at language that unambiguously reflects functional requirements and optimal design principles. After a brief history of the company and the evolution of its national and international virtual collaboration practices, we turn to the role of text across particular task cycles, exploring the uses of writing in generating, designing, and refining plans and products. Focusing on a series of three composing sequences, we highlight the incremental process by which the team moves toward a shared sense of understanding and linguistic precision. We argue that in contrast to common conceptions of texts as simple containers for preformed ideas, these episodes provide a more nuanced picture, as writing comes to play a central role in constituting and fine-tuning meaning and in maintaining strong working relationships throughout the processes of developing and refining products. We close with implications for preparing diverse virtual teams for participation in tasks that demand exacting uses of the written word.

Chapter 4

Patti G. Wojahn, New Mexico State University, USA
Kristin A. Blicharz, IBM Corp., USA
Stephanie K. Taylor, IBM Corp., USA

In this chapter, we discuss factors useful for virtual collaborators to consider when initiating a new writing project. We identify the importance of and challenges common to getting to know others through virtual means. We then address issues associated with establishing expectations and protocols for the collaborative processes to be used for a given project. We do so by drawing from the literature on and our own experiences with virtual collaborative writing, as well as from communication logs and survey responses gathered from a small pilot study conducted in 2007. This pilot study focused on behavior and perceptions related to multiple types of communicative tools for interacting in daily workplace practice. We argue that behaviors, perceptions, expectations, and previous practice all can inform rules of engagement that may benefit teams working in virtual contexts. Time spent planning for the collaboration by defining common goals, rules, and guidelines in early stages of a virtual project can improve the collaborative experience: subsequent efficiency; role, task, and deadline delineations; and group satisfaction.

This chapter explores collaborative writing in virtual teams and, particularly, trust formation in virtual writing teams, to help those who create or work in virtual writing teams to understand the importance of trust. In order to build the case for trust as the key component in teams, the chapter presents important background on teams as a general concept. In particular, it considers the constituents of quality teams, which include small team size, diverse team membership, interdependent relationships, shared team vision, articulated processes, and performance orientation. The chapter then elaborates on the role of trust in teams, presenting it as the key feature for any type of team environment. Based on this background, the chapter differentiates the general concept of teams from virtual teams in particular, arguing that virtual teams must address specific considerations in order to build trust. Such considerations include the composition of the team, where team members possess a propensity to trust; the proper use of technology in the virtual team, so that the medium matches the communicative need; and social presence, or the ways that virtual teams can build trust by using communication behaviors to demonstrate to others that they share understanding. The chapter combines the general team considerations with the virtual team considerations into a rubric for building strong virtual teams based upon four major categories: team traits, team actions, individual traits, and environment traits.

Section 3
Managing Team Dynamics

This chapter features a case study of a collaborative project among a team of writers and a team of multimedia designers, and it examines their intersections. The chapter's central question is: What does it take to enable collective collaboration in a virtual writing environment? The chapter is based in part on a study that found that building and strengthening social presence is integral to effective collaboration. The spoken and unspoken social contracts of working toward a common goal in a respectful environment are important. Also important are the implications that the technologies must be adoptable, adaptable, and they must enable anywhere/anytime collaboration. Therefore, collaboration using technologies is a complex process involving social presence, availability, and adaption/adoption of technologies with the changing needs of the collaborative team.

Chapter 7

There are some obvious rewards of virtual collaboration. However, technological, organizational, and psychological barriers to effective collaboration exist. First, familiarity with the media used for collaboration and opportunities for practice are essential. Next, organizational concerns can hinder successful collaboration. Huws (2005) suggested that traditional face-to-face hierarchical organizations or even those with a degree of hybridity can subvert successful collaboration of any sort but also contain features that might enhance collaboration, if used correctly. Additionally, making work roles clearly defined and making the collaborative endeavor explicit and transparent can ensure positive outcomes. Finally, knowledge of the personality traits and values of the participants in a collaborative project is necessary for project managers. This chapter discusses these three potential barriers; provides examples from higher education and the U.S. Army; and suggests possible solutions.

Chapter 8

With the right combination of writers, collaborative writing may grow organically in a team. But it is more likely that managers need to set the expectation that collaboration is required, provide strong leadership in an organization to make it happen, and put strategies in place to measure its effectiveness. Managers need to lead writers down the path to writing collaboratively, finding effective ways to support the implementation of new writing methods. This chapter provides practical approaches that will help develop a manager's skills for leading virtual collaborative writing teams. The techniques described in this chapter were developed and tested by actual collaborative writing teams, most notably by the Information Engineering team at NetApp, Inc.

Section 4
Planning and Making Decisions Virtually

Chapter 9

Content management technology provides a flexible environment for virtual collaboration for technical and business writing. Internationally, small and large organizations in various industries are using content management system (CMS) technology to improve their communications while lowering their production and translation costs and enhancing the quality of their writing. The following case studies provide a look at how small and large writing teams are really doing it. These teams have successfully implemented content management technology and improved virtual collaboration in varying environments—within a department, between multiple departments, within a division, and across several divisions of their respective organizations.

Chapter 10

Increasingly, collaborative writing occurs in distributed work environments. Collaboration is essential for technical writing teams that develop and share content using content management system (CMS) technology. Technical writers must be proficient not only developing content that can be shared but also in how to carry out complex writing tasks virtually. However, research indicates that asynchronously distributed collaborative writing can lead to productivity losses unless teams implement detailed processes for interacting and using computer-mediated communication (CMC) technology. With highly structured processes to guide their efforts, teams are more likely to see productivity gains. To achieve these gains, effective collaboration must address six key areas: (1) targets to guide team performance, (2) assessing collaborative writing skills in virtual teams, (3) role delineation, (4) process scripts to promote efficient virtual collaborative writing, (5); training framework, and (6) performance measurement and recognition framework for reinforcing team accomplishments. Organizations must be willing to create a culture that supports a team environment committed to these specific areas. This chapter explores how to establish an infrastructure that promotes collaborative writing efficiency in virtual settings.

Chapter 11

When it comes to team decision making, people are more likely to carry out decisions they have helped make (Weisbord, 1987). However, some key decision-making differences in roles, processes, and tools between virtual and traditional writing teams exist. This chapter uses the experiences of Symantec's decision-making process for purchasing a content management system (CMS) as a primary example for how people can make decisions in virtual settings. However, those with other decision-making goals in various virtual collaborative writing settings would benefit from such understanding as well. In particular, this chapter examines how virtual writing teams move through the decision-making process: knowing who has authority, deciding how to decide, using the right decision-making model for a particular decision, doing the groundwork, sharing the information, evaluating the information and making the decision, capturing the decision in a place available to all, and following up on decisions and resulting actions. It also provides a list of tools that can help when making decisions virtually. Finally, keeping the audience—readers or product users—in mind throughout the decision-making process can assist with all of these tasks by keeping decision makers focused on those who most benefit or suffer from writing-based decisions.

The Technical Publications team at Sybase, Inc. maintains many thousands of pages of user documentation and online help topics for a diverse set of software products. Writing teams work in nine locations around the globe; a given project often involves writers from multiple locations. To achieve greater efficiency, increase opportunities for reuse, and improve user experience, the department is moving to the Darwin Information Typing Architecture (DITA) from a variety of source formats. Early adopters realized the need for more detailed information models for several types of content than required by the DITA standard. This chapter discusses why models are a critical component to successful collaborative writing, especially for topic-oriented content. It then describes the collaborative processes and tools by which Sybase® Technical Publications team members propose, evaluate, develop, test, and enforce new content models, challenges encountered, and key success factors.

Unlike mathematicians who have a quasi-universal language for expressing formulas and other mathematical expressions, writers can express ideas in many different ways. Differences in style appear at multiple levels: in the section and chapter organizational patterns, in the syntax, in the complexity of the vocabulary, and in formatting. Consistency is required to produce publications of quality in a collaborative environment; moreover, writers must find efficient ways collaborate as a team. This chapter explores the methods, advantages, and challenges of developing standards—rules related to content, work processes, and the choice and configuration of tools to support collaborative writing and content reuse in virtual environments.

The need for reusing content and automating the writing process to gain efficiency in workplace environments is a priority in many work settings. Writing teams seek effective strategies for integrating reuse principles, and increasingly they need to accomplish this work virtually. Reusing content across an organization requires coordinated collaboration both in terms of establishing standards and ensuring that all team members follow those standards. In view of this high-level requirement, setting up a reuse environment seems familiar; that is, developing and implementing a style guide to promote consistency always has been central to good technical writing. Also familiar is the fact that as long as there have been style guides, adherence to them has been difficult to achieve. What makes a reuse environment different from those less focused on reuse is that degree to which standardization among writers must occur. Whereas style guidelines typically have emphasized word or phrasing nuances, standards for reuse move beyond terminology or syntax, involving all aspects of the writing process. An effective reuse environment thus depends on collaborative input from writing teams, which poses significant challenges in virtual environments. This chapter provides insight into the principles of reuse and how virtual collaboration is essential to making content reusable.

Section 6
Supporting Quality Writing through Virtual Collaboration

Chapter 15

Kent Taylor, acrolinx® North America, Inc., USA

The application of quality management tools in the content development process provides a range of benefits to writing, production, and program teams. This case study of a Natural Language Processing (NLP)-based information quality management solution developed by acrolinx® GmbH describes the results that real-world virtual collaborative writing practitioners have realized, and provides a roadmap for applying quality management strategies within writing organizations. When information products have consistent style, voice, terminology, and brand identification no matter where, when, or by whom the materials are written, they are easier to read, understand, translate, and use. Quality management tools support collaboration within writing teams by centralizing access to the standards as writers are creating content and providing objective quality metrics and reports at handoff points in the information supply chain. This process ensures consistency and clarity across information products, which makes them easier for writers to develop and for customers to use.

Chapter 16

Robbin Zeff Warner, Independent Scholar, Belgium
Beth L. Hewett, University of Maryland University College, USA
Charlotte Robidoux, Hewlett-Packard Company, USA

One aspect of writing in government, business, and academia that always has been collaborative is the document review process. In this process, all persons with a stake in the final writing product are invited to help shape the piece in terms of content, style, or structure. Their review work has primarily been both serial and parallel. However, problems and perils of document review can strike at any stage in the review process: from the reviewer not knowing how to give useful comments to the writer not knowing how to interpret and use comments constructively. In today's Web 2.0 world, what once was a more closed and controlled collaboration review process becomes open and organic because digital and online information is accessible to intended and unintended audiences alike for commenting, ranking, and reviewing. Response to this new openness in review has been mixed among and within institutions. And yet, the momentum for open and even unsolicited reviews is not only impossible to stop but also difficult to manage. While computer-mediated communication (CMC) and content management system (CMS) tools have automated the writing process, the review process has lagged in terms of being efficiently collaborative. This chapter explores collaborative review in a user-empowered Web 2.0 world, including how CMC tools can facilitate the review process.

Chapter 17

Mirhonda Studevant, Ceridian Corporation, USA

Writers often are challenged to measure the effectiveness of their deliverables. Measurement is frequently difficult because the writer is expected to act as a reader advocate without direct customer or audience input. Fortunately, this trend is changing. Today, technical writers have a wealth of opportunities to seek input directly from the internal or external consumers of their deliverables. In today's globally competitive marketplace, organizations constantly strive to deliver high-quality goods and services. Many companies are recognizing customers as a critical strategic partner in their product development and quality improvement programs. This recognition of customers as development and quality partners extends to documentation resources such as training materials, web-based help, support knowledge bases, user manuals, quick-reference guides, and virtual tours and tutorials. More and more, the voice of the customer is becoming the most important consideration in product and process decisions, including the delivery of documentation. Collaborating with customers goes beyond fostering goodwill. Employing various methods to invite customer collaboration accelerates documentation development and significantly improves documentation quality. By considering strategic partner values, organizational culture, cost and complexity, and availability of resources, technical writers can develop customer feedback programs that increase customer retention and positively impact revenue. This chapter explores methods and processes that help to ensure successful virtual collaboration with customers.

Chapter 18

Pavel Zemliansky, James Madison University, USA

This chapter offers practical strategies for instructors, trainers, and managers to use while preparing writers for virtual collaboration. It first considers various existing barriers to successful virtual collaboration, both in the writers' individual preparation and in organizational structures within which they work. Next, the chapter offers a set of specific guidelines designed to prepare writers for virtual writing collaboration and to facilitate their work. In order to prepare writers for virtual collaboration, instructors and trainers must develop trust among members of virtual teams, carefully structure writing assignments, and design learning spaces that promote collaboration and interaction.

Section 7
Using New Media in Virtual Collaborative Writing

This chapter presents a case study of virtual collaboration that focuses on a research and production team's approach to making choices about the most appropriate technologies to support the team's interactions. The study highlights the importance of establishing clear, well-defined roles for collaborators as well as the importance of explicitly acknowledging the institutional context within which the work was undertaken. The chapter concludes with a series of recommendations based upon the experience of this virtual collaboration.

Virtual collaborative writing must acknowledge and encourage a range of symbolization practices because textual products simply are likely to be hybrids of words (discursive) and visual images, aural images, haptic images, olfactory images, and even gustatory images (all nondiscursive). Though digital technologies are still limited to aural and visual technologies, we must theorize collaboration for and within media that are as yet not widely developed or possible. Today's collaborative environments require more from interfaces if we are to invent texts that become edited images, Web pages, films, and/or animations. This chapter argues that virtual collaborative environments must accommodate the invention of non-traditional, multimodal texts.

This chapter examines virtual collaboration, including the production and use of writing between doctors at different hospitals mediated by RP-7, a robot that enables a specialist at one hospital to evaluate the vital signs of and provide diagnosis for a patient at another hospital. Analysis of RP-7 is situated in a theoretical deliberation about the shift from print to digital texts and technologies. I argue that a consequence of this shift is the loss of mutual presence—the alignment of materiality, practice, and expertise—in the production and use of texts. This alignment is transparent and intrinsic to print texts but is lost in digital environments precisely because they afford access to texts irrespective of a user's background, location, or access to and familiarity with other tools, technologies, or workplaces. Study of the writing used and generated during the collaboration between doctors mediated by RP-7 is grounds for the claim that the future of virtual collaborative writing in professional contexts will involve the re-alignment of mutual presence. In other words, the success of digital writing technologies in social practice will depend on the extent to which they bare similarity to, rather than differ from, print texts and technologies. The chapter concludes by emphasizing the value of this research to both academia and industry.

Section 8
Collaborating Virtually to Develop This Book: A Discussion

Chapter 22

Charlotte Robidoux, Hewlett-Packard Company, USA
Beth L. Hewett, University of Maryland University College, USA

This chapter describes how the writers and editors of this book attempted to employ virtual collaborative writing strategies, including those described throughout this text, in the process of developing and writing this book. The discussion reflects on the processes we used to write collaboratively in a virtual environment, as well as strategies and tools that facilitated or hindered our efforts. The discussion draws on the six principles underlying virtual collaborative writing that ground this book (described in Chapter 1) to evaluate the experience of using remote technology to develop content collaboratively. In so doing, we present recommendations that workplace writing teams can use to manage virtual collaborative writing more effectively. This chapter provides a practical example of success and failure that will guide professionals immersed in and committed to improving virtual collaborative writing in range of workplace environments—whether they are building collaborative writing teams, overcoming barriers to collaboration, managing teams of writers virtually, planning and making decisions collaboratively about writing tasks, establishing standards and structured processes for developing content collaboratively, or preparing novice virtual writing teams to collaborate more effectively.

Foreword

I have worked with Charlotte Robidoux, one of the editors of *Virtual Collaborative Writing in the Workplace: Computer Mediated Communication Technologies and Processes*, since 2000. At the time, we were just starting on our single sourcing adventure. We were faced with many skeptics and did our best to present the facts and gain support. We couldn't get through to everybody. Change and innovation can be a huge challenge. At that time I used to say, "You have to make a choice. This is the bus we're getting on. You can either get on the bus or get run over by it." Needless to say, that frank position didn't go over well with many staff and some in management. Some questioned the lack of the "getting out of the way" option, while others just didn't want to see the bus at all. In any case, I got my point across. Since Charlotte had been on the bus for a while, we were able to work together to help make single sourcing work at Hewlett-Packard Company.

In April 2005, Charlotte and I presented *CMS Solutions: Six Important How To's* at the CIDM Content Management Strategies conference in Annapolis, Maryland. The following year, we turned that presentation into a 3-hour workshop. We engaged in virtual collaborative writing at that time with Charlotte located in New England and me in Colorado. Little did I know that this teamwork would be another step along the virtual collaboration journey and that step would be one in the path of Beth and Charlotte publishing this book.

Beth Hewett also was on the proverbial bus, but with the particular focus that whether an organization single sourced content or not, collaboration among writers had to become a priority and, since writing so often occurs in distributed virtual settings, collaboration had to be addressed within that context. Beth's work developing and directing a large online writing program and as co-editor of an online journal where all the staff were geographically distributed had taught her much about the benefits and challenges of virtual collaborative writing, training, and team management. Beth and Charlotte have known each other since they met in 1993 in graduate school working on their doctorates in rhetoric. Over the years, they recognized that writers struggle in moving to this new virtual environment and that they badly want to collaborate successfully on writing projects. Beth and Charlotte talked about how they could combine their interests, experience (both academic and business), and knowledge on collaboration into a book. This book is the result of their years of experience and friendship.

As a trained Lean-Sigma Black Belt (an offshoot of Six Sigma), I currently serve as my group's process improvement program manager. Each day, like you, I am challenged on how to collaborate effectively with a variety of people. Five years ago, I worked in an office and had daily face-to-face contact with most of the people I needed to interact with. Today, I work from a home office and 100% of my business is conducted virtually. *Virtual Collaborative Writing in the Workplace: Computer Mediated Communication Technologies and Processes* mirrors some of my experiences, validates others, and introduces new ideas and concepts. The six middle sections of the book cover the key elements facing writers, editors, and managers in today's globalized business environment. These elements include how to build a virtual writing team, how to manage team dynamics, how to plan and make decisions virtually, how to develop content virtually, and how to support quality.

As a member of the University of Colorado at Colorado Springs Professional Writing Advisory Board, I will advocate the use of this book to help influence academic program content. This book will be valuable to a wide audience including academics and business professionals. It will serve as a resource for anyone thinking about or currently engaged in a virtual collaborative writing project. From virtual team novices to experts, readers will be able to learn new techniques and apply them to their own situations or environments. I invite you all to get on the bus and enjoy the ride.

Patrick Waychoff
Process Improvement Manager
HP Enterprise Servers, Storage and Networking
Technical Documentation Group

Preface

COLLABORATION AS A CHANGE AGENT

Collaboration changes how people view and understand their contributions in any project. Suddenly, it is not the individual's work that is most valued, but that of the team. Yet the individual's work remains crucial as a necessary part of the whole. Without each part competently developed, the whole suffers.

Increasingly, distributed work settings have prompted the need to collaborate virtually on writing tasks. Collaborative writing, the subject of this book, is a process that often occurs both asynchronously (for example, by sharing a document) and synchronously (for example, in face-to-face or telephone communication). It increasingly occurs in virtual, distributed work settings. Those who write virtually distribute their processes across geographic locations and within the colocated space of an office or institutional setting. Unlike traditional document sharing and face-to-face or telephone interactions, virtual collaborative writing requires participants to communicate using computer-mediated communication (CMC) technologies, which include everything from instant messaging (IM) and e-mail to interactions that take place using Web pages, webcasts, and graphical user interfaces. Common virtual activities that make use of these technologies include sharing documents and desktops via virtual classrooms, developing content on wikis, writing and responding to blogs, talking through technical bulletin boards and chat rooms, videoconferencing, and developing and integrating information in content management systems (CMS).

This book investigates the use of CMC technologies and particular collaborative processes to facilitate effective, interdependent collaboration in writing projects, especially in virtual workplace settings.

To this end, this book identifies and theorizes how CMC technologies and explicit collaborative processes can promote interdependent virtual collaboration, particularly collaborative writing. The kinds of writing addressed herein typically occur in work-based settings, such as academic institutions, private and for-profit industry, and the government (including the military), in which the purpose of the writing is to convey information or argue a position rather than to socialize or entertain. The chapters in this book specifically define collaboration and collaborative writing relative to virtual settings. They present core principles for how to collaborate in technology-based virtual settings, and they suggest practices for effective virtual collaborative writing that include rhetorical strategies, roles, and activities among participants. Additionally, these chapters identify practices that use CMC technologies for building consensus so that people can function in integrated and interdependent virtual settings to create texts. Finally, in a meta-analysis of CMC technologies and processes, this book explains how such practices and technologies were used by the editors and writers to develop a coherent, collaboratively written book.

VIRTUAL COLLABORATIVE WRITING

It seems fitting to examine the subject of virtual collaborative writing during the information age, a time with unprecedented access to knowledge through technology. Information is important to us—whether it is an end product, a means to an end, or something in between. No matter the scenario, workplace professionals rely on technology to use, manage, and exchange information. And while technology makes accessing information seem quick and easy, knowing what technology works best to develop and share information is not so easy. Nor is it straightforward to manage, update, and archive information even knowing that the right a combination of tools is available.

Positioning *information* in the context of an *age* underscores the vast nature of the term *information* and the array of overlapping meanings related to the word. In his book, Boiko (2005) suggested that the term *information* is broader, more complex, and richer than the term *content*, which in contrast to information presupposes an underlying aim or use. Insofar as content is contextualized information, it is more streamlined and thus more easily managed by a computer (pp. 11-12). Hackos (2002) made a similar distinction when describing the concept of the information model, a framework for organizing content. Her stratified view of the information model placed content units, the smallest building block use to create documents, at the center of the model (p. 126).

Interestingly, theorists and practitioners alike frequently draw distinctions between the terms *information* and *content* while using the terms interchangeably. For instance, both terms are used to modify *developer*, a role used to define the work of the technical writer, who is gaining more skill in computer programming by using XML technology and content management software.

In this text, we follow the lead set by Boiko (2005) and Hackos (2002), treating *information* as the broader term and *content* as one that is more specific. We have sought consistency in the use of these terms throughout the book. That said, because growth continues in the area of workplace writing, as it should, we understand the importance of ever-changing terminology and recognize that these terms may evolve accordingly.

It is not only the increasing incidence of distributed work settings that prompts a need for a book such as this one, however. The fact is that in many venues, the very nature of written products is changing from that of a completed book individually "owned" by one writer to that of specialized writers who produce particular chunks of content, or *topics*, in a CMS. This change stems, in large part, from technological advances that enable writers to produce information products more efficiently and readers to demand information in multiple formats and for a range of media. These technological advances, in part, have encouraged reader to request documents in digital formats. From Web pages and online help to mobile devices, these formats present information in short, content-rich chunks. Such tools as Web-ready cell phones and laptop computers with wireless access enable readers to access the information they need anytime and anyplace, thus creating a demand for text that is chunked in smaller bits.

NEED FOR A PARADIGM SHIFT

The distributed writing process represents a paradigm shift with respect to a writer's relationship to the written material. As such, it requires a similar paradigm shift in terms of the writer's relationship to other team members writing content and to those who manage that content for the group. Hence, to varying degrees, the chapters in this book emphasize this paradigm shift as paramount in virtual collaborative writing, and all of the chapters within can be understood best as guidance for moving virtual collaborative writers toward embracing and working within the constraints of that shift.

The use of technologies to manage the production and distribution of information thus requires carefully honed and collaborative skills. By collaboration, we mean that writers who contribute virtually to a text must learn to work interdependently using rhetorical strategies. To the extent that individuals typically are more accustomed to producing whole texts rather than smaller pieces of content, many writers do not understand how to contribute efficiently to jointly developed written materials. Furthermore, many geographically distributed writing teams lack guidance and experience on how to coordinate complex activities across space and time. Because they have honed their skills differently over the years, they now need new ways to write collaboratively. Expertise in virtual collaborative writing entails knowing how and when to interact, and how and when to work independently so that the team reaches its goal of developing coherent texts. Guidance on an interdependent writing process that effectively combines contributions from various writers thus is essential for writing collaboratively. Writers must synchronize their thinking, activities, and values about their work and make the CMC technologies serve their mutual goals. Despite geographical distance, they must learn how to work closely with each other, trust and respect each other's ideas, and to depend symbiotically upon each other's feedback to develop ideas and integrate textual elements into a whole. Writers must come to understand their roles and to contribute accordingly. Thus, in a virtual setting and using synchronous tools in particular, writers can learn to express their ideas simultaneously rather than serially to help shape the direction and development of ideas. Interdependence does not mean that writers cannot work independently at times, but that the contributions they make to the overall goal shape more efficient, effective, and collaborative texts.

When writers do not know how best to use technology to communicate collaboratively *and* interdependently, several problems may ensue. The writing process may be strained; the text may not accurately represent the team's intended purpose; the product and the information may not be useful; and, ultimately, the intended audience may be confused or poorly served. The circumstances that create these communication problems are not going away and will continue to multiply in complexity as long as globalization and the use of online media to develop and receive texts persist. For example, companies both are hiring staff from other countries and encouraging their staff to work from home; similarly, academic institutions are providing more distance-based educational opportunities for both teachers and students. These working situations require that writers make the best use of the CMC tools and collaborative processes available to them. Consider also that the reliance on database technology, especially the CMS, to create information products out of small, reusable units of information promotes a great need for effective collaborative techniques. Yet, insofar as many writers still e-mail each other about the development of content as a way to collaborate, they rely primarily on asynchronous practices, which can be less efficient for coordinating activities. More effective collaboration would entail purposefully engaging both synchronous and asynchronous CMC modes while choosing among a wider variety of technologies and collaborative processes. For example, engaging effective virtual collaborative writing processes would entail defining and developing various roles among writers on a team, roles that align with their skills and abilities so that they are prepared adequately for those roles. Effective virtual collaborative strategies would also entail assessing and rewarding staff for how they perform in these roles as members of a working team.

PRINCIPLES OF VIRTUAL COLLABORATION

Documenting the development of an interdependent writing process requires engaging a variety of technology-savvy writers who have imagined and practiced such interdependency in their collaborative writing. Therefore, this edited collection presents the thinking and experiences of writers from a variety of disciplines, such as academics, corporate work, nonprofit enterprises, online journal editing, and the like. Together, we explore interdependent virtual collaboration from a variety of perspectives and our chapters comprise topics that identify, synthesize, and theorize the convergences among them. From our collaboration for the development of this book, we have synthesized six principles for virtual collaborative writing as based on this paradigm shift from a single document, or book, to content chunks, or information. These six principles, outlined here, ground the chapters of this book to provide guidance for writing collaboratively in virtual work settings so that despite the rapidly changing technology and the increase in globalization that writers encounter, they can have a stable baseline for being productive in various workplace environments.

- **Principle 1: Develop a Culture of Collaboration.** The shift to a topic-based paradigm requires a culture that supports virtual collaborative interactions. Growing such a culture takes time, as writers learn (1) how to plan working as a team, (2) how to become skilled working interdependently, and (3) how to value the time spent cultivating this expertise. The cultural shift will not occur in the short term but requires a commitment to longer-term thinking—that in time, the virtual collaborative interaction will produce greater efficiencies than when writers work independently on books.

- **Principle 2: Find and Promote Leadership.** Only with effective leadership will a collaborative culture form. Effective managers will value both the importance and benefits of collaboration, imparting their values to inherent talent within the team, who will support collaboration throughout the organization. Writers who understand the paradigm shift that is required can gather feedback from the teams and shape team behavior during the course of writing projects. Leaders need leaders to establish a new writing context.

- **Principle 3: Establish Trust.** To write collaboratively, writers need to achieve a level of comfort with the abilities, competencies, and intentions of fellow team members. They must be confident that teammates will pull their own weight and produce high-quality content so that the whole team can focus on completing tasks rather than on protecting individual interests. To achieve trust requires ample communication among all participants and consistent processes to ensure effective interactions.

- **Principle 4: Use Tools and Collaborative Modes Effectively.** For writing teams to collaborate efficiently in distributed environments, they must have a sophisticated command of virtual technology and of the types of collaboration needed for topic-based writing. Moving beyond the standard use of tools is essential to create interdependent work habits. Writers must understand not only when to interact with key players on their team but what forms of virtual collaboration will best serve the goals of their team.

- **Principle 5: Create Structure.** Writing teams need structure to collaborate virtually. If new habits are not established, the culture will not grow, trust will unravel, and collaborative work will become unstable. Structure means having scripted processes that articulate what tasks are required and what tools and techniques optimize performance. Structure entails effective work patterns, practice sessions to find the right patterns, repetition—"the new autopilot"—discipline, accountability, and an infrastructure for normalizing perspectives.

- **Principle 6: Measure and Track Performance.** Expectations about how performance is measured guides performance itself. If teams do not have clear expectations about how to write collaboratively in virtual environments, their chances for success are slim. To move past the book paradigm, teams need to know the new rules of the game and how their performance will be assessed and tracked. Good performance deserves recognition; without it, teams will lack motivation to do well. For years, writers have taken pride in owning their books. Finding a new collaborative paradigm depends on recognizing team performance—appreciating the whole as well as the sum of its parts.

UNIQUE QUALITIES OF THIS BOOK

Not only does this book focus on the CMC technologies and processes necessary for implementing and managing collaborative writing in virtual settings, but it does so *using* CMC technology in a collaborative manner—engaging virtual collaboration among the editors and writers. Prior to writing a single chapter, the writers and editors talked by phone in small groups about our ideas and attempted to blend the chapters more seamlessly than is found in most edited collections. We used virtual communications and various CMC technologies and collaborative processes throughout the fifteen months of the book's development—to varying degrees of success—in order to enact the virtual collaborative writing principles that we propose and to discern the challenges that readers will themselves encounter in their own virtual collaborative writing settings.

The reasons for this actively collaborative process include helping the writers to think metacognitively about their chapters' subject matter, providing opportunities for them to see and discuss each other's chapters before submission for publication, and enabling the editors to develop a more coherent book overall. Additionally, this actively collaborative process provided the opportunity to learn more about virtual collaborative writing—to learn by doing, so to speak. We knew that there would be challenges and that we would hit substantial roadblocks and make mistakes. We hoped, of course, that we also would find some successes. Hence, the very process of writing the book has led to organically developed chapters, and the end product exemplifies the book's underlying themes.

In sum, the book provides practical information, poses theoretical questions, and addresses implications of virtual interdependent collaboration that occurs through CMC technologies. The final section of the book, written by the editors and encapsulating their experiences and those of the writers, pulls together and interprets the uses of virtual collaborative writing technologies and processes. Consequently, this book both describes theory and demonstrates practice through the actual CMC technologies.

INTENDED AUDIENCE FOR THIS BOOK

While journal articles are available, few comprehensive discussions exist about technologies and practices for virtual collaborative writing in various work settings. Yet such writing is a part of a wide array of workplaces, multinational companies, nonprofit business, and academic institutions. Indeed, writing provides the glue for the communications and products of such enterprises. And writing collaboratively presupposes a uniform mindset, which in reality is hard—if not impossible—to achieve. Writers need effective rhetorical strategies that enable them to work interdependently so that they can collaborate effectively. While the CMC technologies and virtual collaborative processes for writing are the subject of this book, the guidance that we provide for virtual collaborative writing might apply to any discipline.

To this end, a range of fields—such as business, technical writing, information science, technology, and management—share a need for a book that examines strategies for using virtual tools to create a culture of collaboration and interdependence necessary for working (and writing) in the twenty-first century. The intended audiences for this book include professional writers and editors in both corporate and nonprofit sectors, scholars whose work is focused on writing collaboratively, scholars of technical communication, researchers with academic appointments, and technology professionals. Individuals from these diverse backgrounds will benefit from understanding how best to improve virtual collaborative writing enterprises that rely on CMC technologies. Finally, we hope that readers will find this book to be an important managerial resource in business settings, reference libraries, upper-level technical writing courses, and various academic and nonacademic training settings.

HOW TO USE THIS BOOK

As Pullman and Gu (2009) have suggested, there is a gap between theory and practice as it relates to workplace writing. Industry needs strong technical writers who are trained in school and who have a strong foundation for being effective in the workplace. Academic scholars and instructors need to be able to believe that they have the right tools to prepare students for business and workplace writing. It is important that they have the right tools because much is changing rapidly in terms of how writing is created, the tools that are used, the processes that work effectively, the means and types of delivery, and the expectations for how it will be received. Undoubtedly, a more integrated approach to theory and practice would be especially helpful for industry and academic institutions alike.

Underlying many changes, as this book illustrates, is the idea that the writing often is accomplished virtually and needs to be more collaborative. As a result, we have drawn on the knowledge and expertise of a combination of professionals in industry and research so that we can contribute to the process of bridging the gap. Working together with the two different cultures fully exposed that gap, which might be readily apparent in some of the chapters presented—in other words, some chapters are more theoretical and reflective while others are more action-oriented and check list-based (all chapters, however, provide some form of takeaway for writers in both types of profession). Although we have worked to find a common voice, integrate the material, and create a sense of balance among the chapters, the professional cultural differences we have experienced were pronounced nonetheless. To assist our readers, we offer some recommendations about the ways to use this book depending on preferences or background and on the practical applications readers might have in mind.

Chapter 1 offers a good overview for all readers; it has a minimal review of literature on the subject of virtual collaboration, and it provides a full discussion of definitions and principles that guide our understanding of virtual collaborative writing. Chapter 2, on the other hand, provides a more in-depth framework of theory for those who want to connect workplace writing to theory. Regarding the rest of the book, readers can expect to gain a sense of place and experience from the case studies that lead Sections 2 – 7. Following each case study are two or three chapters that address the types of issues raised in the case study. As often as they could, writers made chapter connections among the other book chapters. They also made connections to the six principles of virtual collaborative writing that ground this book, as described earlier in this Introduction and more completely at the end of Chapter 1.

Virtual Collaborative Writing: Computer-Mediated Communication Technologies and Processes is organized to help readers understand and use the grounding principles of the book. Chapters can be read in the order presented or more randomly according to readers' needs and/or interests. In each chapter, there is a mix of practice and theory while others are more theory-based.

Table 1 provides a roadmap for accessing content in this book. Some might argue that the use of a roadmap to guide readers who might be seeking either practical or theoretical information might seem to conflict with the idea of bridging a gap. In providing a roadmap, however, we are not inviting readers to limit their experience only to a specific kind of information. Rather, the roadmap is intended to achieve the opposite; that is, if readers can orient themselves in the information that is familiar to them, they might be more willing to consider information that seems foreign, insufficient, or irrelevant in some way. We make this assumption having observed disparity in our own team between writers from industry and academia. Practitioners admitted to feeling intimidated by theoretical constructs advanced by researchers, who conversely believed that their frameworks were a logical place to begin writing. To that end, we offer the roadmap both as a way to access topics of interest and as a way to penetrate differing approaches to virtual collaborative writing.

Table 1. Roadmap for using this book

Chapter	Area of focus
Topics with an industry focus	
1	Addresses the nature of collaboration, virtual collaborative writing, basic principles for effective collaboration.
3	Presents a case study that highlights the importance of writing in solving problems and inventing new ideas even when developing software.
4	Illuminates factors useful for virtual collaborators to consider when initiating a new writing project, including the challenges common to getting to know others virtually.
8	Outlines practical methods that will help develop a manager's skills for virtual collaborative writing teams.
9	Offers CMS case studies involving collaboration within a department, between multiple departments, within a division, and across several divisions.
10	Considers the essential components needed to establish an infrastructure that supports virtual collaborative writing efficiency.
11	Examines how virtual writing teams move through the decision making process and what teams can do to improve their decision-making abilities, drawing on experiences implementing a CMS at Symantec.
12	Addresses why information models are a critical component to successful collaborative writing, including how to propose, evaluate, develop, test, and enforce new information models.
13	Considers the methods, advantages and challenges of developing rules around content, work processes, and the choices and configuration of tools to support virtual collaborative writing and content reuse in a virtual environment.
14	Explains why an effective reuse environment depends on collaborative input from writing teams and it provides insight into the principles of reuse.
15	Presents a case study that describes the results that real-world virtual collaborative writing teams have realized when using a quality management tool.
16	Examines collaborative review in today's user empowered Web 2.0 world, including how CMC tools can facilitate the review process.
17	Reviews methods and processes to ensure successful virtual collaboration with customers.
19	Offers a case study of virtual collaboration that focuses on a team's approach to making choices about what technologies support interactivity for an academic online journal.

Chapter	Topics with an academic focus
1	Addresses some theoretical underpinnings related to virtual collaborative writing, including basic definitions and principles for effective collaboration.
2	Provides a theoretical discussion of some of the rhetorical, social, and media-based theories relative to virtual collaborative writing.
3	Offers a case study that points up the important role between language and meaning in the development of software products.
5	Examines the concept of a team, the constituents of quality teams, different types of teams, importance of and social presence in creating shared understanding.
6	Provides a case study about the value of social presence in a collaborative multimedia project preparing content to teach faculty various strategies for improving their students' reading comprehension among.
7	Draws some conclusions about technological, organizational, and psychosocial barriers to effective collaboration based on observations of the TOPIC / ICON project at Texas Tech University and of Army personal at Fort Sill, Oklahoma, using collaborative writing software.
16	Examines collaborative review in today's user empowered Web 2.0 world, including how CMC tools can facilitate the review process.
18	Reviews methods and processes to ensure successful virtual collaboration with customers.
19	Considers a case study of virtual collaboration related to technology choices for the online journal, *Kairos*, highlighting the need for well-defined roles and understanding the institutional context to connect to the goals and expectations of the journal's editors and readers.
20	Examines the idea that collaborative environments require more from interfaces if texts are to be invented that become edited images, Web pages, films, and/or animations.
21	Explores the role of virtual technology and the use of collaborative writing among doctors at different hospitals mediated by the RP-7 robot to evaluate vital signs and diagnose a patient.

Finally, Chapter 22 in Section 8 speaks to all readers who are interested in the practical lessons that we have learned about virtual collaborative writing from the CMC technologies and processes engaged in this book.

A glossary of terms, a list of references used, and an index complete this book.

Section 1: Intersections of Virtual Settings, Collaboration, and Writing

The chapters in Section 1 present an introduction to the nature of collaboration and virtual collaborative writing as we understand them. Section 1 opens with a vignette that describes how the editors, Beth and Charlotte, came to recognize the need to develop this book: "Insight into Virtual Collaborative Writing: Learning by Doing." This scenario leads to questions about the nature of collaboration and virtual collaborative writing that the first two chapters of the book attempt to address.

- **Chapter 1, "Principles for Exploring Virtual Collaborative Writing"** is written by Beth L. Hewett, Charlotte Robidoux, and Dirk Remley. It defines and discusses the nature of virtual collaborative writing. It provides a detailed discussion about the principles that we believe are necessary to effective virtual collaborative writing in any kind of workplace setting.
- **Chapter 2, "Frameworks for Talking about Virtual Collaborative Writing"** is written by Beth L. Hewett, Dirk Remley, Pavel Zemliansky, and Anne DiPardo. It provides a theoretical discussion of some of the rhetorical, social, and media-based theories relative to virtual collaborative writing.

Section 2: Building a Virtual Writing Team

- **Chapter 3, "Case Study: "Can You See Me?" Writing toward Clarity in a Software Development Life Cycle"** is written by Anne DiPardo and Mike DiPardo. This case study details how geographically dispersed software developers employ collaborative writing in the process of creating and troubleshooting products for use in the healthcare industry. It focuses on their efforts to arrive at language that unambiguously reflects functional requirements and optimal design principles.
- **Chapter 4, "Engaging in Virtual Collaborative Writing: Issues, Obstacles, and Strategies,"** is written by Patti G. Wojahn, Kristin A. Blicharz, and Stephanie K. Taylor. They discuss factors useful for virtual collaborators to consider when initiating a new writing project, identifying key challenges common to getting to know others virtually.
- **Chapter 5, "Forming Trust in Virtual Writing Teams: Perspectives and Applications,"** is written by Sean D. Williams. This chapter explores collaborative writing in virtual teams, and, particularly, trust formation in virtual writing teams, including the importance of social presence in creating shared understanding within teams.

Section 3: Managing Team Dynamics

- **Chapter 6, "Case Study: A Collaborative of Content Designers and Developers,"** is written by Beth Brunk-Chavez and Sunay Palsole. This case study considers the value of social presence in a collaborative multimedia project preparing content to teach faculty various strategies for improving their students' reading comprehension among.
- **Chapter 7, "Removing Barriers to Collaborating in Virtual Writing Projects,"** is written by William Carney. This chapter considers some technological, organizational, and psychosocial barriers to effective collaborative writing, draws conclusions based on observations of the TOPIC/ICON project at Texas Tech University and of Army personnel at Fort Sill, Oklahoma, using collaborative writing software.
- **Chapter 8, "Facilitating Virtual Collaborative Writing through Informed Leadership,"** is written by Catherine Lyman. This chapter captures practical methods that will help develop a manager's skills for virtual collaborative writing teams; the techniques described in this chapter were developed and tested by actual collaborative teams, most notably by the Information Engineering team at NetApp, Inc.

Section 4: Planning and Making Decisions Virtually

- **Chapter 9, "Case Study: Putting their Heads Together Virtually: Case Studies on Collaboration using Content Management Technology,"** is written by Suzanne Mescan. This series of case studies provide a look at how some small and large writing teams have successfully implemented content management technology and improved collaboration in varying environments—within a department, between multiple departments, within a division, and across several divisions of their respective organizations.
- **Chapter 10, "Optimizing Team Performance: Virtual Collaborative Writing,"** is written by Charlotte Robidoux. This chapter explores the essential components needed to establish an infrastructure that supports collaborative writing efficiency in virtual settings.

- **Chapter 11, "Making Collaborative Writing Decisions Virtually,"** is written by Alexia P. Idoura. Drawing in experiences implementing a CMS at Symantec, this chapter examines how virtual writing teams move through the decision making process and what teams can do to improve their decision-making abilities.

Section 5: Developing Content Virtually

- **Chapter 12, "Case Study: Advancing New Authoring Strategies through Virtual Collaboration"** is written by Judith Kessler. This case study discusses why information models are a critical component to successful collaborative writing, especially for topic-oriented content. It also describes the collaborative processes and tools by which Sybase® Technical Publications team members propose, evaluate, develop, test, and enforce new content models, challenges encountered, and key success factors.
- **Chapter 13, "Using Standards to Promote Collaboration among Writers,"** is written by France Baril. This chapter addresses how consistency is required to produce publications of quality in a collaborative environment; it explores the methods, advantages and challenges of developing rules around content, work processes, and the choice and configuration of tools to support virtual collaborative writing and content reuse in a virtual environment.
- **Chapter 14, "Developing Content in a Reuse Environment,"** is written by Norma Emery. This chapter explains why an effective reuse environment depends on collaborative input from writing teams and it provides insight into the principles of reuse and how virtual collaboration is essential to making content reusable.

Section 6: Supporting Quality Writing through Virtual Collaboration

- **Chapter 15, "Case Study: Managing Content Quality and Consistency in a Collaborative Virtual World,"** is written by Kent Taylor. This case study of a product developed by acrolinx GmbH describes the results that real-world virtual collaborative writing practitioners have realized in by applying quality management principles and processes to their information supply chains.
- **Chapter 16, "Caution! Empowered Reviewers Ahead: The Challenges of the Review Process in Collaboration,"** is written by Robbin Zeff Warner, Beth L. Hewett, and Charlotte Robidoux. This chapter explores collaborative review in today's reader-empowered Web 2.0 world, including how CMC tools can facilitate the review process.
- **Chapter 17, "Collaborating with Customers Virtually to Improve Content,"** is written by Mirhonda Studevant. This chapter explores the methods and processes to ensure successful virtual collaboration with customers.
- **Chapter 18, "Preparing Writers for Virtual Environments,"** is written by Pavel Zemliansky. This chapter offers practical strategies for instructors, trainers, and managers to use while preparing writers for virtual collaboration.

Section 7: Using New Media in Virtual Collaborative Writing

- **Chapter 19, "Case Study: Writing, Rhetoric, and Design: A Virtual Collaboration Case Study,"** is written by Douglas Eyman. This case study focuses on a research and production team's approach to making choices about the most appropriate technologies to support the team's interactions for the online journal, *Kairos*. The chapter highlights the need for well-defined roles and understanding the institutional context to connect to the goals and expectations of the journal's editors and readers.

- **Chapter 20, "Inventing Nondiscursive Text in Collaborative Environments,"** is written by Joddy Murray. This chapter considers how today's collaborative environments require more from interfaces if texts are to be invented that become edited images, Web pages, films, and animations.
- **Chapter 21, "The Mutual Presence of RP-7 and the Future of Collaborative Writing,"** is written by David W. Overbey. This chapter examines virtual collaboration, including the production and use of writing, among doctors at different hospitals mediated by RP-7, a robot that enables a specialist at one hospital to evaluate the vital signs of and provide diagnosis for a patient at another hospital.

Section 8: Collaborating Virtually to Develop This Book: A Discussion

- **Chapter 22 completes the vignette begun before Section 1.** It offers a metadiscussion about the technologies and processes involved in the virtual collaborative writing of this book, providing both writers' feedback about these and a list of recommendations for virtual collaborative writing that has emerged from our hard-earned experiences.

Back Matter

The book ends with a glossary of important terms, a list of general references, and an index.

REFERENCES

Boiko, B. (2005). *The content management bible* (2nd ed.).New York: Wiley.

Hackos, J.T. (2002). *Content management for dynamic web delivery*. New York: Wiley.

Pullman, G. & Gu, B. (2009). *Content management: Bridging the gap between theory and practice*. Amityville, NY: Baywood Publishing Company.

Beth L. Hewett
University of Maryland University College, USA

Charlotte Robidoux
Hewlett-Packard Corporation, USA

Acknowledgment

Many people have contributed to this book's completion and—we hope—its success. First, we thank Christine Bufton, the Editorial Communications Coordinator at IGI Global. She has been an advocate for us as we developed the collaborative processes used to produce this book. Because the methods we used to develop the book are highly unusual in the book publishing world, she deserves much credit for being forward thinking. She and other key IGI publishing staff have worked with us when we encountered challenges; we found solutions together, which has made collaborating with IGI Global pleasant and productive. From the Hewlett-Packard Company, we offer warm appreciation to Bobbi Gibson, who gave Charlotte the support and encouragement to pursue this project as a way to find and establish best practices for virtual collaborative writing.

We also thank our editorial review board members who read portions of the book-in-progress and provided us with thoughtful advice and encouraging words. We certainly appreciate their time and energies taking from their own busy work lives. Two text editors entered our collaborative process to help us to edit the disparate chapters into a cohesive, interrelated volume. We are eternally grateful to both Sandy MacLeod and Christina Lengyel for their sharp eyes and equally sharp wits in a harried editing period. We would be remiss not to thank Kent Taylor and Todd Ettelson. Kent provided us with unlimited use of the acrolinx® IQ to help us use terminology clearly across the book, while Todd taught us how to establish and manage a terminology base to standardize our use of terms.

Colleagues of chapter writers also have contributed their knowledge and experience to this book, both directly in reviewing draft chapters, and indirectly as practitioners whose collaborative work has made our chapters possible. We are grateful to them for their kindness in doing so, for they have made this a stronger book through their efforts.

Finally, we must acknowledge all of our writers in this book. They committed to us in an unusual book development process, stuck with us through glitches and successes, and they willingly gave over their chapter authorship in a collaborative process that enabled anyone involved in the book to read their work and suggest or make revisions. All of this work was accomplished through virtual technologies and collaborative processes. Their work enabled us to recognize inductively the six principles of collaboration that ground this book. The future of virtual collaborative writing in the workplace depends on writers like them. To our fellow collaborators: we admire your insights and thank you for generously sharing them with us and our readers.

Opening Vignette

INSIGHTS INTO VIRTUAL COLLABORATIVE WRITING

Learning by Doing

Two writers—one primarily a scholar and the other primarily an industry-based technical writing manager—have been friends since they met in 1993 in graduate school. Beth worked on her PhD in English, with rhetoric and composition as her specialty, while Charlotte worked on her PhD in English, with rhetoric and the public life as her specialty. Over the years, they talked about collaborating on a book that would meld their linked rhetoric-based interests in online teaching and learning, writer training, and collaboration. In 2008, they finally embarked on a collaborative writing project that they hoped would enlighten them and others about the nature of collaboration in virtual, computer-mediated communication (CMC) writing settings.

They planned a book in which expert collaborative writers would contribute their knowledge and experiences. The writers would commit to the book project—providing parts of the whole as content writers and cross-pollinating the work by collaboratively editing and commenting upon each others' content. When the call for chapters yielded a strong mix of topic expertise and commitment, Beth and Charlotte then committed to the writers in a manner that rarely happens in academic book development. Typically, writers are accepted provisionally and then judged by outside reviewers and the editors based on the promise (or lack thereof) in early drafts. There is little-to-no interaction among writers and even less assurance that, once they have met as part of the book's team, they will be able to continue as collaborators throughout the book development process.

To simulate a more true-to-life workplace writing scenario, Beth and Charlotte promised writers that they would work with them throughout drafting and idea development, thus enabling the entire writing team to enjoy a sense of stability that would contribute to developing trust and relationship in a distributed writing setting. Although some writers dropped out of the project, no one was eliminated by the editors for weak early writing or content, and everyone had multiple chances to address how the content fit the whole book under development. Beth and Charlotte encouraged the entire writing team to comment on and edit each other's content as it was distributed virtually, first on a wiki and later on a Web-based document workspace.

In essence, Beth, Charlotte, and the book's other writers considered their collaboration to be an ideal case study of the paradigm shift that virtual collaborative writing requires—from that of ownership of a whole book to authorship of content parts that fit with and comprise the whole. Although chapters are attributed to various writers for practical reasons related to traditional ways of receiving credit in the writers' various workplace settings, everyone gave up the idea of sole ownership in an attempt to discover the challenges of virtual collaborative writing through this book's process. The very need to be able to claim credit is one of those challenges of different value in various settings. Additionally, their choices of CMC tools were determined by this collaboratively owned process, which highlighted how challenging it is to find the best technologies and processes that work for any given virtual collaboratively written project. They used, among other tools, a collaborative wiki for initial topic and book development, a shared online document storage space, phone conferencing, a dedicated listserv, e-mail, and IM for interacting with each other and with the writing team as a whole.

This book tells that story, which—despite the writers' backgrounds—is one that occasionally involves extreme culture shock. The story is revealed both in individual chapters regarding virtual collaborative writing and in Chapter 22, which details the team's own successful and failed processes.

Beth L. Hewett
University of Maryland University College, USA

Charlotte Robidoux
Hewlett-Packard Corporation, USA

Section 1
Intersections of Virtual Settings, Collaboration, and Writing

Chapter 1
Principles for Exploring Virtual Collaborative Writing

Beth L. Hewett
University of Maryland University College, USA

Charlotte Robidoux
Hewlett-Packard Company, USA

Dirk Remley
Kent State University, USA

ABSTRACT

This chapter defines collaboration in some of its many variations and settings, and then it locates collaboration in the virtual world of contemporary writers connected through digital technology. In this way, it offers a snapshot of the kinds of collaboration about which this book's writers write in Sections 2 – 7, while it also uses that collaboration in its own development. In other words, the understandings reflected in this chapter are the product of intense collaboration among this book's writers, who have brought to it their own expertise in this subject matter. This chapter addresses (1) the literature of collaboration and collaborative writing in general, (2) the move from traditional collaborative writing efforts into that of virtual collaborative writing, and (3) six principles inherent to virtual collaborative writing. Taken together, they help us to develop the definitions on which we have based this book's approaches to virtual collaborative writing.

INTRODUCTION

Collaboration is a slippery concept. Ask ten people what it is, and ten different definitions will emerge. Ask ten people to collaborate on a writing project, and the result often will be like herding cats or lassoing fish. People tend to have strong feelings about their writing, and while they may claim to want to collaborate, they can hold onto their own words with a tight fist, fighting valiantly to save them from a subject matter expert's (SME) correction, an editor's cut, or a colleague's revision. Yet collaborate they must. The world of workplace writing—whether corporate, academic, government, public, or private—increasingly calls for collaboration among writers to develop and produce complex documents and to do so efficiently and

DOI: 10.4018/978-1-60566-994-6.ch001

effectively. Information products have changed as single sourcing and metadata (labels assigned to content) lead to content reuse in multiple—often unforeseen—ways. That is, writers may use metadata to search for content in a database and locate material that they can reuse, even though it was never written to be included in a particular information product. But it can be included because the content relates to a subject or product discussed elsewhere. The paradigm of the single owner of a document necessarily is giving way to writing content chunks or information that will be reused in various documents and distributed in multiple settings.

This chapter defines collaboration in some of its many variations and settings, and then it locates collaboration in the virtual world of contemporary writers connected through digital technology. In this way, Chapter 1 offers a snapshot of the kinds of collaboration about which this book's writers discuss in Sections 2 – 7, while it also uses that collaboration in its own development. In other words, the understandings reflected in this chapter are the product of intense collaboration among this book's writers, who have brought to it their own expertise in this subject matter. This chapter addresses (1) the literature of collaboration and collaborative writing in general, (2) the move from traditional collaborative writing efforts into that of virtual collaborative writing, and (3) six principles inherent to virtual collaborative writing. Taken together, they help us to develop the definitions on which we have based this book's approaches to virtual collaborative writing.

COLLABORATION AND COLLABORATIVE WRITING

Why Review the Literature Anyway?

Consider the expression "Why do I need road signs? I know where I'm going." Familiarity with anything at the local level—whether it is navigating a map, making a phone call, or planting a garden—is relatively unambiguous. However, venture out into a new place or area of knowledge, and what made sense before can seem foreign or more difficult to contextualize. The same is true when thinking about collaborative writing in terms of the ways it can be defined and the many terms that are associated with it. Within the context of a writing team, collaboration may mean one thing; in another context, it can take on a very different meaning. For example, one of the writers conducted an informal poll of some technical writers, which revealed diverse approaches to collaboration, with some focused on interactions related to the planning and review phases of writing, others focused on interactions relative to the roles writers perform, and still others focused on when to interact and when to work independently to ensure productivity. In the context of this book project, academics and industry professionals had difficulty reaching agreement on the nature of collaboration, cooperation, communication, teams, content, information, and virtual tools. At times, the difficulty defining terms seemed to be a dividing line between theory and practice. That is, how we understand a term relates to a set of values, whether it be valuing a theoretical construct—"art for art's sake"—or valuing the meaning of a term because of its applicability to ensure productivity and quality in a particular work setting.

Given the wide variability in the way different groups approach terminology, it is important to arrive at least at a provisional understanding of the concepts invoked throughout this text to achieve some degree of consensus on the terminology. How, then, can the key concepts be understood as if everyone were all viewing them at the local level? This chapter attempts to achieve a common view of the many dimensions of virtual collaborative writing by reviewing literature that establishes definitions and explanations of key terms. Lowry, Curtis, and Lowry (2004) highlighted the importance of arriving at a standard language:

"To write collaboratively and build supportive technologies, practitioners and academics need to use a consistent nomenclature and taxonomy of collaborative writing" (p. 66). The more global the practice of virtual collaboration becomes, the more honed the terminology needs to be to enable fluency and familiarity with terms and to be able to optimize best practices.

Nuances of Collaboration

Collaboration as a general term means that more than one person is involved in a generative activity, such as inventing or discovering ideas, solving problems, or engaging a process. Vygotsky (1978; see also 1962) provided the theoretical structure for considering collaboration as a social process in which meaning is constructed from discussion among group members. Belenky's definition (as cited in Ashton-Jones & Thomas, 1995; p. 84) contained traces of Vygotsky's (1978) message in that she defined collaboration as a broad "conversation" with a "scope that reflects a wide range of experiences" that a single person could not have created (p. 280). Such a conversation is a process of give-and-take to which individuals submit their ideas and terminology as they strive to develop ideas in collaboration with others. The individual's ownership of ideas and terminology become subservient to the overall shared goal. Schrage (1990) defined collaboration as "the process of *shared creation*: two or more individuals with complementary skills interacting to create a shared understanding that none had previously possessed or could have come to on their own" (pp. 40-41).

Bruffee (1984, 1993) also drew on Vygotsky's (1978) work and encouraged educators to use collaboration in learning strategies for writing development. Bruffee (1984) stated: "If thought is internalized public and social talk, then writing of all kinds is internalized social talk made public and social again. If thought is internalized conversation, then writing is internalized conversation

re-externalized" (p. 641). Thus, he suggested that writers would benefit from a social context for writing in terms of peer tutoring and peer groups. Bruffee (1993) explained that students need to be able to engage in conversation that allows one to cross the boundaries of one's current knowledge community into the unfamiliar community of another; the task he described is one required not only of students, but of all task-bound writers, such as those who are the primary audience for this book. He believed that to accomplish this task, people need "willingness to grant authority to peers, courage to accept the authority granted to one by peers, and skill in the craft of interdependence" (p. 24).

This notion of interdependence is pertinent to all kinds of writing in which people collaborate. Writers need to listen to, consider, rely on, and use each other's knowledge when they collaborate, particularly in settings where no one person has the authority or singular responsibility for that knowledge. Such is the collaboration most often described in this book and toward which this chapter is written. Ironically, given Bruffee's (1984, 1993) apparent intentions of empowering students to work interdependently, it is important to remember that in educational settings, whether discussed with peer tutors or peer readers, most writing remains in the authority of a single writer who is responsible for the final writing decisions and who receives credit in terms of rewards or corrections based on that singular authority. Yet the kinds of collaboration that this book addresses often take the credit out of the hands of individual writers and place it in the purview of a writing team (and its manager), which together will succeed or fail based on both individual and collaborative contributions.

Introducing a sense of structure to the process, Thomson et al. (2007) determined the following:

Collaboration is a process in which autonomous or semi-autonomous actors interact through formal and informal negotiation, jointly creating rules and structures governing their relationships and ways to act or decide on the issues that brought them together; it is a process involving shared norms and mutually beneficial interactions. (p. 3)

The fact of negotiation itself highlights that collaboration is not easy and that one person cannot determine the entire process for the team, although individual leadership is important as discussed later in this chapter.

Suggesting that there is a distinction between "true collaboration" and more or less cooperative projects, John-Steiner, Weber, and Minnis (1998) developed the following definition for collaboration:

The principles in a true collaboration represent complementary domains of expertise. As collaborators, not only do they plan, decide, and act jointly; they also think together, combining independent conceptual schemes to create original frameworks. Also, in a true collaboration, there is a commitment to shared resources, power, and talent: no individual's point of view dominates, authority for decisions and actions resides in the group, and work products reflect a blending of all participants' contributions. (p. 776)

This definition tends to be useful in contemporary educational settings, in which an ideological preference for particular social values suggests that it is important to distinguish between the abilities of team members to blend perfectly, fading away as individuals, and to contribute equally. While such a state is idealistically attractive, it is difficult to achieve. Yet this definition allows for the reality that such negotiation is messy and challenging for people to learn, particularly in academic settings, where grading creates an environment that can be intolerant of mistakes. Furthermore, it creates an implicit opposite to true collaboration such as cooperative projects, which seem to emerge often in educational settings as students parse

their group work into "yours, mine, and ours" for grading and learning purposes.

If this definition were to be applied in business settings, it would strongly suggest that collaborative work is extremely rare in industry and that cooperative work is the norm. For example, in a writing project where more than one writer is involved—what we call a team of writers—in some cases, the only people who are likely to collaborate with writers on a single text are editors or SMEs. Particularly where industry writing produces discrete documents fewer than 5000 words, and where book-length documents have been replaced by help systems and websites created by assembling many short articles, collaboration may mean contributing items to some collection of information or series of topics about particular content. In such settings, the collaboration may more resemble cooperation in that the team's responsibilities include ensuring coverage, avoiding duplication, creating links, and ensuring consistency of organization.

As this book demonstrates, however, our experience is that the nature of collaboration is applicable more broadly than its measure as a social value. Collaboration's scope, as well, is broader than that of cooperation. Indeed, although cooperative opportunities might be a norm for some business activities, collaboration increasingly is called for by management in education, government, industry, and private sectors (Lowry et al., 2004, pp. 66-67).

Collaborative Writing

Ede and Lunsford (1990) defined collaborative, or group, writing as "any writing done in collaboration with one or more persons" (p. 14). Such activities widely included "written and spoken brainstorming, outlining, note taking, organizational planning, drafting, revising, and editing," any of which yield a similarly wide variety of completed "written products," such as notes, directions, forms, reports, and any other published materials (p. 14). An understanding of collaborative writing can range from the readily perceived to the complex. For example, collaborative writing can be seen as a simple blending of writers' voices to produce a document; yet, as needed, deliberate limits can be set to enable writers to retain their own "voices" or writing styles even when sharing and expanding the ownership of ideas (Ashton-Jones & Thomas 1990, p. 280).

From a more theoretically complex perspective, some people have seen all writing as collaborative. The theory of deconstruction, for example, assumes that on an unconscious level every reader rewrites the text being read through the act of interpretation, which would make all texts—from this standpoint—multi-authored. Crowley (1980) explained that "from a Derridaean point of view, editorship of a work-in-progress, or any reading of it, counts as part of its writing" (pp. 37-38). Taking that perspective to its natural conclusion, in a writing classroom, the students who read their peers' works-in-progress and comment on them are as much a part of the composition as is the "original" writer; this assumption also would be true of a teacher's, workplace editor's, or writing team's readings. By assuming that each reader and commenter unconsciously adds to the body of a written work because the writer's collective experience is affected by such readings and commentaries, collaborative writing becomes the conscious employment of this theory. Crowley believed that "the public nature of writing … supports the notion recently advanced by some composition theorists that all writing is collaborative" (p. 37). However, by presuming that broad a definition of "all writing" as collaborative, so-called "collaborative writers" become merely those who make more conscious and deliberate choices for their writing than are those who believe their products to be singly authored. This perspective, while ideologically interesting, is not very satisfying regarding the practicalities of collaboration overall.

Another perspective about collaborative writing concerns the people who do the collaboration. Theorists who view all meaning as being decipherable only among the interpretive community—or group of people—within which it was written would understand collaborative writing as a process of negotiation, which certainly echoes Thomson et al. (2007) and John-Steiner, et al (1998). Bleich (1983) described a process of negotiating one's written meaning within a group: participants must talk together, ask questions, and ascertain the writer's intentions to fully understand the message. Similar negotiation must occur for two or more people to agree on a single document or work product as representative of their collective thoughts. With regard to reading and providing a writer with feedback, Bleich stated:

To understand the "meaning" of any single language act, other acts are needed to create a context, and negotiation is necessary to verify and clarify the author's motivational bearing—and thus the intention and intentionality. Put another way, no single essay is self-explanatory, and people cannot understand its language in a consequential way just by reading the essay .... Negotiation discloses the context and reaches a provisional, collective decision, corroborated by the author as to the meaning, purpose, and intentions of the language. (pp. 87-88)

What Bleich described here is a group or collaborative way of *viewing and understanding* the writer's message—which is not the kind of collaboration that occurs with a multiply authored piece. In other words, he looked at the collective voice of those who commented upon a piece of writing and who, in a sense, were the audience for that writing. When writers attempt to negotiate meaning within a classroom (for Bleich) or in any task-bound writing setting like the workplace, they open the way to hear others' thinking about the writing's meaning. Additionally, they open the way for that meaning to sharpen or to change as the writers' thoughts become infused with readers' thoughts. According to Bleich, this theory of negotiated meaning stemmed from a desire to understand a person's language system; such understanding is good only for that particular moment in time and must be renegotiated for subsequent utterances or writing (pp. 94-95). Another way to describe this process is as a collaboration of thinking or idea development in the acts of reading and writing.

While such a collaboration of thinking has its own appeal, this theory does present a problem when it comes to the practical work of writing collaboratively because it suggests that the meaning can never be pinned down or held as complete. Ideologically, that may be a debatable case, but it is not a useful approach to most workplace writing, where the expectation is that ideas can, indeed, be communicated and that writing in all of its shapes and forms—as expressions of the writers' thinking—can do the communicating. Thus, other theoretical approaches might serve the real-world needs of collaborative writers more practically.

Regarding the professional world, Ede and Lunsford (1990) presented evidence of how business and industry uses groups to create written products. Their research developed out of an attempt to refute "the pervasive and common sense assumption that writing is inherently and necessarily a solitary, individual act" (p. 5; see also Smith, 1981, p. 796). As academic researchers studying business writing, one of their questions was whether writing teachers should "be encouraged to prepare their students for on-the-job collaborative writing" (p. 8). Primarily due to rapid and vast technological advances, this issue continues to be one with which all writing teachers—including the writers featured in this book—must grapple. Indeed, two decades after Ede and Lunsford's seminal study, a recessive economy again suggests that the more skills students gain for securing future employment, the more satisfied they will be with their college educations.

Ede and Lunsford's (1990) study revealed numerous methods of employing on-the-job group writing as well as some difficulties with the process. One survey respondent noted that collaboration can be "'a slow way, a ponderous way,' to get things done" (p. 33). Another noted that she did not always have the leisure and freedom to explore her own thoughts individually while engaged in collaborative writing (p. 41), which raises the question of to what degree the individual writer's ideas and writing should be subsumed by the group. To be sure, conceptual variances between the pragmatic group processes described for on-the-job writing and the view of the academy's English professionals, who tend to see writing more ideologically as "a means of discovery, of getting in touch with the self, of coming to know rather than to report" (p. 44). Whereas industry and most transaction-based organizations are concerned about effectively and efficiently completing a document or project, the academic community very often is concerned first with an individual writer's voice and second with how that voice shifts in collaborative settings. Nonetheless, Ede and Lunsford presciently pointed out that "most [students] will work in situations where they are at least as likely to participate in a group brainstorming session for a proposal or edit a collaboratively written report online as they are to sit alone in their office, pen (or computer keyboard) in hand" (p. 72). We think that Ede and Lunsford's prediction is understated for contemporary task-based writing scenarios even in the academic institutions. One example of the tension between what is expected at the university level and what is expected in workplace settings became apparent as the writers in this volume were working on their chapters. While educational settings promote fluency in writers—indeed, to invent and elaborate—managers in industry require that writers restrict their use of words to ensure productivity and to keep translation costs in check.

Belenky (1990, as cited in Ashton-Jones & Thomas, 1990) recalled that one of the great values of the collaborative process is that "the exchange can keep on going until, like with the writing of our book, the collaborating writers get very, very hardnosed with each other" (p. 289). Becoming "hardnosed," which is as necessary to negotiation as flexibility, is part of a successful writer's maturation process. All of the emotional issues that affect writers are likely to surface just when the "hard nose" is needed most. People tend to attach both ego and self-esteem to what they write, and they may find criticism difficult to accept, a reaction that does not serve writers and editors well in workplace environments. But the reverse also can be problematic. In our experiences with this book alone, writers sometimes appeared to be overly aware of the individual's feelings, potentially nullifying prospective creative contention among the group by trying to avoid overtaking someone else's authority or by seeking to eliminate potential disagreement. We have seen collaborating writers tolerate content with which they disagree and accept text that they find to be substandard to avoid negotiating it with the originating writer. Ultimately, in order to do justice to the quality of content, most collaborators must move beyond sensitivity and ego concerns.

This practical view of the collaborative writer emerges in the definition of collaborative writing provided by Lowry et al. (2004), a view that highlights the social nature of collaborative writing without losing sight of its concurrent goal orientation:

CW [collaborative writing] is an iterative and social process that involves a team focused on a common objective that negotiates, coordinates, and communicates during the creation of a common document. The potential scope of CW goes beyond the more basic act of joint composition to include the likelihood of pre- and post-task activities, team formation, and planning. Furthermore, based on the desired writing task, CW includes the possibility of many different writing strategies, *activities, document control approaches, team roles, and work modes. (pp. 72-74)*

What makes this definition especially helpful is that it considers the breadth of activities beyond writing that encompass a collaborative writing project. Additionally, it allows for the kinds of writing strategies, approaches to documents overall, roles that team members must assume in contemporary work writing, and the increasingly varied work modes—to include distributed work settings—in which writers engage. The paradigm shift discussed in the following section requires that a definition of collaborative writing show understanding of the news ways in which collaboration occurs among writers and for wide varieties of documents.

Collaborative Writing in Workplace Settings: A Paradigm Shift

On the surface, collaborative writing appears relatively simple: people work together to develop and disseminate writing. Collaborative writing involves making joint decisions about the written product, and it requires active thought, input, and writing from each team member. Of the many collaborative activities in which people might engage, however, writing collaboratively may be among the most difficult. One reason that it is challenging certainly is the long-held and somewhat romantic nineteenth-century view of the individual writer composing alone in an attic room. This image encourages people to imagine that what they write is always a singular accomplishment that is original and to be owned by that individual alone. This idea contrasts with the practice of earlier centuries, when writers learned through imitation and copying, and originality was less prized. In transactional collaborative writing settings, originality and creativity still are essential, but imitating and copying for content reuse again are prized as a mutual sharing and creating of content. Furthermore, in transactional settings like the workplace—where the writing plainly is intended to teach, explain, argue, or otherwise accomplish a goal—the individual's written contribution, while important, rapidly is becoming understood as an integral part of a whole rather than as the whole of a document.

This different way to understand transactional writing is coming about largely because of a confluence of technological change at the intersection of the reader's needs and desires and the writer's means to meet those needs. In effect, technology and globalization have helped to create a paradigm shift in the production and use of information. For example, because automated approaches to producing information are now possible and even necessary to make organizations more competitive, writers must learn how to collaborate on written materials. In so doing, they can increase their output because the tools now enable them to publish the same or similar content in multiple formats. At the same time, readers have come not only to appreciate electronic information but also to demand only the specific information needed—not the whole text—to solve a problem, look something up, or understand a concept. Rather than an entire book, smaller chunks of content typically will fulfill their needs. This somewhat truncated sense of content also is true in academic settings—for students, at least, who have grown up using information age technologies, reading Web pages, and communicating socially in pithy utterances. Such students expect similar brevity in their educational materials although, to their benefit we think, they do not always get what they want. Nonetheless, because of technology, readers now can ask for information in different modes and through different media, such as streaming video, cell phones, laptop computers, and book viewers. Increasingly, paper- and print-based products, such as books, magazines, and booklets—while still available—become less important.

To be sure, as far as transactional writing is concerned, technology and the reader's prefer- ences are helping to drive content distribution. The result has been profound for those writers who collaborate to produce that content: it has focused writers on the technologies that enable them to produce these newer and varied content venues. Rather than in days of old, when the writers dictated the content and the story to be told through that content, the readers now dictate the terms of the story: what they need to know, how they want to know it, whether and how they want to store and archive it, and how much they want to manage at any one time. The same technologies that en- able collaborative writers to provide the chosen content in the preferred formats now function to enable readers to make such choices. As a result, parts of a document, which we call *content units*, or topics that comprise information products, are less often produced by one individual. The whole document, which once might have been viewed as a book, is chunked into parts, and group-based writing is respected as a way of involving more minds to the creation of effective and efficiently written documents.

At base, this paradigm shift in the production and use of information is that the very nature of the written product itself is changing because of technology and its vast affordances to reader. The magnitude of changes that a writing team needs to anticipate when reusing content—what we are calling a *topic-based paradigm*—is complex. Teams cannot retrofit the writing of topics into the book paradigm. Writers need a new paradigm to be successful.

Globalization will continue to have a profound effect on the nature of work-based collaborative writing. Those who will use texts may live in any country in the world, and many readers will access documents in a non-native language. Read- ers certainly will have different levels of skills, abilities, and expertise relative to the documents they read, and most people likely will not read whole documents as much as parts of them. Not only are contemporary readers of such documents more globally distributed than at any time in the history of writing, but so also are those who do the writing. The advent of virtual collaborative technology has enabled—sometimes required—that writers work in distributed settings with team members from different writing and technical backgrounds and nationalities.

Virtual Collaborative Writing in the New Paradigm

For the purposes of this book, we define collaborative writing primarily as an opportunity whereby a writing team has the intention, need, and ability to provide input, offer feedback, and receive feedback, as well as to respond to and use that feedback while a text is in process. It involves strategic and generative interactivity among individuals seeking to achieve a common goal, such as problem solving, knowledge sharing, and advancing discovery. Borrowing from Lowry et al. (2004), we include in this definition the broad scope of activities that collaborative writing may engender in the new paradigm we described earlier: Collaborative writing includes a wide variety of writing strategies, pre- and post-writing activities, team roles, and work modes necessary for collaborating in contemporary colocated and distributed work settings (pp. 72-74).

These collaborative writing activities can take place in a wide variety of workplace settings, and we accept as workplace writing any task-bound or transactional writing that is developed in professional settings. Educational settings and documents, for example, often require collaboration of their faculty, administration, and other workers. Faculty constitutions and teaching requirements often are multi-authored; administrative white papers and grant requests tend to engage a collaborative writing process; teaching materials often are the product of more than one writer; and students are asked to learn to write collaboratively. Academic scholarship in various disciplines often is written collaboratively and credits multiple writers. Also, much of the writing accomplished

in contemporary industry requires and rewards collaborative authorship.

The values of collaboration are widely recognized and equally widely are considered difficult to achieve. Nonetheless, as we consider the literature of collaborative writing, it is important to understand that in industry (for example, nonprofit, government, and for-profit organizations)—perhaps more so than in educational settings—productivity is paramount and in some cases to have two writers working on one text might be considered extremely inefficient. As opposed to the somewhat idealistic values held about collaboration found in some of the education-based literature discussed earlier, industry does not value and promote such ideals as much as flout them. Industry does not exist to form minds, but to produce products; collaboration is valuable insofar as it improves product quality or employee productivity. Indeed, in this volume's own development, value-based differences between academe and industry in terms of theory versus practice became apparent and required much discussion among the book's writing team (this difference is addressed in Section 8 of this volume).

We also recognize a variety of collaborative writing models or styles. The act of collaboration may be understood as more than one person working on different parts of a project, which may or may not mean working interactively and may or may not involve negotiation or close cooperation. It simply may mean that each person contributes part of a project, meeting guidelines or designated roles, without ever needing to communicate with other members of the writing team. Collaboration in general—and collaborative writing specifically—might also be understood as a highly interactive activity that involves much negotiation. In other words, collaboration ranges from all members of the team working on all aspects of the project jointly and simultaneously to each member of the team making an individual contribution to the project in cooperation with the general goal but without interacting with the other members. Most projects likely fall between these two extremes at some or all points of the writing process. For example, a collaborative editorial process is one that involves writers refining documents, with the original writer having limited opportunity for input/ before a final draft is published.

The following collaborative writing strategies evolved out of discussions among the writers of this text about a collaborative spectrum. It represents the multiple tasks and different combinations of writers and writing processes that may be employed in any one team-writing project. This spectrum involves three models of collaboration: serial, parallel, and collective.

Serial Collaboration

Serial collaboration occurs when writers work on an information product one after another. Each person works separately on a piece of the writing or the whole document, each performing a distinct function in the creation of the finished work, and possibly in a distinct chronological or hierarchical order. As such, writers may not have a full understanding of the project as a whole. The original writer adds new content to the information product and must wait until the SME in the process completes the review. The writer must then incorporate review comments, send the document to the editor for review, and make more changes before giving the document back to the SME for approval. While this serial process is considered collaborative, it requires each person in the chain to finish before another person can continue working. An example of serial collaboration is a one-writer project, where Writer 1 drafts book A, Editor 1 reviews book A, Engineer 1 reviews book A, and Writer 1 reviews and updates the final copy.

Because Lowry et al. (2004) developed such a useful definition of collaborative writing, which enables discussion of the paradigm shift even if the definition does not overtly refer to a shift, it seems pertinent to note that they did distinguish between single-author writing and "sequential writing," which we identify as serial collaboration (p. 76). They critiqued this kind of collaboration as insufficiently social, however, because different writers' ideas may not be addressed in such settings. Another problem with serial collaboration emerges when there is not appropriate version control, allowing subsequent writers to override the decisions of earlier ones. In serial collaborative settings, they worried that all document sections must be addressed "adequately" and that "documents must be segmented into appropriate work segments" for this process to succeed. As with any collaborative effort, but perhaps more so in serial cases, they expressed concern that a single uncooperative writer could undermine the process. Finally, they pointed to the bias that one writer could bring to the entire document given the particular order in which segments of the document might be written (pp. 76-77).

Parallel Collaboration

Parallel collaboration occurs when writers work on different pieces of the same project simultaneously. Each person works on one piece of the whole, usually based on a set of negotiated standards or requirements, and engages in coordinated communication with other collaborators as required from time to time. In parallel collaboration, writers may find themselves interacting with others on the team because of their common goals. Parallel collaboration assumes serial collaboration. An example of parallel collaboration is a project with more than one writer: Writer 1 drafts book A for the project, Writer 2 drafts book B for the project, Writer 3 drafts book C for the project, Engineer 1 provides input for one or more books of the project, and Engineer 2 also provides input for one or more books of the project.

Lowry et al. (2004) also considered parallel collaboration, which they stated is "work in parallel by multiple writers, and such work does not necessarily have to be partitioned into separate sections" (p. 77). They found benefits to parallel collaboration in terms of efficiency, working autonomy, and anonymity; although they also noted such specific challenges as "oblivious writers," "poor communication," and "stylistic differences and information overload" (p. 77). Interestingly, they further divided parallel collaboration into horizontal and stratified writing, although these do not assume topic-based writing as we do in this volume.

Collective Collaboration

Collective collaboration occurs when writers contribute concurrently to a project through topic assignments based on a writer's knowledge of the product (specialty areas), tracking of the project, and through delineation of specific predefined roles. All members provide equally important contributions to the project and have shared ownership of the overall project success. Collective collaboration also assumes both serial and parallel modes. Furthermore, it assumes an understanding of the paradigm shift from writer of a whole book to that of content chunks, as described in this chapter. An example of collective collaboration shows how tasks are differentiated by projects with more than one writer: Writer 1 drafts content A, B, C to for three books; Writer 2 drafts content D, E, F to for two books; Writer 3 manages book assembly; Writer 4 updates content in all books; Writer 4 oversees project planning, graphics, and inventory; Engineer 1 provides input for the project; Engineer 2 provides input for the project; and so on.

Any collaborative writing project can have some combination of serial, parallel, and collective collaboration. Such a mix of styles can (and often will) be a product of choosing different models of collaboration for different aspects of a project,

rather than an inherent bias toward one model for the project as a whole. Particularly in industry but also in other work settings like education, information products are revised continually from version to version, and they often pass to different writers for each version—or even to a different writer during a single version as workloads are rebalanced. Over the entire life of a given topic, article, or other document, it becomes exceedingly difficult to identify any one individual as its writer and, generally in such settings, it becomes less important to do so.

It is important to note that Lowry et al. (2004) also recognized another mode of collaboration called *reactive writing*, an ad hoc form in which collaboration among writers to create an information product is simultaneous, but has minimal planning to coordinate interactivity (p. 78). The combination of their parallel subdivisions, horizontal and stratified, and reactive writing draw together some of the features of what we term collective collaboration. However, because Lowry et al. (2004) did not address topic-based writing and content development within a CMS, collective collaboration does not have a true equivalent in their strategy.

ENABLING VIRTUAL COLLABORATIVE WRITING

Processes for Using Tools

Finding the right set of tools to fit the modes of virtual collaboration is not always easy. Because patterns are ingrained, familiarity with tools, in fact, can make it more difficult for individuals to learn new ways of interacting virtually. That is, to the extent that they are adept in the technologies used for many years, writers are habitually drawn to the same tools they have already used. So even though e-mail is not considered to be a highly collaborative tool, writers are accustomed to relying on e-mail to interact with each other. Overcoming traditional uses of tools is extremely important if teams are going to be efficient at virtual collaborative writing. Teams, therefore, must understand the key features of various technologies to make the best use of them.

Robidoux and Hewett (2009, pp. 6-8) described the essential features of virtual technologies that must be considered to ensure optimal coordination among team members. These features concern the way that various media relate individuals to one another in terms of time and space. The feature of *time* refers to (1) how present or available individuals appear to one another and (2) how quickly communication occurs among individuals interacting with one another—their synchronicity. The feature of *space* refers to a perceived proximity among individuals, a closeness that can be expressed through (1) a combination of tools or hybridity and (2) a synergistic experience or interactivity among participants. These four features are defined as follows:

Features Related to Time

Presence awareness concerns the degree to which individuals in virtual settings know that others are present or available to communicate. This feature of a tool gives team members a real sense of the status of other individuals, whether they are immediately available, in a meeting, not to be disturbed, and so on. As a result, team members can determine whether others are free to collaborate. Instant messenger (IM) software, for example, provides a status of each participant listed.

Synchronicity pertains to the length of time it takes for individuals to interact using virtual collaborative technology. Asynchronous exchanges have a greater delay among individuals compared to words spoken when team members are colocated. Synchronous exchanges can occur in near–real time, having little or no lag time. When interactions are more immediate, they resemble

face-to-face communication. Often these two features are linked in that increased synchronicity accompanies higher presence awareness.

Features Related to Space

Hybridity involves the use of tools that combine different elements of communication, such as speech and written language. Mixed modes are more like face-to-face interactions and include voice (for example, telephone) and written expressions that enable dialogue (for example, IM). Only when both aspects are combined is the communication considered hybrid. Increased hybridity can improve productivity when writers collaborate.

Interactivity pertains to the extent to which individuals can maintain dynamic flow of communication across virtual space and interactions made when a tool seems to diminish spatial distance. Interactivity involves overcoming an interpersonal distance in order to do the work together. Videoconferencing not only combines modes of communication but also enables rich feedback between and among participants, making the experience more like face-to-face interactions.

Teams must understand both how these features make the selection of one tool over another a better choice for a given activity and what rules should exist when using these tools to ensure efficiency. Figure 1, adapted from Robidoux and Hewett (2009, p. 8), juxtaposes communication tools as they relate to these features.

Lowry and Nunamaker (2002, p. 4052) provided a similar illustration, termed "Collaborative Writing Work Modes," with proximity on the Y axis and synchronicity on the X axis. Teams can begin to build processes and rules around the tools that will support their goals. For instance, new teams have a goal of establishing trust and forming cohesive bonds among members. The tool set that would facilitate team building will include a rich combination of the features that are possible using virtual tools.

Figure 1. Tools and their time and space features

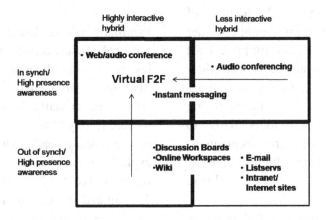

Table 1. CMC tools, time and space, and purpose

Technology	PA	S	H	I	Purpose
Web/audio confer-encing	✓	✓	✓	✓	To enhance team and one-on-one meetings. To present data or demonstrate a point. To reinforce team identity, listen, respond, and build trust. To meet spontaneously to address issues, plan, solve problems, build relationships, and address differences in opinion.
Audio conferences	✓	✓	-	✓	To manage progress with team and individuals as appropriate. To listen, respond, and build trust. To meet spontaneously to address issues, plan, solve problems, build relationships, and address differences in opinion.
Instant messaging, (chat)	✓	✓	-	✓	To engage in spontaneous, informal dialogue. To clarify, question, and respond. Springboard for moving to other modes of collaboration.
Discussion boards	-	✓	-	✓	To facilitate formal deliberation and decision making. To document information about a complex issue. To distribute information equitably among all team members. To seek input about issues needing resolution or clarification for two or more team members.
Online project workspaces	-	✓	-	✓	To post project-related documents, processes guidelines, instructions. To issue organization-wide announcements. To manage team schedules.
Wikis	-	✓	-	✓	To post and collectively edit information.
E-mail	-	-	-	✓	To notify, ask, and answer simple questions. To create a record of actions. To alert team of developments and location of new content.
Listservs	-	-	-	✓	To notify, ask, and answer simple questions. To create a record of actions. To alert team of developments and location of new content.
Internet/ Intranet sites	-	-	-	✓	To provide information about the writing organization for other departments or for outside organizations.

Note: PA = presence awareness; S = degree of synchronicity; H = hybridity; I = interactivity.

Table 1, adapted from Robidoux and Hewett (2009, p.), describes some of the features of CMC tools that writing teams should consider with regard to their overall goals for projects. It provides an overview of many tools to consider when interacting virtually. Lowry and Nunamaker (2002, p.)) also presented a table listing tools, but instead of looking at tools relative to their features, they listed tool requirements as they relate to key thinking patterns: diverge, converge, organize, elaborate, abstract, evaluate, build consensus.

Success in the use of virtual tools depends on three elements, especially for new teams, changed teams, and teams with individuals who are not experienced with working remotely: (1) facility among all members of the team in how to use all of the tools that enable virtual communication, (2) explicit documented procedures and rules that indicate to all team members what tool to use for various types of communication, and (3) leadership that ensures compliance with the processes established by the team. An example of a rule might be that e-mail will not be used to transfer files, ask questions, or provide comments. Instead, online workspaces will guide the transfer of information from one team member to another.

Team competence in using required tools is even more crucial when organizations employ single sourcing technology. That is, CMS environments that support the use of XML technology and publishing add another complex dimension to virtual interactivity that is difficult to manage without extensive training and practice within teams. For example, tasks that are automated in a CMS, referred to as workflow, trigger notifications to designated members of the team. If the team members do not understand what action is required upon receiving the notification, the flow of activity can be disrupted by just one person.

Processes for Interacting Effectively

Familiarity with tools and technology is only one aspect of efficient collaboration. Another is ensuring effective coordination among team members. In a study of novice writing teams attempting to collaborate virtually, Lowry, Nunamaker, Curtis, and Lowry (2005) learned that performance declines dramatically when processes are not explicit: "groups that are left to establish processes for themselves tend to perform suboptimally" (p. 342). In that research, they explained that absent any degree of guidance from a facilitator, teams need highly structured processes to direct cues for interacting: "the value in scripted processes is their ability to recreate the experience of having a facilitator guide activities" (p. 343). Without structured processes, inexperienced collaborative writing teams will struggle to function effectively.

The level and degree of explicitness, of course, depends on the skill of the teams of writers to work with one another. If one or more members are unskilled or new to a team, then they will need exact processes to guide their actions. If a team is newly formed, then the whole team will need highly explicit documented processes. The reason for this extensive level of detail is that even if these individuals are skilled writers and facile with a range of virtual tools, they have limited experience working together and limited knowledge of what activities to perform at a given point in time. On football teams, for example, even though professional football players have technical proficiency, they must practice scripted plays repeatedly to ensure that the whole team's activities are coordinated. Orchestras, too, must practice their various instruments and sections both individually and together to develop harmonious music. From the perspective of collective collaboration, the process of writing becomes a completely different experience, one that is social in nature. Thus, individual performance must be understood in terms of the team as a whole; the group dynamics force the team to adopt different operation norms, including establishing a cohesive team, building trust, negotiating, decision making, coordinating, and measuring and tracking performance.

Addressing the added complexity within teams that may have been more accustomed to serial and parallel collaboration requires scripted activities to ensure process efficiency. What follows are the key elements needed to build a process script and an example of one related to team building and establishing trust.

Key Elements of a Process Script

The goal of preparing scripted processes is to help individuals coordinate their activities so that the team is successful in creating predefined outputs. The primary elements of a process script include:

- An explanation of the rules of engagement

- The purpose of the script in relation to the overall goals of the team and the milestones necessary to meet the deadline
- Expectations for completing the script and how it relates to other tasks
- Background information as needed
- Rules for following the script
- Distinct steps needed to complete a script
- A definition of completion—the output of the script

Table 2 provides an example of a team-building process script that is designed to help a writing team establish trust and determine how they will interact as a team. It would be used for a newly formed team of four to six people to create a team agreement for working together effectively. The idea of asking new teams to complete this process script serves three purposes: (1) setting

Table 2. Example of team-building script to establish trust

Assignment: Create Team Agreement	
Purpose	To help your team members get to know each other better, establish team rules, and set standards for interacting to coordinate collaborative writing activities across the team.
Instructions	Schedule a 90 minute long Web conference for the team to develop a charter and agreement. • Use the first 15 minutes for introductions and to determine roles. During this time, choose a facilitator (makes sure all members have an opportunity to participate), a mediator (keeps the discussion directed), a note taker (records essential discussion points), and a time keeper (ensures discussion covers all topics in the allotted time). • Spend the next 50 minutes brainstorming each of the following topics, which will make up the team agreement. Divide your time to ensure discussion of each item. o Responsibilities and expectations o Communication o Participation o Decision making and problem solving o Managing disagreements o Conduct during and between meetings o Consequences of not completing tasks • Spend the next 20 minutes defining each topic so that the whole team is in agreement. • Use the final 10 minutes to determine who will complete each topic and who will review and assemble the completed document. All team members must review and approve the descriptions. Determine the logistics for completing the draft within a week to present at the next team meeting. Spend no longer than 3 hours completing the agreement.
Ideas to consider	Use the questions that follow to help you develop topics: • How will the team members give feedback to one another? • How will the team clarify new ideas and suggestions? • How will the team manage differences of opinion? • How will the team handle misunderstandings? • How will all team members be included?

the groundwork for productivity throughout the project lifecycle; (2) allowing team members to create relationships, form bonds, and establish trust; and (3) providing an immediate chance to see the team in action, measure performance, and learn lessons for working together on actual information products.

Training for Virtual Collaborative Writing

Training is a way of providing doable learning activities for writing teams. In our view, training is necessary both for the CMC tools that will be used in the virtual collaborative writing and for the processes that the team will engage as they produce information products. In essence, every chapter in this volume presupposes training on various levels, at different junctures, and toward numerous ends. Most chapters provide some elements of training regarding the issues highlighted within. For that reason, and because we believe that training is an ongoing and undeniably necessary process, we do not reduce training to any one chapter but rather suggest its value at all stages of collaboration. To this end, we examine five principles common to strong training programs in order to highlight how they can be used in accord with other guidance in this book.

One way to address training is through process scripts, as described in Table 2. Another way is to take apart the process scripts and uncover the underlying principles that always accompany such training. For these principles, we turn to Hewett and Ehmann (2004) and Ehmann Powers and Hewett (2008), who considered training for online writing instruction and for other training that occurs in virtual workplace settings. Their five principles were investigation, immersion, individualization, association, and reflection. Such principles can sustain the collaborative writing team even in the face of rapidly changing technologies and when teams change members

because they are not bound by particular technologies or people; instead, they are grounded in ways of understanding training that works in online settings. Indeed, such principle-centered training relies on the belief that preparation for online writing collaboration necessitates online training and interaction (Ehmann Powers & Hewett, 2008; Hewett & Ehmann, 2004).

Investigation

Investigation as a training principle recognizes that CMC technologies remain too new and unstable for much empirically gained knowledge to exist. There is much that we do not know about how online technologies influence writing, for example, and about the social processes necessary for virtual collaborative writing. Therefore, a training program that engages the principle of investigation would acknowledge that fact and would openly and straightforwardly make use of the day-to-day work as a data fund for study. Using the regular work of the writing team and not the kind of "busy work" that often accompanies training would involve collecting information about how the team's training is received and how well it succeeds in providing doable and learnable tasks. Therefore, feedback from team members by way of informal surveys, e-mail, or frank IM or phone discussions with a manager provides an incredibly useful amount of information (Ehmann Powers & Hewett, 2008, p. 263). Nonetheless, it must always be understood that such feedback cannot be used to discipline or to punish trainers or team members; fruitful and ethical investigation cannot occur in a punitive setting.

In the trust-development process script outlined in Table 2, investigation is the job of the team, and their product will be feedback that demonstrates their understanding of what a team is and how trust is developed within the team in the culture of that workplace community. A manager or trainer can analyze the team's responses to the topic development of such issues as providing feedback to one another, how ideas will be developed and shared, and how to be inclusive of all team members. The manager's investigation then can lead to higher-level discussion among managers about the potential for a virtual collaborative writing team's understandings and misunderstandings as the team is imagined ideally within that organization's culture. Hence, investigation is both a training principle and the potential change agent for training that does or does not work.

Immersion

Immersion as a training principle presupposes that adults learn in the context of doing and therefore that they can self-diagnose problems (Apps, 1991; Galbraith, 1991; Galbraith & Zelenak, 1991; Knowles, 1990). For virtual collaborative writing—indeed, for any online work or activity—immersion means that the training should occur in the setting in which the work will occur. In this case, the training should occur through the kinds of virtual tools that a particular writing team will be expected to use. If the team is expected to use a CMS, then the training should involve not only the technological mastery of the CMS but also the writing that is developed and stored in the CMS. Technological mastery is good as far as it goes, but it is insufficient for providing novice writers in a virtual collaborative setting with the deeper understanding of content or topic develop and reuse, for example. Furthermore, trainees should take on the roles that they will be expected to enact as team members rather than simply watch other team members engage their roles (Ehmann Powers & Hewett, 2008, p. 263).

In the trust-development process script outlined in Table 2, immersion is enacted when the team meets virtually for a Web conference. They learn through using the Web conferencing tools, whether phone, voice-over-Internet, or desktop-sharing software. They also enact the processes of defining and selecting roles, working in those

roles (as note taker, for example), and dividing time to make the best use of it and to complete a task within specified time frames. There are no wasted steps in this trust-development process script, which mimics the best of real-life workplace meeting opportunities.

Individualization

Individualization is a principle that "suggests that training be tailored to meet the needs of individual participants. Every online employer must reconcile the operational requirement for standardization with trainees' needs for flexibility or individuality as they progress through training" (Ehmann Powers and Hewett, 2008, p. 264). The need to match the individual with the training is strong, particularly in virtual collaborative writing, because adults have differing learning styles and often can describe the kinds of learning they do best. For example, many adults can say whether they are visual- or audio-based learners and whether they grasp a task immediately or need to repeat it. Further, some adult learners find that they are more social learners and are able to learn best within the group, while others might need to spend some solitary time on task.

In the trust-development process script outlined in Table 2, individualization is enabled by allowing the writers to volunteer for various roles. Solitary learners, though they certainly need to be able to speak up within the context of a writing team, might find themselves initially more comfortable taking on the note taker's role or a document review and assembling role—particularly as the task is to develop trust. For these people, trust may come more slowly, and the quieter tasks may enable them to process the meeting differently. More extroverted team members likely will be more active in the discussions themselves, displaying by their openness how they envision trust to take shape within the context of a particular team.

Association

Association is a training principle that Hewett and Ehmann (2004) and Ehmann Powers and Hewett (2008) named in lieu of using the word *community*. Using Martin Buber's (1923) understanding of an association as a group of people meeting in a transactional setting, they viewed "training as a means of facilitating 'cyber-associations' that are grounded in a *transactional* or *business* purpose—employees developing professional relationships with one another within the context of working toward a shared company mission or goal" (Ehmann Powers & Hewett, 2008, p. 264). In this sense, an association enables virtual collaborative writers—or any distance-based workers, for that matter—to connect with one another. IM often provides a useful synchronous method of connecting because it can be used socially at the same time as it is used for business (Hewett & Hewett, 2008). Other methods include scheduled conferences, dedicated listservs, and distribution groups. The value of phone calls also should not be underestimated in establishing a sense of association among team members and across teams.

In the trust-development process script outlined earlier, association is modeled in the very subject of the process script and the purpose of the meeting. The virtual team members need opportunities for interacting and learning about each other's thoughts, personalities, and work preferences. Such a scheduled meeting is invaluable in providing the team with this opportunity. At the end of the 90-minute meeting, one reasonably could expect people to know each other's names, have a sense of each other's voices, and to begin to associate work concerns and work style preferences with those names and voices. Regardless of this meeting's success, one could expect that the next meeting of this team would be less formal, friendlier, and generally warmer in tone—which can enable more rapid engagement with the work at hand. At the least, teammates likely will have identified at least one person whom they would

feel comfortable calling for assistance in the next writing task.

Reflection

Reflection is the fifth principle that Hewett and Ehmann (2004) and Ehmann Powers and Hewett (2008) outline. This principle "addresses the potential of training to be a reflective and iterative process during which trainees' assumptions about their work product and processes are identified, challenged, and potentially refined. As such, allowing occasions for trainees to alter their practice based on what occurs in the online context is valuable opportunity for individual as well as programmatic growth" (p. 265). Reflection means offering virtual collaborative writers opportunities to go beyond thinking about their writing and collaboration practices. Ideally, a reflective training program would involve the chance to write about what has gone well and what could have gone better; it also would involve using other senses like talking among the team about what must be adjusted both midstream in a project and at its end. Ideally, such reflection would enable conversation between manager and team or individual team members, again without a punitive purpose although that does not mean that skills and abilities could not be assessed for improvement purposes.

In the trust-development process script outlined in Table 2, reflection is addressed only minimally in the potential for the team to meet again with the document containing the reviewed and approved team management descriptions. A more powerful opportunity for reflection might be asking everyone to provide a brief (no more than one-page) memo regarding how the meeting had succeeded in terms of building trust, which was its intent. This memo could be sent only to the manager, or it could be the basis for a time-limited online discussion via a dedicated listserv or IM chat.

Governance Models for Collaborative Writing

Fundamentally, collaboration means that more than one person works on a single piece of writing. Wherever more than one person is working on a project, there is a team. We define a team as a group of two or more people who are assembled (with or without explicitly defined roles) with the specific, shared goal of a material outcome. By extension, a writing team is a group with the shared goal of producing a written product. Lipnack and Stamps (2000) defined a virtual team as "a group of people who work interdependently with a shared purpose across space, time and organization boundaries using technology" (p. 18). A virtual team's processes may be distributed across geographic locations, but also within the colocated space of an office or institutional setting. Unlike traditional document sharing and face-to-face or telephone interactions, virtual writing requires participants to communicate using CMC technologies.

The division of the parts of a project among writers can take any or all of the collaboration model forms—serial, parallel, or collective, as discussed earlier. However, we have learned that wherever a team exists, some division of responsibilities must occur. Team responsibilities can be divided along several possible axes:

- Roles (for example, writer, editor, illustrator, publisher, information architect)
- Parts (for example, separate topic or chapters)
- Authority (for example, some people having more decision-making power than others)

Most likely such division will involve all three axes, as we discovered in the process of working with writers on this book. To this end, we suggest being mindful of ways that teams govern their collaboration. Kasemvilas and Olfman (2009)

observed that "the collaborative writing process needs good governance in order to better organize the process" (p. 94). At some point, the team's responsibilities and the style or model that their collaborative writing follows likely will be constrained by a governance model or method for dividing authority once roles and parts are divided. Although sometimes the authority will be imposed from outside the team, as with a manager tasked with forming a collaborative team, sometimes the team itself will have some choices.

Roles themselves may be confusing to collaborators. Wolfe (2009) for example, indicated that many perceive the project manager as a "boss," or "leader." However, she suggested, "think of the project manager as someone who plays a specific role on the team by keeping the project on course. The project manager's primary responsibility is to track the status of the project and to ensure that all team members know what they should be doing at any moment" (p. 13). Wolfe also acknowledged the importance of clearly defining each member's role: "If they don't have a clear understanding of their responsibilities and deadlines, their work style tends to come into conflict just when the team is under the most pressure to finish" (p. 55).

Five basic governance models emerged from this book's wiki-based discussions. The first is that of a *monarchy*, wherein one person is in charge and the others work for that person and accept his or her decisions. The second model is that of a *hierarchy*, wherein there is a chain of command for authority with people responsible for different parts of the work. Monarchic and hierarchic governance structures may involve the person in charge encouraging subordinates to use one of the other models and may restrain that person from exercising authority on the work. These governance models also include mandating a structure that the subordinates would not naturally choose for themselves and may be reluctant to adopt. The third is that of a *democracy*, wherein each person has a vote and the majority rules; to be frank, that is the model with which we first started to talk with writers, but we quickly learned that however idealistically attractive that option might be, at some point there is a need for someone to make a decision with which not everyone will agree. However, a team charter, which includes how impasses and other events that require someone to make a decision with which some may disagree will be handled, can help maintain a democratic approach because such a charter is developed democratically (Wolfe, 2009, pp. 34-35). Where producing a product is a goal, democracy may not be a sustainable team governance model. A fourth model for governance is that of *consensus*, wherein everyone has to agree with the decisions; in certain situations, this option also can make for slow going in decision making and can, in effect, halt the work process. Finally, the fifth model that we identified is that of an *anarchy*, wherein anyone can make any change at any time. For us, this model also failed the "get the project done" test, in part because most of the writers did not venture to make the changes that their given authority allowed.

Some scholarship on virtual collaborative writing, while not esteeming one model over any others generally, considers governance structures relative to the tools collaborators use and the potential for face-to-face interaction. Cerratto and Rodriguez (2002) noted that "people involved in collaborative activities are inexorably interdependent in terms of strategies, heuristics, perspectives, goals, motives, etc. The more distributed the activities of a given cooperative work arrangement, the more complex the articulation of the activities of that arrangement" (p. 140). They also asserted that for writing that involves collaboration from a distance, the need for some coordination design to be in place is paramount (p. 140). Discussing results related to studying differences in collaboration using a wiki-like tool and face-to-face methods, they observed that: "First CSCW groups concentrated exchanges on their actions. It became essential for them to know about the ongoing organization of the collaboration (cf. who is doing what, when and

where in the document). Others' actions became the principal object of the CSCW groups' communication" (p. 142).

Further, with respect to the use of wikis in collaborative writing, Kasemvilas and Olfman (2009) stated that "wikis that support collaborative writing cannot be open or arbitrary ... [readers] need to have specific roles and have to finish their tasks in a certain time period" (p. 90). The more clearly each team member understands his or her role in the design of the project, the more each can focus on that role and on related responsibilities.

Weng and Gennari (2004) noted that "collaborative writers communicate with each other in a variety of ways, such as e-mails, phone calls and face-to-face meetings. Therefore, decision-making and communication are often disconnected from the writing itself" (p. 579). They observed that the use of a writing tool that facilitates annotations, such as MS® Word's "track changes" feature, rather than a wiki, may facilitate a more democratic process. By providing "threaded annotations throughout the document," it is possible to facilitate discussion, letting the text as well as annotations evolve in a dynamic way (p. 579). However, they also espoused a hierarchic model, arguing that cross-role communication awareness is also part of the collaboration. While team members are aware of the group's work, they also are aware of each others' role in that work. So, a well-defined governance design should be in place at the outset of the project. Indeed, while a project manager supervises the work of the team, the remaining structure can vary depending on the distribution of the work relative to the document and members' specializations, or even distance between collaborators.

It is important to note that— despite the preferences of individual writers—no one way of constructing a collaborative writing project is inherently preferable to another because of the highly contextual nature of each project. What seems most common to all teams is not the actual set of roles, parts, and authority models but rather the need to develop rules that work for the team. Without such rules, it will flounder. As with the football team described earlier, without a coach and a series of assistant coaches, the players would be left to making decisions on the field, a situation that is less than desirable because no one player on the field has other than his own tunnel-vision view of the game in process. From a broader perspective, it seems clear that different projects with different goals and different constraints may benefit from different models of collaboration. For example, a project to devise an advertising campaign may favor a model in which people in different roles work collectively under the monarchic authority of an account executive who encourages an anarchic approach to brainstorming campaign ideas. On the other hand, a project to compile an application programming interface or code reference for a programming language may favor several people working in parallel and using a consensus governance model to determine the template they will use to develop the reference. It is therefore important for project managers to understand the benefits and costs of each way of structuring collaboration so that they can make the right choices for their projects.

Among other factors, physical conditions can limit the forms of collaboration that are available to a team. For instance, a team in which members are physically separated from each other may make collective collaboration difficult, especially if they live in different time zones. Technology can be used to remove physical barriers to different models of collaboration, enabling project managers to implement different assignment of roles, different partitioning of work, and different governance models than would be possible without the technology. When selecting technology, therefore, it is important to be aware of the different collaboration modes that are possible and to consider whether and how technology could enable a more productive mode of collaboration for the project.

In some cases, technology can make forms of collaboration possible that would not be possible even to a team that is physically present to each other without technological help, or it can be used to make their collaboration significantly more efficient. Whenever roles are delineated, work is partitioned, or authority is delegated, communication among the members of the project team becomes essential. Team communication is, in formal terms, an overhead—that is, it is an activity that is required to make the collaboration work rather than an activity that directly creates the product. As such, the amount of communication overhead should be kept to the minimum required to achieve the project objectives, and the value of each communication should be made as high as possible. To make this team communication as high-value as possible, several factors must be considered:

- The project must be organized in the way that makes communication efficient.
- The content of the communication must be efficient and effective.
- The communication skills of the team members must be of a high level and must be appropriate to the type of work they are doing.
- The right technology must be chosen and it must be used correctly.

For example, in the business setting described in chapter 12 of this volume, there is a general movement to topic-oriented content in which each writer is assigned topics to write, and the role of organizing that content falls primarily to the information architect, an individual who develops and manages the structural design of information that is shared in a digital environment. In any setting, however, writers and architects *must* coordinate their work so that all topics are covered without gaps or duplication. Large projects may have multiple information architects, so there must be agreement on a consistent means of organizing the content across the product. Some content truly is shared across different components or products, so we need to agree on its suitability for all even if one writer is the "owner." Such shared content may exist at the topic level, or as a group of topics, or as something smaller than a topic.

Finally, it is important to acknowledge that writers on a virtual collaborative writing team have to be willing participants—engaged in the project and willing to work as a team. The spoken and unspoken social contracts of working toward a common goal in a respectful environment are very important for any project. Indeed, the incorporation of technologies that enable anywhere/anytime collaboration is a complex process involving both social learning among collaborators in their interchange of ideas and learning of new technologies. Where writers are unwilling to work collaboratively, they need either to discern what is stopping them (for example, fear of shared responsibilities or unwillingness to share credit or blame) in order to correct the problem or they may need to find other more solitary writing jobs. The culture shock of virtual collaborative writing may be too much for some writers, particularly if their organization has not acculturated them in helpful ways. However, the advent and increasing reliance on virtual technologies in various workplaces, discussed at the outset of this chapter, may limit unwilling team members in their continued role as workplace writers. There can be no doubt that virtual technologies and the globalization they enable make collaborative writing more important than any time in human history.

SIX PRINCIPLES FOR COLLABORATIVE WRITING IN THE NEW PARADIGM

We close this chapter with the identification and discussion of six key principles that underlie the process of writing in a topic-based or otherwise collaborative paradigm. As described earlier, the process of collaborating virtually on this book led to identifying these principles; in fact, to the extent that these principles are central to writing collaboratively, they permeate in varying degrees all the chapters contained in this volume. Taken together, these principles serve as overarching guidance for organizations to consider when investigating automated technologies for managing content and how best to prepare virtual writing teams.

Principle 1: Develop a Culture of Collaboration

If changing a culture entails altering a closely held system of values and often tacit assumptions (Schein 1999), then creating a culture of collaboration involves finding a way to access, understand, and change those values (p. 16). Creating a culture of collaboration is essential when moving away from the development of whole books toward a topic-based paradigm. The challenge underlying cultural change can be neither underestimated nor measured on a quarterly basis. Changing a culture takes time.

An argument can be made that it would be easier to work with staff not trained as technical writers than to encourage seasoned writers to adjust their writing practices. In other words, it might be easier to learn a new skill than to break hard-worn habits, an occurrence described by Schein (2009): "Changing something implies not just learning something new but unlearning something that is already there and possibly in the way" (p. 116). Understanding this reality is essential when creating a culture of collaboration. Writers know their craft, value their proficiency, and take great pride in their accomplishments. A necessary starting point for organizations, then, is to appreciate that the impact of this change is equivalent to upending the professional ethos of workplace writers, which ultimately can threaten their professional identities.

Changing a culture is a process that occurs in stages. Schein (2009) identified three stages, which he labeled "unfreezing," "learning new concepts," and "internalizing new concepts" (p. 117). In the first stage, individuals can experience unfreezing with the help of a "change leader," a motivating force typically located higher in the organization. Leaders work with what Schein called "change agents," who can motivate individuals to move beyond the threatening circumstances that create anxiety (p. 118). The threats or disruptions that prompt upset in individuals can cause them to question cultural assumptions directly. For many of today's workplace writers, the concern is twofold, pertaining to (1) a technology that if avoided will eliminate their jobs and (2) an internal distress over a change that stands in their way of their goals and aspirations (p. 118). Effective leadership, the second principle we consider, is needed to help transcend the anxiety. Culture is thus tied to leadership, the second principle involved in creating a culture of collaboration, both of which emerge in Section 2 and 3 of this volume.

Principle 2: Find and Promote Leadership

To compete in the global marketplace, writing organizations continually must transform themselves. Because transformation involves cultural change, organizations need leaders to help guide individuals through the changing cultural circumstances. The principles of leadership and culture are overlapping, which suggests that effective leaders must appreciate the implications of the paradigm shift, the cultural disruption that can trigger skeptical responses among writers. Leaders must grasp the worrisome nature of a change that undermines the very identity of writers. In addition to a loss of identity, writers might resist change because they fear being incompetent or unproductive (and then being reprimanded) or being different from others members on the team. Organizations need strong leaders to help writers address these insecurities so that change

agents can help writers learn new concepts and then internalize them.

Schein (1999) identified eight elements that leaders should address in organizations undergoing change to help teams unfreeze, learn, and internalize concepts (p. 125). These concepts dovetail with the five principles of training outlined earlier in this chapter.

- **A compelling positive vision.** The vision must be clearly defined and endorsed by senior management, and individuals must be convinced that the change is good for the organization.
- **Formal training.** Training must be provided if organizations want individuals to adopt new assumptions, values, and ways of thinking and conducting their work.
- **Involvement of the learner.** Make sure that new ideas are taking root by working directly with individuals to observe and optimize progress.
- **Informal training of teams.** Because cultural beliefs are embedded in teams, leaders need to work with whole teams to promote change. Individuals do not want to seem different.
- **Practice sessions and feedback.** Individuals require feedback from mentors to feel like they are making progress in adopting new methods or processes.
- **Positive role models.** If the new processes are complex, individuals must observe how expected behavior and actions are carried out. Otherwise, they will have no way of imaging how to do the work.
- **Support teams.** Individuals need a forum for venting their frustrations and to see that others may be experiencing similar problems.
- **Consistent systems and structures.** Strong leadership means that the organization has implemented a definite framework

that guides individual activities, including a plan for issuing rewards and punishments, especially at the team level.

According to Schein, all eight elements are necessary to prevent failure from occurring. Leadership thus entails finding ways to address underlying anxiety and to mobilize change agents who can ensure the implementation of these eight elements so that learning can be internalized. Ultimately, change agents transform their valid concerns into motivation. If this outcome is to occur, individuals must realize that not changing is more distressing than the change itself. Schein referred to this dilemma as one related to learning: "The motivation to unlearn and learn something new comes from the realization that if you continue in the present way, you will not achieve your goals; you will experience survival anxiety [which] must be greater than [its opposite] learning anxiety" (p. 188). In other words, writers when motivated will be less anxious about learning new technologies and adopting new practices.

Principle 3: Establish Trust

Writers need to feel comfortable with the skills, experiences, and intentions of team members in order to collaborate virtually. We all have had the experience working on teams and quickly distrusting the experience because someone on the team does not follow through on the assignments. If writers believe they cannot depend on teammates, they will be reluctant form bonds and to work effectively together. As described more fully in Chapter 5, establishing trust involves many dimensions. What follows are some high-level considerations related to the principle of establishing trust:

- **Social interaction.** Getting team members to know each other is crucial.
- **Shared leadership/roles.** Give team members areas of responsibility to manage and

they will "own" a portion of the end goal the team is trying to meet. Rotate roles to build team competence and ensure inclusion.
- **Communication and predictability.** Ample communication enables teammates to learn predictable patterns to ensure effective interactions.
- **Inclusion.** Writers must be included if they are to feel connected and to reach consensus on methodologies. Team members must be a part of key decisions and important announcements.
- **Consistent processes.** Consistency ensures that everyone on the team can be confident that all team members are carrying out tasks as planned.
- **Team concept.** Teams must be evaluated for their collective contributions. Setting team expectations and measures that enable teams to function effectively is crucial for building the relationships that support collaboration.

Principle 4: Use Tools and Collaborative Modes Effectively

Writing teams must be proficient in the use of virtual technology and in the types of collaboration needed for topic-based and other collaborative writing projects. Inefficiencies and failures arise if writers collaborating virtually use the wrong tool for particular kinds of interactions. Although we have covered some of the ways to develop efficient processes for using tools and collaborative modes effectively in this chapter, looking at these concerns through the lens of a principle enables a broader understanding. In order for teams to use tools effectively, for example, training is critical. Otherwise, it can be difficult for trust to form or strengthen. In particular, the training principles of immersion and individualization are essential for enabling tools-based training opportunities. The following are some overarching considerations related to the principle of using tools and collaborative modes effectively:

- Conduct nonthreatening training for improving each team member's uses of the virtual technology and collaborative modes.
- Select tools and collaboration modes that enable efficiency for most people in the organization. In other words, whenever possible, select stable technology that supports the goals of the organization and the types of writing it produces.
- Similarly, determine what kinds of collaboration are needed for particular projects or types of projects and adapt the available technology to the collaboration (rather than vice versa).
- Thoroughly prepare writers new to an organization or the team in ways that are appropriate to the collaborative culture as developed with principle one.
- Similarly, offer frequent professional development opportunities so that current team members can be empowered to do their best and continue to improve their skills in all areas necessary to the job.

Principle 5: Create Structure

As described earlier, writing teams need high degrees of structure to guide the practice of collaborating virtually. Without efficient work habits, teams will struggle to form bonds, establish trust, and create a stable collaborative writing environment. Structure entails delineating processes precisely so misinterpretations will not occur, ultimately reducing the margins for error. The aim of creating structure is to ensure optimal productivity. Key to this principle is the idea that providing rules, techniques, and recommended strategies to teams will improve their chances of succeeding in their tasks.

While process scripts offer one excellent way to create structure for virtual collaborative writing teams, there are others. Structure, for example, can be established in a number of ways:

- Developing work plans that document exact assignments
- Defining roles with specific sets of responsibilities
- Providing guidelines for project management
- Setting up practice sessions that help teams learn how to coordinate activities
- Integrate closed-ended rather than open-ended work configurations, such as workspaces, that make participation easy, so that individuals do not start from scratch when contributing
- Documenting rules about how to share information related to writing projects

Furthermore, by creating an environment that values repetition, habits, and patterns, the team has an internalized sense of structure in the ways that they should learn and interact. Such structure enables change because it allows new writers to learn quickly by imitating the team as their model. Because a clear social structure provides a safer environment for relating to one another and addressing tasks, the principle of structure may increase the likelihood of everyone on the team contributing and participating, even those who would consider themselves introverted, solitary, or shy.

Principle 6: Measure and Track Performance

Expectations about how performance is measured guides performance itself. If teams do not have clear expectations about how to write collaboratively in virtual environments, their chances for success are slim. To move past the single-writer, one-book paradigm, teams need to know the new rules of the game and how their performance will be assessed and tracked at the team level.

In many ways, the concept of measuring and tracking overlap with structure because measure and tracking should operate as a well-structured system that guides high performance. Spitzer (2007, pp. 15-16) outlined the essential functions of performance measures:

- **Measures that regulate behavior.** When individuals have a definite understanding of how their work will be evaluated, they will know what behaviors will be recognized. The key is finding a system of measurements that apply to the team environment, a topic discussed further in Chapter 11.
- **Measures that enable the visibility of performance**. When processes and procedures are put into place to ensure efficiency, seeing them in action is not easy. With measures in place, teams can see their progress and managers have the ability to track good performance.
- **Measures that focus attention.** When individuals struggle with competing priorities, measures that are carefully selected can help them concentrate on the most important priorities.
- **Measures that clarify expectations.** Most individuals want to do a good job. If they know exactly what is expected of them, they will be more likely to perform well.

Teams must be recognized for an organization to see consistently good performance. For years, writers have been recognized for owning and producing their books. New recognition structures are central in organizations to achieve success in the collaborative paradigm.

REFERENCES

Apps, J. W. (1991). *Mastering the teaching of adults*. Malabar, FL: Krieger.

Ashton-Jones, E., & Thomas, D. K. (1995). Composition, collaboration, and women's ways of knowing: A conversation with Mary Belenky. In Olson, G. A., & Hirsh, E. D. (Eds.), *Women writing culture* (pp. 81–101). Albany, NY: State University of New York Press.

Bleich, D. (1983). Discerning motives in language use. In Horner, W. B. (Ed.), *Composition and literature: Bridging the gap* (pp. 91–95). Chicago: The University of Chicago Press.

Bruffee, K. A. (1984). Collaborative Learning and the 'Conversation of Mankind.' *College English, 46*, 635–652. doi:10.2307/376924

Bruffee, K. A. (1993). *Collaborative learning: Higher education, interdependence, and the authority of knowledge*. Baltimore: The Johns Hopkins University Press.

Cerrato, T., & Rodriguez, H. (2002). Studies of computer supported collaborative writing: Implications for system design. In Blay-Fornarino, M., Pinna-Derry, A., Schmidt, K., & Zarate, P. (Eds.), *Cooperative systems design* (pp. 139–154). Amsterdam: IOS Press.

Crowley, S. (1989). *A teacher's introduction to deconstruction*. Urbana, IL: NCTE.

Ede, L., & Lunsford, A. (1990). *Singular texts, plural authors: Perspectives on collaborative writing*. Carbondale, IL: Southern Illinois U P.

Ehmann Powers, C., & Hewett, B. L. (2008). Building online training for virtual workplaces. In St. Amant, K., & Zemliansky, P. (Eds.), *Handbook of research on virtual workplaces and the new nature of business practices* (pp. 257–271). Hershey, PA: Information Science Reference.

Galbraith, M. W. (1991). The adult learning transactional process. In Galbraith, M. W. (Ed.), *Facilitating adult learning: A transactional process* (pp. 1–32). Malabar, FL: Krieger.

Galbraith, M. W., & Zelenak, B. S. (1991). Adult learning methods and techniques. In Galbraith, M. W. (Ed.), *Facilitating adult learning: A transactional process* (pp. 103–133). Malabar, FL: Krieger.

Hewett, B. L., & Ehmann, C. (2004). *Preparing educators for online writing instruction: Principles and processes.* Urbana, IL: NCTE.

John-Steiner, V., Weber, R. J., & Minnis, M. (1998). The challenge of studying collaboration. *American Educational Research Journal, 35,* 773–783.

Kasemvilas, S., & Olfman, L. (2009). Designing alternatives for a mediawiki to support collaborative writing. Journal of Information. *Information Technology and Organizations, 4,* 87–105.

Knowles, M. (1990). *The adult learner: A neglected species* (4th ed.). Houston, TX: Gulf.

Lipnack, J., & Stamps, J. (2000). *Virtual teams people working across boundaries with technology* (2nd ed.). New York: John Wiley & Sons.

Lowry, P. B., Curtis, A., & Lowry, M. (2004). Building a taxonomy and nomenclature of collaborative writing to improve interdisciplinary research and practice. *Journal of Business Communication, 41,* 66–99. doi:10.1177/0021943603259363

Lowry, P. B., & Nunamaker, J. F. (2002). Synchronous, distributed collaborative writing for policy agenda setting using Collaboratus. In *Hawaii International Conference on System Sciences* (HICSS), (10), (pp. 4051-4060).

Lowry, P. B., Nunamaker, J. F. Jr, Curtis, A., & Lowry, M. (2005). The impact of process structure on novice, virtual collaborative writing teams. *IEEE Transactions on Professional Communication, 48,* 341–364. doi:10.1109/TPC.2005.859728

Robidoux, C., & Hewett, B. L. (2009). Is there a write way to collaborate? *Intercom, 56*(2), 4–9.

Schein, E. (2009). *The corporate culture survival guide* (2nd ed.). San Francisco: Jossey-Bass.

Schrage, M. (1990). *Shared minds: Then new technologies of collaboration.* New York: Random House.

Spitzer, D. (2007). *Transforming performance measurement: Rethinking the way we measure and drive organizational success.* New York: Amacon.

Thomson, A. M., Perry, J. L., & Miller, T. K. (2007). Conceptualizing and measuring collaboration. *Journal of Public Administration Research and Theory, 36.* Retrieved April 3, 2009 from http://jpart.oxfordjournals.org/cgi/reprint/mum036v1

Vygostky, L. (1978). *Mind in society: The development of higher psychological processes.* Cambridge, MA: Harvard UP.

Weng, C., & Gennari, J. H. (2004). Asynchronous collaborative writing through annotations. In *Proc of ACM Conference on Computer Supported Cooperative Work (CSCW'04),* Chicago, (pp. 578-581).

Wolfe, J. (2009). *Team writing: A guide to working in groups.* Boston: Bedford.

Chapter 2
Frameworks for Talking about Virtual Collaborative Writing

Beth L. Hewett
University of Maryland University College, USA

Dirk Remley
Kent State University, USA

Pavel Zemliansky
James Madison University, USA

Anne DiPardo
University of Colorado, USA

ABSTRACT

This chapter draws on various rhetorical, media-based, social presence–based, activity-based, and systems-based frameworks for understanding virtual collaborative writing. Such theoretical understanding is helpful to bridging the gap between those who study virtual collaborative writing to develop theories of the practice and those who draw on theory to develop effective practices.

INTRODUCTION

This chapter provides information to help readers understand how virtual collaborative writing has been theorized so that readers can make informed decisions about what tools they may use, how roles may be assigned, and what processes they may use in specific situations. To this end, it addresses some issues relevant to bridging the gap between theory and practice—academic scholars and business-based writing practitioners—and the theories that

DOI: 10.4018/978-1-60566-994-6.ch002

ground some of the conceptions of virtual collaborative writing as discussed in this book.

In Chapter 1, we identified definitions of collaborative writing and principles associated with collaborative writing in virtual settings. We also acknowledged that virtual collaborative writing can occur in a variety of ways in terms of the tools that writers can use and the processes teams choose to use to produce a given text. As teams try to ascertain the best tools and approaches to use for their particular writing situations, they need to consider a number of factors that can influence the efficiency of virtual collaborative writing. Researchers have studied these factors, using real workplace projects as their case studies and surveying practitioners about their perceptions of certain dynamics in their collaborative writing. From this research, a body of literature exists concerning the issues of media choice, roles of team members, and approaches to writing. Theories drawn from these studies can inform decisions that project managers and those who participate in virtual collaborative writing projects generally face.

It is important to note that the language and terminology discussed in this chapter's literature review may not always match that of Chapter 1, but that many of the concepts are similar and will be identified as related. These theories are interdisciplinary and, as a result, the writers may not be using the same term for a similar concept given different perspectives from different disciplines. Much as Table 1 in Chapter 1 provided a general understanding concerning how certain tools can facilitate collaboration relative to presence awareness, degree of synchronicity, hybridity, and interactivity, this chapter reviews the theories most pertinent to discussing virtual collaborative writing. Indeed, some of the theories described in this chapter contribute to a discussion of information in that same table. For example, elements pertaining to *presence awareness* have been discussed in this literature using the term *social presence theory*, and dynamics associated with *interactivity* have been discussed using the term *media richness theory*.

A Gap between Theory and Practice

Much as professional writers learn general skills through formal education, educators try to learn about specific practices and problems that professional writers experience in order to inform pedagogy and to refine instruction, helping students become well prepared for their workplaces (see Chapter 18). As the editors discussed in the Introduction to this book, academics and business writers need to support each other, to write

to and with each other, to explore practice from a theoretical standpoint, and to explore theory from the position of practice. Therefore, differences between what academic professionals and practitioners value are woven into the very essence of this book. Some of our contributors are academics, while others are practitioners; however, some work within both settings and their tend to blend the perspectives. Miller (1989) linked research findings associated with technical writing workplace practices with those of rhetorical education; she acknowledged: "We seem, that is, uncertain about where to locate norms, about whether the definition of "good writing" is to be derived from academic knowledge or nonacademic practices" (p. 15). She observed a perceived gulf between the instruction that teachers tend to provide and what actually happens in business writing practice, seeing a "discrepancy between practices that are supposed to be effective and those that are actually preferred and accepted" (p. 15).

Research into workplace writing practices contributes to new directions in writing instruction. Miller explained this link between workplace practice and writing education: "Understanding practical rhetoric as a matter of *conduct* rather than of production, as a matter of arguing in a prudent way toward the good of the community rather than of constructing texts, should provide some new perspectives for teachers of technical writing and developers of courses and programs in technical communication" (p. 23). For example, it was through such research that scholars and teachers learned the importance of providing students with opportunities to experience collaborative writing situations in their educational settings—to give students practice with the kinds of writing they likely would experience in the workplace. Now, educators who plan to teach business writing or technical writing courses regularly read the research of collaborative writing dynamics. Finally, Miller asserted that research into workplace practices informs new directions in education: "We [the academy] ought not, in other words, simply design our courses and curricula to replicate existing practices... we ought instead to question those practices and encourage our students to do so, too" (p. 23). Likewise, research findings also can inform practice toward identifying more efficient ways of doing tasks and theorizing about processes to develop concepts that help managers make decisions.

Researchers—academics and practitioners—have used empirical methods in studies of real, workplace writing tasks and the kinds of challenges those involved in collaborative writing projects face. Some of this research was identified in Chapter 1. However, a more extensive review of related theories can help readers to understand frameworks based on these studies for making decisions that affect virtual collaborative writing projects. Such a view can help develop ways to evaluate a project's efficiency and dynamics with the goal of improving the involved processes. These theories include those pertaining to issues that affect collaborative writing processes; those associated with computer-mediated communication (CMC), which affects writing processes within virtual forms of collaboration; and those specific to how technology affects communication. Other theories are associated with the rhetorical dynamics involved as writing teams consider their audiences and their needs. Finally, some theorists have discussed socio-economic elements that impact available tools and the ways that tools are used. These elements also are discussed in this chapter.

WRITING IS RHETORICAL IN NATURE

Writing both Informs and Represents Collaborative Thinking

The centrality of collaboration to twenty-first century workplace success has been proclaimed widely (see, for example, IBM, 2008; Partnership for 21st Century Schools, 2006; Rainie, 2006;

Rosen, 2007), prompting institutions of higher education to produce glossy ads declaring their capacity to teach future workers the art and skill of teamwork. Although proficiency in written communication commonly is regarded as central to effective collaboration, the precise dynamics of its role often are left somewhat vague. Given the ubiquitous demands to produce work that is both high quality and on schedule, the efficacy of collaborative processes typically is judged by the quality of resulting products. Virtually authored texts, then, frequently are seen as important clues to the functionality of a particular writing team.

Given the fast pace of the digital workplace, writers understandably may be tempted to assume a linear view of the virtual collaborative writing process, thereby casting efficiency as a prime virtue. An alternative perspective more in keeping with insights from research on writing envisions the role of writing rather differently—not simply representing the product of collaborative thinking but, through multiple iterations and discussions, serving as an important heuristic in developing and sustaining substantive joint work. Kalmbach (J. Kalmbach, personal communication, 2009) called this process *emergent activity* because it leads to new thinking that neither party might have perceived prior to the collaboration; in effect, emergent activity is a type of idea invention. The process of responding collaboratively to successive drafts becomes part and parcel of collaborative thinking, as team members develop and refine ideas; recognize flaws; and improve the clarity, detail, and accuracy of textual content.

Despite a great deal of attention in recent years to fostering readiness for workplace collaboration in schools, colleges, and workshops, substantive joint work in idea and content development may be a relatively unfamiliar process to many novice employees. In her ethnographic study of workplace writing, Beaufort (1999) noted an emphasis on collaboration and consensus building (often supported by extensive oral communication and social networking) that stood in striking contrast to the norms of discourse in academic communities Further, as workplace writing tends to encompass a greater array of forms and functions than commonly is the case in schools (Beaufort, 1999; Hull, 2000), the task of developing content collaboratively also demands that team members either reach consensus regarding genre and goals or are provided with process scripts and standards, which is a way of developing structure (see Principle 4 in Chapter 1). Workplace writing, then, brings into sharp relief the affordances and demands inherent in collaboration more generally, thereby providing opportunities to identify challenges and foster more productive collaborative relationships.

Rhetoric and Collaborative Writing

While there has been emphasis over the past 30 years on writing's potential to generate, extend, and enrich thought, novice writers entering today's workplaces are likely to embrace a rather traditional view, shaped more by writing on demand in testing situations than by sustained collaboration over complex and longer-term writing intended for real-world audiences. That is, twenty-first century virtual collaborators may regard the development of a given piece of writing in old-fashioned terms—as something akin to setting up an efficient filing system to sort and sequence ideas and information, with the challenge of revision limited largely to ironing out flaws in grammar or usage. Missing in such a conception are the complexity and potential of writing as a recursive and rhetorically situated process of *meaning-making* as well as *meaning-communicating*. Even such online tools as Google Docs™ (http://docs.google.com), Writeboard™ (http://www.writeboard.com), and Zoho™ Writer (http://writer.zoho.com) software provide enriched opportunities for geographically dispersed writers to collaborate in developing and refining ideas, the persistent notion of writing-as-container threatens to undercut the generative potential of such innovations.

What do virtual collaborators need to know about the process of writing collaboratively to maximize the quality of their ultimate products? If written content is about more than transferring ideas into organizational templates, then it is important to consider what this "more" might be. The study of rhetoric as first articulated by Aristotle helps in considering such issues. At the least, according to Eble (2009), a study of rhetoric indicates that the process should include attention to the canons of rhetoric:

- *Invention*, or content creation. What needs to be written and delivered to an audience.
- *Arrangement*, or layout. How the document or text is structured or organized to meet the audience's needs; how the interface will be accessible and friendly.
- *Style*, or design. What content should look like; and how to make it look appropriate to the medium in which it is delivered.
- *Memory*, or database and archives. Written material, user interface, Web page, stylesheets storage, labeling, and taxonomy.
- *Delivery*, or interface/distribution. What is public and what is private; how it is shaped to meet the requirements of the medium in which it is delivered, such as online (Web page or searchable database) or printed, and whether it is delivered in components or completed text. (pp. 94-95)

Furthermore, with regard to writing as a rhetorical act, in any writing setting, there is a person who writes and one who receives the writing; it is impossible to ignore the rhetorical implications of this reciprocal act. Ultimately, writing is about the *audience*, the readers of the text, which makes writing a rhetorical endeavor. When writers, their working contexts, and the organizational culture do not consider the audience, texts often show this lack of consideration by being unreadable, incoherent, or otherwise less than useful. All the principles and theories about virtual collaborative writing become meaningless without a careful consideration of audience and its effects on the writing. Despite the transactional nature of workplace writing—whether in academic, government, for-profit, or nonprofit settings—writing is about the humans on the other side of the document or information product. It is about the real needs of real people whose real goals the writing will help to meet. And it is for this reason that rhetoric matters to virtual collaborative writing as it is discussed in this book. Geisler, et al. (2001) explained that "Central to rhetorical theory is the idea that audience determines the appropriateness and success of communication. The expectations, task needs, immediate situation, values, interests, and presumptions of readers affect how they understand and respond to a text or message" (pp. 271-272). In other words, the needs of the audience are a primary consideration for thinking about how to write collaboratively in virtual settings.

In addition to audience, the ideas of *purpose* and *occasion* are central to a rhetorical understanding of the collaborative writing act. Purpose refers to the goals for the written product, whether it is a standard document, webtext, or multimedia-based text. Occasion refers to the event or reason for carrying out a particular goal or purpose. For example, the inauguration of a president leads to the need (purpose) for speeches, original literary texts like poems, and even new musical arrangements. As Geisler, et al. (2001) said: "Finally, rhetorical theory directs us to the rhetorical situations in which writers and readers co-exist: the occasions that draw them together, the motives they bring, the tasks they are engaged in, the rules of engagements they operate within, and the communities they affiliate with" (p. 272). Collaborating writers need a comprehensive understanding of the contexts—audience, purpose, and occasion—for which they write.

To say that writing is "rhetorically situated" is to reference the various aspects of the contexts that inform composing processes as well as products

(Ewald & Burnett, 1996). A world of possibilities fraught with both peril and promise exists in this concept. Take, for instance, writers themselves, with their particular understandings of the purpose of a given task, its communicative challenges, and their grasp (or lack thereof) of particular modes of communication (for example, terminology, style, and ways of organizing and presenting information and ideas). And then there are the writers' relationships with and understandings of their intended audiences—that is, the extent to which they can accurately assess readers' background knowledge, biases, needs, and levels of receptivity. Finally, one must consider the larger institutional contexts in which writing is situated, including such factors as the relative urgency, controversy, and novelty attending a given writing event.

The notion that writing takes shape in the context of rhetorically situated events carries several implications in terms of idea and content development in virtual collaborative writing. First, if the purpose and demands of a given writing task are not objectively stipulated but rather interpreted, fine-tuned, and taken up by writers throughout the composing process, then ongoing checks for mutual understanding among members of a writing team become not just advisable, but critically important. If we understand the acts of reading and writing as parallel processes of meaning-construction (Tierney & Pearson, 1983, Tierney & Shanahan, 1991), then writing teams also must understand their intended audiences, carefully assessing and re-assessing potential points of misunderstanding and resistance as well as readers' current background knowledge and needs. Especially where new participants enter a reading-writing cycle—whether as fresh additions to a writing team or as audiences endeavoring to understand text apart from the context in which it was created—special consideration must be given to monitoring the potential for disparate understandings, confusion, and controversy.

The process of developing one of the chapters in this book provides a telling illustration of the importance of close attention to rhetorical context.

When the editors convened a conference call that included all of the writers working on the section of this book devoted to developing content virtually (see Part V), discussion of the rhetoric of content focused to a large extent on the notions of reuse and repurposing (Robidoux, 2008). Referencing the strategic reuse of particular topics across documents and rhetorical contexts, these terms essentially were new to one writer, as was the use of XML markup and XSL transforms (style sheets) to render documents (Robidoux, 2008, p. 115). Some refer to these tools or technological dimensions of creating content as "egoless" writing (Weiss, 2002, p. 3). This addition to the writer's understanding of potential readers' orientations is important because workplace writers increasingly associate the phrase *content management* with the use of software intended to facilitate such purposeful reuse of particular chunks of text (for example, Vasont Systems, 2009).[1]

For the above-mentioned writer, formulating a chapter about content entailed an iterative attempt to reach shared understandings of the nature of content in determining what kinds of discussion might be most useful to targeted readers. Cognitive psychologists refer to such mental constructions as *schema*—that is, representations of ideas or phenomena that are fine-tuned and expanded as new information and understandings become available (Alexander, Schallert, & Hare, 1991; Rumelhart, 1980). Only after the writers for Part V refined their understandings of the content development process through their discussion did the construct of content, the needs of virtual collaborators, and their own purpose as writers become mutually clear. At that point, they were able to begin talking constructively about content development.

Finally, we would be remiss if we did not at least touch on the critical concept of *values*. Perelman and Olbrechts-Tyteca (1969) offered a neo-Aristotelian approach to rhetoric or probable reasoning, examining degrees of adherence to opinion. Their views about opinion, particular

their understanding of values, becomes a useful construct for examining how culture influences virtual collaborative teams. Perelman and Olbrechts-Tyteca's classification of opinion revealed that some types of opinion induce more universal agreement than others, such as what statements or views seem factual. Suppositions about reality that are less universal, though still potent, pertain to preferences or attitudes about reality—what people value or their commitment to a system of beliefs (p. 74). Accordingly, there is an emotional aspect to the concept of values to the extent that when individuals are drawn to something, the experience is not strictly a logical response.

A consideration of values is essential for understand virtual collaborative writing because attitudes about writing are embedded in culture, which is the first principle articulated in Chapter 1. As Schein (2009) suggested, workplace behavior is consistent with the prevailing attitudes or values, which ultimately are reflections of the culture: "Culture matters because it is a powerful, latent, and often unconscious set of forces that determine both our individual and collective behavior, ways of perceiving, thought patterns, and values" (p. 19). If organizations seek a paradigm that supports virtual collaborative writing, they must influence the culture and thus the attitudes and values that drive writing behavior. In essence, then, the process of shaping corporate culture is one that is rhetorical.

It also is one that employs the rhetorical ideas of *ethos*, *logos*, and *pathos* (Miller, 2004, p. 204; see also 1979). *Ethos* refers to the credibility of writers who convey knowledge or information to people who need to use it. Writers need to understand that they are people writing to other people who are trying to carry out daily activities of which their particular document is but one part. The more credible a writer is in terms of his or her ability to present reliable information, based either on his or her own expertise with the topic or references to others who are experts, the more a reader can depend on the information to be accurate. *Ethos* implies a human dimension to virtual collaborative writing both in terms of the end product and in the way that team work is conducted. *Logos* refers to the accuracy of the information that is being conveyed, which in turn helps to secure the writer's own ethos. Finally, *pathos* refers to the attitudes that motivate people to write and write well, but also it refers to the excitement and urgency related to the people who will use the documents to carry out work tasks, to use products, and to make decisions large and small.

Writing is Cultural and Social

Because writing is inherently rhetorical, it is also cultural and social. While the rewards of virtual collaboration are obvious, there exist a number of technological, organizational, and psychosocial barriers to effective collaboration. First, familiarity with the media used for collaboration and opportunities for practice are essential. Dede (1995) asserted that immersion in virtual environments is key to successful collaboration (see also Hewett & Ehmann, 2004). Next, organizational concerns can hinder successful collaboration. Huws (2005) suggested that traditional face-to-face hierarchical organizations or even those with a degree of hybridity can actually subvert successful collaboration of any sort. Additionally, Foray (2004) suggested that making work roles clearly defined and making the collaborative endeavor explicitly transparent and democratic can ensure positive outcomes. Finally, knowledge of the personality traits and values of the participants in a collaborative project is necessary for project managers. Daughtery and Funke (1998) and Rovai and Jordan (2004) demonstrated that face-to-face and virtual collaboration will be difficult for participants whose personality characteristics lead them to occupations in which individual efforts are rewarded.

To say that the rhetorical situatedness of writing renders it inherently social is to tell only part of the story, for in these transactions among writers, readers, and institutional contexts reside assumptions that further shape emerging understandings and their results. Often largely tacit, these assumptions can nonetheless hold important and sometimes highly charged consequences for those seeking to participate in a given writing event. For several decades, literacy researchers working from sociolinguistic and anthropological perspectives have documented the central role of culture in determining access to and meaningful participation in linguistic events (Gee, 2008; Heath, 1983; Street, 1995). These insights take on new urgency in virtual collaborative writing, in which writers often compose jointly across divides of language, geography, and culture.

The challenge of formulating content in virtual collaborative writing events lends fresh resonance to insights gleaned over the past several decades from research examining the dynamics of language use in particular groups—that is, how culturally and socially shaped linguistic practices signal membership in certain communities, grant or deny access, and produce potential for misunderstandings and diverse interpretations (for example, Gee, 2008; Heath, 1983; Street, 1995). Early on, much of this work focused on the dynamics of particular cultural groups' discursive practices, exploring their associated interactional dynamics, politics, and valuing systems (Erickson, 1987). More recently, as "community" has come into use as a metaphor for geographically dispersed participants sharing common interests or goals, researchers have begun exploring how such groups both reflect and achieve a sense of "affiliation" (Gee, 2004, p. 79) and provide opportunities for the development of memberships that transcend culture and nationality (Lam, 2006).

While it has always been the case that what counts as textual quality in one context may be regarded as aberrant or inappropriate in another—and that social, cultural, and power dynamics determine what gets articulated and how it is valued—these notions take on multiple complexities with the advent of virtual collaborative writing. Content development teams, for example, increasingly comprise colleagues who bring diverse cultural and linguistic backgrounds to their work, thereby presenting opportunities to incorporate a broader array of perspectives while also demanding mindful attention to the potential for conflicting understandings of textual norms and practices. Further, as virtual collaborative writing often takes place across institutional entities, the task of content development can involve additional challenges in terms of arriving at shared understandings of textual purposes, norms, and priorities (Hull, 2000).

Getting content developers on the same metaphorical page becomes trickier than ever when team members engage in joint writing across familiar divides of culture, nationality, and space. Although virtual collaborative writing remains relatively unstudied, several insights from earlier research on technologically assisted writing point to some relevant dilemmas. First, while technological advances can invite wider and more democratically robust participation (Selfe, 1992), those with the greater share of relevant technical knowledge can come to dominate a team's work (Forman, 1990). Further, as the digital integration of sound, image, and video with written text is increasingly second nature to younger workers, virtual collaborative writing teams must reach consensus on what counts as text and how diverse participants can work together toward the development of effective content (see Chapters 20 and 21). Finally, even as they endeavor to establish shared values concerning the nature and purpose of a given set of textual content, it is critical that virtual collaborative writing teams also allow ample space for the play of disparate perspectives.

Some years ago, DeMarco and Lister (1987, p. 4) made the important observation that problems often labeled technological are in fact fundamentally sociological, an insight that is particularly apt where writers employ virtual tools across spatial and cultural distances. When it comes to virtual collaborative writing, what may at first seem a set of purely technical and linguistic challenges turns out to be fundamentally human after all—rife with opportunity for both conflict and cohesion, for enlarged or diminished understandings, and for inclusion or exclusion.

Social and Economic Conditions Relative to Collaboration in the Workplace

In order to understand the ways in which virtual collaborative writing in the workplace has developed into a phenomenon, it is necessary to understand some of the rhetorical contexts in which it takes place. Because the need for and possibility of extensive writing collaboration have been created by larger social and economic forces, we must look at those forces in some detail.

Literature that discusses the connection between business and workplace practices on the one hand and writing collaboration on the other can be broken down into two broad categories. The first category includes literature that emphasizes the current economic and business realities, but mentions workplace writing collaboration only in passing or treats it implicitly. Nevertheless, these works are important because they show how workplace writing collaboration is connected to larger economic and social forces. The second category comprises works produced by writing and communication specialists that, while analyzing the changing nature of the twenty-first century workplace, place a higher importance on writing and writing collaboration theory. While analyzing the present and future of writing and communication, however, these writers do so against the backdrop of larger economic, social, and political forces that influence the work of collaborating writers. For example, the onset of the content management system (CMS) is an attempt to make content development more efficient so that information products can be priced more competitively. Very often, the writers in the second category borrow heavily from the writers in the first, which demonstrates a tight connection between current theories of the workplace and of workplace collaborative writing.

One economic and social trend that is important for discussing workplace writing collaboration is the increased globalization and interconnectedness of national and regional economies and the need for companies to reorganize them to meet the requirements of a world economy. Reich (1992) argued that, as the world economies become more connected, a new "Web of enterprise" is created (p. 87). According to Reich, the new enterprise "need not be organized like the old pyramids that characterized standardized production, with strong chief executives presiding over ever-widening layers of managers... all following standard operating procedures" (p. 87). Here, Reich spoke about the increased need for members of business organizations to engage in collaboration and to see each other as members of a team with the same goal. Clearly, such a structure not only allows but necessitates new relationships among workers and new ways of communication among them. This communication is complex; it includes not only hierarchy, but also multi-directional, horizontal, and even messy communications with people from all over the world.

A key component in Reich's argument was the notion of "symbolic-analytic work"; symbolic-analytic workers' jobs included "problem-solving, problem identifying, and strategic brokering" (p. 177). They "manipulate symbols—data, oral, and visual representations" (p. 177). According to Reich, symbolic-analysts: "solve, identify, and broker problems by manipulating symbols. They simplify reality into abstract images that can be rearranged, juggled, experimented with, communicated to other specialists, and then, eventually, transformed back into reality" (p. 178). Although some symbolic analysts may not see themselves as writers or even communicators, it is easy to notice that much of the work they do is very similar to the work done by people who do call themselves writers or communicators.

That connection to writing is what makes Reich's concept of symbolic-analysts and the use of this term particularly relevant (see Chapter 18).

Tapscott and Williams (2006) built on Reich's (1992) argument. They claimed that in recent years people have entered "the age of participation," and they argued that the widely available and low cost (or free) tools for online collaboration, among which they named "free Internet telephony, open source software [and] global outsourcing platforms" that enable people both to access new markets and to participate in economic production (p. 11). Indeed, as Chapters 16 and 17 indicate, customers can and do participate in reviewing and recommending different document development strategies to meet their needs better. Tapscott and Williams stated:

Though egalitarianism [in this new economy] is the general rule, most peer networks have an underlying structure, where some people have more authority and influence than others. But the basic rules of operation are about as different from a corporate command-and-control hierarchy as the latter was from the feudal craft shop of the preindustrial economy. (p. 25)

One of the examples that they offered to support their claims was the well-known computer repair outfit The Geek Squad®, which is owned by the popular technology store Best Buy®. According to the writers, the company's founder, Robert Stephens, attributes the success of the Geek Squad® to a high level of collaboration among employees. One instance of such collaboration was the decision by the "geeks" to use online multiplayer games to stay in touch after the number of people employed by the company surpassed 12,000 (p. 243).

Tapscott and Williams described what they called the "the rise of the wiki workplace" (p. 245). According to them, the change in the structure of many companies became necessary because the nature of work itself had changed: "Work has become more cognitively complex, more team-based and collaborative, more dependent on social skills, more time pressured, more reliant on technological competence, more mobile, and less dependent on geography" (p. 246). If this argument about the changing structure of the corporate workplace and the changing nature of work itself is, indeed, correct, then the importance of virtual workplace collaboration for business success becomes clear. Such "weapons of mass collaboration" (p. 247) as community blogs, wikis, social networks, and so on are changing the nature of doing business and increasing the role of collaboration in the workplace.

Both Reich's (1992) and Tapscott and Williams' (2006) arguments are applicable to the economy at large while writing and writing collaboration are mentioned in those works only in passing and indirectly. As such, they belong in the first category of texts outlined earlier. On the other hand, Johnson-Eilola (2005) looked at the impact that the new networked economy may have on writers and communicators more closely. His argument proceeded along two main lines: Work in the twenty-first century—especially online work—is and will remain nonlinear and nonhierarchical. Such work will require multiple location and spaces, both computer- and non-computer-based, and will ask workers to multitask; to identify, manage, and broker multiple problems; or, in Reich's (1992) terms, to engage in symbolic-analytic activity. An example of differences in workplace activities is the increased use of Twitter or blogs among corporate officers as a public relations tool. For example, Step2, a manufacturer of toys, teamed with Case Western Reserve University to develop a blog to help parents understand how to use toys in assisting children with developing various skills. While the blog site does not include advertisements pertaining to toys manufactured by Step2, there are links on the site to Step2's product Web site. Prior to the development of such social networks,

this kind of collaboration would be limited to an advertisement or public service announcement.

These writers demonstrate two important shifts in the nature of twenty-first century work and workplace. They show that the nature of work may be shifting to a more interactive environment, and these texts demonstrate the role of Internet-based communication tools in that shift, leading to the need for more discussion of virtual collaborative writing.

In summary, globalization has been a contributing factor to a host of changes in workplace environments. Just as some changes have been welcomed, some of the same changes have been equally unwelcomed by particular countries, groups within organizations, and individuals within those groups. A general discussion of the many effects of globalization—such as the positives and negatives, advantages and disadvantages, and rights and wrongs—is beyond the scope of this book. With regard to the impact of globalization on writing teams specifically, we do not pretend to have addressed all the ways in which the global economy has influenced the day-to-day activities of writing teams. Our goal in raising issues related to the workplace writing in a highly technical global environment is twofold: (1) technological advancements put many demands on writers to collaborate virtually on writing projects in more deliberate ways and (2) when workplaces are highly automated as, for example, with those using a CMS or machine translation, topic-based writing practices are essential, and these practices in turn presuppose increased productivity and the need for collaboration. Yet the emphasis on reusable topics is not only a function of technological advancements in the workplace; technology also has prompted readers to look for content anytime, anywhere, and though various media. While not all individuals may like this approach to writing, if writers are interested in working in larger industry settings, it is important that they acquire the skills needed to remain competitive in the workplace because automation is reducing staff within writing teams. In particular, writers working in the large-scale enterprises should understand that the risk to losing their jobs is very real as companies increasingly rely on technological solutions (along with lower paid staff in other countries) to reduce costs.

OTHER FRAMEWORKS FOR VIRTUAL COLLABORATIVE WRITING

As technologies that writers use change, thereby affecting how collaborative writing occurs, it is important to consider certain theories pertaining to technology and its impact on communication. Theories of technology and CMC are valuable to understanding virtual collaborative writing because they help to frame and describe certain dynamics of this writing model. Often-cited theories include media richness, social presence, activity, systems, and new media theories.

Media Richness Theory and Collaborative Writing

The objects of study within *media richness theory* are the task being performed and the media used to facilitate it. The assumption is that given media will facilitate effective communication for a given task. Rice (1993) argued that different media are required for different tasks, which are distinguished by the amount of uncertainty associated with information and the potential for multiple definitions or interpretations to exist in a single exchange. Rich media may be able to minimize reader uncertainty and multiple interpretations by providing a sufficient number of cues; allowing for immediate feedback, it uses language naturally and it facilitates some degree of personal focus (Bouwman, et al., 2003, p. 97). Generally, traditional face-to-face communication is considered the richest medium. For example, if two people are communicating with each other in a face-to-face

setting, the listener is able to see the communicator's visual cues and hear voice inflections that help to understand a message, while the speaker is able to see the listener's reaction and respond to any potential confusion immediately. The ability to minimize ambiguity in a given message is what makes a medium "rich." Relative to given tasks, a rich medium would be encouraged for tasks that involve much potential for uncertainty of information and multiple meanings. Tasks that involve less potential for such occurrences could be supported by less rich media. However, it is impossible to determine objectively which combination of task-media is best for a given event, unless relationships within a given task organization are well defined (that is, people involved know each other well and understand each other's communication styles). Human factors, such as different proficiencies with certain media and a lack of understanding of other team members involved in the task affect the potential for ambiguity to occur.

Several studies document the difficulty of ascertaining whether a particular technology can facilitate the most effective communication (Dennis and Kinney, 1998; D'ambra, et al., 1998). D'ambra et al. especially called attention to the fact that equivocality cannot be objectively defined. They stated: "The results obtained provide evidence to suggest that equivocality may not be unidimensional, and that media richness is perceived multidimensional in terms of the information carrying capacity of media. The findings on dimensionality of equivocality raise doubts as to the basic assumptions of this concept and media richness theory" (p. 164). Relative to virtual collaborative writing, if relationships between collaborators are well defined and everyone in the team has equal proficiency with a given medium, all participants may be able to use that medium for all tasks. However, if relationships are not well defined and collaborators have different proficiencies with media, they will need the richest media available to them to facilitate communication. The less knowledge collaborators have of each other's behavior and ways others will react to a given message, the more they need to have richer media available to avoid ambiguities or misunderstandings.

With the vast number of technologies available, virtual teams must consider carefully which technologies suit their purposes. Media richness theory points the way here, examining which types of technologies are most suitable for which type of work (Andres, 2002) because not all writing activities are accomplished equally well by all media. In short, media richness theory gauges how much content a particular medium can carry, hypothesizing that one reason virtual teams succeed (or fail) rests on the team's choice of technology. Individual technologies vary in the amount of feedback they allow; the number of verbal, nonverbal, and back-channeling cues available; and the emotional communication possibilities. Media richness theory research suggests that virtual teams face significant challenges because of the technology, positing that:

- Electronic communication leads to increased negative communication, including assertive hostile language.
- Electronic communication can create a sense of depersonalization due to lack of social context cues.
- Electronic communication is perceived as less warm than face-to-face interaction.
- Consensus building is easier in face-to-face teams than in similar teams working through computer-mediated technology.
- When given a limited time frame, face-to-face teams outperform virtual teams. (Andres, 2002)

Social Presence Theory and Collaborative Writing

Another framework that attempts to account for the relationship between media used in communi-

cation and the people involved is *social presence theory*. Many users perceive differences between the kinds of communication that can occur with different media: more "social" communication can occur when communicators are physically present to each other, as in face-to-face communication; while more formal communication is likely to occur when that physical presence is lacking, as in e-mail. Social presence theory attempts to understand to what degree certain media facilitate social presence, and therefore more effective communication. The more a medium facilitates communication attributes associated with physical presence—such as nonverbal cues or an image of the person with whom one is communicating—the more social the communication may be (Bouwman, et al., 2003, p. 96).

While high social presence is desired for communication, the more proficient one becomes with a given medium and with collaborators, the less the feeling of social presence may be needed. If those who are communicating to each other using e-mail or IM technology, for example, know what the others look like and understand each others' use of emoticons to represent nonverbal cues, then the perception of social presence can be very high. If the communicators do not know what the others look like and do not know the others' usage of emoticons, social presence will be low.

Consequently, social presence cannot be objectively identified relative to a given technology or medium. Felt social presence depends on the communicators' relationship with each other and the technology used for communication. Much as in the case of media richness theory, one may be less sensitive in communicating a given message when in the presence of another because the other person may understand the message better with the speaker's nonverbal cues or voice inflection. Such paralinguistic features are absent from the message in an e-mail.

Given that media richness and social presence theories often are considered together, an example that combines them would involve two team members who have access to each other face-to-face but do some work electronically. They are able to understand each other well when speaking face-to-face; however, they sometimes misunderstand each other's meaning when e-mailing each other about certain issues with the project. One e-mails the other the following message in an effort to encourage the reader to revise a particular graphic:

Writer 1: *"I'm not sure that we can use the graphic showing a diagram of the entire system because it seems very convoluted."*

The second writer perceives this to suggest that the diagram, which he developed, is weak and becomes troubled by the suggestion.

Writer 2: *"Well, if you don't think it can work, we can get rid of it."*

While the first writer may have been able to offer a nonverbal cue or respond immediately to the second member's response by reassuring him that she thought the graphic would be useful but needed to be modified, the fact that the messages were exchanged asynchronously via e-mail slows that potential response, and the second writer feels disappointed and begins to give up on the graphic entirely.

In this example, the lack of presence associated with e-mail makes it a less-rich medium for that particular situation; part of that lack of richness is due to its asynchronous nature, as Chapter 1 discusses. Face-to-face communication would be richer in that it would provide an opportunity for more clarity in the message and facilitate immediate feedback if there were any misunderstanding; this richness is not surprising because face-to-face communication is the most immediate of all synchronous communication types.

Activity Theory and Collaborative Writing

Activity theory provides another framework that is associated largely with social and cultural considerations of uses of available technologies in writing practices. This theory considers that the contexts—or cultures—in which people work—including their technological tools, environment, and social structure—shape their behaviors. Leont'ev (1978) and Vygotsky (1978) introduced a framework for analyzing variables associated with human activity; these included an understanding of the subject's internalization of external events and experiences and the externalized processes associated with the activity, an understanding of the object of the subject's efforts—that is, what is motivating the activity toward some end, and an understanding of how the subject uses tools to accomplish that object. Figure 1 shows this representation relative to a team of writers using a wiki to collaborate on a particular document.

The team's goal is to develop the document, and they use a particular wiki to mediate the activity of performing that task. The tools can be broken down into tools for writing and tools for collaborating. The boundary between these two functions—writing and collaborating—in team writing projects is blurred, so scholarship has discussed tools relative to both functions. As Nardi (1996) stated, "the object of AT [activity

Figure 1. Original diagram of activity theory applied to VCW

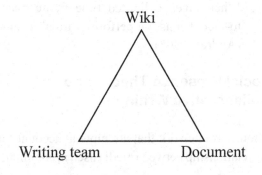

theory] is to understand the unity of consciousness and activity" (p. 7). In activity theory, artifacts are mediators of human thought and behavior. Artifacts, here, are the tools—material and intellectual—used by humans to complete an activity. Relative to human-computer interaction (HCI), an activity theory analysis would consider how subjects use computer tools to mediate an activity.

Engeström (1987) introduced the notion that certain external factors influence how the subject might use tools. While the original model (Leont'ev, 1978; Vygotsky, 1978) placed the subject with the mediation tools and object, it did not consider some external social elements that affect the subject's choice and use of tools and how the subject addressed the object. Engeström argued that one's community, the generally accepted or established rules associated with how that community might behave in completing a given activity, and how work on an activity may be divided all influence how a team uses tools to complete a task. Engeström's diagram added the three generalized components of community, rules, and division of labor. Figure 2 shows this conception of activity theory, expanding on the example provided in Figure 1.

The first three constructs are the same as Leont'ev (1978) and Vygotsky's (1978); however, Engeström (1987) recognized that work on a writing project may be divided into different subtasks such that each writer on the team may have different responsibilities, that the company (or community) affects how one uses the wiki to mediate the activity, and that there may be certain rules or parameters applied to the activity that affect how one can accomplish the task. For instance, the following list breaks down the different parts relative to an example pertaining to virtual collaborative writing:

- **Tool:** Wiki used among all of the team members to compose a single document: a user manual for a new piece of software.
- **Object:** Final version of the manual under development.
- **Writing team:** Those involved in the collaboration and their respective backgrounds. One may be expert in document design, and two may be engineers who developed the software specifically.
- **Rules:** Parameters the project manager develops, in consultation with team members or not, that members will use to guide their work. In this project, the members are to collaborate collectively.
- **Community:** The company or the industry in which the team is working. This also may include the markets to which the team is trying to appeal or the users of the software.
- **Division of labor:** Each member has his or her own specialty and proficiency with the writing tools such that the document

Figure 2. Engeström's diagram of activity theory applied to VCW

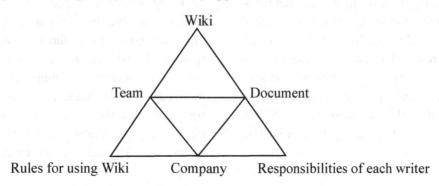

designer understands best how to use a word processing program to integrate images and graphics that will enable the reader to understand the software. The engineers may have their own expertise with the software's development and can contribute that information. A fourth member of the team may not be expert with the technology and can act as a test user and provide feedback to the group developing the document.

Some elements of Engeström's diagram of activity theory are useful for analyzing activity associated with virtual collaborative writing because it considers more variables and levels of actions. Activity theory proves useful for understanding and analyzing dynamics of virtual collaborative writing. Prior studies that have applied activity theory to an analysis of collaborative writing specifically have focused attention on the relationship between task and team, assuming a common understanding among participants of the tools used in this activity, and on distributed knowledge within such systems. That is, researchers have approached the study of collaboration and application of activity theory to this study assuming that the subject is a group and that each member has similar background to the others, though each with his or her own perspective. The study, then, focuses on how the group uses certain tools to mediate their actions toward completing the task. Activity theory is used in the analysis to try to understand the relationship among the actors; the tools they use; what rules, if any, affect the performance or use of tools; and how the work is divided. Activity theory is not applied as a prescriptive analysis—attempting to predict behaviors or outcomes. Instead, it is used as a descriptive analysis relative to a particular case in order to understand how the actors may apply a given set of tools in a particular writing situation.

This analysis can help in developing technologies that accommodate certain activities among actors. Bracewell and Witte (2003) attempted to refine constructs that consider psychological elements of collaborative writing in the workplace. They observed that activity theory research into collaborative writing has "aimed to capture the influence and interaction of cultural, historical, and social factors for particular human acts, including that of producing and using written text" (p. 513). Acknowledging some confusion over the unit of analysis of activity theory, Witte and Haas (2005) indicated that the unit of analysis is the tool used to mediate activity. In virtual collaborative environments, the collaborative writing technologies would be those tools.

Schendel, et al. (2004) identified four axioms associated with CMC and collaborative literacy. Two of these have immediate application to activity theory: "Processes of collaboration shape technology even as technology shapes collaborative processes" (p. 202), and "online collaboration produces artifacts that can be used for systematic analysis and theory building" (p. 205). Beck (1995) presented a case that demonstrates these axioms: two writers working collaboratively from different locations some distance apart established rules, or syntax, of interaction when the network they were using failed on a couple of occasions. The writers were not able to receive messages that had been sent, and when they realized this, they decided to build redundancy into their process. They explained: "Repeating issues was a way of keeping them salient. Given that the technology could not be fully trusted to deliver messages, an amount of double checking may have ensured that important points really did get communicated" (p. 59). The writers also used e-mail messages for certain kinds of communication: they summarized comments made in a manuscript, which was attached to the message, and they also highlighted certain comments included in the attached manuscript. Throughout this case, the writers saved drafts to document any changes, which enabled them to refer to a previous draft in case the dynamics of the anticipated output changed, facilitating use of text from a previous draft (p. 64). This example illustrates how the tools used in virtual collaborative writing can disrupt the collaborative writing process. Activity theory would help people understand what tools negatively or positively affected collaboration and why. A future application, then, can integrate this understanding toward optimizing use of the tools within the collaborative framework.

Activity theory's consideration of how artifacts are culturally mediated and how artifacts mediate activity opens the door to applying it to understanding how technology is used in an activity. Technology can be both a facilitator and a constraint. How people use technology also may be influenced culturally by interactions with others in their community; one user may be more technically astute than another and, consequently, more likely to use a certain technology for certain purposes than another would use that technology. Haas (1996) observed that users shape technologies through their thinking about and discussing them; artifacts are not static. A particular writer may understand that he can use Word in certain ways, not having any experience with the diagramming tools available within Word; however, a second writer may understand how to use graphic tools to create diagrams in Word effectively. The two writers use a single tool in different ways because of their perspectives about that single tool. Pargman (2003) also observed the relationship between the user and the technology; a tool becomes "an instrument only when the subject is able to... subordinate it as a means to accomplish his/her ends" (p. 5). Technological artifacts are shaped through sociological dynamics. Users perceive certain possibilities and limitations of a given artifact, and they attempt to work around perceived problems within the framework of their understanding of an artifact's potential.

Because the ways that people use certain tools is affected by how they perceive they can use those tools, it is important to consider a theory that addresses such perceptions. Norman (2002) observed that visual cues inform users of a given technology's abilities, and they also shed light on what that technology cannot do. Norman emphasized visibility of tools and functions and how affordances and constraints are relative to what the user can or cannot see of potential functions and ways to operate the artifact. Affordances and constraints of a given tool are relative to the user's previous experiences with similar tools or technologies; that is, an affordance may be derived from a physical, visible attribute that readily assimilates the user's past experience with another technology, while a constraint may be derived from an attribute of the other, referent technology that is not visible in or readily transferred to the newer technology. Using the earlier example of the two writers who use a word processing program in different ways, the first writer perceives that the program cannot create diagrams effectively because he has not learned how to use it for that purpose; he sees it as being constrained in that he cannot use the tool to create a diagram. However, the second writer has learned the capability of the program to create diagrams, and she applies her understanding of its affordances to create effective diagrams.

Norman stated that "Affordances can signal how an object can be moved, what it will support.... Affordances suggest a range of possibilities, constraints limit the number of alternatives" (p. 82). A constraint can be a visual cue that suggests a limitation (that is, it tells us in some way not to use it a certain way or limits how we can use it), but if we integrate the notion of perception into consideration, then it may suggest a perceived limitation that does not actually exist. For example, a swinging door has on either side a plate, indicating that it should be pushed. As one approaches it for the first time, not knowing that it is a swinging door, one sees the plate and understands that it ought to be pushed, but also may assume that it can only be opened by pushing from that side and the other side has a handle to pull the door open from that particular side. This perception of it as opening only one way may be a constraint (87-88). Again, the first writer in the earlier example perceives a constraint in the word processing program's ability to generate diagrams that does not actually exist. Consequently, this perception limits how he uses it, while the second writer, who is able to use the program to create diagrams, perceives no such limitation and uses it freely to create diagrams.

When analyzing how collaborators use particular tools to facilitate collaborative writing, it is important to consider how users perceive a given tool's affordances and constraints. These perceptions will affect how the tool itself is used. This activity analysis also is useful in designing collaborative technologies. Usability testing may be considered a form of affordances and constraints analysis.

Systems Theory and Collaborative Writing

Generally, *systems theory* considers the interrelationship of variables that influence a given organizational system. The goal of a systems theory analysis of a given phenomenon is to understand how a change in one variable may affect the rest of the components in the system and, consequently, the outcome or product of the system's processes. The nature of the systems, then, is a component of whether the organization functions in various ways. As such, it might be useful to consider the system as the organizational culture that, as the first principle that grounds this book (see Chapter 1) indicates, needs to adjust to accommodate effective collaboration among writers and other team members.

Systems analysis, which uses systems theory principles, is a practitioner-oriented approach to developing efficient processes. If one part of a given system is changed, then the outcome of that system may be affected. Systems analysis recommendations may provide alternatives for a more efficient process or more effective method of arriving at a given, desirable outcome. For example, if a four-person writing team is using serial collaboration, each writer represents a single step in the writing system. It may be possible, though, to combine two writers into a single step, thus making the system more efficient.

Systems can be characterized as either *closed* or *open*. A *closed system* limits the number of variables that may affect it to those that come into immediate contact with the various parts of that system. Examples of variables in a closed system within a collaborative writing system include the members of the group, their respective departments or units, and the methods they use to interact and draft text. An *open system* allows for consideration of indirect variables and their impact on the system. An example of an open system would extend the prior closed-system example variables to include the amount of money an organization could invest in certain technology to facilitate collaborative writing; the relationship among the organization and its competitors, customers or suppliers, and any Federal policies that affect competition or innovation.

Bouldin and Odell (1993) called for systems theory approaches to analyzing writing in workplaces, recognizing the collaborative nature of writing in such settings and that one's understanding of a phenomenon should be holistic. Generally, many factors affect how communication occurs in the workplace including, but not limited to, the general macro-economy, positions held by communicators, and relationships with each other as well as office politics. Further, a writer who is nervous about losing a job may be inclined to avoid using a certain technology that could negatively affect his or her performance, such as one with which he or she has little experience. Again, using the example developed in the discussion of activity theory earlier, the first of the two writers with differing experiences with the word processing program's diagramming abilities may not integrate a diagram into a given document, or will copy and paste from a different tool with which he created a diagram to develop a needed diagram; whereas the second writer is able to compose entirely with the program. Dias, et al. (1999) applied a form of systems theory—distributed cognition—to understanding how writing and collaboration act to disseminate knowledge within organizations.

Based on an extensive system theory–related study in which face-to-face collaboration was compared with distance, synchronous collaboration, Cerratto and Rodriguez (2002) recommended that collaborative writing tools should support sharing of information and work. Additionally, collaborative writing tools should:

- Support focused discussion on two levels with one level taking the document as a whole and the other on a particular part of the document.
- Allow them to continue to use the word processor they are used to and not detach writers from their working environments.
- Inform about co-writers' activity and about the writing pace of co-writers.
- Allow the audience to have different views of the document in relation to their interests in the document. During the writing process, it may occur that one writer is more linked to or interested in certain parts of the document.
- Support the integration of co-writers so that they are incorporated smoothly with the process in ways that minimize transition-based delays.
- Support individual or private work. (pp. 149-151)

Generally, a systems theory approach to analyzing virtual collaborative writing combines consideration of the variables influencing those

who collaborate on a given project relative to understanding how each component contributes to the system in a particular way. The following discussion identifies theories that consider collaborative writing within a system, although each takes a different perspective toward that analysis. Rhetorical theories tend to focus attention on the audience and its needs. Social theories focus attention on interaction among participants, whether that interaction is among writers and readers or just among writers. Other theories examine how the particular technology involved influences the activity and communication dynamics. However, even some of these theories integrate social attributes of the system of collaborative writing activity.

New Media Theory and Collaborative Writing

Authors writing about virtual collaboration in the twenty-first-century workplace typically use the framework of either *new media theory* or rhetoric, sometimes a combination of both. New media theory is useful because it helps people understand the changing nature of both the composing process and product. According to new media theory, the composing process is even more multidirectional and nonlinear than the "pre-digital era" theorists of the writing process would have us believe. Simultaneously, new media theory recognizes that twenty-first-century writing moves beyond words alone; it often uses images, video, hyperlinks, and even sound (see especially Chapters 19, 20, and 21). Thus, composing in the twenty-first century may mean operating not just with words but also with other media. Manovich (2007) provided several compelling examples of texts that mix different media and genres to considerable rhetorical effects.

Generally, new media theory attempts to answer the question of what happens to writing and communication when it is done through means other than traditional print-linguistic forms of representation such as audiovisual media or Web tools with which one can develop various page designs. This framework considers the rhetorical and communicative effects of using images, video, sound, hypermedia, or a combination of those and other media.

Barton (2008) used new media theory to discuss workplace collaboration. He built his argument from Reich's (1992) ideas and invoked the notion of the symbolic-analytic worker. More importantly, however, Barton's (2008) essay illuminated the five hallmarks of the so-called new media and their relation to the practices of the virtual workplace in general and collaborative writing in particular: play, space, identity, simulation, and collaboration (pp. 389-390; see also Manovich, 2007). For Barton (2008), the ability of writers in the virtual workplace was closely linked to the design of their workspace space and to the extent to which their managers allow and encourage "play" at work. Influenced not only by new media theory but also by post-modern ideas about the collaborative nature of reading, writing, and communication, Barton stated that "New Media theory has much to offer anyone interested in building, maintaining, or participating in virtual workplaces" (p. 392). Among future trends in workplace collaboration, Barton considered the increased role of the symbolic analyst, whom he calls "the individual most fit for survival in the virtual workplace" (p. 393). One important competency that symbolic analysis possesses, according to Barton, is the ability to "arrange symbols and algorithms in exciting new combinations; to forge new connections and possibilities for collaboration" (p. 393).

On the other hand, Brewer (2008) called rhetoric "the main unit of exchange" in the virtual workplace (pp. 3-5). This attention to rhetoric suggests Brewer's concern with the effectiveness of workplace communication. Brewer claimed that when it comes to movement of information, virtual workplaces have both significant advantages and drawbacks. The most significant advantage that the virtual workplace affords writers is the ability to "cross boundaries of space, time, organizations and hierarchies, enabling organizations to assemble teams that are best suited for the task" (p. 4). Brewer also claimed that the virtual workplace is "more democratic and less centralized" (p. 4); if true, then all these gains certainly would be important for the collaborating writer. At the same time, however, Brewer argued that virtual workplaces have significant negative implications for the collaborating writer. Among these negative aspects, she counted loss of trust and loss of social engagement among members of virtual teams (p. 5). This lack of face-to-face social engagement and interaction, Brewer wrote, can cost virtual teams success in a given project (pp. 5-6). Also important to Brewer was the loss of face-to-face intercultural communication, which currently may be replaced with an e-mail exchange or a video conference. In order to ensure success of virtual workplace collaboration, Brewer called for further research into "new types" of rhetoric that virtual workplaces can afford and into better configurations of virtual workplaces, which would allow better information exchange (p. 12).

In using rhetoric as the theoretical framework, Brewer joined a number of other thinkers. Zappen (2005) wrote that the concept of digital rhetoric "encompasses a wide range of issues, including novel strategies of self-expression and collaboration, the characteristics, affordances, and constraints of the new digital media, and the formation of identities and communities in digital spaces" (p. 319). Referring to work by Gurak (2001, 1997) and others, Zappen (2005) stated that digital rhetoric allows us to understand "the transformation of the old rhetoric of persuasion into a new digital rhetoric that encourages self-expression, participation, and creative collaboration" (p. 321). According to Zappen's analysis, the essence and the primary goal of digital rhetoric may be not "moving audiences to action or belief," but "participation and creative collaboration for the purpose of building communities of shared interest" (p. 322). Of course, examples of such "communities of shared interest" are numerous: community blogs, wikis, social networking groups, parts of virtual worlds like Second Life, and so on. Zappen concluded by suggesting that this new rhetoric's emphasis on participation and collaboration can challenge and transform some long-established professional and academic practices (pp. 323-324).

Johnson-Eilola (1999) made clear the idea of "networked writing" and of digital rhetoric's attention to the compositing process over product. The primary audience for his work was writing teachers, but practicing workplace writers have much to learn from the argument, too. Drawing on social constructivist rhetoric and hypertext theory, Johnson-Eilola argued that texts should be seen primarily not as fixed and stable products but as fluid and ever-changing networks of ideas. Acknowledging that writers increasingly use hyperlinks and hypertexts, Johnson-Eilola nevertheless argued that such use usually promotes "traditional notions of authorship" as an individualistic activity (p. 19). He called, instead, for an increased attention to seeing writing as a process of networking and connection rather than simple production of texts (pp. 19-25). Such a process is congruent with this book's understanding of a paradigm shift from that of whole book/single writer to content units/multiple writers (see Chapter 1). Although his work did not mention workplace writing collaboration directly, he suggested that writers need to pay more attention to what happens when texts are created from many parts and by many people. To be a successful collaborator, one must, to a degree, squelch one's own writer's ego: "Reconfiguring writing as social construction requires a corresponding recognition of deep responsibility to communities that extends beyond merely asking students to collaborate on producing a text" (p. 26). Such responsibility to communities is necessary in virtual collaborative workplace writing.

CONCLUSION

This chapter has considered a variety of frameworks with which to understand virtual collaborative writing. It has taken the position that writing is first and foremost a rhetorical act, although not all frameworks directly acknowledge this primary rhetorical nature. There are, to be sure, many ways to bridge the gap between the primarily theoretical focus of academic educators and workplace-based writing professionals. These frameworks provide but a beginning. Ongoing collaboration between academic and business professions is needed to study virtual collaborative writing and to find frameworks that help to identify and describe best practices in virtual collaborative writing.

Various chapters in this book integrate elements from one or more of the frameworks discussed in this chapter. Chapters that integrate elements of activity theory include Chapters 4, 6, and 19. Chapters that integrate elements of social presence and media richness theories include Chapters 3, 5, 7, and 21. Chapter 17 integrates elements of affordances and constraints analysis. Chapter 20 discusses elements involved with new media theory, while Chapters 19 and 21 use this theory more implicitly.

Writing is heavily situated within specific contexts; what works in one setting may not work in another. Consequently, it is very difficult to pinpoint specific guidelines to facilitate decision-making in particular cases that consistently will meet a collaborative writing team's needs. To this end, however, the remaining chapters in this book offer specific cases and experiences to which these frameworks can be applied. Additionally, by combining the principles discussed in Chapter 1 with theories of virtual collaborative writing and the cases and processes described in the following chapters, project managers and writers may be able to generate their own company's or team's principles to guide decision-making.

REFERENCES

Alexander, P. A., Schallert, D. L., & Hare, V. C. (1991). Coming to terms: How researchers in learning and literacy talk about knowledge. *Review of Educational Research, 61*, 315–343.

Andres, H. P. (2002). A comparison of face-to-face and virtual software development teams. *Team Performance Management, 8*, 39–48. doi:10.1108/13527590210425077

Aristotle. (1975). *The art of rhetoric. (Trans. John Henry Freese). The Loeb Classical Library.* Cambridge, MA: Harvard University Press.

Barton, M. (2008). New Media and the virtual workplace. In Zemliansky, P., & St. Amant, K. (Eds.), *Handbook of research on virtual workplaces and the new nature of business practices* (pp. 382–394). Hershey, PA: IGI Global.

Beautfort, A. (1999). *Writing in the real world: Making the transition from school to work.* New York: Teachers College Press.

Beck, E. (1995). Changing documents/documenting changes: Using computers for collaborative writing over distance. In Star, S. (Ed.), *The cultures of computing* (pp. 53–68). Oxford, UK: Blackwell.

Bouldin, T., & Odell, L. (1993). Surveying the field and looking ahead: A systems theory perspective on research on writing in the workplace. In Spilka, R. (Ed.), *Writing in the workplace: New Research perspectives* (pp. 268–281). Carbondale, IL: Southern Illinois University Press.

Bouwman, H., van den Hoof, B., van de Wijngaert, L., & van Dijk, J. (2005). *Information and communication technology in organizations. Adaption, implementation, use and effects.* London: Sage.

Bracewell, R. J., & Witte, S. P. (2003). Tasks, ensembles, and activity: Linkages between text production and situation of use in the workplace. *Written Communication, 20*(4), 511–559. doi:10.1177/0741088303260691

Brewer, P. E. (2008). Gaines and Losses in the rhetoric of virtual workplace. In Zemliansky, P., & St. Amant, K. (Eds.), *Handbook of research on virtual workplaces and the new nature of business practices* (pp. 1–14). Hershey, PA: IGI Global.

Cerratto, T., & Rodrigues, H. (2002). Studies of computer supported collaborative writing: Implications for system design. In Blay-Fornarino, M., Pinna-Dery, A., Schmidt, K., & Zaraté, P. (Eds.), *Cooperative systems design* (pp. 139–154). Amsterdam: IOS Press.

D'Ambra, J. G. (1995). *A field study of information technology, task equivocality, media richness and media preference.* Dissertation. The University of New South Wales, School of Information Systems.

Daugherty, M., & Funke, B. L. (1998). University faculty and student perceptions of web-based instruction. *Journal of Distance Education, 13*(1), 21–39.

Dede, C. (1995). The evolution of constructivist learning environments: Immersion in distributed, Virtual worlds. *Educational Technology, 35*(5), 46–52.

DeMarco, T., & Lister, T. (1986). *Peopleware: Productive projects and teams.* New York: Dorset House.

Dennis, A. R., & Kinney, S. T. (1998). Testing media richness theory in the New Media: The effects of cues, feedback, and task equivocality. *Information Systems Research, 9*, 256–274. doi:10.1287/isre.9.3.256

Eble, M. F. (2009). Digital delivery and communication technologies: Understanding content management systems through rhetorical theory. In Pullman, G., & Gu, B. (Eds.), *Content Management: Bridging the gap between theory and practice* (pp. 94–95). Amityville, NY: Baywood Publishing Company, Inc.

Engeström, Y. (1987). Learning by expanding. Helsinki: Orienta-Konsultit.

Bracewell, R. J. & Witte, S. P. (1987) Tasks, ensenbles, and activity: Linkages between text production an situation use of the workplace. *Written Communication, 20*(4), 511-559.

Erickson, F. (1987). Transformation and school success: The politics and culture of educational achievement. *Anthropology & Education Quarterly, 18,* 335–356. doi:10.1525/aeq.1987.18.4.04x0023w

Erkins, G. (2005). Coordination process in computer supported collaborative writing. *Computers in Human Behavior, 21,* 463–486. doi:10.1016/j.chb.2004.10.038

Ewald, H. R., & Burnett, R. E. (1996). *Business communication.* New York: Prentice Hall.

Forman, J. (1990). Leadership dynamics of computer-supported writing groups. *Computers and Composition, 7,* 35–46. doi:10.1016/S8755-4615(05)80025-8

Gee, J. P. (2004). *Situated language and learning.* New York: Routledge.

Gee, J. P. (2008). *Social linguistics and literacies: Ideology in Discourses* (3rd ed.). New York: Routledge. (Original work published 1990)

Geisler, C. (2001, July). IText: Future directions for research on the relationship between information technology and writing. *Journal of Business and Technical Communication, 15*(3), 269–308. doi:10.1177/105065190101500302

Gurak, L. J. (1997). *Persuasion and privacy in cyberspace: The online protests over Lotus MarketPlace and the clipper chip.* New Haven, CT: Yale University Press.

Gurak, L. J. (2001). *Cyberliteracy: Navigating the Internet with awareness.* New Haven, CT: Yale University Press.

Haas, C. (1996). *Writing technologies: Studies on the materiality of literacy.* Mahwah, NJ: Lawrence Erlbaum Associates.

Haas, C. (1999). On the relationship between old and new technologies. *Computers and Composition, 16,* 209–228. doi:10.1016/S8755-4615(99)00003-1

Heath, S. B. (1983). *Ways with words: Language, life, and work in communities and classrooms.* New York: Cambridge University Press.

Hewett, B. L., & Ehmann, C. (2004). *Preparing educators for online writing instruction: Principles and processes.* Urbana, IL: NCTE.

Hull, G. (2000). Critical literacy at work. *Journal of Adolescent & Adult Literacy, 43,* 648–652.

IBM. (2008). *The new collaboration: Enabling innovation, changing the workplace* (white paper). Accessed August 9, 2009 at http://www-935.ibm.com/services/us/cio/pdf/new-collaboration-white-paper.pdf

Johnson, T. S., Smagorinsky, P., Thompson, L., & Fry, P. G. (2003). Learning to teach the five-paragraph theme. *Research in the Teaching of English, 38,* 136–176.

Johnson-Eilola, J. (1999). Negative Spaces: From Production to Connection in Composition. In Taylor, T., & Ward, I. (Eds.), *Dialogic Spaces* (pp. 17–33). Urbana, IL: NCTE.

Johnson-Eilola, J. (2005). *Datacloud: Toward a new theory of online work.* Creeskill, NY: Hampton Press.

Lam, E. (2006). Culture and learning in the context of globalization: Research directions. *Review of Research in Education, 30,* 213–237. doi:10.3102/0091732X030001213

Leont'ev, A. N. (1978). *Activity, consciousness and personality. (Translated from original Russian by Marie J. Hall).* Englewood Cliffs: Prentice-Hall.

Manovich, L. (2007). *Understanding hybrid media*. Accessed October 28, 2009 from http://www.manovich.net/DOCS/hybrid_media_pictures.doc

Miller, C. R. (1979). A humanistic rationale for technical writing. *College English, 40,* 610–617. doi:10.2307/375964

Miller, C. R. (1989). What's practical about technical writing. In Fearing, B. E., & Sparrow, W. K. (Eds.), *Technical writing: Theory and practice* (pp. 14–27). NY: MLA.

Miller, C. R. (2004). Expertise and agency: Transformations of ethos in human-computer interaction. In Hyde, M. (Ed.), *The ethos of rhetoric* (pp. 197–218). Columbia, SC: University of South Carolina Press.

Nardi, B. (1996). Studying context: Comparison of activity theory, situated action and distributed cognition. In Nardi, B. (Ed.), *Context and consciousness: Activity theory and human-computer interaction* (pp. 69–102). Cambridge, MA: MIT Press.

National Writing Project, & Nagin, C. (2003). *Because writing matters*. San Francisco: Jossey-Bass.

National Writing Project. (2008). *Research brief: Writing project professional development for teachers yields gains in student writing achievement*. Retrieved July 23, 2009 from http://www.nwp.org/cs/public/download/nwp_file/10683/NWP_Research_Brief_2008.pdf?x-r=pcfile_d

Norman, D. A. (2002). *The design of everyday things*. New York: Basic Books.

Northwest Regional Educational Laboratory. (2009). *6+1 trait writing*. Retrieved July 23, 2009 from http://www.thetraits.org/index.php

Pargman, T. C. (2003). Collaborating with writing tools. Retrieved March 9, 2007 from http://journals.ohiolink.edu/ejc/xml_ft.cgi/Cerratto_Pargman_Teresa.html

Partnership for 21st Century Schools. (2006). *Are they really ready to work?: Employers' perspectives on the basic knowledge and applied skills of new entrants to the 21st century U.S. workforce*. Retrieved August 9, 2009 from http://www.21stcenturyskills.org/documents/FINAL_REPORT_PDF09-29-06.pdf

Perelman, C., & Olbrechts-Tyteca, L. (1969). *The new rhetoric: A treatise on argumentation*. Notre Dame: University of Notre Dame Press.

Rainie, L. (2006). *New workers, new workplaces*. Retrieved August 5, 2009 from http://www.pewinternet.org/Presentations/2006/New-Workers-New-Workplaces.aspx

Reich, R. (1991). *The work of nations: Preparing ourselves for 21st century capitalism*. New York: A.A. Knopf.

Rice, R. E. (1993). Media appropriateness: Using social presence theory to compare traditional and new organizational media. *Human Communication Research, 19*(4), 451–484. doi:10.1111/j.1468-2958.1993.tb00309.x

Robidoux, C. (2008). Rhetorically structured content: Developing a collaborative single-sourcing curriculum. *Technical Communication Quarterly, 17*, 110–135. doi:10.1080/10572250701595652

Rorschach, E. (2004). The five-paragraph theme redux. *Quarterly of the National Writing Project, 26*(1), 16–25.

Rosen, E. (2007). *The culture of collaboration*. San Francisco: Red Ape.

Rovai, A., & Jordan, H. (2004). Blended learning and sense of community: A comparative analysis with traditional and fully online graduate courses. *The International Review of Research in Open and Distance Learning, 5*(2). Retrieved October 27, 2009 from http://www.irrodl.org/index.php/irrodl/article/view/192/274

Rumelhart, D. E. (1980). Schemata: The building blocks of cognition. In Spiro, R. J., Bruce, B. C., & Brewer, W. F. (Eds.), *Theoretical issues in reading comprehension* (pp. 33–58). Hillsdale, NJ: Erlbaum.

Schein, E. (2009). *The corporate culture survival guide* (2nd ed.). San Francisco: Jossey-Bass.

Schendel, E., et al. (2004). Toward a theory of online collaboration. In B. Huot, B. Stroble & C. Bazerman (Eds.), Multiple literacies for the 21st Century (pp. 195-209). Cresskill, NY: Hampton.

Selfe, C. (1992). Computer-based conversations and the changing nature of collaboration. In Forman, J. (Ed.), *New visions of collaborative writing* (pp. 147–169). Portsmouth, NH: Boynton-Cook.

Sharples, M. (1993). Research issues in the study of computer supported collaborative writing. In Sharples, M. (Ed.), *Computer supported collaborative writing* (pp. 9–28). London: Springer-Verlag.

Street, B. (1995). *Social literacies: Critical approaches to literacy development, ethnography, and education*. Reading, MA: Addison Wesley.

Tapscott, D., & Williams, A. D. (2006). *Wikinomics: How mass collaboration changes everything*. New York: Portfolio.

Tierney, R., & Pearson, P. D. (1983). Towards a composing model of reading. *Language Arts, 60*, 568–580.

Tierney, R., & Shanahan, T. (1991). Research on the reading-writing relationship: Interaction, transaction, and outcomes. In Barr, R., Kamil, M. L., Mosenthal, P., & Pearson, P. D. (Eds.), *Handbook of reading research* (*Vol. II*, pp. 246–280). White Plains, NY: Longman.

Vasont Systems. (2009). *Software: Vasont CMS*. Retrieved July 26, 2009 from http://www.vasont.com

Vygotsky, L. S. (1978). Mind in Society: The development of higher psychological processes. (M. Cole, V. John-Steiner, S. Scribner, & E. Souberman, Eds). Cambridge, MA: Harvard UP (Russian original work published in 1930).

Weiss, E. (2002). Egoless writing: Improving quality by replacing artistic impulse with engineering discipline. *Journal of Computer Documentation, 26*, 3–10. doi:10.1145/584731.584733

Wesley, K. (2000). The ill effects of the five paragraph theme. *English Journal, 90*, 57–60. doi:10.2307/821732

Witte, S. P., & Haas, C. (2005). Research in activity: An analysis of speed bumps as mediational means. *Written Communication, 22*, 127–165. doi:10.1177/0741088305274781

Zappen, J. P. (2005). Digital rhetoric: Toward an integrated theory. *Technical Communication Quarterly, 14*, 319–325. doi:10.1207/s15427625tcq1403_10

ENDNOTE

[1] See Robidoux (2008) for a discussion of reuse and repurposing that takes up the rhetorical dynamics of writers' intention, readers' uptake, and institutional context of use.

Section 2
Building a Virtual Writing Team

Chapter 3
Case Study: "Can You See Me?"
Writing toward Clarity in a Software Development Life Cycle

Anne DiPardo
University of Colorado, USA

Mike DiPardo
Chezelle Group, USA

ABSTRACT

This chapter presents a case study detailing how geographically dispersed software developers employ writing in the process of creating and troubleshooting products for use in the healthcare industry. It focuses particularly on their efforts to arrive at language that unambiguously reflects functional requirements and optimal design principles. After a brief history of the company and the evolution of its national and international virtual collaboration practices, the authors turn to the role of text across particular task cycles, exploring the uses of writing in generating, designing, and refining plans and products. Focusing on a series of three composing sequences, the authors highlight the incremental process by which the team moves toward a shared sense of understanding and linguistic precision. They argue that in contrast to common conceptions of texts as simple containers for preformed ideas, these episodes provide a more nuanced picture, as writing comes to play a central role in constituting and fine-tuning meaning and in maintaining strong working relationships throughout the processes of developing and refining products. They close with implications for preparing diverse virtual teams for participation in tasks that demand exacting uses of the written word.

INTRODUCTION

Back in the dawn of the digital era, an IBM® training film featured a classic Muppets sketch in which a wild-eyed, fang-toothed creature named Wheel-Stealer encounters a talking computer blandly reciting its own technical manual. The hungry Muppet proceeds to eat the machine, blowing up just as the computer can be heard explaining that its purpose is to create a huge explosion (Henson, 1971/2006). Then as now, it seems, when it comes to presenting technical information, clarity and timing matter quite a lot.

DOI: 10.4018/978-1-60566-994-6.ch003

An array of technical writing handbooks has flooded the market in the years since, each imploring readers to adopt a concise, easy-to-follow, and precise prose style (for example, Alred, Brusaw, & Oliu, 2003; O'Keefe & Pringle, 2000; Van Laan, Julian, & Hackos, 2001; Young, 2002). Given the ubiquity of such admonitions, one might hope that Wheel-Stealer would enjoy a happier outcome today. Then again, perhaps the enduring market for such resources testifies to the tenacity of the problem—for despite these efforts at fostering clarity, most of us know all too well the experience of intending to communicate one thing and being understood as meaning quite another. In contemporary geographically dispersed, high-technology workplaces, efforts to develop unambiguous prose—whether to inform in-house collaboration, to share information and ideas, or to provide guidance to clients—are fraught with uncertainty and complexity. As workers collaborate across divides that are linguistic and cultural as well as spatial and national, casting shared understandings in transparently precise prose remains an often elusive goal. It is one thing for self-help writers to call for writing that defies misinterpretation, but producing such prose can be quite another. As cross-national virtual collaborative writing becomes commonplace, workers must be closely attentive to the potential for miscommunications that, if left undetected, can result in confusion, time delays, and even project, product, or enterprise failure. Such miscommunication can be alleviated in part by considering ways to address the first and third principles that ground this book, which are to develop a culture of collaboration and to establish trust among team members. This chapter further illuminates these principles through an exploration of how these principles were realized in the working dynamics of a particular collaborative team.

The question of whether written texts can stand as unambiguous representations of meaning—representations, that is, that mean the same across places and times—has been hotly debated

for many years among scholars of literacy. In the latter twentieth century, several now-classic works argued that the advent of alphabetic literacy and explicit prose styles made possible new ways of thinking and reflecting. These were said to include not only the capacity to look back critically at one's own earlier words and deeds, but also to contemplate and critique history *writ large* (Goody & Watt, 1963; Havelock, 1980; Olson, 1977). In the decades since, many literacy researchers have taken issue with the notion that written texts can ever be so unambiguously explicit as to ensure stable meaning across readers and contexts (Olson, Bloome, Dyson, Gee, Nystrand, Purcell-Gates, & Wells, 2006). As writing scholars have turned to the importance of culture in shaping how texts are constructed, understood, and used, the field has come to recognize that no text—let alone drafts produced in the press of a workday—can ever be entirely safe from unintended interpretations and responses.

While the challenge of clearly communicating shared understandings has vexed writers through history, twenty-first century virtual workplaces are adding a formidable new set of wrinkles. Much remains to be learned concerning how geographically dispersed and culturally diverse collaborators use their interactions around written documents to recognize differences in their understandings, and how they go about formulating common language as they reach shared understandings. If achieving clarity in technical communication is a matter of moving incrementally toward less ambiguous language, then we need to know more about what this process entails, how collaborating writers think their way through it, and what is involved in helping new team members move into full participation.

Toward this end, this chapter presents several examples of virtual collaborative writing among members of an international software development team. We begin with a brief account of the company's history and evolving goals, tracing the evolution of its telecommuting workforce as emerging tools have supported increasingly substantive virtual collaboration. We then provide a few glimpses of the team's work at various points in the software development cycle, providing narratives that describe movement toward greater specificity and clarity in particular collaborative writing events. Finally, we reflect on the challenges this process dramatizes and its implications for preparing a new generation of digital workers for the demands of collaborative, team-based writing.

BACKGROUND: TELECOMMUTING WITH THE CHEZELLE GROUP

A global company headquartered in the western United States, The Chezelle Group (all proper names except for Mike's are pseudonyms) develops software for use in the healthcare industry. Founded by a small group of entrepreneurs in the mid-1980s, the company has since gone public and currently employs about 80 employees across the continental US, a workforce supplemented by approximately 20 international employees, based primarily in Eastern Europe.

One of the company's first telecommuters, Mike began working for Chezelle in 1991 from a home office in the Midwest. His tools at the time were reflective of a still-emerging Internet frontier: A 2400-baud modem, an early version of e-mail, and Gopher, a then newly released character-based Internet search engine. Given the limitations of these resources in fostering and sustaining close collaboration, Mike undertook a series of essentially independent tasks, supplementing digital communication with weekly analog phone conversations and quarterly visits to Chezelle's headquarters.

When Mike entered code into the company's West Coast server in the early 1990s, response time was so slow that he often had trouble sustaining a line of thought. File transfers were even slower, and responding to written texts involved the painstaking use of strikeout and manual inser-

tion of bolded or italicized comments. Because the computers of the day allowed only a single Internet-based application to run at any given time, shifting from coding to e-mailing required terminating one program and opening a new window.

Despite such limitations, written text figured prominently even then in Chezelle's software development life cycle (hereafter SDLC), which encompasses both initial product development and updates to existing products. The process involves the following series of five recursive steps, each carefully documented in continuously revised written texts:

1. **Defining requirements:** Identifying what the software needs to accomplish in a particular context of use, developing a clear analysis of project scope and intended functionality, and speaking with domain experts to ensure use of precise and mutually understood terminology.
2. **Analysis:** Determining how to bring to fruition a product that will fulfill the identified needs.
3. **Design:** Defining product architecture appropriate to clients' requirements and project scope.
4. **Development:** Writing code for the project.
5. **Testing:** Detecting bugs and assessing the efficacy of the program with reference to requirements and design.

Before the mid-1990s, much of the necessary collaboration throughout the SDLC occurred at Chezelle's headquarters, as workers met face-to-face to hammer out understandings, formulate progressively exacting written accounts of each stage in the process, and troubleshoot and refine the software. As the turn of a new century approached, improved and new technologies were enabling ever-closer long-distance collaboration. Coding and file transferring could be accomplished in the blink of an eye, the advent of change-tracking software was easing the burdens of collaborative writing, and multitasking across programs had become the norm. By the first years of the new millennium, Mike and his Chezelle colleagues were using such affordances as instant messaging (IM), desktop sharing, and free voice-over-Internet, as well as accessing a vast array of public and private online resources. Suddenly, distant colleagues could record Internet voice conversations and retain transcripts of IM sessions, using these artifacts as aids to memory and understanding. Having already experienced success with more cumbersome telecommuting relationships, Chezelle was well poised to carry long-distance collaboration to a new level.

This new intensity would involve not only colleagues across the U.S. but globally as well. By 2004, Mike was negotiating the SDLC through the frequent exchange of written texts with internationally based workers. At this writing, he has been working closely for several years with developers in Eastern Europe, holding daily voice-over-Internet and desktop-sharing meetings, corresponding many times daily by e-mail and IM, and collaboratively authoring documents specifying plans and refinements at each stage of the SDLC. Although Mike takes a lead role in facilitating the team's work, the Eastern European workers report to supervisors in a local company that arranges contracts with U.S. companies. All of the Eastern European team members speak English as a second or third language, while Mike knows only English. In recognition of the challenges inherent in the team's cross-cultural communication, Chezelle has provided coaching by management and intercultural-communication experts as well as funding opportunities for Mike and other Chezelle staff to work for extended periods at the Eastern European workers' offices.

The team's work is exacting, time-pressured, and often intense. Intended for use in the healthcare industry, the software that they produce is considered a medical device and is therefore subject to rigorous review in order to receive Federal Drug Administration clearance. Func-

tioning in a competitive global market, the team must meet demanding deadlines while maintaining an exceedingly high level of precision and responsiveness to feedback. Facilitated by strong relationships, a shared work ethic, and a wealth of daily communications, the team in many ways provides a best-case scenario—an instance, that is, of closely shared purpose, processes, and commitment to formulating common understandings. And yet, as we will see in the following snapshots of their work as a collaborative writing team, the need to negotiate misunderstandings and to move together toward an optimal degree of shared clarity is persistently present.

GETTING IT RIGHT: MOMENTS IN THE SDLC

We turn to brief portraits of three collaborative writing episodes situated at various points in the recursive SDLC, each illustrating challenges—interpersonal, cognitive, communicative, and technical—that the team negotiates on a regular basis. As these vignettes illustrate, the team's movement toward precise written language is enmeshed in its pursuit of shared conceptual understandings and closely connected to its commitment to fostering long-distance working relationships that promote a sense of solidarity and mutual understanding.

Thinking in Two Languages: A Project Scope Analysis

In addition to designing new products, the team regularly addresses client-reported issues and problems in existing software, which constitute an important source of input to the SDLC. As in the initial design process, this type of problem-solving activity begins with efforts to define requirements and assess the scope of a given issue. After Chezelle's client-support office has notified the team of a particular problem, a collaborative document is initiated in which team members record in detail their efforts to understand and address the issue until a resolution is reached. Progressively accurate and precise descriptions of a given problem are recorded in a left-hand column, while appropriate solutions are brainstormed and eventually finalized in a right-hand column; by clicking on a "history" link, users can view a time line of the project to date, including detailed information concerning which team members have entered project descriptions and solutions. Any team member can check out a given version history from a shared repository (referred to by the Eastern European team members as "the vault"), which is stored on a server at Chezelle's West Coast headquarters.

In this instance, a client had reported a problem with entering a small portion of its available healthcare data. Acting as project director, Mike initiated the task cycle by establishing a version history (initially a 9-page document, growing to 20 pages by the time the problem was resolved) and by asking the Eastern European team to discuss the document and record a proposed solution intended to generate further reflection and conversation. Through the group's daily voice-over-Internet meetings, Mike was aware that this task had fallen to a relatively new colleague—Karole, an analyst who happened to be one of several women who had joined the predominately male team just two months earlier. After an initial conversation about the problem, Karole noted that she would send Mike an updated version of the document as well as a testing protocol to guide further investigation of the client-reported concern.

What arrived in Mike's e-mail inbox the next day was an updated version with a new entry written by Karole in the solution column. Below an earlier comment that Mike had written indicating that the issue involved a particular type of coding problem, Karole had written a 5-line entry in her native language—save, that is, for periodic company-specific words in English. This marked the first time that a team member had written a version-history entry in a language

other than English, and Mike wrote back in a spirit of friendly protest: "I like this very much," he began, "but I am not smart enough to understand it! Could you translate it for me?" A few hours later, he sent a follow-up message in an attempt to assure his new colleague that his request did not imply disapproval:

☺ ☺ ☺ ☺ ☺

I am going to have to get enrolled in accelerated language lessons!!

Karole, just so you know, I am not criticizing you at all. Joska and Laszlo can confirm that—they have seen me and know my sense of humor and know that I am not criticizing!!

I always feel bad that I only know one language. You all know at least two languages and probably more. I am the one that I am criticizing because I only know English—and I do a fairly poor job of it!!!

In a voice-over-Internet conversation the next day, Karole explained that she had taken no offense, adding that to "get things clear," she often wrote initially in her native language, and had forgotten to translate this particular entry into English.

In subsequent messages and version-history entries, Karole and Mike documented (consistently in English) their many efforts to duplicate the reported problem. In her own attempts to reproduce the client's issue, Karole would sometimes playfully enter the names of American celebrities well-known in Eastern Europe (on one occasion, her voice-over-Internet conversation with Mike featured the actor Nick Nolte as a test case for whom the software was working just fine). As they systematically eliminated possibilities, Mike and Karole eventually detected a coding error that prohibited entering data from client groups with names of less than four characters (thereby explaining Nick Nolte's trouble-free experience). Because this was a coding rather than design issue, the team moved directly to the development and testing stages of the SDLC, entering their ultimate "solution" comments in the version history as the issue was successfully resolved. Mike then closed the version history—"locking it in the vault," as the Eastern Europeans put it.

Given the need for a strong sense of camaraderie among team members, Mike was engaged in this episode of collective collaboration in fostering interpersonal rapport as well as solving a particular software problem. (For information about collective collaboration, see Chapter 1.) Similarly, Karole was not only searching for a coding error, but learning the norms and procedures of long-distance collaboration both reflected in and constituted by English-language writing. Along with a solution, the episode yielded mutually enhanced understandings of their working relationship, including the realization that there was ample room for whimsy amidst the rigors of long-distance problem solving.

Further Development: Fine-Tuning a Users' Manual

The task of producing and revising software users' manuals falls to various parties within Chezelle: analysts and programmers complete first drafts, which are then reviewed by technical writers and granted final approval by a project director. Because many programming corrections involve requisite revisions to users' manuals, the team frequently engages in recursive efforts to refine or enlarge these documents. In addition to providing precise representations of correct understandings, user documentation must also convey critical information in a clear, accessible, and timely manner. Because users' manuals are integral to the successful implementation of Chezelle's software products, writing and refining such documents is considered part of the development stage of the

SDLC, followed by in-house and often client review.

When a client reported difficulties in changing user-system options, the team was faced with complex programming and documentation challenges. What might seem to be a well-defined set of issues was anything but, as system-option changes involved orchestrating multiple scenarios of use as well as variables related to the operating contexts in which such changes might occur. Having successfully negotiated the SDLC in identifying these challenges and in making and verifying the necessary programming changes, the team turned to the task of revising the users' manual to provide accurate and up-to-date instructions to clients.

Mike worked through this process in collaboration with another Eastern European colleague, Tass. Although they shared an understanding of the procedures involved, Mike and Tass also knew that because different user strategies would be needed across various scenarios, formulating readily comprehensible instructions would not be a simple matter. Only over time, however, did they come to appreciate the multiple and closely related layers of their revision process, as what was intended as a simple grammar check yielded the realization that more substantive changes to the draft document were in order.

As work began on the user-system-options project, a document was once again established in a version-history repository where team members would log a detailed history of their collaborative efforts. Tass completed a first draft of the revised user instructions and e-mailed Mike to let him know that he had uploaded his work to the version history. "Please take a short look on them (in grammar point of view ☺ also)," he requested. The next work day, Mike e-mailed Tass to let him know that he had "changed the wording just a bit," and also noted that he had written a few comments to discuss further during their daily voice-over-Internet call. Indeed, many of Mike's changes were minor—the addition of a word here and there to enhance clarity, slight corrections to grammar and punctuation, and occasional stylistic revisions to render the prose more standardized. But a more substantial issue arose as well, as Mike realized that amidst the demands of composing painstakingly precise English-language text, Tass had overlooked a substantial chunk of what needed explaining.

Using their desktop-sharing affordance, Mike explained to Tass and his colleagues that the problem resulted from approaches to changing system options varying along with contexts of use. In the initial draft uploaded to the version history, Tass had accounted only for procedures to be followed upon an initial installation of the software; changing these options later on, however, required a different set of procedures as well as secondary security measures. Over the course of the meeting, the team discussed the option-changing process and the attendant documentation challenges until all were clear on precisely what was needed and how to capture it in accessible and specific language for the users' manual. Although team members had understood these complexities as they completed the necessary programming changes, the challenge of writing with precision in a non-native language had produced an apparent cognitive overload, necessitating a process of collective collaboration involving lengthy back-and-forth conversation in which understandings could be articulated, played back, and refined.

As crucial as the team's voice-over-Internet conversations were at such moments, they often presented a double-edged sword, serving both to clarify and to remind Mike of his unstoppable penchant for Western idiom. The Eastern European team was known to bring lists of Mike's expressions to their weekly English lessons—"back in the saddle," "it's a wrap," "okey-dokey," and so on—and the team often paused during meetings to wonder what Mike might mean by some new turn of phrase. Because the entire team was assisting Tass in his users-manual revisions, for instance, Mike implored all to "keep crankin' along,"

prompting an extended comparison to the role of meat grinders in the sausage-production process.

Given the multi-layered nature of their own ongoing communication processes, the team's collaborative movement toward precise and comprehensive prose demanded recursive revisiting, as what had seemed a simple proofreading task yielded awareness of the need for more complex and substantive revision. With expanded and refined text ready for the revised users' manual, the Eastern European team arrived at their weekly English class with a strange new scenario to report.

A Mothership Conundrum: When Getting it Wrong is Part of Getting it Right

This final vignette focuses on a more complex project sequence, involving a process of serial collaboration that extended across 10 or more e-mails and a full work week. (For a discussion of serial and parallel collaboration, see Chapter 1.) The issue concerned synchronization between two databases—one a main application database that the team called the "mothership," the other a parallel version used on laptops in the field. In both databases, an audit function allowed users to track data changes, who had entered such changes, and when. The system was designed to trigger a records audit whenever data were entered on laptops, thereby ensuring that the mothership records were continually updated. On this occasion, however, client support notified the team that in a particular circumstance involving a specific field, audit data were not reaching the mothership. In their efforts to duplicate the auditing error, Mike and another Eastern European colleague, Laszlo, made exhaustive use of all the tools at their disposal (e-mail, voice-over-Internet, and desktop sharing) as they described possible strategies in text, examined screen shots, and brainstormed in conversation.

In their early e-mail exchanges concerning how they might duplicate the target problem, Mike inadvertently suggested a flawed testing procedure. Although Laszlo recognized Mike's error, he e-mailed the results with such an abundance of tact that only during the next day's voice-over-Internet conversation did Mike catch his mistake and grasp the implied meaning of Laszlo's earlier explanation. Even so, the problem proved elusive, and Mike and Laszlo sent many more e-mails as they eliminated possibilities and developed further strategies. While the process was lengthy and complex, the tone of their messages increasingly reflected a growing optimism ("Please let me know your opinion of my intended fix"; "It looks like you are totally on the right track").

Through this winnowing process, Laszlo eventually hit upon what seemed to be the key issue, reporting his process of detection in an 8-page letter detailing a series of 10 steps that had led him to this new insight. Combining screen shots, segments of coding, and English-language text, Laszlo's letter related a series of procedures, each of which represented both a failed attempt at problem duplication and an incremental step toward a solution. "Please check my approach if you have time and let me know your opinion," he wrote to Mike; "Please let me know whether my understanding is good or not."

As it happened, Laszlo's understanding was basically sound, although a fully formulated remedy remained persistently out of reach. In a subsequent chain of e-mails, Mike twice suggested approaches that lacked key details. The ever-tactful Laszlo gently pointed out his need for further information. Finally, after a flurry of e-mails and a voice-over-Internet desktop-sharing meeting, Mike and Laszlo reached consensus on the precise issue and what was needed in order to fix it. As was their accustomed procedure, they articulated this understanding in a written text intended to confirm that they were indeed in accord; and, in keeping with the recursive, ever-complex nature of this particular problem-solving sequence, Laszlo and Mike used that confirmation document to identify further mismatches in their understandings, resulting in yet another such

document and, finally, resolution of the stubborn audit-error problem.

As this vignette illustrates, virtual collaborative writing in the SDLC can be profoundly interwoven with problem solving, serving as a support to logical thinking, troubleshooting, error identification, and a check on mutual understandings. Although communicating in a second language certainly makes this process more taxing, these demands do not negate the heuristic potential of the act of writing—as a means of supporting the process of problem solving, with all its setbacks and miscues, as well as representing its fruits.

THE SDLC AS "AFFINITY SPACE": TOWARD TWENTY-FIRST CENTURY LITERACIES

As these vignettes show, Mike and his colleagues came together around shared challenges and problems, using digital writing to generate, refine, and communicate increasingly precise understandings; in doing so, they drew on sensibilities and skills developed on the job rather than through formal instruction in virtual collaborative writing. While the particulars of their school-based preparation varied, the commonalities are so familiar that they scarcely bear comment. In countless classrooms around the world, individual students are graded and scored on their ability to produce acceptable texts independently —texts written for a lone audience of teacher or examiner and for the sole purpose of proving one's individual proficiency.

Many years ago, a pioneering team of British researchers termed such texts "dummy runs" (Britton, Burgess, Martin, McLeod, & Rose, 1975, p. 104), arguing that students would do well to write to a variety of audiences and toward a range of purposes, regularly subjecting their texts to the proving ground of authentic communication. Even now, as literacy educators and business leaders alike are issuing urgent calls for expansive participation in twenty-first century literacies, schools and universities are yet to address the requisite challenges fully (AT&T, 2008; Partnership for 21st Century Skills, 2004; National Council of Teachers of English, 2009; National Center on Education and the Economy, 2006; see also Chapter 18).

Preparing a new generation of workers for the textual practices of workers like Mike and his colleagues demands educational opportunities marked by versatility, mindfulness, and nuance. Take, for instance, our focus in these pages on the Chezelle team's efforts to produce prose that is at once clear, complete, and precise. While a basic ability to produce prose that adequately captures evolving understandings is certainly critical in such work, we would characterize such linguistic skill as necessary but hardly sufficient. That is, the team's movement toward more exacting written language is so enmeshed in attendant conceptual, technical, and interpersonal challenges that it becomes virtually impossible to contemplate writing as a separate activity. Because it is so attached to human interaction as well as technical problem-solving, writing in these scenarios emerged as something much more than a simple conduit or container (see Chapter 2). Rather, these writing processes (encompassing such affordances as desktop sharing, document version control, e-mailing, and instant messaging) became means by which understandings were reached, problems solved, and human relationships sustained.

Gee (2004), a sociolinguist, coined the term "affinity spaces" (p. 85) to describe settings—be they digitally dispersed or face-to-face—where a sense of shared purpose trumps the sorts of differences of background and location that characterize Mike's team. While such spaces are increasingly the norm in today's workplaces, Gee argued, they tend to be strikingly absent in schools:

In the midst of our new high-tech global economy, people are learning in new ways for new purposes. One important way is via specially designed spaces (physical and virtual) constructed to resource people tied together, not primarily via shared culture, gender, race, or class, but by a shared interest or endeavor. Schools are way behind in the construction of such spaces. (p. 85)

Gee's caution echoes a growing chorus of voices calling for educational opportunities that foreground not only real-world writing challenges, but also opportunities to collaborate around shared problems and to apply new understandings in the world beyond the classroom (AT&T, 2008; National Writing Project, Partnership for 21st Century Skills, 2004; Wallis & Steptoe, 2006). Despite great strides over the past quarter century in understanding and teaching writing as a complex social and cultural process (National Writing Project & Nagin, 2003; Sperling & Freedman, 2001) and promising new efforts to foster teachers' capacities to adapt practices informed by new technologies and globalization (National Writing Project, 2009), the challenge of preparing a new generation of workers for the demands of virtual collaborative writing largely remains unmet. As noted in Chapter 18, where institutions of higher education privilege the traditional notion of solitary writer moving linearly toward a finished document, the challenge of traveling the long, slow road to facility in collaborative writing is left primarily to workplaces—where intensifying demands leave scant time for extensive coaching on the nuances of recursive writing processes. Schools, universities, and workplaces alike must address the complexities of writing in a digital age, where collaboration across distances is fast becoming a new norm.

Between Mike's employment with a global software company and Anne's longstanding involvement in the teaching of writing, we find ourselves positioned to witness the possibilities and pitfalls of both school-based writing preparation and on-the-job learning. On the one hand, while we applaud literacy educators' burgeoning interest in "twenty-first century literacies," we sometimes note a tendency toward unqualified celebration of out-of-school participation in new text forms and genres, as if the simple fact of young people's participation in activities such as Twittering, texting, and 'ning-ing represents a substantive advancement over traditional school literacies (for a fuller discussion of this argument, see Dressman, Wilder, & Connor, 2005). Meanwhile, as we have seen, those more particularly concerned with workplace writing tend in their manuals and workshops to focus single-mindedly on facility with tools, grammatical correctness, and clarity. While the difficulty of cross-cultural long-distance collaboration may be given a nod or two, the rich situatedness of writing in relationships, tasks, and activities is typically given short shrift where the focus never moves beyond technical tools and basic linguistic skill.

As the already complex activity of writing is rendered ever more so in today's globalized workplaces, educators, technical writing coaches, and managers must share the challenge of ensuring initial competence as well as developing facility with the demands of virtual collaborative writing. In the context of global companies, such as the Chezelle Group, this clearly involves much more than fostering skill in the use of particular tools or even an ability to encode meanings with clarity and correctness. Rather, being a proficient writer in such contexts encompasses a capacity to foster and sustain rapport, to understand and appreciate difference, to engage in collaborative problem solving, to manage multiple urgencies and deadlines, and to work tenaciously toward an optimal degree of precise and principled design. What is needed, then, is facility not only with language but with understanding and negotiating systems of activity (Kaptelinin & Nardi, 2006)—an ability, that is, to function effectively and smoothly within the affinity spaces through which workplace demands are jointly formulated, explored, and addressed.

Learning how to understand and function within such workplace affinity spaces demands exposure, reflection, and above all, practice. While scenarios such as those we have presented here can serve as starting points for reflection and con-

versation, growing facility demands immersion in these challenges coupled with supportive and ongoing coaching. In these new times, school and university writing instructors face the challenge of creating opportunities for technology-savvy young people to explore the demands of collaborative virtual writing in contexts of real-world problem solving. Technical writing coaches, meanwhile, must continue to encourage verbal clarity while also providing requisite support in understanding and working with geographically dispersed and culturally diverse teams.

We began with the unfortunate saga of Wheel-Stealer, the computer-eating Muppet who fell victim to a poorly sequenced technical manual. Originally intended to underscore the importance of clarity and timing in such documents, in light of the discussion we have provided here, perhaps the sketch says something more besides. Where, after all, are the human beings in this scenario? Who wrote the ill-fated machine's manual, anyway? What if a team of writers had hashed out the needs at hand, engaged in thoughtful design, critiqued and perfected one another's work, and tested it against possible scenarios? We human beings are a mixed bag, to be sure, capable of flawed thinking, faulty communication, and ill-functioning relationships—but at the end of the day, we remain one another's best hope when it comes to developing mutual understanding and enacting complex problem solving. Locating virtual collaborative writing within larger webs of activity and relationship may not solve all our problems, but it sure would make our workplaces and world a whole lot safer.

SOLUTIONS AND RECOMMENDATIONS

This chapter has discussed several levels of engagement in collaborative virtual writing, each with strengths and limitations that demand understanding and adaptation:

1. E-mail represents a most basic level of collaboration and typically yields the least results. If all that is needed is quick clarification of a fairly simple point or a general invitation to begin thinking about an issue in preparation for a future meeting, e-mail can be a good choice. In the fast-paced world of software development, however, e-mail seldom is read at the point of maximal need and often is regarded as interruptive.

2. In a more intense level of engagement, virtual collaborative writers pass documents back and forth, with individuals making changes subject to further review and revision by fellow team members. Although only one writer can revise at any given time, this sequence of parallel collaboration does allow team members to observe how a document is changing over time.

3. Desktop sharing, on the other hand, involves more substantive, collective collaboration in allowing members of a team to participate simultaneously in thinking, writing, and problem solving. Given multiple modes of input—watching, listening, reading—team members can more readily grasp key constructs and adapt shared vocabulary as they focus their distributed expertise on a focal issue. Here, the total problem-solving energy becomes greater than the sum of its parts, as team members synchronously respond to one another's input and move toward informed and expansive strategies and solutions.

These categories are of course not mutually exclusive, as desktop sharing readily can be supplemented by e-mail and serial document sharing. Additionally, technology enabling collective collaboration will continue to evolve in years to come, providing greater challenges and opportunities. Our point in charting these three levels of virtual collaborative writing is to highlight the need for targeted preparation in communicative modes that may be relatively unfamiliar to new workers.

As of this writing, one can safely assume that young employees will bring to their collaborative efforts extensive experience with e-mailing. While it is likely that they have received feedback on their writing using such tools as Word's track-changes and commenting features, they may be somewhat less practiced in using such affordances in the service of joint authorship; and although many will have used a host of virtual tools, the experience of desktop sharing may be relatively unfamiliar. With this in mind, we offer three recommendations to educators and trainers working with student writers and new employees:

- Provide hands-on opportunities to explore the appropriate uses and limitations of various technology-enhanced communicative channels. Such hands-on opportunities are ways of training through immersion (as described in Chapter 1).

- Regularly offer practice in and opportunities to reflect upon the uses of new and emerging virtual collaborative writing tools.

- Emphasize that periodic voice and face-to-face meetings can serve to strengthen team bonds and provide a stronger platform for virtual collaboration. These meetings help both to create a culture of collaboration and to develop trust (this volume's guiding Principles 1 and).

REFERENCES

Alred, G. J., Brusaw, C. T., & Oliu, W. E. (2003). *The handbook of technical writing* (7th ed.). New York: St. Martin's.

AT&T. (2008). *Building a framework for 21st century literacies*. Retrieved April 15, 2009 from http://www.kn.pacbell.com/wired/21stcent/framework.html

Britton, J., Burgess, T., Martin, N., McLeod, A., & Rosen, H. (1975). *The development of writing abilities* (pp. 11–18). London: Macmillan Education.

Dressman, M., Wilder, P., & Connor, J. (2005). Theories of failure and the failure of theories: A cognitive/sociocultural/macrostructural study of eight struggling students. *Research in the Teaching of English, 40*, 8–61.

Gee, J. P. (2004). *Situated language and learning: A critique of traditional schooling.* New York: Routledge.

Goody, J., & Watt, I. (1963). The consequences of literacy. *Comparative Studies in Society and History, 5*, 304–345. doi:10.1017/S0010417500001730

Havelock, E. (1980). The coming of literate communication to Western culture. *The Journal of Communication, 30*, 90–98. doi:10.1111/j.1460-2466.1980.tb01774.x

Henson, J. (2006). Muppets magic (video). (Available from Pegasus Entertainment, Unit 5 Brook Trading Estate, Deadbrook Lane, Aldershot, Hampshire, GU12 4XB, United Kingdom.) (Original "Computer Dinner" sketch 1971).

Kaptelinin, V., & Nardi, B. (2006). *Acting with technology: Activity theory and interaction design.* Cambridge, MA: MIT Press.

National Center on Education and the Economy. (2006). *Tough choices or tough times: The report of the New Commission on the Skills of the American Workforce.* San Francisco: Jossey-Bass.

National Council of Teachers of English. (2009). *21st century literacies.* Retrieved April 15, 2009 from http://www.ncte.org/positions/21stcenturyliteracy

National Writing Project, & Nagin, C. (2003). *Because writing matters.* San Francisco: Jossey-Bass.

National Writing Project. (2009). *National Writing Project receives MacArthur grant: Grant will support new "Digital Is" technology program.* Retrieved April 15, 2009 from http://www.nwp.org/cs/public/print/resource/280

O'Keefe, S. S., & Pringle, A. S. (2000). *Technical writing 101: A real-world guide to planning and writing technical documentation.* Cary, NC: Scriptorium.

Olson, D. R. (1977). From utterance to text: The bias of language in speech and writing. *Harvard Educational Review, 47*, 257–281.

Olson, D. R., Bloome, D., Dyson, A. H., Gee, J. P., Nystrand, M., Purcell-Gates, V., & Wells, G. (2006). Orality and literacy: A symposium in honor of David Olson. *Research in the Teaching of English, 41*, 136–179.

Partnership for 21st century skills. (2004). Retrieved April 15, 2009 from http://www.21stcenturyskills.org/index.php

Sperling, M., & Freedman, S. W. (2001). Research on writing. In Richardson, V. (Ed.), *Handbook of research on teaching* (4th ed., pp. 370–389). Washington, DC: American Educational Research Association.

Van Laan, K., Julian, C., & Hackos, J. (2001). *The complete idiot's guide to technical writing.* New York: Alpha Books.

Wallis, C., & Steptoe, S. (2006, December 6). How to bring our schools out of the 20th century. *Time magazine,* 51-56.

Young, M. (2002). *Technical writer's handbook: Writing with style and clarity.* Sausalito, CA: University Science Books.

Chapter 4
Engaging in Virtual Collaborative Writing:
Issues, Obstacles, and Strategies

Patti G. Wojahn
New Mexico State University, USA

Kristin A. Blicharz
IBM Corp., USA

Stephanie K. Taylor
IBM Corp., USA

ABSTRACT

In this chapter, the authors discuss factors useful for virtual collaborators to consider when initiating a new writing project. They identify the importance of and challenges common to getting to know others through virtual means. They then address issues associated with establishing expectations and protocols for the collaborative processes to be used for a given project. They do so by drawing from the literature on and their own experiences with virtual collaborative writing, as well as from communication logs and survey responses gathered from a small pilot study conducted in 2007. This pilot study focused on behavior and perceptions related to multiple types of communicative tools for interacting in daily workplace practice. They argue that behaviors, perceptions, expectations, and previous practice can all inform rules of engagement that can benefit teams working in virtual contexts. Time spent planning for the collaboration by defining common goals, rules, and guidelines in early stages of a virtual project can improve the collaborative experience: subsequent efficiency; role, task, and deadline delineations; and group satisfaction.

INTRODUCTION

I learned two weeks ago that I have a new manager who works in another part of the country. Talk about needing to interact and create identity "out there"...

I'm going to have to convince my manager that I'm doing a good job, differentiate myself and my work from that of my peers (some who work at his location), all while my current focus is writing for a product that he does not manage. And then there is the writing and communicating I'm already doing

DOI: 10.4018/978-1-60566-994-6.ch004

every day with people in four different locations...
It can get confusing. (A collaborating writer)

For many people, collaborative writing projects are a daily workplace reality, as are collaborative projects that include writers working at remote locations. Members of writing teams large and small interact with colleagues across the globe using such tools as instant messaging (IM), videoconferencing, e-mail, and phone. Collaborating writers now intermittently switch between typing and talking orally in their communications through newer technologies that combine the affordances of screen-sharing, IM, and embedded voice-over-Internet software. They distribute drafts, files, images, and notes through shared databases and content management software. They share professional and personal information with people whom they have never met in person and likely never will. They experience frustration and enjoy successes together and remotely.

When beginning to work on a virtual collaborative writing team, what factors should be considered? In this chapter, we address some of the issues and strategies that can be critical to new groups of virtual collaborative writers. These issues and strategies speak directly to the need to develop a culture of collaboration and to establish trust among writers, which are the first and third principles that ground this book as discussed in Chapter 1. We draw from the literature on and our own experiences with virtual collaborative writing. We also draw in part from a small pilot study conducted in 2001 that focused on three writers working for high-technology firms at three different locations. On specific days, the participants kept logs of every type of interaction they initiated or took part in, noting the nature and purpose of each interaction, its duration, the parties taking part in the conversation, and the medium used to communicate. Participants also responded at length to questions about their remote interactions and the communication tools used to support them. Using these pieces as a

backdrop, we address issues related to unifying remote individuals into a team of writers working on a shared project.

Although some people believe that writing collaboratively makes writing easier, we argue that writing collaboratively requires additional care, coordination, and cooperation and can substantially complicate the writing process. In general, when writers attempt to arrive at a shared understanding of what needs to be said in a piece and how to say it, communication problems and other difficulties seem inevitable (Kraut, et al., 1988). Difficulties can occur as team members try to convey their ideas, agree on goals and purposes, share personal knowledge or perspectives to arrive at common understandings, coordinate individual and shared perspectives, use both individual and collective contributions, and then guide all of the distributed writing to a unified end (Bond & Gasser, 1988). Given such factors, writing collaboratively is not easy to do—even when collaborators are colocated, sitting next to one another in an office (Fleming, Kaufer, Werner, & Sinsheimer-Weeks, 1993). Collaborative writing can be even more challenging when colleagues write and interact in virtual environments.

Communicating online in general can be a difficult endeavor. Virtual communication makes some aspects of communication more difficult, introduces new issues, and mitigates if not reduces others (Siegel, Dubrovsky, Kiesler, & McGuire, 1986; Sproull & Kiesler, 1986). Virtual teaming on collaborative writing projects, we argue, does the same. We know much about teaming and small group work processes from theory, research, and practice (see, for example, McGrath, 1984; Cohen & Bailey, 1997; Hirokawa & Salazar, 1999; Gouran & Hirokawa, 2003; Salas, Priest, Stagl, Sims, & Burke, 2006; Klein, DiazGranados, Salas, Le, Burke, Lyons, & Goodwin, 2009). We know far less about the implications of teaming and small group processes when collaborators write solely or primarily online.

Because of the complexity of both collaborative writing and online communication, we need to focus more explicitly on strategies that can specifically support the processes of virtual collaborative writing. What aspects of group work and development should we especially keep in mind when writing with online collaborators? What factors can play an important role as collaborators establish and maintain teams that write and communicate primarily online? What strategies can assist virtual collaborative writers as they encounter the dual complications of collaborative writing and online communication?

The purpose of our chapter is to share common practices of virtual collaborative writing, to identify challenges of virtual collaborative writing, and to offer strategies to consider when writing collaboratively in virtual contexts. We do so by addressing key factors that affect the building and maintaining of virtual collaborative writing teams, following part of a framework often cited in the literature on teaming. Specifically, Tuckman's (1965) categories of forming, norming, storming, and performing, with the later addition of adjourning (Tuckman & Jensen, 1977), remain some of the most recognizable stages invoked when team processes are considered (Schuman, 2001). We suggest the first two stages—forming and norming—as aspects to consider during the early if not ongoing life of virtual collaborative writing teams. We use these familiar stages to coordinate related material rather than to suggest that all teams experience them in distinguishable phases, linearly, or at all.

We begin by discussing issues related to how team members form and get to know one another online, particularly through virtual text-based means. Next, we consider how virtual writing teams "norm." How can virtual writing teams create a shared understanding of goals for a given writing project while establishing shared expectations about the project they are charged with addressing, the processes they will use to bring that project to fruition, and other "rules of engagement"

to be employed for writing and communicating remotely as a team? We focus on these aspects of teaming because we believe that issues addressed in forming a team and in norming and establishing expectations play a crucial role in shaping subsequent actions and interactions. Elsewhere in this collection, writers address how writing teams handle and resolve the "storm," conflict and misunderstandings, online; issues of "performing" and putting the pieces—communications, plans, drafts, feedback, varied perspectives—together to make the online project a coherent, unified, and complete entity; and "adjourning," bringing a virtual collaborative writing project to a close.

FORMING AS VIRTUAL COLLABORATIVE WRITERS: "GETTING TO KNOW YOU, REMOTELY"

In this section, we discuss aspects related to the ways in which individuals get to know one another as they form or join online writing teams. Teams begin as groups of diverse people with diverse interests and abilities. Forming a group into a team that integrates efforts within a shared task is an important early and ongoing process in the ideal collaborative writing situation.

Awareness of one another's tendencies, assets, and needs can enable team members to be more informed when making decisions and establishing expectations for how the given team will optimally function in the standard workplace. Often this awareness emerges through informal communications. After all, workplace teams rarely take time to formally structure "getting to know you" time. In fact, when communicating online, collaborators might feel compelled to try to increase efficiency by attempting to create routinized and formal interactions (DeSanctis & Monge, 1998). Yet, as DeSanctis and Monge discussed, virtual collaborators ultimately tend to require that their interactions become more intimate and informal so that trust and professional intimacy can be established. The question then becomes how virtual team members can benefit from the positive attributes of informal communication and get to know one another as they establish themselves on a writing team.

In this section, we address the following issues of virtual collaborative writing:

- Managing introductions and impressions online
- Building or maintaining various types of relationships in virtual contexts
- Embedding informal communications into online work processes
- Selecting tools for forming virtual writing teams

Managing Introductions and Impressions Online

When collaborative writers get to know one another online, the "getting to know you" is often initiated when a new project is under way; employees might be working with some people they have worked with in the past while other colleagues will be new to one another as well as to the project.

We see the process of "getting to know you" in virtual space as distinct from the ways in which we get to know colleagues who share a physical space or who interact with us in person as well as online. In the physical workplace, collaborators can become acquainted in any number of face-to-face contexts: in the hallway; next to the coffee machine; during or just before or after face-to-face meetings; and in spontaneous, ad hoc conversations (Fish, Kraut, Root, & Rice, 1993). In face-to-face encounters, we form impressions based on such factors as physical appearance, non-verbal cues and facial expressions, or decor and organization of an office space.

We cannot simply show up online and expect people to be able to discern the same types of characteristics that are drawn quite readily in face-to-face contexts. When colleagues get to know one another through online means only, they still seek out characteristics that can provide cues to personality, attitude toward work, and work styles, presumably because these help to facilitate a working relationship.

In addition, in virtual environments, we have fewer ways of gauging someone's reaction to or impressions of what we say or write, so considering how we help others get to know us is perhaps even more important. Given that, consciously or not, virtual team members are continually offering impressions of themselves to their virtual collaborators, we suggest that collaborators act and react more deliberately during online interactions. It can be productive to consider seemingly insignificant factors that contribute to impressions made during online interactions. We discuss the following as two of the many aspects we can attend to more thoughtfully when we write with collaborators online: word and text choices, including quality, quantity, and timing of responses or contributions; and visual representations of oneself.

Word and Text Choices

Language choices and tone are commonly invoked as factors that convey information about a writer; this remains true for those writing and collaborating in person or online. In our pilot study, one participating writer spoke of situations in which she worried about the tone conveyed in online messages; with local collaborators, she was able to assess her interpretation of tone in face-to-face contact, typically finding that her concerns were unfounded. But with remote online collaborators, that proved more difficult. She found herself weighing her words more carefully and taking more time to communicate more precisely in online interactions.

We have all heard of misinterpreted words and intents proving detrimental to a collaborative writing group. Miscommunication can occur in any context, but without the cues available in face-to-face interactions, it is more likely in exchanges among virtual team members. Consider the following example: During a phone conference an employee has a small concern about a remote collaborator's comment about another team member. After reflecting on how the comment could in a small way negatively impact impressions of the other team member, he decides to approach the comment mildly. If the employee and collaborator had been working together in person, the employee could have smiled and said, "Hey, next time we're in a meeting, would you mind <request>?" Given that they work together remotely, the employee decides instead to write a quick note via IM. The employee writes, "Hey, this is no big deal but <request>." However, because the employee has taken the time to write the comment and request, the collaborator assumes that the issue is quite serious. The collaborator feels bad and apologizes profusely. The employee sees that the issue is now blown out of proportion and subsequently avoids commenting on small issues online, risking that small issues build momentum and eventually do become more of a "big deal."

The quality of remote interactions is but one thing that contributes to impressions virtual collaborative writers gather about one another. Impressions can be based not just on type or quality of communications but also on quantity of interactions. For instance, Cummings (2004) reported that work groups who interacted more frequently and exchanged more information externally were rated more highly by managers. Knowing when to interact and to what extent can help remote collaborators gather information about one another and about the project they share.

Those restricted to online-only interactions can weigh more heavily how physical or visual qualities can contribute to impressions of a writer interacting via text messages. Practitioners and theorists alike have noted how "visual attributes of a document have a subtle and often complex impact extending beyond legibility and readabil-

ity" (Brumberger, 2003b, p. 208). Parker (1997) discussed how an aspect as subtle as a typeface "conveys mood, communicates attitude, and sets tone" (p. 60). Recent studies have found typeface to influence a writer's persona as perceived by readers (Brumberger, 2003a, 2003b, 2004). If typeface itself can contribute in establishing persona, we need to consider the potential impact of other choices we make related to digital messages, including emoticons and adherence to standard written English. In discussing this issue, one member of our pilot study stated:

I tend to lighten up with a colleague who uses emoticons and less-than perfect punctuation and sentence structure. On the other hand, too many smiley faces and indecipherable abbreviations make me worry about how productive the person will be. These factors dictate whether I keep the work focused on project-specific communication or create a more open forum of communication that allows for more dialogue outside of or surrounding the project.

Given the different types of cues people can gather from one another as they write together in virtual environments, we are reminded of the need to take into account rhetorical context—the task at hand, the deadline, the situation, the immediate audience, the medium, the purpose for writing or interacting— as we work and write with virtual collaborators, perhaps even more thoughtfully than we might need to do in face-to-face interactions.

Visual Representation Choices

From informal online social networks to work-related tools for communicating and writing, personal photographs and images have begun to play a more prominent role in self-identification. People might post a current photo or a favorite photo from younger years; they can post a photo where they look mature, polished, and serious or a photo where they look casual, fun, and happy.

Consciously or sub-consciously, we actively "read" as well as "write" these photographs: Should I be formal with this person? Can I stray from the primary writing task when interacting with this colleague? What does the photograph I have posted suggest about me? What do I want it to convey? A participant in our study emphasized the important role of the identity photograph:

I am very aware that I gather information about the people I'm working with from their choice of photo. The pictures my colleagues post to represent themselves online in our organization include (a) the personal (for example, photographs of their children, their pets, themselves at home or work); (b) a default company logo; (c) professional head shots; and (d) playful pictures such as a smiley face emoticon or a shot of themselves wearing a bowler hat or a mischievous grin. When I see someone with a fun-looking hat, I tend to feel more relaxed when introducing myself, and I feel more comfortable breaking the ice with chitchat before focusing on the specifics of a writing project. When I see a user has no picture of himself or herself, I tend to stick to discussing the project. This piece of missing information signals to me formality. Another signal of formality for me is the professionally shot photo. Professional shots tend to suggest to me that... I should stick strictly to business details.

Beyond the identity picture, other photographs can be used to convey information about oneself or one's surroundings as a means of getting acquainted with virtual others. One practitioner on our team reported how the sharing of photographs of surroundings helped her become acquainted with a new team member; at the same time, it led to much smoother coordination as the writing project progressed and subsequent writing projects were launched:

I was pulled last minute into a project that was falling behind in part because of difficulties in virtual collaboration among various teams. I was tasked with helping a team in India catch up, in the midst of other approaching deadlines. The assignment circumstances made me collaborate in a very formal manner. While working out the time zone schedule with the project leader in India, I noticed he was located near the Taj Mahal, a place I had always wanted to visit. We started talking about the beauty of the Taj Mahal, and then the Himalayas, and then he described the physical environment of the company's office in India. He then sent me screen caps of pictures he had taken around the area, and I started to feel much less stress about the project. Our conversation flowed from interest in the places we had visited to a more animated approach to our project. Getting to know my teammate through pictures and a discussion of our mutual interest in traveling made the project feel lighter, and it made our conversation flow better when we transitioned into talk about the project. We were both more gracious in delegating tasks and felt more comfortable to informally "bother" one another about simpler questions related to the writing project. This relationship has carried beyond our initial project together. We now use each other as a resource for updates at meetings we missed or to ask questions when we receive a new process to follow.

To some collaborative writers, taking alternative, explicit steps, such as posting a photograph to foster "getting to know you," might feel inauthentic. Yet if we consider the steps that we take when meeting colleagues in face-to-face encounters, the same claim can be made. When we post representative photographs to be accessed by our remote collaborators, who will otherwise come to know us only through our writings and conversations about writing, we need to consider implications, both personal and professional. We also need to take into account how online collaborators' visual representations can create positive or negative impressions that then guide our interactions and behaviors within virtual teams. As one practitioner on our writer team stated, "This seemingly small detail—the photograph—often dictates how I communicate."

Here we have mentioned just a couple of aspects that can enhance impressions we gather from virtual collaborators who are new to us. Ignoring the importance of human characteristics in virtual collaboration creates the same types of risks that doing so in face-to-face collaborations would. If we want to take more control over the impressions we make online, we can consider both the standard means that colleagues use to get to know one another and their virtual alternatives.

Building and Maintaining Relationships in Virtual Contexts

Increased awareness about collaborators can result in the ability to move more easily and quickly into a project, allowing team members to bypass normal formalities or small talk and get the precise information they need. In an article on virtual organizations, DeSanctis and Monge (1998) explained that when interacting during virtual collaborative writing, "some communication is likely to become more relationship-based. Parties might seek a relational basis for transactions so that intimacy can be created in the face of distance, and trust can be established and maintained" ("Communication in Virtual Organizations" section, para. 2). Strong professional relationships rely on these, among other, factors.

While professional relationships vary and evolve, in our workplace experiences, at any given time our online colleagues fall primarily into one of three categories:

- **Acquaintances.** Colleagues with whom interactions tend to be direct and formal, with few interpersonal elements.
- **Cohorts.** Colleagues with whom one has frequent contact, some informal conversations, and few breaches of professionalism.

- **Intimates.** Colleagues with whom one can, while working and interacting, feel comfortable expressing feelings or attitudes beyond what would be considered primarily professional discourse, to include frustrations, personal information, and humor.

Often the groundwork for these relationships is established when co-workers are getting to know one another online. When we initially meet new collaborators with whom we will work online, circumstances will dictate whether formal or informal introductions are made or whether introductions are made at all. Once the tone and degree of formality are introduced, relationships might stay at the initial levels for a period before team members—or individuals on a team—move into a closer or more distant level.

Each category of professional relationship has its own advantages and disadvantages. For example, working or interacting with *acquaintances* often occurs only on an "as-needed" basis. When acquaintances collaborate on a writing project, they usually request and share information immediately with little small talk. Acquaintances tend to stay on task and often do not attend to others' personalities. They do not know details about each other's work styles, backgrounds, or preferences, and it is likely that they do not want to know such details.

However, *cohorts* know more details about and are more involved with one another. They take part in some exchanges concerning their daily experiences, and they might experience a higher level of comfort in sharing information about work and their personal lives.

Intimates share many personal details and opinions, in addition to work-related information. Intimate relationships go beyond sharing information or gaining mutual respect; often, intimates form a bond by sharing vulnerabilities or grievances. They know one another's predicaments, achievements, concerns, tendencies, and strengths at work, if not beyond.

Of course, getting to know a remote professional colleague at a more intimate level takes time. But in fact, time can be saved and difficulties avoided when collaborators know, trust, and understand one another. For information about building trust in virtual teams, see Chapter 5. Knowing one's writing team members more intimately can encourage informal discussions that enable writers to understand immediate personal or professional constraints and to be aware of others' tendencies in writing and in collaborating. As a result, taking project-related time for informal, "off-task" conversation ultimately can lead to greater efficiency and productivity as a project or future project progresses. Consider the following example from our real-life experiences:

Two very distant co-workers began regular online contact after being introduced and working as remote colleagues. Frequent, brief, and informal online interactions ensued, and they regularly knew what the other was doing both during and after work hours. Frequent, quick interactions led them to develop a solid professional relationship as well as a friendship. Three months into these interactions, the two remote colleagues were assigned to co-lead a large, global-spanning effort related to one of their company's products. Through substantial professional and informal interactions, they had been able to gather that each was a creative thinker and that they could jointly take more risks, working out ways to approach the project with a spirit of energy and fun rather than following the status quo. They enjoyed developing the project together and expanding on ideas for educating and engaging the team virtually. In the end, they were able to create not just a workable process for developing the project but a process that was innovative, interesting, and sustainable. Through many phone calls, Instant Messages, and virtual online meetings, they came up with a clear strategy to implement, which their team received well. They agreed that the successful project resulted in large part because of what they *had learned from and about one another through frequent, informal online interactions.*

This example is not surprising. Research, theory, and practice all point to the importance of informal communication among people who are working together on shared projects.

Tendencies toward one level of relationship or another can result from time constraints, the extent of prior contact, hierarchy, past experiences, or personalities and preferences of team members—all influencing what is said and how it is said. In any case, planning for interactions and accessing tools to support remote interactions among collaborative writers will play an important role in relationship building and, therefore, the life of a team.

Embedding Informal Communications into Online Work Processes

Informal communication is traditionally how people become familiar with one another on interpersonal and professional levels. Informal communication is therefore particularly important to keep in mind on projects carried out with others online. While early research on virtual collaboration indicated a tendency for more on-task interactions than would typically be found in face-to-face collaboration (Sproull & Kiesler, 1991), in the example in the previous section, the collaborators' informal virtual interactions enabled more insight into individual strengths, interests, and approaches to writing projects. These insights helped make it possible for the two distant colleagues to smoothly transition to their new roles as co-leaders of a substantial, global project—and to its success. The informal interactions gave them the confidence to work jointly though at a distance through the risks of breaking from standard practice while seeing an innovative writing project unfold successfully.

Another way that virtual collaborative writers tend to get to know one another is through the informal correspondence that tends to occur after positive and negative catalyzing incidents. We have found that some of our most satisfying and lasting work relationships on writing projects have developed without ever having seen our colleagues face-to-face. Such relationships are instead fostered through interactions using videoconferencing, e-mail, phone, IM, or other interactive tools. Each close collaborative relationship will grow out of different circumstances, but one common circumstance that can bring a relationship into greater intimacy is that of a catalyzing event. Such an incident leads people to take small risks in breaking out of some workplace conventions. The risks usually involve humor or a shared frustration or both.

Most of us have encountered times when an online colleague's behavior serves as a catalyst for bonding among the rest of the collaborators. For example, when an online teammate ignores a deadline, sends a rude message, grandstands in a remote meeting, or does not respond to the rest of the team over an extended period, colleagues might let down their professional guards and commiserate—bonded together against the common problem of the colleague's poor communications. In the pilot study that we conducted on interactions and communicative tools, one of our participants mentioned: "During one frustrating online conference meeting, there was a global storm of angry IMs, kind of like a swarm of angry bees that was going on globally, against the video-conference backdrop of a hosting team that was sitting very seriously in a conference room." Such situations lead to at least some team members feeling more connected to others on the team, and they might learn more about one another personally. The shared experience of a "charged" situation can lead to some level of informality as team members share in a success or attempt to cope with the difficult situation or party.

For example, consider how international colleagues are working with various constraints—distance, time zones, and language—which add up to a potential for communication breakdowns and frustrations. A bit of laughter in the midst of a difficult online writing project or situation such as this can help pull a team together. In our experience, some international colleagues have made light of constraints, for instance, by asking one another about an idiom in one language and then laughing together at the resulting translation in another language. Sharing humorous moments also can allow team members to share in an authentically personal moment. Another result can be writers growing comfortable enough to ask each other to clarify phrases that are confusing without fear of insulting the other person or without the burden of feeling vulnerable for not knowing given terms.

The bonding that occurs as a result of an emotionally charged incident can, but does not necessarily, lead to increasing comfort levels when team members seek clarification or forego normal formalities to get needed information. But when it does, the benefits of increased interpersonal understanding can lead to substantially more efficient and effective collaborations, allowing writers to later rely on one another in productive ways, serve as sounding boards for subsequent projects, or assist one another in a critical and time sensitive task. Such bonding often begins when that first "off-topic" IM is sent or that first complaint or humorous take on an event is launched. At the same time, not all co-workers want or choose to delve into such discussions. Virtual collaborative writers need to become attuned to indications of such moments or preferences, such as a lack of response or a formal response to light commentary.

For collaborative writers, in addition to informal communication, it can also take expertise, the sharing of useful information, and other types of valuable contributions to build substantial impressions among remote collaborators. In their article on virtual status seeking and the role of sharing one's experience, expertise, or solutions among a virtual group, Lampel and Bhalira (2007) referred to such actions as "informational gift giving" ("Online Rating Systems" section, para. 6).

Their results suggested that the practice of virtual informational gift giving can help virtual teams to maintain and unify. We agree and have elsewhere discussed this type of information sharing as "virtual doughnuts" (Taylor, 2005), given that relevant information provided when needed can be seen exactly as would an offering of treats or jokes with co-workers in one's office. The "virtual doughnut" can help establish a productive, if not intellectual, exchange and help the work that has required the relevant information to move forward.

Selecting Tools for Forming Virtual Writing Teams

The medium used to communicate can also affect interactions among collaborative writers. How can virtual collaborative writers adopt strategies and employ tools for communicating at a distance to improve the process of forming a team and getting to know one another?

Both e-mail and IM tools have a reputation for fostering less formal discussion and supporting informal interactions. In part due to the (false) impression of impermanence, IM is a common means for people on virtual teams to get to know one another. For one thing, informal communication tends to occur more readily via IM. Also, because IM is a real-time communication tool in which exchanges occur quickly, speakers often use informal grammar and emoticons to convey emphasis as they would in speech (Hewett & Hewett, 2008). Abbreviated forms of communication, such as "BRB, got a mtg" ("Be right back—I have a meeting") also are typical and acceptable among most writing teams. IM chats are often one-to-one and are rarely forwarded to others, which again encourages less formality.

One advantage of remote as opposed to face-to-face interactions is that they can be asynchronous as well as synchronous. For asynchronous interactions, email is often chosen as a means for launching a virtual project. E-mail provides a record of the announced project and, when sent to all primary collaborators, provides a convenient means for subsequently replying to all team members at once. After an initial e-mail to all team members, collaborators often jump in to say something brief if not informal about what they think of the project or what step they will be taking next.

In some organizations, synchronous introductions are more common than are e-mail exchanges. In these organizations, when a new project is started, teammates reach out to one another through IM within hours of the assignment, whether the collaborators are remote or onsite. Such interactions can begin with a request for project background information or a spontaneous introduction ritual among those team members who have not worked together before. As a participant in our study reported:

I often get to know virtual teammates by sending them an Instant Message as soon as they are hired. I catch them early to start a friendly relationship given that we will eventually be working on projects together. I will send them an Instant Message saying "hello," asking small bits of personal or professional information such as where they live, what their experience in technical writing or programming is, or what their interests are. I will also offer them any help they need getting on board. I then try to follow up with a quick hello on the instant messenger at least once a month just to stay in touch and keep the relationship going.

The participant added that others have similarly initiated the "getting to know you" with her:

When I relocated and began working with my current team, I was immediately IM'd by a colleague. She welcomed me to the team, asking me about my new apartment and the trips I had recently been on. We began instant messaging every week or so and eventually developed a good friendship.

Even at a distance, I was able to discern that she is passionate about her writing and knows how to be a very good team motivator.

These types of interactions can help unify the collaborators and strengthen the social aspects of teams that McGrath (1984) has found to be important to team success. Many collaborative writers concur that informal, synchronous chats foster task-related or informal discussions. Some would argue that the projects at hand therefore tend to be more exciting, more innovative, and more engaging. As one member of our writing team stated, "After some informal, real-time give-and-take, I find that I feel energized and connected to my colleagues. I also feel like everyone is being heard on a project."

When collaborators begin to know characteristics of other team members, this information can help put contributions and conversations in context. For a case study in advancing new authoring strategies for virtual collaboration, see Chapter 12. Knowing who is saying what during the collaborative writing process is important for decision-making and subsequent actions (Neuwirth, Kaufer, Chandhok, & Morris, 1990). For instance, if we know that one collaborator tends to focus attention on a favored aspect (such as usability) to the exclusion of other aspects (such as functionality), it would be advisable to make sure that other necessary aspects are included specifically in the work plan. If we know a collaborator bristles at suggestions about his or her ideas or writing, we can position our recommendations accordingly. If we know a less active collaborator has the most expertise with a topic being discussed in the text, we can attempt to draw out that person to contribute what he or she knows.

Getting to know colleagues, their interests, and their communication styles before actually collaborating on a writing project can help to get an assignment started and completed more efficiently. As writing teams form and the writing task is getting clarified, participants are getting to know more about one another's abilities, capabilities, preferences, potential contributions, expectations, availability, and other characteristics that will contribute to completing the writing task at hand. In short, the ways in which we present ourselves to others and draw impressions about others influence individual and team behavior throughout the life of a collaborative writing project. Virtual collaborative writers should approach remote collaborators thoughtfully in order to build and maintain the type of relationships that will optimize collaborative writing.

In this section, we have addressed just a few factors related to creating and maintaining relationships among writers working virtually on collaborative texts. We argue that teams with collaborators who have not met or worked together before could benefit from taking some time to consider these key factors:

- How individuals are visually presenting themselves (for example, through photographs) so new virtual collaborators can "see" them
- The extent to which emoticons, abbreviations, and "texting-speak" are employed and decipherable
- The notion of critical incidents leading to informal exchanges that can repair or extend interpersonal bonds if not intra- and inter-team cohesion
- Conventions for encouraging team members to initially "get to know" collaborators who have not worked together before
- The need to consider characteristics of the tools selected for initial interactions among professional colleagues

Next, we address factors related to coordinating plans and expectations for collaborative processes and text products.

ESTABLISHING SHARED EXPECTATIONS: "DO YOU HEAR WHAT I HEAR?"

In this section, we focus on many factors related to "norming" a virtual group of writers into a virtual collaborative writing team. Virtual collaborative writers who have not met or worked together before should consider a range of factors, including the following:

- Need to establish collective notions of a project's aims, scope, and audience
- Individual and collective responsibilities
- Tendencies for the best laid plans and for team membership to evolve
- Benefits of publically documenting changes in project conception, direction, decisions, and agreements
- Conventions and protocols to solidify practice and expectations and to guide team actions and behavior
- Levels and amount of interaction required, including information communication
- Strategies for asking and answering questions
- Interdependencies within collaborative work, particularly in virtual settings
- Characteristics of the tools selected for providing and procuring information as well as for maintaining relationships among professional colleagues.

As we have suggested, the development of online team relationships is important for collaborative work. This is particularly true for collaborative writing team members whose writing depends on input from other team members and who frequently work under tight deadlines (Kraut & Streeter, 1995). With many online writing teams, there is no explicit plan for initiating relationships, and the fostering of bonding, if it occurs, is implicit and unplanned. But maintenance of successful online writing team relationships has

to be deliberate—online team members do not spontaneously run into people virtually. Similarly, efficient progress on a shared online project is reliant on many factors that can be deliberately addressed.

In this section, we share results from the literature, from our pilot study, and from our own experiences as collaborators. We focus on using various digital media to establish or maintain a common understanding about the reasons for and the aims of an online writing project. We also attend to the ways in which we might use various online tools to share both individual and collective notions of purpose and audience and to establish procedures, tasks, and responsibilities for completing a given project. We begin by addressing strategies for establishing and maintaining the purpose and scope of a given writing project.

Sharing Project Aims and Scope

Before moving forward on a writing project, team members should try to establish a clear notion of what the project is: its purpose; scope; stakeholders; and connection, if any, to other projects. (For a discussion of removing barriers to virtual collaboration, see Chapter 7.) This is not to say that a conception for a project is (or can be) carved in stone from the start. Collaborative writing projects are typically assigned to teams because of the complexity or scope of the project, the multiple expertises required to complete the project, or the need for parallel work so multiple components can be completed at once. Flower (1988) wrote that purposes and aims evolve as texts are created, observing that a "web of purpose... may remain under construction throughout composing" (p. 534). For virtual collaborative writers, however, this process is more complex than that. As Flower stated, "maintaining a meaningful hierarchy of one's own goals can be difficult" (p. 534). Consider multiple individuals collaborating on an information product, with multiple and at times conflicting goals of individual team members, not to mention the evolving nature of many projects as well as smaller projects that are embedded within larger projects, and it is clear why virtual collaborative writers face challenges.

Projects as well as plans evolve. A key factor in efficiency and effectiveness, then, is communicating evolving plans and decisions among all involved members and notifying others of updates. More tools are available for allowing remote collaborators to track changes and keep updated with a project. As addressed in other chapters in this volume, industry-specific software and shared databases as well as publically available collaborative writing tools, such as the Google Docs™ program or wikis, can allow people to share documents; view and work on the same documents synchronously or asynchronously; and insert comments, updates in plans, and other notes into ongoing written projects and plans. Some organizations provide intra-office databases, content management systems, and other online tools for such sharing and updating to occur as well (see Chapters 9 and 19). Ideally, teams if not organizations will establish protocols for publishing or posting, tracking changes and versions, identifying who changed a text and when, and so on. A number of strategies are recommended in Chapters 12 and 13. These strategies have the best chance of succeeding when members of the collaborative writing teams are able to contribute to the decision making and to deliberate about what is working and what is not.

Assuming Tasks and Responsibilities

Given that trust has proven to be an important factor in collaborative projects, virtual writing teams should explicitly aim to develop shared expectations about the project, the subtasks, the deadlines, and each individual's role. As Jarvenpaa & Leidner (1998) explained, trust is initially extended quite quickly in virtual teams, but that trust can be quite tenuous and more readily weakened, for instance,

when response time is unpredictable. This suggests that teams take time to track and display in writing the task, the names of those involved in each task, and the anticipated deadlines. It also suggests that team members notify one another of likely (or certain) delays or changes in assignments, deadlines, and the like. Drawing primarily on McGrath (1991), Jarvenpaa & Leidner (1998) stressed the importance of relationships among successful virtual teams:

Effective groups are engaged simultaneously and continuously in three functions: (1) production (problem solving and task-performance), (2) member-support (member inclusion, participation, loyalty, commitment), and (3) group well-being (interaction, member roles, power, politics). Member-support and group well-being relate directly to relationship development. ("Developmental View" section, para. 2)

Individuals on a collaborative writing team should be encouraged to extend trust as well as earn trust by doing what they commit to or are assigned in the proposed time frames. As needed, they should notify other team members of new deadlines or shifts in direction. Chapter 5 discusses the importance of trust in more detail, listing such characteristics as a "high tolerance for ambiguity" that can contribute to success in virtual collaborative writing.

Incorporating New Team Members

One complication of teaming is the tendency toward membership changes within a team—or within the external teams upon which another team must rely. Research and practice indicate that team behaviors are markedly different in teams that are formed for ad hoc purposes as opposed to teams that have a history and a future (Sproull & Kiesler, 1991). Similarly, evolving membership on teams can impact behaviors (Gersick 1988). When new people join a team or when new external teams are added to the picture, there is a strong benefit in introducing new members not just to the writing project but also to the other writers. Not doing so can lead to the new individuals and their questions being ignored because the established team members have no idea who they are; indeed, in such cases, new team members are at risk of being seen as a distraction or intrusion rather than as welcomed assistance for the team.

For example, consider a team that has been working on a project for an intense seven months. Imagine some change occurs (a new deadline or a somewhat new direction for the written document) requiring that the team work closely with an external and remote group. Members of the remote group might have a difficult path to tread. They must ask questions so they can learn about the project without seeming critical about decisions that have long since been made and instituted. Similarly, they must appear confident without portraying an unearned air of authority. Finally, among other things, they must become part of a review process that is not necessarily relevant to their late role in the project yet is valuable for understanding the project from a more global perspective.

When new, support members join a team, longer-standing team members nonetheless face additional obligations, such as taking preliminary steps to ease new collaborators into developing relationships and understanding the project. Not doing so risks ultimately adding to task time given the potential for mismatched expectations about the project, tendencies toward tolerating rather than resolving conflicts, and the possibility of derailing one another's efforts rather than merging toward a shared goal (Grudin, 1988).

Staying on Track

When virtual collaborative writers launch a project, how do they coordinate and stay on track? What factors are likely to impact the collabora-

tors' abilities to stay on track? What strategies for virtual collaborative writing can help?

Determining Amount and Types of Informal Interaction

Research on informal communication suggests it is the glue that can help turn a group into a team (McGrath, 1984). Research and theory support the need for informally communicating with one's collaborators, virtual collaborators in particular. But how much is too much? How much is "enough"? What is "not enough"?

E-mail, IM, and Twitter in particular have potential for leading to too much interaction. Dabbish & Kraut (2006) define e-mail overload in the workplace as a situation that occurs when users "receive and send more e-mail than they can handle, find, or process effectively" (p. 431). This definition might well apply to IM overload as well. Certainly, getting "pinged" with a message every few minutes can disrupt thought processes and the type of focus that writing requires. As a participant in our pilot study mentioned. "The little blue blinking square at the bottom of my screen has the same effect as a ringing phone—I cannot let it go unanswered." Because in her workplace IM is not used heavily for work purposes, IM messages tend to be "chatty." As the participant stated, "This use of IM can definitely be a distraction from my work. IM can definitely be a hindrance if I am trying to complete a task and a co-worker IMs me to gossip." Another participant in our pilot study mentioned that IM used for chatting can severely interrupt her work: "Sometimes I have seven IMs from co-workers just wanting to ask what my lunch plans are or even just what I'm up to. This [communication] definitely hinders my job." So, one measure of "too much" can relate to the relevance to the collaborative project and the likelihood of interruption. Is the invitation to interact a means for the initiator to take a break? If so, is the invitation extended at a time that will not interfere with the flow of the recipient's work? Communicating with collaborators as a needed break, to bond, or even to discuss the collaborative task does take time away from the individual work that is also required in writing collaboratively (Perlow, 1999). And, as suggested here, communicating with collaborators does not necessarily facilitate the process of producing an effective text or artifact.

While interaction and information overload are concerns for virtual collaborative writers relying on communicative technologies that allow for quick interactions, equally pressing is the ability to maintain venues for informal communication. Long-standing studies of collaborative work suggest that for complex tasks requiring input from multiple team members, interpersonal and informal communication are key to success (Van de Ven, Delbecq, Koenig, 1976). Sproull (1984) found informal communication to be the main means managers used to gather information, receive or share opinions, and ultimately make more informed decisions. Perhaps it is not surprising, then, that teams that communicate more often—gathering and sharing knowledge externally—are subsequently rated more highly on performance (Cummings, 2004).

As we have suggested, insufficient communication, however defined or determined, has been found to impede collaborative writing and other collaborative work (Kraut, Galegher, Fish, & Chalfonte, 1993). How can we know whether shared information has been understood or whether it is sufficient for a collaborator who needs to work with it? Determining whether understanding has been achieved is a common difficulty in online interaction. We are not able to see a look of confusion or notice hesitancy as we go our separate ways to embark on a task. Particularly in virtual work, teams should establish that asking for and asking questions are critical practices. For information about the process of decision making in virtual teams, see Chapter 11. When communicating synchronously, this means taking

time after new details are introduced or after extended explanations are shared to check whether anyone has questions. It also means creating space for discussion so that thoughts and questions can occur more naturally, well before collaborators proceed with erroneous assumptions. Using tools such as IM allows writers to ask questions and quickly gather small pieces of information at the point of need. The ability for spontaneous chats, for instance, enables writers to request information from other collaborators when they need it.

Whether or not remote collaborators create a space for questions, we should not hesitate to ask questions when they occur. The strategy of avoiding questions when we have them in order to present ourselves as informed on all issues can and does backfire. If we continue as though we know or understand, our contributions in a document will not likely reflect that we did. No single writer's education can be monolithic enough for a person to know exactly how to address a given issue, write with the voice of a team or organization, or understand or follow processes that will best facilitate any given project. In the long run, asking questions early on and as they occur can save time; if someone does not understand where a project is going and proceeds on the wrong road, the person will get somewhere but not where the project needs to go. Backtracking takes time, as does starting over or trying to work from the wrong road and find a path to the main road.

When the contributions to a shared document indicate that a writer is misunderstanding some aspect of a project, collaborators might hesitate to "correct" the writer whom they know only virtually. But clarifying earlier rather than later can help save time and ultimately allow for more goodwill than would ignoring the issue while one or more people work with incorrect information.

For virtual collaborators concerned about interrupting co-workers, teams can be encouraged to establish protocols, such as indicating whether or not one is available for questions or interaction. We can use technology's indicators to let team members know we are in heads-down mode, "in" but working and not interruptible, in a physical meeting, and so on. Some organizations require writers to make themselves available for IM during all work hours.

Establishing protocols such as this among a collaborative writing team can divert the potential for too many small interruptions and instead encourage team members to feel comfortable asking questions and interacting when they need to do so, before they lead to additional if not larger problems.

Considering Interdependencies

Another consideration for keeping on track is the interdependencies that exist within teams, and between teams and the external people with whom they must interact. Collaborative writers tend to work under conditions of substantial interdependency. In many organizations, technical communicators and others who spend a great deal of time writing are reliant on others who hold information critical to sections of text that must be produced, integrated, or revised. Collaborative writers in industry often find this to be true—and problematic. As Kraut (2002) explained, team members experience greater stress under conditions of "synchronization problems" (p. 340). This problem can occur when the timing between providing and receiving information is off and when the "outputs offered by one individual in a group do not meet the inputs need to another" (p. 340). We argue that this problem is especially true for collaborative writers, given their common reliance on people who have pieces of information they need. This issue is further complicated for virtual collaborative writers who cannot walk down the hall to urge someone to provide information or sit next to and work with someone to procure a needed piece of information.

Another critical complication related to the interdependencies of online collaborative writing occurs when documents are written for external

target audiences or customers. Chapter 17 discusses strategies for interacting with customers virtually to align the document goals with the audience needs. But sometimes the collaborative teams themselves have to make decisions for and about the target audience. In such cases, tensions can build when different parties assume the role of advocating for a target audience. Developers of a product or system, for instance, might believe they know more about the uses for a feature they are adding. Technical communicators working with the developers might argue that the feature will likely be used in another manner or not at all. Arguments may ensue over what should be noted in the supporting documentation, what should be emphasized, and what should be explained in more—or less—detail. One participant in our study mentioned a situation such as this in which a remote collaborator wrote a long note of complaints about a text with one paragraph in red. From the technical writer's perspective, this paragraph was suggesting something that the team at large had discussed and addressed earlier. The technical writer quickly e-mailed the remote collaborator about her "fundamental misunderstanding of the file structure...." The technical writer shared that "The person who wrote in red later told me she was offended by my response, to which I said I was offended by her red paragraph." In this case, the two who collaborated closely but remotely for some time worked out the issue via the telephone. At times, the circumstances of the virtual setting mitigate this type of disagreement; sometimes the circumstances exacerbate it. In any case, to stay on track, collaborators who are local and remote have to recognize the extent to which they are dependent on one another. They therefore need to work to clarify and make explicit the agreements, aims, and scope of a project. A content management system or shared database can work to keep decisions and agreements about scopes, aims, and guiding principles posted for all to see.

Another complication of staying on track can occur when various collaborators hail from different places. Each writer is embedded in his or her own organizational culture; even in large, multinational corporations, the organizational culture varies from site to site. Variations in features of workplace socialization can potentially impact given writers' perspectives on the roles of the document, the organization, and the target audience. The issue can be further complicated when remote teams are reliant on outside consultants or employees who are part of outsourcing. Because of interdependencies, team members might not even realize when arguments result not just from individual differences but also as a result of distinct organizational cultures among other virtual collaborators. Kraut, Egido, & Galegher (1990) addressed the importance of collegial interactions in bringing distinctions to an explicit level: "When people communicate in ways that allow them to assess their partners' view of the world... and to use this information to change their conversational tactics, their communication becomes more effective and efficient than it might be when this feedback is lacking" (p. 169).

Yet another aspect of interdependencies relates to timing and the type of information that is needed by other team members. Collaborative writers themselves need to take into account the stages of a given project and to offer suggestions and commentary about a draft that are aligned with those stages. For example, when writing a document for a beta version of a product, a technical writer would not want to offer fine-grained analysis or fine-grained critique about a collaborator's use of an abbreviation. Similarly, when a writer has a serious concern about a feature of a product, that concern should be raised as early in the process as possible and not left waiting until, for example, 48 hours before the document is due.

Another important element related to interdependencies relies on individual contributions. Despite the shared effort, individuals collaborating nearly always need to work individually on components of a given information product. This factor is important to keep in mind as well when we consider the need to stay on track. Individuals need to know what their individual responsibilities and tasks are and what deadlines are required to keep the collaborative project moving forward. Teams can take time to establish these expectations and at least one person on the team can take the lead on seeing that individuals are contributing along the agreed-upon lines so that no one piece is holding up the progress of others. This is particularly important because of the interdependencies of collaborative writers. Text written by one member of the team might be required for a subsequent piece of text to be created or expanded. To add to the complications, in many collaborative writing projects, some people on the team are "idle" on a given project, while others are working quite frantically (Kraut, 2002). While writers are currently idle on one project, they might be in a frantic stage with another project with its own deadlines that need to be taken into account. Here is where the public calendar and the shared database can play important roles, allowing others to see and coordinate schedules.

Considering Issues for Selecting Appropriate Tools

To put it simply, projects are easier to complete when we can get the information we need when we need it. Selecting appropriate tools for a given purposes or junctures in a project and establishing protocols with other collaborators can be key to being able to do the getting what we need when we need it.

When virtual collaborative writers must communicate with other team members, many factors play a role—the relationship one has with the parties one needs to communicate with, time zones, urgency, complexity, and so on. These factors—and more—contribute to the decisions we make each day about the media we use to communicate with collaborators. An orchestration of factors can shape our choices and the purposes for which we primarily use one medium over another. Some media (such as IM) afford more immediate and spontaneous one-to-one interaction; other media (such as videoconferencing) afford a broad reach and synchronous discussion. More studies are identifying factors related to matches between media and purpose, for instance.

Dabbish, Kraut, Fussell, & Kiesler (2005) studied e-mail messaging behaviors and e-mail message content and identified such primary purposes for e-mail as "action requests, status updates, reminders, information requests and responses, scheduling requests and responses, and social content" (p. 693). Similarly, in our study of the use of interactive tools in daily workplace practice, writers listed appreciating affordances of IM for the following purposes:

- Allowing for quick exchanges
- Taking a quick break from work to chat
- Providing updates
- Checking on where a latest version might be
- Checking on a collaborator's status to determine how best to communicate at a given point
- Sending quick reminders
- Answering quick questions or receiving answers to them
- Establishing contact ("Are you busy?" "OK if I call you now?")
- Getting clarification about something that was said or done
- Sending examples
- Checking quickly on a definition
- Tracking who on the remote team is available at a given time
- Following up on important issues
- Getting attention from a person who tends to lag behind in response time
- Allowing a writer to "force" an immediate response

For online collaborative teams that rely on such practices, IM can be a good choice when protocols

are established and expectations are shared with the team. Without protocols established in given work teams or organizations, IM status will not prove useful for tracking people or documents. Even if someone is not "in" according to a status icon, he or she may very well be at work and available for a phone call or other interaction.

Hill, Yates, Jones, & Kogan (2006) discussed how larger tasks can become more unmanageable with the use of multiple quick reply tools, such as the phone or IM. Indeed, sometimes what a writer needs to say to others on the team is too complex or formal for IM. When collaborative writers suspect their question requires complex answers, they might want to choose e-mail or some alternative medium that better supports reflection.

The nature of the information needing to be discussed will also guide decisions about communication tools. Based on their research, Walsh and Maloney (2007) suggested that with e-mail and communication tools allowing for interacting asynchronously, with detail, a collaborative team can facilitate coordination and help writers keep on track. Collaborative writers can make note of their progress and provide rationale for changes, additions to the collaborative text, revisions of other writers' work, and so on.

Asynchronous online communication can also provide team members time for reflection as they compose notes to one another and time for clarifying or specifying information with care. As a technical writer in our study mentioned, "Because IM implies immediacy, not necessarily accuracy, I often find myself having to revise what I've previously typed because it has been misunderstood or questioned. In these situations, a longer in-depth email or phone conversation probably would've worked just as well and in the same amount of time as the IM communication." When explanations or details are complex or need to be precise, an asynchronous medium will tend to be preferred.

The project deadline is often used as a starting place for determining the communicative tools that are used. A participant in our pilot study emphasized using the deadline for just that purpose: "Look at the deadline first. Then look at the tasks required to complete the project to meet that deadline. Take into account the quality being aimed for in this deadline." In the early stages of a project, when colocated team members tend to meet face-to-face, remote collaborators might choose to use videoconferencing tools. But when the deadline approaches and many members are polishing their respective contributions, a videoconference could be interruptive to many participants. In that case, such asynchronous options as announcements on a shared database, content management system (CMS), or e-mail system might be preferable. As a technical writer in our pilot study mentioned, "On days when deadlines are near, I email rather than IM to keep my interruptions to a minimum."

When selecting media for communication, we should also take into account the historical and organizational memory requirements of given collaborative documents. Depending on the medium used to communicate, we might lose track of our "project memory" conducted online. If virtual collaborators rely on phone conferencing for interacting and decision making, they might have divergent notions about why a decision was made or who was assigned a given task. If teams establish a protocol for communicating about and sharing drafts with a given CMS, they will have better, more immediate access to decisions made, task deadlines, role assignments, and external reminders. For case studies on collaboration using CMS technologies, see Chapter 9.

We also need to consider whether and when a system that supports interactions with multiple collaborators is required. Interacting with multiple collaborators allows all team members to keep track of where the project is, what issues are arising, what decisions are being made, and what progress on the information product looks like.

With one-to-one discussions between remote collaborators, information can be shared with specific people who most need it, but that too comes with potential issues. It can become challenging to remember who possesses what information. As the writing project proceeds, erroneous assumptions can be made about the rest of the team possessing information that had been shared one-to-one. Information shared in one-to-one interactions can ultimately be pivotal information that the subsequent work of the team should rely on: a change in direction, a section that should be highlighted in a text, a turn in the plans for an artifact a given text is supporting, and so on.

A robust online medium should allow collaborative writers to complete most of their tasks—initial or ongoing planning, discussions about the writing processes or products, drafting, revising, interacting, scheduling, and so on. The quickest form is not always the most advantageous. Hill et al. (2006) discussed complications of what they call "information scatter" when online collaborative writers use such tools as IM outside of the main software systems. Anecdotally, people are not likely to file instant messages, which can also prove problematic. If much of the interaction among collaborative writers takes place in IM, it is likely to be more difficult for the writers to later find what these researchers found in terms of people filing or retaining in emails: "status updates, reminders, or scheduling messages... retained... for later reference" (p. 693). These are the types of messages that typically do not require a reply, so e-mail is also likely a preferred medium for such purposes. In fact, Dabbish, Kraut, Fussell, & Kiesler (2005) reported that a majority of e-mail messages are filed in targeted folders or left in an inbox.

Interfaces and screen real estate can also impact virtual collaborative writing. As we write, we often need to multitask with multiple media at the same time or on the same project. One writer can have multiple screens open at one time and be working in each screen, composing text, reading, chatting in IM, and e-mailing almost simultaneously. We refer to this multitasking as *writing bounce*. Issues that arise with writing bounce include the limitations of the screen real estate—room for only so many screens and the challenges of focusing attention between them.

Clark & Brennan (1991) suggested other aspects related to the importance of screen real estate—the need for collaborative writers to "ground" their conversations while interacting. A study by Gergle, Millen, Kraut, & Fussell (2004) on collaborative grounding found two primary aspects related to screen real estate to play an important role for online collaborating:

- The ability to maintain online interactions for review by all participants
- The ability to share the screen remotely so all virtual collaborators can simultaneously see the same text or artifact being discussed

Teams working without established protocols will have to take a guess when selecting media for interacting with collaborators. For information about infrastructure tools to support virtual collaboration, see Chapter 10. Even in teams with established protocols and expectations about media choices, personalities can dictate what tools are used to interact and when. Sometimes a writer is tired of typing and chooses to call a collaborator. A person who is shy might prefer IM to avoid telephone or face-to-face interactions. Or a person might tend to choose e-mail more frequently because he or she feels more able to control his over her message with the additional time it allows for composing messages as compared to the allowance provided in synchronous communication (IM, phone, face-to-face).

In this section, we described the many factors related to norming in a virtual collaborative writing team. Taken together with the factors shared in the section on forming, it is all too clear that virtual collaborative writing is a challenge. Of the principles that ground this book, it is clear that Principle 1, developing a culture of collaboration, and Principle 2, establishing trust among team members, both help with the forming and norming processes. With attention to the issues we have raised, the virtual collaborative writing process can also lead to remarkable products, products far beyond the initial aims and expectations that brought the team together in the first place.

CONCLUSION

For virtual collaborative writing to succeed, team members have to agree on shared purposes and understandings. They have to coordinate their work with the work of others and piece the contributions together. After addressing issues related to forming virtual collaborative writing teams, this chapter has focused on the first two aspects mentioned here: developing shared goals and establishing rules for integrating the work of multiple remote collaborators.

As organizational contingency theorists would agree, no group of virtual collaborative writers can establish rules of engagement that will be effective if applied universally, whether for the same team of writers or for others. Similarly, the best choices for using communicative media for effective expression will vary from team to team and from context to context (Timmerman & Scott, 2006). Nonetheless, we have attempted in this chapter to raise issues that all virtual team members can consider as they or others enter a new remote team or begin a new task within the same team. In their study of virtual teams, Timmerman and Scott (2006) found that communication practices more strongly correlated with virtual team outcomes (identification as a team, cohesiveness, trust, and satisfaction) than did structural factors, such as team size, dispersion of team members, or type of organization. When explicit attention is devoted to considering development of not just the task but also the team, the outcome of virtual collaborative writing is more likely to be a stronger product and a more productive and satisfying experience overall.

REFERENCES

Bond, A. H., & Gasser, L. (Eds.). (1988). *Readings in distributed artificial intelligence*. San Mateo, CA: Morgan Kaufmann.

Brumberger, E. R. (2003a). The rhetoric of typography: The awareness and impact of typeface appropriateness. *Technical Communication, 50*(2), 224–231.

Brumberger, E. R. (2003b). The rhetoric of typography: The persona of typeface and text. *Technical Communication, 50*(2), 206–223.

Brumberger, E. R. (2004). The rhetoric of typography: Effects on reading time, reading comprehension, and perceptions of ethos. *Technical Communication, 51*(1), 13–24.

Clark, H. H., & Brennan, S. E. (1991). Grounding in communication. In Resnick, L. B., Levine, R. M., & Teasley, S. D. (Eds.), *Perspectives on socially shared cognition* (pp. 127–149). Washington, DC: American Psychological Association. doi:10.1037/10096-006

Cohen, S. G., & Bailey, D. E. (1997). What makes teams work: Group effectiveness research from the shop floor to the executive suite. *Journal of Management, 23*, 239–290. doi:10.1177/014920639702300303

Cummings, J. N. (2004). Work groups, structural diversity, and knowledge sharing in a global organization. *Management Science, 50*(3), 352–364. doi:10.1287/mnsc.1030.0134

Dabbish, L., Kraut, R., Fussell, S., & Kiesler, S. (2005). Understanding email use: Predicting action on a message. In *CHI 2005, Proceedings of the ACM conference on human factors in computing systems* (pp. 691 - 700). New York: ACM Press.

Dabbish, L., & Kraut, R. E. (2006). Email overload at work: An analysis of factors associated with email strain. In *Proceedings of the 2006 ACM conference on computer supported cooperative work* (pp. 431 - 440). New York: ACM Press.

DeSanctis, G., & Monge, M. (1998). Communication processes for virtual organizations. *Journal of Computer-Mediated Communication, 3*(4). Retrieved from http://jcmc.indiana.edu/vol3/issue4/desanctis.html.

Fish, R. S., Kraut, R. E., Root, R. W., & Rice, R. (1993). Evaluating video as a technology for information communication. *Communications of the ACM, 36*(1), 48–61. doi:10.1145/151233.151237

Fleming, D., Kaufer, D. S., Werner, M., & Sinsheimer-Weeks, A. (1993). Collaborative argument across the visual/verbal interface. *Technical Communication Quarterly, 2*(1), 37–49.

Flower, L. (1988). The construction of purpose in writing and reading. *College English, 50*(5), 528–550. doi:10.2307/377490

Gergle, D., Millen, D. R., Kraut, R. E., & Fussell, S. R. (2004). Persistence matters: Making the most of chat in tightly-coupled work. In *CHI'04: Proceedings of the Conference on Human Factors in Computing Systems,* (pp. 431-438). New York: ACM.

Gersick, C. J. G. (1988). Time and transition in work teams: Toward a new model of group development. *Academy of Management Journal, 31*(1), 9–41. doi:10.2307/256496

Grudin, J. (1988). Why CSCW applications fail: Problems in the design and evaluation of organizational interfaces. In *Proceedings of the ACM 1988 conference on Computer-supported cooperative work.* (pp. 85-93). New York: ACM.

Hewett, B. L., & Hewett, R. J. (2008). *Instant messaging (IM) literacy in the workplace* (pp. 455–472). Hershey, PA: IGI Global.

Hill, C., Yates, R., Jones, C., & Kogan, S. L. (2006). Beyond predictable workflows: Enhancing productivity in artful business processes. *IBM Systems Journal, 45*(4), 663–682. doi:10.1147/sj.454.0663

Hirokawa, R. Y., & Salazar, A. J. (1999). Task-group communication and decision-making performance. In Frey, L. R., Gouran, D. S., & Poole, M. S. (Eds.), *The handbook of group communication theory and research* (pp. 167–191). Thousand Oaks, CA: Sage.

Jarvenpaa, S. L., & Leidner, D. E. (1998). Communication and trust in global virtual teams. *Journal of Computer-Mediated Communication, 3*(4). Retrieved from http://jcmc.indiana.edu/vol3/issue4/jarvenpaa.html.

Klein, C., DiazGranados, D., Salas, E., Le, H., Burke, C.S., Lyons, R., & Goodwin, G.F. (2009). *Small Group Research, 40*(2), 181-222. doi:10.1177/1046496408328821

Kraut, R., Galegher, J., & Egido, C. (1988). Tasks and relationships in scientific research collaborations. *Human-Computer Interaction, 3*, 31–58. doi:10.1207/s15327051hci0301_3

Kraut, R., & Streeter, L. (1995). Coordination in large scale software development. *Communications of the ACM, 38*(3), 69–81. doi:10.1145/203330.203345

Kraut, R. E. (2002). Applying social psychological theory to the problems of group work. In Carroll, J. (Ed.), *Theories in Human-Computer Interaction* (pp. 325–356). New York: Morgan-Kaufmann Publishers.

Kraut, R. E., Egido, C., & Galegher, J. (1990). Patterns of communication and contact in scientific collaboration. In Galegher, J., Kraut, R. E., & Egido, C. (Eds.), *Intellectual teamwork: The social and technological bases of cooperative work* (pp. 149–171). Hillsdale, NJ: Lawrence Erlbaum Associates.

Kraut, R. E., Galegher, J., Fish, R. S., & Chalfonte, B. (1993). Task requirements and media choice in collaborative writing. *Human-Computer Interaction, 7*(4), 375–408. doi:10.1207/s15327051hci0704_2

Lampel, J., & Bhalla, A. (2007). The role of status seeking in online communities: Giving the gift of experience. *Journal of Computer-Mediated Communication, 12*(2), article 5. Retrieved from http://jcmc.indiana.edu/vol12/issue2/lampel.html

McGrath, J. E. (1984). *Groups: Interaction and performance.* Englewood Cliffs, NJ: Prentice-Hall.

McGrath, J. E. (1991). Time, interaction, and performance (TIP): A theory of groups. *Small Group Research, 22*(2), 147–174. doi:10.1177/1046496491222001

Neuwirth, C. M., Kaufer, D. S., Chandhok, R., & Morris, J. H. (1990). Issues in the design of computer support for co-authoring and commenting. In *Conference on Computer Supported Cooperative Work* (CSCW '90) (pp. 183-195). New York: Association for Computing Machinery.

Parker, R. (1997). *Looking good in print. Research Triangle.* NC: Ventana Communications Group, Inc.

Perlow, L. (1999). The time famine: Towards a sociology of work time. *Administrative Science Quarterly, 44*(1), 57–81. doi:10.2307/2667031

Salas, E., Priest, H. A., Stagl, K. C., Sims, D. E., & Burke, S. (2006). Work teams in organizations: A Historical reflection and lessons Learned. In Koppes, L. L. (Ed.), *Historical perspectives in industrial and organizational psychology* (pp. 407–438). Mahwah, NJ: Lawrence Erlbaum Associates.

Schuman, S.P. (2001). ed. "Editor's note," Special issue on group development. *Group Facilitation: A Research and Applications Journal, 3*, 66.

Siegel, J., Dubrovsky, V., Kiesler, S., & McGuire, T. (1986). Group processes in computer-mediated communication. *Organizational Behavior and Human Decision Processes, 37*(2), 157–187. doi:10.1016/0749-5978(86)90050-6

Sproull, L. (1984). The nature of managerial attention. *Advances in Information Processing in Organizations, 1*, 9-27. Greenwich, CT: JAI Press.

Sproull, L., & Kiesler, S. (1991). *Connections: New ways of working in the networked organization.* Cambridge, MA: The MIT Press.

Sproull, L. S., & Kiesler, S. (1986). Reducing social context cues: The case of electronic mail. *Management Science, 32,* 1492–1512. doi:10.1287/mnsc.32.11.1492

Taylor, S. K. (2005). *Preparing technical communicators for the software industry: Teaching technology or teaching theory?* Paper presented at the Association for Teachers of Technical Writing. San Francisco, CA.

Timmerman, C. E., & Scott, C. R. (2006). Virtually working: Communicative and structural predictors of media use and key outcomes in virtual work teams. *Communication Monographs, 73*(1), 108–136. doi:10.1080/03637750500534396

Tuckman, B. W. (1965). Developmental sequence in small groups. *Psychological Bulletin, 63*(6), 384–399. doi:10.1037/h0022100

Tuckman, B. W., & Jensen, M. A. (1977). Stages of small-group development revisited. *Group Organizational Studies, 2,* 419–427. doi:10.1177/105960117700200404

Van de Ven, A. H., Delbecq, A. L., & Koenig, R. Jr. (1976). Determinants of coordination modes within organizations. *American Sociological Review, 41,* 322–338. doi:10.2307/2094477

Walsh, J. P., & Maloney, N. G. (2007). Collaboration structure, communication media, and problems in scientific work teams. *Journal of Computer-Mediated Communication, 12*(2), 19. Retrieved from http://jcmc.indiana.edu/vol12/issue2/walsh.html. doi:10.1111/j.1083-6101.2007.00346.x

Chapter 5
Forming Trust in Virtual Writing Teams:
Perspectives and Applications

Sean D. Williams
Clemson University, USA

ABSTRACT

This chapter explores collaborative writing in virtual teams, and, particularly, trust formation in virtual writing teams, to help those who create or work in virtual writing teams to understand the importance of trust. In order to build the case for trust as the key component in teams, the chapter presents important background on teams as a general concept. In particular, it considers the constituents of quality teams, which include small team size, diverse team membership, interdependent relationships, shared team vision, articulated processes, and performance orientation. The chapter then elaborates on the role of trust in teams, presenting it as the key feature for any type of team environment. Based on this background, the chapter then differentiates the general concept of teams from virtual teams in particular, arguing that virtual teams must address specific considerations in order to build trust. Such considerations include the composition of the team, where team members possess a propensity to trust; the proper use of technology in the virtual team, so that the medium matches the communicative need; and social presence, or the ways that virtual teams can build trust by using communication behaviors to demonstrate to others that they share understanding. The chapter combines the general team considerations with the virtual team considerations into a rubric for building strong virtual teams based upon four major categories: team traits, team actions, individual traits, and environment traits. The chapter concludes with suggestions for future study.

DOI: 10.4018/978-1-60566-994-6.ch005

INTRODUCTION AND BACKGROUND

Imagine this situation as I experienced it:

A contract technical writer is hired as an outside expert to manage a documentation project for a large bank; the bank management hopes to bring some order to the documentation concerning a specific internal product. The team brings together a group of subcontracted writers and some members of the internal communications group from the bank—12 people in all—with a goal of delivering 900 pages of documentation in less than 3 months. The subcontracted technical writers are located in three different states, the client is in another state, and the project manager resides in a fifth state—all of which make face-to-face collaboration nearly impossible. To complicate matters, some of the documents provided by the bank are in "old" word-processing formats, such as Word Perfect® format, while others are handwritten or in PowerPoint®, MS® Word, or Adobe® PageMaker® format. Finally, the documents contain large numbers of figures and tables, all of which are numbered inconsistently at best. Combine the complexity of the documents facing the team with the multitude of formats, the challenges of working remotely, and the pressures of completing the project under a tight deadline, and one can imagine the stress the team feels as it squanders hours debating inconsequential things, such as how to format headings or what software to use for creating figures. These small stresses escalate into disagreements about the distribution of work within the team, some members resorting to silence as a form of protest and outright competition between the team of internal bank employees who "know the bank way" and the contractors who know "the best way." As a result of the team's various dysfunctions, key deadlines pass and ultimately the team fractures into two autonomous work groups. The project manager is left compiling the separate pieces into some cohesive documentation over a series of three very long weeks without assistance from the other team members, who by this point have all but given up on the project. Let us say that the result of this chaos is that the documentation is substandard and that the project manager never will be invited to bid on another project for this client.

Admittedly, this situation is about as bad as it gets: A group of individuals who are supposed to work together to achieve a shared purpose instead compete with one another and undermine each other's work as bad feelings mount and communication breaks down among the team members. The team misses deadlines and blame-based e-mails fly from keyboards because individuals feel like their expertise is not being respected. Compound these challenges with the difficulties of collaboratively writing through electronic media—with the choice of collaboration medium itself a point of dispute—and we have all the ingredients for the catastrophic failure that befell this writing team.

Yet, virtual teamwork does not need to be that way. Successful teams appear in almost every facet of society and workplace. From athletics to industry, to government and nonprofit agencies, there are myriad different incarnations of cooperative groups. Groups such as, "committees, task forces, blue-ribbon panels, quality circles, employee-participation groups, joint union/management leadership teams, action committees, project teams, supervisor councils, autonomous or self-directed work teams," and collaborative writing teams are a few examples (Huszczo, 1990, n.p.). Most often, teams are implemented because they are perceived to possess a wide array of benefits including increased employee buy-in, greater responsibility, improved productivity, better product quality, increased employee satisfaction, higher quality of work life, and enhanced efficiency (Gustafson & Kleiner, 1994; Neck, Manz, & Anand, 2000; Purdum, 2005). Companies use teams because the advantages of teamwork translate into increased cost savings and greater employee satisfaction—assuming that the teams are well-conceived and managed, unlike the writing team profiled in the opening scenario.

A multitude of disciplines influence current theories on teamwork. Psychologists (social, industrial, organizational, mathematical, human factors, cognitive, military, and engineering) as well as sociologists, anthropologists, and workplace writing scholars all contribute research to the field. In fact, one study found that more than 130 labels are used to describe the knowledge, skills, and attitudes that teams must possess to function effectively (Salas & Cannon-Bowers, 2000, p. 326). Additionally, some of the newest research suggests that virtual teams are becoming a favorable alternative to teams built and supported in a single location (Jarvenppa & Leidner, 1999; Robey, Khoo, & Powers, 2000). Virtual teams have great potential for success; however, virtual teams also possess certain complexities that can hinder progress, as we witnessed in the opening scenario. Chief among these complexities is *trust* (or lack thereof)—the trust that every team requires to be successful—and it one of this book's six core principles for writing in virtual teams. In this chapter's opening example, the bank employees mistrusted the contractors and vice versa, which resulted in the team's failure. As virtual teams become more prevalent in the workplace, the need for research that examines trust in virtual teams becomes more relevant in order to avoid the type of dysfunction exhibited by the writing team in the opening scenario. Therefore, the purpose of this chapter is to explore collaborative writing in virtual teams, and particularly trust formation in virtual writing teams, to help those who create or work in virtual writing teams to understand the importance of trust.

This chapter provides some background on the general concept of teams, including a brief history of teams, what comprises teams, and the role of trust in teams. After this introduction, it discusses virtual writing teams in more detail, outlining the difference between virtual teams and traditional teams and discussing the specific types of trust involved in successful virtual teams whose primary role is collaborative writing. Finally, the chapter ends with a practical overview—a checklist almost—for building strong virtual teams. It concludes with some future research directions.

A BRIEF HISTORY OF TEAMS IN THE UNITED STATES

Conversations about teams in the workplace began in the early twentieth century in the United States. At that time, scientific management principles held the most dominant position until at least mid-century. These principles were characterized primarily by time and task measures of performance; a regard for employees as expendable brutes who could be replaced at a whim by another brute to do the same repetitive work; and strict, unbreakable hierarchies. For example, much research published in the 1920s argued in favor of scientific management principles by demonstrating that teams, rather than increasing productivity, diminished individual productivity in team efforts. Support for this position came from social psychology studies, such as the Ringelmann Rope-Pull Paradigm, that found in team rope pull exercises, teams of three performed at 85% of their potential while teams of eight reached only 49% of their potential (Porter & Beyerlein, 2000, p. 5). Based on evidence like this, many believed that individuals could not be held accountable for team output, and so management in American companies continued to focus on task simplification, task efficiency and individual performance rather than developing team-based models in which workers held collective responsibilities within a horizontal structure (Huszczo, 1990; Gustafson & Kleiner, 1994). Clearly, this chapter's opening scenario supports the position that teams degrade performance.

This negative position toward collective responsibility held firm through the 1950s as American industry prospered following World War II while other industrialized nations struggled just to recover from the war's aftermath (Schneider & Stepp, 1998, n.p.). However, by the mid-1970s, industrialization had improved in those countries ruined by the war and those countries began producing superior goods at costs lower than American businesses. The influx of these foreign products caused declines in profitability for U.S. companies, and the American firms began to examine the practices of their foreign competitors, and Japan in particular, where the concept of had become rooted. These quality circles were the earliest forms of modern teams because members were given the autonomy to collaboratively analyze workplace problems and then propose solutions to management for solving those issues. Quality circles differ from teams, though, because they were not focused specifically on accomplishing assigned tasks or work. Instead, quality circles focused on improving the workplace or processes within the workplace, thus contributing as much to improving efficiency as to improving the work climate. Additionally, unlike teams, quality circles remained intact over time because they focused on improving the workplace overall and not on completing specific jobs that might come and go (Gustafson & Kleiner, 1994, p. 16).

Despite Japanese success with quality circles, "U.S. manufacturers were slow to follow Japan's example" (Huszczo, 1990, n.p.). The first American businesses to experiment with team structures on the Japanese model were Lockheed Manufacturing, Proctor and Gamble, and General Foods (Gustafson & Kleiner, 1994, p. 16). For example, the General Foods Topeka Kansas plant opened in 1971 with a revolutionary structure designed for maximum employee participation. It featured flattened hierarchies, interrelated employee teams with flexible task responsibility, a learner-centered environment upheld by a monetary bonus system, and participative decision making at the lowest levels in the organization (Lee, 1990, p. 25). While today in the United States, this would be an exemplary model of a team-oriented organization, in the early 1970s, this structure was radical.

By the 1980s, news of the successes demonstrated by this type of structure had spread and companies like Digital Equipment Corporation, TRW, and Cummins Engine were also reporting 30 to 40% productivity gains (Huszczo, 1990, n.p.). By the 1990s and moving into the twenty-first century, teams have become so commonplace that their existence has become transparent and popular press books such as Katzenbach and Smith's *The Wisdom of Teams* (1993) have become required reading in business circles. Katzenbach and Smith summarized the position that evolved in the 1990s, stating—in direct opposition to positions in the early twentieth century—that teams "outperform individuals acting alone or in larger organizational groupings" (Katzenbach & Smith, 1993, p. 3).

This position holds only if teams are constructed and managed well. As illustrated in the chapter's opening scenario, teams do possess the potential for failure if those who use them are unaware of the complications and requirements that they entail. In the sections that follow, I discuss the components that would have improved the collaboration of the documentation team in the opening scenario, had the team been constructed and managed with these concepts in mind.

CONSTITUENTS OF A QUALITY WRITING TEAM

Because teams are now transparent for most people regardless of job type, whether in industry, in government, or in the nonprofit sector, it is helpful to step back and defamiliarize the constituents of teams. Research shows that teams succeed best when they are composed of specific characteristics—ones that mirror this book's six core principles—and include, for example, certain types of environments, individual characteristics, group processes, networked behavior, and goal-oriented outcomes. As outlined famously by Katzenbach and Smith (1993), teams are "a small number of people with complementary skills who are committed to a common purpose, performance goals, and approach for which they hold themselves mutually accountable" (p. 45). To place the commonplace concept of teams specifically within the context of collaborative writing and to prepare to examine its relationship to trust, it is helpful here to outline six essential characteristics of successful writing teams:

- Limited team size
- Diverse team membership
- Interdependent relationships
- Shared Team Vision
- Performance orientation
- Articulated team processes

Limited Team Size

Team size influences writing teams socially, psychologically, and logistically. In groups that are too large or too small, uneven distribution of the workload can occur; small groups might not offer the range of skills needed to complete the task, but a large group might encounter logistical constraints and negative group behaviors, such as "groupthink" or "social loafing" (Blickensderfer, Salas, & Cannon-Bowers, 2000). For this reason, Katzenbach and Smith (1993) recommended a limited group size of no more than 20 to 25 members. Expanding these numbers, they cautioned, makes it difficult to perform important functions can impede the evaluation process and cause crowd or herd behaviors that reduce team productivity (Katzenbach & Smith, 1993, p. 46). A version of this kind of behavior was illustrated in this chapter's opening scenario, as the bank team reacted negatively to the contractors. Granted, the bank team was small and the overall team was relatively small at 12 people total, but the bank subgroup was large enough to set it at odds with the goals of the larger team. In fact, recent research suggested that 20 to 25 may be too large a team; Blickensderfer, et al. (2000) argued that

teams composed of three to five members are most successful (p. 257).

Within the context of writing teams, these smaller teams of up to five writers usually are more efficient due to the complex interactions necessary to write collaboratively. Writers must share and discuss drafts and often work through nuanced stylistic differences. When too many writers become involved, the team reaches a point of diminishing returns because debating the merits of using commas versus dashes, for example, can negatively affect productivity. And, when productivity declines, then social cohesion also declines.

Diverse Team Membership

Whether the team is a product development team, specialized-job group, or writing team, diversification of skill sets within the team is necessary to reach team goals and maintain group function. For teams to prosper, "team members must possess certain knowledge, skills, and attitudes to facilitate teamwork" (Salas & Cannon-Bowers, 2000, p 327). Team members must demonstrate a mix of technical, problem-solving, decision-making, and interpersonal skills. For example, research on team membership has shown that diverse teams are more accurate, more efficient, more adaptable, and require less training than their more homogenous, and less skilled, counterparts (Blickensderfer et al., 2000, p. 262).

Writing teams are no different from other teams in this respect. Individuals with complementary skills produce the best teams. For example, I recently participated in a grant proposal writing team that successfully achieved its goal of receiving a $1.5 million award. The team consisted of a seasoned professional grant writer as project manager; a computer scientist and computer engineer who provided much of the domain knowledge; a technical writer who translated the technical knowledge into approachable language; an information designer who created the argumentative structure of the proposal; a graphic designer who created a professional appearance in the document; an editor who performed comprehensive and copy editing tasks; and a proofreader who ensured the quality of the final document. This team assumed a "divide and draft" approach to writing that worked well because each team member knew what was expected based on negotiations prior to beginning the collaboration. Each team member also relied on the work of the others to create the final document because no one individual could do individually what the team could accomplish together.

Interdependent Relationships

As the anecdote about the grant writing team demonstrates, team members must be interdependent. Having a diverse team enables interdependence. In 1949, Deutsch theorized this concept, calling it "social interdependence." This theory sought to explain the underlying motivation for group behavior based on cooperation and competition. Deutsch defined interdependence as "behavior that depended not only on whether individuals were in a group but also how they believed their goals were related to each other" (qtd in Tjosvold & Johnson, 2000, p. 133). This and later research showed that interdependent exchange leads to responsible decisions, productivity, and success due to the mutual affirmation of group members. As the grant writing anecdote shows, individual accountability is needed to achieve results, but team members must also accept responsibility for the fulfillment of team goals—each individual must see how his or her contribution advances the goals of the entire team. The opening scenario with the bank shows what happens when teams do not possess social interdependence; when individuals do not view their own contributions in light of the larger team goals, they fail. Because of this duality, team members should be held ac-

countable independently and teams also should be evaluated as a unit according to the outcomes of the product. When teams *and* team members are simultaneously held accountable, team members will see their actions as simultaneously individual and collaborative, enhancing a sense of interdependence.

Shared Team Vision: Centralized Group Goals

Clear understanding of the overall team vision assists in developing a meaningful direction, strong momentum, and sustained commitment. The grant writing team shared a vision that the bank documentation team clearly did not share. When team members share a group goal, the common identity builds cohesion, and cohesive teams generally perform better than noncohesive ones. In fact, a meta-analysis of hundreds of studies showed that "cooperative goals promote communication and exchange," while individual goals promote unhealthy competition and can even create an environment for openly counterproductive behaviors (Tjosvold & Johnson, 2000, p. 131).

Writing teams often struggle with a shared team vision, suggesting that teams should articulate—literally write down—their purpose early in the collaborative process. For example, all team members should know the context of the document, such as the problems the document will address and its intended audience. In general terms, the team must also share a vision about the rhetorical nature of the document: Is it a persuasive piece or an expository piece? What are the appropriate genres allowed within the general purpose, rhetorical purpose, and organization? To paraphrase a commonly circulated truism, writing teams must "begin with the end in mind." If team members know where they are going and negotiate their differences based upon a sense of mutual interest, then the team becomes far more efficient.

Performance Orientation

In addition to the structure that a centralized group vision provides, teams also need to focus on action. Simply saying what the plan is does little to solidify a team; it needs actual activity directed toward that goal. According to Katzenbach and Smith (1993), "Most small groups can deliver the performance results that require and produce team behavior... by focusing on performance—not chemistry or togetherness or good communications or good feelings" (p. 3). In other words, a bias toward action can bring teams together better because focusing on the goals separates the people from the problem, to paraphrase Fisher and Ury's (1983) method of conflict resolution (p. 11). In turn, everybody directs their attention to accomplishing the shared objective, and therefore communication, actions, and morale itself all stem from progress toward the single goal. In the opening scenario, we saw that as performance degraded, team cohesion likewise degraded, initiating a vicious cycle of increased animosity and decreased productivity.

The emphasis on tasks, however, does not mean that teams should not enjoy their time together. Quite the contrary, as social information processing theory teaches. Specifically, teams must have a level of social engagement that supports the task requirements. The highest functioning teams, in fact, simultaneously socialize *and* pursue instrumental outcomes (Walther & Bunz, 2005, p. 832). Writing teams, then, must pursue their shared team goal, but they must also allow for some extracurricular socializing. I address the particulars of social information processing later in this chapter, in the discussion of building strong virtual teams.

Articulated Team Process: Standardized Group Functions

As Principle 5 from Chapter 1 suggests, people often feel most comfortable moving from task-based activity to socializing when they know the rules of the game. For example, Nilsson (2000) advocated a structured approach to internal team function so that all the team members know what is expected and how the team will collaborate (p. 284). This standardization allows groups to set predictable patterns of behavior and understand their roles in helping the team achieve its outcomes. Additionally, articulated processes also ensure that the team produces uniform products because everybody understands the criteria against which their work will be judged. Developing standardized working approaches, therefore, go hand-in-hand with meeting goals because common approaches that incorporate social, economic, and administrative elements help teams achieve success by prescribing a clear model for how team members will work together.

For writing teams, these processes can take many forms. For example, clear expectations about who will be accountable for particular activities on a specific schedule give team members transparent goals to achieve. Likewise, creating style sheets and style guides prior to writing—and agreeing that all team members will adhere to those guidelines—streamlines later editorial decisions. Additional decisions regarding software use and interoperability, methods of sharing files, approaches to naming files, and appropriate times for synchronous activity all aid team members in sharing a process. In the story that opened this chapter, such processes were not articulated, and what should have been small inconveniences erupted into full-scale conflicts as the tension mounted and deadlines approached.

Physical Collocation

Many of the characteristics of successful teams discussed earlier imply that team members are physically present with one another—that they inhabit a shared physical space. Sharing space causes workers to influence each other intentionally and unintentionally, sometimes positively and sometimes negatively. Routine tasks benefit significantly from shared space, while more complicated tasks often are hindered by another person's presence. The length of time that team members spend together also contributes to the development of team identity. That group identity in turn creates routines that become the basis for commonality, which itself then enables teams to become more productive as complex tasks become routine. In other words, collocation can transform the complex into the routine, leading to greater productivity and worker satisfaction as the team develops the culture of collaboration articulated in 1 (see Chapter 1). This process suggests that individuals working in physical proximity synchronize their work cycles, work rates, interaction patterns, communication timing, and even breathing patterns. Proximity also influences the development and maintenance of group identity though group culture, authority, and norms (Tjosvold & Johnson, 2000; McGrath I Hollingshead, 1994). If writing teams are physically colocated, they benefit from easy interactions: John walks down the hall to talk to Sarah about what she meant when she wrote such and such. This interaction engenders shared understanding of the project as John and Sarah talk about their respective contributions; it also establishes patterns of interaction—it is okay for Sarah to question John now. These two have built a relationship—they trust each other—largely because they share the same physical space and can interact in real time through the richness of face-to-face conversation. Those who work in virtual teams, however, have to work hard to build such trust because the markers present in conversation are much less visible. But the role of trust is no less important for virtual teams. The next section outlines the components of trust in teams, so that those who work virtually can build an understanding of just how important trust is for their success.

THE ROLE OF TRUST IN TEAMS

Communication, cooperation, shared social norms—indeed all the concepts outlined earlier—provide the foundation for trust, the single most important component of successful teams regardless of the team's goal. Mayer, Davis, and Schoorman (1995) defined trust as "the willingness of a party to be vulnerable to the actions of another party based on the expectation that the other will perform a particular action....irrespective of the ability to monitor or control that other party" (p. 712). For them, trust represented one of the most essential constituents of successful teams and represents the third of the six core principles for virtual collaborative writing, as described in Chapter 1. When trust exists, especially in an ego-threatening activity like writing, where writers often feel individual ownership of their texts, teams perform tasks to a higher standard because the team members believe in the good intentions of their collaborators. Because this concept of trust is so important for teams of every type—and writing teams are no different—the following discussion develops this concept more fully by discussing the components of trust.

Components of Trust in Teams

Mayer, Davis, and Schoorman (1995) argued that trust is comprised of characteristics on both the part of the "trustor" and the perceived character of the "trustee" and empirically demonstrated that the following factors contribute to trust in organizational teams:

- **Ability.** A set of skills, competencies, and characteristics that enable a party to have influence within some specific domain. Ability depends on the trustee.
- **Benevolence**. The extent to which one party believes that another wants to do the

right thing aside from any egocentric motives (such as a profit motive). Benevolence depends on the trustee.

- **Integrity.** The perception that the trustee adheres to a set of principles that the one who is doing the trusting finds acceptable. Integrity depends on the trustee.
- **Propensity to trust.** A natural predisposition toward or away from trust or a party's inclination to believe that others will not harm him or her.
- **Risk-taking action.** Willingness on the part of the trusting party to be vulnerable and to choose risk even when there are other options. (p. 715)

These factors that contribute to trust are called *antecedents,* and they exist prior to a trusting relationship. These antecedents do not form trust, but they facilitate the process of building it. Most individuals also exhibit a continuum of trusting behavior, ranging from those who "repeatedly trust in situations that most people would agree do not warrant trust" to those who are "unwilling to trust in most situations regardless of circumstances that would support doing so." Mayer, Davis, and Schoorman (1995) suggested that propensity combined with ability, integrity, and benevolence result in trusting action (p. 715). Finally, these different attributes manifest themselves more prominently at differing stages of the relationship. Prior to interaction or during the initial meetings, when one team member knows little about the other team members, propensity to trust becomes the primary determinant in trusting behavior; this is a concept I return to when speaking about virtual teams. After interactions begin, individual contributions heavily influence trust development; however, in later exchanges, benevolence tends to influence trust more than individual action (p. 722). These elements broke down in the scenario that opened this chapter. The members of the writing team entered the collaboration with a distrustful stance—demonstrated low propensity to trust—

and the bank employees questioned the integrity of the contract employees. The bank employees also might have questioned the benevolence of the contractors because, after all, contractors are often derided as being motivated solely by individual rewards. Finally, the collaborators questioned the abilities of others on the team, and this questioning combined with other failures quickly led to a dysfunctional team.

Types of Trust

Based on the antecedents, or the necessary precursors of trust, researchers also have characterized various types of trusting behaviors that teams demonstrate. One particularly coherent model comes from Lewicki and Bunker (1996), who proposed a three-stage model in which trust moves from action-oriented trust to what we might call *thick trust*:

- **Stage 1:** Deterrence-based trust
- **Stage 2:** Knowledge-based trust
- **Stage 3:** Identity-based trust (p. 118)

In *deterrence-based trust*, team members trust each other because if they do not, negative consequences can occur, and so the fear of punishment initially unites parties. When parties have united, they continue acting together for fear of reprimand, creating a cycle of negative reinforcement. Trust at this stage is fragile and subsides easily because the parties do not feel any significant responsibility to one another outside of the consequence. The team in the chapter's opening scenario never progressed beyond this phase, if they even achieved it in the first place.

Knowledge-based trust builds through recurrent interaction, as parties coordinate cycles of work, form common values for their work, and structure their interactions consistently. This trust evolves from predictability and frequent communication, both of which strengthen bonds. The grant writing team in the earlier anecdote acquired this type of trust through its compressed time line and frequent interactions to meet the tight deadline.

The final stage of the trust relationship, *identification-based trust*, represents the most secure stage. Parties can anticipate and act on the behalf of others because their values and norms align so closely. In short, each party understands and appreciates the other's wants, needs, and values and acts to realize these things because they share the same ideas. Because this trust is so "thick," it also is the most difficult to repair when it has been breached (Lewicki & Bunker, 1996, p. 128).

VIRTUAL TEAMS

In opposition to the concept of "thick" trust, the very name "virtual team" implies that such teams are shadows of so-called "real" teams because they do not have the deeply embedded identity that might characterize long-standing work teams. Yet, as the twenty-first century opens, globalization and the demands for improved performance and cost efficiency are challenging traditional, colocated team structures. One study of teams, for example, concluded that traditional models of teams have become less profitable in the face of the changing business environment that requires successful teams to evolve quickly and be adaptable (Lipnack & Stamps, 2000, pp. 175-78). Additionally, virtual teams are advantageous because of their "flexibility, responsiveness, lower costs, and improved resource utilization" (Jarvenpaa & Leidner 1999, p. 791). In short, organizations ranging from Fortune 500 companies to the U.S. Army have implemented virtual teams, resulting in significant cost savings, improved decision quality, and improved worker dedication to outcomes (Tullar, Kaiser, & Balthhazard, 1998, p. 53). Clearly, the idea of virtual teams, and the unique form of trust that characterizes them, is quickly becoming the new "normal" model of teamwork—particularly for writing teams—as individuals make the transition from long-standing

models of trust in teams to more dynamic and temporary models facilitated by technology.

Differences between Traditional Teams and Virtual Teams

Even though at their core virtual teams should embody the best practices that characterize traditional teams, the character of a virtual team differs enough from traditional teams that understanding the nuances of the difference will help in building stronger virtual teams. In its simplest form, a virtual team could be characterized as a group of individuals in different locations who work interdependently using technology (Lipnack & Stamps, 2000, pp. 39, 44, 48). Under scrutiny, this definition reveals how virtual writing teams might differ from traditional writing teams based upon their composition, their use of technology, and the role of social presence. I discuss each of these as a prelude to a more expansive discussion of trust formation in virtual teams, one of the key differences between virtual and traditional teams.

Composition

Because both colocated and virtual writing teams are created to produce documents, they share many qualities. However, fundamental differences exist between the two types of teams. For example, due to the dispersed membership and technological environment in which they operate, members of virtual writing teams need to possess a higher tolerance for the unexpected (Porter & Beyerlein, 2000, p. 18). Similarly, because virtual team members are not physically present—and therefore not accountable in the same way as colocated teammates—ideal virtual team members are self-sufficient, reliable, and good communicators (Robey, Khoo, & Powers, 2000, p. 58). Membership in virtual writing teams also should be highly selective, allowing participation only from writers who are self-motivated with unique skills and favoring those who can work interdependently while sharing a goal with others (Suchan & Hayzak, 2001, p 175). Approaching the composition of virtual writing teams in this way means that these types of teams can exhibit a highly diverse set of possible configurations that respond to specific, local needs within specific organizations, as writers with different areas of expertise, yet stable characteristics, collect into a writing team. For example, Majchrzak et al. (2004, p. 132) studied virtual teams across 54 companies and found that the virtual teams they studied had a variety of similar qualities. Those teams:

- Had members from more than one company
- Were occasionally long term
- Had been set up for a single project
- Were global
- Were regional
- Included people from at least three time zones
- Relied on a virtual work space to communicate
- Almost never met with all team members face to face

This list indicates that members of virtual teams represent a highly diverse set of people, ranging from those across different companies to those across continents and from different regions. Additionally, virtual teammates share the ability to collaborate without the connections enabled by face-to-face contact. In short, the composition of virtual teams embodies the definition of virtual as people work across organizational boundaries, space, and time using technology.

Technology and the Virtual Team

Due to the distributed nature of virtual teams, technology assumes a central role in the work of virtual teams because virtual teams simply cannot exist without some technological means of collaborating. These technologies can vary across organizations, but usually include e-mail, teleconferencing, videoconferencing, Web conferencing, online bulletin boards, instant messaging, and document sharing systems, to name a few. Most recently, there are 3D virtual worlds, wikis, and social media for virtual teams to collaborate both synchronously and asynchronously through the Internet (Kraut et al., 2002). Because these largely text-based methods of communication are familiar to writers, virtual teams can draw on the expertise of people across the globe, where the sun literally does not set on the work being accomplished. The presence of these technologies, then, makes virtual teams possible and writers are especially well-equipped to work within parameters restricted by technology.

With the vast number of technologies available, virtual teams must carefully consider which technologies suit their purposes as Principle 4 in Chapter 1 articulates about effective use of tools and collaborative modes. Media richness theory, described in Chapter 2, points the way here. This theory examines which types of technologies are most suitable for particular types of work because all writing activities are not accomplished equally well by all media. In short, media richness theory gauges how much content a particular medium can carry, hypothesizing that one reason virtual teams succeed (or fail) rests on the team's choice of technology. Individual technologies, that is, vary in the amount of feedback they allow, the number of verbal, nonverbal, and back-channeling cues available, and the emotional communication possibilities. Media richness theory research suggests that virtual teams face significant challenges because of the technology, positing the following:

- Electronic communication leads to increased negative communication, including assertive hostile language.
- Electronic communication can create a sense of depersonalization due to lack of social context cues.
- Electronic communication is perceived as less warm than face-to-face interaction.

- Consensus building is easier in face-to-face teams than in similar teams working through computer-mediated technology.
- When given a limited time frame, face-to-face teams outperform virtual teams. (Andres, 2002, p. 41)

This chapter's opening scenario is a perfect example of the ways that technology only amplified challenges that the team faced in their collaboration. One important strategy for mitigating the possible negative aspects of virtual teams is choosing the right technology for the right purpose; they must assess the particular purpose of a specific communication event and determine which medium will most likely achieve the desired outcome. For example, a team might select e-mail for task-related items and videoconferencing for conflict resolution or discussing complex issues. Chapter 10 more deeply addresses the issue of appropriateness in selecting the right virtual media for the task.

Social Presence

Perhaps the most important aspect for overcoming some problems of virtual teams rests with the concept of *social presence*, which Chapter 2 details. Social presence represents the concept of "being there" with other people, of feeling that you are working together with other real people. Virtual teams challenge most of the conventional standards of presence because the technology must enable the participants to "feel" the presence of their collaborators, which explains the rise of richer media, such as 3D virtual worlds that enable collaborators to "see" their partners and to see "emotions" through avatars. Likewise, videoconferencing and even instant messenger clients encourage team members to feel that others are present because these media require ongoing attention. In other words, if you are

here with me now, whether in a virtual world, in a videoconference, or in an online chat, then you cannot be somewhere else at the same time—you are present with me. Three-dimensional virtual worlds are particularly good at this because avatars enable certain nonverbal cues that approximate physical presence between real people, which further strengthens the sense of social presence. For example, avatars enable learners to approximate such cues as gaze, gestures, and proximity (Bronack, et al., 2008, p. 265).

Even with the challenges posed by technology and the mitigation of those challenges through social presence, research still points to the benefits of using electronic communication for teams. For example, virtual teams are sometimes the most focused teams because their physical distribution leads to infrequent face-to-face meetings. As a result, a virtual team may have:

- Fewer prejudgments about team members based on their looks
- Less influence of high-status members on the conformity of others
- Decreased distraction from non-verbal elements (gestures, and so on)
- Streamlined verbal exchanges that focus the message and use greater precision
- Depersonalized context (McGrath & Hollingshead, 1994; Gustafson & Kleiner, 2000)

In short, the difference between face-to-face teams and virtual teams resides primarily in the ways that the technologies can overcome the weaknesses of traditional teams. Using these technologies correctly, as Principle 4 recommends, also will help create a sense of presence, which likewise helps to achieve the goals of creating a culture of collaboration, the first principle of virtual, collaborative writing. These two principles must work together in virtual teams.

TRUST IN VIRTUAL TEAMS

Trust is the chief of all concerns for virtual teams. In the self-directed, sometimes isolated, virtual environment, trust becomes a pivotal element of success. Without trust, or with low levels of trust, virtual workers may engage in dysfunctional behavior that avoids interaction with other team members. Such symptoms as low commitment to a project, lack of information sharing, and focus on processes rather than outcomes might indicate low levels of trust, which limits the overall effectiveness of the group and decreases the productivity of a virtual team. Clearly, the workers in the chapter's opening scenario exhibited such behaviors. Trust invisibly, but markedly, facilitates the overall success of a team and understanding how it functions in virtual teams becomes paramount for ensuring the team's success. Without it, virtual teams may look and behave like the dysfunctional bank documentation team.

Solid performance of a virtual team cannot be achieved without trust, but how exactly does this trust come to exist? Virtual teams are not afforded the usual interaction opportunities that contribute to trust building, such as colocation (Jarvenpaa & Leidner, 1999; Coutu, 1998), and spontaneous communication (Tijosvolod & Johnson, 2000). To form traditional trust, it is necessary to have time, shared values, empathy, shared experience, reciprocal disclosure, fulfilled promises, and non-exploitation of vulnerability (Meyerson, Wieck, & Kramer, 1996; Lewicki & Bunker, 1996). Virtual teams, then, not only face the challenge of building trusting relationships like their face-to-face counterparts, but they must also build relationships through technology and across space and time (Robey, Khoo, & Powers, 2000, p. 63). Moreover, the issue of building trust in writing teams is especially challenging because writers often feel attached to their contributions. That is, writers must work a little harder to build trust in writing teams than in other types of teams because of the emotional investment that writing

commonly requires. The next section focuses on two important approaches to building trust in virtual teams, social information processing and *swift trust*, as ways of understanding how to build trust in writing teams.

Social Information Processing Theory

Perhaps the most important theory that describes how trust operates in virtual teams is social information processing (SIP). This perspective contends that "the restrictiveness of the computer medium, while hindering relational intimacy among unfamiliar participants, will dissipate over time" (Chidambaram, 1996, p. 145). Empirical research demonstrates that virtual teams are able to overcome the barriers of computer-mediated communication primarily through extensive cycles of communication. Walther and Bunz (2005) offered a compelling demonstration of SIP's effectiveness and presented six rules of virtual teams that can overcome difficulties related to trust:

- **Rule 1:** *Get started right away.* Because virtual teams have a harder time building rapport, they must begin working on tasks more quickly than colocated teams. Doing so provides adequate time for more social interactions.
- **Rule 2:** *Communicate frequently.* Trusting behaviors often are correlated to frequency of communication—we trust those we interact with more. Likewise, more communication enables a distribution of tasks over time.
- **Rule 3:** *Multitask by getting organized and doing substantive work simultaneously.* Organizing tasks often occur at the beginning of a team's work. However, if too much time is spent organizing and not enough on execution, the substantive work is overlooked. Teams should begin work on substantive tasks early, before the tasks

are fully developed, and by comparison, not extensively over-plan less important tasks.

- **Rule 4:** Overtly *acknowledge that you have read another's messages.* Because virtual teams do not enable teammates to read each other's faces, members must confirm verbally and immediately what is understood through nonverbal means in face-to-face settings. Acknowledging others not only clarifies meanings, but it also indicates that others matter, which contributes to the formation of trust.

- **Rule 5:** *Be explicit about what you are thinking and doing.* As media richness theory teaches, online technologies enable relatively little extra-verbal or body language content, such as head nods, to show agreement. Team members should overtly state their agreement and disagreement, as well as the intentions of their contributions, such as proposing a topic change. Without these explicit interactions, distant team members might be left wondering what another collaborator is doing, thereby introducing doubt into the team. Doubt never enhances trust.

- **Rule 6:** *Set deadlines and stick to them.* Accomplishing tasks along the way reduces the anxiety that the project will exceed deadlines by giving the team small victories along the way. The small victories increase trust as teammates can validate their expectations that others will perform work. As teammates accomplish tasks, they begin to have more confidence that future tasks likewise will be completed. (pp. 833-36)

These six rules focus on balancing task messages and social messages such that teams oscillate between socializing and doing work. For example, confirming receipt of another's message shows interest in the teammate's response and provides the opportunity to provide task-based feedback on the response. Walther and Bunz's study demonstrated that these six rules increase the effectiveness of teams as reported by outside evaluators and—most importantly—increased the teammates' sense of enjoyment and trust in working with other participants. Consequently, the six SIP rules give an indication of what constitutes trust throughout a virtual writing team's life cycle as teammates oscillate between cycles of vulnerability and validation. They contribute and have others confirm their value, which are key components of trust and are components that are particularly central in the (often) emotionally charged writing environment. Perhaps most significantly, a team that agrees to follow the SIP rules builds accountability into their process, the sixth of this book's principles of virtual, collaborative writing teams. The team members know what to expect from one another, and by explicitly stating communication intentions, meeting deadlines, or overtly acknowledging others' messages, for example, trust begins to form as the team members demonstrate that they hold themselves and others accountable to the process.

Swift Trust

SIP addresses the long-term trust building process in virtual teams; thus, it is an important part of successful virtual teams. However, virtual teams need to form trust quickly at the outset of the collaboration because they have short life spans. The concept of *swift trust* helps in understanding how team members form trust in a short time at the beginning of their collaborations. According to Jarvenpaa and Leidner (1999), swift trust relies on teammates demonstrating trusting behavior and individual propensity to trust by initiating and responding to communication with those they have not met before. These teams are temporary, face-to-face work systems characterized as highly task-focused, forming around a clear purpose for a finite life span (p. 794). To explain how swift trust functions in a temporary system, Meyerson Weick, and Kramer (1996) explained:

Trust that unfolds in temporary systems is more accurately portrayed as a unique form of collective perception and relating that is capable of managing issues of vulnerability, uncertainty, risk, and expectations. For these groups, trust depends less on feeling, commitment and exchange and more on action, cognition, the nature of the network and labor pool, and avoidance of personal disclosure, contextual cues, modest dependency, and heavy absorption in the task. (p. 167)

The focus on tasks and action rather than on individual relationships separates swift trust from the other types of trust because in these teams, the collapsed time frame of the project leads individuals to enter the team expecting to act rather than expecting to build relationships. Swift trust earns its name because teams develop this trust early in the team's life according to these factors:

- Participants with diverse skills are assembled by a central figure to enact expertise they already possess.
- Participants have a limited history working together.
- Participants have limited prospects of working together again in the future.
- Participants often are part of limited labor pools without overlapping networks.
- Tasks are often complex and involve interdependent work.
- Tasks have a deadline.
- Assigned tasks are nonroutine and not well-understood.
- Assigned tasks are consequential.
- Continuous interrelating is required to produce an outcome. (Meyerson, Weick, & Kramer, 1996, p. 169)

These conditions coordinate to form trust that relies on the interconnection of the individuals toward achieving a purpose and a personal disposition of members, enabling them to assume that others share the same goals. In a way, swift trust collapses all three stages of deterrence-based trust, knowledge-based trust, and identity-based trust because team members must assume that others wish to avoid negative consequences, must engage in frequent communication, and must believe that others genuinely believe in the same goals. Jarvenpaa and Leidner (1999) added that virtual teams require more than merely predisposition to enact trust and that trust in virtual teams tends to be established—or not—right at the outset (p. 808). This *modified swift trust* bears a resemblance to the type of swift trust discussed by Meyerson, Weick, and Kramer (1996), but it also has some unique features. Specifically, modified swift trust and swift trust share the proposition that teams are temporary, with no history or anticipated future association, and that team members use complex skill sets to work interdependently on specific tasks.

However, the differences between Meyerson, Weick, and Kramer's conception of swift trust, originally developed for temporary face-to-face teams, and Jarvenpaa and Leidner's (1999) modified swift trust, developed for virtual teams, demonstrates some differences as well. Specifically, communication in modified swift trust occurs through electronic media, and team members come from weakly defined professional networks rather than from strong overlapping networks. In other words, not only have the team members probably never met, but the team members' networks might not overlap either. Because writing tasks require tight alignment of the participants, a virtual writing team requires individuals who might be completely disconnected to come together through electronic media in a short period of time to accomplish a specific task. This alignment challenges face-to-face writing teams as it is, but when the added complication of electronic media is introduced, the importance of selecting the "right" team members to participate on a virtual writing team assumes even greater importance.

Specifically, because these team members have no history and no common understanding, the individual's disposition and history in other teams plays an even more significant role in modified swift trust than in other conceptions of swift trust (Jarvenpaa & Leidner, 1999; Iaccono & Weisband, 1997). In other words, team members form trust in the opening stages of an interaction based almost exclusively on their own personalities and experiences, without regard to the others in the team. Ensuing interactions either maintain or weaken this predisposition as others on the team communicate effectively (or not) and accomplish tasks (or not). Individual initiative, coping with technical uncertainty, persistence in the face of crisis, and positive leadership form the basis of modified swift trust because "in the absence of individuating cues about others, individuals build stereotypical impressions based on limited information" (Jarvenpaa & Leidner, 1999, p. 793). In short, trust is first formed through the depersonalized pre-judgments of team members in the initial contact—team members enter an interaction *already* trusting an image—a stereotype—of others rather than waiting to build trust through cycles of vulnerability and validation as in regular trust. After this initial interaction, trust is influenced by communication and action, which confirms either that the trust was appropriately assigned to others or that others are not trustworthy. In the chapter's opening scenario, the manager at the bank who assigned her subordinates to the documentation team and the contracted project manager share responsibility for failure in this regard. Neither person chose the "right" team members for their documentation team; as a result, the parties entered the collaboration lacking trust, and the lack of trust grew more intense as tasks went unaccomplished.

The bank manager and the project manager should have recognized that modified swift trust requires participants to possess some specific characteristics in order for the team to succeed.

Specifically, individuals who collaborate on virtual teams should have had positive experiences in the past with this type of collaboration and should be willing to suspend doubts about others at the outset of the collaboration—that is, they should understand the "culture of collaboration" before entering the team. Some members of the bank documentation team had worked on a virtual team in the past, and some had not. Teammates should also have experience implementing the rules of SIP in order to validate that the initial trust was given appropriately to others. The responsibility here falls primarily on the project manager because that person could have set the precedent from the beginning for how the team would interact. The trust that sustains virtual teams, then, is action-based, categorical, and highly fragile (Myerson, Weick, & Kramer, 1996; Jarvenpaa & Leidner, 1999; Coutu, 1998). Meyerson, Weick, and Kramer (1996) added that "To trust and be trustworthy, within the limits of a temporary system, means that people have to wade in on trust rather than wait while experience gradually shows who can be trusted and with what" (p. 170). Add the complications of collaborating through electronic media over distances, and the complications of working with complex writing tasks, and it becomes clear how urgent it is that those who build virtual teams carefully consider whom they select to work in this manner. Not everybody succeeds on a writing team using virtual collaboration and authoring tools.

Building Strong Virtual Teams

In the previous sections of this chapter, I discussed the general theory and components of teams and then set virtual teams against traditional teams by revealing some of the unique component of virtual teams, focusing on SIP and swift trust. I also used a real scenario to highlight the importance of the concepts and linked the concepts I present to the six core principles of collaborative virtual writing teams, described in Chapter 1. In this section, I build on these sections to develop practical guidelines for building strong virtual teams. These guidelines synthesize the literature on teams and virtual teams, and they are presented here as a rubric for ensuring the quality of virtual writing teams.

1. Virtual writing teams share some components with all types of teams. Specifically, the team must be small enough to enable meaningful interaction, yet large enough to allow for the diversity required to complete complex tasks. The team members must depend upon one another to achieve goals, which should be shared by all the team members. The members of the team should record the processes for interacting to ensure clarity among teammates, and the team should be focused primarily on accomplishing tasks. Hence, these are the essential components of teams:
    - Small team size
    - Diverse team membership
    - Interdependent relationships
    - Shared team vision
    - Articulated team processes,
    - Performance orientation
    - Social presence

Together, these components form the most essential condition for successful teams—trust—which is defined here as the willingness of one party to be vulnerable to another party with the expectation that the other will validate the trust. In traditional face-to-face teams, trust forms over long periods in physical proximity and moves from deterrence-based trust to knowledge-based trust to identity-based trust as individuals gradually grow closer together. Because virtual teams have no physical proximity, the seventh component in traditional teams is omitted and social presence replaces it; the purpose of social presence is to approximate physical colocation and simulate the sense of being present with others.

2. This discussion of teams, however, diverged from the literature on the general concept of teams when I discussed the complications of teams formed over large geographic spaces. Traditionally, teams are colocated, but virtual teams develop across time zones, organizations, and expertise. Therefore, virtual teams, by definition, rely on electronic communication technologies to complete their work. These teams require that members possess some specific characteristics to succeed. Specifically, those who work on virtual teams should possess the following seven characteristics:
    - High tolerance for ambiguity
    - Self-reliance
    - Excellent communication skills
    - Self-motivation
    - Unique skills within the team
    - Strong goal-orientation
    - Collaborative spirit

Without a healthy dose of these traits, workers in collaborative virtual team situations will not succeed because they will not have the structure or direction that they might expect in other work situations. Because not everybody will succeed in virtual teams, those placed in positions to create them, such as managers or teachers, must be careful about whom they ask to collaborate this way. If writers are not comfortable in this environment, their work will falter, and because virtual teams are primarily goal-oriented, the poor performance will significantly degrade trust formation, initiating a cycle of degrading trust and poor performance.

3. Working with appropriate technologies represents a third set of concerns for building successful virtual teams. As media richness theory suggests, not all media are suitable for all activities because some media, like e-mail, provide less finely distinguished information than other media, such as videoconferencing or 3D virtual worlds. This

information deficit is especially true in writing teams, as writers negotiate nuanced differences in their approaches to problems. Additionally, media must be chosen to help build a sense of social presence to overcome some of the challenges of working at distances and across cultures. The following recommendations arise from the discussion of technology and social presence:

- Lean media (for example, e-mail) should be used for routine or mundane tasks.
- Richer media (for example, video-conferencing) should be used for complex tasks.
- All team members should have access to the same suite of technologies and possess facility using them.
- To the extent feasible, synchronous (for example, instant messaging) technologies should be used to create social presence, especially in conflict resolution or other interpersonal negotiations.

If those working in virtual teams use the wrong media at the wrong time, then communication will falter as teammates begin to misunderstand one another. When misunderstandings occur, communication decreases, and because the teammates in virtual writing teams rely solely on electronic communication to do their work, both the work and the trust it requires will suffer. If virtual collaborators use technologies wisely, however, it can increase trust and performance by focusing on the contributions of individuals rather than identity markers, such as age or gender.

4. The previous three categories of concerns all contribute to the central concern of successful teams: trust. Without trust, nothing else matters in a team. However, unlike their colocated counterparts, virtual teams cannot rely on repeated physical interaction or

long periods to develop trust because these teams are, by definition, distributed and short term. Social information processing theory becomes a mechanism for helping to build trust in virtual teams, and the theory's six rules contribute to the core actions that virtual teams must perform:

- Get started right away.
- Communicate frequently.
- Multitask by getting organized and doing substantive work simultaneously.
- Overtly acknowledge that you have read another's messages.
- Be explicit about what you are thinking and doing.
- Set deadlines and stick to them.

These rules are core to virtual writing teams because they overcome the difficulties inherent in virtual team settings. When team members follow these rules, they decrease the opportunities for misunderstandings to occur. Likewise, these rules enable members to build rapport while focusing on tasks and, by definition, all teams must have both social and task-based activities because their integration builds trust—the core component of teams.

5. The final concept discussed in this chapter was swift trust. In a way similar to the mirror that SIP theory holds to the core aspects of all teams, swift trust holds a mirror to the core traits that those who work in virtual teams must possess. Specifically, swift trust relies on individuals possessing the following traits:

- Strong propensity to trust
- Experience with virtual collaborations that leads to forming trusting opinions of others from the outset
- Ability to launch into action immediately without knowing teammates well
- Persistence in the face of stress

Given all of these factors necessary for success in virtual collaboration, we begin to see why many have said that virtual teams, and writing teams in particular, can never be as successful as face-to-face teams and why the writing team in our opening scenario failed. Yet, when virtual teams are conceived and managed properly and when they contain the right types of people, such teams can be just as successful as traditional teams. Indeed, when virtual teams succeed, they can surpass regular teams in performance because they can draw on expertise from across the globe rather than from one city or organization. Ideally, then, the best of the best can collaborate to solve complex problems efficiently and effectively. Finally, when virtual teams succeed, not only are they potentially more successful at problem solving than traditional teams, but they also may cost an organization less money. Given the appropriate technological infrastructure, the team does not require any physical space to meet or expensive airfares to gather. The trick, however, in achieving these possibilities comes from heeding the concepts presented here.

In summary, Table 1 presents these characteristics as a checklist of the components for creating strong virtual teams.

IMPLICATIONS AND FUTURE RESEARCH DIRECTIONS

Undoubtedly, writing teams have become firmly rooted in American institutions. The military, private corporations, and educational organizations all use them, to name just three examples. Because teams are so pervasive, they now function almost transparently in workplaces and have begun to be used in many work settings. However, with the advent of sophisticated electronic communication technologies, virtual writing teams have become subject to scrutiny as their complications require analysis of processes for creating successful interactions and products. Virtual teams originally

Table 1. Elements of strong virtual teams

Team Traits	
• Small team size • Diverse team membership • Interdependent relationships • Shared team vision	• Articulated team processes • Performance-orientated • Social presence
Team Actions	
• Get started right away. • Communicate frequently. • Multitask getting organized and doing substantive work simultaneously.	• Overtly acknowledge that you have read another's messages. • Be explicit about what you are thinking and doing. • Set deadlines and stick to them.
Individual Traits	
• High tolerance for ambiguity • Self-reliance • Excellent communication sills • Self-motivation • Unique skills within the team • Strong goal-orientation • Collaborative spirit • Strong propensity to trust	• Experience with virtual collaborations that leads to forming trusting opinions of others from the outset • Ability to launch into action immediately without prior knowledge of others • Persistence in the face of stress
Environment Traits	
• Lean media used for routine or mundane tasks • Richer media used for complex tasks	• Same suite of technologies available to all team members • Synchronous technologies used to create social presence

emerged to meet needs for increased output in shorter time frames by drawing on geographically distributed resources. But as these teams have expanded their scope across the globe, complications have arisen that challenge the core component of teams—trust. When writing teams form across cultures, across time zones, or across organizational boundaries with specific goals and compressed time frames, forming trust—in its traditional sense—becomes difficult. As discussed, challenges for developing trust arise from the temporary nature of virtual teams, geographic distribution, lack of shared history of norms, and technological barriers.

Yet, in spite of such trust-based challenges, virtual teams still manage to succeed. As researchers have tried to understand this phenomenon, they have speculated that alternative types of trust, such as swift trust, which appeared in face-to-face temporary teams, could likewise apply to virtual teams. With Jarvenpaa and Leidener's (1999) contribution of modified swift trust, which adapts the swift trust for virtual teams by accounting for the complexities of electronic communication, it is possible to see that trust does exist in virtual teams. This type of trust, though, differs from "thick trust" or more traditional forms of team-based trust, such as deterrence-based, knowledge-based or identity-based trusts, because swift trust accompanies a participant into the collaboration. The trust does not emerge from sustained interactions over time.

This difference represents the single most important trust-based distinction between traditional teams and virtual teams, and presents the beginning of significant research questions regarding virtual writing teams. Those who work on virtual writing teams must enter the collaboration *already* trusting their counterparts. Swift trust is an abbreviated form of trust that forgoes the traditional trust-building process, and instead relies on stereotypes, enthusiastic communication, and individual predisposition to form trust from the initial moment of contact with collaborators.

Because trust in virtual writing teams relies on these initial moments and upon individual predisposition to trust, it is important to consider whom we ask to work on these types of teams. If the wrong people are chosen, suspicion or concern will mark the first moments of a virtual collaboration, and overcoming the challenges of these negative impressions can be difficult in the compressed time frame and electronically mediated context of virtual teams.

Because trust represents the most important aspect of successful teams—writing and otherwise—and because virtual teams have a different set of characteristics than traditional teams, researchers need to develop more appropriate models to examine swift trust in virtual teams. Swift trust in virtual teams has only received limited attention in formal research settings, and that research has been conducted primarily in academic settings that rely on student work teams as the model. Such studies need to be extended to collaborative writing in the work context. An appropriate model for virtual writing teams should step outside the controlled academic environment to the complexities of real workplace writing settings, and the model should be designed to uncover the complexities that office politics and stresses add to the formation of trust in virtual teams. Possibly, when transported into workplace settings, the concept of swift trust would require substantial modification and guidance to enhance trust development.

Maintaining a separation between academic institutions and the workplace preserves the pedigree of the theory; however, collaboration benefits both disciplines. Every attempt at communication across boundaries, such as working together on research and education or planning and executing events together, has the potential to create deeper understanding and more effective cooperative work relationships. Academic studies cannot predict all of the complexities that influence a virtual writing team in the workplace merely by studying the response of graduate or undergraduate students. One researcher summarized this point well in a report of a 14-year case study: "We have always to ask the question about the frontiers of knowledge above all else but we run the risk that our frontiers are constructed inside the academic process world view rather than inside of the managers' applied areas" (Macbeth, 2002, p. 397).

Trust building in all virtual teams is a complex process, and it needs to be understood in different contexts—particularly within the nuanced arena of workplace writing. The skill sets of students, the influences on their performance, and the networked relationship among students cannot necessarily stand in place of the skills that workers need or the concerns that they harbor about virtual collaboration. Developing a theory of trust in virtual writing for the workplace, or one that applies equally to academic or other applied settings, cannot be predicted without research in nonacademic settings. Although academic research has provided a starting point to hypothesize about the traits that individual team members need to possess, the technological factors to consider, and the ways teams should structure their work in virtual settings, questions about the role—and perhaps validity—of swift trust in the virtual workplace still exist. One purpose of this chapter has been to provide a foundation from which this exploration can begin.

REFERENCES

Andres, H. P. (2002). A comparison of face-to-face and virtual software development teams. *Team Performance Management: An International Journal, 8*(1), 39–48. doi:10.1108/13527590210425077

Blickensderfer, E., Salas, E., & Cannon-Bowers, J. (2000). When the teams came marching home. In M. Beyerle. In Teams, W. (Ed.), *Past, Present and Future (Social Indicators Research Series)* (pp. 255–274). Amsterdam: Kluwer Academic Publishers.

Bronack, S. C., Cheney, A. L., Riedl, R. E., & Tashner, J. H. (2008). Designing Virtual Worlds to Facilitate Meaningful Communication. *Technical Communication*, 261-69.

Chidambaram, L. (1996). Relational development in computer-supported groups. *Management Information Systems Quarterly*, (June): 143–165. doi:10.2307/249476

Coppola, N. W., Hiltz, S. R., & Rotter, N. G. (2004). Building trust in virtual teams. *IEEE Transactions on Professional Communication, 47*(2), 95–104. doi:10.1109/TPC.2004.828203

Coutu, D. L. (1998). Trust in virtual teams. *Harvard Business Review, 76*(3), 20.

Fisher, R., & Ury, W. (1983). *Getting to Yes: Negotiating without giving in*. New York: Penguin Books.

Gustafson, K., & Kleiner, B. H. (1994). New developments in team building. *Work Study, 43*(8), 16–19. doi:10.1108/EUM0000000004316

Huszczo, G.E. (1990). Training for team building. *Training and Development Journal, 44. 2, 37*(7). Academic OneFile. Gale. Clemson University Libraries. 16 Sept. 2009.

Iaccono, C. Z., & Weisband, S. (1997). Developing trust in virtual teams. In *Proceedings of the 30th Annual Hawaii International Conference on System Sciences*. Retrieved from http://uainfo.arizona.edu/~wiesband/Hiccss-97

Jarvenpaa, S. L., & Leidner, D. E. (1999). Communication and trust in global virtual teams. *Organization Science, 10*(6), 791–815. doi:10.1287/orsc.10.6.791

Katzenbach, J. R., & Smith, D. K. (1993). *The wisdom of teams: Creating the high performance organization*. Boston, MA: Harvard Business School Press.

Kraut, R. E., Fussell, S. R., Brennan, E., & Siegel, J. (2002). Understanding effects of proximity on collaboration: Implications for technologies to support remote collaborative work. In Hinds, P., & Kiesler, S. (Eds.), *Distributed Work* (pp. 137–162). Cambridge, MA: The MIT Press.

Lee, C. (1990). Beyond teamwork. *Training: The Magazine of Human Resources Development, 27*(6), 25–33.

Lewicki, R. J., & Bunker, B. B. (1996). Developing and maintaining trust in work relationships. In Kramer, R. M., & Tyler, T. R. (Eds.), *Trust in organizations: Frontiers of theory and research* (pp. 114–139). Thousand Oaks, CA: Sage.

Lipnack, J., & Stamps, J. (2000). *Virtual teams: Reaching across space, time, and organization with technology*. New York: John Wiley.

Macbeth, D. (2002). From research to practice via consultancy and back again: A 14 year case study of applied research. *European Management Journal, 20*(4), 393–400. doi:10.1016/S0263-2373(02)00059-2

Majchrzak, A., Malhotra, A., Stamps, J., & Lipnack, J. (2004). Can absence make a team grow stronger? *Harvard Business Review, 82*(5), 131–147.

Mayer, R. C., Davis, J. H., & Schoorman, F. D. (1995). An integrative model of organizational trust. *Academy of Management Review, 20*(3), 709–734. doi:10.2307/258792

McGrath, J. E., & Hollingshead, A. B. (1994). *Groups Interacting with Technology: Ideas, Evidence, Issues and an Agenda*. Thousand Oaks, CA: Sage Publications.

Myerson, D., Weick, K. E., & Kramer, R. M. (1996). Swift trust and temporary groups. In Kramer, R. M., & Tyler, T. R. (Eds.), *Trust in organizations: Frontiers of theory and research* (pp. 166–195). Thousand Oaks, CA: Sage.

Neck, C., Manz, C., & Anand, V. (2000). Self-managing teams in a crystal ball: Future directions for research and practice. In Beyerlein, M. (Ed.), *Work Teams: Past, present, and future* (pp. 311–322). Amsterdam: Kluwer Academic Publishers.

Nilsson, T. (2000). A history of teams. In M. Beyerle. In Teams, W. (Ed.), *Past, Present and Future (Social Indicators Research Series)* (pp. 275–288). Amsterdam: Kluwer Academic Publishers.

Porter, G., & Beyerlein, M. (2000). Historic roots of team theory and practice. In Michael Beyerle. In Teams, W. (Ed.), *Past, Present and Future (Social Indicators Research Series)* (pp. 3–24). Amsterdam: Kluwer Academic Publishers.

Purdum, T. (2005). Teaming take 2. *Industry Week/WI, 254* (5), 41-43.

Robey, D., Khoo, H. M., & Powers, C. (2000). Situated learning in cross-functional virtual teams. *Technical Communication, 47*(1), 51–66.

Salas, E., & Cannon-Bowers, J. A. (2000). Teams in organizations. In M. Beyerle. In Teams, W. (Ed.), *Past, Present and Future (Social Indicators Research Series)* (pp. 323–332). Amsterdam: Kluwer Academic Publishers.

Schneider, T. J., & Stepp, J. R. (1998). The evolution of U.S. labor-management relations. In J. A. Auerbach, (Ed.), *Through a glass darkly: building the new workplace for the 21st century* (148). Retrieved from http://www.restructassoc.com/case/06.pdf

Suchan, J., & Hayzak, G. (2001). The communication characteristics of virtual teams: A case study. *IEEE Transactions on Professional Communication, 44*(3), 174–186. doi:10.1109/47.946463

Tjosvold, D., & Johnson, D. (2000). Deutsch's theory of cooperation and competition. In M. Beyerle. In Teams, W. (Ed.), *Past, Present and Future (Social Indicators Research Series)* (pp. 131–156). Amsterdam: Kluwer Academic Publishers.

Tullar, W. L., Kaiser, P. R., & Balthazard, P. A. (1998). Group work and electronic meeting systems: From boardroom to classroom. *Business Communication Quarterly, 61*(4), 63–65. doi:10.1177/108056999806100407

Walther, J. B., & Bunz, U. (2005). The rules of virtual groups: Trust, liking, and performance in computer-mediated communication. *The Journal of Communication, 55*(4), 828–846. doi:10.1111/j.1460-2466.2005.tb03025.x

Section 3
Managing Team Dynamics

Chapter 6
Case Study:
A Collaborative of Content Designers and Developers

Beth Brunk-Chavez
The University of Texas at El Paso, USA

Sunay Palsole
The University of Texas at El Paso, USA

ABSTRACT

This chapter features a case study of a collaborative project among a team of writers and a team of multimedia designers and examines their intersections. The chapter's central question is: What does it take to enable collective collaboration in a virtual writing environment? The chapter is based in part on a study that found that building and strengthening social presence is integral to effective collaboration. The spoken and unspoken social contracts of working toward a common goal in a respectful environment are important. It also found that the technologies must be adoptable, adaptable, and they must enable anywhere/anytime collaboration. Therefore, collaboration using technologies is a complex process involving social presence, availability, and adaption/adoption of technologies with the changing needs of the collaborative team.

INTRODUCTION

This chapter draws on and exemplifies the three models of collaboration introduced in Chapter 1:

- **Serial collaboration** occurs when writers work on a product one after another. Each person works separately on a piece of the writing or the whole document. In turn, each writer performs a distinct function in the creation of the finished work, possibly in a distinct chronological or hierarchical order.

- **Parallel collaboration** occurs when writers work on different pieces of the same project simultaneously. Each writer works on one piece of the whole, usually based on a set of negotiated standards or requirements.

DOI: 10.4018/978-1-60566-994-6.ch006

- **Collective collaboration** occurs when writers all work on the same piece of writing at the same time. Everyone works together on one piece of the work, or the whole work, with no segregation of ownership

Additionally, this chapter illustrates the need for adhering to Principles 1 and 4 that ground this book (Chapter 1). First, it is necessary to develop a culture of collaboration for writing teams to work. Second, Principle 4 indicates that it is important to select and use the right tools and any of the three discussed models of collaboration in ways that serve both the project at hand and the people who undertake it.

The first two models listed above, serial and parallel collaboration, can be equated with cooperative work: something a little quicker and a little less messy than collective collaboration. In these collaborative settings, team members complete the project by dividing it into discrete parts and then splicing those parts into the agreed-upon framework. There are many contexts in which such features as the nature of project, time, personalities, and relationships make serial and parallel collaboration appropriate. However, collective collaboration, the focus of this chapter, can be more challenging to achieve. In collective collaboration writing projects, writers work simultaneously to create, revise, and edit the same text or project with the goal of creating a seamless, univocal product. Such collaboration may be difficult to embrace in business settings where the culture promotes and rewards competition among individuals and may recognize individual writers separately from the team. However, we believe that collective collaboration is desirable in virtual writing contexts because it can lead to more cohesive and higher quality products than other forms of collaboration.

Using the case study of a collaborative grant project to build interactive teaching modules, this chapter considers the following questions:

- What does it take to enable collective collaboration in a virtual writing environment?
- What are the characteristics of the collaborative team that enable strong collective collaborations?
- What are the characteristics of the technology that enable effective collective collaboration?

BACKGROUND

The multilayered collaboration discussed in this chapter was the result of a competitive grant awarded by the Texas Higher Education Coordinating Board to the University of Texas at El Paso (UTEP). This project produced 14 digitized modules, the purpose of which was to teach various strategies for improving their students' reading comprehension to faculty who were not trained in reading instruction. The collaborative team consisted of faculty writers, graphic designers, instructional technologists, and programmers working in two separate teams that often intersected with one another. The first team of collaborators wrote the content for the modules. This team included four faculty members who taught a range of courses related to rhetoric, writing, and reading. The second team of collaborators created the multimedia elements of the modules to make them "work." Finally, the third collaboration was between these two groups—the content writers and the technology designers—who collaborated to integrate the content and design in the modules. Bridging these two groups were the authors of this chapter and the principal investigators of the grant: Brunk-Chavez represented the content side, and Palsole represented the technology side of the project. To facilitate the virtual collaboration, the writers used PBWiki, the programmers and designers used Adobe® Buzzword®, and the entire team used Zoho™ Projects, an online service that enables work teams to plan, track,

Figure 1. Intersections of the different collaborative technologies used by the team

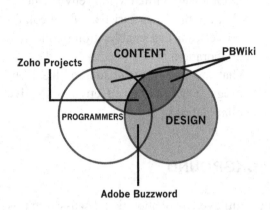

and collaborate to develop the project. Figure 1 shows how these products interrelated.

This grant project involved, to some degree, all three kinds of collaboration defined earlier. The teams collaborated serially when the writing team gave the text to the production team, who then transformed it into the interactive modules. The teams engaged in parallel collaboration when the content and production teams discussed interactive options early in module development and worked at the same time to create them. For the purpose of this chapter, however, we are most interested the collective collaboration process. For this case study, we map the different activities or events that lead to collective collaboration. Before we do, we want to discuss more deeply the characteristics of collective collaboration.

Vygotsky (1978) provided the theoretical structure for considering collaboration as a social process in which meaning is constructed from discussion among group members. Schrage (1990) defined collaboration as "the process of *shared creation*: two or more individuals with complementary skills interacting to create a shared understanding that none had previously possessed or could have come to on their own" (p. 140). More recently, Thomson et al. (2007) derived the following definition of collaboration:

"Collaboration is a process in which autonomous or semi-autonomous actors interact through formal and informal negotiation, jointly creating rules and structures governing their relationships and ways to act or decide on the issues that brought them together; it is a process involving shared norms and mutually beneficial interactions" (p. 25). While we will draw on each of these definitions, John-Steiner, Weber, and Minnis (1998) proposed a definition that we use as the framework for this study:

The principles in a true collaboration represent complementary domains of expertise. As collaborators, not only do they plan, decide, and act jointly; they also think together, combining independent conceptual schemes to create original frameworks. Also, in a true collaboration, there is a commitment to shared resources, power, and talent: no individual's point of view dominates, authority for decisions and actions resides in the group, and work products reflect a blending of all participants' contributions. (p. 776)

In other words, collective collaboration is a highly complex process; the end product is the result of collective intelligence shared by all members of the collaborative group, and the work presents a "perfect blending" in which individual components do not stand alone in thought or form. In short, we believe that, collective collaboration occurs when the individual members fade away, when there is equal contribution, and when the result is highly blended. The question, then, is how collective collaboration can be accomplished in a virtual writing environment. While collective collaboration can be difficult to achieve and sustain, we argue that it occurs most effectively when particular traits of what is termed social presence and technology converge (see Chapters 2, 4, and 5 for discussions of social presence; Chapter 21 addresses concerns of mutual presence).

Convergence of Social Presence and Technology

Collective collaboration in virtual settings is a complex process involving:

- Social presence among collaborators in their interchange of ideas and learning of new technologies
- Availability and adaptation or adoption of technologies with the changing needs of the collaborative team

While these two points may seem relatively simplistic, achieving social presence and locating the appropriate technologies are, in fact, complex processes.

First, the collaborators must invest in the purpose of the project, and they must be willing to work as a team. (See Chapters 4 and 5 for helpful guidance toward developing effective and efficient teams.) However, we do not suggest that the team members must agree on all ideas from the outset. To mitigate conflict and a cacophony of ideas, the theory of social presence is important.

Social presence has been defined as "the ability of participants in a community to project themselves, socially and emotionally, as real people through a medium of communication" (Garrison & Anderson, 2003; see also Bouwman, et al., 2003, p. 96). The spoken and unspoken social contracts of working toward a common goal in a respectful environment are, we believe, foundational to creating social presence. Kehrwald's research (2007) supports this position. He cited several "social relational mechanisms" that, when individually present, work to strengthen the impact of social presence. These mechanisms include commonality, feelings of safety, respect, rapport, and interdependence (pp. 504-506). Kehrwald further explained that "relations and ties between individuals develop over time based on the number of interactions and transactions between them, the intensity of those interactions, and the working

of the social-relational mechanisms within those transactions. As the number of transactions between individuals increases, the combination of social presence cues and social-relational mechanisms contributes to the overall development of the ties between these social actors" (p. 507). Additionally, social presence is relative. Therefore, social presence is not something that develops immediately, nor can it be forced: "Relations are emergent and dynamic, in state of constant flux, sometimes developing, sometimes waning" (p. 507). As with any face-to-face collaborative relationship, virtual social presence is subject to change and therefore must be maintained.

For example, when a collaborative team charged with accomplishing fixed tasks works face-to-face, there is an open exchange of ideas in brainstorming sessions. When each member contributes ideas to create an idea set, immediate verbal and nonverbal feedback helps to develop and narrow these ideas. A possibility that arises in this setting is that strong opinions and personality conflicts can easily derail the efforts of the collaborative team, at which point social-relational mechanisms—commonality, safety, respect, rapport, and interdependence—must be considered.

In asynchronous virtual settings, the collaborative team is still charged with accomplishing fixed tasks; however, the immediacy of feedback is missing, and the development of social presence takes place in a time-delayed and nonverbal setting. Instead of verbal and nonverbal feedback, social presence is maintained following rules of "Netiquette," or online etiquette. When working collaboratively in a virtual environment, the collaborative team must ensure that the time lines are not too short. They must also understand that the slower pace of online collaboration can make conflict visible and simultaneously productive. Rather than glossing over conflicts or letting them dominate communication, team members can negotiate conflicts, in which everyone's voice now contributes to the final product, which in turn may lead to stronger social presence.

While strong social presence is desirable to begin the collaborative process, proficiency with the collaborative technologies is equally important. Therefore, the second factor important for creating collective collaboration is to use technologies with the following characteristics: easily adoptable (ease of use), adaptable (fits the needs of the project), available and dependable (anywhere/anytime). Hence, the technology must be simple enough to be used by the collaborative team members. Obviously, the members may have attained different levels of technological literacy, so it is important to locate and use a technology that either can be used immediately or learned quickly and easily. Second, the technology must be appropriate to, or adaptable for, the project. The nature of each collaboration and the tasks required to complete the project will vary, so it is necessary to find a virtual workspace that facilitates the project's goals. Finally, because virtual collaboration can, at least in theory, occur anywhere and anytime, the technology must be available and dependable, not subject to unreasonable downtimes, to all team members.

As members of a collaborative team work with the selected technology, they perceive and encounter both its possibilities and limitations. O'Reilly (2005), in defining Web 2.0, looked at the architecture of newer technologies geared for greater user participation. He suggested that these new technologies allow groups to harness the collective intelligence of all participants for increased productivity. Not surprisingly, then, Tapscott and Williams (2006) proposed that the harnessing of these new technologies would contribute to the most effective harnessing of human skill, intelligence, and ingenuity. One way that ingenuity becomes evident is through the collaborative group's conscious and subconscious invention of workarounds within the technology's framework to adapt it to the needs of the project. One of the four axioms Schendel, et al. (2004) associated with computer-mediated communication and collaborative literacy has immediate application

to our case study: "Processes of collaboration shape technology even as technology shapes collaborative processes" (p. 202). Accordingly, the technology shapes the working patterns of the collaborative team, and the working patterns shape the use of the technology.

In sum, we argue that over time, collective collaboration can be achieved through a convergence of social presence and technology. As the nature of collaboration changes from embryonic states to more mature stages, not only do the collaborators have to change, but the technologies must change as well.

CASE STUDY: THE COMPLEX COLLABORATIVE PROCESS OF UTEP'S READING COMPREHENSION MODULES

As mentioned earlier, what makes this grant-funded academic project unique is the use of collaborative technologies to provide a visualization space in which textual information interplays with the development of interactive elements and graphic design. We summarize the nature of these collaborations as:

- **Content creation.** The writing and development of textual content that was used for the modules;
- **Interactive content.** The brainstorming and creation of interactions that were used to engage end users in meaningful dialogue;
- **Creation of visual elements.** The design and development of the "look and feel" of the modules.

The Collaboration Process

Using an anonymous online survey tool, we questioned all members of the collaborative team about their processes and about the characteristics of the collaboration. When asked to describe the process of constructing the modules, everyone agreed that a recognizable collaborative pattern emerged over time. Most respondents described the process in the same way: "Brainstorm subtopics for each module, create goals and objectives, research both the theory on each module... as well as best practices from many sources... write explanatory material that distills the information, and then create exercises and activities... and then create handouts." Additionally, three of the four writers used the word *role* to describe the ways they work. Writers made such comments as "Each of us gradually grew to take on a different role" based on different "interests, willingness, and expertise," and they added the point that this "sounds fragmented, but actually is very collaborative."

Through the survey responses, we noticed a clear notion that when the content developers were done with the content of the module, it ceased to belong to them anymore. They passed it on to the design and production teams with few expectations for interaction. Therefore, in this sense, the content-writing process represents a serial collaboration because a clean break exists between the writing and the production. Interestingly, one writer said, "Sometimes I wish I could see [the production team] more f2f [face-to-face] to ask more immediate questions as I'm working on content, but by and large, what we write and what is produced matches." It is not that there was no

collaboration between the two teams; however, such collaboration generally took place between the two team leaders via phone or e-mail rather than among all the participants. These leaders discussed solutions or revisions that generally were implemented immediately rather than sent back to the writing team. The writing team leader described this step as "still collaborative," although not as "close or intense" as the writing team's collaboration.

When the content was complete, the designers and programmers looked over the content individually and then tried "to understand the concept completely." They reported sitting "down [to] brainstorm ideas from all the team members to make the interpretation of strategies simple." As indicated by the phrase "sit down," the designers created a different model of collaboration because most of them are colocated in the same or adjacent offices. They could pull chairs together and talk about ideas or challenges. They also used e-mail, tools, such as Adobe® Buzzword® software, and a combination of forums and commenting tools in Zoho™ Projects.

Based on the survey responses, we visualize the collaborative process as shown in Figure 2.

From these process-oriented survey responses, we conclude that the team found collaboration in various forms to be important, but its importance was not related to getting the work done quickly. Rather, it was important for leveraging the

Figure 2. A map of the collaborative process

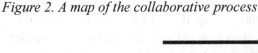

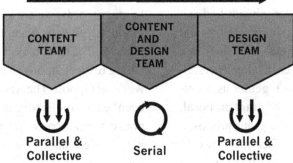

strengths of all participants to create modules and an overall project that was seamless—one that brought everything together as a whole rather than each module having a strong overprint of the principle creator. Again, reaching this level of virtual collaboration is dependent upon a strong social presence and an efficient technology.

Social Presence

As noted earlier, social presence is an important factor in influencing the nature and success of virtual collaborative writing. In our case, the reading comprehension writing team had the advantage of being on the same campus, but the reality is that they rarely saw each other, much less had schedules that enabled them to meet and write together. The majority of their collaboration was done asynchronously online. The design and technology teams, however, tended to work collaboratively in a colocated setting except in inter-team collaborations, where they used online tools to supplement their interactions. With all the groups, the spoken and unspoken social contracts of working toward a common goal in a respectful environment were foundational, we believe, to creating a strong and productive social presence. When asked in the survey about the characteristics of the collaboration, the group members' responses aligned well with Kehrwald's (2007) positive traits of social presence: commonality, feelings of safety, respect, rapport, and interdependence (p. 504-506).

Members joined the writing team by responding to a call for interest e-mailed by their department chairs. Although the writers already had met face-to-face through teaching similar courses and interacting at campus workshops—and therefore were somewhat familiar with each other's personalities—they had not worked together as a collaborative team until drafting the grant proposal. After committing to submit the grant proposal, the team held several face-to-face meetings. In the survey, everyone commented that knowing

the group members previously did make the collaborative process easier to manage: "I think the initial meetings were important to establish a group rapport, to really get to know who each group member is and how he/she thinks with regard to the subject matter with which we are dealing." Another pointed out that "I also think that establishing f2f rapport has also allowed us to function without interfering ego issues or fear of criticism." Additional similar responses from the content developers lead us to conclude that the content collaboration was effective and efficient because all members of the content collaborative came from *common* disciplinary backgrounds. Additionally, because there was a unifying grant proposal to work from, the common goals of the project were clear. These commonalities allowed for less negotiation of what would be presented and more attention to how it was going to be presented. Therefore, the collaborative team experienced an active interchange of ideas. As one member said: "I've learned a great deal from everyone, and when parts are completed, it's inspiring to continue."

Feelings of safety, respect, and rapport also have been identified as important to the development of social presence, and the survey responses illustrate these characteristics as well. No team members mentioned feeling like their writing was heavily critiqued or that their ideas were second-guessed. At the same time, most expressed comfort with giving and taking suggestions for improvement; they felt *safe* articulating their ideas: "We have self-confident group members who do not have competitive, ego issues which interfere with development of ideas within the modules. In other words, we are kind to each other but not afraid to give or accept critique, suggestions, revisions." The survey responses also indicate a strong respect among members as well as a good working rapport. The writers mentioned that it has been "easy to collaborate—lots of mutual support, praise, thanks, 'okay, let me help you think about it' type of collaboration going on in the comments section." Additionally, the "suggestions one member puts into the comments section or within the current module draft in color font inspires further ideas." When asked whether they were surprised by any of the collaborative process, three of the four commented on how easy it has been to work together collaboratively, "how mutually cooperative and supportive we are as a team. There does not seem to an interfering competitive spirit, which is what makes this collaboration such a pleasant, inspiring experience. We do not seem to hesitate to suggest and take others suggestions—the ego thing does not interfere with the creation."

These testimonials illustrate the positive traits of effective collaboration. However, although most of the group responded positively to accepting suggestions and having their writing revised to meet collaborative goals, others also indicated that they "tend to hold back on editing because I worry that I may be too 'assertive' in my own views and that tendency has to be monitored so that I am not the cause of friction." In other words, the desire to self-monitor was strong and may have affected the quantity or quality of the collaboratively edited pieces overall. Conversely, though, another writer said, "I don't revise major ideas," but [I am] "quite comfortable" revising and editing others' writing. "It might help that [in the wiki] we don't know who wrote exactly what—so it's not like targeting someone else's writing." In fact, this respondent says that she might not "directly recognize when [her own writing has] been revised."

The designers made similar comments about their work—that the work is "easy and inspiring. I think the reason is due to a great development team who [is] motivated and innovative." They also suggested that even though there are deadlines, the "relaxed" atmosphere helps to keep the collaboration positive: "Everyone understands their part in development and no intense overlook on the process is required."

Interdependence, as discussed in Chapter 5, is a vital social presence trait for working toward collective collaboration. If the team members were

not interdependent, they easily could divide the work and then cobble it together at the end. Similarly, if one person was doing most of the work, the other members would not feel any ownership of the final product or feel like productive team members. Thus, interdependence is an important trait for building highly productive collaborative teams. While the survey responses do not mention interdependence specifically, they do refer to the importance of it. For example, one writer reported being surprised at enjoying the virtual collaborative writing process so much: "I've worked on projects where wheels spin and nothing ever gets done. With this project, every wheel spinning is useful and applicable, and [it] gets done. I guess it's also surprising how so many people, with such diverse lives and schedules can still collaborate and share a 'workspace' with such effectiveness." This sense of productivity is a strong indication that collaborative teams think that interdependence enables the project's completion and success.

The strongest case for building social presence emerged from a participant who commented on how the wiki helped to create it: "It [the wiki] builds virtual closeness and trust among team members who may see each other only rarely, but work together every day." We believe the collaborative team's experience mentioned here speaks to the power of having technologies that are flexible and easily adoptable/adaptable in their use. The wiki, by its very nature, helps enhance the social nature of the collaborative team by making the product of the collaboration transparent, visible, and moldable by all members. The wiki's commenting feature is useful when members think that they do not have enough expertise to change content but can provide a voice in the molding of the content. This likely helps build feelings of commonality, respect, rapport, and interdependence among the content writer collaborative team.

Technology

The selected technology has a significant role in building social presence, as indicated earlier. Thus, the technology used must be well suited to both the collaborative team and the project itself; in other words, it must be easily adoptable, easily adaptable, as well as available and dependable. The grant team went through a 3-month-long process of finding the technology that worked best for them and the project. After the whole team was assembled, they had several face-to-face meetings to discuss the project's overall objectives. Half of these meetings included both the writers and the production teams for a total of eight people. After they had a general idea of what direction the grant proposal would take, the face-to-face meetings became less frequent, and content collaboration primarily occurred between two members, using WebCT, an educational course management system that can house an entire course's activities. Because the writing team was teaching with it and was therefore already familiar with WebCT, they requested an empty shell to house and exchange the proposal documents. However, using WebCT to collaborate did require the writers to log into the system, access the document, download it, change it, and then upload it for the next person. Although this asynchronous process worked relatively well when just two people were responsible for the proposal, it was unwieldy, and it quickly became apparent that the serial collaboration was not helping the team to achieve the ideal results. After the grant was awarded, the writing team agreed to search for technologies that would enable us to collaborate collectively, which was an appropriate step in keeping with Principle 4 that grounds this book.

The technology team suggested moving the collaboration from WebCT to Zoho™ Projects, a Web-based project management software that incorporates document management, discussion forums, and management dashboards. In Zoho™ Projects, the writers and developers tracked proj-

ect progress, recorded their time, and exchanged documents all inside one digital space. The team quickly found, however, that while this application was fine for storing documents and logging time, it had a significant learning curve and required extra steps to edit and exchange documents. Even when working side-by-side in a computer lab, the writers had a difficult time exchanging documents; simultaneously, they began to create more and increasingly complex content. They realized that this software was insufficient for achieving their collaborative goals, and they decided to adopt technologies that would let them leverage the anywhere/anytime affordances of the Web with the power of the read-write Web, which is exemplified best by a wiki. Ultimately, the entire team migrated to a more flexible environment, a wiki set up to enable collective collaborative activities. Instead of the constant cycle of uploading and downloading, writers could access the shared space, edit, write, and save without opening additional applications.

The development team also started using the wiki to communicate design ideas with the writing team. All new designs for the website, icons, and related graphics were shared on the wiki, and user comments were used to modify the images and send them back to the entire team. For the internal work, the development team found it better to keep using Zoho™ Projects because they could use Zoho™ Writer to build collaborative documents and project manage the entire development process. The graphic design team found the wiki to be restrictive because of their need to able to annotate and comment on the content directly, and they adopted Adobe® Buzzword® software for the collaboration between the graphic design team and the development team. Hence, the entire team found itself using technologies that met its needs, albeit different technologies for different subgroups and purposes at different times.

In the survey, team members responded directly to the issues of adoptability, adaptability, availability, and dependability. One person stated,

"The wiki is very easy to use to store the research and shape the material and provides a good reference to previous material." The features most mentioned were instant notifications of changes, message board capabilities, edit lockout when someone is currently working, ability to make changes without uploading and downloading documents, and comment boxes. The edit lockout was an important feature for several writers. With Zoho™ Projects, unless they left messages for one another, such as "Beth is writing now. Beth is done writing now," the software enabled more than one person to write or edit at the same time—a collaborative document nightmare! The wiki software locks the page while someone else is composing, which saved much frustration. The team also appreciated that the wiki saves previous versions of the document so "we don't have to fear deleting or changing something other group members may decide was better left as it was."

The wiki, the writing team determined, is adaptable to the nature of the collaboration. When asked about how the technology contributed to the project, one responded, "In developing content, there is always the challenge of brainstorming and developing ideas. Discussing possibilities both inside the drafts on the wiki and on the comments section has worked, I think, quite well for collaboration." Another made a similar comment—that the challenge of finding time to work was "easily resolved because we are able to work and have access to this project anytime we want it."

A feature of the wiki that has proven useful for "spurring on" the writers is that it provides updates of who has recently used it. Users can set the frequency of updates, and most of them choose to receive daily e-mails highlighting the updates that another team member has made. Several writers found that these kept them engaged in the project. After receiving the notice, they checked in to see what someone else had done and that often lead to time spent writing.

Although the writers left Zoho™ Projects behind for the most part, the designers commented

that they liked using it to "see where everyone else was on the project even if I couldn't ask that person in person." They found it to "improve the efficiency of the development process." There is good reason for this preference because the design team's process was not collectively collaborative but more of a parallel collaboration. Additionally, they were working in highly technical software applications and were, therefore, not as unsettled by moving in between them. There is a strong possibility that with a collaborative team composed of diverse working subgroups, each subgroup may decide or need to adopt different technologies to facilitate their work. Forcing such diverse subgroups to adopt the same technologies may be counterproductive to the entire collaborative process. That said, the whole team found that there needed to be a standardized element to the adopted technology that enables collaboration among the diverse subgroups of the overall collaborative group.

This adoption of various technologies fit in well with Bracewell and Witte's (2008) idea that while technology facilitates more diverse collaboration, it also acts to constrain collaboration and to modify it. Users may use tools differently from others in the team, and this variance may affect the overall processes. Pargman (2003) also observed the relationship between the user and the technology; a tool becomes "an instrument only when the subject is able to... subordinate it as a means to accomplish his/her ends" (p. 5). Technological artifacts are shaped through sociological dynamics. This reality is well supported by our case of different subgroups adopting technologies that they perceived as being useful for their work even if another subgroup was using a different technology.

ISSUES AND PROBLEMS

While we would not suggest that drastic changes needed to be made to the collaborative process demonstrated in this case study, our analyses have led to suggestions for creating and sustaining efficient virtual collaborations, some of which we implemented as a result of this study. In this section, we discuss the issues that our analysis of the case study reveals. We have grouped these issues into categories: social presence, technology, collaborative process, and sustainability. In the next section, we present our suggestions for improving the collaborative process.

Social Presence Issues

As indicated by our survey, some writers had problems with editing the collaborative work because they were concerned about coming across as being pushy. While this difficulty did not seem to be a debilitating problem, it does indicate the interesting situation that some writers were comfortable having their own work revised or edited, but they were not comfortable editing others' writing. There may be several reasons for this that would be worth exploring further. One reason might be the power dynamics of the team that existed both within and outside of the collaboration interactions. Another might be that because the changes are traceable through the wiki's stored pages, a writer might be afraid that someone would track the changes and be offended. To what degree this is problematic, we do not yet know.

One missing element in the collaborative process was an effective integration of project assessment into the design loop. While this missing element might not seem initially like a social presence issue, we believe that project assessment affects the traits of commonality and safety. Because the writing team did not have immediate access to the three sets of assessment data, they did not have a good sense of their success at conveying the material. Interviews with the design team, however, indicated that they created an internal feedback loop among the team for all elements associated with putting modules together. Their feedback process created a stronger sense of own-

ership because they felt challenged and energized to develop creative ways to engage the users. This sense of ownership was diminished with the writing team because they were not part of a feedback loop that provided end-user information with potential to influence their revision process.

Technology Issues

While the selected individual applications (PbWiki for the writers, Adobe® Buzzword® for the designers, and Zoho™ Projects for project management) appeared to work well for the writing team and the design team, they were not efficient for the project administrators. For them, the use of multiple applications created a technological dissonance; they needed to access three different applications to manage the project. Figure 3 shows one possible view of a tighter integration of the tools for future projects.

The project managers also realized that because each team used different technologies to enable their work, there were gaps in the feedback loop. For example, because the writers did not use Buzzword®, there was a gap in the feedback loop between the designers and writers. We think that if this loop were closed, as illustrated by the dotted line in Figure 3, it would help the writing team see the problems that the design team faced in visualizing the content.

Collaborative Process Issues

In terms of collaboration, the problem with the work iteration described here was that occasionally the content was difficult to design for electronic delivery in the time allocated for each module. In such cases, the content team received feedback from the design team, and the content was edited and re-edited as many times as needed to meet the design constraints. This recursive process lead to expansion of the development time line, and often the content team was not fully aware of these constraints and challenges.

Figure 3. Final project workflow

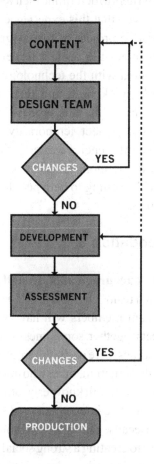

Problems Sustaining Collective Collaborations

We find that while the grant team has achieved collective collaboration to some extent, it was a difficult process to sustain over an extended period. The grant period ran for 2 years, with a majority of the writing to be completed over 14 months. As the team started approaching the end of its first year, there was some degree of writing fatigue among a few of the content developers. This created some fragmentation in the collaborative because other members expressed feeling as if they have an added burden to ensure quality and timely completion of the project. This

fragmentation resulted in a smaller collaborative team that still functioned collectively, while the rest of the content development team distinctly moved away from collective to a combination of serial and parallel collaboration. Letting these shifts occur naturally was in keeping with using the collaborative modes effectively and to the team's advantage—rather than adhering to some outside ideal—as discussed in Principle 4 that grounds this book.

Over the same period, however, our interviews suggested that the technology designers continued to follow the collective collaboration model. We believe that this team continued to collaborate and not experience fatigue because they were challenged constantly to develop creative ways to engage the learners in the new modules. The technology designers also were constantly communicating with the entire group, leading to a stronger feeling of commonality, interdependence, and rapport among all members of this group and, thus, leading to stronger social presence.

SOLUTIONS AND RECOMMENDATIONS

We make the following recommendations to promote, establish, and sustain collective collaboration with the understanding that these recommendations may need modification based on the needs of the unique collaborative group.

Recommendation 1

Find the technology that is most adaptable and adoptable to the project and that supports the virtual collaboration most effectively.

Before the project begins, project managers should research appropriate technological tools. The problems of technological dissonance faced by the project leaders in this case study, the time delays introduced in the development process due to diverse technological adoptions, and the need to build stronger social presence between the writers and designers indicate the need to locate and use an integrated technological solution that can be adopted by the whole collaborative team. It is recommended that a needs survey be distributed before the work is assigned to help define the characteristics of the technology that will need to be adopted for the collaborative team to function.

The grant team started looking at other wikis or wiki-like tools that can be used in conjunction with Zoho™ Projects. Zoho™ has updated the Zoho™ Writer product and has now incorporated a wiki in the Zoho™ Projects tool with similar functionality as the PBWiki. In the ideal situation, the team hopes to move all three working teams to a single technological tool that meets the criteria of being adaptable, adoptable and anywhere/anytime enabled. Such technology would bridge the gaps that exist within and between the design and content teams and also bridge the gaps within the feedback cycle from the assessment to the content team. Figure 4 indicates the final migration pattern.

Recommendation 2

Survey technological fluency of collaborators and follow up with targeted assistance. Be sure

Figure 4. Future plan for a common technology adoption for the different working groups

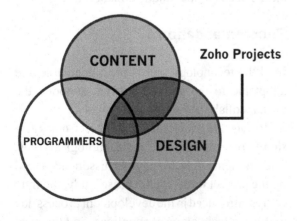

to survey the writers to determine their technological fluency. Given that this experience was their first collaborative project of this magnitude for everyone involved, the project leaders located and experimented with the technology that they thought would work best, and then asked the members to join. While this process served the purposes of the project temporarily, it would have increased efficiencies earlier in the process if there was a common adoption of tools that was paired with training to help people make the necessary shifts.

Recommendation 3

Find ways to encourage and strengthen social presence. Each team, obviously, will be different. Sometimes team members will have worked on several projects together, sometimes everyone will be new. Sometimes there will be a core group of collaborators with one new member who might feel left out. Sometimes they will know each other through previous face-to-face interactions, and sometimes they will not. Because of so many variables, there is no one answer to creating a strong social presence. Team leaders and members, however, must work toward creating a virtual environment that fosters commonality, feelings of safety, respect, rapport, and interdependence. These social presence traits will contribute toward creating a seamless project.

Recommendation 4

Promote team ownership. Strong individual ownership can impede collective collaboration. Therefore, before the start of the project, writing teams should have an exercise or activity that helps the members of the collaborative team understand that the ownership and reward is in the final product and not just in individual contribution. It follows, then, that managers need to create a working environment in which collaboration and not just individual achievement is acknowledged and rewarded.

Recommendation 5

Create a short timetable. We find that collective collaboration is possible but difficult to sustain over a lengthened period. This experience may vary depending on the nature of the project and the members of the collaborative team. However, there may be greater success with shorter timetables in terms of keeping team members' interest and participation levels high.

Recommendation 6

Be flexible. When collective collaboration lags, be willing to move into other forms of collaboration—especially that of serial collaboration. It is possible that some member may need to take charge of the collaboration to complete the project. While this management-level engagement may have the problem of disrupting the collaborative process, it does have the advantage of enabling tasks to be accomplished so that the overall project stays on track.

Recommendation 7

Map the collaborative process. Before the project begins, create a visual map of the desired collaborative process. This should be done prior to development of the project timeline. Then, in order to improve efficiency, make careful observations of the project and survey the collaborators as they work to assess successes and to determine gaps in the process.

Recommendation 8

Ensure an effective closed-loop assessment system along with transparency in the feedback process. For the project outlined in this case study, one module was completed and the writing team jumps to the next and then to the next without sufficient feedback. The assessment data was reported to the design team, but limited feedback was provided to the writers. Both negative and positive comments would have helped to solidify the common goals of the project; additionally, such feedback would have helped the writers feel safer in the content development and in their revisions and comments in the collaborative document. Therefore, the feedback loop could be shortened, making the content development more efficient. While doing so might have lengthened the content development time line, it would have also introduced efficiencies in the overall development process.

FUTURE RESEARCH DIRECTIONS

There has been an increase in the adoption of collaborative techniques in academia and industry. The advances and proliferation of communication technologies also have increased the possibilities of long-range collaborations among distant team members. Our study of this localized collaboration has led us to examine the question of whether we can map the development of social presence and the necessary adaption/adoption of technology to define the mediated collaborative space. As the European Commission Group on Future and Emerging Technologies (2002) stated, "We need to develop a deeper understanding, both in theory and in practice, of how people interact with each other and virtual others through communication of media. The experience of social presence.... this becomes a concept of central importance" (IJsselsteign, Harper, & Group, n.p.).

We propose expanding our localized study to a long-term, broad study to map the intersection of the development of social presence and the characteristics that technology needs to adopt to enable successful collaborations in virtual settings. We think that creating structures to map these developments will enable us to create predictive models. Such models will facilitate the mapping of the entire collaborative process and project the success of the collaborative based on user tracking data. While this goal is far-reaching, the process of collaborating on this book itself has shed new light for us on the definitions and possibilities of adaptable technologies and collaborative work.

CONCLUSION

Principles 1 and 4 (see Chapter 1) are exemplified in this chapter. Effective collaboration in virtual settings requires (1) the intersection of social learning and social presence, in which the members of the collaborative view each other with respect and as contributing members of the collaborative team, and (2) adoption of the appropriate technologies. The selection of the proper technologies is crucial to engaging diverse teams in a meaningful dialogue for shaping the product of the collaborative. If we are to adopt the definition of collaborative products as being those that are homogeneous and reflect the entire collaborative team rather than any one individual, then these technologies have to enable social presence and also must be easily adoptable/adaptable by all the members of the collaborative team. The sequence in the development of strong collaborative teams has to start with the development of social presence first, followed by a mapping of the needs of the collaborative team, and leading to adoption of the appropriate collaborative technologies. The development of social presence and adoption of the proper technologies can lead to highly productive collaborative teams.

REFERENCES

Bouwman, H., van den Hoof, B., van de Wijngaert, L., & van Dijk, J. (2005). *Information and communication technology in organizations. Adaption, implementation, use and effects*. London: Sage.

Bracewell, R. J., & Witte, S. P. (2003). Tasks, ensembles, and activity linkages between text production and situation of use in the workplace. *Written Communication, 20*(4), 511–559. doi:10.1177/0741088303260691

Garrison, D. R., Anderson, T., & Archer, W. (2000). Critical inquiry in a text-based environment: Computer conferencing in higher education. *The Internet and Higher Education, 2*(2-3), 87–105. doi:10.1016/S1096-7516(00)00016-6

IJesselsteign. W., Harper, B., & Group P. W. (2002). Virtually there? A vision of presence research, (pp. 2000-31014). Brussels: Presence—Information Society and Technology, European Community Public Deliverable.

John-Steiner, V., Weber, R. J., & Minnis, M. (1998). The challenge of studying collaboration. *American Educational Research Journal, 35*(4), 773–783.

Kehrwald, B. (2007). The ties that bind: Social presence, relations, and productive collaboration in online learning environments. In *ICT: Providing choices for learners and learning. Proceedings Ascilite Singapore, 2007*, 502–511. Retrieved from http://www.ascilite.org.au/conferences/singapore07/procs/kehrwald.pdf.

O'Reilly, T. (2005). *What is Web 2.0? Design patterns and business models for the next generation of software*. Retrieved from http://www.oreillynet.com/pub/a/oreilly/tim/news/2005/09/30/what-is-web-20.html

Pargman, T. C. (2003). Collaborating with writing tools. Retrieved March 9, 2007 from http://journals.ohiolink.edu/ejc/xml_ft.cgi/Cerratto_Pargman_Teresa.html

Schendel, E., et al. (2004). Toward a theory of online collaboration. In B. Huot, B. Stoble & C. Bazerman (Eds.), Multiple literacies for the 21st century, (pp. 195-209). Cresskill, NY: Hampton.

Shrage, M. (1990). *Shared minds*. New York: Random House.

Tapscott, D., & Williams, A. (2006). *Wikinomics: How mass collaboration changes everything.* New York: Portfolio.

Thomson, A. M., Perry, J. & Miller, T. (2007). Conceptualizing and measuring collaboration. *Journal of Public Administration Research.* Published online 1 Dec. 2007.

Vygotsky, L. S. (1978). *Mind in society: The development of higher psychological processes* (Cole, M., John-Steiner, V., & Souberman, E., Eds.). Cambridge, MA: Harvard UP.

Chapter 7
Removing Barriers to Collaborating in Virtual Writing Projects

William Carney
Cameron University, USA

ABSTRACT

While there are some obvious rewards of virtual collaboration, technological, organizational, and psychosocial barriers to effective collaboration certainly exist. First, familiarity with the media used for collaboration and opportunities for practice are essential. Next, organizational concerns can hinder successful collaboration. Huws (2005) suggested that traditional face-to-face hierarchical organizations or even those with a degree of hybridity can subvert successful collaboration of any sort but also contain features that might enhance collaboration, if used correctly. Additionally, making work roles clearly defined and making the collaborative endeavor explicit and transparent can ensure positive outcomes. Finally, knowledge of the personality traits and values of the participants in a collaborative project is necessary for project managers. This chapter discusses these three potential barriers, provides examples from higher education and the U.S. Army, and discusses possible solutions.

INTRODUCTION

Higher education commonly uses graduate students as teaching assistants. They work with undergraduate students as one way to earn their tuition through graduate school. Some have never taught before they begin to teach first year college writers, and most of them, once trained and prepared for this work, leave their particular graduate institutions

after only two to five years on the job. The system leads to an annual revolving door of new graduate assistants who become novice instructors.

In 2002, the First Year Writing Program administrators at Texas Tech University (Texas Tech) unveiled an innovative method for delivering writing instruction. TOPIC / ICON used locally written software to support what the developers and program administrators hoped would be more "objective" grading of undergraduate student writing; additionally, the software and new practices were intended

DOI: 10.4018/978-1-60566-994-6.ch007

to offer students more opportunities to practice writing. Specifically, the program attempted to address two challenges faced by first-year writing programs. First, TOPIC / ICON sought to address an increase in the number of incoming first year students who demonstrate varying degrees of writing preparation at the high school level and often even greater variations of English proficiency. Second, the program provided a response to the reality that providing writing instruction for these students increasingly becomes the responsibility of graduate students.

The TOPIC / ICON program addressed these instructional needs in a rather unique manner. Students submitted drafts anonymously online; two graduate student instructors then read and assessed the writing. Usually, both instructors provided commentary on the draft (although it was only mandatory that the first reader do so). In this way, instructors graded student writing without knowing the student's identity. The program's developers and administrators hoped that this practice would create more accurate and "objective" grading for students. Additionally, because instructors could grade and comment on a greater number of drafts than they could have under more traditional classroom settings, there was a clear expectation that through a "practice effect," instructors would become more skilled (and faster) in grading and providing commentary for student writing.

Most importantly, the collaborative nature of TOPIC / ICON promised to make the process of grading more transparent for both student and instructor alike. The fact that second readers had access to the commentary of the first reader (although not to the numerical grade assigned by this reader) promised more uniform and useful commentary for the undergraduate students as well as a conduit for the transmission of grading skill from experienced-to-novice teaching assistants. Thus, the TOPIC / ICON program offered graduate instructors practice in the sort of "workplace writing" that is required in higher

education by allowing instructors to collaborate on grading commentary, a written by-product of the grading process.

Sadly (but, perhaps, not so surprisingly), things did not go as planned. Rickly (2006) reported that TOPIC / ICON did meet many of its instructional goals, but the program itself was mired in controversy from its inception. Graduate teaching assistants were almost uniformly dissatisfied with the system. The transparency was perceived as surveillance, the anonymity was widely seen as "de-contextualizing" the student writing and allowing instructors to eschew responsibility, and the opportunities for collaborative writing of commentary were dismissed—in the words of one instructor—as "more meaningless work." Although TOPIC / ICON was designed to be a "recursive" system (that is, feedback from users could lead to system modification), many instructors viewed the program as static and immovable and, thus, in many cases they refused to do any more than the minimum required of them. Here, the intentions of the First-Year Writing Program administrators could not readily overcome the perceptions of the graduate teaching assistants.

As the editors and contributors to this volume discuss throughout, collaborative writing increasingly occurs in virtual settings. While many of these settings involve the composition of documents across geographic regions, many times the virtual collaborative writing process occurs within the colocated space of an institutional or office setting. An exploration of these more localized settings enables collaborative writing managers and team members to understand and address those barriers to successful collaborative writing in virtual settings. Such understanding is essential to managing team dynamics for the greatest efficiency and efficacy.

This chapter explores four types of barriers to effective collaboration:

1. Those that arise from the media/technology used to facilitate collaboration (either as a

result of unfamiliarity with the media being used or with a choice of media and software that do little to facilitate collaboration);

2.	Those organizational factors that result from the institutional setting itself;

3.	Those that have to do with the personality characteristics and values of the participants in the collaborative endeavor; and

4.	Those arising from the actual make-up of the collaborative writing group.

Using the specific settings of higher education and the U.S. Army, to contextualize these four barriers, this chapter explores and considers each of them. Specifically, these venues demonstrate that barriers to virtual collaborative writing are common obstacles that need to be addressed in overt ways. The first venue is the TOPIC / ICON program at Texas Tech, which provided the chapter's opening anecdote. The second venue reflects some recent training efforts by the U.S. Army. To these, I add occasional insights drawn from recent research in organizational behavior in private enterprise.

To ignore the barriers raised in this chapter can lead not only to the failure of one particular collaborative writing project, but also to the mistaken belief that virtual collaboration (and sometimes collaboration itself) provides too little benefit to workplace to justify its use. This result is particularly unfortunate because, as Baumard (1999) and others have suggested, the collaborative environment is the place where tacit knowledge is both created and disseminated. To attain this collaborative environment, this chapter tacitly invokes Principles 1, 3, 4, and 6 of the principles that ground this book (see Chapter 1). A culture of collaboration must be cultivated by those who value and want it to be a part of their organizational structure. To cultivate this culture, trust must be established and collaborative performance must be measured so that it can be rewarded appropriately. The chapter concludes with a list of specific actions that can be taken to remove some of these barriers to virtual collaborative writing projects.

BARRIERS TO COLLABORATING IN VIRTUAL WRITING PROJECTS

Barrier 1: Training and Technology

A first barrier to virtual collaborative writing emerges from the media/technology used to facilitate the collaboration. Obviously, familiarity with Computer-Mediated Communication (CMC) technologies in general and with the specific one chosen for a particular institutional endeavor is key to the success of a virtual collaborative writing project. As far back as the 1990s, participants' lack of familiarity with technology and lack of opportunity to learn the technology adequately has been identified as a primary significant barrier to effective collaboration. Steeples, et al (1996) suggested, for example, that inadequate experience with e-mail due to the lack of training opportunities provided a significant barrier to its adoption in institutions of higher education. Billings and Watts (2006) studied the use of CMC in online dispute resolution and concluded that familiarity with the actual dispute resolution software was a factor in practitioner success in the field. Fuller, Vician, and Brown (2006) suggested that computer anxiety and a separate construct, CMC anxiety, could be alleviated through intensive and formal training in the technologies employed by a particular institution for virtual collaboration purposes.

One particularly ambitious CMC project was the TOPIC / ICON program at Texas Tech University, which was outlined earlier. Faculty in the English Department's First-Year Writing program developed this hybrid program to address the problems created by burgeoning freshman enrollment and static university budgets as well as the fact that freshman writing courses are taught primarily by a transient labor pool (graduate students). The ICON (Interactive Communication Online) program used locally written software (TOPIC) to support more "objective" grading of student assignments, larger composition classes, and more frequent writing assignments. Indeed, in the 2002-

2003 academic year, the ICON program served 4,394 students (an increase of about 8% over the previous academic year), and provided numerical grades and commentary for 139,704 pieces of student writing. For each student, this meant that he or she would be writing and submitting twice as many documents as a typical student had done in the previous academic year. Each student essay draft was submitted online, and the drafts were graded by two anonymous "Document Instructors," who assigned numerical grades and provided commentary. This commentary was mandatory for the first reader but optional for the second reader of any draft although such second reader commentary was encouraged because program administrators believed that novice writers would benefit from commentary on their writing that covered a variety of perspectives.

Surprisingly, while TOPIC / ICON received much attention on the Writing Program Administration and Technical Writing listservs, it was the subject of almost no systematic published research. During the 2005-2006 academic year, I interviewed a sample of 20 instructors in the Freshman Composition program at Texas Tech University as part of a grounded theory study of TOPIC / ICON. One detail I noticed when studying the corpus of student documents in the Freshman Composition archive was how few of these documents contained any sort of commentary from the second reader even in those cases where numerical grades were widely divergent (that is, more than 8 points apart). The interview subjects, most of whom were graduate instructors (teaching assistants) in the Composition program, suggested that they were essentially "thrown to the wolves" as both Classroom Instructors and Document Instructors. In the initial year of the TOPIC / ICON program, students entered the program with fewer than three days of training on the new procedures. This training was combined with the regular new graduate student orientation. Many of the interview subjects, thus, complained of feeling overwhelmed with both the system and the software and more

than half of them suggested that, because of this, they were unwilling to provide any commentary that was not required explicitly. The fact that the Composition faculty offered frequent face-to-face and online training sessions and other resources to help new instructors master the software and the procedures seemed to do little to change this perception and the instructors' strategy of "doing the bare minimum." More than half of the interview subjects reported that what they perceived as inadequate training at the beginning of the semester seemed to result in an unwillingness to master the procedures. It appears that despite these team-building strategies, the faculty failed to develop a culture of collaboration that would sustain the TOPIC / ICON processes. Steps taken by the Composition faculty at Texas Tech to provide formal training and earlier exposure to this hybrid system are discussed later in this chapter.

Issues of usability testing and content management are significant here. Chapter 9 offers four case studies from industry settings that detail the need for an empirically grounded understanding of the needs and behaviors of any system that supports collaborative writing. In the case of TOPIC / ICON, a relatively small pilot study was undertaken prior to the system being introduced on a large scale in the fall 2002 semester. Few in the pilot study could be termed "typical" graduate instructors, those who would ultimately have to use the system since all but one of them would be teaching upper division courses instead of freshman composition. More thorough usability testing prior to the department-wide introduction of TOPIC / ICON and a more user-centered design approach to the development of the system might have made for greater satisfaction with the system and greater willingness on the part of the graduate instructors to use the more collaborative aspects of the system, which is a failure of using the tools effectively, as discussed in Principle 4 that grounds this book. More thorough usability testing involving those instructors slated to use TOPIC / ICON might have uncovered and addressed aspects of the system that they ultimately found difficult to manage, unattractive, or objectionable. Curiously, the usability testing that was performed was limited to the First-Year Writing faculty and a few select graduate instructors who were involved in the development of TOPIC / ICON rather than those instructors who would be tasked with using the system. The participants in the pilot study and usability testing were individuals with significant technological expertise and an investment in hybrid instructional systems requiring a high degree of collaboration. Absent were graduate instructors with fewer computer skills and no clear understanding of what the system required.

In another setting—that of the U.S. Army—usability issues created similar problems. The Center for Management of Information at the University of Arizona has been actively developing new online collaborative writing tools for the United States Army and other government agencies for well over 20 years (Lowry, Albrecht, Nunamaker, & Lee, 2002). Early efforts in virtual collaborative writing in the military focused almost solely on writing policy manuals but more recently, virtual collaborative writing appears in many other forms in military settings. For example, Orvis, Wisher, Bonk, and Olson (2002) discussed the use of online collaborative writing software in military training courses. Presently, the U.S. Army relies on virtual collaborative writing teams to perform a wide array of tasks from writing policies, to training, to the evaluation of special projects (see also Cohen, 2009).

To this end, I am in the process of conducting focus group research with civilian instructors at Fort Sill, Oklahoma detailing their experiences with collaborative writing software and the willingness of senior Non-Commissioned Officers (NCO) to participate in virtual projects that require collaborative writing. Specifically, these NCOs are tasked with the writing of training manuals and the establishment of training sequences for various NCO schools. Preliminary results suggest that willingness to participate in these projects

and satisfaction with the content of these projects seems to be related to proximity to Ft. Sill itself. In other words, NCOs at more remote sites seem less willing to participate and the instructors indicate that this unwillingness may be related to less access to face-to-face interaction in learning and troubleshooting the CMC software. The NCOs stationed at Ft. Sill and those who have opportunities for regular Temporary Duty (TDY) assignments to Ft. Sill seem more satisfied and have a higher degree of proficiency with the software than those at more remote sites. While this satisfaction undoubtedly is related to a number of factors, the instructors I interviewed indicated that different methods of training are necessary to achieve full participation in these collaborative writing projects. Boczkowski (1999) suggested that the user's perception of adequate training also is vitally important in encouraging a sense of community and "sociability" in CMC projects. Indeed, the NCOs seem more satisfied with those projects that offer opportunities for face-to-face interaction between participants or that employ supplemental software that provides other opportunities for interaction (such as Skype, Yahoo Messenger, or text messaging). This concern is discussed in greater detail later.

While training in the software used in the collaborative writing project is essential, the choice of the software itself can determine the success of the project. Noting that most collaborative writing projects are asynchronous, Lowry, et al. (2005) suggested that Group Support Systems (GSS) are essential for creating structure in virtual collaborative writing, particularly with novice team members. McKenzie and Potter (2004) indicated that, if face-to-face meetings are not feasible during a virtual collaborative writing project, supplementing the writing software with other media that will enrich the project can achieve the desired effect. Oral and visual media can facilitate relationship issues that arise from the collaborative process. Thus, supplementing whatever software is used to write the text with media that offer ways to provide reflection, questioning, and conflict resolution can assist in the virtual collaborative writing process. Baker (2004) demonstrated better results for virtual collaborative writing projects that feature other "supplemental" technologies. The instructors I have interviewed at Ft. Sill tend to agree. One staff sergeant I interviewed mentioned the difficulty he encountered when collaborating with people he could not see. For him, the occasional conference call did not provide the necessary personal interaction he needed for successful collaboration. Another NCO had expressed satisfaction with his participation in a project that used Skype for meetings among the collaborative writing participants. Still another NCO who had participated in several projects noted that he felt a greater attachment to members of virtual collaborative writing teams who used text messaging as a supplement to whatever writing software the team used. He even suggested that he found himself texting jokes and news from Ft. Sill to his virtual collaborators even after the project was complete.

Face-to-face interaction among virtual writing collaborators also was identified by the instructors in this sample as something that seemed to guarantee cooperation in collaborative writing projects, even in instances when meetings were brief. Certainly, face-to-face meetings may be preferable for gaining cooperation, but, in the case of Army NCOs, it is often impossible. Laru and Jarvela (2008), however, demonstrated a high degree of "buy-in" to collaborative projects through more extensive use of Personal Digital Assistants (PDAs), something some of the instructors in my sample also have used in their virtual collaborative writing projects. In the end, technology may not be as important as the writers' buy-in to participate in a virtual collaborative writing group. Sakellardis, et al. (2008) suggested that there really are no electronic technologies that better enable virtual collaborative writing in each and every case. Rather, the most important quality may be the willingness of all participants

in a particular project to agree on the technology to be used.

Barrier 2: Organizational Factors

A second barrier to virtual collaborative writing involves the characteristics of the organization or institution itself and how the shape of the organization affects participants' perceptions. In effect, it involves the organization's success or failure in developing a culture of collaboration, Principle 1 (Chapter 1) that grounds this book. Huws (2005) categorized institutions according to where they fall within the "3 Fs" framework—formal, foot loose, or fractured. Each of these types of organizations creates different opportunities for collaboration but also creates its own set of barriers to collaboration, virtual or otherwise. According to Huws, a formal organization is one that features a high degree of face-to-face contact (for example, "brick-and-mortar" schools and businesses). While employees in such settings might show some initial resistance in moving from the face-to-face to virtual modes of collaboration, these organizations offer "rich" interaction opportunities and, thus, contain structural aspects that might better facilitate training and socialization for other ways of collaborating. Community building is easier as participants frequently interact with each other in ways that, arguably, CMC technologies can only mimic. If, however, the goals and expectations of virtual collaboration are not made explicit to the participants, there is the very real probability participants will choose to focus less energy on the virtual projects. One of the FYC faculty at Texas Tech, for example, admitted that he and his colleagues did not "sell" the value of the collaborative nature of TOPIC / ICON to the graduate instructors as well as they might have. "Instructors wondered why they couldn't just go to someone else's office to talk about a draft they were both grading," he said. "We never really told them that their online writing provided an archive that other instructors could potentially use as well as feedback that might be helpful to the student."

On the other hand, a "foot loose" organization is one characterized either by predominantly temporary or contract workers, virtual workers, or both. While these organizations might seem best situated to encourage virtual collaboration, the fact that they use "transient" workers (many of whom are concerned about subsequent opportunities with the organization) actually makes collaboration more difficult. For example, adjunct instructors in higher education, whether they teach in traditional classrooms or in distance education venues, tend to be transient workers whose impermanence leads them to remain aware of future work possibilities. Kezim, Pariseau and Quinn (2005) studied adjunct instructors in a college of business and found that they assigned students higher grades than did more permanent faculty because of their concern for future teaching opportunities. Moore and Trahan (1998) found similar differences and suggested that, because of their situations, adjuncts would be less likely to participate in any departmental activities regarding collaboration. Often, adjuncts and other temporary and transient workers believe that "too much" participation actually creates opportunities for social blunders. Thus, their temporary status leads these workers to avoid collaboration. These are issues of trust, as described in Principle 3 (Chapter 1). In such cases, involving these kinds of workers in virtual collaborative writing might be something that employers could mandate. More-or-less "voluntary" collaborative writing might be something that temporary and transient works will opt out of. If, however, employers or project managers privilege virtual collaborative writing and make it the primary part of the job assignment, such workers will have no choice but to participate.

Huws' (2005) "fractured" organization, however, might offer greater opportunities for virtual collaboration. These organizations combine elements of the first two types, formal and footloose. There is a team of permanent employees with day-to-day or, at least frequent, contact with each other and teams of temporary and contract employees who work in face-to-face or virtual settings. For the permanent employees, this contact with other types of workers provides a model both in theory and in the practice of virtual collaboration. Many collaborative writing teams, both virtual and face-to-face, are comprised of individuals of different ranks, with different levels of job tenure, and with different types of expertise. Thus, the "fractured" organization might actually lend itself to the formation of virtual collaborative writing teams. Indeed, Pisano and Verganti (2008) noted that different types of members in these teams can encourage better outcomes. Certainly, differences in motivation exist between temporary and permanent employees. The temporary participants have a greater potential interest in being hired for subsequent projects and, thus, may not be as willing to engage in critique of the work of other participants. For permanently employed participants, there might exist less willingness to accept the input of transient workers with whom a personal familiarity does not exist. Still, with explicit guidelines (clear expectations regarding outcomes and an explanation as to why the project in question needs to be conducted in either a virtual or face-to-face environment), this sort of organizational structure might well encourage collaboration.

Most likely, both permanent and temporary employees who work from home or another remote setting will possess a high degree of proficiency with the organization's CMC software and all the participants will share the virtual milieu. Because such an organization uses temporary workers, conduits that are more sophisticated than those used by fixed organizations often exist for transmitting information. These organizations make use of technologies that place employees on a more level playing field in terms of their input into virtual collaborative writing projects simply because they have to do so. In order to accomplish what they need to, such organizations will use software and provide training that all participants can use, something the First-Year Writing program at Texas

Tech has done (see "Overcoming Barriers" that follows). Huws (2005) also suggested that these organizations offer a "two-edged sword" in terms of employee identity. While it is more difficult for employees in these organizations to define their work with traditional labels, there are more tasks that all workers perform in common and, thus, a potential for more "democratic" participation in collaborative projects. Similarly, Warshauer (1997) noted that virtual collaboration actually does lead to more equal levels of participation for team members.

There is, however, no guarantee that such an organization will automatically breed collaboration. For this "fractured" organizational structure to successfully facilitate collaboration, virtual or otherwise, the organization's particular culture must be disseminated to all team members. McKenzie and Potter (2004) believed that the perceptions about work and the loyalties team members bring to a virtual collaborative writing project often may be antithetical to the needs of a particular project. Clearly defined expectations for the project and the development of shared experiences among team members suggests that adequate time must be devoted to any virtual collaborative writing endeavor. These concerns emerged in the Texas Tech study. First, the "fixedness" of the university and the fact that the graduate instructors were, by their own admissions, drawn to graduate study because of their own positive experiences in traditional face-to-face undergraduate settings suggests that the graduate instructors brought with them rather "traditional" expectations of graduate student life and work. Indeed, Lindholm (2004) indicated that students who pursue graduate education do so because they have had positive experiences in endeavors that encourage a high degree of autonomy and independence. Further, Golde (2005) studied attrition from doctoral programs and indicated that disappointed expectations played a significant role in determining whether a student will abandon or complete his or her graduate work. In the hu-manities, undergraduates often are not exposed to the work of teaching in meaningful ways. These psychological factors will be discussed in greater detail later, but they bear mentioning here as they seem to have provided a barrier to the development of a culture of collaboration at Texas Tech. While new graduate instructors had experienced instruction as "consumers," few initially understood the demands of instructional delivery in this very different and novel context. Indeed, the fact that TOPIC/ICON-based instruction looked so different from traditional instruction seems to suggest that novice instructors were being introduced to a milieu in which their traditional expectations were disappointed. The very novelty of TOPIC/ICON was something with which many of my interview subjects expressed disappointment. In Huws' (2005) terminology, the English Department at Texas Tech University was more fractured and, thus, bound to create some confusion and disappointment for those who expected a more formal and traditional graduate student experience. Pisano and Verganti (2008) suggested that much effort needs to be invested in such a setting to encourage collaboration. Such effort might include more time in training and more "realistic" previews of the work involved, issues that will be discussed later under "Psychological and Social Barriers."

The organizational structure of the Texas Tech University English Department and the often-conflicting roles that graduate instructors play within the department provided another example of these institutional barriers. Most of the instructors who agreed to be interviewed for the study believed that the First Year Composition program at the university offered a number of opportunities for meaningful collaboration. The year after TOPIC/ICON was launched, an online chat room feature was installed to the grading interface so that instructors could collaborate on the work they were doing. Additionally, grading teams were formed so that those instructors teaching in the classroom could interact with those who were only grading documents. In this way, through collaborative processes, information could be disseminated and grading practices could be made more explicit. These results failed to happen immediately as instructors tended to experience a rather uncomfortable confusion in their roles. As most of the instructors in the program were also MA and PhD students, many of those interviewed expressed a concern that collaboration with others would be self-defeating because they were competing with other graduate students for awards, scholarships, and fellowships, One PhD student stated rather bluntly, "Why should I help anyone else and make them as good as me?" This questions reveals the extent to which trust had not been established within a culture of collaboration.

Another expressed source of reluctance to collaborate came from the "outsourcing" of grading. Graduates of the English program (and, indeed, some instructors affiliated with other institutions) were allowed to continue grading and responding to student documents for remuneration even after their formal affiliation with Texas Tech had ended. A number of the instructors interviewed expressed dismay at this practice and shared a concern that these graders would have less access to grading information than would the on-site graduate instructors. This concern led a few of those interviewed to suggest that those "outsiders" who were contracted to grade essentially would be paid for inferior work. A few suggested that, when administrators at the university encouraged a more rapid completion of graduate degrees and fewer guarantees of graduate employment for those who completed the degree at a slower pace, outsourced employees would be those with whom they would be least likely to collaborate. This line of thinking led a number of those interviewed to refuse to engage in the collaborative virtual writing (grading commentary) that TOPIC / ICON made possible.

A few of these concerns (as well as a degree of frustration) also were expressed by my sample of civilian army instructors at Ft. Sill. In some military units, active duty military personnel work alongside civilians and, in some cases, report to civilian Department of Defense (DOD) employees. One complaint from the focus group participants was that senior NCOs, especially those who had line responsibilities, often were unreceptive to collaboration, virtual or otherwise, and especially to collaboration with civilian workers. Those soldiers with line assignments are involved in day-to-day operations (for example, supply, artillery, and maintenance). Staff positions may be thought of as "middle management." These positions typically sustain those with line responsibilities by providing support, advice, and knowledge. Not surprisingly, for those with line assignments, line responsibilities needed their attention first. Collaborative projects were considered to be secondary to the mission. Staff NCOs, on the other hand, work in a more explicitly defined "culture of collaboration," and they seemed to see collaboration as part of the job. Those who had staff responsibilities were more receptive to virtual collaborative projects. Of course, staffs NCOs are those who will more likely have TDY assignments to places where their collaborators work, which enabled them to meet each other in face-to-face settings. Thus, while organizational structure certainly has an impact on the outcome of virtual collaboration projects, some of the psychological factors briefly mentioned above also can act as potential barriers to virtual collaboration. These are discussed below.

Barrier 3: Psychological and Social Factors

In the Texas Tech study, many of the interview responses tended to support what previous research regarding the personality characteristics of graduate students in the humanities has demonstrated. For one, as I discussed above, graduate students in the humanities enter such programs because they value independence and autonomy (Lindholm 2004). But with the value they place on independence, there seems to exist a simultaneous and almost paradoxical belief in authority and hierarchy. Weaver and Qi (2005) suggested that graduate students in the humanities place a significant reliance on authority figures and often engage in behaviors described as "passive withdrawal" when instructions are not made explicit. A number of the instructors in the Texas Tech sample suggested that, because they perceived the Composition faculty as lacking interest in their professional development, they did the minimum amount of work required of them. In such cases, finding ways to employ reasonable ways to measure and track performance could provide feedback both to the faculty and to the students who essentially refused to collaborate as required. Doing so employs Principle 6 of the principles that ground this book.

Wang and Newlin (2000) studied the personality characteristics of graduate students who experienced success in online environments and found that they exhibited a greater locus of control and a strong belief in personal efficacy. Friedman (2004), however, found that graduate students in the humanities showed significant tendencies toward introversion and exhibited a more-or-less theoretical orientation toward work in their academic specialties and toward academia in general. Indeed, there is research that suggests that those characteristics that lead to effective teaching service work in any environment are often at odds with the personality traits of scholars in the humanities (Rushton 1982). These dynamics seemed to be in operation with the Texas Tech sample as a number of the instructors expressed significant dissatisfaction with the TOPIC technology as well as with the fact that they were expected to work online collaboratively. While Wang and Newlin (2000) indicated that exposure to online environments can improve locus of control, it seems that many in the Texas Tech sample did not care to spend time learning the capabilities of the software. Knowing the personality characteristics of "typical" graduate instructors in the humanities

might have led the First-Year Writing faculty at Texas Tech to spend more time in exposure to and training on the TOPIC / ICON software to encourage graduate instructors to use the system more fully.

Another personality characteristic exhibited by students in liberal arts and humanities graduate programs is what Onwuegbuzie (1997) terms a "socially prescribed perfectionism." Such students' anxiety over the perceived high standards of faculty mentors in terms of their writing is manifest in procrastination. A number of the Texas Tech instructors expressed both dissatisfaction with the "scarce" feedback they themselves received on the commentary they had written and the admission that they put things off and, thus, gave themselves little time to comment collaboratively with other instructors. Many expressed that, not only was their work ignored but also that their perception of the limited feedback they were provided meant that the task of teaching composition itself was devalued. In the context of introducing the new software at Texas Tech, the First-Year Writing faculty might have allayed some of the anxiety instructors experienced by "modeling" collaboration in the system themselves and by providing more immediate feedback to the instructors. Parenthetically, a couple of the staff NCOs in my Army sample indicated that they spend the early part of any training class in virtual collaborative writing working with the participants in a series of exercises using the software that will be used in the project—a practice that appears to work for them in overcoming barriers.

In the military setting, the instructors at Ft. Sill also expressed concern that line NCOs possess personality traits that might be opposed to those skills and traits needed for success in online collaborative projects. Even though military personnel typically have no problems with collaboration or hierarchy, per se, there are still aspects of the "typical" line NCO that might not make virtual collaborative writing an easy task.

Church and Waclawski (2001) found that line managers in industry were significantly weaker at relationships, openness to new ideas, demonstrating respect, and adaptability to change. Carlstedt (1998) suggested that a degree of rigidity and field dependence are characteristics of a "good" NCO. It seems that such traits might be at odds with what is required for success in virtual collaboration. Hurley & Eberharter (1995) explained that there may be different types of competencies that are affiliated with success for staff and line NCOs, respectively. Staff NCOs tend to have adequate technical skills but are lacking in tactical knowledge while the opposite seems to be the case for NCOs on the line. His or her personality make-up, then, might lead an NCO to choose staff over line responsibilities and postings (and vice versa). The trend, however, according to the instructors in my sample, is that the Army in general is requiring greater collaboration, virtual or otherwise, from all of its NCOs, which means that even those who are less drawn to collaboration by virtue of their personality traits also must overcome the barriers.

Finally, there is a growing corpus of research that explores psychological aspects of collaboration in industry, which can provide some insight into the academic and military settings that contextualize this chapter. Brown, Poole, and Rodgers (2004) found that successful outcomes in virtual collaborative writing projects in e-commerce firms were more likely to occur when the participants had a disposition toward trust and affiliation. In a similar study, Holton (2001) suggested that team building was essential for any sort of successful collaboration. Hertel, Geister, and Konradt (2005) suggested that, beyond the factor of trust, those employees who tend to excel in virtual collaborative writing projects (or in virtual collaboration of any sort) might be those who exhibit a high degree of "external motivation." They expect extrinsic rewards (if only public recognition for their participation) and thrive in work settings that offer such rewards.

Barrier 4: Team Composition

The way the virtual collaborative writing team is constituted also can become a barrier. Certainly, the technical, organizational, and psychological can influence on virtual collaborative writing projects, but there are other factors that also influence the outcome of a project for better or worse. First, a virtual collaborative writing team composed of novice members will require significantly more time to achieve cohesion than will a team with one or two "veterans." Lowry, et al. (2005) argued for the necessity of technological and social supports for novice team members, especially in those projects where the document is composed asynchronously. These supports include explicit step-by-step instructions and objectives for the completion of the document or project and a discussion board in which members can discuss the progress of the collaborative team. The degree to which the virtual collaborative writing team is "open" is another factor that can help to facilitate the outcome of a project. Pisano and Verganti (2008) discussed four types of collaborative teams ranging from elite circles in which membership is selected by management and closed thereafter to "innovation communities" in which membership is voluntary and fluid. While there are collaborative writing projects that might benefit from open outside input, accountability may be harder to establish for team members. A more finite team, chosen by managers, might make team expectations more transparent but also might limit the types of input into a particular project. The choice of which model to use depends upon factors such as the expertise of the potential participants and how clearly defined the outcome is.

Another factor discussed at length by Pisano and Verganti involves the degree to which team composition is hierarchical. Flat hierarchies certainly can enhance the willingness of participants to participate, but some degree of hierarchical structure may be necessary when the completion of the document depends upon the knowledge and expertise of a particular participant. In other words, having a project supervisor who is ultimately accountable for the project might be necessary in certain cases. A third factor to consider involves the "space" of the virtual collaborative writing project. If the team members are geographically distant from each other, a degree of "forgetting" is often likely with team members having to spend some amount of time revisiting the project goals and objectives every time they write. Henderson and DeSilva (2006) indicated that in such cases the team members should spend time creating what they call a document narrative. This piece of writing clarifies the objectives of the document under construction and lists the duties and intentions of each writer. They found that such a practice also served to assist in making the final document more coherent. Parenthetically, the contributors and editors of this volume made use of collaborative reviewing and editing practices designed to enhance the consistency of this book. Through frequent virtual meetings, a transparent editorial process, and the adoption of shared terminology and objectives across the chapters, a more cohesive volume has been produced.

The Texas Tech study participants expressed some of these group composition barriers. One of the reasons for the development of TOPIC / ICON was to provide novice graduate instructors a way to gain expertise in grading as well as a way to assess student writing more efficiently. Yet, for all the recursive elements that the software featured, a number of the participants complained that it was a "top-down" system—hierarchical in nature and based on teaching expertise that the developers refused to share. Certainly, experience plays a role in the structure of any collaborative team. As Chapter 18 indicates, much of the collaborative virtual writing that occurs in academic settings involves time spent in invention on the part of the participants and a fairly high degree of supervision from those with expertise. In industry, as Chapter 9 suggests, team members appear to

have a higher degree of fluency with the virtual collaborative writing process. In academia or in the case of an innovation, some degree of expertise and hierarchy is necessary. Yet, the graduate instructors interviewed at Texas Tech believed that there were few opportunities for any input into the initial or ongoing development of TOPIC / ICON. Additionally, several expressed dismay that some of the instructors who graded in the system were outside the region and, thus, were not party to recent developments in the use of the software as were those instructors on the Texas Tech campus. Similarly, the instructors in the U.S. Army sample did not identify hierarchy as a barrier to successful virtual collaborative writing outcomes—which makes sense based on the hierarchical nature of the military organization—but they did express a concern that geographic separation among members affected their collaboration.

OVERCOMING BARRIERS TO VIRTUAL COLLABORATIVE WRITING

How, then, can we overcome these rather significant barriers to effective virtual collaborative writing?

- Make sure that all the participants in a particular writing project are familiar with the software being used in the project. The experience of the first-Year Writing faculty at Texas Tech demonstrates just how important expertise can be especially if the software itself is brand new. The time spent training the participants on the use of the software ultimately is time well spent.
- Be certain that the software chosen for the project fits the goals and objectives of the project. In any case, project managers might consider supplementing the software with other media that provide other venues for interaction between the participants.

- Understand why a project employs virtual (as opposed to face-to-face) collaboration. Is it that the participants are separated by geography or is it that virtual collaboration creates an archive of the process itself, as was the case with TOPIC / ICON? Understanding the reasons behind the choice of virtual collaboration and communicating those reasons to the participants is essential in getting those participants to commit to the project.
- Know and understand the participants in the project. What other responsibilities do they have? In my sample of Army NCOs, those with line responsibilities tend to see writing in general and virtual collaborative writing in particular as a task of secondary importance. Understanding this thinking and being able to communicate the importance of the writing project can lead to greater commitment on that part of all the participants. One of the NCOs involved in artillery training admitted that it was not until he understood how the writing of a policy manual impacted the actual training that soldiers receive that he actually "bought in" to the process.
- Choose participants for a project who have the potential for being successful collaborators. It may be the case, for example, that more-or-less "typical" graduate students in the humanities might never be ideal participants for virtual collaborative writing. It might also be the case that effective collaboration is a possible outcome but that these participants will have a fairly steep "learning curve" and that they will need to be deliberate about setting an intention to be collaborative in such writing projects. In either case, it is essential that the virtual collaborative writing team managers have some understanding of the potential participants.
- Finally, both provide frequent feedback and revisit the objectives of the project often. Project managers should clarify what is expected from each participant whether or not his or her participation is based on a particular expertise that the other participants may not possess. Each participant needs to understand the desired outcome and his or her role in reaching that outcome.

CONCLUSION

What can be done to make virtual collaborative writing successful in the specific settings described in this chapter? How can we remove some of the barriers discussed above? As detailed above, some adherence to Principles 1, 3, 4, and 6 of the principles that ground this book might help.

The First-Year Writing faculty at Texas Tech University made some substantive changes that have led to greater collaboration. To enhance familiarity with the TOPIC / ICON interface (now called "RaiderWriter"), prospective graduate students now are introduced to the software during a pre-enrollment orientation weekend. Prospective candidates can now decide whether working in a hybrid setting meets their needs and personalities and, if they do decide to attend Texas Tech, they are familiarized more deeply with the system. Organizational and even personality factors are addressed through mandatory professional development workshops for students enrolled in the doctoral program. Issues and expectations of collegiality and collaboration are discussed and doctoral students learn that, although individual scholarship is still the "gold standard" in the humanities, classroom practice is a large part of the work of an academic and collaboration is expected for success in the field. Parenthetically, in a number of subdisciplines in the humanities (linguistics and technical communication, for example) collaborative scholarship is becoming more widely accepted. These professional development workshops encourage participants to become involved in collaborative endeavors in graduate school and in their careers. Decentralized "grading groups" have been instituted, and these groups enable graduate instructors to collaborate face-to-face and in virtual settings with other graduate instructors that they get to know over the course of a semester. These collaborative teams allow more experienced members to "mentor" those less experienced and to encourage collaboration. All these things have led to an increased willingness to collaborate not only in writing grading commentary but also in many aspects of the teaching of composition.

And, what of the U.S. Army instructors? Of course, my research is in a formative stage so, without a clear picture of the state of virtual collaboration in that milieu, recommendations seem premature. It does seem, however, that any solution or, at least, any modification will involve a deeper understanding of the technologies involved as well as an understanding of how to make the organization structure mimic face-to-face communication for both staff and line NCOs. As the military itself engages in virtual collaborative writing in the writing of policies and in newer venues such as the use of virtual collaborative writing in training scenarios, the insights gleaned from the study of these endeavors might yield some insights for virtual collaborative writing in industry and other large, hierarchical organizations.

REFERENCES

Baker, G. (2004). A study of virtual teams. In Khosrow-Pour, M. (Ed.), *Advanced Topics in Information Resources Management* (pp. 333–352). Hershey, PA: Idea Publishing Group.

Baumard, P. (1999). *Tacit knowledge in organizations*. London, UK: Sage.

Billings, M., & Watts, L. (2006). The model of relational communication: Explaining difficulties encountered through the use of technology in alternative dispute resolution. In *Proceedings from the 8ᵗʰ Australian Mediation Conference*.

Boczkowski, P. (1999). Mutual shaping of users and technologies in a national virtual community. *The Journal of Communication*, *49*, 86–108. doi:10.1111/j.1460-2466.1999.tb02795.x

Brown, H. G., Poole, M., & Rodgers, T. (2004). Interpersonal traits, complementarity, and trust in virtual collaboration. *Journal of Management Information Systems*, *20*, 115–138.

Carlstedt, L. G. (1998). Prediction of fitness for service in UN military units. *Storming Media*. Retrieved 19 May 2009 from http://www.stormingmedia.us/31/3122/A312263.html

Church, A. H., & Waclawski, J. (2001). Hold the line: An examination of line vs. staff differences. *Human Resource Management*, *40*, 21–34. doi:10.1002/hrm.4013

Coen, N. (August 13, 2009). Care to write Army doctrine? With ID, log on. *The New York Times*. Accessed October 28, 2009. http://www.nytimes.com/2009/08/14/business/14army.html?_r=1&em

Friedman, A. A. (2004). The relationship between personality traits and reflective judgment among female students. *Journal of Adult Development*, *11*, 297–304. doi:10.1023/B:JADE.0000044533.75067.ee

Fuller, R. M., Vician, C., & Brown, S. A. (2006). E-learning and individual characteristics: The role of computer anxiety and communication apprehension. *Journal of Computer Information Systems*, *46*, 103–115.

Golde, C. M. (2005). The role of department and discipline in doctoral student attrition: Lessons from four departments. *The Journal of Higher Education*, *76*, 669–700. doi:10.1353/jhe.2005.0039

Henderson, P., & De Silva, N. (2006). A narrative approach to collaborative writing: A business process model. In *8th International Conference on Enterprise Information Systems (ICEIS)*, Cyprus.

Hertel, G., Geister, S., & Konradt, U. (2005). Managing virtual teams: A review of current empirical research. *Human Resource Management Review, 15*, 69–95. doi:10.1016/j.hrmr.2005.01.002

Holton, J. (2001). Building trust and collaboration in a virtual team. *Team Performance Management, 7*, 36–47. doi:10.1108/13527590110395621

Hurley, J., & Eberharter, S. (1995). CMF 12 advanced Noncommissioned Officer Course program of instruction. *Engineer, 25*, 1–17.

Huws, U. (2005). Fixed, footloose, or fractured: Work, identity, and the spatial division of labor. *Monthly Review (New York, N.Y.), 57*, 23–39.

Kezim, B., Pariseau, S. E., & Quinn, F. (2005). Is grade inflation related to faculty status? *Journal of Education for Business, 80*, 358–363. doi:10.3200/JOEB.80.6.358-364

Laru, J., & Jarvela, S. (2008). Social patterns in mobile technology mediated collaboration among members of the professional distance education community. *Educational Media International, 45*, 17–32. doi:10.1080/09523980701847131

Lindholm, K. (2004). Pathways to the professoriate: The role of self, others, and environment in shaping academic career aspirations. *The Journal of Higher Education, 75*, 603–635. doi:10.1353/jhe.2004.0035

Lowry, P. B., Albrecht, C. C., Nunamaker, J. F., & Lee, J. D. (2002). Evolutionary development and research on Internet-based collaborative writing tools and processes to enhance eWriting in an eGovernment setting. *Decision Support Systems, 34*, 229–252. doi:10.1016/S0167-9236(02)00119-7

Lowry, P. B., Nunamaker, J. F., Curtis, A., & Lowry, M. R. (2005). The impact of process structure on novice, virtual collaborative writing teams. *IEEE Transactions on Professional Communication, 48*, 341–364. doi:10.1109/TPC.2005.859728

McKenzie, J., & Potter, R. (2004). Five keys to better virtual collaboration. *Knowledge Management Review, 7*, 8–9.

Moore, M., & Trahan, R. (1998). Tenure status and grading practices. *Sociological Perspectives, 41*, 775–782.

Onwuegbuzie, A. (1997). Writing a research proposal: The role of library anxiety, statistics anxiety, and composition anxiety. *Library & Information Science Research, 19*, 5–33. doi:10.1016/S0740-8188(97)90003-7

Orvis, K., Wisher, R., Bonk, C. J., & Olson, T. (2002). Communication patterns during synchronous web-based military training in problem solving. *Computers in Human Behavior, 18*, 783–795. doi:10.1016/S0747-5632(02)00018-3

Pisano, G., & Verganti, R. (2008, December). Which kind of collaboration is right for you? *Harvard Business Review, 10*, 78–86.

Rickly, R. (2006). Distributed teaching, distributed learning: Integrating technology and criteria-driven assessment into the delivery of first-year composition. In Yancey, K. B. (Ed.), *Delivering college composition: The fifth canon* (pp. 183–198). Portsmouth, NH: Boynton/Cook.

Rushton, P. (1982). Moral cognition, behaviorism, and social learning theory. *Ethics, 92*, 459–467. doi:10.1086/292355

Sakellariadis, A., Chromy, S., Martin, V., Speedy, J., Trahar, S., Williams, S., & Wilson, S. (2008). Friend or foe? Technology in a collaborative writing group. *Qualitative Inquiry, 14*, 1205–1222. doi:10.1177/1077800408324210

Steeples, C., Unsworth, C., Bryson, M., Good-year, P., Riding, P., & Fowell, S. (1996). Technological support for teaching and learning: computer-mediated communications in higher education. *Computers & Education, 26*, 71–80. doi:10.1016/0360-1315(95)00082-8

Wang, A., & Newlin, M. (2000). Characteristics of students who enroll and succeed in web-based psychology classes. *Journal of Educational Psychology, 92*, 137–143. doi:10.1037/0022-0663.92.1.137

Warschauer, M. (1997). Computer-mediated collaborative learning: Theory and practice. *Modern Language Journal, 81*, 470–481. doi:10.2307/328890

Weaver, R., & Qi, J. (2005). Classroom organization and participation: College students' perceptions. *The Journal of Higher Education, 76*, 570–601. doi:10.1353/jhe.2005.0038

Chapter 8
Facilitating Virtual Collaborative Writing through Informed Leadership

Catherine Lyman
NetApp, Inc., USA

ABSTRACT

With the right combination of writers, collaborative writing may grow organically in a team. But it is more likely that managers need to set the expectation that collaboration is requirement, provide strong leadership in an organization to make it happen, and measure its effectiveness. Managers need to lead writers down the path to writing collaboratively, finding effective ways to support the implementation of new writing methods. This chapter provides practical approaches that will help develop a manager's skills for leading virtual collaborative writing teams. The techniques described in this chapter were developed and tested by actual collaborative writing teams, most notably by the Information Engineering team at NetApp, Inc.

INTRODUCTION: WHEN COLLABORATION NEEDS HELP

The writing team has been assembled carefully for "the big project." There are several strong first-line managers who know the technical material in their respective areas. They understand their writers and are respected by them; in fact, in many cases, they have worked together for many years. Equally important, the managers can work the politics of the company. The writers are a diverse group

bringing varied skills. They have different areas of product expertise, tools knowledge, leadership, and emotional intelligence. The writing team recently has moved to a collaborative work environment, and most of the team members are over the initial training—thankfully, they "bought in" to the new system. Everyone seemed excited about this shift in practice.

Well, everyone *was* excited and everyone *was* making progress, but something has changed and the excitement has diminished. Perhaps people are somehow feeling stuck because suddenly stress signs have been popping up in various places—

DOI: 10.4018/978-1-60566-994-6.ch008

short tempers and irritated comments. Stress is also apparent within subgroups of the overall team. For example, managers have gotten testy about work not being completed by some writers in *other* teams. Writers are becoming territorial and complaining about not letting other writers put content in their books because of improper planning. What is going wrong? And, what can be done to set things right?

FACILITATING VIRTUAL COLLABORATIVE WRITING AMONG LEADERS

Some writers and writing teams have not ventured far down the collaborative-writing road, but they notice that projects are taking longer to get started. In fact, these projects seem to require that writers cover more ground in the published deliverables than ever before. In such cases, writing teams may benefit from putting virtual collaborative techniques in place. This chapter provides suggestions for helping the team optimize virtual collaborative practices and to identify pitfalls before venturing too far down this road. One key way to get virtual collaborative writing teams up and running is to develop the skills of managers and other leaders as well as the uses of tools and processes. Accordingly, this chapter addresses a number of the principles of collaboration that ground this book—creating a culture of collaboration (Principle 1), finding and promoting leadership (Principle 2), using tools effectively (Principle 4), creating structure (Principle 5), and measuring and tracking performance (Principle 6).

Model the Solution

"How can I expect my team to work collaboratively when I don't know what they are experiencing?"

"We just aren't getting anywhere with this project even though we have a bunch of people on it. What is wrong?"

Designated team managers and leaders are a big part of the solution, but so is every manager and leader-without-a-title of-leader on the team. By identifying how the entire leadership team (including the leaders doing the identification) can work collaboratively and by modeling those changes to the team, change will filter down. The efforts that leaders make in learning virtual collaboration themselves will help all writing team members to develop trust in their managers and in each other, but most of all in themselves. All of the suggestions in this chapter directly apply to the manager and leadership team—by providing specific ways to apply collaborative techniques especially during initial learning phases. What follow are suggestions for helping mangers lead and helping them understand what signs point to the need for more collaboration.

Be (and Practice) the Change

Create a collaborative workspace for the management team. As Chapters 9 and 10, this volume, suggest, there are many computer-mediated communication (CMC) tools available for virtual collaborative writing teams. Among the ones most often employed in various work settings are content management systems (CMSs), e-mail, instant messaging (IM), desktop sharing, and voice over the Internet conferencing. After reviewing the discussion of CMC tools (particularly see Chapter 1) and speaking with the information technology (IT) staff about what is affordable and available in the organization, it becomes possible to choose the tools for starting the collaborative process.

Beginning to work virtually *and* collaboratively means developing a culture of collaboration, one of the first principles that ground this book (see Chapter 1). Such a culture requires training in the virtual collaborative setting, which means immersive training for all involved. Immersion as a training principle (see Chapter 1; see also Ehmann Powers and Hewett, 2009; Hewett and Ehmann, 2004) requires that all team members—including managerial level staff—experience real collaborative projects by using the available CMC tools whether or not they are geographically distributed. In this way, managerial staff are directly involved in both the technological and the collaborative learning processes, and they will be investigating the processes at the same time. In a very real sense, they will research the necessary practices and learn some pitfalls to help their writing teams make wise choices and avoid as many negative and nonproductive experiences as possible (see investigation as a training principle in Chapter 1; also see Ehmann Powers and Hewett, 2009; Hewett and Ehmann, 2004).

To facilitate these processes, it helps to choose a project in which the managers as leaders are personally involved and for which they have significant responsibility. Such a project helps to keep things real and enables them investigate virtual collaborative writing processes on meaningful tasks with genuine deadlines—in the same way that such writing will occur for the writing team as a whole. It is useful to keep the tools, processes, and the designated project simple initially. Following are some practical suggestions for getting a collaborative project started and moving among the management and leadership staff:

- Identify a report or presentation that the leadership team needs to create in the next month.
- Analyze the content and assign ownership of each portion to a different team leader.
- Have someone create an outline of the deliverable and upload it to the selected collaborative workspace.
- Create a plan including a proposed work method to the team of how everyone will

work together on the material using the collaborative workspace.

Review Chapters 3, 4, and 5 for discussions about how to build the writing team and develop the structures within the teams that enable healthy and productive interactions. This plan should contain—at minimum—answers to the following questions:

- Who owns what?
- When will participants do the work?
- What work can be done as serial or parallel collaboration?
- What work must be done as collective collaboration?
- When and how will each writer know that the project is complete?
- What does "complete" or "finished" mean in the context of this project?

After sufficient planning, the leadership team needs to implement the plan. It is important to notice when the team runs into problems and when the work goes smoothly. What impediments arise? At different set check points, bring the team together quickly to communicate about the impediments, identify fixes, and then integrate these fixes into the process. Tables, charts, or spreadsheets often work well to track the impediments; a form similar to the one shown in Table 1 can help in tracking how the team has worked around the problem and in understanding why a workaround was successful, if it was. Of course, it also is helpful to debrief the team about its successes and to understand why they occurred.

Once the initial collaborative project is complete for the leadership team, draw on the sixth principle that grounds this book by measuring the team's performance and discussing what the team learned. All writers in this project need to apply these lessons as they manage virtual collaborative efforts of their teams. This process is a way not only of establishing trust but also of developing

Table 1. Problem solution chart

Frustration Point	What Was Tried Before the Solution Was Found?	What Worked?	Why Do You Think It Worked?
The project got off to a slow start. The manager posted the outline and nothing happened for weeks.	Reminding the team via e-mail.	Reviewing who owned what, what tasks depended on other tasks. Getting owners of early tasks to notice dependency and commit.	Writers felt assured that the whole team understood the work, and they felt good about dependencies among the tasks.

an appropriate structure and habits for future projects. Team members will find it helpful to publish the list of problems and their corrections in a virtual collaborative space that can grow as the entire writing team's understanding of virtual collaborative work grows.

Furthermore, it is important to expand and continue using the collaborative workspace in other projects. Individuals on the leadership team will see the usefulness of CMC tools grow through practicing together. It is helpful to notice and commend the team when they expand the use of virtual collaborative tools and processes. Also, it is helpful to speak positively to the broader writing team by way of encouraging and preparing them for using such practices as well. In this way, leaders are modeling the collaborative processes and the attitudes that are most helpful for making it work (see Chapter 8). Watch collaborative magic happen in the collective practice.

NOTICE WHERE COLLABORATIVE WORK EFFORTS CAN BE EMPLOYED

A major challenge to working collaboratively is identifying when a writing project might benefit from explicitly applying collaborative techniques. Therefore, leaders need to engage in self-education about the types of writing projects that benefit most from collaborative writing techniques so they can apply them from the start of a project. Signs that such collaboration will be helpful include:

- Skills are required from multiple writers;
- A team is assigned, but the project is stalled;
- Team members are working, but work is being repeated; and
- There are clear areas where one writer can reuse work that another writer has already finished or is planning to do.

In a full-scaled documentation process, these signs typically are apparent in an architectural review of the project deliverables. It is less formal in smaller projects.

Manage Collaborative Work

"I love my assignment and my technical team, but the project manager tells me one thing and my manager doesn't seem to know what they mean!"

"I absolutely can't put that material into my document this late in the game. It wasn't in the plan. Period."

Notice Breakdowns

In a less technologically complex time, once a writer created a work plan, the manager interacted on a regular basis and assessed the project's progress. As the one-book, one-writer paradigm has shifted to the new paradigm of collaboratively written and produced content that can be reused, this type of interaction between managers and writers has changed, too. Whereas progress used to be as easy as communicating through a simple status report of completed sections and problems were resolved, the new paradigm invites new challenges.

With virtual collaborative work, writers must depend on each other much more, and their projects move quickly. Often, however, projects are stressed by problems that would not be identified through a traditional status report. As a manager, it is vital to analyze the team's progress and success more deeply than the typical status report allows by watching for places where collaboration is breaking down. Here are questions to ask that can help in identifying weak areas, thus helping the team to fix them.

As work begins, address the following questions:

- Have content or architecture plans been created? Have the right people reviewed them?
- Has work been divided among writers in an understandable way and with some structure applied to the division?

- Has work been divided into small modules or chunks of work with clear delivery schedules, preferably weekly?
- Have areas of shared work been identified in the content plans?
- Has a clear methodology for shared work been agreed upon by all participants?
- Has someone on the management team met with all writers who will be sharing content or working closely together? The purpose of the meeting is to review how content will be created and shared and to ask the writers about their concerns.

Table 2 provides some signs to look for as projects progress. Being aware of these signs can help to shore up a project before it fails or to resuscitate it once it has begun to fail. As the project progresses watch out for the following danger signs:

It is important, too, to determine how the team leaders will know that the collaborative work is getting done effectively and efficiently. In other words, what does success look like? Table 3 pro-

Table 2. Warning signs for collaborative writing projects

Warning Sign	Question to Ask	Potential Resuscitation Action
A writer withdraws material that was designed to be reused downstream	What would this material look like so you could reuse it? What prevents you from writing the material so the other writer can reuse it?	Get both parties together and identify the block. Two known causes of such block are (1) inadequate understanding of the customer and of the down-stream writer and (2) incomplete understanding of how to write for reuse.
A writer announces that he or she cannot make changes to the plan to include the work of another writer.	Why are you having problems using the material developed by the other writer? Does the material not meet the needs of the customer? Does it not fit in with the other material?	Address the writer in a safe "place." This problem could be a reaction to quality issues, concerns that the other writer's content does not meet certain standards.
Are e-mail storms erupting frequently and sucking energy from the team?	What started the storm? Who needs to work together to address and fix the issue?	Notice the storm and call for another medium through which to collaborate (for example, a telephone call, a meeting, a discussion on a shared forum space, or other). Empower all team members (not just managers) to notice storms and to call for a discussion.
Have once-lively meetings via phone or in person become passive events or mostly passive events that seem to be taken over by one or two writers? Are participants grumbling?	Does the meeting cover what the team needs? Does the meeting method support everyone and encourage all team members to participate?	Assign someone to manage meetings virtually and actively so all participants are heard and so that overly dominant participants are managed.

vides some markers of success against which to measure the work.

Enabling Multiple Managers to Help with Collaborative Projects

If a collaborative team is large enough to include multiple managers, then matrix management may be part of both a problem and a solution. Loyalty to managers, differing management styles, and the possibility of mixed-messages may weaken the team's enthusiasm for collaboration. Here are some signs to look for:

- It is not clear which managers are responsible for what in a project.
- Managers are complaining about each other and are expressing such sentiments as, "Other team members are not towing the line" or "meeting their targets."
- Managers are quiet in project meetings. That is, they are not stepping in to agree with statements made by other managers. They may agree or disagree with statements, but they are not voicing their position.

It is important to watch and listen carefully for any of these behaviors and to work with all team managers to change it. Assuming that these managers are working for the success of the team, they probably do not see what how their actions are influencing the team's work overall. Peer managers must feel comfortable identifying ways

that shared management is not working. Table 4 offers some corrective actions to apply.

Making Meetings Support the Team

Virtual collaborative writing typically means that people work closely using CMC to share plans, topic architecture challenges, and to adjust goals. Talking more often means more meetings. Unless the entire team is colocated at one site, this need for meetings means more time on the phone and using Web collaboration tools. Despite the fact that writers are great with written words, they not always great at meetings. Great meetings require that people listen carefully to each other, that they notice when they are not fully communicating, and that all who have an opinion feel safe and appreciated enough to participate fully. Meetings also usually have decisions and actions items as a by-product, and great meetings deal with these in an effective way.

Team leaders can make a big difference in this area by structuring virtual meetings to be effective. While some of these techniques are not new, they have been helping people to collaborate for years. The most effective techniques use various principles that ground this book, such as developing a culture of collaboration, finding and promoting leadership, establishing trust, using tools and collaborative modes effectively, creating structure (see Chapter 1). Dust off those notes from the old "effective meetings" course taken years ago and apply those principles here. Table 5 presents corrections for typical meeting problems:

Table 3. Markers of success

Practice	Question to Ask	Positive Action
Material is being written and reused according to schedule.	Is the team making progress as planned? Is the material useable as written?	Post your Progress to a collaboratively shared space.
Problems are identified by team members and given to the team for resolution.	What problems occurred this week? How were they addressed? Were they corrected?	Keep and post to the collaboratively shared space a list of the problems and solutions so teams do not have to redevelop the solutions later.

Table 4. Matrix management pit falls and solutions

Peer Management Problem	Questions to Ask	Solution
Writers spend much time getting direction from the management team.	Ask key writers what they see as the problem. Ask managers if they find themselves needing to constantly repeat instructions to the team. If so, have them analyze where they are repeating themselves.	Unclear management responsibilities or unclear communication may be the cause. Determine whether it is clear to writers to whom they should go to get different types of project information. Determine whether managers are contradicting other managers outside of collaborative discussion.
Peer managers on a project are complaining that a manager is not doing their job.	Focus on the success of the project and ask what the "offending" manager would be doing differently if they were supporting the project fully. Also ask what the writers on the other team would be doing differently.	Remind managers that they have different styles and expectations but shared goals. Have the managers talk to each other and share best practices. Particularly for a virtual work setting, use phone conferences and Web meetings to share experiences and practices. Get commitments from all individuals. Reflect those commitments in the "roles and responsibility" list for managers that was created as part of the project plan.
Complaints that the writers reporting to a peer manager are not doing what is required.	Ask both managers what they see happening and what they believe that the other writers need to do for a successful project outcome.	Adjust direction to your manager appropriately.
Continuing complaints about a manager as after you suggested and implemented solutions.	Review what the managers need from each other.	Continuing communication is needed! A technique effectively used by one management team has been for managers to ask other managers or project leads explicitly (and daily during crunch times): "What do you need me to do today?" or "How can I support you today?" These questions can open the communication channels.
Peer managers not voicing positions.	Ask "what does it say to your team when you do not explicitly support a request from your peer manager?"	Give "permission" to all managers and collaborative writers to ask actively for agreement in a discussion or meeting for the sake of clarity. Make it clear that this is a requirement of working on the team.

Table 5. Corrections for virtual team meetings

Problems that Occur in Virtual Team Meetings	Potential Corrections
Writers are complaining that meetings are being dominated by a few participants and their input is over-run.	Tell participants that you need input from everyone (if that is the case) and you will be structuring meetings so that everyone will be heard. Build in a way to ask people privately to stop talking and take questions, perhaps through IM or a similar private synchronous tool. Actively reach out and seek input from each participant, calling them by name either through voice or textual communication. Prepare agendas that include key team members' work and that allow for multiple team members to provide ideas and feedback.
Not everyone is physically present at the meeting and some people cannot understand what is going on. This often happens when some of the people are in a room together and some of the people have "called in" to the meeting virtually.	Put everyone on the phone from each person's office so that everyone is at approximately the same geographic advantage. At most, have only two people in a room, which prevents side conversations from happening and one roomful of people breaking up into laughter that excludes others.
People cannot identify what decisions were made or they cannot remember all the action items for the meeting.	Make sure there is an official note taker and that the notes are displayable in a common virtual space.
People are not prepared to speak on a topic.	Create and share the agenda ahead of time. Identify who will introduce the topic, and give people assignments to address it.
Despite having good meetings, team members do not take action.	Identify someone to follow up with individuals on action items several days before the next meeting. Personal contact makes a difference. It may also be helpful to include such follow-up as part of virtual team performance reviews.

Create an Environment that Fosters Virtual Collaborative Work

"How can I possibly get my work done when I have to have all these meetings?

"It is a challenge to figure out who I need to talk to and work with to get my work done."

"Nothing is easy around here anymore!"

"I have to do it all…. It is too much."

"These tools are powerful, but they are complicated. I need help figuring out how to use them wisely."

It is necessary to change more about the writing environment than just what type of material writers are asked to create. Most likely, the job descriptions of team members will need to change to accommodate virtual collaborative work. Managers need to help lead this change and support writers.

Require (or Ask) Managers to Adopt New Practices

A manager's job in the collaborative world includes building structures into the work environment so people can see the role they play, understand the dependencies team members have on each other, and keep work going smoothly. It is also a manager's job to enable team members to appreciate and feel good about what other people are doing or will do. Managers are the oil that makes processes work smoothly. With collaborative work and especially collaborative writing that occurs in virtual settings or using CMC tools, managers can shoulder the burden of getting projects off to a good start.

A variety of ways exist that managers can support writers:

- Build time into writers' schedule (daily!) to handle reviews and collaboration check points.
- Set up regular check-in meetings (daily or weekly); post progress in the collaborative online setting for each participant.
- Build trust by getting people to share what they are doing, as a part of building the collaborative culture by making such sharing a natural and normal part of their daily work.
- Set up review meetings for jointly developed work, and include all the involved writers in those meetings.
- Make sure all review processes (architecture and quality) are streamlined and work well. Define clear roles and responsibilities for each type of review.
- Create templates or checklists to help writers know what is expected of them.
- Make sure writers are looking at the work of their teammates and collaborators. Set the expectation that such reading is not an optional activity. Create review structures such as peer reviews and module reviews that formally support collaborators in this area.
- Ask "what can I do to support you?" at each collaboration check point. The result may be identifying a resource, linking with someone else in the company, figuring out how to make a tool, or doing something so that the writer does not need to stop writing to do it. If team members are uncomfortable asking for help, give examples to get their creative energies flowing, which is one way of teaching them that they can have the assistance they need.
- Identify key metrics to measure for defining "progress." How will writers know when they are finished? Collect those metrics regularly and share them with the writers, as described in Chapter 10.

Celebrate progress and call for a problem-solving conversation when things seem to be stuck.

- Post goals and progress regularly in a shared, virtually accessible space.
- If there are specialized roles in the team like architect or tools specialists, make sure that writers are asking them questions and not making up their own answers on the fly. Those specialists exist to ensure that the entire team is being consistent.
- Ensure that writers create detailed architecture and delivery plans. Make certain that those plans are reviewed by all participants in the project, as well as shared by writers who will be reusing content "downstream." These plans should cover the following information:
- What topics or modules are individual writers delivering and why? Who is the audience? How is the product alignment among writers?
- What content maps or submaps will use the selected writing topics (as best as can be predicted at planning time)?
- Include:
- strong short descriptions
- explicit index entries
- explicitly identified metadata
- For delivery plans, break work into small segments that can be committed to *and* be monitored. If people do not keep to schedule, trust is eroded If work is in small pieces, schedule can be monitored and adjustments made. Writers and downstream users feel less anxiety, which means that they can trust in a positive outcome.

Develop Clear Roles and Responsibilities

Small teams can write collaboratively without fancy specialization. However, some individuals take on specialized roles naturally. For example, one team member will identify a great tools solution to a problem. Another will create the metadata list for the product area. It is likely that managers will need to take note of new work that needs to be assigned and completed while people are working on particular projects. Writers may not have a special title, but they all have a special responsibility. With larger teams of more than five people, managers likely will need to be very clear about roles and responsibilities. Table 6 provides one working set of roles from which individual managers can develop their own role sets appropriate to their own work settings. See Chapters 10 and 12 for additional discussions of roles.

Build Skills and Trust in Every Way Possible

"That material does NOT belong in MY book! Ever!"

Words along the lines of "not in my book, ever" indicate a serious trust problem. Trust among the collaborators—as Chapters 1 and 5 indicate—is key to making virtual collaborative writing work (indeed, it is key to making any collaborative writing work). Some trust issues arise because team members do not know each other very well. Chapters 3 and 4 address getting to know other members of a virtual writing team. Other trust issues arise because sometimes team members recognize before managers that the material being created is inadequate, but they do not have a healthy and manager-approved way to deal with that problem.

Many management practices are effective because they build or support the trust that can be developed among individuals. Both developing collaboration skills across the team and holding public quality reviews will improve trust.

Table 6. Writing team roles and responsibilities

Role	Responsibilities
Information Architect, high level	Manages information types at the broadest levels, looking out for consistency and customer interaction. Assures that decisions made at product level are workable.
Information Architect, product level	Manages information types at the product level, looking out for consistency and customer decides about how to use tools to share content. Makes final decisions about what content goes into what deliverables.
Project lead	Works with architects to define collections of deliverables at high level for project. Monitors progress and interacts with non-writing functions such as project managers or assemblers.
Writers/Subject matter expert	Writes content. Makes final decisions about what a content module includes, usually based on the needs of the reader.
Assembler	Builds deliverables. For example, builds on-line help and PDF files. Identifies broken builds and calls on writers to fix components as necessary. Publishes as required.
Illustrator	Creates specialized illustrated content with input from writers
Editor	Collaborates with writers to set standards. Evaluates material for usefulness and application of standards. Identifies trends in writing to architects and managers. Identifies writing weaknesses and helps writers improve them.
Manager	Creates collaborative methods and keeps them working for the team. Supports all project players.

Develop a Broad Set of Skills

Collaborative environments in which content reuse or re-purposing is prevalent tend to fall apart when one or more members of the team cannot pull their weight. To this end, training is extremely important.

Make information widely available to the writing team. Statements like the following suggest that the writers in question have not had sufficient training or supervised practice doing real-life virtual collaborative writing using whatever tool or process is in question.

"I can't remember how to do THAT!"

"Our support team is great because they listen to us and improve our processes... but since we are always changing I can't just know all our procedures"

As a remedy, the following are some suggestions for how to give team members easy access to process and training information:

- Use a tool like Captivate to create training modules for tools-based work. That way, writers can go back and review procedures at any time. Whenever a writer seems to flounder using a particular tool, request or require that writer to review the training module.
- Use a wiki to document roles, responsibilities, and approved collaborative writing technologies and processes. Empower all teams to update the material as they see the need.
- Create self-help guides that list problems that arise regularly in your type of work and how writers can fix them.

Do not let people go solo until they are ready. Although writers might be itching to start writing on their own, provide them both with training and support until they appear ready from a management perspective. Make sure that the schedules developed for the "real" project activities account for the required training so that everyone acknowledges its importance and the team understands that they are being credited with the training they undergo.

One effective way of training people is to identify what they do not know and match them up with a team member who is strong in that same area. Once the advisor/writer pair is established, this process can be applied to bring other team members up to speed. For example, one way of using pairing to train individuals on relatively simple tasks follows: After each pair has addressed particular training concerns, each can be re-paired with another individual, thus increasing exponentially the number of writers who can train on a particular technology or collaborative writing process. Table 7 provides examples of typical training pair combinations.

It is important to provide time for the advisor to do intensive reviews of early work prior to the initial phase of the project. Also it is useful to include time in the schedule for the advisor and writer to have time to discuss the work together.

For most pairings, the process that follows can work or be adapted:

1. Writer writes.
2. Writer sends work to advisor, editor, and manager for review, giving a reasonable amount of time such as two days.
3. Together they review, write up comments and send to writer and manager, and note trends and project issues. The trend information can be used to improve department training checklists. The project issues will need to be escalated to a project manager.
4. Advisor, editor, writer, and manager come together in a face-to-face or phone/internet meeting to discuss questions and trends found in the writer's work product. The focus of the meeting is for the writer to ask the advisor questions, so the writer must come prepared to do so. Adequate preparation on the writer's part enables the writer to set the tone and prevent the session from giving the appearance (or reality) of being a scolding.
5. The advisor tracks how much time they devote to reviewing material and interacting with the writer so that the time is recognized formally.
6. Repeat the process with subsequent portions of the deliverable until sufficient knowledge is passed on and the writer can address the technologies and processes without this level of individual support.

Review What is Written

Implement content and quality reviews regularly, which is a way of addressing the sixth principle six that grounds this book regarding measuring and tracking performance.

"Code review? I can barely get material reviewed by the subject matter experts and you want me to do a code review? It will take too much of my time."

On some level, everyone knows that reviewing a certain amount of source material will assure consistency. But how can this process be done efficiently and effectively? Who does the reviews? How can it be made into a learning experience and not a waste of time?

Table 7. Training pair combinations

Advisee	Advisor	Techniques to Improve....
Junior writer	Senior writer	Customer usability, clarity, richness of content, indexing, and SEO/metadata terms.
New DITA writer	Experienced DITA writer	Organization, tagging, indexing and SEO/metadata terms.
Inexperienced tools user	Experienced tools user	Processes and correct use of tools.

Engaging the entire virtual collaborative writing team to review content does more than assure quality. It builds trust among writers, which in turn enables them to depend on each other and on the content they write. Content reviews can be scary if teams are not used to sharing material with peers or going through formal quality review process. Therefore, managers need to make sure they build an environment where it is safe to offer work for review and safe to identify problems. It is important that the team knows that it is to their advantage to identify problems before they get to upper management or the client as reader. Content review—as Chapters 15, 16, and 17 make clear—requires an investment of time. But this investment pays off with strong written information products in the end.

To make sure the work load and benefits are widespread, set participation goals for reviews and keep track of participants. When implementing a review process, it is important to include the following tasks:

- Define what the content review is looking for and optimize the review process around that goal. Here are three types of reviews:
- **Content source reviews:** Are writers employing the right tagging techniques?
- **Short description reviews and content reviews:** Is material reusable by others?
- **Technical reviews:** From a non-writer's perspective, is the content accurate for the final reader?
- Identify the format of the review, roles of the reviewers and writers, and responsibilities required of all participants.
- For each type of review, track the results and have a feedback loop for comments to reviewer.

Remember to acknowledge great reviewers and the brave submitters who model the kind of collaborative attitude and behavior that managers most want in a virtual collaborative writing team!

FUTURE DIRECTIONS

The important role of managers in leading the change from book- to topic-based writing cannot be underestimated as indicated by the second principle of collaboration that in this volume. Because teams of writers have firmly established behaviors for writing linearly and owning complete books, they need leaders as role models helping to redefine processes and coaching them throughout the experience of adopting new strategies. Managers, like the teams they lead, need to share the vision of writing collaboratively, understand the roadblocks in the way, and find creative solutions for helping teams implement effective strategies. The future of topic-based writing depends largely on the leaders that create and shape a culture of virtual collaborative writing. Just as writing teams need feedback for making improvement, managers need feedback on their methodologies and just as much guidance when confronting numerous challenges that emerge. For this reason, it is essential that industry leaders worldwide learn from each other about what strategies enable teams to be successful in some workplace settings and not in others, what tools support certain topic-based writing practices and not all of them, and what solutions take root in addressing problems at certain times of the life cycle and not at other times. An ongoing dialog among leaders not only about successes but also about failures can help managers to understand better how to lead teams more effectively. Studying what happens within organizations is essential for moving teams forward and for employing a new paradigm for workplace writing.

CONCLUSION

There is much that a manager or director or leader in a collaborative writing environment can do to shape, model, and lead collaborative writing practices. A writing team leader can strategically influence how a team works by influencing the planning, learning, reviewing, meeting, and management practices in the team. The structure that the manager brings to the team allows the writers to use their time to write effectively.

REFERENCES

Ehmann Powers, C., & Hewett, B. L. (2008). Building online training for virtual workplaces. In St. Amant, K., & Zemliansky, P. (Eds.), *Handbook of research on virtual workplaces and the new nature of business practices* (pp. 257–271). New York: Information Science Reference.

Hewett, B. L., & Ehmann, C. (2004). *Preparing educators for online writing instruction: Principles and processes*. Urbana, IL: NCTE.

Section 4
Planning and Making Decisions Virtually

Chapter 9

Case Study: Putting their Heads Together Virtually:
Case Studies on Collaboration using Content Management Technology

Suzanne Mescan
Vasont Systems, USA

ABSTRACT

Content management technology provides a flexible environment for virtual collaboration for technical and business writing. Internationally, small and large organizations in various industries are using content management system (CMS) technology to improve their communications while lowering their production and translation costs and enhancing the quality of their writing. The following case studies provide a look at how small and large writing teams are really doing it. These teams have successfully implemented content management technology and improved virtual collaboration in varying environments—within a department, between multiple departments, within a division, and across several divisions of their respective organizations.

INTRODUCTION

The task of writing content in an organization has shifted from one in which a writer (who might also do the work of an editor) works alone on an entire document (that is, a white paper, report, or a chapter or book) to a collaborative effort among colleagues to develop and refine topics within the document. Increasingly, organizations are finding value when colleagues can share their ideas and skills during the writing and editorial process to perfect

their content before processing it for translation and/or multi-channel publishing. One proven tool to create and facilitate an interconnected virtual writing environment in an organization is a content management system (CMS).

The creation and management of content using computer-mediated communication (CMC) technology is not new. Writers in all kinds of environments rely on tools beyond pen and paper to create content—whether they are employees in business or government workplaces, students or scholars in academic workplaces. From word processors and XML authoring tools to wikis, blogs, and social

DOI: 10.4018/978-1-60566-994-6.ch009

networking software, writers depend on technology to develop content and deliver information to readers. The increasing sophistication of the tools used to create and manage information has made writing more and more virtual, and the use of virtual technology to publish content has had differing goals and outcomes depending on the purpose or occasion for writing. While CMC technology provides limitless opportunities for writers to publish an unlimited number of words in collaboration with a world audience, the same kinds of technology in business settings helps to contain words strategically so that content can be translated and distributed on the Web, through mobile devices, and in or alongside products across the globe. Given the contrasting goals for communicating and given the aim of this book to create links between diverse readers working in industry and academia, it is important to understand the contexts and tools that influence various approaches to writing. Understanding these differences can ensure that writers have the suitable skills needed to write effectively in a range of workplaces.

Comparing the context of writing in a CMS to that of writing in academic settings provides insight into the use of technology to write collaboratively. In an academic environment, writing often begins with a rehearsal of texts read by students, who are absorbing new ideas and learning to develop original content. Originality of thinking and writing is prized in the classroom and as ideas develop across Web-based environments, as described more fully in Chapter 7, which addresses how novice writers use technology to develop ideas. Such writing often is a creative process in which one or more writers compose a document and then deepen and extend it through review cycles with peers. Collaborative input from other students is intended to help students enhance the accuracy, fluency, and academic value of their papers. The writer's focus is to emphasize the primary points of the work they have read with sound facts and references regardless of the

length of the work. In many academic writing projects, the writing neither costs the institution financially nor does it overtly generate revenue for either the writer or the institution; its value is intrinsic in terms of knowledge development, idea dissemination, and prestige.

In contrast, the writing environment of many non-profit and for-profit organizations focuses more on efficiencies and cost savings, and less on originality of thought. A technical documentation team that produces user guides and other product documentation is a *cost center* for the organization. The technical documentation is necessary to support their products by providing customers with accurate instructions or parts information, making it easy for customers to install, use, or fix products. Good technical documentation not only reduces costs in the organization's customer support area by minimizing help calls and returned products, but also it is useful to customers who want to use products, not wrestle with or return them.

Technical documentation typically does not generate additional revenue for the organization, making the department a target for reducing costs from management. Therefore, writers must focus on producing accurate, reusable topics that become building blocks for generating many different kinds of publications that deliver a consistent message. This work requires all writers on the team to collaborate by following an established writing style and applying the approved corporate terminology, as explained in detail in Chapter 15. In organizations that do business internationally, writers also must focus on writing in a minimalist style—writing as succinctly as possible and eliminating unnecessary verbiage—to keep the cost of translations lower, since translation services are charged by the number of words translated.

Likewise, organizations that publish and sell reference books, such as dictionaries, encyclopedias, and standards manuals have similar writing environments. Production and translation costs are continuously scrutinized by management teams to ensure that they generate a profit on their publications. Therefore, writers in these editorial departments must collaborate effectively and adhere to strict writing guidelines to maintain lower production and translation costs.

Virtual collaboration in an organization's technical writing team goes beyond the writing task itself. Writers must collaborate with co-workers in other departments; with subject matter experts (SMEs) outside of the organization; and with their vendors. When developing technical documentation or reference publications, writers do not necessarily create new content as it is in the academic environment; instead, often they inherit content from a previous version of a product or from another department, which starts the process of collaboration. For example, the engineering department that develops the products may provide specifications about the products to the writers, who then transform those specifications into user manuals, catalogs, service bulletins, online knowledge centers, and other publications. SMEs (for example, engineers, doctors, usability experts, scientists, and quality assurance staff) collaborate with the writers to refine the content's integrity through the documentation review process, the subject of Chapter 16. The writers also must collaborate with translation services vendors to ensure that the preparation and delivery of the base content is optimized for translation to avoid unnecessary additional fees. Therefore, even though the focus of technical writers is broader in scope than in the academic environment, technical writers must streamline their writing to accommodate reader preferences and business goals. That is, instead of inventing new content, writers must concentrate on creatively and collaboratively managing the development, production, and delivery of content to lower or maintain the cost of publishing in a global economy.

This chapter provides four case studies of how content management technology has facilitated virtual collaborative writing in different organizations. The case studies include one involving our own company, Vasont Systems, and three of our long-standing clients, all of whom use our Vasont CMS to manage content and collaborate with their co-workers, colleagues, and vendors. The chapter focuses on the successful experiences that these organizations have had using content management technology to improve their communications and the quality of their writing. Principles 1, 2, 4, and 5, the principles of collaboration that ground this book, underlie the use of content management technology concerns in these case studies. They are: creating a culture of collaboration, providing leadership to guide teams, using tools and collaborative modes effectively, and creating structure.

These case studies illustrate the flexibility of content management technology to enable virtual collaboration in technical and business writing settings ranging from small companies to large, international organizations. Scenarios include:

- **Inter-departmental collaboration:** How a small writing group of four people who sit in neighboring cubicles within a large, international organization benefitted by using a CMS to write and update their reference publications, demonstrating that virtual collaboration also can facilitate better organization and communication among colocated people. (See Case Study 1.)
- **Inter-divisional collaboration:** How a 25-person division of a small business used a CMS to integrate their development team with their technical documentation and marketing groups to keep their software manuals up-to-date and accurate with new features and product enhancements for one primary product line with ongoing releases. (See Case Study 2.)
- **Cross-departmental collaboration:** How an international Fortune 500 company initially used a CMS to collaborate on their user assistance initiatives in one department, and then, by "thinking outside the box," discovered how, with very little effort, it also could provide positive

collaboration with other departments in their division of the company. (See Case Study 3.)

- **Cross-divisional collaboration:** How a CMS fostered collaboration between two divisions of an international Fortune 500 company to write and update their content and translate it into 21 languages. (See Case Study 4.)

CASE STUDY 1: SIZE DOESN'T MATTER? SMALL WRITING GROUPS BENEFIT FROM VIRTUAL COLLABORATION

Background

This global publisher (referred to herein as "Company A") of science and health care information produces books, journals, patient education materials, and a variety of online information sources and solutions tools. Company A is a partner with the scientific, technical, and health communities; it delivers information products and services that foster communication, build insights, and enable individual and collective advancement in scientific research and health care. A department of four writers creates and maintains Company A's English-language medical dictionaries and coordinates with reviewers and translators around the globe to produce international versions.

Challenges

In 1984, Company A was using 5 x 8-inch index cards to manage the entries for their medical dictionaries— a system perfected in the 1750s that could be considered a primitive CMS. The data were chunked, and each dictionary entry had its own card. Each entry also had metadata that described and categorized it: a specialty code, the book and edition, a sequence number, and a source.

This data management process was a labor-intensive system. It involved walking around the office and retrieving cards from drawers. It also required a full-time secretary to type and file cards. Content was typed twice—once to create the card from handwritten copy and once to put the card's data into the typesetting system.

In 1990, Company A installed a mainframe database to hold the data, which eliminated writing the cards out by hand. Instead, the writers entered information into the database and extracted content to feed into the typesetting system. It was a huge improvement over the primitive index card process. The database eliminated the cards, the walking, and the need to type the content twice. Company A was able to produce more publications without increasing staff size.

However, in the sense of individual storage containers, the content still lived in silos. The writers edited one component of one product at a time, making it difficult to work on multiple publications simultaneously. Additionally, the writers could not identify what changes other writers had made or who made them. The silo system created problems in terms of efficiency and efficacy.

Multilingual editions of Company A's documents appeared much later than the English editions. The translators waited for the printed book, and then manually compared the old and new editions to determine what must be translated. Sometimes that time-consuming process meant that a translation was published as much as two years later—just when the next English edition was published.

Company A's list of publications kept growing, but—as is true in many organizations—the staff size did not. At the same time, the life of each edition was shrinking, requiring more frequent editing and publishing of new editions. It was a classic case of writers needing to do more with less. How could they continue to produce excellent documents and yet solve these ongoing content management problems?

Solutions

In 1993, Company A implemented a CMS to control their content better. The features of a CMS—single sourcing, component level management of content, a shared repository, and metadata management—enabled the writers in the department work together in new, efficient ways and provided better collaboration with their external reviewers and translators.

Company A stored their content as components in the CMS; for example, the content was broken down into headword, definition, and pronunciation components that acted as reusable building blocks that, when combined in a specific sequence, created the dictionary entries. Each component was stored only one time, and every writer could write, edit, and reuse these components in their publications. This single sourcing of content provided one copy of content that the writers could trust to be accurate and up-to-date when they needed to reuse it to build other dictionary entries or produce new publications. The CMS tracked every change made to the content, allowing others to see what had been changed, who changed it, and when it was changed. The system itself served as a vehicle for collaborating virtually, providing valuable information for other writers on the team.

This single-sourced, componentized content authoring method enabled the writers to specialize in different pieces of content, which eventually enabled greater efficiency. Whereas the index card system forced one person to shift gears constantly and work on one entire entry at a time, the CMS enabled one person to write cross references or phonetics by sharing content in the database. This process saved time because writers were developing dictionary entries by collaborating on them simultaneously.

The CMS allowed writers to become rules experts in their areas of expertise. Their specialist in phonetics could insure that pronunciations were written consistently both within and across all dictionaries, and she knew the rules for applying their phonetic respelling system. The writer developed solutions to difficult situations without searching through the style guide to find an obscure rule. On rare occasions when the writer needed to look up rules, she knew where to find them. Company A's editorial group collaborated more efficiently on writing their content by focusing writers on their areas of expertise.

Company A also found value in using metadata to collaborate with colleagues. At times, definitions written and recorded in the previous database iteration would look odd; writers wondered what the original writer was thinking when she wrote it. Sometimes that writer was no longer around to ask. If the writer still worked at Company A, she might not remember what her intentions were since she had written thousands of definitions for each edition. With the new CMS, when writers wrote new entries that might be questioned later, they attached notes to the content using metadata—virtual sticky notes that are permanently attached to the content to which others could refer at any time. The metadata provided key information about content so that writers working serially could collaborate effectively.

For their dictionaries, the metadata allowed writers to classify their content by medical specialty automatically, making it easy to share content with the appropriate specialists; for example, a cardiologist reviews heart entries and a dermatologist reviews skin disease entries. Previously, the writers created a giant stack of typeset sheets, manually organized by specialty, at great expense. Now they shared digital content for each specialty simultaneously with the reviewers, an effective use of parallel collaboration. This automated, digital method saved the writers many hours of time compiling information, printing and sorting paper copies and distributing them via mail delivery to the reviewers, as well as the expensive typesetting and mailing costs.

Metadata also controlled which content was extracted for translation, saving Company A time and money in translation cycles and costs.

Using metadata in the CMS allowed writers to supply the translators with only the content that was changed in the new edition, eliminating the labor-intensive task of manually comparing books after the English edition was published. Now, they collaborated with the translators pre-publication and ultimately reduced their translation cycle from two years to two months. Naturally, this reduced translation cycle benefited their non-English reading customers by getting updated information to them in a more timely manner.

Summary

Despite sitting together in a room and working face-to-face, processes and communication between small teams can be inefficient. By implementing a CMS, Company A's team used virtual technology to improve their collaboration in several ways:

- The writers shared a common repository of single-sourced content components, enabling them to write simultaneously—using collective collaboration—while specializing on pieces of content. Now they saw each other's changes and achieved consistency across their content.
- Using metadata, writers documented the content's purpose for other writers to reference and understand, making the most of serial and parallel collaboration.
- External reviewers who specialized in certain medical fields collaborated in parallel more easily on relevant content with the writers since it was classified by medical specialties using metadata.
- Editors quickly provided only changed content to the translators, thereby reducing translation cycle times from two years to two months, both lowering translation costs and improving content dissemination dramatically.

The CMS allowed Company A's staff of four to work together more effectively, producing a greater volume of quality content. It also provided better collaboration with their external reviewers and translators, resulting in much shorter production cycles of their multi-language editions. Company A's smooth transition into a CMS resulted in part from their implementation of a mainframe database initially, helping the team to adapt to a centralized approach to managing content. Moving iteratively into content management helped Company A advance a culture of collaboration, the first principle of collaboration. This case study also helps to underscore the importance of collaboration Principles 4 and 5: using tools and collaborative modes effectively and establishing underlying processes that can be supported by technology.

CASE STUDY 2: "EATING OUR OWN DOG FOOD" FOR INTER-DIVISIONAL COLLABORATION

Background

In 1992, Vasont Systems developed a CMS as a project for a client who needed help with managing the content for its medical dictionary and multiple spin-off publications. By 1997, Vasont Systems officially launched a CMS as a product called Vasont and sold it to reference publishers. Soon, manufacturers of a wide range of products used this CMS to manage their user's guides, parts catalogs, training materials, and online knowledge centers, and to publish them in various formats and multiple languages. By 2008, Vasont Systems was named four times to *EContent* magazine's *EContent 100* list of "companies that matter most in the digital content industry" (Manafy, 2008).

In 2007, Vasont Systems consisted of 25 people who worked in groups that were scattered throughout a building shared by three other divisions of the overall organization. This case study illustrates how Vasont Systems' technical documentation group used virtual inter-divisional collaboration to overcome the challenges created when their workload increased six fold. Indeed, the CMS itself helped in producing new documentation related to the more frequent updates to the CMS system.

Challenges

Every 18 months, Vasont Systems delivered a major release of their CMS. The corresponding documentation, consisting of 10 manuals for the software and its extensions, was produced using XML, stored in our CMS, and published to PDF and context-sensitive Help formats.

As the CMS was enhanced, the technical documentation group did not receive any information from the developers from which to create the needed documentation. As a release deadline approached, the writers hunted for features that were new to this release, initiating many phone calls, e-mails and discussions with the developers, interrupting them from programming tasks and wasting the writers' time overall. The writers were never certain that they had documented all of the new features—especially those that were developed early in the cycle—because there was no information about the new features provided from the developers.

Additionally, there was no review process to ensure that the documentation was accurate, a common problem among documentation teams. The management and marketing staff wanted to review the documentation, but by the time it was written, there was no time for a review cycle. Ultimately, this unfinished production process affected our clients when they looked up instructions and the documentation was incomplete. Their problems and dissatisfaction circled back to our support group, who received more e-mails and phone calls when the documentation was not as helpful as it should have been.

As the features list for our CMS grew longer, a formal release schedule was created that included six interim releases between each major release to accommodate enhancements, special requests, and immediate clients' needs. This schedule better organized the development efforts.

However, it also created new problems. For example, it required a set of documentation (10 manuals) for each interim release of the software, creating a 600% increase in documentation to be published during a major release cycle. No staff was added to handle this increased workload, and the writing team quickly fell behind. Furthermore, management had trouble tracking the status of all the documentation since it was a manual process.

Our writing team faced a growing list of challenges, and we realized that our problems stemmed from a lack of collaboration among the groups. Of course, the answer to the problems was right at our fingertips—literally.

Solutions

Remember the saying, "The cobbler's kids have no shoes?" We fell into the same trap of not providing for ourselves what we provided to our clients. Although we used our CMS to manage our content, we were not taking advantage of its collaboration features to manage our revision processes. Configuring our internal system for our own use always fell to the bottom of the priority list. As the challenges grew, we decided it was time to "eat our own dog food."

Collaboration between and among departments was our biggest challenge. The groups involved—development, technical documentation, management, marketing, and support—were located in different areas of the building, making it easy to forget to include the other groups when important tasks were due.

To conquer these challenges, we implemented a multi-tiered workflow process, automated in the CMS, that defined each task to be performed, who

Figure 1. Conceptual diagram of the multi-tiered workflow implemented for virtual collaboration between five groups within the division

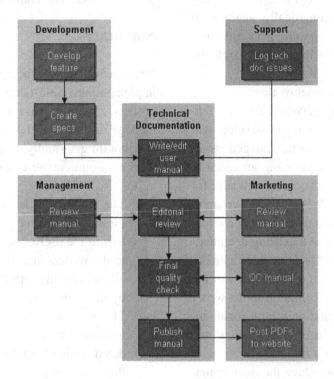

was responsible for each task, and when each task was due. (See Figure 1.) This automated workflow included the entire process and involved every group, enabling us to collaborate more efficiently and inclusively on our documentation and ensure that every task was performed. User roles, such as writers and non-technical reviewers, were created and assigned to each task, and several business days were allotted for each task to be completed. When the workflow was launched, an e-mail was automatically sent to a user, notifying him of an assigned task, providing information about performing the task as well as its due date. As each user completed a task, the CMS automatically notified the next user of their pending task, and so on until the workflow reached the end of the process. For each project, workflow information fed into the project management window in the CMS, allowing the management team to track the overall status of

projects quickly and to take action on projects that were falling behind schedule.

This multi-tiered workflow process worked in the following way, combing the three modes of collaboration — serial, parallel, and collective collaboration:

- **Development workflow tier:** The workflow was launched on a project when the manager assigned a new CMS feature to a developer for programming. The developer received notification of a task and due date. Upon completion of this task, he was then given the task to create specifications for the new feature in a Word document and store it in the CMS.

- **Support workflow tier:** The workflow also was launched on a project when the support group logged a customer issue that related to unsatisfactory documentation. If the support group flagged a support call as a documentation issue, the editorial workflow launched automatically again with a link to the information from the support call so the documentation could be improved.

- **Documentation workflow tier:**
  - **Editorial cycle:** When the new feature was completed in development or when a support call flagged issues with the documentation, an editorial workflow launched automatically for the technical documentation group to write documentation for the new feature or to improve existing documentation. The first task included a link to the development specifications or the support call information so the writer had the information for the documentation immediately, eliminating the need to hunt for it.
  - **Review cycle:** Once the documentation was completed, a review process launched automatically for a review of the documentation by the technical and non-technical reviewers: the department manager and the marketing staff. Using the CMS's built-in review tool, reviewers suggested changes and made comments on the content. Employing collective collaboration, each reviewer not only made changes but also could see other reviewer's suggested changes simultaneously and comment on those as well. When the reviewers completed their tasks, an editor accepted or rejected the suggestions from the reviewers, allowed the CMS to update the content in database automatically, and completed the review process.
  - **Publishing cycle:** The documentation was sent through a final quality check that included the marketing

staff, and then it was published to PDF and context-sensitive Help files.

Summary

We improved many process and product steps by implementing a multi-tiered, automated workflow process, a synchronous review cycle, and project management capabilities to solve our difficulties collaborating virtually in our own face-to-face work environment to create information products:

- The content needed to document new features or to improve unsatisfactory information in the user manuals was now supplied to the writers in a timely, automatic method, eliminating information-gathering time by the writers and developers.
- The writers were now confident that the information products were thoroughly updated with *all* of the new features since they were automatically notified in their workflow queue when any new development occurred.
- A synchronous review cycle—referred to in this volume as collective collaboration—included the manager and marketing staff, who were tasked with reviewing the updates and helping to improve the quality and completeness of our information products.
- Management team members could now track the progress of the updates synchronously. Using the CMS's project management capabilities, the manager could see what was running late and reassign tasks to staff with smaller workloads.
- Clients saw an improvement in the quality of the documentation, and fewer documentation issues were reported, thus saving time at the support group level.

The collective collaboration among various teams, including technical documentation, development, marketing, management, and support groups improved our process and information products dramatically. The advancements in technology supported the efforts of the writers and extended teams not only to establish but also to implement fundamental information development processes. The automation of our processes in the CMS, and the development of features to support more effective processes made efforts to collaborate more successful. In the end, incorporating synchronous technology ensured that every important step occurred in the process to improve the quality and timeliness of our documentation. See Chapters 13 and 16 for more information about tools that support processes and about managing efficient reviews. Using the collaboration capabilities within the CMS—including project management, automated workflow, and collaborative review—we supported the 600% increase in workload that was required from the new release schedule without increasing staff. This case study helps to underscore the importance of collaboration Principles 4 and 5: using tools and collaborative modes effectively and establishing underlying processes that can be supported by technology.

CASE STUDY 3: EXTENDING CONTENT MANAGEMENT ACROSS DEPARTMENTS FOR CORPORATE-WIDE GAIN

Background

This global Fortune 500 company (referred to herein as "Company C") is a provider of software, services, and technologies for healthcare provider organizations. They provide complex information associated with patient care and the business issues that surround it. To help customers lower healthcare costs and improve the quality of care, Company C's information technology (IT) business provides comprehensive clinical and financial IT solutions, including enterprise and departmental Information Technology products, Radiology Information Systems/Picture Archiving and Communication Systems (RIS/PACS) and Cardiovascular Information Systems (CVIS), revenue cycle management and practice applications.

This case study discusses how Company C initially used a CMS to collaborate on their user assistance initiatives within the documentation department of their Clinical Business Solutions division of their IT business. With some creative thinking and little effort, they later discovered how the CMS also could provide positive collaboration with other departments in their division.

The nature of Company C's business required the organization to provide documentation and training support for new products to their customers quickly and efficiently. The Documentation department had a core of good information, but it was scattered and in too many formats to easily maintain and distribute. Company C purchased a CMS in 2003 to consolidate and organize this information. The CMS allowed them to develop an infrastructure that centralized information, improving virtual collaboration, so that it could be reused and quickly delivered it in appropriate formats to their customers. More people could work together on their content synchronously, and they eliminated the time to compile multiple formats of information.

While shopping for a CMS, the documentation department got the idea to create an online knowledge center for their clients that went beyond the reference manuals and online help they had been providing. It would also provide a vehicle for collaborating with customers, a topic described in more detail in Chapter 17. The CMS would allow them to develop and maintain the user assistance Web site with more up-to-date information for their clients—something they could not have done without the CMS. The knowledge center was successfully developed shortly after their purchase of the CMS, and Company C's clients, who benefitted from more accurate and accessible information.

Challenges

As the documentation department within Company C used the CMS to produce their documentation, they realized that other departments in their division were recreating similar information in other formats:

- The installation department was producing Dictionary Worksheets in Word and Excel for their customer installation projects. These worksheets contained similar information being produced and maintained by the technical documentation department.

- The upgrades department captured information for the Customer Test Log by extracting it from a Lotus Notes database and cross-referencing it with similar information created by the documentation department in the CMS. Other information for the Customer Test Log was retrieved manually from PDFs of the New Features Guides. It took 40 hours to compile the raw information into a usable form—researching and resolving discrepancies and updating information; then, they still had to produce the deliverable. The information was often inaccurate and uncoordinated, causing customers and staff to become frustrated.

The writing redundancies and lack of content coordination across the departments was obvious to the documentation staff when they implemented their content management and reuse strategy.

Solutions

With a new focus on content reuse and consolidation of content assets, the documentation department realized that they could collaborate with these departments to consolidate their content into a single, trusted source—the CMS. By sharing content that was managed in one repository, they could eliminate many of the formats (including Lotus Notes®, Word™, and Excel™) in which the content was stored, reduce the inaccuracies within the published documents across these departments, and save each department the time spent recreating and maintaining similar information.

Thinking beyond their own department, the documentation staff realized that the efforts to collaborate with other departments using the CMS would be minimal. Because no formal previous collaboration existed among the departments in the division, the documentation team needed to develop a plan and a structured process for approaching the other departments that would be well-received as a means to improve productivity among the teams. The upgrade team was already feeling the pain from the content inconsistencies among the departments through the customer complaints that were received. However, the installation team was not aware of the duplicated efforts and internal inefficiencies across the departments. So, the documentation staff developed criteria with which to approach the other departments for better collaboration. They realized that they could:

- Take advantage of content they already have;
- Take advantage of structure they already have;
- Address pain points for business and/or customers; and
- Leverage reuse, consistency, and increased accuracy.

The results of their efforts to collaborate with the other departments saved Company C time and money while improving the quality of their content across their publications. For example, they worked jointly with their installation department to finalize the design and time line for the Dictionary Worksheet Word and Excel deliverables that would be managed through CMS rather than multiple tools. From that point forward, the documentation department took on the responsibility for maintaining those deliverables for each product release. This project significantly improved the accuracy of the information for the Dictionary Worksheets and eliminated the duplicate efforts that were going on previously.

In addition, they established the CMS as the trusted source of the Customer Test Log information, creating a scenario where the upgrades department could collaborate with the documentation department to determine the plan for going forward. They implemented specific metadata as content attributes to query the database and pull an accurate set of starter content to produce the Customer Test Logs, replacing the raw data that had been pulled from the Lotus Notes database. The upgrade department's effort to get the raw data to a usable, trusted state for each major product release was reduced from 40 to 4 hours. It was a big win for Company C's customer satisfaction levels, too. Both internal and external customers now received more accurate information, eliminating the frustration of discrepancies within the content being distributed to customers by the two departments.

Summary

Company C was able to save time and money in multiple departments by using a CMS as the trusted source for their content. They consolidated their content creation efforts, then shared and reused the information across multiple departments.

They were able to meet their goals by focusing on reusing content that existed in the CMS across the various departments. The CMS allowed content reuse to happen almost instantaneously because the other departments could use the content that was already structured in the CMS by the documentation department. This content reuse made their messaging consistent in the published documents from all three departments.

By collaborating through one system, Company C obtained its goals and achieved better information management and publishing. The result was not only a huge time savings across multiple departments, but also more satisfied cli-

ents because consistent information was provided from all areas of their organization.

Company C indicates that they see more opportunities to collaborate effectively with other departments. To continue to improve the quality of the information delivered to their clients, in the near future, they plan to develop processes with the marketing and development departments to share content and cut duplicate writing efforts. The principles of collaboration operating in this case study include Principle 1, creating a culture of collaboration across the company and Principle 5, establishing structured processes for managing collaborative interactions with many teams in the organization.

CASE STUDY 4: TEAMING UP ACROSS CORPORATE BUSINESS UNITS

Background

This case study explains how a CMS fostered collaboration between two divisions of an international Fortune 500 company (referred to as "Company D") to write and update their documentation and translate it into 21 languages.

Company D is a manufacturer of medical equipment, with divisions located across the globe, and with worldwide customers that include hospitals, physicians, and patients. Company D is divided into several businesses that provide medical equipment in various medical specialties. This case study focuses on one of these manufacturing business units, located in the U.S., which has a team of 20 people who produce technical documentation for their medical devices (referred to as "Tech Docs" throughout this case study). These documents are then translated into 21 languages by their sister division (referred to as the "Translator" throughout this case study) located in Europe. The Translator has 25 employees who work directly with Tech Docs to manage, translate, and compose the global publications for inclusion in the product packages sold in the different countries and geographies.

Challenges

When Tech Docs completed writing their technical documentation for their medical devices, they sent files containing this content to the Translator to be translated into 21 languages for their multilingual publications. The files were not always sent to the Translator in a consistent way, causing the two divisions to spend extra time coordinating, fixing, and resending files. Collaboration between Tech Docs and the Translator needed improvement because too much time was wasted in this process of transferring content back and forth, causing them to miss publishing deadlines and costing the organization money, a problem discussed in Chapter 15. They realized that they needed to improve the communications and collaboration between the groups to better facilitate an efficient workflow and meet deadlines, as well as to work together to provide content in a more consistent fashion across the divisions. For example, the Translator had tools for their translation memory and translation processes in place. These tools contained a project management feature that minimized the deviations in the way content was received for translation from different users, but they felt more could be done to improve these inefficiencies.

When Tech Docs implemented the CMS, it gave them the perfect opportunity to collaborate more effectively with the Translator. Tech Docs was challenged to create a process to deliver content that was prepared consistently for translation. Since the Translator already had processes in place that were working well, they needed to create a workflow around the translation process that did not force the Translator to change their current methods. They also wanted to create a translation workflow process that would provide information back to Tech Docs regarding the status of the translations.

Solutions

Company D used the workflow feature in the CMS to unite the Translator with Tech Docs and allow the staff to collaborate better throughout the production and translation process. Using the CMS's workflow to assign tasks with specific due dates to appropriate users, all content could flow through the translation process in the same way. The workflow defined the proper steps that the content must take to ensure the Tech Doc writers and the Translator team all followed the same process for preparing and sending content back and forth every time.

Tech Docs learned that they could design their workflow to front-end and back-end the project management that was already in use in the translation tool without duplicating it. The Translator now became a part of Tech Doc's workflow process. This change would enable the teams to collaborate virtually with greater synchronicity. The Translator interfaced with Tech Doc's staff using the CMS to access the content needed for translation, thereby standardizing the interface with which the Translator accessed the content and minimizing their training time to learn the process. While the authoring portion of the workflow could be tailored for Tech Docs, the Translator could still use one consistent workflow to process content for translation rather than different workflows from each writer. The data were delivered from the CMS in the same format each time and processed and loaded back in the same way, regardless of from which writer the content originated. With a consistent workflow process in place, these divisions saved hours of coordination time and were better able to meet their publishing deadlines. Customizing technology to meet the information development demands allowed the teams to maximize the use of serial and parallel activities when handing off translation content.

They also implemented the use of attributes in the content management system as a way to collaborate on translation processes. Translation status attributes on the English content inform the Tech Docs team of the translation workflow's progress for their documents. Now, as stages of the translation workflow are completed, attributes are automatically updated on the English content in the content management system, alerting the writers of the English content that all translations for the document have been completed.

Summary

The implementation of a single, collaborative writing and translation CMS provided several efficiencies for Company D now and in the years ahead:

- Less training time is needed for the Translator staff to learn to process content from Tech Docs for translation. All writers see the same software interface every time they work on content using the content management system. This standardization saves training time, and it enables effective knowledge sharing among translation staff.
- Improved teamwork between the Tech Docs and the Translator teams due to a collaborative content management environment and shared, automated workflow. The teams have a higher degree of collaboration because they are linked virtually through shared content, task flows, and system-triggered status information. This electronic connection leads to improved partnering on projects, greater efficiencies in processes, and less virtual throwing work back and forth over cubicle, office, and worldwide walls.
- More timely translation cycle adjustments due to automated notification of changes to English. In cases where translation work is underway on a project, the automated workflow and system-triggered status updates automatically alert the Translator team when changes have been made to the English content. This automatic update ensures that the translators are made aware

of last minute English updates, enabling them to inquire with the Tech Docs team as to how to integrate those updates into the translated documents.

The increased collaboration between Tech Docs and the Translator has had an impact on both groups, leading to improved efficiencies in their overall processes for producing product documentation. For the U.S. Tech Docs staff, for example, it has meant having a broader focus than only the English content, so that the translations can do their work more efficiently. For instance, greater attention now is paid to using the correct Unicode characters so they do not continue to send files with the wrong characters to the Translator, making the files cleaner for composition in other languages. For the Translator team, increased collaboration has meant increased communication with the Tech Docs team to ensure that the content passed back and forth between the writers and translators is clean and usable for optimal processing by both groups. By automating their processes and information delivery, these groups work more effectively together to translate English content and process revisions for publishing their multilingual documents. Overall, the increased collaboration and awareness of the needs of the other divisions has paid off for Company D in time and cost savings for the organization. The principles of collaboration at work in this case study include Principle 1, creating a culture of collaboration across departments, Principle 4, using tools and collaborative modes effectively, and Principle 5, establishing structured processes for managing collaborative interactions within and between.

RECOMMENDATIONS AND FUTURE DIRECTIONS

Although CMSs were developed originally to organize, consolidate, and store content more effectively, they have evolved into collaborative writing tools as well. Features such as workflow and collaborative review have been built into CMSs to give writers the ability to easily gather the information that they need to refine their content from colleagues by assigning them specific tasks with due dates. Writers can then use this information to write their documentation and process it effectively and consistently while managing the costs associated with the editorial, translation, and publishing cycles. They can share content virtually with colleagues in review cycles to solicit feedback and improve the fine details of their writings. Virtual collaboration on writing assignments extends to managers using project management capabilities. Writers and managers can monitor the progress of each writing assignment and ensure it will be completed accurately and on schedule.

While CMSs can provide huge benefits in collaboration, efficiencies, and cost savings, many writers lack the knowledge needed to work in a content management environment. There is a great need for more education about content management and topic-based writing for reuse so writers can be more prepared to move into the technical documentation field. For example, education in structured writing skills and content management concepts in colleges and university can greatly help novice business writers to understand better the differences between writing in an academic environment, where they most likely were introduced to business and technical writing, versus a business setting.

Similar skills training is needed for writers who have business-setting experience to learn to write differently with such virtual collaborative tools as a CMS. For writers who work in the technical documentation field, the transition to a content management strategy can be an uncomfortable change. Writers who were taught to focus on creating and extending content as an entire work, as in the academic environment, now must change their focus to topic-based writing methods that result in lower editorial, production, and translation costs.

One recommended key for a successful transition is *training*: Writers must receive appropriate and timely training in skills, tools, and concepts to successfully transition to a content management culture. Another key is *communication*: Regular communication from management that conveys their support of such collaborative strategies, a culture of collaboration, as well as their goals and status will keep the writers informed. Frequent, small bits of information are more easily digested and accepted by writers rather than overwhelming them by throwing the entire strategy at them in one shot. Training and communication can ease the fear of the change in virtual collaborative writing settings.

A third key to success is to *manage a CMS implementation properly*. If an organization attempts to roll out a CMS across the entire team and/or the complete documentation set all at once, the implementation will have a lesser chance for success. It is recommended leaders in organizations roll out the implementation in small steps by starting with one or two projects and/or with one group of lead writers. This method provides an opportunity to test and tweak the configuration, workflow, and collaboration processes with a small subject before opening it to the entire team or documentation set, making for a smoother transition to the new content management strategy.

CONCLUSION

Collaboration in business and technical writing environments traditionally has been achieved through manual methods—phone calls, e-mails, or visits to colleague's cubicles—if it existed at all. As more and more writing groups are dispersed in various locations or become home-based, it becomes harder to work collaboratively and by default, writers tend to work in silos.

Technologies have provided new, virtual methods for collaboration, allowing people to interconnect during the writing tasks as well as during the corresponding editorial and production processes that complete the entire publishing cycles. Specifically, CMSs provide solutions to share content, document supporting information, track project statuses, review content and provide feedback, track versions, and implement efficient workflow processes to help everyone work together more effectively. This use of CMS technology can help to support the structured processes described in Chapter 10. Automatic notifications about pending tasks or available information can be provided to writers to ensure they stay in the loop, perform their duties on time, and get the information they need to do a quality job while eliminating time-consuming manual methods.

CMSs support effective virtual collaboration in many ways. Colleagues within a department work more effectively together. Communications and processes across departments and divisions of the organization can become more efficient and eliminate duplicate efforts while improving the quality of the publications produced by these varying groups. External groups, such as subject matter experts or translation vendors, can be integrated into processes that were once secluded from content or information sharing, making the processes more efficient. With virtual collaboration using a CMS, organizations see significant quality improvements and time and cost savings in all areas of the editorial, translation, and publishing cycles.

REFERENCE

Manafy, M. (2008, December). Welcome to the eighth annual EContent 100—Our list of companies that matter most in the digital content industry. *EContent, 31*(10), 26–57.

Chapter 10
Optimizing Team Performance:
Collaborative Virtual Writing

Charlotte Robidoux
Hewlett-Packard Company, USA

ABSTRACT

Increasingly, collaborative writing occurs in distributed work environments. Collaboration is essential for technical writing teams that develop and share, or single source, content using content management system (CMS) technology. Technical writers must be proficient not only in developing content that can be shared but also in carrying out complex writing tasks virtually. However, research indicates that asynchronous-distributed collaborative writing can lead to productivity losses unless teams implement explicit processes for interacting and using computer-mediated communication (CMC) technology. With highly structured processes to guide their efforts, teams are more likely to see productivity gains. To achieve these gains, effective collaboration must address six key areas: (1) targets to guide team performance, (2) assessments of collaborative writing skills in virtual teams, (3) role delineation, (4) process scripts to promote efficient virtual collaborative writing, (5) a training framework, and (6) performance measurements and a recognition framework for reinforcing team accomplishments. Organizations must be willing to create a culture that supports a team environment committed to these specific areas. This chapter explores how to establish an infrastructure that promotes collaborative writing efficiency in virtual settings.

INTRODUCTION

An Unplanned Collaboration

Consider a team of four writers who have worked together successfully for a few years, revising a set of documents for a well-established computer product. When the documentation is ready to be revised, each team member ensures that the book she has been assigned is updated to reflect new or changed product features. In this scenario, the writers are able to revise the documentation efficiently. Now imagine what would happen if the process for

DOI: 10.4018/978-1-60566-994-6.ch010

making updates changes dramatically, and only one writer fully understands the new process. Under these circumstances, the chance for success could diminish rapidly depending on the team's ability to learn and adapt to unfamiliar tasks and to redefine their interactions with each other. That is, team members could flounder when the writers do not have an expected set of assignments and a defined approach to revising content. They could waste time trying to carry out tasks that other writers might have implemented or disrupt each other by trying to carry out the same tasks.

A scenario like this overwhelmed a team of Hewlett-Packard Company (HP) writers, who unexpectedly were forced to update individual chunks of content that would become the source material for a set of documents. Team members working in different locations were required to work collaboratively when one team member prematurely divided whole books into small, modular pieces of content that then could be reused, or single sourced, across the documentation set. While this writer thought she would improve the efficiency and quality of the content by making this change, she did not realize how difficult it would be for the team of writers to learn how to collaborate with one another under these circumstances, how to coordinate an effective flow of tasks, and how to adjust to an entirely new process. She made decisions about how the content would be updated as if she were working on her own and without understanding the consequences for the team at the point when the content would be shared. The consequence of this decision for the rest of this team was that the once-familiar experience of a single writer owning and updating a complete book would not be possible.

Although sharing reusable pieces of content had been a goal for HP writing teams, plunging a team without preparation into the process of reusing topics in different books was never the intent. In the end, the writers could not adapt quickly enough, and the only way to avoid delaying the shipment of the product was for the content management administrator to reverse the writer's actions—to unlink the referenced topics and embed them into separate books.

This scenario revealed important information about the nature of collaboration. While teams of writers working in the book paradigm collaborate with each other, the type of collaboration employed typically is serial or parallel collaboration, not collective collaboration as described earlier in this volume. The experience also underscores the need to establish an environment that enables writers to collaborate collectively within distributed work settings. This type of environment must provide explicit, scripted processes to address the unique challenges faced by virtual collaborative writing teams.

Retrofitting the Book Paradigm

Working individually on a piece of writing has been a mainstay strategy in technical writing for many years. Before technology made automated reuse possible, writers typically took ownership of whole books and the updates within them (see Chapters 13 and 15). From this standpoint, collaborative writing entailed the assignment of particular books across a writing team, which in this volume is defined as serial and parallel collaboration (see Chapter 1).

As the practice of single sourcing increases, so does the need for collaborating virtually on writing projects. Under these circumstances, writers no longer are expected to own whole books. Yet their inclination to seek out familiar roles rooted in the book paradigm persists, leaving writers wondering how to find effective frameworks for collaborating—how to have multiple authors write topics that can be reused across many books. Assumptions still linger that information grows sequentially, that writing is essentially a collocated, solitary activity, and that "owning" a complete document is the natural order of producing documentation. An instinctive response to this situation involves attempting to retrofit topic-based writing into the book paradigm. Unfortunately, as the earlier scenario illustrates, reinventing the status quo only invites problems because the book paradigm cannot anticipate all the complexities of sharing content across virtual space and time. Writers need a new paradigm to be successful.

In recent years, experts have identified the need for teams to work collaboratively when sharing content in a database (Hackos, 2002, p. 350; Hackos, 2007, p. 493; Rockley, 2003, pp. 365-367). Even so, explicit collaborative writing strategies seem to be elusive, and our understanding of virtual collaborative writing is lacking (Lowry, et al., 2005, p. 341). What researchers do know is that while the need for virtual collaborative writing is a "competitive advantage" in global environments, this approach to writing "is generally performed suboptimally" (Lowry, et al., 2005, p. 341). Knowledge of this potential outcome is important because organizations are increasingly anticipating increased productivity because of single sourcing strategies. However, if unfavorable results are a real possibility, managers need to appreciate the challenges that writers confront when immersed in virtual collaborative writing environments, especially as globalization drives teams to work remotely and topic-based writing requires what we describe in Chapter 1 as collective collaboration. For this reason, managers need to provide the leadership that will ensure the success of teams writing collaboratively; writers must have the skills needed to coordinate complex activities and to contend with countless changes related to CMC technology. Without explicit processes that guide interactions among writing teams, as described by Lowry et al. (2005), process efficiencies may be undermined, leading some organizations to conclude that single-sourcing, while a great idea in theory, cannot live up to the many promises advanced over the years. The shift away from the book paradigm requires leaders of organizations to create a culture of collaboration, abiding by the first two principles outlined at the outset of this book.

Finding a New Collaborative Paradigm

The difficulty in conceiving of co-authored content is that multiple minds cannot combine to formulate a sequence of words simultaneously. Thoughts do not collectively span many minds or hands when being documented. While a team can throw out ideas and some individuals can write down what they hear or interpret, this way of writing is not particularly practical or efficient, especially in industry settings where productivity is paramount. For this reason, creating an infrastructure that can help writers conceive of and engage in a different paradigm is essential.

The aim of this chapter is to provide organizations that require virtual collaboration with practical strategies for building strong collaborative writing teams. These teams will be adept not only in the use of tools but also in the different modes of collaboration—serial, parallel, and collective forms, as described in Chapter 1. This chapter discusses six areas that managers should address to establish an infrastructure that supports effective virtual collaborative writing: (1) targets to guide team performance, (2) assessments of collaborative writing skills in virtual teams, (3) role delineation, (4) process scripts to promote efficient virtual collaborative writing, (5) a training framework, and (6) performance measurements and a recognition framework for reinforcing team accomplishments. These areas embody all the principles of collaborative writing that ground this book.

STRATEGIES TO OPTIMIZE VIRTUAL COLLABORATIVE WRITING

Targets to Guide Team Performance

Identifying a set of targets, or objectives, to shape performance in organizations is a common practice. When individuals can focus their attention effectively, they are more likely to realize some improvement related to a specific area of focus. The challenge with targets is findings ones that will produce good results for a team of writers, especially in organizations that typically has recognize individual performance. In order for writing teams to collaborate effectively, managers must identify a set of targets that includes the whole team and guides synchronized performance.

If choosing the right targets underlies good performance, how do we know which ones to consider? The key to this process, as indicated by Spitzer (2007), involves: (1) identifying a few meaningful targets that will have a large impact on the organization and (2) clearly defining the targets so that the team being measured understands how the targets relate to the overall success of the organization (pp. 111-112).

Lowry et al. (2005) defined categories related to the performance of virtual collaborative writing teams. Inexperienced teams that were given highly scripted processes performed better in five different areas than those that were given less explicit processes to follow: document production, document quality, process satisfaction, relationship quality, and communication quality. These areas can serve as a basis for selecting targets that are appropriate for virtual collaborative writing teams. Adapted from the Lowry study, Table 1 describes five targets that can be used to evaluate writing team efficiency (Lowry et al., 2005, p. 344).

In this study, researchers learned that relationship and communication quality are central to productivity. That is, improved social interactions contribute to team efficiency. This research underscores the value of including targets related to team dynamics. If group well-being and team member support are poor, individuals will have a harder time coordinating tasks and performing effectively as a team (p. 353).

Accordingly, the categories in Table 1 can serve as a basis for selecting targets that will guide collaborative writing teams as they move away from the book paradigm. Teams can adapt the categories to meet the needs of a specific organization. Once defined, these targets should help individuals understand the criteria for interacting as a cohesive team—that performance depends on team-oriented contributions.

To make the targets meaningful, teams can discuss the nuances of each item, ways of adapting them to arrive at agreement, and how best to maintain performance throughout the life cycle of the project. Team members, in fact, can discuss working examples to test the targets. For example, writers can explore what it means to be productive when developing topics. The team might agree that topics must comply with standards, as suggested in Chapters 13 and 15, ensuring that topics are structured consistently and meet the criteria for reusability, that the text adheres to minimalist principles (as described by Hackos (1999)), and that word selection complies with terminology lists. Concurrence on these points means that the team should see itself as less productive if topics do not meet these standards. The Measurement

Table 1. Targets for assessing collaborative writing team performance

Target	Description
Production	• Number of topics, word choice, structure, reusability, and discussions • Group-formation, brainstorming, outlining, and time to write topics • Time spent on the various collaborative writing activities
Document quality	• Perceived value of documents or information products
Process satisfaction	• Perceived satisfaction with their team's work processes
Relationship quality	• Ability to negotiate with team members, positive feedback, and teamwork
Communication quality	• Discussion quality, appropriateness, involvement, group support, task discussion effectiveness

and Recognition Framework section discussed later considers how teams might measure performance against targets and recognize team accomplishments.

Assessing Collaborative Writing Skills in Virtual Teams

In addition to establishing targets that guide team performance, managers and team leaders should perform an assessment to anticipate how the team and its members might interact together. Assessing teams will help managers determine how they can support team performance more fully—what areas need improvement to enhance collaborative interactions in virtual settings. Knowing how best to gauge the strengths and weaknesses of a team is an essential starting point. This process can be likened to evaluating the performance of members on a sports team, considering how each individual functions individually and in the context of the whole team. For instance, returning to the "unplanned collaboration" at the opening of this chapter, it is possible to see how an assessment would have benefitted the manager and project leader overseeing this team. Even observing that the one writer made decisions without informing other team members would have revealed how inexperienced the team was in terms of collective collaboration.

Assessing teams and their members is also an important tool for managers and project leaders, given that staffing levels expand and contract to balance costs with the demands of product development. In fact, it is increasingly difficult to find collaborative writing teams that remain together continually. Team leaders should use the assessment to determine how much experience a team has writing collaboratively in distributed settings so that structures can be established to help ensure team success.

If a team has extensive experience collaborating in virtual environments, an assessment may not be needed unless a new team member is added or if the complexity of the work increases dramatically. When working with novice or less experienced teams, it seems useful to conduct a more formal assessment that addresses many indicators related to high team performance. Table 2 illustrates generally how a manager and project lead might rate the experiences of a team and its members.

Based on the experiences uncovered in this assessment, managers can determine how much structure a team and its members will need to coordinate activities efficiently—to prevent mistakes like those described earlier in the opening scenario. The aim of the assessment is for managers to gather as much knowledge as possible about a team's strengths and weaknesses to determine what degree of structure is needed to ensure productivity.

Role Delineation

Delineating roles is essential when writers share content and need to collaborate. Teams have to find effective ways to divide the work—to determine a system of roles and responsibilities around developing topics into complete deliverables. The discussion of roles that follows can help teams plan and assign work based on the functions required throughout a project and on particular skills needed on a writing team. (Unlike Chapter 12, this discussion of roles is not specific to a DITA environment.)

Placing roles into categories helps to ensure a complete understanding of the complex interactions underlying the virtual collaborative writing process. The roles that writers assume are not always specific to writing topics per se; however, so-called non-writing tasks are still fundamental activities needed to carry out writing projects. I recommend dividing roles into categories: (1) the project life cycle, (2) technical or skill-based knowledge, and (3) product knowledge expertise. Table 3 elaborates on the roles related to the three categories. The many roles included presuppose

Table 2. Assessment tool for managers

Area	Indicator	Low	Medium	High
Background	• Roles played on a team	✓		
	• Knowledge of project-planning processes		√	
	• Interactivity with other team members, teams, and organizations		✓	
	• Practice leading teams		✓	
	• Familiarity with single-sourcing practices, collaborating online			✓
	• Use of XML-related technologies	✓		
Past performance	• Project management, understanding of different roles		✓	
	• Success working effectively with others		✓	
	• Implementation of initiatives, such as structured writing			✓
	• Commitment to team objectives		✓	
	• Skill level		✓	
	• Quality of work			✓
Experience collaborating virtually	• Modes of collaborating			
	• Serial			✓
	• Parallel		✓	
	• Collective	✓		
	• Virtual interactions			
	• Synchronous (discussion boards)		✓	
	• Asynchronous (e-mail)		✓	
	• Presence (instant messenger)			✓
	• Interactivity (online workspaces)	✓		
	• Hybridity (video conferencing)			✓
	• Processes for using various tools		✓	
Group dynamics/ trust	• Diversity, experience, interactive skills, decision making		✓	
	• Overcoming conflicts, barriers		✓	
	• Flexible work style to support team		✓	
	• Knowledge of product being documented			✓
	• Understanding of work styles, patterns, norms		✓	
	• Shared vision, values	✓		
	• Formal agreements, negotiation, and communication strategies	✓		

a large and complex project and team size. As a result, some roles—administrative ones, for example—take up a portion of person's time in addition to writing activities. The writing output expected of a person who has administrative du-

ties will not be as high as someone whose sole responsibility on the team is writing. Determining who takes on what role depends on different factors, including project requirements, the strengths and weaknesses of team members on given tasks,

Table 3. Functional roles to plan effective virtual collaborative writing

Function	Description	Collaboration
Project Life Cycle Roles		
Project lead	Assesses scope of work to plan allocation of resources. Oversees project planning and management, including team formation and agreements, measures of success.	Conducts team assessments with team coordinator; creates work plans; and implements measures, training, customized process scripts with input from senior writers.
Team coordinator	Oversees collaborative writing processes, maintaining process scripts, tool selection, team configuration needs.	Before project start, sets up mentoring for new team members; gathers feedback for improvements.
Project tracking administrator	Oversees project and deliverable progress. Maintains status updates for review internally and with engineering.	Works with project lead and team to address shortfalls and required staff redeployment.
Online workspace administrator	Uploads and maintains project-related information needed for team to access and carry out day-to-day operations.	Sets alerts on workspace to notify team immediately of status, scope, and timetable changes.
Localization coordinator	Posts file for localization; assesses need for part numbers; maintains localization tracking and file management; and facilitates approval.	Coordinates with regional staff, engineering, and writers to meet localization regulations.
Release administrator	Creates the CD index; submits files to manufacturing and Web administrators; and tracks any issues raised.	Confers with writers to validate final information products. Confers with manufacture to ensure CD accuracy.
Technical/Skill-based Roles		
Information architect	Obtains technical understanding of managing and publishing content, as well as how identical and similar content can be combined, linked, and reused to form various information products. Oversees the classification, organization, and assembly of content to ensure the creation of a complete set of information for the project.	Works with writers on updates required and content mapping. Identifies impact of new or obsolete content. Seeks team agreement for the best strategy for conveying information and changes to customer. Ensures that tools are configured to support processes.
Build or publishing architect	Oversees all technical aspects of publishing digital information products on the Web, for integration into user interfaces, online help files, and for CD production.	Works with writers to create accurate interim and final build/publication of information products for reviews and delivery to release administrator.
Tools specialist	Oversees tools-related issues, including the troubleshooting related to the XML editor, style sheet administration, DTD management, loading and extracting files to and from the CMS.	Assists team with tools issues that arise during the project; logs issues needing tools or developer support; and follows up on critical fixes as necessary.
Product Knowledge Related Roles		
Content Developer	Creates and revises topics and building blocks for complete documents.	Works with engineers to validate new features; confers with other writers about division of labor and product expertise.
Update specialist	Updates existing topics.	Works with engineers to validate updates; confers with other writers about product knowledge and division of labor.
Content assembler	Validates topic assembly, cross references, and content quality.	Works with writers to validate accuracy of topic relationships and links across the set of information products.
Editor	Oversees compliance with standards, style guide, and requirements for content reuse.	Works with writers and project lead. Consults with team on strategies for writing reusable content.

and their overall experience. While it is important to encourage individuals to pursue areas of interest, it is equally beneficial to rotate roles so that team members can build trust as they come to appreciate the work from different perspectives.

In terms of the first area, project life cycle, the roles assume three stages of writing: pre-writing project tasks, writing (forming, planning, development, review, production), and post-writing tasks. As Lowry et al. (2004) suggested, the emphasis on various writing stages is useful because work carried out effectively during each phase helps the team form, build alliances, establish trust, and participate equally (p. 72).

Gradually, team members learn that many different roles—rather than one writer on one book throughout the project—contribute to the creation of information products. Figure 1 illustrates that when assigned specific roles, writers can work across documents and projects rather than on single documents or books. Working in a CMS simplifies this process because writers can add or modify pieces of content rather than accessing a whole book. When assigned to document new features, writer A can create topics needed for any book (1, 2, 3) or project (A, B, C), writer B can update existing content, and writer C can focus on administrative or technical tasks.

The primary concern with this process is that the members of the writing team collaborate with each other to gain agreement on key processes for carrying out the work, such as on additions, modifications, and deletions of content. As described in Chapter 1, this process is called collective collaboration. The interactions that the team agrees to will affect performance, as Lowry et al. (2005) suggested: "The processes and tasks a team chooses (for example, using agendas, taking turns in communication, and determining how decisions are made) can affect team relationships, outcomes, and underlying agreement" (p. 345). If the rules for handling tasks are not specified, individuals will follow their own typical processes, which may not be the most efficient way to collaborate.

Process Scripts for Efficient Virtual Collaborative Writing

Lowry et al. (2005) promoted the importance of highly scripted processes to direct virtual collaborative team interactions: "Groups with high levels of process structure had better results in terms of production, document quality, satisfaction, relationships, and communication" (p. 341). The importance of structure is underscored by the fact that even teams working face to face are more effective when guided by explicit processes: "Increasing process structure for FtF [face-to-face] teams has been shown to decrease process losses and increase process gains" (Lowry, 2005, p. 342). As depicted earlier in the opening scenario, collaborative writing conducted in virtual settings is exceedingly more difficult to carry out than single-author writing. Collaborative writing is so challenging because of the required level of interdependence, interactivity, and coordination. Without explicit processes and practice, writers can encounter numerous problems that not only can compromise the quality of documentation but also delay projects

Figure 1. Collective collaboration model for writing

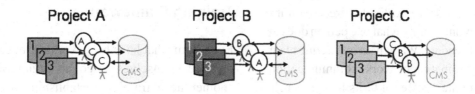

Several factors can contribute to inefficiencies in virtual collaborative writing teams. First, collaborative writing transforms the process of authoring into a social undertaking which interposes a whole set of activities related to team dynamics: "building consensus… communicating, negotiating, coordinating, group researching, monitoring, rewarding, punishing, recording, socializing, and so forth" (Lowry et al., 2004, p. 72). Second, the virtual aspect of collaborative writing—authoring in distributed asynchronous environments—requires teams to interact effectively to keep tasks on track before a process can go awry (Lowry, et al., 2005, p. 342). Newly formed or inexperienced teams have fewer experiences or established patterns to draw on for handling complex team dynamics. Third, teams need more than technology; while tools are important, teams either become overly dependent on them or need procedural guidance for using them effectively. Inexperienced teams that lack structure will have strained relationships, and as a result difficulty communicating. If the team begins to doubt that its members can complete the work together, the willingness to engage with one another dissipates, which in turn will impede production.

Accordingly, new teams, reconfigured teams, or teams unfamiliar with writing topics that are shared need structure to collaborate effectively. Lowry et al. (2005) defined process structure as the "rules and resources such as agendas, organizational norms, training, corporate culture, group experience, and knowledge that are used to coordinate the flow of a group's processes" (p. 342). Process structure refers to a framework of repeatable practices that facilitate the flow of communication and tasks needed to make the team function effectively. The more novice the team, the more structure it will need. Highly structured processes are ones that explicitly direct team interactions beyond simply what one person does to carry out a procedure. Written scripts define team rules, the coordination of work, communication practices, and the transfer of tasks from one role

to another. What makes scripted processes so valuable is their ability to recreate the experience of having a facilitator guide activities (p. 343).

While many organizations may have documented procedures, the use of scripts extends beyond a set of steps to follow. If a set of procedures can be likened to a two-dimensional appearance on a screen, a process script functions more like a three-dimensional experience. Process scripts expose assumptions and provide guidance on how to coordinate activities across time and space for individuals as they relate to each other as a team. Consider, for example, a football coach's playbook, which illustrates player formation and how individuals will move with, around, and in coordination with each other. Organizations, naturally, will want to determine the most appropriate form and specificity of the script. In some cases, a streamlined checklist will suffice for experienced teams. Table 4 illustrates what a process script outlining a prescribed sequence of interactions might look like for a less experienced team needing to write and update topics. Note that the procedural information describing the use of the tool is only one aspect of the script; instructions for interacting with others are equally important.

This process script example, which links competence in creating modules with social interactions among team members, helps teams practice collective collaboration and move past using just serial and parallel modes of collaboration. It supports the basic task by providing thinking patterns that help individuals engage in more advanced modes of interacting. The concept of the process script draws on the fourth and fifth principles of collaboration (using effective modes and creating structure) to establish a new framework for working in a topic-based environment.

Training Framework

Even teams that have been working together and that see themselves as collaborating with one another need training. Establishing a training

Table 4. Process script example

Process Script for Planning the Development of New Topics	
Task	Creating new topics: • Alternative Backup to a System Disk • Migrate Volumes under I/O Load
Roles	Primary: product knowledge Secondary: life cycle, technical/skill
Objective	Teach writers to collaborate virtually to develop content that can be shared across information products
Task	1. Create a module in Arbortext Editor: • Select the appropriate module template. • Create your content in the module as you would any other XML document. • Run a completeness check and save the file to your extract folder. • Load the file into the appropriate collection into CMS. • Create references to this new module (see Reusing modules). 2. Reuse module: • Open and tile two Navigator windows in the CMS: one for the book and one for the appropriate modular collection (such as Sections—Working). • Copy and paste a module from a modular collection (such as Sections—Working) to the desired location in the book using the right-click Copy and Paste menu items. • The Drag and Drop Wizard dialog box opens. • In the Select the Action to perform box, click Copy. • In the Select the destination component box, click the row that contains the reference name (such as SectionRef) in the Component column, and Sibling in the Relationship column. • Click Finish. The module is now referenced (as SectionRef) in your book file.
Temporal and social cues	• Before creating topics, determine who will: Validate content requirements with engineers. Post any notes from engineers on team workspace for central team access. Verify that a set of topics on this subject are not already in the CMS. • If no topics exist, schedule a video conference (synchronous communication) for team to discuss strategy for writing topics that can fit the context of multiple information products. Consider: Are there multiple audiences for the topics? What is the best topic organization to meet audience needs? Do the topics require the need for any glossary terms? • Schedule video conference (synchronous communication) for team to determine: How these new topics will relate to other existing topics and what relationships and links will be necessary to add. Who will write what topics based on subject expertise, including description, requirements, procedure, and troubleshooting. How the new topics may affect existing material. Who will update existing material. The metadata strategy and values selected. • Coordinate with project tracking coordinator regarding assignments. • Establish schedule for ensuring proper coordination of serial, parallel, and collective collaboration. • Employ rules for using instant messenger to coordinate any changes. • Post all questions on the workspace to ensure central access to answers. • Address any tools-related issues with troubleshooting specialist. • Coordinate with build specialist to coordinate draft builds. • Coordinate with editor for review of drafted topics, metadata, and deliverables with topics added. • As a team: Review editorial feedback to coordinate consistent changes across topics. Confer with project tracking administrator on the progress of the development. Update and upload all new topics to the CMS. • Fill out performance measures survey on workspace when first draft is complete for review at lessons learned.

framework is essential because the team dynamics change dramatically when teams need to employ collective collaboration. HP writers who have been preparing for single sourcing and content sharing for at least five years have provided feedback that highlights how important training is to address a number of challenges related to communicating, negotiating, overcoming conflicts, and coordinating tasks virtually:

Good communication among team members will be key [in collaborating]. I think team leads (project leads) will play a key role in facilitating the communication and team work. They would benefit from facilitation and conflict resolution training. Also some communication training might be useful for all team members. For example, introverts need to realize they need to speak up and extroverts need to realize they need to "yield the floor" more....Communication through a work plan (Excel spreadsheet) seems to be survival for us. It would be nice if we could improve on this by using SharePoint and make it a more dynamic communication point using a database or something. I say this because we need to perfect our system of understanding who has made what changes and when those changes were made. Everyone's still learning the tools so many are not comfortable using comments in the XML, version labels in [the CMS]. (Unpublished survey response, March 7, 2009)

This employee indicates that "everyone is still learning," which underscores the need for overall team competence. Expertise comes from guiding teams consistently in the process of writing collaboratively in virtual environments. Recall from Chapter 1 that learning new strategies base on changed operating norms involves cultural change. As Schein (2009) revealed, the three steps of changing a cultural include "unfreezing" or unlearning old behavior, learning new behavior, and "refreezing" or internalizing new concepts and standards (p. 106). It is important that managers help teams to feel secure about overturning writing practices that have been deemed effective over time. Learning to write in a new way means believing that it is safe to leave the old practices behind (see also Chapter 8).

A training framework for virtual collaborative writing teams falls into two categories: technology and process structure. Of the two categories, technology, while more complex in some cases, generally is clear-cut in terms of finding courses and materials. Building competence with tools—both tools for interacting virtually and for writing—is a basic starting point. Lowry et al. (2005) learned that teams can perform more efficiently when they do not spend time trying to adapt to particular uses of the technology, especially when learning to interact with each other. Moreover, the study revealed that skill in using the tools enabled team members to relate to one another more effectively (p. 353). This outcome suggests that if team members are not skilled in the use of the tools, relationships may become strained, which in turn may have an impact on trust and thus productivity. The second category, process structure, is less straightforward than tools training because organizations have unique contexts for carrying out activities. Even so, as indicated by Lowry, et al. (2005), teams need explicit guidance on how best to carry out tasks collectively.

Some organizations, however, do not always have training resources available to them. How can a team establish a training framework if it does not have a trainer to guide writers? Lowry et al. (2005) revealed "that accurate, sufficiently explicit process scripts can be used to train members of virtual teams" (Lowry et al., 2005, 354). Similarly, Neff and Whithaus (2008) recommended the use of process scripts for training purposes: "Process scripts are effective pedagogical tools in distributed-learning environments because they [scripts] account for the differences in context between e-learning and conventional, face-to-face classes...Process scripts are themselves one way of teaching that takes complex social conditions and institutional structures into account" (pp. 83, 102). While process structure cannot take the place of basic qualifications and competence, scripted processes can direct activities related to ways of using technology to coordinate writing tasks (see also Chapter 18).

The best way for organizations to establish a training framework is by drawing on their operating procedures to determine what basic instructions related to both tools and processes may need to be scripted. Figure 2 illustrates that implementing this framework begins by assessing each team's ability to collaborate.

Starting with an assessment helps leaders to determine how much guidance the team will need. Advanced teams will need less structure, and changed or novice or teams will need more. Teams can adjust levels of structure, as appropriate, whether a task requires more or less specificity. Lowry et al. (2005) used the term "decompose" to refer to more detailed processes. Inexperienced teams require more fully decomposed instructions for coordinating tasks with other writers, while experienced teams can rely on compressed scripts (p. 344).

The goal of drawing on structure for training purposes is to create a cognitive tool set that supports team coordination. When constructing process scripts, certain principles apply:

- Make scripts self-explanatory;
- Specify the minimum number of participants;
- When possible, describe participant involvement explicitly, such as "each," "all," and "at least";
- Refer to the roles of participants when assigning activities or allocating resources;
- Highlight interdependencies among participants;
- Use verbal descriptors to clarify the guidance; and
- Consider hierarchies of tasks when needed, classifying larger tasks into smaller ones.

While writing organizations themselves are not instructional designers, they do have the process knowledge to articulate the structure that encompasses the complex social, temporal, and spatial complexities needed to coordinate virtual collaborative writing. Accordingly, the teams themselves should collaborate on the explicit processes that can guide efficient performance. Such work entails the first two principles of virtual collaborative writing, effective leaders who promote a culture of collaboration.

Performance Measurement and Recognition Framework

In business, results-related axioms are ubiquitous: "You're good at what you emphasize," "Energy follows attention," and "You can't improve what you don't measure." When teams set expectations or targets, as described earlier, they have a basis for tracking, monitoring, and recognizing performance. The importance of acknowledging teams for their collaborative work cannot be underes-

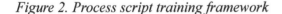

Figure 2. Process script training framework

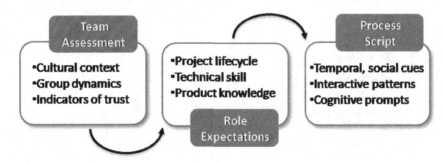

timated. Individuals feel good about performing well and having their peers and managers notice. For years, writers have taken pride in owning their books. Finding a new collaborative paradigm depends on recognizing team performance—appreciating the whole and the sum of its parts.

Once targets are established, managers need to reinforce the concept of tracking team accomplishments—an essential dimension of transforming the culture and moving to a topic-based paradigm. A well-designed system of measuring performance and recognizing accomplishments will begin the process of establishing new norms so that teams feel secure when learning and practicing new behavior. Spitzer (2007) suggested engaging team members and encouraging discussions to establish what I call a performance measurement mindset:

- Ensure early involvement of those individuals who are interested in being innovative, so called early adopters, and

- Find opportunities to measure and discuss progress so that individuals integrate the data collected into knowledge that can be used to transform other members of the organization (pp. 132-134).

The underlying concept suggested by Spitzer (2007) involves finding ways to encourage and develop new behaviors in an organization. As individuals show success in the process of writing collaboratively, managers can reflect on these accomplishments across the organization so that the other teams can observe how new methods are producing high-quality information products. Project leaders can also improve performance by inviting teams to monitor their own collaborative performance. Figure 3 illustrates how the targets described earlier can be adapted into an online survey for teams to measure their ability to work as a team. The aim of the survey is not to assign blame but rather to focus on the effectiveness of overall team contributions.1

Figure 3. Excerpt of survey: virtual collaborative writing team productivity

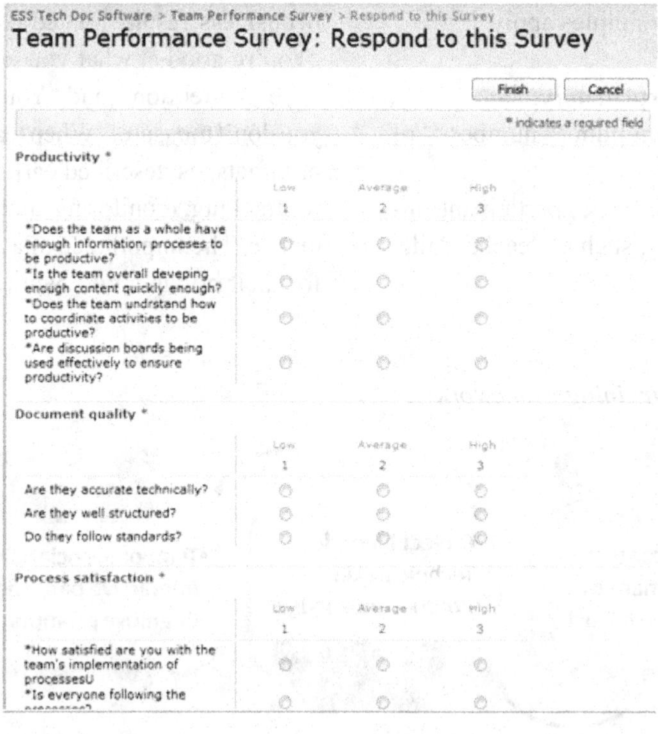

Recognizing successful team performance creates reinforcement. Measuring and recognizing thus are integrally related. An effective recognition framework is fair, motivating, and clear-cut in terms of what matters in the organization. *The HR Specialist* (2009) promoted eight rules related to recognition, which are so simple that they might be overlooked. Table 5 adapts these rules to virtual collaborative writing. Project leaders can share survey results to recognize team contributions. As teams measures their own performance at key points during the course of working together, they can gather feedback to make improvements along that way. This process can lead directly to high performance and obvious accomplishments to recognize.

Teams can overcome the challenges of writing collaboratively if they have clear targets that can be measured and if managers recognize the value of collective efforts.

FUTURE RESEARCH DIRECTIONS

Virtual collaborative writing will continue to have significance as long as technology makes content reusable and thus writing more efficient and as long as readers demand digital information at any time, any place, and on all types of devices. While the tools may range from basic to elaborate and the scale of implementation may extend from small operations to enterprise-wide initiatives, managing shared content always requires effective interactions among teams of writers. As technology improves, teams will benefit from new features that better support collaboration. Even so, sophistication across tools creates yet another opportunity for learning and then for assimilating new knowledge. Virtual writing teams need ongoing validation that team members are skilled in the use of ever-changing tools. And teams increasingly

Table 5. Eight rules for recognizing performance

Rule	Description
1) Specify the recognition criteria	Typically, these criteria relate to the performance measures. Targets that guide virtual collaborative writing would involve recognition related to accomplishments in five key areas: • Production • Document quality • Process satisfaction • Relationship quality • Communication quality The benefit in recognizing measures is that they have been linked to increased performance in virtual collaborative writing.
2) Recognize everyone who meets the criteria	Use the word "everyone" literally to signify all the roles that significantly contributed to a given performance measure.
3) Tailor recognition to what an employee values	Each writer places a high degree of importance on certain aspects of the work. Recognize what each team member values and highlight his or her special contribution. For example, recognize the person who takes pride in getting every detail right and actually achieved this end.
4) Say "thank you" frequently	Being appreciated is a basic human need at work or outside of it, and individuals rarely tire of hearing, "thank you." Encourage team members to thank each other for making collaborative work successful.
5) Nurture self-esteem	Make the most of cultivating what typifies a team member's sense of worth on a project. For instance, writers have high regard for good quality; acknowledge the team for its commitment to quality.
6) Foster intrinsic rewards (self-motivation)	This item pertains to what we value and relates to motivation. Consider the motivating factors that inspire good performance and draw on these factors when assigning particular roles to team members. The writer who enjoys learning the nuances of tools is a good candidate for the troubleshooting role.
7) Recognize the whole team	Effective collaborative writing entails the whole team. Showing favoritism can undermine the performance of the team collectively. Even though some sports figures become icons on teams, they are rewarded for helping to make the whole team successful.
8) You get what you reward	If you do not reward the team and its members, virtual collaborative writing will suffer. Performance measures must become the basis for recognizing team accomplishments.

need technical writers who literally are technically savvy in the process of managing computer code, databases, and publishing engines (Pullman and Gu, 2009, p. 9; McShane, 2009, p. 83).

As this chapter has shown, a sound methodology also is crucial for teams having to navigate shifting technology, especially when tools go offline and breakdowns are unavoidable. The more inexperienced teams are with virtual collaborative writing, the more they need high degrees of structure to guide their interactions. Additional research should examine more fully how scripted processes are helping teams write collaboratively in various writing environments. Such examination would consider how scripts used in the classroom help prepare students for the workplace. Additionally, research might investigate how the application of targets and measures are helping to shape cultural change in writing organizations.

CONCLUSION

The increased frequency of virtual collaborative writing reflects a growing trend in workplace settings. Globalization and technological advancements shrink time and space and make working with team members across distances a common experience, as revealed in Chapters 3 and 12. While the idea of collaborating is not new, the importance of working effectively with team members across distances brings the concept of collaboration into the spotlight. When teams are colocated, collaboration may seem more ad hoc as individuals make connections in hallways, in the cafeteria, and in cubicles. When teams can no longer take advantage of chance conversations on site, they have to be strategic and deliberate about interactions online. Virtual collaborative writing teams cannot afford to be inefficient.

Gaining collaborative writing proficiency is especially challenging for individuals who are accustomed to working independently. Fostering a sense of interdependence in writing environments will help writers to see themselves as valuable contributors to a writing project and their ideas as fully reflected in the whole of the work. The process of guiding teams to value interdependence takes time and adherence to the six principles of virtual collaboration as described in Chapter 1. Leaders across the organization must cultivate a culture of collaboration. Such a culture is built on trust so that the team as a whole truly believes that its members will contribute equally, enabling the team to succeed. This change in mindset can only occur (1) if teams gain proficiency in the use of technology and collaborative modes, (2) if they have enough structure to guide complex interactions, and (3) if they have performance measures and recognition that help them adapt to a new culture.

REFERENCES

Chrislip, D. D., & Larson, C. E. (1994). *Collaborative Leadership*. San Francisco: Jossey-Bass.

Hackos, J. T. (1999). An application of the principles of minimalism to the design of human-computer interfaces. *Common Ground, 9,* 17–22.

Hackos, J. T. (2007). *Information development: Managing tour documentation projects, portfolio, and people* (3rd ed.). Indianapolis: Wiley.

Lowry, P. B., Curtis, A., & Lowry, M. (2004). Building a taxonomy and nomenclature of collaborative writing to improve interdisciplinary research and practice. *Journal of Business Communication, 41,* 66–99. doi:10.1177/0021943603259363

Lowry, P. B., Nunamaker, J. F. Jr, Curtis, A., & Lowry, M. (2005). The impact of process structure on novice, virtual collaborative writing teams. *IEEE Transactions on Professional Communication, 48,* 341–364. doi:10.1109/TPC.2005.859728

McShane, B. J. (2009). Why we should teach XML: An argument for technical acuity. In Pullman, G., & Gu, B. (Eds.), *Content management: Bridging the gap between theory and practice* (pp. 73–85). Amityville, NY: Baywood Publishing Company.

OMNI Institute. (n.d.). *Working together: A profile of collaboration, an assessment tool*. Retrieved October 11, 2009, from http://www.omni.org/instruments.aspx

OMNI Institute. (n.d.). *Working together: A profile of collaboration, a companion to the assessment tool*. Retrieved October 11, 2009, from http://www.omni.org/instruments.aspx

Pullman, G., & Gu, B. (2009). *Content management: Bridging the gap between theory and practice*. Amityville, NY: Baywood Publishing Company.

Robidoux, C., & Hewett, B. L. (2009). Is there a write way to collaborate? *Intercom, 56*(2), 4–9.

Rockley, A. (2003). *Managing enterprise content: A unified content strategy*. Indianapolis: New Riders Press.

Schein, E. (2009). *The corporate culture survival guide* (2nd ed.). San Francisco: Jossey-Bass.

Spitzer, D. (2007). *Transforming performance measurement: Rethinking the way we measure and drive organizational success*. New York: Amacon.

The HP Specialist. (2009, March 26). *8 Rules for Recognizing and Rewarding Employees*. Retrieved on 6/24/2009, http://www.thehrspecialist.com/26695/8_rules_for_recognizing_and_rewarding_employees.hr?cat=tools&sub_cat=memos_to_managers

ENDNOTE

[1] To employ a more formal tool that measures collaboration effectiveness, refer to the OMNI Institute's "Working Together: A Profile of Collaboration." This assessment tool was designed to be statistically valid and reliable for measuring the effectiveness of collaboration processes. The research underlying the tool is based on the work of David D. Chrislip and Carl E. Larson, *Collaborative Leadership*.

Chapter 11
Making Collaborative Writing Decisions Virtually

Alexia P. Idoura
Symantec Corporation, USA

ABSTRACT

When it comes to team decision making, people are more likely to carry out decisions they have helped make (Weisbord, 1987). However, some key decision-making differences in roles, processes, and tools between virtual and traditional writing teams exist. This chapter uses the experiences of Symantec in making decisions, such as the decision for purchasing a content management system (CMS), for how people can make decisions in virtual settings. In particular, this chapter examines how virtual writing teams move through the decision-making process: knowing who has authority, deciding how to decide, using the right decision-making model for a particular decision, doing the groundwork, sharing the information, evaluating the information and making the decision, capturing the decision in a place available to all, and following up on decisions and resulting actions. It also provides a list of tools that can help when making decisions virtually. Finally, keeping the audience—readers or product users—in mind throughout the decision-making process can assist with all of these tasks by keeping decision makers focused on those who most benefit or suffer from writing-based decisions.

INTRODUCTION

What can be done when trying to streamline a budget for managing information products and costs only seem to escalate? How can translation costs be managed when the price per word to translate starts to make translation unaffordable—even though localized information is essential in a global economy? How can companies merge, combine information products authored in different applications, and publish the combined information quickly? How can information products be created quickly for rapidly configured products? How does one respond to immediate demands from customer for product information?

DOI: 10.4018/978-1-60566-994-6.ch011

These questions reflected a significant set of challenges for Symantec, which was growing significantly because of its purchase of various companies. At one point, the company was absorbing an average of two major and at least six minor acquisitions a year. The organization became geographically distributed with almost 200 writers, a number of whom are in located in India. The result was multiple tool sets, no common design template, no common editing standards, and no common information model. Relying on these circumstances, writers had to develop information products suitable for seven kinds of help systems, PDF files, print publications, and HTML output. And the localization requirements were substantial, with some of the materials needing to be translated into more than 30 languages.

Symantec had to find more effective ways to work globally and deliver information to customers requesting it in multiple formats. The company needed a streamlined approach to developing and providing information. It seemed that the best way to address these challenges was to consider automating the information development process. This realization gave rise to seemingly endless decisions as the company investigated different tools for single sourcing. Teams worked collaboratively to perform content audits, develop information models, and reexamine tools, templates, and standards. Symantec identified complex reuse goals, and given the large amount of content being shared, it seemed logical to purchase a content management system (CMS). But the many questions and issues that were raised prompted intense deliberation and decision making that employed more than logic alone. The whole process of investigating automated reuse strategies tapped strongly held beliefs about the best ways to develop information products. The need to make decisions required strong leadership, a deep sense of trust, and collaborative teams with a willingness to shift technical writing paradigms.

This chapter uses the experiences of Symantec's decision-making process for purchasing a CMS as a primary example for how people can make decisions in virtual settings. However, those with other decision-making goals in various virtual collaborative writing settings would benefit from such understanding as well. Principles 1, 4, and 5 that ground this book have particular pertinence in this chapter. Without developing a culture of effective collaboration, making good decisions virtually is difficult to impossible. The right tools and models of collaboration also are necessary to accomplish the decision-making task. To that end, Principle 5's emphasis on creating structures by which collaborative writers can make decisions virtually is a crucial consideration.

BACKGROUND

By definition, the writing process is about decision making—deciding on a topic, why it is important, who might be interested in it, how it will be used, how it should be organized, and what words to choose. Writers make, unmake, and remake decisions. It is not uncommon that writers second guess their decisions. A whole new set of decisions arises after a piece is reviewed—how to address reviewer comments, what to do if they are in conflict, and how to combine far-flung feedback, as suggested in Chapter 16. In workplace settings, decision-making becomes formalized as writers consider what tools to use, what style guidelines to follow, and how to gather review comments. The magnitude of the decisions escalates at the enterprise level when organizations investigate options for single sourcing, including whether or not to employ advanced single sourcing technology, such as managing content in a CMS. And at the point of purchase and implementation, the number of decisions seems to spiral out of control.

When it comes to decision making and virtual collaborative writing in the workplace, a key question to ask concerns who should benefit from the decisions that are made. The hope would be that the audience—the reason for creating information products—ultimately would benefit from the decision-making process. With this goal in mind, how can writers working collaborative ensure that decisions are made with the best interest of the audience in mind? This question is so important because it is easy to make a whole host of decisions that primarily are about an organization—with little consideration as to how those decisions will impact the audience, customer, or end user. When collaboration entails decision making, it is not implausible to imagine the individuals being more concerned about their own opinions than about the very reason for their writings—to inform readers. If the decision making process actually can help collaborators make good decisions for both the organization and the audience, then that process is worth investigating. In the end, the decision-making process should support the overall purpose for the writing, the circumstances for delivering it, and the concerns of people for whom it is written.

Virtual collaborative teams need to have a good decision-making process because so many decisions that must be made affect every person on the team, as described in Chapter 10's opening vignette. Surprisingly, it is not unusual for virtual teams to lack basic processes for functioning effectively. In discussing one study undertaken by her firm of 48 virtual teams across industries, DeRosa (2008) noted that they found that many of the teams struggled with basic issues such as not having clear roles and responsibilities or not having a shared process for decision making (pp. 6-7). A wrong decision can be disastrous for a team and thus for the information products that readers depend upon to be clear and accurate. Preventing poor decision making is essential for the overall success of virtual teams.

Given this array of decision making opportunities, writers and writing organizations not only need to know how to make decisions but also how to make good decisions that benefit the team, the organization, and the audience. Virtual collaborative writing teams face a number of challenges from logistics to cultural differences to the decision making process itself. The aim of this chapter is to examine how virtual collaborative writing teams can move more effectively through decision making, drawing on the right decision-making model for a particular decision, understanding the types of decisions that impact virtual collaborative writing teams, knowing how to factor in decision-making authority, deciding how to decide, doing the groundwork, sharing the information, evaluating the information and making the decision, capturing the decision in a place available to all, and following up on decisions and resulting actions.

CHALLENGES THAT AFFECT DECISION MAKING

Virtual collaborative writing teams face a number of challenges when making decisions, some of which involve logistics, cultural differences, conflict, process maturity, and problems specific to the decision-making process itself that are magnified by the virtual nature of the team.

Logistics

Logistical challenges often are the most obvious ones attended to by teams and include:

- **Geographic distribution:** Having virtual team members located in different countries, for example
- **Time zone differences:** A side effect of geographic distribution, often stressful to all involved because, especially for synchronous decision making, someone is going to be inconvenienced
- **Travel restrictions:** Being limited from even periodic face-to-face meetings to facilitate decision making

However, while important to address because of the stress they add to individuals and teams, logistical challenges often are the easiest to identify and correct. At Symantec, distributed writing teams have experienced difficulties related to basic logistical tasks, such as setting up conference calls when all participants could attend. Team members have had to participate during meal times, in the middle of their night, or the early hours of their morning. Difficulty coordinating team schedules can strain decision making if all the members cannot be present. In addition, teams with limited experience working virtually may find it hard to make decisions virtually. In this case, leaders should increase the opportunity to simulate face-to-face interactions through technology that uses the synchronous modality, as described in Chapter 1. Even so, it is important to note that logistical challenges may not always be the source of true difficulty when collaborative writing teams are trying to make decisions virtually.

Cultural Differences

Cultural differences, which may be linked to the logistical challenge of geography, also can contribute to decision-making difficulties. Geographic "distance," however, can occur even when individuals are relatively close to one another; this outcome may be related to the following factors:

- Power (authority) distance dimension
- Short- and long-term orientation
- Uncertainty avoidance
- Individualism and collectivism (Hofstede, 2005, p. 23)

Regarding the power distance dimension, two types of social structures emerge based on size. In smaller power-distance societies, hierarchies are less formal and superiors and subordinates have more or less equal status. Accordingly, subordinates expect to be consulted before decisions are made. In contrast, in larger power-distance societies, no such consultation or negotiation is expected. At Symantec, the concept of power became evident several times in multicultural teams. In one case, when discussing simple style issues (the use of bold for a particular type of content), some people on the team wanted an authority to make the decision, while others were outraged at the suggestion that a decision would be made without their full input and participation. The facilitators were caught in the middle of dynamics related to the power distance dimension. Chapter 1 further considers issues of governance and power.

The second item, short- and long-term orientation, pertains to the amount of time expected for a decision to be made. Teams that have a very short-term orientation tend to set goals and make decisions relatively quickly based on the bottom line and quarterly results. This style is common in the U.S. for individuals focused on quick results. Teams with a long-term orientation expect to have time and resources when making decisions—even at the expense of immediate returns. This decision-making style is focused on future investments. Cross-cultural teams need to be aware of the style difference when implementing structured authoring and CMS solutions. Even though moving to a structured writing environment is a long-term project, companies based in the U.S. typically expect to track progress and make decisions from quarter to quarter. It can be difficult to meet this expectation during the initial implementation, especially when working with team members who are accustomed to a more methodical style.

In terms of avoiding uncertainty, cultures that are uncomfortable with ambiguity may have a high level of uncertainty avoidance. Individuals with this cultural orientation are less optimistic about their ability to influence decisions. In contrast, cultures that are comfortable with ambiguity have low levels of uncertainty avoidance. Individuals with this cultural bent want to be involved in the details around decisions and will argue aggressively as necessary. Huijser (2006) suggested that while societies with high levels of uncertainty avoidance do take longer to analyze input and make decisions, it is not due to a fear of uncertainty, but due to not wanting to make mistakes from hasty short-sighted decisions. When considering these perspectives, team managers would benefit from simultaneously considering both uncertainty avoidance and long or short-term orientation.

The last item regarding individualism and collectivism concerns the relationship between an individual and a group. In an individualistic culture, such as the U.S., the interests of the individual tend to take precedence over those of the group. For this reason, individuals are comfortable working on their own and like having their names attached to their task. Such a preference may make the need to give up ownership in a team more difficult. In collectivist cultures, such as China, the group prevails over the individual. As a result, individuals do not mind working in a group or being anonymous. Another difference is the need in an individualistic culture for details and contracts, both of which are assumed in a collectivist culture.

These types of differences matter when working in a topic-based writing environment given that the sense of ownership changes dramatically, as described elsewhere in Chapters 1, 10, 12, 14, and 18. This sense of ownership around decision making can be a real challenge for those in individualist cultures accustomed to being the sole owner of a book. A structured content environment puts the group goals above those of the individual and writers no longer own their work as they did in the past. The magnitude of this change requires leaders who will promote change, defining new roles for writers, and creating a culture of collaboration. Just as important, however, is the need to keep in mind the audience for whom the decision is being made. With regard to the fourth issue of individualism and collectivism, the team may not be able to help its cultural background as individual people with preferences for independent action or collective action. But they can be guided to focus on whether the information product's reader will benefit most from individually written books, for example, or single-sourced material. When the audience is drawn explicitly into the discussion, the decision-making process is contextualized to the writing product as well as the process.

Conflict

Conflict on any team can be a barrier to effective decision making, of course, but in virtual teams, conflict must be managed more carefully to avoid destroying team-member trust—essential to a successful virtual collaborative writing team. When people do not have opportunities to develop relationships in face-to-face settings, the challenges of settling conflicts can seem insurmountable even when they are not. Issues related to conflict and trust are discussed more fully in Chapters 4, 5, and 7.

Process Maturity

Knowledge of the organization's process maturity—what work patterns are in place that are indicative of a particular stage of development—is important to consider when making decisions related to any kind of virtual collaborative writing decision. In Symantec's case, this knowledge was pertinent to moving into single sourcing and content management. Hackos (2007) described five levels that characterize an organization's process maturity:

- **Level 1.** Ad hoc: lacking structured process
- **Level 2.** Rudimentary: early stages of implementing structured process
- **Level 3.** Organized and repeatable: established process structure
- **Level 4.** Managed and sustainable: structured processes are apparent in upper levels of the organization
- **Level 5.** Optimizing: structure processes entails innovation (pp. 35-37)

Deciding to implement a systematic approach to managing content in a CMS requires a minimum of a Level 2 organization because some semblance of organizational structure is necessary to consider the structuring of the writing process. At Level 1, the organization or team is beginning to implement standard processes and models; even so, strong leadership is needed to ensure that the organization continues to advance and will not be tempted to slide into an ad-hoc way of doing things again. A Level 3 organization is better suited to making more effective decision about whether and when to formalize the information architecture and whether, for example, to implement a CMS. Structure is extremely important in an organization committed to an automated information development process. Collaborative teams must agree not only upon the standards used to structure information products, as described in Chapter 13, but also how to formalize social practices—group dynamics and coordination—within teams by creating highly structured processes that support productive team interactions, as described in Chapter 10.

Problems with the Decision-Making Process

Virtual teams need a clearly defined decision-making process even more so than do face-to-face teams. This need stems from the challenges of communicating virtually. When negotiation is necessary in virtual settings, as discussed in Chapter 5, trust must exist and that trust is developed differently when done virtually. Symptoms of an ineffective decision-making process include multiple decision points in the process, no or poor decisions being made, a lack of support for decisions made, and a lack of follow-up and action. The process scripts that are described in Chapters 1 and 10 may prove a helpful beginning point for correcting these symptoms or avoiding them before they arise.

Sometimes, decision-making problems result from incomplete knowledge, which may be caused by a failure to seek information—such as feedback from users that would illuminate the concerns that need to be addressed in the decision. Chapter 17 addresses how get the feedback from customers in ways that will make them collaborators in the product development process. Problems also can be caused by a failure to share information. One of the most valuable lessons learned at Symantec, for example, was that teams should not jump into problem solving or decision making too soon, but rather to ask more questions first to learn what information might be missing.

Often, requests from virtual teams relative to a major decision seem simple on the surface. For example, a team might ask whether it can roll back the content to a previous version, but after asking questions of the team, managers might learn that a "roll back" will not solve the real problem. In Symantec's case, the underlying issue pointed to a communication problem about the changed content. These experiences of uncovering more information are an important dimension of decision making as described by Qiu, Chui, and Helander (2004): "The knowledge necessary for decision making is attained with different degrees of confidence at different stages of decision making, and sometimes, incomplete knowledge is acquired... knowledge is shared with inadequate understanding. Decisions are made under the influence of many uncertain factors" (p. 556). Whenever possible, uncertainty should be eliminated by seeking more information prior to making the decision.

When faced with decisions, collaborative writing teams can strengthen the decision-making process by identifying the degrees of knowledge they have or do not have by asking questions. Qui, Chui, and Helander (2004) recommended probing uncertainty using a technique that echoes the journalistic questions: "know-what," "know-who," "know-why," and "know-how" (p. 558).

Table 1 illustrates how these terms can be used in practical ways regarding different aspects of a decision.

When virtual collaborative writing teams show signs of an ineffective decision-making process, they may need to engage in a questioning process, like the one described in Table 1, to help them fill in missing gaps. Ways to accomplish asking and answering these questions virtually include listserv discussions, team-based online surveys, questionnaires, synchronous meetings, and small-group synchronous or asynchronous breakouts; see the end of this chapter for a partial list of available tools. An important dimension of the questions they ask should be whether the proposed decision benefits their writing processes but also their readers.

Other Organizational Challenges

Other factors to consider regarding the decisions-making process in virtual collaborative writing teams include team lifespan and size.

While Levi (2007) claimed that virtual members may experience themselves as less committed to team decisions (p. 266), I would argue this experience might be truer for a temporary virtual team brought together for a specific purpose than for long-standing distributed teams. For example, it is not hard to imagine that a team brought together briefly to restructure content on an Agile development project might show a lack of commitment

to team decisions after resuming their "real" jobs. More permanent or primary tasks often take priority over temporary ones, as Chapter 7 indicates. However, cohesive geographically distributed teams that work together on a daily basis, such as a support group for distributed collaborative writers, cannot escape to other priorities or ignore key decisions related to primary organizational goals when those goals also affect their daily tasks.

Team size influences decision making as it does trust building (Chapter 5). Levi (2007) suggested that when issues are complex or too many people are involved in decision making, virtual team discussions may get so confusing that no issues get resolved (p. 266). Here again, strong role definition, team structure, and structured processes help with this problem, as described also in Chapters 5, 10, 12, and 13. Collaborative teams at Symantec experienced difficulties both with roles and structure. A strong team leader with good virtual facilitator skills is essential for keeping the group focused on the goal of the discussion and its decision-making charge. Whether the facilitator works with the team asynchronously or synchronously, working with too large a group can keep some team members from speaking out, and in that silence, it can allow one or two members too much opportunity to speak to the detriment of the group. Also, deciding who on the team is best suited to collaborate on an issue and arrive at a decision can improve team efficiency. For example, opening up a style issue to discussion

Table 1. Points to consider when uncertainty exists

Decision point	Description
Know-what	When more information is needed, find out on what additional knowledge will provide clarity about a decision: *What* is the goal? *What* is the problem? *What* is already known? *What* still needs to be known?
Know-who	When others have the information needed to make a decision, ask: *Who* has the information that the team needs? *Who* has what kinds of information? *Who* is available to provide needed information?
Know-why:	When it is unclear why a problem occurred and what decision could be made to address it, ask: *Why* did the problem occurred in the first place? *Why* do some approaches to resolving it have more merit than others?
Know-how:	When more information can help provide insight into alternatives, ask: *How* does this information shed light on previous solutions that may have been benefitted from a different solution? *How* will the information help generate different decisions and new solutions? *How* will the information help teams choose from alternatives?

with all the writers in an open conference call is much less effective than handing the topic over to a smaller representative workgroup that can make a decision and report back to the larger team.

Types of Decisions Virtual Writing Teams Face

Understanding the challenges that affect the virtual team decision-making process is central to helping writers arrive at a number of decisions that pertain, for example, to organizations committed to single sourcing and topic-based writing. I have separated these decisions into two groups,

technical and managerial. After adjusting for their own contexts, these categories can assist virtual writing teams in other decision-making settings.

Technical

Technical decisions about whether to purchase and use a CMC include decisions about the content being created, how the content is formatted and delivered, what tools are used to create the content, and what standards must be followed in creating the content. Symantec faced a number of these specific technical decisions. It is interesting to note that as the company has moved more to a

Table 2. Technical categories for making decisions

Category	Description
Content and architecture	• Who the audiences are (usually by role and goal) for various pieces of content • How will they be affected both positively and negatively by the decision to be made?
	• What content needs to be developed? o This question considers the architecture design for all the content a customer receives o The individual parts must be coherent and add up to a meaningful, usable whole, which may require cross-functional coordination to accommodate content convergence in online media such as forums, portals, and so on
	• Whether reuse is indeed a goal and at what level: library, deliverable, section or cluster, topic, element (paragraph, table, graphic), segment, and term
	• How structured elements must be structured, written, and reused (Rockley, 2003, p. 365)
	• How the source content must be organized (whether distinct from that of the final deliverable or not, for example)
	• Quality criteria for the content
	• Other requirements for the content, such as machine-translation readiness
Format	• What deliverables audiences need
	• How the deliverables should look
	• What is known about what is not known—how content may be used in ways that cannot be anticipated, thus informing decisions about formatting
Models and standards	• Content models task flow models
	• Style and content-development guidelines
	• DTD, in the case of XML
Tools	• What planning and design tools to use (such as documentation plans, user-topic matrices, Task Modeler, and so on) and how
	• What collaboration tools to use (such as wikis and group decision-making tools) and how
	• What content-management tools to use and how
	• What authoring tools to use and how
	• What language quality checker tools to use and how
	• What delivery tools to use and how

structured writing methodology and environment, decisions such as style and formatting have become much less important—certainly when compared to the former, more traditional writing process. The lists provided in Tables 2 and 3 represent a sample of the types of decisions collaborative teams need to consider.

Managerial

Managerial decisions are not necessarily made by the manager. Instead, they concern how projects and people are managed and what overall processes are needed to ensure efficiency across virtual collaborative writing teams. Some managerial decisions pertain to process and workflow decisions, best practices, who develops what content,

how the team works together (including how they make decisions as a virtual team), how the project is managed, and so on. Table 3 provides only a sample of managerial types of decisions relative to the primary example of acquiring a CMS, but these decision types can become the basis for an expanded list pertinent to the reader's organizational context.

Decision-Making Models

When making technical or managerial decisions, virtual collaborative writing teams benefit from understanding standard decision-making models and applying the right approach to the right situation. The primary decision-making models are described in Table 4.

Table 3. Managerial categories for making decisions

Category	Description
Business rules for content and strategy	• Smallest unit of reuse is the section • Content owners keep content locked • Goal is reuse, not creativity • Structure is enforced by DTD (DocBook or DITA), scripts, and architects • Overall setup of CMS for content storage • Stability of choice is important for high-level content containers • As general as possible
Processes and best practices	• Analysis • Design • Creation • Quality • Delivery • Archiving
Communication	• Team work practices • Team agreements • Decision making • Content sharing • Meeting protocol
Project management	• Goals • Scope • Roles and responsibilities (including who should develop what content) • Estimates and schedules • Priorities • Pilots—criteria, what to start with
Human resources	• Hiring (agreeing on criteria and who to hire based on criteria) • What skills to keep in-house, what to outsource, what to centralize, what to push out to decentralized teams, and how the source content must be organized (whether distinct from that of the final deliverable or not, for example)

Table 4. Primary decision-making models

Model type	Description
Majority or Most vote	• Everyone votes for one option and whichever option gets the most votes, wins o Used for simple issues that do not require a great deal of buy-in o Not a good option for more complex issues or issues that require buy-in and commitment
Multi-voting	• Multi-voting gives everyone multiple votes to use (often one vote for every person voting plus one) o Can assign one or more votes to as many options as they want, resulting in a clear sense of priority o More effective than a straight majority vote o For example, when determining agenda items for key annual three day face-to-face meetings, may use multi-voting to prioritize and narrow a list of possible agenda items
Unanimous vote	• Unanimous vote requires that everyone agrees on the final vote
Consensus	• Reaching consensus is one of the most important decision-making skills o Does not mean reaching unanimous agreement o Team members agree to support the decision that has been made, even if they think it was not the best possible decision (Rockley, 2003, p. 372)
Leader/authority decides	• Some decisions do not need much discussion and can be handled quickly and effectively by the manager o For example, within a directly managed permanent team as opposed to a team of peers that has come together for a particular purpose
Minority/small group decides	• With this option, a decision is handed off to a small workgroup (ideally fewer than eight people) o Investigate the options and make a recommendation o May be the final decision or a strong recommendation for a leader to make the final decision o For example, for a style change that is likely to affect a number of groups, representatives from those groups can investigate and agree on a solution o However, for a large purchasing decision (such as for a language quality checker, as described in Chapter 15) workgroup can make recommendation, but the leader with purchasing authority makes final decision

Different Types of Decisions Use Different Models

As suggested in the minority and small group decision-making model, it is possible to combine and mix models. No team is going to use the same decision model for every decision, nor should they. Part of making effective decisions is agreeing on what model or combination of models to use and in what circumstances. Some of the decision making that was formerly reserved for management can move to the writing team in a virtual collaborative setting. In fact, Salomon Brothers found that when they moved decisions from management to the team, "involving all team members in the decision-making process turned up problems that an individual manager might have overlooked" (Fisher, 1998), which suggests that including teams in any setting might be good for decision making. It is even more important to do so in a virtual setting because managers cannot see all of

the facets of the work and the challenges that are affecting the team when they are geographically distributed. The key to success is to be clear about what are the expectations of the team so that writers can understand their roles in the decision-making process. For example, asking writers to provide input about technology decisions—like purchasing a CMS—can yield useful information, but the team needs to realize that even the manager must get approval to make the purchase.

One question that arises is how to decide what decisions to turn over to the virtual collaborative writing team and when. The Tannenbaum and Schmidt Continuum is a simple model that shows the relationship between the level of freedom that a manager chooses to give to a team, and the level of authority used by the manager (Martin, 2005). By illustrating how the manager's role can change from *telling, selling, consulting*, or *joining* with the team, this continuum demonstrated that managers can hold appropriate amounts of control in any of these levels of authority sharing, which means that the team also can have an appropriate level of authority (p. 352-353). As a result, it can be a useful tool to determine what parts of the writing process should be more manager-directed and what others should be less so. The model gives the manager a range of possibilities and criteria to evaluate which level best suits the situation and the team. However, even when involving their teams, managers need to take responsibility for the ultimate decisions made, as Chapman (1995) indicated: "Delegating freedom and decision-making responsibility to a team absolutely does not absolve the manager of accountability." Not surprisingly, as Chapter 1 discusses, most governance models do involve someone who has ultimate authority and responsibility for making decisions.

Research suggests that there are benefits to sharing the decision-making process with teams. According to Fisher (1998), the overall team also is involved in decisions that would have been limited in the past to team members with special areas of expertise. For example, in the past at Symantec, standardized terminology was the domain of a small centralized group, but as groups are more geographically distributed and as resources become rarer, some standardized terminology responsibilities have been pushed out to distributed teams who have come together as a virtual workgroup with the central group providing support to them. This work, in turn, has increased the buy-in across the company from teams to use standardized terminology. Their increased role in making decisions has created a stronger adherence to the decisions overall. In describing similar experiences from a course in business school in which virtual teams made decentralized decisions, Saarinen (2008) said that

Van der Vegt [et al.] note that when representatives from all relevant areas of expertise are brought together, team decisions and actions are more likely to encompass a full range of perspectives and issues that may affect the success of a col-

lective venture. Teams combine the expertise and talent of many people, and can thus exceed the limits of personal performance. (p. 327)

Understanding the available decision models, the context of the teams (team leaders and team members), and the situations in which the models are being applied help to ensure that the appropriate models are being used toward effective decision-making.

THE PROCESS OF MAKING COLLABORATIVE WRITING DECISIONS VIRTUALLY

The overall decision-making process follows eight generally accepted best-practice steps that apply to all kinds of teams and are used as a basis by a number of group decision support systems:

1. Know what authority you have
2. Decide how to decide
3. Use the right decision-making model for a particular decision
4. Do the groundwork
5. Share information (and find the information that has not been shared)
6. Evaluate information and make the decision
7. Capture decision in a place available to all
8. Follow up on decisions and resulting actions

By following these eight steps, the potential rises for effective decision making in terms of good decisions that are fully supported and successfully carried out. In

Step 1: Know What Authority You Have

Before making any decisions about whether and how to involve the virtual team in making decisions, be sure the team understands what authority it has. Can the team make purchasing decisions?

Or just recommendations? Does the team have the authority to make company-wide terminology decisions? Or tools usage decisions? Or content model decisions that affect other teams? Much time can be wasted deliberating decisions that the team does not have the authority to make, which results in frustration and a lack of trust in the team as well as in the leadership.

Even when a team does not have the authority to make a particular decision, it does not mean that the team cannot express its informed opinion or otherwise affect the decision. The team can be part of the information sharing process and they can work with the person or team that does have the authority to make the decision.

Step 2: Decide How to Decide

For a particular situation, a virtual writing team must decide what decision-making model they are going to apply. In my opinion, the best way to make that decision is to come to consensus about which model to use. Recall that consensus does not imply unanimity and that it involves a buy-in or team agreement to abide by the decision. Therefore, if the process is fair, people are likely to accept a decision even if they would have made a different decision alone. Merry (2002) listed types of issues that the team needs to agree upon:

- Who decides who should be involved?
- Who makes the various decisions?
- When should we ask everyone; when should we ask just a small group?
- How do we account for cultural values in our decision-making procedure?
- Who enforces and sets boundaries for decisions?
- What methods of decision making will be employed?
- What form of communication will be used during the decision making process?

Once these decisions about decisions are made, they must be documented and stored in an accessible place so that people can retrieve them to remind themselves of their decisions and rationale so they do not have to be reconstructing them. Colocated teams are challenged to remember why and how decisions were made. Because they cannot turn to a colleague face-to-face or go to a local file drawer for reminders, virtual teams have an even greater challenge to document and share those group decisions to maintain both efficiency and trust. Virtual centralized tools can help in these situations, as discussed at the end of this chapter.

Example 1 is a decision-making agreement developed by individuals with a stake in technical writing standards at a company where I worked formerly. As will become apparent, that company was not yet in a structured-writing environment. This example illustrates the decision-making principles addressed in Steps 1, 2, and 3.

Example 1: Standards for decision-making This is the decision-making code for the Standards group (a virtual team of volunteer stakeholders). Our objective in writing this code is two-fold:

- *To set down our decision-making process for all the different kinds of work that we do together, with a sensitivity to the type and importance of the decision*
- *To codify how standards decisions and changes are disseminated to the entire Tech Pubs community*

We stand to gain clarity about how decisions are to be made and, thus, increased efficiency and buy-in when making them. And we minimize the amount of hair torn out.

The code consists of the following sections:

- *Decision-making matrix*
- *Decision categories*
- *Definitions of decision-making styles*
- *Our decision-making toolbox*

Table 5. Matrix

	Template changes (FM and WWP)	Workflow, procedural changes	Writer standards, style guide	Tools issues (how to use the templates and tools)
Unilateral	Necessary fixes (owned by tools person)	Technical fixes (owned by tools person)		Necessary changes (owned by tools person)
Consultative	Styles & formats (owned by tools person)	Interdepartmental changes (owned by central standards body)	Terminology issues (owned by editor)	Substantial changes (owned by central standards body)
Working Group	Developing boilerplate content; changing EDD structure		Style guide areas, like indexing or graphics usage	
Consensus	New templates; evaluating biannual update incidents	Intradepartmental changes (TechPubs-only procedures)		

- *How decisions are disseminated*
- *History of this code*

The matrix below (table 5) matches decision categories to decision-making styles. The categories are broken down further in the matrix rows. The categories (including an explanation of the specific styles chosen for it in the matrix) and styles are defined in detail beneath the matrix.

Decision Categories

Here are the categories of what the Standards Group has to make decisions about, with recommendations for decision-making styles. The definitions of the decision-making styles are at the end of this document.

Template Changes

Necessary template changes like bug fixes will unilaterally be done by the tools person. Style and format decisions will be Consultative, where the tools/templates person develops a recommendation with the help of other writers (ex. font sizing for headings). If a change has effects writers' work in a broad way, or is outside the tools/template person's expertise, a Working Group will develop and present a recommendation (ex. changing the look and feel of a particular help output).

For our biannual template updates, writers will log bugs and enhancement request incidents against the templates. The Standards group will use Consensus to sort the incident list into the above categories.

Workflow, Procedural Changes

For necessary technical fixes, such as updating our PDF-generation procedure, the tools person can make a unilateral decision.

For interdepartmental workflow changes, where writers are working with another department like Localization or Release Engineering, a Consultative process will be managed by the central standards body. The central standards body will report on progress to the Standards group to get feedback and direction (for example, how part numbers are disseminated).

For intradepartmental workflow changes having exclusively to do with writer procedures, Consensus decisions will be made by the group during Standards calls (for example, how to request a template change).

Writer Standards, Style Guide

Terminology standards, like deciding when to use "FTP" as opposed to "ftp," should be consultatively owned by Editorial. For broader style guide issues (and this would be most of the style guide), a Working Group method will be managed by Editorial (for example, guideline for when/when not to use a graphic in a topic; style guide issues).

Tools Issues

Some tools standards are keyed directly to the tools themselves—in this case a unilateral decision can be made (ex. updating Distiller job options files). Otherwise a Consultative method should be managed by the central standards body to develop broader tools usage guidelines, like the standard procedure for how to place a graphic in an FM document.

Definitions of the Decision-Making Styles

- **Unilateral:** One person makes the decision, acting alone. The assumption here is that the person empowered to make this decision has appropriate expertise.
- **Consultative:** One person makes the decision, after consulting with others. These "others" can be writers or people from other departments, chosen by the person empowered to make the decision for their expertise and help.
- **Working group:** A small group (2 to 5 people) with expertise on or interest in a specific issue is assembled to research and develop a recommendation. They present their recommendation to the Standards group for feedback toward ratification by a vote by the entire group. A revised recommendation can also be requested of the working group. Their recommendation is voted upon by the Standards group—majority rules.

- **Consensus:** The entire Standards group discusses an issue in detail, with each member getting a chance to air views and try to influence others. The decision is shaped and modified to reflect different member views. Members hold out until the team reaches a decision they can support, even if it wasn't their first choice. We discuss until we get something upon which 100% of the group can support.

Our Decision-Making Toolbox

- **Voting:** A vote is used to finalize a Working Group decision. A simple majority (more than 50%) carries a vote.
- **Multi-voting:** This is the same as voting, but each team member is allowed to vote for several ideas, prioritizing them by number of votes assigned to each.
- **Polling:** A poll is taken during a call or via e-mail to get a quick opinion on a single specific issue, such as feedback on an example PDF posted on InfoNet.
- **Survey:** A survey is used to gather specific information needed to make a decision.

How Decisions are Disseminated

When decisions and changes are made in the Standards call that affect all writers, a high-importance e-mail will be sent with "WRITER ALERT" in the subject line. Additionally, the change will be mentioned in a weekly e-mail as well as in relevant sections of our web site. Standards group attendees also have the responsibility to spread the word about decisions made in the calls to the other writers in their groups who were not in attendance.

History of this code: On 6 August the Standards group categorized the areas we have to make decisions on and discussed what styles were best for each category. Writers agreed that most categories had degrees of scope and importance that each required different decision-making styles. A draft code was compiled and posted on our web site. On 20 August we reviewed this code and proposed substantial changes. On 3 September we clarified a few minor points.

Step 3: Use the Right Decision-Making Model for a Particular Decision

As Example 1 regarding the description of models indicates, to be successful, teams need to understand the different decision-making models and when to use each one. Discussing the different models and when each is appropriate can "eliminate some of the confusion and frustration often associated with making team decisions over time and space" (Fisher, 2001, p. 82).

Step 4: Do the Groundwork

Not all decisions need large amounts of time invested in them. Take the necessary and appropriate time needed to investigate the question. Then prepare to discuss the decision to be made and the possible options.

Groundwork includes identifying possible options to be evaluated against the decision criteria. See Chapter 10 for information on creating a structured process that guides teams on how to split up tasks and collaborate across the team. Groundwork also includes understanding the decision to be made. Everyone should be working on making the same decision. That sounds very obvious, but without absolute clarity on a virtual writing team, individuals or subgroups actually can be working on solving different problems, and they may not be aware that they are looking at different issues until a much time has been wasted.

For example, one virtual writing team at Symantec was given a set of slides to review from the user-centered design team. They were to determine whether they could borrow some of the same concepts and visuals to communicate

similar types of information. Part of the team started working on making decisions around what sort of content was the same and could be communicated in the same way. Another part of the team started working on decisions around how to apply what the user-centered design team was doing to their writing. These were both useful and interesting sets of decisions, but they were two different sets of decisions, and the lack of a common understanding caused initial confusion over what was being requested. Their groundwork should have included clarifying the decision they were addressing.

Step 5: Share Information (And Find the Information That Has Not Been Shared)

Virtual teams have to rely on fact-based decision making, which means that information sharing is essential. For example, teams might make the mistake of making decisions based on what the competition is doing—assuming that the competition is doing what customers prefer—rather than finding out from customers themselves what content they need and how. Just because the competition does something a certain way does not mean that is what customers want. Chapter 17 provides useful guidance for getting feedback from customers and learning what they want so that writing teams can make decisions to the audience's benefit. This type of information sharing actually is enhanced in virtual settings because of the wide range of technologies that are available.

Additionally, it is easy to focus on information that has been shared and to ignore the information that has not been shared—out of sight, out of mind. However, finding information that has not been shared can be important, and "when decision-making groups fail to uncover key pieces of information, they make poorer-quality decisions" (Dennis, 1996, pp. 532-549; Stasser and Titus, 1985, pp. 81-93). At Symantec, for example, a writing team once made a set of decisions based on the assumption that all content would be delivered for all languages via the Web. However, the product manager had decided to ship certain languages on CD-ROM. The manager, unfortunately, did not inform the team. If the team had known this information, they would have made different decisions around their process and schedule for that release.

Information does not get shared within virtual teams for three key reasons (Gibson and Cohen, 2003, p. 224):

1. The person or group that has the information assumes that the others already know it or that they do not need to know it. In the virtual setting, the writers truly are out of sight of each other, so without a thoughtfully developed information flow, writers will be operating in the dark, as with the earlier CD-ROM example.

2. The person or group that has the information tried to share it, but there was some failure to transmit the information (human or technical), and no one realized it. For example, a key piece of information about a new localization requirement or process went to an incorrect distribution list, missing the people who needed to know about it.

3. The person or group receiving the information does not recognize it as new information or information that they need to know or evaluate. A number of times, for example, writers still in an unstructured writing environment have assumed they do not need to know about or have not paid attention to decisions relevant to the new structured writing environment until it was their turn to move to it. Then, long after decisions have been made, they raised new concerns that could not be addressed easily, if at all.

Collaborative writing teams need to put into place processes to address these three possible information-sharing failures. Such processes might include the following actions:

- Post shared information in a single central place (that is, a central workspace like a Wiki rather than e-mail, which can be lost). Hold team members accountable for accessing centrally located information. One way to do this is to provide them with a process script, as described in Chapters 1 and 10 or to employ affordances like a message alert when new information is placed in the shared virtual space.

- Develop and enforce conventions that signal levels of importance for team members. Because so much virtual work is accomplished by text rather than video or audio modes, it is critical to provide ways to indicate clearly the priority level of shared information.

- Ask the team:
  - Are you assuming that others know what you know?
  - Do you have information that you need to share with them?
  - Have individuals not responded to information you have shared?
  - Do you know whether they received it?
  - Do you know whether they recognize it as important?

Whether they work as distributed or colocated writing teams, it is important that collaborative teams overcome obstacles to sharing information if they are to work together effectively. Assumptions often are made that virtual teams have greater information-sharing challenges than colocated teams. However, Lam and Shaubroeck (2000) disputed this assumption and suggested that virtual teams using tools called group decision support systems (GDSSs)—such as GroupSystems Think-Tank™—actually are more likely to find and share previously unshared information. Vathanophas and Liang (2007) supported this finding:

Decision-making groups collectively have a larger information pool than any individual within the group. When groups employ group support systems (GSS) for discussion, task-relevant information that is common to all is exchanged more frequently than information that is unique to one person alone..... Results indicated that regular GSS groups tend to pool more common information and partially shared information as compared to unique information. When role-assigned, GSS groups pooled more unique information during discussion and retained more unique information after discussion than non-role-assigned groups.

One company, Rocketdyne, used collaborative technology to manage information sharing and, in fact, even prohibited face-to-face discussions among teams because oral discussions could not be captured and recorded and shared easily (Majchrzak, et al, 2004, pp. 131-137). If the information sharing conventions are put into place, the technology has been selected for ease of sharing, and the team has received adequate training for using tools and collaborative models appropriately (see Principle 4 in Chapter 1), then it is likely that information sharing problems can be alleviated for virtual writing teams.

Interestingly, the least effective team organization with regard to information sharing and decision making may be the partially co-located and partially distributed team. In at least one study, the "colocated group formed an in-group, excluding the isolates. But, surprisingly, the isolates also formed an in-group, mainly because the colocated people ignored them and they responded to each other" (Bos, et al., 2004, pp. 429-436). At Symantec, we have struggled with this problem a number of times and resorted to asking the colocated members to call in to conference calls or participate in meetings individually from their own desks or homes rather than from

a conference room as a group. In fact, as more of the colocated members started telecommuting over time, we found communication improved among the overall group and with that improved communication came improved collaboration.

Step 6: Evaluate Information and Make the Decision

The process of evaluating the information and actually making the decision involves a number of points, all of which are important for ensuring that team members collaborate effectively and make the best decision for the organization and audience alike. These points pertain to: understanding everyone's starting positions, determining decision criteria, defining the alternatives, evaluating the alternatives against the decision criteria and making the decision, and discussing the decision.

Understand Starting Positions

Ask everyone: "With the information I have today, what alternative would I choose today?" The quality of the answers is likely to be better when the information is provided anonymously. Follow this step with a discussion of the responses, which can expose the informal criteria (and initial bias) that people used to make their choice. This discussion can take place asynchronously via discussion boards or listservs, or it can occur synchronously by voice, video, shared desktops, and instant messaging (IM). The modality and media chosen may have an effect on the quality of the discussion. Much depends on how familiar the team is with the selected technologies for discussing these positions. See the end of this chapter and Robidoux and Hewett (2009) for more information about choosing the right tools for the communicative need).

Determine Decision Criteria

To make a good decision, the team must agree on what the critical criteria are for making the decision. Are the key drivers related to cost savings? Information architecture considerations? Customer information needs?

Also, consider that the criteria may change over time. In the past, translation technology meant that a key criterion for deciding whether to change a piece of content was whether it had been localized already. If it had been, it was too expensive to touch unless there was a clear need to correct the technical accuracy of the information. However, at Symantec, with the move to machine translation, we gained a small degree of freedom because the cost of translation decreased. We still did not want to go overboard changing existing content, but we redefined our criteria to allow for more flexibility, such as allowing changes when the content was going to be translated into additional languages.

One helpful way to determine what the criteria should be for a particular team or setting involves brainstorming. Using the appropriate technology and keeping in mind the decision to be made, brainstorm criteria as a team. Group criteria together and clarify why particular considerations are in each group. Come to consensus over three to five major criteria that can be described clearly and briefly. Consensus is entirely appropriate for this step; again, although unanimity is not required, everyone must understand and agree on the criteria to make a good decision about the real issue at hand.

Define Alternatives

Identify the alternatives from which team members will choose. Do not rush this step—even when the alternatives seem obvious. There may be details that need to be clarified that can change the choices or how they are measured against the decision criteria. For example, design decisions such as what deliverables will be developed and how they should be structured often are rushed

through. The pressure is always on to make a decision and move on to what seems like a more "productive" stage. However, by moving too quickly through the design process, writers tend to jump into the modular writing process and may need to revisit architecture decisions that should have been made earlier or that were made hastily and not in the best interest of the content and readers of the content. Revisiting those decisions later means more time and money lost to redesigning content after it has been written. Sometimes, those changes are necessary, but most often they could have been prevented.

This pattern is so common that it has become something of an archetype for technical writers: they insist that they do not have time to make thorough early architecture decisions, but they seem to make time later to correct things that could have been done correctly the first time through better planning.

According to Burkhardt (2009), Jill Nemiro, author of several books on virtual teams and collaboration, described in an interview how she guides her student teams, "who have a tendency to move too early to a modular approach" to work through the idea generation stage thoroughly first." The interviewer asked whether virtual teams are destined to be less creative than colocated teams because of pressures (from leaders or the members themselves) to "find quick solutions" rather than take the proper time to "define the problem, generate ideas for possible solutions, and adequately assess alternatives to determine the "best" solution. While Nemiro acknowledged the pressure that "moves us to quick solutions," she asserted an optimistic view that there are teams and companies that appreciate the need for working through the design process before jumping into solutions. As discussed earlier in this chapter, particularly given the coordination needed to make meetings happen fruitfully, in virtual settings it seems especially prudent to think and decide first before writing.

Evaluate Alternatives Against Criteria and Decide

Evaluate the alternatives against the criteria, discussing each in turn. Allowing people to change their votes through the discussion using the appropriate tools (listed at the end of this chapter) can be helpful in moving towards consensus, if the plan is to reach a consensus decision.

Discuss the Decision

After the decision has been made, discuss it to give team members a chance to identify any possible blocks to implementation. Identify both positive thoughts and areas of concern about the decision. Clarifying these might create a stronger adherence to the final decision within the group. The team will more than likely experience themselves as having been heard on all important points.

Step 7: Capture Decision in a Place Available to All

It is crucial to document decisions and make them available in a place accessible to the people who made the decision as well as people affected by the decision. At the time, the decision may seem obvious and self-explanatory. Or the team may have it documented in individual e-mails. However, questions may arise later, and it can waste everyone's time to have to revisit the decision because no one could remember it or the reasons behind it. It is easy to do this research with more trivial decisions, such as many style decisions—but time spent resolving those so-called trivial issues repeatedly adds up and increases everyone's frustration, not to mention affecting a team's sense of trust. Perhaps of greatest importance, however, there always is change in any organization and even stable or long-standing teams can have turnover or attrition. By placing the decision documents in a centrally located online space, the organization's

historical memory is preserved for others who will not know the events and thoughtful discussion surrounding critical decisions.

Step 8: Follow up on Decisions and Resulting Actions

One of the worst things that can happen following the making of a decision is to not act on it or to fail to follow up. That failure will frustrate the people who needed the decision to be made and will demoralize the people who were involved in making it. When a decision is made, identify the follow-up and action items needed immediately and turn those into an action plan that is reviewed regularly until the items have been completed successfully. When and where necessary, reconsider the action plans to make adjustments to the decisions, always remembering to record and post any changes made, as discussed in Step 7.

Solutions and Recommendations

Based on the available research as well as experience, several actions can help address the challenges of decision-making on virtual teams:

- Address logistics, but not at expense of other bigger issues. Make sure people are treated fairly so that no one becomes resentful, burned out, or feels less than a part of the team.
- Be aware of cultural differences and discuss explicitly why writing decisions on the virtual team are being made in a particular way so that people understand why things may be handled differently than they are accustomed. People are more adaptable when they understand the reasons for an action.
- Build trust within the virtual writing team, described in Chapter 5. Be aware of and manage conflicts to protect that trust.

- Continue building process maturity to help virtual writing teams make better quality writing decisions.
- Establish a clearly defined decision-making process for the virtual writing team. Provide useful tools for the team. Then, trust the team to make good decisions.
- Carry out decisions using action plans. Review regularly the plans to see whether they are being addressed and whether they require any adjustments.

Establishing a clearly defined decision-making process is a multi-dimensional effort, including:

- The process itself
- Roles
- Tools, which are discussed in the next section

The Decision-Making Process

Several steps in the decision-making process itself lead to better decisions, including:

- Have different people or groups initiate and approve the decision to make sure discussions are complete and to avoid a non-collaborative, "silo mindset" that focuses on the individual alone (for example, have the requestor bring the issue—a change to the DTD, for example—to the group that will review and make the decision for discussion to make sure all relevant concerns are discussed)
- Clarify who is responsible for implementation and involve that person in the decision-making process (the owner of the DTD, for example, who has both the technical expertise and experience to contribute significantly)
- Encourage participation based on individuals' skills or experiences rather than just group membership or formal role

- Rely on transparent approval criteria for the decision so everyone understands when and how a decision will be made
- Discuss the decision as part of the bigger portfolio of decisions (for example, often decisions within the writing team affect colleagues in localization; decisions should be made with them in mind)

In short, for strategic decisions in particular, "ensure that participants in the discussion about any decisions are included on the basis of skills and experience, that decision criteria are transparent, and that the decision is discussed in relation to the organization's other strategic decisions" (Garbuio, 2009).

Are Face-to-Face Meetings Necessary?

Pauleen (2004) claimed that "leadership challenges are magnified in a virtual environment" and recommended required face-to-face meetings. However, while face-to-face meetings can be very important and productive, in today's economy they are not a reality for many organizations—particularly those with geographically distributed writers. Majchrzak, et al. (2004) countered that claim and provided several examples of successful teams that have never met face-to-face.

In fact, I have at least one person on my team who has worked for me for several years whom I have never met face-to-face. However, we have used communication technologies from phone to IM to communicate almost daily and have established a trusting relationship. We make a point of sharing information with each other so we can better support each other in doing our jobs. Another team member and I had not seen each other for over two years and recently attended a conference together—again, because of almost daily communication over a number of channels, we did not feel like strangers. We jumped right into our work in person as if we were simply using another communication option.

Face-to-face meetings are a "bonus" in today's world—work can be accomplished without them, if and whenever necessary.

Tools to Support Virtual Decision-Making

A good decision-making process is essential to successful decision-making by virtual collaborative writing teams. However, tools can help, too. I would recommend establishing the process before introducing tools, though. The temptation is strong to expect the tool to solve all problems magically.

Several types of tools can be useful in helping a virtual writing team make better decisions:

- Tools to support relationship building and informal communication, such as social networking technologies and IM
- Tools to support information sharing, such as wikis, GoogleDocs, and Microsoft™ SharePoint®
- Tools to support decision making, such as decision matrices and flowcharts, and group decision support systems such as GroupSystems ThinkTank™

These tools are particularly helpful because they increase a sense of social presence (see Chapter 2), which provides a sense of being present to the one with whom one is communicating. Generally, synchronous tools provide a higher degree of social presence than asynchronous ones (Robidoux and Hewett, 2009). According to Nemiro (2009), "Using communication methods with high levels of social presence" is important to build connections. As I mentioned earlier, I have a team member who has worked for me for several years whom I have never met. But we communicate regularly and casually via IM, e-mail, and phone, so I know he has a penchant for *The Beatles*, plays polka music, commutes on a bike when weather allows, bakes bread, and has eclectic reading interests. Those details may not help us specifically when we work together to

make decisions, but certainly the relationship we have established has helped us to work together more effectively when we need to make decisions.

A number of simple online decision-making tools are available. More complex GDSSs are more appropriate for more complex decision making. Overall results of studies "suggest that the use of a GDSS improves decision quality, depth of analysis, (and) equality of participation" (Fjermestad, 2004). Technology is advancing quickly in this area. An online search for decision tools and group decision support systems will yield the latest available tools.

One thing to note when choosing a system is whether the system will support text-only, audio, or video. One study suggested that: "While the results of the study found no significant difference between the quality of the decisions for teams using text-only versus audio-only communication, the addition of video to audio-only communication resulted in a significant improvement in the quality of teams' strategic decisions" (Baker, 2003, pp. 79-93).

FUTURE RESEARCH DIRECTIONS

Some of the research consulted for this chapter seems to assume that a virtual collaborative team is a cross-functional team that comes together for a finite period of time to address a particular issue. It would be interesting to see more research on the contemporary reality of globally distributed virtual teams working together in place of a traditional colocated team (see Chapter 2 for a discussion of such teams). For example, in the past, we had writing teams that were within themselves colocated at various sites and representatives would participate in a virtual team to determine standards issues. However, now the teams themselves are distributed as well. There are, of course, advantages to long-standing virtual teams. For example, trust is easier to develop over time on a long-standing team than it is on a temporary team. Also, with a long-standing team, members are more likely to prioritize commitments than they are on a temporary team. Certainly, the dynamics of a long-standing team with more-or-less "permanent" relationships established differs from a temporary coalition, and those dynamics affect decision-making and the assumptions around decision-making. Nonetheless, the contemporary reality is that writers who collaborate virtually are likely to have at least one person on the team that they will not meet in a face-to-face setting. Such distributed teams merit further study in terms of decision-making processes.

CONCLUSION

As shown, some key differences in roles, processes, and tools for decision making for virtual writing teams exist. Clear roles and a good decision-making process is essential for better decisions and, overall, for more successful virtual teams. Once roles and the process have been established, tools are available that can help support and make the teams more effective.

Virtual teams are not a panacea—they will not magically fix other problems within the team. In fact, virtual teams can magnify problems such as a lack of leadership or trust, which will, of course, affect effective virtual decision making. However, it is important to remember that working with virtual collaborative teams is not all challenge and no benefit. Virtual writing teams offer both advantages and disadvantages when it comes to making decisions in particular. Some of the advantages include:

- Virtual team members may be more focused on facts and logic rather than hierarchy and status (Roch and Ayman, 2005), not to mention irrelevant social information such as gender, orientation, age, race, and so on.
- Virtual teams may be better at "weighing the quality of the opinions of individual

members and folding this information into a group decision" (Levi, 2007).
- Virtual teams may give rise to better critical thinking: "Dispersed, asynchronous teams generated more diverse perspectives, conducted more in-depth analyses, and produced higher quality decisions than face-to-face groups" (Ocker, et al 1996).
- Virtual teams, according to Majchrzak, et al. (2004), make constant decision making online possible, "whereas normal settings required postponing decision making until face-to-face meetings could occur."
- Virtual teams, compared to individuals, may be less likely to continue to support a failing project. According to Schmidt, et al. (2001), in evaluating the success of a project, virtual teams were most effective, followed by face-to-face teams, with individuals being least effective (pp. 575-600.).

The advantages of working with virtual writing teams in decision making and other processes are enhanced when they are developed with the principles that ground this book in mind. In particular, Principles 1, 4, and 5 speak to the needs for creating a culture of collaboration, choosing and learning to use the best tools and collaborative models for the job, and creating structures—such as those for virtually based decision-making processes. Additionally, any decision making in virtual or face-to-face settings should be accomplished with the audience in mind. Whenever possible, the reader or user's needs should guide the team's decisions.

REFERENCES

Baker, G. (2002). The effects of synchronous collaborative technologies on decision making: A study of virtual teams. *Information Resources Management Journal, 15*(4), 79–93.

Bos, S., et al. (2004). In-group/out-group effects in distributed teams: an experimental simulation. In Proceedings Computer Supported Cooperative Work, (pp. 429-436). doi: 10.1145/1031607.1031679

Burkhardt, V. (2009. Virtual teams. *Idea Connection*. Retrieved from http://www.ideaconnection.com/articles/00117-Virtual-Teams.html

Chapman, A. (1995). *Tannenbaum and Schmidt—Model of delegation and team development*. Retrieved from http://www.businessballs.com/tannenbaum.htm

Dennis, A. (1996). Information exchange and use in small group decision making. *Small Group Research*, *27*(4), 532–549. doi:10.1177/1046496496274003

DeRosa, D. (2008). *Collaborating from a distance: Success factors of top performing virtual teams*. OnPointConsulting. [white paper].

Fisher, K., & Fisher, M. D. (1998). *The distributed mind: Achieving high performance through the collective intelligence of knowledge work teams*. New York: AMACOM.

Fisher, K., & Fisher, M. D. (2001). *The distance manager: A hands-on guide to managing off-site employees and virtual teams*. New York: McGraw Hill.

Fjermestad, J. (2004). An analysis of communication mode in group support systems research. *Decision Support Systems*, *37*(2), 239–263.

Garbuio, M., et al. (2009). How companies make good decisions: McKinsey Global Survey Results. *McKinsey Quarterly*. Retrieved from https://www.mckinseyquarterly.com/Strategy/Strategic_Thinking/How_companies_make_good_decisions_McKinsey_Global_Survey_Results_2282

Gibson, C. B., & Cohen, S. G. (Eds.). (2003). *Virtual teams that work: Creating conditions for virtual team effectiveness*. San Francisco: Jossey-Bass.

Hackos, J. (2007). *Information development: Managing your documentation projects, portfolio, and people*. Indianapolis: Wiley.

Hofstede, G., & Hofstede, G. J. (2005). *Cultures and organizations: Software of the mind. Intercultural cooperation and its importance for survival*. New York: McGraw Hill.

Levi, D. (2007). *Group dynamics for teams*. Los Angeles: SAGE Publications.

Majchzak, A. (2004). Radical innovation without collocation: A case study at Boeing Rocketdyne. *Management Information Systems Quarterly*, *25*(2), 229–249.

Martin, J. (2004). *Organizational behavior and management* (3rd ed.). London: Thomson Learning.

Merry, P. (2002). *Effective online decision making*. Retrieved from www.genderdiversity.cgiar.org/EffectiveOnlineDecisionMakingMerry2.doc

Pauleen, D. J. (2004). An inductively derived model of leader-initiated relationship building with virtual team members. *Journal of Management Information Systems*, *20*(3).

Qiu, Y. F., Chui, Y. P., & Helander, M. G. (2004). Knowledge-based decision making in virtual team environment. In *Proceedings IEEE International Engineering Management Conference*, (Vol. 2, pp. 556-560). doi: 10.1109/IEMC.2004.1407440

Robidoux, C., & Hewett, B. L. (2009). Is there a write way to collaborate? *Intercom*, *56*(2), 4–9.

Roch, S., & Ayman, R. (2005). Group decision making and perceived decision support: The role of communication medium. *Group Dynamics*, *9*(1), 15–31. doi:10.1037/1089-2699.9.1.15

Rockley, A. (2003). *Managing enterprise content: A unified content strategy*. Berkley, CA: New Riders.

Saarinen, E., Lainema, T., & Lahteenmaki, S. (2008). Experiencing virtual team membership decentralized decision-making processes leading to meaningful learning. In *Proceedings of the Seventh IASTED International Conference Web-based Education*, Innsbruck, Austria, March 17-19, (pp. 328-332).

Schmidt, J. (2001). New product development decision-making effectiveness: Comparing individuals, face-to-face teams, and virtual teams. *Decision Sciences*, *32*(4), 575–600. doi:10.1111/j.1540-5915.2001.tb00973.x

Stasser, G., & Titus, W. (1985). Pooling of unshared information in group decision making: Biased information sampling during discussion. *Journal of Personality and Social Psychology*, *48*(6), 1467–1478. doi:10.1037/0022-3514.48.6.1467

Vathanophas, V., & Liang, S. (2007). Enhancing information sharing in group support systems (GSS). *Source Computers in Human Behavior*, *23*(3), 1675–1691. doi:10.1016/j.chb.2005.10.001

Weisbord, M. R. (1987). *Productive workplaces: Organizing and managing for dignity, meaning, and community*. San Francisco: Jossey-Bass.

Section 5
Developing Content Virtually

Chapter 12
Case Study:
Advancing New Authoring Strategies through Virtual Collaboration

Judith Kessler
Sybase, Inc., USA

ABSTRACT

The Technical Publications team at Sybase, Inc. maintains many thousands of pages of user documentation and online help topics for a diverse set of software products. Writing teams work in nine locations around the globe; a given project often involves writers from multiple locations. To achieve greater efficiency, increase opportunities for reuse, and improve user experience, the department is moving to the Darwin Information Typing Architecture (DITA) from a variety of source formats. Early adopters realized the need for more detailed information models for several types of content than required by the DITA standard. This chapter discusses why models are a critical component to successful collaborative writing, especially for topic-oriented content. It then describes the collaborative processes and tools by which Sybase® Technical Publications team members propose, evaluate, develop, test, and enforce new content models, challenges encountered, and key success factors.

INTRODUCTION

It is 4:00 PM in Paris, 3:00 PM in London, 10:00 AM in Boston and Waterloo, 8:00 AM in Denver, 7:00 AM in California, and 11:00 PM in Singapore. The Technical Publications (Tech Pubs) team for Sybase Proposed Product—information architect, authors, editor, build expert, and project lead—gather by phone and Web meeting to discuss how

DOI: 10.4018/978-1-60566-944-6.ch012

they will develop content for their new project. The Tech Pubs director has announced that, to facilitate content reuse and reduce localization costs, the team will be adopting the DITA architecture for this highly visible project. The information architect notes that the new product will share some of his existing several-thousand-page doc set; he also has found some redundant content and plans to apply minimalist principles and DITA's topic-oriented approach to make the information more effective. The authors in Singapore, California, and Colorado say they are pleased about learning the DITA standard, but they also are very nervous about the major learning curve it involves. The editor would like to see greater consistency among installation guides for different products. The build expert has learned that the product requires Eclipse output for CD, Web, and dynamic product help, two types of Microsoft® help, as well as PDF files. And, as if things were not exciting enough, the project lead warns everyone that the agile development process the company is adopting means they no longer have 12 or 18 months to document a major new release, but instead must deliver customer-ready content for a series of breathtakingly brief 8-week sprints through a long roadmap of new product features.

Sybase Tech Pubs develops user documentation for dozens of products. Our audience is technically sophisticated, including database, system, and security administrators, data and business process modelers, enterprise software developers, and mobile business application developers. Sybase technical writers must be comfortable not only with writing text and using authoring tools, but also with testing the software they document—creating databases, developing applications, performing complex installations. Most Sybase authors have more than 10 years of experience in the industry; many have far more than that.

The information products we deliver also are increasingly complex and diverse. They include not only traditional user guides and reference manuals, but an ever-increasing number of online help formats that require greater integration with the product user interface. We still produce PDF files for electronic and printed books, but we also provide HTML, several Microsoft® help formats, and Eclipse®-based information centers delivered in the product user interface (UI), on CD, on the public Website, and by download. (Eclipse® is an open-source integrated software development environment that also supports software and information deployment.) Some content is localized in as many as 10 languages, sometimes with simultaneous delivery of English and translated content.

In the past, writers have developed source content for these multiple delivered formats using a variety of common authoring tools. Much of our legacy content was developed in Structured FrameMaker®, which allows us to do single-sourcing for multichannel publishing (see Chapter 14), but does not readily support the level of content sharing across components and products that we are required now to provide. The ability to reuse content at varying levels of granularity has become critical not only to stretch our resources, but also because the products themselves share components at many levels. Some project teams approached this challenge by using the DocBook standard to manage document structure. But our director was convinced that the new DITA standard was gaining momentum among leaders in the technical writing industry. Driven by changing product requirements and the need for ever greater efficiency, Sybase Tech Pubs has adopted DITA as its standard, and is using a content management system (CMS) to develop and manage a growing repository of DITA content.

The transition to DITA and enterprise content management is a multi-year process, requiring writers to train for new roles as well as learn new tools and practice new approaches to developing information. It requires them to share responsibility for overall content to a degree that is new to most of them. Virtual collaborative writing Principles 1, 2, and 3—developing a culture of collaboration, promoting leadership, and establishing trust—are keys to success at this shared responsibility. Moreover, DITA itself requires a high degree of collaboration. To create deliverables, for example, writers must organize independent topics into maps. The maps define the order of topics and their relationship to each other for a particular set of user goals. At Sybase, while writers develop the topics, information architects design and develop the DITA maps, and a build architect develops the build manifest, which our build system uses to produce output deliverables from the content in maps and topics.

To accomplish all this while still serving the needs of our user audience requires extensive collaboration, both within and between project teams, and at all stages of a project from planning through writing, building, review, and release. Without sufficient collaboration, organizations may find that some of their content is redundant, or has gaps or inconsistencies; furthermore, their end users may have difficulty finding the information they need. Inconsistencies and redundancies can be a challenge to resolve within a single project; inconsistencies between project releases and among products pose an even greater challenge. Addressing these challenges is crucial to achieving our goal of creating reusable information components for a product set that is increasingly componentized.

A key enabler of our collaboration on DITA content is our CMS. DITA maps and topics, along with images and other resources needed to build output, are stored in a common repository. All aspects of content development and release take place in the CMS under the control of CMS-defined roles and workflow. Virtual collaboration is inherent to this environment. And it is a good thing, too: with writers, subject matter experts (SMEs), and managers located all over the world, face-to-face communication is a luxury that most teams no longer have.

In addition to the changes in structure from book chapters and sections to DITA maps and topics, writers must adjust to changing roles. While some roles are specific to our organization, as shown in Table 1, the need to distinguish author, architect, editor, and build- or tool-developer roles and expertise is an accepted best practice in the DITA user community (Fisher, 2008). Managers can begin the transition to topic-based documentation and content management by assigning most of these roles for all projects before conversion to DITA.

BACKGROUND

In discussing the mature information-development organization, Hackos (2007a) advocated for consistent structuring of content and for elevating information planning from the province of individual authors, to the realm of an enterprise activity. Information models, content plans, a topic-oriented architecture based on user scenarios with linking architected in a relationship table, and a metadata strategy are all aspects of this approach, along with management that encourages collaboration (see especially Chapters 2, 17, and 20 in Hackos, 2007a).

Industry best practices increasingly lean towards a structured approach to information development, both in the content and in the methodologies and tools used to produce it. Jones and Schell (2007), among others, have made the case for architected reuse and a model-driven architecture with standards, tools, processes, and collaboration as key components of a "content ecology." The Rockley Group (2005) has written about the distinction between implementing a standard—for example, DITA—and developing a complete content model. The model represents the design of each information product down to the element level, and it is an essential guide for authors in developing information collaboratively and defining how content can be reused.

Adopting these new strategies is a sea change for writers, their managers, and everyone else in a publications group. Bottitta, Idoura, and Pappas (2003) addressed the need to manage changes in teams, and to support teams in adjusting to evolving roles when moving to single sourcing. Indeed, Chapter 13 discusses the critical role of standardization for collaborative writing and content reuse, and considers the challenges it entails. In addition, Chapter 14 describes the role of a well defined information product architecture and content architecture in implementing a single-source strategy with reusable content objects.

Table 1. Roles for collaborative information development

Role	Definition	Collaboration
Information architect (IA)	Define overall architecture for a single product and its components. Know what goals and tasks users need to accomplish. Design and develop DITA maps and relationships. Apply reuse mechanisms.	Work with authors to ensure that the information architecture accurately reflects product features and user scenarios. Develop content plan in collaboration with authors, and with feedback from technical SMEs, editor, and other information architects. Develop documentation project plan in collaboration with the project coordinator. Work with (or serve as) DITA mentor to help other IAs and authors learn and apply best practices.
Author	Create minimalist content objects according to architecture. Act as SME on a component or feature set. Write task, concept, and reference topics according to plan outlined by information architect. Clean up converted legacy content. Create screen shots or other images in accordance with standards.	Work with information architect to validate architecture for assigned components. Work with editor to ensure topics are edited. Work with other authors as peer reviewer, and to maximize topic reusability. Work with engineers, support staff, and other SMEs to ensure accuracy. Work with DITA mentors to learn and apply best practices.
Editor	Edit topics in accordance with style guidelines. Set editorial and style policies.	Review documentation project and content plans to help information architects and authors follow best practices and provide high-level feedback on information organization.
Build architect (subclass of Information architect)	Oversee technical implementation of information architecture that represents the final information product (electronic bookshelf for Web and CD, and product UI; help files in various formats). Set up documentation builds. Create resource files required for builds.	Work with information architect to ensure build reflects all product requirements. Work with production staff on the build and release plan. Work proactively with doc tool experts to ensure that product delivery requirements can be met. Work within and across teams to help determine metadata strategy.
Project coordinator	Manage all aspects of project and time line. Coordinate project time lines and track deliverables.	Work with program management to coordinate project planning. Support the information architect in developing the documentation project plan.
Manager	Primary advocate for team, to ensure overall success of the Tech Pubs organization. Assign staff to projects, ensuring that all project roles are filled and tasks performed. Work with information architect and build architect to produce release deliverables. Knowledgeable on doc planning and estimating practices, DITA, and CMS to assist with educating and supporting staff.	Mentor team members in adapting to new ways of working, and ensuring they complete training. Manage expectations with development, quality assurance, product management, and program management, working as an equal partner and ensuring that documentation is represented in product development discussions. Review documentation plan, content plan, and schedules. Encourage collaboration within the team and across teams.

continued on the following page

Table 1. continued

Role	Definition	Collaboration
Production team	Generate final information products for delivery to Web, CD, and download. Manage documentation release process. Monitor customer feedback.	Review documentation plans for production impact. Work with the build architect to complete the build and release plan, and ensure output deliverables are ready for release. Serve as liaison with Tech Pubs management, program management, localization vendors, legal department, and media production department.
Tool and process developers	Develop and document tools, training, and best practices.	Work with project teams to ensure that tools, training, and guidelines are effective and meet project requirements. Support and mentor teams in applying best practices and resolving issues.

DEVELOPING INFORMATION MODELS FOR COLLABORATIVE WRITING

An information model describes the information types, content units, metadata, elements, and naming conventions that are required or recommended for a particular type of information (Hackos, 2007b). A model may be associated with a template, or it may consist entirely of guidelines and examples (see Chapter 13). Information models help address the architectural, textual, and reusability issues that arise when developing DITA content, ensuring consistency and quality, and boosting efficiency. But they cannot be developed without significant input from all project teams. In a global organization, with enterprise content stored and managed in a CMS, virtual collaboration is essential to developing useful information models.

This chapter uses a case study approach to describe the virtual collaborative process by which Sybase develops its information models through a group of enterprise-wide councils and applies them in information products.

In the book-oriented environment that preceded our move to topics, information is developed linearly. Books have chapters; chapters have sections. Some sections include semantic structures like procedures, tables, and reference pages, but the assumption is that chapters are delivered to users as a unit. If chapter 1 tells users how to connect to a server, the author knows she can link from the text to information for system administrators in chapter 10 on how to set up new users. Within chapter 10, she can include sections on how to create a new user, define privileges for users, and set up groups of users; each of those sections can refer to the others in text because the entire chapter remains intact as a unit. If another product must use one of those chapters for some other purpose, it may be copied and maintained separately. When organizations follow this practice, they find that it leads to duplicated effort and eventually to inconsistencies. While writers may be responsible for describing a feature across different documents, often, each author works on his or her own book and coordinates with other authors only at a very high level. There is little or no need to coordinate with authors working on similar content for other products. This book orientation is described in Chapters 1 and 14.

In this book-oriented legacy environment, all authors in the department follow the same style guide, but most document types have no standard content requirements. Each author is, for the most part, free to include and organize information as he or she sees fit, achieving quality by careful review of individual documents or document sets. Coordination with writers across products is rare.

For example, although all products have some sort of installation guide, in our pre-DITA environment there was no requirement for a standard order of information. To ensure maximum reusability in a collaborative environment, stricter standards are needed, as discussed in Chapter 13.

LIFE WITH DITA: REUSE AND COMPONENTIZATION DRIVE NEED FOR COLLABORATION AND INFORMATION MODELS

A few years ago, Sybase Tech Pubs recognized the need for sharing content among different products more effectively. This requirement was partially driven by product evolution that included ever-greater componentization of previously independent products, as well solution platforms that need customized versions of documentation sets. And like all organizations in the recent economic climate, we constantly look for ways to improve efficiency. Localization cost is another factor: we can achieve considerable savings by reusing localized information units at varying levels of granularity.

For all of these reasons, we chose DITA as the new standard for all content development. In DITA environments, authors develop topics that exist independently of a book structure, and can be reused in maps. But these topics do not exist in a vacuum. Each is developed with a particular product or component in mind. The challenge, then, is to develop content that is genuinely reusable—whether at the map, topic, or subtopic level—and still makes sense to the end user. For example, various questions arise when moving to a DITA environment:

- How should all projects document a particular type of information (for example, installation, troubleshooting, new features)?
- Is each audience for an information type identified? Do the content and structure serve audiences with different roles or experience levels?
- What metadata should be in each DITA topic, map, and image to support internal needs of finding content in the CMS and supporting production requirements (e.g., consistent title pages and conditional filtering), as well as facilitating end-user searches?
- Are topics ordered and linked according to end-user goals and scenarios? Is there any consistent linking pattern, or is it haphazard according to the information architect's or author's individual preferences?
- Is there a topic flow that follows the user's task flow through the product, component, or feature?
- Does it support users by providing a reliable path through similar types of information, between tasks and concepts, from high-level composite tasks to low-level component tasks?
- If a user employs multiple products—or multiple components of a single product— is there sufficient consistency that users can readily find the information they want?
- Are topics named or searchable according to the way users conceive of the task or concept rather than by product feature or user interface names?
- How much conceptual or reference detail is allowed in a task topic before it must be split off into a separate concept or reference topic?
- Does conceptual material support users in performing the task effectively, or does it merely get in the way?

When a product with multiple information components is developed by multiple authors in various locations across a dozen time zones, or when there is an opportunity for different products to share reusable information, clearly the information developers—authors, information architects, even editors—must collaborate on answers to these questions. Some of that collaboration occurs within project teams, as members grapple with project-specific issues. But some of that collaboration must occur in the broader organization, using a variety of virtual collaboration tools and methods appropriate to the problem, the participants, the level of urgency, and the information and resources available.

In the DITA environment, we still have a style guide. We also provide extensive instructions and training to assist authors, editors, and information architects in developing content using the new tools, in following the DITA standard, and in applying a minimalist approach to writing, in which information is focused on user goals and experience rather than product features, learning by doing more than by reading, and error recovery (Hackos, 2004). But these guidelines, while critical, are not enough to ensure a consistent approach to information development. And they are not always the most efficient way for organizations to support writers being asked each year to do more with less—fewer writers and editors, more content to deliver, new help formats, and shorter release cycles.

Once they begin working in DITA, writers continually ask for ways to make their job easier. They want more to start with than just a standard DITA task template with steps, reference templates for commands and properties, or a concept template with room to freely expound on anything that's neither task nor reference. They want something to help them get started on writing and revising the hundreds or thousands of topics they are responsible for maintaining, and they want help architecting them in a meaningful and consistent structure. As managers, editors, and DITA evangelists press them to write reusable, minimalist content, they push back for more efficient means of developing topics, and for identifying reusable content in the CMS. In this way they demonstrate the need for Principle 5, creating structure.

INFORMATION MODELS: STRATEGY FOR PRODUCTIVITY

Table 2 shows differences between a style guide and an information model. See Chapter 13 for a different look at how style guides, information models, and templates compare. Information models, sometimes also called content models, are an important piece of the strategy for improving both writer and end user productivity:

- Authors and information architects can be more productive when they have a supply of reusable or partially reusable topics and a reusable architecture, in addition to base topic templates and guidelines.
- End users can be more productive because information is structured according to their own goals, easy to find, consistent, and complete without being excessive.

Thus, while some might argue that information models take away writers' freedom, most writers see them as an important means of providing better, more consistent information for end users, as well as a critical aspect of supporting the internal need for greater productivity. Even so, writers are going to comply only if there are models that truly satisfy their needs. If the teams for Projects A and B both say "We need to write troubleshooting information," both teams are urged to participate in developing a set of requirements for troubleshooting information that meet not only their immediate needs, but also the needs of Projects C, D, and E that have not yet made the transition to DITA but see it looming ahead.

PUBS COUNCILS: COLLABORATION FORUM

Councils provide a forum for collaborative decision making, and an opportunity to discuss a broad set of issues affecting information developers

Table 2. Style guide compared to information model

Characteristic	Style Guide	Information Model
Structural requirements for a document (for example, title page, table of contents, chapters, and index)	Describes or lists required elements, typically in a fairly generic way, for example, book/chapter/section. May give examples.	Includes a comprehensive list and detailed description of required elements, and the context in which each is permitted. The description may take the form of a template or sample of each required element. May include optional elements. May specify content required for a particular type of document or segment of a document.
Stylistic guidance (for example, capitalization, pagination, numbering, use of notes, use of images, and style of index entries)	Describes or lists acceptable styles and practices.	Less likely to address general writing concerns such as capitalization.
Terminology guidance	May specify approved terms, their spelling, or approved definitions for a product or for all products.	May specify approved terms, their spelling, or approved definitions for a product, for all products, or for a particular type of information.
Content guidance	Limited content guidance. May provide general guidance for the type of information a particular document can include.	More likely to provide content guidance. For example, may state that administration guides should include a separate chapter with troubleshooting information, or that troubleshooting information should be included with every command in a reference manual.

enterprise-wide. As technical publications organizations adopt DITA, they typically recognize the need to adopt a formal structure for ensuring input to decisions from a representative set of team members and stakeholders, for educating writers in new approaches, and for charging some team or individual with responsibility for tool sets (Doner and Hood, 2008; Mescan and Robidoux, 2008). Councils have both the power to make decisions, and the responsibility to do so in a way that meets real project requirements and deadlines for information deliverables. They may determine policy and strategy in advance or in response to issues that arise.

Sybase adapted its approach from one used at IBM® (Jones and Peterson, 2007). Each Tech Pubs project or team may send a representative to any of our five councils. Most councils have about six active members. One council whose mission includes educating all of Tech Pubs on the new role of information architect has opened its meetings to the entire organization. Besides bringing personal expertise to discussions, each council representative is the voice for his or her

project or team in decisions and should solicit the team's input on important issues. Some councils may include members from outside Tech Pubs, where collaboration with engineering, product marketing, or other voices in the enterprise is appropriate. In the interest of effective decision making, leaders may set up working groups within their council, but must ensure that decisions represent enterprise needs.

Each council's role is to:

- Collaborate on issues that affect Sybase users' total information experience;
- Research when appropriate, to inform decisions and recommendations;
- Make binding policy decisions;
- Provide input to tool and process developers on policy decisions, recommendations, requests, and requirements; and
- Ensure that decisions meet the needs of diverse groups across the enterprise.

A separate group of in-house experts develops tools, scripts, guidelines, and training. This group implements council decisions, taking into account technical concerns, research results, and department priorities.

The Models and Templates Council:

- Researches and develops templates and information models for topic-based content to ensure consistency and quality;
- Considers existing information models and templates and how to best represent them in DITA;
- Ensures that models and templates are suitable for all potential output deliverables;
- Provides information models that aid the gradual transition from book-oriented to topic-based content;
- Works with Information Architects Council to create appropriate information models;
- Works with Usability Council to ensure that information models are usable and meet customer needs;
- Works with Style Council on stylistic aspects of information models and templates; and
- Works with internal tool developers to ensure that models and templates are technically feasible, and produce expected results.

Figure 1 shows the role of each council in the overall collaboration process. For example, when Project Team A submits to the Models and Template Council a request for an enhanced troubleshooting information model, the council collaborates internally on model details, but also may gather additional requirements from the Information Architects Council, work with the Style Council on visual formatting and editorial issues, and approach the Usability Council for support in user research and testing of the model.

Note that while the council approach to collaborative decisions includes broad-based participation, it is a representative democracy, not a pure one. Moreover, council leaders have the authority to move the process to conclusion. As noted in Chapter 11, "Consensus doesn't mean reaching unanimous agreement—what it does mean is that team members agree to support the decision that has been made."

IMPLEMENTING AN ENTERPRISE ARCHITECTURE BY AND FOR VIRTUAL COLLABORATION

Each information model developed at Sybase includes:

- A sample DITA map that defines overall topic organization and makes recommendations for linking;
- A set of topic models or templates that define topic type, required and optional structural elements, and required and optional information;

Figure 1. Council collaboration

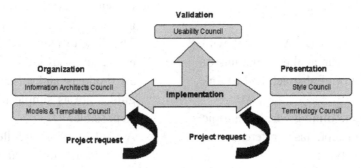

- Where possible, reusable topics, or reusable content units that are smaller than a topic (for example, boilerplate notes, steps, or bullet items that can be referenced from topics);
- Instructions in our internal authoring guide, and in comments and guide text embedded in model topics and templates;
- Examples of content developed according to the model; and
- Where appropriate, a specialization of one of the base DITA topic types.

Each model defines one category of information: for example, an installation guide, a release bulletin, or a new features document. These information types are generic enough to apply to many different products. They are also, in most cases, larger than a single topic.

There are also models at the topic level. The base DITA topic types—concept, task, and reference—are the underpinnings of our information models. We also have taken advantage of DITA's principle of inheritance to specialize information types for some reference content. Reference specializations have been developed to simplify legacy conversions for extensive existing reference material: command reference, functions, and so on. For the most part, the semantic structure and guide text within these specializations, in concert with conversion scripts and post-conversion cleanup documentation, provide sufficient guidance for using them.

We also have guidelines in our internal documentation for items such as:

- Title conventions;
- Short descriptions (a DITA element with text that can appear at the beginning of every topic as a brief abstract, and in link previews);
- Topic typing: determining whether a topic should be a concept, task, reference, or specialized topic type;

- Tables: deciding when to use each of the supported table types;
- Indexes;
- Images;
- Metadata; and
- Reuse strategies: for example, determining when and how to nest maps, apply conditional text, or use content references (also known as *conrefs*, which are a DITA mechanism to reference standard reusable text units maintained outside the topic).

Developing the Models: Collaboration Process, Participants, and Tools

As noted in Chapter 13, implementation and adoption go hand-in-hand. The road from a proposal to an effective and widely accepted model loops through early trials, multiple iterations of development and implementation, and multiple calendar cycles. This section lists the steps in our process at Sybase and describes how we developed one model. The process and tools represent our application of Principle 4, using tools and collaborative modes effectively.

Needs Identification

Project teams identified needs and sometimes also proposed solutions for those needs. Such needs typically emerged during planning and content development, for example:

- All products require an installation guide. Depending on the product, the installation process can be very simple or complex. The director identified the need for a model that imposes greater consistency across all products and ensures that installation guides are as simple to maintain and use as possible.
- An information architect saw that troubleshooting content may require a set of

related topics for diagnosing and resolving a user-identified problem that can have multiple symptoms, multiple causes, or multiple solutions. She proposed formalizing that in an information model.

- The Information Architects Council discussed the need for greater consistency in how teams approach new features content, especially given the challenges of evolving product release types.
- A customer reported an issue relating to some standard release bulletin content. The tech support representative created a documentation bug in the company-wide tracking system.

Collaboration mechanisms for this phase included the following: Proposals originated in e-mail messages, and in virtual team or council meetings; face-to-face discussion sometimes occurred among colocated team members, but was always followed by some sort of online vetting before a formal proposal emerged. If the proposal included a solution, it might take the form of a document, an e-mail message, a drawing, or any form the user was comfortable with and had time for. At this early stage, the form was less important than initial consensus that a model for a particular type of information was desirable, who needed it, and why. If the council needed broad input to answer even those questions, we posted an article on our internal wiki so that any member of Tech Pubs could contribute to the discussion.

Formalizing the request required that the requestor must use the appropriate electronic forum and attach supporting documents for the request to enable the work to be prioritized and tracked.

Work Prioritization

Project teams, managers, and the tool implementation team prioritized the work. While all of the model requests had merit, realistically we could address only one or two in the initial time frame.

Since release bulletins and installation guides are used most broadly and the benefit from consistency is great, the Models and Templates Council, in consultation with requestors, managers, and implementers, decided to address those first. Factors that they considered included:

- **Quality factors:** How significant were differences in what was already delivered, and what, if any, was the impact of those differences on end users? For other requested models, could we provide only general guidelines and the basic DITA concept/task/reference structure with the assumption that enhancements would come in the future?
- **Organizational factors:** Visibility (that is, was it required for a strategic product release?), breadth of application (that is, how many teams need this model?), and other management priorities were an important influence.

Collaboration mechanisms for this phase included the following: Project requests were recorded in a shared virtual notebook, sometimes with attached spreadsheets or other documents. Reports could be generated from the change tracking system. Discussion took place on e-mail, in phone calls, and via virtual team meetings (phone, Web, or both). All of these methods were used to help prioritize work and determine which models to address first.

Requirements Refinement

The Models and Templates Council gathered and refined requirements.

To develop the initial installation guide and release bulletin models, the council met several times. Several council members volunteered to research existing patterns in various products, to gather input from colleagues outside of Tech Pubs who work directly with end users, and to do some competitive analysis. The entire council discussed the topic hierarchy, linking, the degree to which content for each section should be standardized, and where a template was appropriate versus a descriptive model and guidelines. A proposed topic hierarchy was recorded in the virtual notebook and updated during and after live discussion.

Social factors involved in this phase included: Some members had worked together previously, but others were introduced for the first time. Mutual respect developed in previous encounters and over the course of this collaboration helped members develop the trust that allowed us to get broad participation in the discussion, and to reach consensus on a DITA map structure.

Collaboration mechanisms involved in this phase included: All meetings were virtual in that they were by phone and often included Web participation. Meeting notes and research findings were recorded in a shared virtual notebook. All council members had access to the notebook, and they entered comments before, during, or after meetings. Multiple users could simultaneously have the notebook open, view others' entries in near-real time (synchronization every five minutes), and enter their own comments; or they could view others' notebook updates in near-real time through the Web meeting application, which exposed the meeting leader's shared desktop.

Challenges involved in this phase included scheduling above all else. Active participants were located in four North American time zones, France, the U.K., and Singapore. (According to the World Clock Meeting Planner, http://www.timeanddate.com/worldclock/meeting.html, in February 2009, 10 AM in Boston (U.S. EST) is 4 PM Paris, 3 PM London, 7 AM San Francisco (U.S. PST), and 11 PM Singapore.) Remarkably, all council members participated "live" at least sometimes. We occasionally shifted meeting times to accommodate different participants. Some of those participating from home had only phone access during meetings.

Model Development

Tool implementers developed the initial models in our pre-CMS DITA environment.

Implementation work for the initial versions of these two models included:

- Creating a DITA map with model topics and topic templates or models;
- Creating instructions for authors and information architects in the topics, a readme file, and our authoring guide; and
- Creating reusable elements for DITA conrefs.

Collaboration mechanisms involved in this phase included: The initial models and instructions were created in our first DITA environment, a file-based repository with source control. The two implementers each took one model and worked independently to create the DITA maps, topics, and conref sources, guided by prior discussions and by personal interpretation of what the model should look like.

Model Prototypes

Councils weighed in on a prototype of the models.

The Models and Templates Council invited the leaders of Information Architects Council, Usability Council, and Style Council to Web meetings where the models were reviewed. The model implementer demonstrated how the release bulletin and installation guide models could be used to produce a DITA map with a high-level topic hierarchy that IAs and authors could develop with their project-specific content.

Collaboration mechanisms involved in this phase included: Discussion and approval took place mostly during the live Web meeting; some council members later listened to a recording of the meeting and provided feedback via e-mail.

Model Adoption

Early project teams adopted initial models.

On a pilot basis, a few project teams adopted the initial release bulletin model, and one project team adopted the initial installation guide model. All IAs and authors made good faith efforts to follow the models, making adjustments where needed.

Collaboration mechanisms involved in this phase included: All model content was stored in a common folder in the repository. IAs and authors created maps and topics in project folders in the repository. They relied on documentation for using the models, but they also consulted with the Models and Template Council leader by phone and informal Web meetings to pose questions and resolve issues.

Adopter Feedback

Early adopters gave feedback.

The models were intentionally designed to allow for variations in content. Most content adjustments were well within the expected range.

Challenges involved in this phase included: In the pilot adoption cycle, technical limitations quickly became apparent. The release bulletin model needed a way to use variable conrefs in shared topics, for which there was no support. The number of topic templates in the installation guide model became a usability issue for content creators.

Collaboration mechanisms involved in this phase included: Group discussion took place between the Models and Templates Council and Information Architects Council.

CMS Involvement

With input and assistance from the Models and Templates Council, implementers enhanced the model content, structure, and documentation when we adopted a CMS. The CMS, which replaced the earlier content repository, gave us the ability to

clone topics and maps, and to create and find reusable content units and where they are referenced in topics more efficiently. We updated the models and documentation to take advantage of these capabilities. At this point, we also had gained a better understanding of where the models needed more structural and content flexibility.

Challenges involved in this phase included: As more teams adopted the models in both expected and unanticipated ways, the need for better metadata became clear. Metadata requirements extend beyond the scope of any one information model to our broader uses of the CMS and DITA, but they do affect the models. Other environmental and substantive changes sometimes affect the models as well. For example, some content that we assumed applied to all products needed adapting for evolving product distribution methods. Some authors informed Models and Templates Council of changes they made to the model, while others simply did what they felt they needed to do. We learned that it is important to establish an ongoing feedback loop.

Collaboration mechanisms involved in this phase included: With all maps and topics readily accessible in the CMS, it was easy to compare examples while working on the model update. It also was easy for any Tech Pubs CMS user to view any content. This review allowed tool experts and mentors to provide support and guidance, as well as allowing authors and IAs both to use the model map and topics and to see how others have applied the model.

Model Enforcement

The editor, tools team members, and DITA mentors enforced the models.

Ideally, mentoring and review take place early and throughout the project. In the planning stage, a DITA mentor provided guidance in developing the table of contents, and an editor or another information architect reviewed it. The Models and Templates Council leader and other knowledgeable staff were always available for support. A DITA code review gave authors and IA's early feedback on how well they were applying the models and other DITA best practices. An editor reviewed all new content.

Collaboration mechanisms involved in this phase included: Planning documents were posted and accessible from a document sharing site. The CMS was the primary mechanism for content collaboration. Editors and SMEs used the CMS or other electronic reviewing facilities to enter comments, view others' comments, and vote to approve or not.

DITA code reviewers entered comments directly in topic files; the code review took place in a Web meeting between a small number of code reviewers and a small number of authors working on the same project team or on similar projects. We adopted this process from a paper by two presenters who were experienced in helping IBM writers become skilled in using DITA (Inkster and Rouiller, 2008). They recommended a face-to-face meeting for code reviews, as the process can be intimidating, but we are so geographically dispersed that face-to-face code reviews are unlikely ever to occur. We made a strong effort to present recommendations in a positive and unintimidating way. The first code review gave authors an opportunity to offer feedback on the model.

Challenges involved in this phase included: We have strongly encouraged best practices, but realistically, time and resource constraints, pressure from SMEs, and other factors have sometimes prevailed. As our models have matured and our writers have gained experience with DITA and the CMS, project teams are finding it easier to use the models.

Model Testing

The Usability Council initiated a user survey and testing for some aspects of models.

Challenges: We have gleaned some end-user input on how best to approach certain types of information from a brief Web survey. We plan eventually to validate our models by performing usability testing on released product documentation and by analyzing user feedback collected through direct feedback links in our online documentation.

For reference specializations, we followed a somewhat different process:

- A Reference Council, run by our lead editor, gathered and refined requirements. The lead editor requested representative reference chapters from each product representative. From those chapters, she created a spreadsheet that identified all the elements (semantic tags) that were consistently used across products.
- Tool implementers developed and tested the DTD and style sheet for the specializations.
- Leaders of Reference Council, Style Council, and Models and Templates Council evaluated results.

The key issue here was how to resolve differences between existing structured content, and to adapt the content for DITA. We already have a large body of reference content that follows a generally consistent structure and uses semantic elements (for example, command, syntax, variable, parameter, and usage). Agreement was needed on how to reconcile differences and whether it made sense to try to convert everything to the more complex DITA syntax coding, or to develop a specialization that would simplify conversions of this relatively stable, reasonably consistent content. We did not need to develop model DITA maps, as our conversion scripts produce a fairly clean map, and reference content rarely exhibits excess, missing, or hybrid content (that is, task/concept/reference all mixed up). Differences to resolve were minor. The main sticking point between two teams with extensive legacy content was the order of sections within reference topics.

The Reference Council leader and the tool and script developer decided to allow either within a given doc set, as the structure was similar enough that it could be reused.

Virtual Collaboration Tools Used

Table 3 describes the types of virtual collaboration tools used throughout our process, and briefly summarizes our experience with them. It is not intended to be a comprehensive tool review. Other organizations' experience with and configurations of the same tools may differ. For more information about virtual tools, see Chapter 1.

In addition to all of these virtual collaboration tools, sometimes there is no substitute for picking up the telephone and talking to someone in real-time. See the discussion of hybridity in Chapter 1.

ISSUES, CONTROVERSIES, PROBLEMS

As indicated in Chapter 2, technical and linguistic challenges may turn out to be fundamentally human issues. Like all organizations attempting to bring about a change in culture, in developing and applying information models we needed to address not only technical and logistical issues, but also human challenges.

Technical Issues

DITA is a relatively new methodology; the specification and toolkit are evolving. Our pilot models were too restrictive, and did not scale. We have made significant progress since that time. Our models continue to mature over time.

Some models are more template-like. IAs, for example, can generate a map and initial set of topics automatically. In other cases, more manual effort is needed. Our tool development process is an agile one, and each incremental release brings better automation.

The content reuse that we hope to facilitate with content management and information models requires an effective metadata strategy. Chapter 14 further discusses the critical role of metadata.

Logistical Issues

It takes time to develop a complete, full featured set of models. Once a model is developed, training and fine-tuning must also be completed.

Global meetings can be difficult to schedule due to time differences. Virtual tools are important, but sometimes there is no substitute for being an active member of a real-time conversation.

Additionally, as Chapter 7 discusses, "lack of familiarity with technology and lack of opportunity to learn the technology adequately has been identified as a primary significant barrier to effective collaboration." A staff gains experience with collaboration tools over time. We provide instructional materials to help users get started with new tools and roles, project and design checklists, training for advanced users and managers. We collaborate with our CMS vendor on adding features and enhancing usability.

Human Issues

When collaborating to make decisions and there is no agreement, how will disagreements be resolved? Relationships and trust developed over time, whether by virtual or face-to-face experience, certainly help in having fruitful collaboration. Virtual tools may also be helpful, for example, by allowing a "majority rules" solution. Occasionally, when opinions are fiercely held, it may be necessary to prevail upon managers to weigh in, or even make a final decision. Chapters 10 and 11 address these issues.

Sometimes, important contributors may not participate or pay attention to discussions about model development until they actually need to use the model. Even with broad product representation, it can still be difficult to envision or to devote the

Table 3. Virtual collaboration tools: use, advantages, drawbacks

Purpose/Description	How we use it	Advantages/ Disadvantages
Collaborative environment for sharing unstructured information in a set of electronic notebooks for near-synchronous and asynchronous communication	Share council and project team discussions. Record meeting notes and status reports. Share research. Link to shared documents. Semi-public: no special password needed, but notebooks are typically shared only within a project team or a council.	Pros: Integrates easily with other common tools. Very intuitive. Cons: Synchronizing large notebooks in near-real-time can slow machine performance. Notebooks can grow rapidly and become unmanageable; need to impose some organization.
CMS for DITA Repository for content and related resources DITA map, topic, and relationship table development Source control/version control Workflow for authoring, localization, and publishing Collaborative review Ad hoc output generation Project coordination	Information architects develop maps and relationship tables. Authors develop topics and referable content units. Model developers create maps and topics that can be reused, cloned, or used as examples. All users manage workflow. Editor and some SMEs review content. Project leads track projects. Tools team develops documentation in DITA for authoring, architecting, building, reviewing, and publishing content from DITA source. Tools team provides sample resources for reuse or cloning.	Pros: In a large organization doing topic-based content development, eventually a CMS becomes a necessity. Ability to share, search, and version content, including model content, is essential to our reuse strategy. Cons: It is a lot to learn; takes training and patience. CMS environment is evolving; we have worked closely with our vendor on functionality and usability enhancements.
DITA Open Toolkit, required to build output from DITA maps and topics.	Tools team created a map specialization for defining a build manifest, and an editing environment for it. The build manifest defines how DITA maps and related resources are to be processed by the DITA Open Toolkit. Style sheets refine output format specifics such as fonts.	Pros: The toolkit is a critical productivity tool, and an essential advantage of DITA over other XML environments. Cons: Capable tool developers are still needed to use the Open Toolkit. Our build manifest and editor simplify build definition, but it is still challenging to define a build for some of our required outputs. For this reason we have adopted a build architect role, and are working on templates and examples.
Wiki, a collaborative Web site	Internal wiki site for asynchronous collaboration. Councils publicize membership, meetings, current issues, and decisions Councils and tools team solicit discussion and feedback. Tools team posts internal authoring guide. Tools team provides training curriculum downloadable training materials, and recordings for on-demand use. Announce upcoming events. Link to recordings of past events and training. Download nightly builds for all designated DITA content.	Pros: Accessible to anyone in Tech Pubs, 24x7. Easy to search for posted information. Easy to solicit, post, and find others' comments. Cons: Users forget to look at the wiki, except for the authoring guide and nightly builds. Editing is much less sophisticated than many other authoring tools, so only a few users feel comfortable doing more than basic commenting. Login is required to edit or comment; users sometimes forget their logins. For a tool that is not our primary collaboration method, requires significant planning to avoid a hodge-podge of pages.
Common file-system repository with version control, and check-in/checkout of topic, map, and image files	Source control and repository for DocBook and DITA content and models prior to adopting the CMS.	Cons: File-based system did not scale to enterprise needs for DITA content development and reuse.
DITA-enabled XML authoring tool	Develop DITA maps and topics. Stand-alone tool used to prepare legacy content during conversion.	Pros: GUI XML authoring environment adapted for DITA is much easier to use than a simple text editor. Cons: Can be expensive.

continued on the following page

Table 3. continued

Purpose/Description	How we use it	Advantages/ Disadvantages
Corporate e-mail tool Shared calendar	Asynchronous discussion among global teams Announcements Informal sharing of ideas and issues Large group communication via listservs and aliases Scheduling meetings	Pros: Used by nearly all employees for e-mail and calendar. Ability to schedule meetings and see others' availability. Simple, intuitive, and ubiquitous. Easy to address a group. Cons: Any e-mail excludes those not on the list. Can be hard to find information discussed previously. Users may delete old mail that may be needed for later reference.
Instant messaging	Quick informal 1:1 or small group communication Often used to initiate unscheduled phone calls with developers or with anyone in a different location. For extended discussion, we usually switch to phone or sometimes to an on-demand Web meeting.	Pros: Easy to have a quick conversation with minimal interruption; either party can ignore while engaged in other work. Chats can be saved for later reference. Cons: Incompatible IM systems hamper access. One must remember to save a chat before closing a session; otherwise, it is gone.
Web-based meetings	Training (leader and participant) Council, project team, and "All Pubs" meetings Demos and discussions with vendors	Pros: Easy to demonstrate applications to dispersed groups. Allows user interaction. Training sessions and meetings can be recorded. Cons: Delayed response can be annoying. Most users and presenters do not have time to learn advanced capabilities (for example, interactivity, graphic markup, and polling).
Conference calls and audio for Web meetings	Formal and informal meetings	Pros: Live discussion helps build trust and encourage participation. Cons: Some leaders are more skilled than others at facilitating discussion, though most get better with practice. Tends to exclude users in some time zones.
Graphical tool for task modeling and information architecture with DITA map output	Develop task models and export to DITA maps (used by a few information architects to develop models for their projects; not used to develop information models but may be in the future).	Pros: Excellent way to design, share, and evaluate task models in preparation for map design. Cons: Hard to learn, so only a few users have tried it. Have not yet found a good way to integrate task models with actual content in our CMS and use the tool's ability to do roundtrips between map and model.
Browser-based collaboration and document management tool	Download shared planning documents. Enterprise-wide, secure sharing (between engineering, Tech Pubs, program management).	Pros: Because it is used enterprise-wide, we can leverage corporate support and knowledge of the environment.
Web surveys	End user input on documentation	Pros: Inexpensive way to get focused input from users. Cons: Survey design requires skill. Getting survey participants can be challenging. Survey data must be analyzed.
User feedback links in public documentation Web site	End-user input. Enhanced means of soliciting, analyzing, and responding to user feedback are in development.	Pros: End users can contribute directly to improved content. Cons: User feedback requires attention, response, and analysis.

continued on the following page

Table 3. continued

Purpose/Description	How we use it	Advantages/ Disadvantages
Software usability testing tool that captures all user interactions with the interface of the software being tested. In combination with Web meeting and verbal feedback, allows usability experts to facilitate usability tests by remote, external testers, while others in remote locations can observe user actions during or after the test session.	We plan to use this tool in the future to validate delivery mechanism and information models as applied in released documentation.	Pros: Invaluable benefit to writers to watch real users interact with the product and use documentation to perform real tasks, or even just to navigate the documentation. Cons: Expensive and time consuming. Requires skilled facilitator and access to end users willing to participate.
Web site for planning global meetings. Specify a meeting date and time in up to four time zones, and the planner shows you meeting times in UTC and all requested zones over a 24-hour period, color-coded for workday, evening, and late night.	Determine best meeting time for all locations before scheduling global Web or phone meetings.	Pros: Easy to use, free tool Cons: None

time necessary for a thorough evaluation until a problem is immediate. Suddenly, the question of exactly how to make this process work for a multiplatform product, or how to handle developer requests to include materials that violate the spirit of the model, becomes urgent. Chapter 11 indicates that sometimes "the person or group receiving the information does not recognize it as new information." Similarly, individuals may not recognize until long after decisions have been made that this new information affects their content, either now or in the future.

In any organization, some authors and reviewers are reluctant to let go of older designs and methods. We have found that giving more authors a voice in model development can help them feel ownership, and it can add to the richness and appropriateness of the models—though it is not reasonable to include everyone in developing every model.

Full adoption of information models grows over time, as users gain experience and confidence with the models and with minimalist topic-oriented information development in general, and as the models themselves mature. There is a major learning curve for adopting models; over time we have developed more internal experts who can mentor

new DITA users. Particularly when converting legacy content, a phased adoption plan can be the best approach.

SOLUTIONS AND RECOMMENDATIONS

Key Success Factors

Leadership

Effective leadership at all levels is essential to successful collaboration on the implementation of information models. If there are authors who are not convinced of the value of consistent models, who are unhappy about the available model, who may not want to relinquish control over how to present information, or who are uncomfortable with the idea of collaborative writing, they consciously or unconsciously may circumvent the model. When it is clear that technical publications managers—both directors and immediate supervisors—fully support the effort, individuals are far more likely to participate in developing an effective model, and applying it consistently. Leaders of model development teams must make every effort to encourage broad participation, develop trust across the team, and do the iterative work required to work through issues. Collaboration Principle 2, finding and promoting leadership, cannot be emphasized enough.

Business Requirements for Content and Delivery Mechanism

Business requirements may come from customers or from internal sources. Customers may communicate—via technical support, user surveys, site visits, product managers or even executives—that they want more troubleshooting information for their complex usage scenarios or that they need a quick installation document rather than a comprehensive guide with lots of conceptual information. Engineering may require that content be provided in a particular online help format; some developers may want to include more technical detail than users need. It is important to evaluate and prioritize requirements.

Milestones and Deadlines

Collaborative model development can stretch on interminably without imposed deadlines. Typically, the ultimate driving factor is a documentation release, but to deliver the model when it is needed, interim milestones are critical. Set dates for establishing the team, determining requirements, developing the model, reviewing it within the team and with a broader group, testing it, documenting it, and releasing it.

Roles

When developing topic-based information models, whether using DITA or some other standard, it is critical that everyone understand who is responsible for each aspect of content development and delivery. The information architect who develops the DITA map must rely on the model to know

what topic types are needed, the order in which they occur, and how they should relate to each other. The author needs to know the content and structure that is required within a given topic model. The build architect must design a build that meets all delivery requirements. Even if the same person fills all roles, it is important to separately consider the goal of each role.

Tools for Global Collaboration

Sybase Tech Pubs was fortunate to obtain budget approval for a CMS that is proving essential to enterprise level content development, reuse, and information model implementation. Be prepared to argue appropriately for the necessary tools. In addition to the tools needed for developing and sharing content, one or more collaboration mechanisms are necessary to propose, discuss, evaluate, and test the model itself. Several chapters in this book discuss characteristics of tools that support these goals most effectively. To overcome issues with collaboration in real-time, use tools that offer high degrees of presence awareness, interactivity, and synchronicity (see, for example, Chapters 1 and 10). Consider shifting meeting times both to get broader participation and to gain respect and trust from long distance participants.

Broad-Based Participation

To the extent possible, solicit input from customers or from people who work directly with them. Customer input should help drive the organization's requirements gathering, but is also helpful to validate the model; as suggested in Chapter 17, collaboration with customers can help with this endeavor. Look at what competitors are doing. Include writers who work on a broad set of products to ensure that the needs of both new and legacy products are satisfied. Include members from different geographies, who may offer a different perspective and may reflect the global audience

233

for the information deliverables. Consider beta testing models by having different teams try them out on real products.

FUTURE RESEARCH DIRECTIONS

Adoption of DITA is growing, not only within the traditional technical writing community for which it was developed, but increasingly for other purposes such as requirements documents and governmental documents. Some vendors and experts are proposing a DITA Maturity Model that looks at DITA adoption beyond the technical writing team to marketing, engineering, and other players in large corporate environments (Priestley and Swope, 2008).

As larger organizations adopt DITA, they can make their own transition process smoother by paying careful attention to how they apply this broad standard—developing information models, ensuring broad collaboration, and building trust into the process. The ideal tool for a particular type of collaboration may be rejected in favor of the one preferred for other purposes by the broader organization. Research into how a very large, broad-based set of participants for whom writing is not the major responsibility can agree on information models would be welcome.

Also, while there are some usability studies on minimalist, topic-based writing, more studies on content developed as DITA maps and topics and with particular architectural approaches might offer insight into best design practices. It would be interesting for a contingent of DITA experts to collaboratively develop a usability study mechanism that resource-strapped documentation teams can easily implement.

For optimal effectiveness, how detailed should an information model be? "Optimal" is likely some mix of a model's usefulness for content consumers and challenges for content creators. Research into optimal model detail for different content creators and content consumers would be welcome.

CONCLUSION

Information models are an important means for technical writing teams to ease adoption of DITA and other new authoring strategies. Broad-based, focused collaboration during the model development phase, using readily available virtual collaboration tools, and with trust built into the process, is essential to successful information model adoption. Follow-up activities to support model implementation and ensure that models remain current also are essential. A CMS is ideal for this phase in terms of planning, developing, and reviewing content. Ongoing communication and training also are critical.

Sybase is a registered trademark of Sybase, Inc. in the United States and/or other countries. Microsoft is a registered trademark of Microsoft Corporation in the United States and/or other countries. IBM is a trademark of International

Table 4. Optimal model detail concerns

Content Creator Factors	Content Consumer Factors
Difficulty for authors in creating and maintaining the content and associated metadata. Experience level of authors with subject matter, technical writing, and the particular mode of writing. Availability of live, trained editors performing developmental edits, copy edits, or no edits. Automated tools for checking consistency, terminology, linking. Project environment, such as resource and time constraints, agile projects, commitment and support within the organization. CMS with goal of content reuse.	User work environment. Urgency or criticality of user tasks (for example, inserting a pacemaker or operating a nuclear power plant, versus developing game software). Complexity of user tasks. Experience level of content consumers.

Business Machines Corporation in the United States, other countries, or both. Adobe and FrameMaker are registered trademarks of Adobe Systems Incorporated in the United States and/or other countries. OASIS is a registered trademark of OASIS, the open standards consortium where the DocBook and Darwin Information Typing Architecture (DITA) specifications are owned and developed. SourceForge and SourceForge.net are registered trademarks of SourceForge, Inc. in the United States and other countries. Eclipse is a trademark of Eclipse Foundation, Inc. All other company and product names mentioned may be trademarks of the respective companies with which they are associated.

REFERENCES

Bottitta, J., Idoura, A. P., & Pappas, L. (2003). Moving to single sourcing: Managing the effects of organizational changes. *Technical Communication*, *50*(3), 355–370.

Doner, S., & Hood, L. (2008) A democratic approach to overcoming DITA and CMS issues. *Proceedings of CMS Strategies/DITA North America 2008*. Santa Clara, CA: Center for Information-Development Management.

Fisher, L. (2008). Staffing information architects for a world of topic-based information. *Best Practices*, *10*(5), 105.

Hackos, J. (2004, August). *Pursuing a minimalist agenda*. Web seminar, Comtech Services & Vasont Systems.

Hackos, J. (2007a). *Information development: Managing your documentation projects, portfolio, and people*. New York: John Wiley & Sons.

Hackos, J. (2007b). *Information modeling. Comtech Services, Inc. Workshop at CMS Strategies/DITA North America, April 2007* (pp. 1–48). Boston: Center for Information-Development Management.

Hackos, J., & Priestley, M. (Eds.). (2007, August 1). *DITA Version 1.1 Architectural Specification OASIS® Standard, OASIS Darwin Information Typing Architecture (DITA) TC*. Retrieved from http://docs.oasis-open.org/dita/v1.1/OS/archspec/archspec.html

Hahn, M. (2004, August). *Vasont and the minimalist agenda*. Web seminar, Comtech Services & Vasont Systems

Henry, C. (2007). Ensuring quality coding in your data source. *Best Practices*, *9*(2), 40–43.

Inkster, C., & Rouiller, S. (2008). Improving code quality with DITA code reviews. In *Proceedings of CMS Strategies/DITA North America 2008*. Santa Clara, CA: Center for Information-Development Management.

Jones, E., & Peterson, D. (2007). Total information experience: Defining an IBM-integrated approach to developing information in a flat world via effective global collaboration. *Best Practices*, *9*(2), 29–34.

Mescan, S., & Robidoux, C. (2008). All I really need to know about successful content management I learned in kindergarten. In *Proceedings of CMS Strategies/DITA North America 2008*. Santa Clara, CA: Center for Information-Development Management.

OASIS Darwin Information Typing Architecture (DITA) Technical Committee FAQ. (n.d.). Retrieved August 17, 2009 from http://www.oasis-open.org/committees/dita/faq.php

OASIS DITA. (2007). *Version 1.1 Language Specification, OASIS Standard*, August 1, 2007. Retrieved from http://docs.oasis-open.org/dita/v1.1/langspec/ditaref-type.html

Priestley, M., & Swope, A. (2008). *DITA maturity model: A JustSystems white paper*. JustSystems, Inc. and IBM Corporation. Retrieved from www.na.justsystems.com/files/Whitepaper-DITA_MM.pdf

The Rockley Group, Inc. (2005, February 15). *The role of content standards in content management.* Jones, E. & Schell, D. (2007). Delivering the right content to the right person at the right time: defining the total information experience. In *Proceedings of CMS strategies/DITA North America conference,* Boston.

Van Raaphorst, A., & Johnson, D. (2007, April 18). *DITA Open Toolkit User Guide,* (3rd ed.). Retrieved on June 22, 2009 from http://dita-ot. sourceforge.net/doc/ot-userguide131/xhtml/ index.html. All files are copyright 2006-2007 by VR Communications, unless otherwise indicated. Licensing and usage of this document and related materials is regulated by a Common Public License (CPL) granted by OASIS (Organization for the Advancement of Structured Information Standards).

World Clock Meeting Planner. (2008). Retrieved from http://www.timeanddate.com/worldclock/ meeting.html

ADDITIONAL READING

Carroll, J. M. (Ed.). (1998). Minimalism beyond the Nurnberg funnel. Cambridge: The MIT Press, with Society for Technical Communication.

Hackos, J. (2002). Content management for dynamic Web delivery. New York: John Wiley & Sons. In Gilbane Report 10 (1), February, 2002, *What is an information model & why do you need one?* Retrieved from http://gilbane. com/gilbane_report.pl/69/What_is_an_Information_Model__Why_do_You_Need_One.html

Hackos, J. (2006, August) Transitioning your technical publications team to DITA. Web seminar, Comtech Services & PTC, Inc.

Hackos, J. (2006, August) Developing a strategy for minimalism: Creating manuals people can use, workshop, Comtech Services.

Hackos, J., & Redish, J. (1998). *User and task analysis for interface design.* New York: John Wiley & Sons.

Hargis, G., Carey, M., Hernandez, A. K., Hughes, P., Longo, D., Rouiller, S., et al. (2004). Developing Quality Technical Information: A Handbook for Writers and Editors (2nd Edition). Upper Saddle River, NJ: Prentice Hall PTR.

Linton, J., & Bruski, K. (2006). *Introduction to DITA: A user guide to the Darwin information typing architecture.* Denver: Comtech Services.

Chapter 13
Using Standards to Promote Collaboration among Writers

France Baril
Architextus Inc., Canada

ABSTRACT

Unlike mathematicians who have a quasi-universal language for expressing formulas and other mathematical expressions, writers can express ideas in many different ways. Differences in style appear at multiple levels: in the section and chapter organizational patterns, in the syntax, in the complexity of the vocabulary, and in formatting. Consistency is required to produce publications of quality in a collaborative environment; moreover, writers must find efficient ways to collaborate as a team. This chapter explores the methods, advantages, and challenges of developing standards—rules related to content, work processes, and the choice and configuration of tools to support collaborative writing and content reuse in virtual environments.

INTRODUCTION

Computer networks, document repositories, databases, and communication technologies can make documents and their content accessible to multiple writers independently from their various geographical locations. Content management systems (CMSs) can manage access rights, versions, and the workflows that support the cycles of document creation, maintenance, and publishing. These systems also have the ability to notify writers other collaborators when changes are made to the content or status of documents.

Because it is common to find similar content within many documents, many tools even enable writers to manage content reuse across multiple publications. For example, a product's training manual may contain many of the tasks or feature descriptions defined in the user's reference guide. The same is true when products of the same family share similar functionalities or physical components. With access to a decent search engine, writers can find and reuse content that has been written by others. They may even review and propose changes to

DOI: 10.4018/978-1-60566-994-6.ch013

existing content within the common virtual work environment.

With today's technologies, it is possible to *reference* existing content instead of using the traditional cut-and-paste feature (see Chapter 14). When content is referenced, a permanent link that pulls content in, as opposed to a hyperlink that directs the reader to a new location, is maintained, allowing all publications to be updated when the original content is modified and updated. Depending on the rules and regulations of the technology used in each organization and industry, the updates to content may or may not require approval before changes are applied. Besides increased consistency, the most obvious advantage of reuse by reference is decreased time and cost needed for maintaining and localizing content: write it once, update it once, and localize it once.

In the technical publication industry where maintenance (modify + re-localize) is often as big a part of the publication process as creating original content and where the ability exists to publish updated content as soon as the product is ready for release, reuse can become quite a competitive advantage. However, technologies alone are insufficient to make reuse happen. Computer mediated communication (cmc) technology opens the door to collaborative writing. Because collaboration among writers is not easy to achieve, as indicated in Chapter 10 about optimizing team performance, their publications can become compromised if team interactions are not effective. In this way, creating good publications is like baking muffins. Publications and muffins are made of multiple ingredients, but both are actually greater than the sum of their parts. Muffins are all made of similar ingredients that are measured and mixed until they have good consistency. Similarly, publications are made of content units (chapters, sections, paragraphs, sentences, phrases, and words) that are put together in publications that should have a consistent writing style and a uniform look and feel.

Discrepancies in writing styles limit collaboration. They make it difficult to create a single publication without extensive re-editing cycles. If the differences are not smoothed at the outset, they will have to be done later in the process. In the technical publications industry where the documentation is one of the last things to be finalized before a product can be put on the market, cleanup at the end of the production line usually means publishing incomplete information, pushing up deadlines, dealing with higher costs, or learning to live with low quality publications that may increase the number of e-mail and support calls, or affect the perception of the product.

Inconsistent content also reduces opportunities for reuse by reference. Good writers who work collaboratively to ensure consistency and quality in general will not include content in their deliverables if it does not match their writing styles or their reader requirements. At best, writers will copy-and-paste the desired information and modify it to meet their own needs. At worse, they will recreate the entire information set. But neither of these options is efficient. To ensure efficiency, the organization must constantly and consistently support writers in their effort to collaborate and reuse content. If they cannot find content or share it easily, they will focus on their own content, processes, and deadlines.

These challenges demonstrate the need for having standards that are recognized and shared among writers collaborating, particularly in virtual settings like that made possible through a CMS. How a team can work together to improve work practices and reduce inconsistencies is what standards are all about. Ensuring consistency and effective collaborative interactions requires a culture of collaboration and strong leadership, the first two principles of virtual collaborative writing.

IMPLEMENTING STANDARDIZATION PROCESSES AS PART OF A COLLABORATIVE ENVIRONMENT

Once a collaborative writing team is convinced that standardization is necessary, or at least desirable for collaborating on one or multiple publications, the need for articulating those standards emerges. Teams can choose among the many existing standards or create their own. Their decision will be driven by many aspects, such as:

- The team's objectives and priorities, such as removing the bottle necks in the publishing process because of last-minute cleanup work, improving user support, improving content quality, lowering costs, or increasing the number of served locales;
- The internal work environment, such as the organizational structure, the tools and processes already in place, and the culture.
- The external environment, such as the industry in which the organization functions and its relationship with business partners;
- Access to technologies, such as a CMS, central repository, or other authoring tools;
- The skill sets of the team members, like their knowledge of methodologies, tools, and their abilities to learn them; and
- The resources such as the time, money, and human resources that can be engaged to plan, deploy, and maintain the collaborative process and the virtual environment that supports it.

From a project management perspective, these considerations influence both the implementation of collaboration and standardization processes. Just as the move to a collaborative writing prompts the need for standardization, the need to conform to standards creates a fertile ground for collaboration; if writers have common work practices and work with a common tool, the team is already halfway to its collaboration goal.

Collaboration and standardization processes are so closely linked that it is as if they are different sides of the same coin. On the one side, standards should be chosen for their ability to support the objectives that are driving the adoption of the collaborative process; on the other side, the implementation of the standards influences the way writers and other team members collaborate.

WRITE STANDARD CONTENT

When baking muffins, the availability and quality of the ingredients are key; quality flour, good oil, and something to sweeten the mix are all necessary. In terms of content, there also are key ingredients; three main ingredients that influence the quality of the publication:

- *The content organization.* The organization defines the general content structure like the chapters, the sections, the reusable components, and text blocks such as notes, lists, and regular paragraphs.
- *The writing styles: grammar, voice, and vocabulary.* The style defines how to write content. Is the audience addressed at the second or third person? Singular or plural? Are there syntactic and, grammar rules that everyone should follow (for example, spelling, abbreviations, the use of punctuation)? Is there a standard terminology base? Should some information be highlighted with specific tagging or style (for example, font style, font size, or heading 1 preset template style)?
- *The delivery.* The delivery defines the processes that enable writers to turn content into deliverables, as well as the delivery formats, the navigation patterns (for example, lists, indexes, links, and other references), and the levels of interactivity necessary for readers, learners, or any other kind of audience.

It is important to understand these three items from a number of perspectives—design, implementation, and workflow. However, in practice, it is essential to keep in mind that these elements are closely related. And even if the organizational structure is *physically* defined first, structure supports the writing and delivery processes. Therefore, these last two items must be included from the initial planning stage forward.

For example, to be able to generate a list of figures automatically at the time of publishing, writers must plan to provide titles for the figures in their content: there must be structural elements that provide the ability to insert these titles at a consistent place in the document. Then there needs to be a way to extract these titles to create and deliver the desired list of figures. From this perspective, the need to standardize delivery drives the requirements for both the standardized structure and the writing rules.

The standardization process called information *modeling* involves creating standards that writers will follow. These standards must support and be supported through all aspects of the documentation process, from creation to delivery. From the information architecture perspective, it is important to consider a tool's ability to manipulate and transform content. For this reason, *transform content*

appears as separate item in Figure 1. However, as far as the collaborative writing team is concerned, the architecture of information is translated into rules that govern the writing styles; therefore, transformation is hidden under the writing style item of the list of ingredients that influence the quality of the publication.

COLLABORATE: STANDARDIZE WORK PRACTICES

A well-written muffin recipe and quality ingredients are essential for baking good muffins. But there is more to baking than these components. If the muffins are to be made by more than one person, it also becomes important to define who does what and how the work is coordinated. Does everyone participate in creating and writing the recipe? Do all the bakers choose and buy their own ingredients based on their own perception of quality and price? Does everyone mix and bake their own muffins? While it is possible that multiple bakers will make separate batches of muffin, it is more likely that one person or team will be in charge of selecting and buying the ingredients, another one in charge mixing them, and another one in charge of inspecting the different aspects for quality.

Figure 1. Information architecture and how it relates to the documentation process

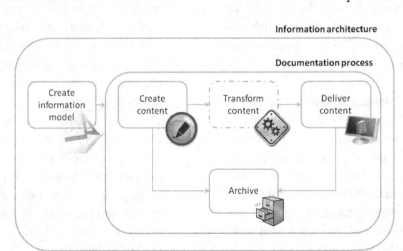

This analogy works in the context of collaborative writing, where collaboration drives not only the need to standardize different aspects of content, but also how people work together:

Roles and Responsibilities (Who Does What)

When a writer works alone, that writer defines the general structure for the publication and also defines the content hierarchy and the order of different subjects. He or she does the research; writes the content; draws the graphics and charts; reviews the content, syntax, and grammar; handles the document's look and feel; and so on. However, to profit from a collaborative writing team, as well as to leverage the many different strengths, skills, and interests that the team presents, someone should assign different roles to participants. Writing—perhaps the skill that brought most people to the team—may not remain everyone's main activity. Some may take on more writing, while others will handle some of the other tasks that they used to perform as single writers. As indicated also in Chapters 10 and 12, there are common roles to consider when preparing writing teams for collaborative work:

- Content architects (organize content),
- Designers (design layouts for deliverable and/or graphics and charts),
- Writers (create content),
- Reviewers (review and comment on content),
- Editors (review and comment on or modify content and layout),
- Programmers and system administrators (set up and manage the virtual work environment and often the publishing process), and
- Coordinators or project leads (optimize the work of the collaborators and makes sure that nothing falls between the cracks).

Some team members may be responsible for tasks related to the standardization process itself, such as defining and maintaining the main content structure and the templates used by others, defining and maintaining a manual of style for text, and defining and maintaining a terminology base, which also is considered in Chapter 15.

Working as a team enables the writers to contribute what they do best and also to optimize the distribution of the work based on the production needs, such that a person may take on different roles based on the most immediate needs. Accordingly, having roles does not mean that a writer cannot make different types of contributions to different projects; each member may play more than one role. For example, collaborators may review each others' work, and a tech-savvy coordinator could manage the virtual work environment.

However, letting members take care of their own pieces from beginning to end, instead of structuring work into various roles and assignments, is like trying to bake a dozen muffins with each team baking one or more muffins in an individual process from selecting the ingredients to taking them in and out of the oven. The muffins are not likely to be as consistent as they would be if the different tasks were split among the team members. In terms of efficiency, if everyone does everything from gathering ingredients to cleaning the pots and pans, the task requires more energy, more dishes, and more uses of the oven, which is the equivalent to working overtime.

As with all things, the team will need to find its own equilibrium between being too strict and too flexible in the roles and responsibilities, where the scope of work is precise enough to limit confusion and the duplication of efforts, but flexible enough to enable team members to be creative and bring innovative ideas to improve the quality of the work. Such balance enables the team to improve productivity, make the collaboration more pleasurable, and create opportunities for members to develop new professional skills for long-term sustainability of the system.

Creating new work practices is a process and managing change may become one of the main tasks when a team moves to either collaborative writing or a virtual environment. If both the collaborative writing practices and the virtual environment change at the same time, handling change may become as much a priority as implementing the standards, which is the reason why the principles of good leadership and the culture of collaboration are linked and so important. In fact, good change management will help the team choose, develop, and implement good standard information models, collaborative work practices, and virtual tools.

Workflow and Work Processes (When to Do What)

Just as ingredients must be bought, combined, and mixed before the muffins can be put into the oven, there are many steps from the initial request to the publishing of documents or Web publications, and some steps must be completed before others. As a team becomes more functional, it learns to trust one another and finds that splitting roles is useful to overall team productivity. The concept of team productivity is considered more fully in Chapter 10. Over time, team members have the opportunity to rely on others for support at some level, but they also start to depend on each other in positive ways that get the job done.

In order to keep the production lines flowing and to reduce bottlenecks, coordinating efforts becomes important. Standard processes are the result of discovering what works best and implementing it on a large scale.

In collaborative writing, processes normally evolve around the document life cycle. From planning to writing to translating, up to delivery and maintenance, standardized processes specify how the work is performed and then assigned to the next person or team. Both content ownership and rules regarding reuse may be defined. For example, it is useful to specify what happens when

a piece of content that is used in many deliverables is modified. Do changes apply everywhere automatically or do they need to be reviewed and approved for each publication? Are owners of the deliverables notified before changes are made, when they are made, or at the point that they are ready for publishing? Is there a pre-defined approval process that delineates what is ready for publishing?

The more repetitive the activities and the bigger the team, the more sense it makes to have standard processes and integrate them into CMC technology. Standard processes that support the production life cycle also support the collaborative effort in terms of the decision making process and other collaborative aspects that are necessary whether the collaboration occurs in face-to-face or virtually.

In computer science, methodologies that are used to design work cases identify the *system* as one of the actors in the work process. In virtual collaborative writing settings, since the system can take on some of the writers' workflow tasks like managing dependencies between content units or handling roles and the status of the content, it is useful for writing teams also to think of the system as a team member with whom they can exchange and collaborate. The more dynamic the system, the more it can become a player in the virtual team. This player can be the standard expert that supports guidelines, rules, and quality markers; the manager that dispatches work based on standard business rules and raises the red flag before it is too late; the reviewer that checks link validity; or the content master that helps the team find and manage reusable pieces of content.

Storage, Access, and Transportation (Where and How)

By definition, virtual collaboration cannot happen outside the virtual world. When baking muffins, everyone needs to be at the same location or to be connected to that location by some means: the farmers do not need to make it to the kitchen, but the flour, oil, and sweetener do.

In the virtual collaboration environment, the storage area for content can be likened to the kitchen and the communication systems are the means for people and ingredients to make it there. Content may travel by e-mail, and some details may be stored in a database, while others are stored in an old mainframe system before they make it into the deliverables. Yet, in the end, writers must be able to access the content and bring it together to a single location to create the desired end results. Having a central virtual location, at least for delivery and good communication between different storage locations, plus a means for people to access and manipulate the content is what makes the environment virtual.

It is no surprise that the standards of the virtual environment are technical in nature: standard communication tools and protocols, storage facilities and their application programming interfaces (APIs), as well as compatible writing tools and file formats are important components of the mix. While the main purpose of this chapter is to focus on standards that are closer to the collaborative team's activity (since tools are used to support the collaborative process), it is vital to ensure CMC compatibility. For example, if encoding—and therefore special characters—are not handled the same way by different systems, writers will have to replace the changed characters and will be less efficient. Also, if systems cannot be integrated, collaborators will have to export content from one system before they actually can write.

VIRTUALIZE: SUPPORT THE STANDARDS

In virtual collaborative writing, the virtual quality is the new affordance. Writing and collaborative work have always been possible in face-to-face settings. The CMC tools have made collaborative virtual writing possible. In fact, for information

management teams that already have been collaborating in the non-virtual world or that have evolved in regulated industry where standards regarding content and processes have been present for a long time, the virtual aspect of new tools may be the element that has led to the most significant changes for writing teams.

Still, there are good reasons for taking the time to explore successful standards that ground existing content and collaborative perspectives before integrating virtual elements. Because tools, with all their features and gizmos, are the new aspect in this environment of change, there is a risk that they will get all the attention at the cost of other standard aspects that may be taken for granted or forgotten altogether. Indeed, if the tools are adopted at the same time as the team takes their first steps into the virtual environment, there is a risk of unrealistic expectations that these tools can do it all and that team members no longer need to worry about writing standards or collaborative practices. However, as seen with the muffin analogy, there is more to making muffins than getting an oven, molds, and ingredients. The people who use these tools are as important, if not more so.

That said, beside storage and communication, today's CMC tools when coupled, often seamlessly, with the right software can play an important role in supporting the different aspects of content (the structure, text, and delivery), as well as the collaborative process (people and the way they collaborate). Therefore, they do influence both the writing and the collaborative processes.

The choice of CMC tools and software applications is large, but with choice comes the need to make decisions, a concept discussed in Chapter 16. It is important, therefore, to be able to evaluate tools in reference to the way they support, enhance, or limit each aspect of the virtual collaborative writing (see Table 3 in Chapter 12) process in order to make the best possible decision.

This section offers insight into major approaches and technologies that apply to standardization in the virtual collaborative environment.

Rather than trying to provide an exhaustive look at specific tools, its purpose is to explore different approaches and strategies offered by families of tools and to provide some criteria to orient teams in their selection and definition processes for choosing existing standards or developing their own, and for implementing them in their environment. Note that not all tools are technological in nature and that some time-honored approaches, such as the use of a common terminology base (or glossary) and manuals of style, still apply to the virtual environment.

XML/SGML and Structured Authoring in General

What it Is

XML and SGML are markup languages that provide and support a standard structure for content. They define the order and hierarchy in which elements may appear. Structured authoring tools offer the same type of support, but are based on proprietary languages. The main difference between XML and SGML is that XML has a more rigorous syntax that makes it easier and a lot less expensive to use for Web publication. They support semantics identification of content within the text and can support structures that provide context for interpreting the semantic elements.

What it Does

Structured languages, as the name indicates, are especially strong when it comes to controlling structures. Many standard structures exist, like DocBook, DITA or S1000d; yet structured tool languages are flexible enough to let teams define their own structure and therefore their own standard rules. Most importantly, structured tools and languages provide the mechanisms necessary for tools to support and validate content rules; they can ensure that content follows the defined content structure. XML and SGML are good examples of

technologies that enable the development of standards and that provide the means to support them.

Elements in the structured authoring environment may be defined to meet different objectives. Here are some of the reasons for defining a more specific structure:

- *Build consistency in the general organization of content.* Build consistency in how content is defined and ordered; define what type of information is mandatory, what type is optional, and where it should appear in the text.

- *Manipulate pieces of content.* Support content extraction or the ability to reference specific pieces of content. For example, identify all topic short descriptions in order to extract them to create a summary, or identify pieces of content that can be reused.

- *Describe the information for more powerful usage.* Provide extra context for understanding or searching content. For example, use an author element to support the ability to search for content written by Shakespeare instead of content that mentions or cites Shakespeare.

- *Manage the content, workflow, and delivery.* Keep track of anything related to life cycle, workflow, or use. For example, content could be mined with metadata that is not published but is used by writers and systems.

- *Format pieces of content.* Even with the separation of content and presentation, it is important to identify information that needs to have a special look. For example, highlight the button names of a user interface not only in a reference guide but also in other publications. Identifying the information by type instead of formatting still provides separation of content and presentation in the sense that it does not say "bold"; instead it just identifies the element as something that can be formatted. It can be bold, but also italic, colored, or not formatted at all depending on the different context, media, and publications.

Structured languages not only enable the writing team to identify any piece of information with extra meaningful tags or metadata, but also automation of the processes that manipulate content. In that regard, it is helpful to involve team members who have a good technical background. They can optimize processes from the creation to the delivery process with reuse of content through different types of referencing, as well as automated content manipulation.

Limitations

Structured authoring is only as good as the implementation mechanisms that support it. To address limitations, define a structure that supports the objectives defined for the implementation. For example, a team could choose XML for its ability to separate content and presentation and yet include XML elements that allow users to bold or italicize text.

Defining standard structures and processes is a hard task. A structure that is too strict and that does not provide enough XML elements may prevent authors from including some information that may be useful to their audience, or it may force them to break the rules and use whatever element gives them a desired look (which may apply only to a specific authoring environment since XML allows different formatting in different publications). On the other hand, defining too many semantic elements creates confusion for the team and means that each new team member has to undergo a steep learning curve.

The costs associated with implementing structured authoring as well as the learning curve that most team members must make are substantial. Even though organizations are increasingly emphasizing structured writing practices, both

cultural change and strong leadership—the first two principles of virtual collaborative writing that ground this book—still are needed to encourage writers and to help them become proficient and effective collaborators.

How it Affects the Work

Switching to a structured authoring environment represents a big paradigm shift at many different levels. First, writers must adjust to the fact that the separation of form and content prevents them from being able to control fully the look and feel of documents produced. Second, writers need to learn how to think of structure separately and to define it explicitly to support more than one publishing processes. Finally, writers should be prepared to work with semantic elements, which add complexity, a concept explored in Chapter 14.

Examples

If writers want to reinforce standard rules about how steps in a procedure should be written, they can create a structure that achieves the following:

- Tell the writer what to do in the mandatory element <command>.
- Prompt them to enter optional details about the step in <details>.
- Prompt them to indicate the outcome of the optional step in the <result>.

The results will be something like the procedure shown in Figure 2.

Content Modularity and Information Typing

What They Are

Content modularity is the practice of dividing large pieces of content into smaller pieces, often called modules or topics, can be understand-

Figure 2. Procedures

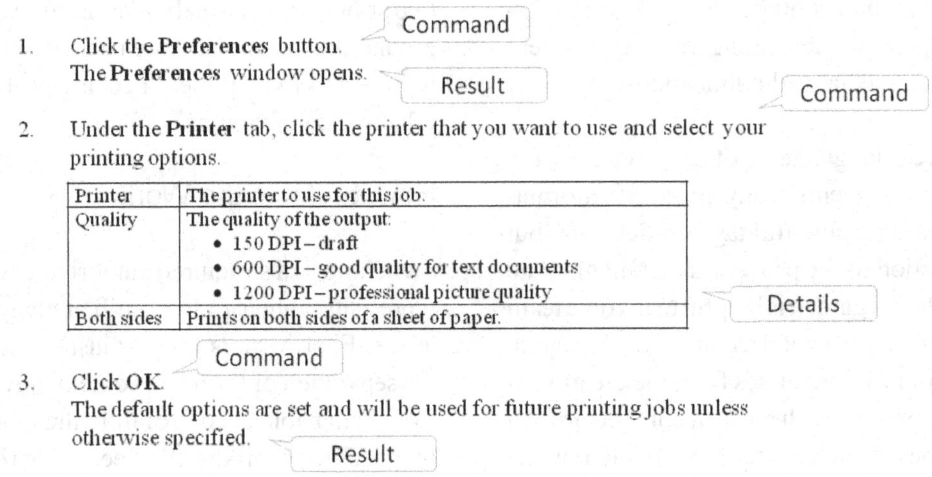

1. Click the **Preferences** button. | Command |
   The **Preferences** window opens. | Result | | Command |

2. Under the **Printer** tab, click the printer that you want to use and select your printing options.

Printer	The printer to use for this job.
Quality	The quality of the output: • 150 DPI – draft • 600 DPI – good quality for text documents • 1200 DPI – professional picture quality
Both sides	Prints on both sides of a sheet of paper.

| Details |

| Command |

3. Click OK.
   The default options are set and will be used for future printing jobs unless otherwise specified. | Result |

able on their own. Or, from the perspective of those who create the content, it is the creation of small pieces of standalone, comprehensible content that can be put together to create larger publications. (See Chapter 14 for more information about content units.) Defining content units of similar sizes that handle specific types of information can improve consistency through the standardization of form.

This methodology relies on writing techniques that reduce the organizational dependencies between the different modules or topics to improve their ability to fit into different contexts. The simplest example is that if content is going to be presented in a different order, one has to stop referencing sections in terms of their locations: "The previous chapter showed us XYZ; this chapter shows ABC."

What They Do

Creating modular content makes the different pieces easily digestible so that users can quickly find the specific information needed. This practice has little value for writing a novel, for example, but it useful for the Web where people are often looking for an answer to a specific question and do not wish to read many pages of contextual

information before they can get to what they want.

Modular content, when implemented with tools that allow the manipulation of modules as separate physical entities, such as structured authoring tools, is critical to content reuse and repurposing since it allows modules to be placed in different hierarchies in various publications.

Modularity often goes hand in hand with creating structure and with identifying the nature of the content, referred to as *content type*, so that it can be reused. It also allows the team to define different rules for structuring each type. Common types used in technical documentation include task or procedure and concept or definition, but types can be made more specific, such as a task related to troubleshooting, scheduling, a bug report, or a training exercise. Identifying content types helps to determine how modules should be separated. This process standardizes the content components so that published information is more consistent, easier to locate and read, and thus more usable for audiences.

Accordingly, modularity requires collaborative writing practices so that different writers can work collectively to create the modules that will be used and reused across publications. CMC tools can help writers if they reinforce the structure, purpose, and form for each type of module.

Example

Figure 3 illustrates how processes for developing content concurrently can speed up the creations and delivery of publications because each module can be handled independently. That is, one module can be reviewed and translated while another is still being written. However, writers must work together to ensure that each module can stand alone and does not refer to any sequential ordering.

Modular content creation makes it easier to for managers to define the scope of work for writers especially if they do not have to figure out the entire context of a book or subject area and if the status of the different pieces is already known (for example, 80% of the content is already approved). If modules are standardized, is easier to estimate the average time to complete a module and the impact of changing the content. Moreover, it is easier to manage resources efficiently just prior publication when modules are standardized.

Limitations

The entire information set must be modularized to allow for the manipulation and reuse of all the pieces, a process that requires time and resources.

Writers also must agree to follow collaborative writing practices, including syntax and rules for referencing content. These practices are hard to implement without support from managers and other leaders, who can ensure a culture of collaboration One the one hand, specific writing practices can make it difficult to bring on temporary staff or those familiar with other standards; on the other hand, when standards are documented, it can be easy to direct new staff to these guidelines. The more writers become familiar with topic-based writing, the easier it is for them to adapt to new modular practices.

In the context of reuse, the biggest limitation pertains to the lack of access to tools that have the capacity for locating and manipulating smaller pieces of content (that is, to create, save, find, aggregate, and so forth). When a team works with a few large publications, a good online folder structure usually is sufficient. However, if each publication is made of dozens of small modules, each saved as a separate physical entity, then more advanced CMC tools are critical. To the extent that technical standards vary, it is important to choose a standard that best supports the goals of an organization. Some standards like shareable content object reference model (SCORM, used

Figure 3. Concurrent work processes

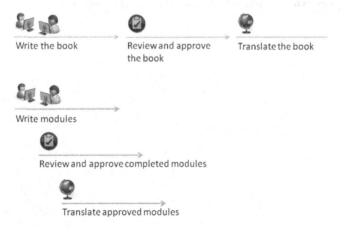

Write the book   Review and approve the book   Translate the book

Write modules

Review and approve completed modules

Translate approved modules

mostly for computer-based training) that do not define the details of the content architecture will require content to be delivered in lesson-like modules. What constitutes a module may differ from one standard to another (for example, DITA, S1000D, and home-grown standards).

Smaller content units are more flexible, making it is easier to aggregate them to create larger publications. However, the smaller the content unit, the greater the support that is required to manipulate and track the content creation and delivery processes. Teams that are focused on multichannel publishing to deliver information on the Web, computers, and mobile phones require this support to administer effective processes.

How They Affect the Work

Web-based teams have greater familiarity writing modular content. For teams accustomed to book-based texts, the shift away from linear, to modular writing is difficult. Writers must learn how to split up their work tasks while staying coordinated with other writers so that the different pieces can be used independently.

Modularization is at the heart of the need to collaborate, when writing content that can be shared. It requires writers interacting not only to create modules but also to oversee the organization of the various parts so that a publication has coherence. This kind of work requires different roles and co-ownership of tasks to ensure that the information products make sense to audiences. Modularization can be a powerful approach to writing, but establishing the modular framework requires overhead both to develop and implement effective standards.

Example

Figure 4 provides an example of how standalone modules can be reused in publications with different purposes. In a training guide, users expect a scenario-based approach on how to use a collaborative platform to create a team project; steps are in the order in which the user is likely to perform them. In a reference guide that is used as needed, such as when users have forgotten how to perform a task, tasks are organized by feature to simplify the search process.

Manuals of Styles

What They Are

Style guides or manuals of style serve as reference for an explicit set of standards for organizing and writing content.

Figure 4. Content repurposing enabled by modular content creation

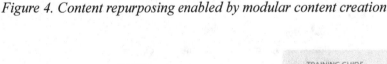

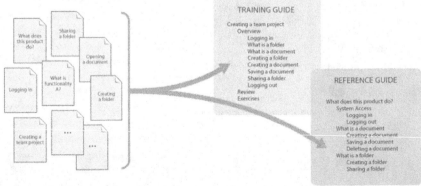

What They Do

Guidelines focus on different aspects of content creation from structure rules, grammar, punctuation, terminology, and spelling to visual and presentation requirements. These manuals usually serve specific functions, such as to increase consistency, reusability, and readability for a specific type of media, such as the Web or mobile phones. For further information about how style affects quality, see Chapter 15.

Limitations

The greatest limitation of style manuals is the need to rely on writers to implement guidelines consistently. Such work requires strong leadership to convey the importance of adherence to the style for topic-based writing to be successful.

How They Affect the Work

Manuals of style are themselves expressions of standards. They affect the work primarily by requiring the writing team to learn and follow rules related to the writing itself. A variety of strategies help make implementation easier:

- Some teams rely on editors and reviewers to be the "style police," addressing this requirement through a role assigned to team members.
- Some teams will implement specialized tools that can help with support (as described in Chapter 15). While configuration may be involved, implementation generally is not complicated, assuming that the tool can be integrated with the rest of the team's toolset.
- Many teams include specific, often agreed-upon rules as instructions in their template to guide authors.

Example

Simplified English is an interesting example of a standard style guide that focuses on reducing ambiguity to increase the reader's comprehension, including those whose first language is not English. Simplified English is used widely in the aerospace industry to ensure that confusion does not lead to life threatening situations (see, for example, ASD-STE1000, 2004-2005).

Another well-known standard of the technical documentation industry is the Chicago Manual of Style, which also is available online as a virtual tool handy for collaborative writing teams (see The Chicago Manual of Style Online, 2007). Other industries that involve writing teams also have standards, of course. The Associated Press (AP), for example, requires journalists to follow their style guide, and their style has been adopted by other industry writers as well. Interestingly, the AP also offers online services for external teams to add their own custom standard information that can then be accessible along with the main standard information (see, for example, AP Stylebook, 2009).

Document Templates

What They Are

In the context of content creation, templates are either documents with predefined sections or fields to be filled by users or style templates that define the look for content such as blocks of text, titles, list items, and paragraphs or inline elements. They also may be a combination of both. The equivalents in structured authoring are templates that include the elements (tags) that are mandatory or most often used in the structure.

What They Do

Templates are a low cost and simple way to provide standards by way of guidelines for writers. They standardize collaborative writing by providing the basic building blocks (structure) for writers at the moment where writers need them. Templates also may provide pre-defined styles for formatting content and written guidelines to help writers comply with the standard writing practices. Their efficiency depends on the tools that support them; some of them offer writers more flexibility than others.

Limitations

There are few limitations to document templates, but templates that are too complete or too strict may be more cumbersome than useful for writers who are used to the rules. An efficient implementation focuses on the most important aspects of the standards. Access to templates must be central to ensure consistency among a writing team. Too often if templates are saved on the individual user's local drive and, updates are not implemented. Moreover, if writers can override basic rules, consistency will be compromised.

How They Affect the Work

Templates may give writers a head start in terms of structure, grammar, and display style because they provide hints along the way. However, the complexity of some templates makes them a liability; they may become cumbersome if too much information is provided, especially in combination with the learning curve of new standards.

Examples

For example, when documenting a user interface with a document template, instead of applying the bold style to the names of buttons in a user interface, writers would apply the "button" to the "term" styles. The main advantage is that presentation decisions can be delayed or changed, which increases maintainability and the ability to publish content to different outputs with different styling.

Another example is that if the design team decides to make terms italic instead of bold in Web help, they can define "term" as italic, and all these instances will be updated from bold to italic, while all button names from the documented user interface will remain bold without necessary human intervention on every single term in the content.

Terminology Base

What it Is

A terminology base is a bank of terms with optional definitions and rules for use. The terminology base can be as simple as list of terms documented on paper or it can take the form of an electronic base integrated in the authoring tool in order to offer tips and suggestions to writers as they create content. The terminology base provides standard wording and expressions. It prevents writers from using the same expression for two separate means, and from using too many expressions for the same concept. Terminology tools are extremely important when trying to manage translation costs. For a complete discussion of a particular type of terminology base, see Chapter 15.

What it Does

The objective of a terminology base is to standardize the use of terms and to avoid creating confusion for the reader and to ensure efficiency when translating or localizing content.

Limitations

Compliance to the rules of a terminology base is most often on the shoulders of the writing team. Unfortunately, their learning curve can be rather large if the size of the base also is large. There are, however, tools that can support authors with guidelines and suggestions. The use of these tools is not yet widespread.

How it Affects the Work

The writing team must be consistent in its use and in their maintenance of terminology. Most CMC tools that can support the use of pre-defined terms and rules are easy to use and require little effort to learn.

Example

A glossary is the simplest and most well-known form of a terminology base.

Delivery Formats

What They Are

Standards for delivery can be as simple as a well-known document format like rich text files (RTF) or portable document format (PDF). Delivery standards can be more complex and specify rules about how the information should be delivered with other files in a specific format and hierarchy and with specific mechanisms for navigating and referencing content.

What They Do

The delivery rules focus on the audience, the context in which they use content (that is, reference, learning, making a purchase) and various media. The rules may define navigation and searchability. For example, most publications have a table of contents, some have lists of figures and tables, and others have indexes or reference to topics found on other book or Web pages.

How it Affects the Work

Delivery is the ultimate purpose, and hopefully the objective is to create a deliverable that reaches the audience within the scope that was set for the project. Therefore, standards are crucial for a virtual collaborative writing to ensure that the team delivers the information as specified.

In the case of semantic-based structure, for example, the structure should be defined to support the requirements for delivery. Writers then are responsible for following the structure within the pre-defined guidelines and for providing the necessary cross-referencing information when they create the content. Automated transformations tools, XSLTs, and processing can take care of the rest of the referencing information. If the use of structured tools is new to the team, some members of the team may need to specialize in maintaining the transformation processes.

In other cases, writers must be aware of the requirements for delivering and creating content within the specified toolset and within the specified guidelines, especially in reference to content organization and formatting. Moreover, they may have to make some last-minute adjustments if mistakes could not be caught before the transformation to the final delivery.

Example

The SCORM is a good example of a standard focused on a specific goal, in this case, training. SCORM defines how to deliver modular content for learning purposes in the form of what it calls "learning objects." The notion of a "shareable content object" is about writing and managing units of training material for online delivery, such as where the content units can be shared across systems.

The focus of SCORM is not the regulation of the writing process, but the regulation of the delivery. In this sense, most, although not all, of the responsibility for standard compliancy relies on the developers instead of the writers. What is defined in the delivery standard?

- The *packaging* and the description of the content; how all the pieces are aggregated into a single deliverable.
- Sequencing, the *navigation* paths available to the learner between different parts of the course.
- The *interaction* (run-time environment), which in SCORM specifies how the content is controlled and presented by the learning management system that delivers content to the learning audience.

Even when standards focus on delivery, they may require that the content be built following some basic architectural rules that can include creating modular content and specific navigation patterns.

Content Management Systems

What They Are

A CMS is a computer application that manages the content creation and publishing life cycle as well as the workflows related to the collaborative work that takes place. In a large environment, the CMS is the main system around which the rest of the tools are integrated. CMSs support standard collaborative work processes, but since there are many different kinds of CMSs, such as ones to manage complete documents or Web content, choose one based on its ability to support the standards established for managing modules or content components. For example, in a modular writing environment, the CMS should manage small pieces of content and their dependencies in terms of managing the life cycle and workflow during the creation and manipulation of the modules as well as the creation and manipulation of the aggregated piece. For more information on

CMSs, see Chapter 9; Chapter 16 also provides information about the use of CMSs to conduct document reviews.

What They Do

The functionality of a CMS includes many of the following: content creation process management, review and approval management, versioning, indexing, searching features, file loading and extracting, translation management, publishing, and archiving. Some systems manage only a few types of formats, like text and html, while others can handle almost any media type including audio and video files. Moreover, since CMSs have a strong focus on workflow—the interplay of work tasks as they affect different members of the writing team—most manage security and access rights. A few even control delivery and interaction with users, such as a specialized CMS called learning management systems (LMS) that can help learners return to one place to review ideas that were not well understood and even to follow their progress and keep score. Some CMSs also offer means to communicate such as wikis, blogs, and chats—offering the advantage of allowing writing teams to choose how to collaborate.

To summarize, the main goal of the CMS is to orchestrate the writing process from planning to delivery. They function as powerful tools for managing collaboration among writers, for example, by notifying them if changes are made, indicating who has content checked out, and allowing them to compare versions and find out where certain content is being used.

Limitations

The cost of a CMS often is the biggest limitation. Not only is the purchase price high, but also configuration and integration costs are significant to get the system fully functioning. Ironically, if CMSs are not configured and structured properly, the ways they are used in an organization can grow organically and defeat the primary purpose of being able to manage content effectively.

There are other challenges to working with standards in a CMS. Some common ones include:

- *Not finding the right balance between implementing an organization's work processes and adapting to the system's "out of the box" set up (including optimized storage, search, and management, for example).* Even when working with a CMS specialist there are difficulties: the team knows what it does, the consultant understands what the system can do, but it's hard for one to grasp the entire context of the other's work practices.
- *Choosing the wrong CMS for the job.* CMSs are like cars: a small car will save money on gas, but a van is better for moving large quantities. As mentioned earlier, it is important to start with the needs of the organization and then choose the toolset to fit those needs. The hard fact is that if one has experience with the toolset, it is hard to understand how to use the power of the tool to improve content manipulation and collaboration. Prototyping or working with experts can be useful in that case.
- *Trying to do it all at once.* If the IT team needs to adapt the system to the people and the people need to learn how to work with the system, a phased approach may facilitate learning for smoother implementation. It is easier to adapt along the way than after the whole thing has been built.
- *Not allowing for enough training.* The best CMS can do no good if people do not know what it can do. While the CMS advanced search feature can help one find a document, if one does not feel confident using the feature, it has little benefit. It is the difference between baking one's first muffins and starting to be creative with ingredients to create new varieties. Writing teams can integrate variety after they have the basic knowledge and experience.
- *Neglecting existing content or feeling the need to include everything.* Some content may be near the end of its usefulness, for example, when a product will be replaced soon, if few updates are needed, and if reuse opportunities are limited. On the other hand, when one has relevant content or content that may need to be updated regularly, the system can be useful.
- *Neglecting usability and performance of the CMS.* The CMS should make the team more productive. A slow system or one that is not maintained may reduce performance and increase the frustration levels. Moreover a bad integration with other tools could create extra work for users instead of automating the part of their work that does not require their active, ongoing thinking.

How They Affect the Work

The CMS is often the center of the collaborative virtual environment. It has a major impact on collaborative process relative to content development and manipulation and on establishing a virtual space. As with many of the items discussed earlier, the implementation of a CMS represents an enormous paradigm shift for writers. While writers typically access content through a hierarchy of files and folders when working outside of a CMS, the approach changes dramatically when working inside one. A CMS transcends common hierarchical classification methods. With advanced searching and indexing capabilities, not only can writers in a CMS display content in a custom hierarchy that meets the need of the moment, but they can reorder content by project, department, subject, and date. With a few clicks, it can be reordered by work assigned to writer, due date, and department; and then reordered again by due date and by alpha order of the person to whom it is assigned. Focusing too much on folder hierarchies and naming conventions during a CMS implementation is like buying a car to get to work yet taking the bus route, following its schedule, and making all the stops. While one is assured to get a seat, it seems that the person is missing out on some of the main advantages of buying a car. Such writers might say: "I just bought it to ensure I'd get a seat every morning. I don't really care for changing my ways to take advantage of the other opportunities." For writers who are willing to make the needed adjustments, CMSs offer many additional options for classifying and accessing information.

Example

Providing an example for a CMS is like trying to provide an example for intelligence. The difficulty is that the CMS manages what happens behind the scene. The CMS is the coordinator or manager that knows everything and everyone. It is the tool that manages the relationships among content pieces and among people. It is the central tool that communicates with all others—the authoring tool, the storage, the delivery system, the people that create content, and sometimes the people who access content for consumption.

Choosing an Approach

Few teams will choose to work with a single approach or methodology for standardizing the development of information. The most important rules to consider when making choices for particular virtual collaborative writing teams are:

- The content comes first. It is the primary resource for creating deliverables that readers can use.
- Good collaboration improves content creation, and collaboration practices should be adapted to the type of content created and delivered.

- Tools support content and collaboration in the virtual world; however, these tools must be chosen based on goals and objectives to ensure that they facilitate work processes and do not create new barriers.

Table 1 provides a comparison of tools and approaches that support standards. It identifies what these approaches can do, but also how much is based on the ability of the team to comply with those standards, how complex the technology is, and how costly using the approach can be (often closely related to complexity).

The following paragraphs explain how the tools and approaches illustrated can be understood in terms of standards.

Support Standards in Terms of...

Collaborating writers need to select CMC tools that will support the standards identified by the organization. Once the organization documents the required standards, identify what the main advantage the tool provides: Does the tool support standard content structures? Does the tool help to even out writing styles? Does the tool support standardized work processes? Does the tool support information product delivery?

Separating Content and Format

Keeping the formatting technology separate from the content allows for more flexibility when implementing multi-media or multi-branded publishing. It is especially useful when organizations undergo a change of image either for marketing reasons or following a merger because the look can be developed and applied automatically to each piece of content in every single document. Success lies in the quality of the implementation and in the ability of the team to develop an information model that integrates the use of semantic structures.

Some tools are more limiting in regard to semantic tagging features. For example, many

Table 1. Tools and approaches that support standards

Approaches to standardization	Support standards in terms of...	Can separate presentation from content (scale of 1 to 3)	Complexity of the technology (scale of 1 to 3)	Reliance on authors/editors (scale of 1 to 3)	Costs (scale of 1 to 3)
XML/SGML and Structured Authoring in General	Structure	3	3	2 to 3	3
Content Modularity and Information Typing	Structure	Depends on implementation	1 to 3	2 to 3	3
Manuals of styles	One or many of: structure, syntax, grammar, terminology.	n/a	1	2	1
Document templates	Structure and sometimes syntax and terminology*	Depends on implementation**	2	2	1
Terminology base	Vocabulary	n/a	1	2 to 3	1 to 3
Delivery formats	Delivery		1 to 3	2 to 3	3
Content management systems	Storage and work processes		2 to 3	1 to 2	2 to 3

* Templates can support syntax and terminology with instructions or labeled sections.

** Efficiency in content/presentation separation depends on the tool's ability to support context and to prevent style overrides.

applications ask writers to identify what is a level 1 or a level 2 heading, which limits the ability to move pieces around without reapplying different formatting styles on titles. Look for structured authoring tools that allow writers to identify titles as titles so that XSLTs can apply the right formatting for the right title level.

Technical Complexity

The evaluation of the technical complexity is based on the need for configuration and computer programming skills.

The complexity of tools that is relevant at the time this book is published, may no longer apply ten or even five years from now. Complexity tends to decrease over time as vendors automate processes and create nicely designed visual interfaces to handle what started as a complex task. Plus, as writers increase their computer literacy, the skill to carry out certain automated functions becomes more common. Just think of how many people knew how to use word processors 15 years ago compared to today.

The Scale

1. At a minimum, team members must know how to create content in word processors and other tools available in today's office settings.
2. Advanced knowledge is necessary for tool configuration, but intermediate knowledge is enough for use (for example, typing and formatting is basic, while using predefined styles consistently is more complex).
3. Programming skills are required for implementation.

Reliance on Writers/Editors

Reliance on writers is related to the support that tools can provide. When no tool is available to support a standard, the responsibility to meet expectancies and follow the rules and guidelines falls on the writers and other team members.

The Scale

1. At a minimum, tools guide team members through the documentation process, and they can measure compliance to some extent. Team members are expected to know the rules and not to bypass the tools.
2. Templates and a number of styles are available to limit the differences between writers, but tools make few suggestions to team members and provide mechanism for validation.
3. Guidelines are provided in writing, but it is up to people to apply them all.

Costs

The costs are evaluated in terms of money, time, and the number of people who need to implement the standard and the related tools. These resources are often interchangeable. For example, a group with little time may be willing to pay more, while a group with a knowledgeable team but little money to buy tools may use its people to reduce the cost of change and the time it takes to implement the solution.

The Scale

1. At a minimum, there is a short learning curve (basic training, practice, change management) and the cost is low (common for tools already available) or affordable for many groups.
2. Some members need to develop advanced skills for tool configuration, which may imply the use of a specialized toolset. The skills necessary to operate the tools are not as common on the market and training is more likely to be required. The costs are affordable in one form or another to most groups.

3. There is a need for specialized tools that can be expensive and that are likely to require more intensive training. These are affordable to larger groups, specialized small groups, or when the benefits can be proven to justify it in the organizational context.

SUMMARY AND CONCLUSION FOR A FAST EVOLVING WORLD

Approaches to collaborative virtual writing can apply at three basic levels—content, life cycle, and workflow—as well as the tools that make the environment virtual. Standards exist to ensure that everyone's work fits into the larger picture of delivering information to an audience.

The tools that virtualize or digitize the virtual world exist to support the writing and collaborative processes, but they also create an opportunity for improving content organization and work processes. Still, familiarity with the technology often is more crucial than appears at first glance. Not using the tools to the team's advantage is like buying a car to get to the bakery mentioned earlier, but using it to resolve a single annoyance instead. Not using virtual tools involves letting everyone drive the car to the bakery without standard rules—without roads, street signs, regulations, parking spaces, and even without policing— "Please do stop at that red light!"—which can be a risky adventure.

This chapter has explored the elements that can be standardized when creating content collaboratively in a virtual environment. Standards improve cohesion. How much standard and control is good enough? There is no single answer. Once most team members have acquired enough knowledge for baking muffins, they may want to start being creative with ingredients and make their own necessary adjustments to bake new and differently tasty muffins (missing a batch once in a while is not so bad compared to creating the next best seller). No risk, no gain.

As with everything in life, the conclusion is open: play, explore, try, hit the wall, learn from your successes by making the recipe repeatable, learn from mistakes by making some necessary adjustments, improve until the new opportunity or challenge comes around and you need to adjust again. And if you want new collaborators, make sure that they can join in easily: be accessible (beware of tool compatibility issues), show them the ways of your world (your standards), and let them contribute to the development or implementation of standards with their own suggestions for improvements. Doing so will enable you to get the best from everyone's unique skill set and abilities. Virtual collaborative writing is a complicated journey—not only in terms of employing complex tools, but also in terms of defining and implementing the standards that make tools functional and the information delivered to readers usable. The crucial step when implementing standards is to ensure that the organization employs the first two principles that ground this book—creating a culture of collaboration and ensuring strong leadership to change the culture.

REFERENCES

ASD Simplified Technical English. (2004-2005). ASD Simplified Technical English Maintenance Group. Accessed October 1, 2009, http://www.asd-ste100.org/INDEX.HTM

Stylebook, A. P. (2009). The Associated Press. Accessed October 1, 2009. http://www.apstyle-book.com/

The Chicago Manual of Style Online. (2009). (15th ed.). Accessed October 1, 2009 http://www.chicagomanualofstyle.org/home.html

ADDITIONAL READING

CMS do's and don'ts. (2005). *Alt Tags*. Accessed October 1, 2009. http://www.alttags.org/content-management/cms-dos-and-donts/

Rockley, A. (2004). Why start with analysis and design? *The Rockley Bulletin* Accessed October 1, 2009. http://www.rockley.com/TheRockleyReport/V1I1/Best%20Practices.htm

Rockley, A. (n.d.) Best practices. *The Rockley Group*. Accessed October 1, 2009. http://www.pubexec.com/article/launching-new-content-management-system-can-disaster-without-right-plan-place-experts-share-their-advice-help-you-better-manage-process-401358_1.html

Chapter 14
Developing Content in a Reuse Environment

Norma Emery
Alcatel-Lucent, USA

ABSTRACT

The need for reusing content and automating the writing process to gain efficiency in workplace environments is a priority in many work settings. Writing teams seek effective strategies for integrating reuse principles, and increasingly they need to accomplish this work virtually. Reusing content across an organization requires coordinated collaboration in terms of both establishing standards and ensuring that all team members follow those standards. In view of this high-level requirement, setting up a reuse environment seems familiar; that is, developing and implementing a style guide to promote consistency always has been central to good technical writing. Also familiar is the fact that as long as there have been style guides, adherence to them has been difficult to achieve. What makes a reuse environment different from those less focused on reuse is that degree to which standardization among writers must occur. Whereas style guidelines typically have emphasized word or phrasing nuances, standards for reuse move beyond terminology or syntax, involving all aspects of the writing process. An effective reuse environment thus depends on collaborative input from writing teams, which poses significant challenges in virtual environments. This chapter provides insight into the principles of reuse and how virtual collaboration is essential to making content reusable.

INTRODUCTION

Whether to Rewrite or Reuse Content

For writers who have had to remember every document that contains the same content, the possibility of reusing what is already written—not having to document material from scratch—sounds like a vast improvement in the practice of developing content. What value is there in having numerous writers create the same content multiple times? Not only is such a practice inefficient, but doing so risks confusing readers if each writer offers a slightly different view

DOI: 10.4018/978-1-60566-994-6.ch014

of the same concept. Unfortunately, this outcome is inevitable without the strategic reuse of content; an even worse outcome would be contradictory content created by two different writers.

Consider, for example, the customer who purchased both a personal computer and a printer that has advanced features for handling graphics. The computer arrived and was easy to set up, but the printer posed problems. Because it was not a standard printer, the cable included would not fit any of the ports. This setback prompted a call to customer support, and, after much discussion, the customer learned that a dongle was needed to connect the printer to the computer. Once the necessary adapter arrived, the customer read the instructions about how to use it to connect the printer and the computer. Somewhat confused by what she read, the customer also looked at the original instructions that came with the printer. The instructions that came with the dongle completely contradicted the instructions that came with the printer. Because neither set of instructions helped her connect the printer, her only recourse was to contact customer support again so someone could walk her successfully through the process.

This experience highlights the problem that occurs when there are relationships between products, but the writers who create documentation about these products do not collaborate. In this example, if the writer who wrote the printer content spoke with the writer who wrote the dongle content, they may have been able to develop reusable content in support of both products that would have helped the customer connect her printer. Yet, collaboration between writers working on related products or even the same product is sporadic for the many reasons indicated in this book. Finding ways to enable collaboration so that writers can create reusable content is essential for establishing an effective reuse environment.

This chapter provides writers and writing teams who are considering implementing content reuse background information on the meaning and evolution of reuse. It describes principles underlying an information development methodology that incorporates reuse and single-sourcing as fundamental precepts. It reveals that collaboration among writers, who often work virtually, is an essential requirement for making reuse possible. Writers must work together to determine the architecture required to operate in such an environment. For instance, what types of information products are needed to address customer questions: user guides, configuration manuals, installation instructions, and online help? More specifically, writers must collaborate to determine what units of content are required to make up the information products, and how the units will be organized. As shown in the example earlier, if writers do not collaborate during the process of developing content, the information about products that are related can be conflicting, inaccurate, and contradictory—all of which can have a negative effect on readers. As mentioned elsewhere in this book, the move from book writing to writing reusable topics is a shift in paradigm for writers. Accordingly, the principles of collaboration that are most relevant to developing reusable content include creating a culture of collaboration and providing effective leadership to help writers accustomed to working independently to adopt this different approach to developing content (see Principles 1 and 2, Chapter 1).

Thus, this chapter provides virtual collaboration guidance about how to implement the principles of reuse and single-sourcing in order to implement reuse across information products. Because collaboration among writers is an essential component of a reuse strategy, the sections that follow refer to methods of collaboration and critical points in the reuse process where close collaboration is needed. The example considered later pertains to a project involving three writers who are documenting the information products for a matching washer and dryer. This example is best considered in the context of various elements of reuse.

THE ELEMENTS OF CONTENT REUSE

The Evolution of Reuse

A term often used, but not universally understood, *reuse* is one aspect of a content development, maintenance, and delivery methodology in which content is developed and maintained—not as a whole "book"—but as modular content units. Content units may be any type of digitally stored information, such as text, graphics, or multimedia and they can be reused in multiple delivery contexts, such as documents and training courses.

Writers and writing teams may believe that they are not ready to reuse content in their projects or organizations. Yet, without realizing it, they have been reusing content since they first put pen to paper. As we look at the levels and evolution of reuse and examine its potential for collaborative writing, it is helpful to keep in mind four primary aspects: (1) granularity, (2) meaning, (3) collaboration, and (4) storage.

Primary Levels of Reuse

Writers can even consider that they already are reusing letters and symbols that have evolved over centuries. Each letter in the alphabet has a specific use. Combined, letters can form morphemes, which also have a specific use and meaning as do, in large part, words. Take, for example, the text shown in Figure 1.

As Figure 1 shows, in these primary levels of reuse, there are varying levels of granularity.

- At the first level of reuse is the letter. In the above example, there are 25 instances of the letter "e" being reused.
- The second level of reuse is the morpheme. In this example, the morpheme "ing" has been reused three times.
- The third level of reuse is the word. Again, using the above example, there are two instances of the word "they" being reused.

Note that the lower the level of granularity, the greater the amount of reuse that typically occurs. In moving to higher levels of granularity—in this case, the word level—fewer opportunities exist for reuse.

Conveniently for writers in the 21st century, the symbols, meaning, and spelling employed in these three levels of reuse have, for the most part, been resolved and to some extent fixed over time in the English language. From the Proto-Indo-European language through Old English, Middle English, Early Modern English, and now

Figure 1. The primary levels of reuse

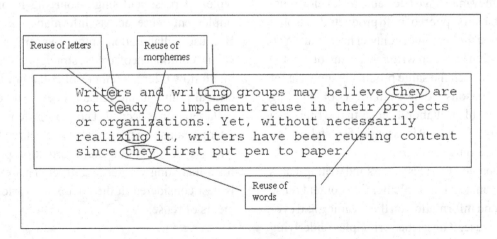

Modern English, these units of information that we now use to convey meaning were arrived at collaboratively among speakers of those languages. In many cases, such collaboration took place in a serial fashion through the natural evolution of language. An example of such serial collaboration is the gradual abandonment of the inflectional system during the Middle English period. In serial fashion, the evolution of the plural noun ending *–en* to *–es* began in the north of England during the Middle English period and spread over time to the south, ultimately leading to our current *–s* ending. (Barber 157–158). In other cases, such as the codification of words and their meanings, some degree of parallel collaboration took place. Willingly or not, the morphology of the English language evolved collaboratively, albeit under hostile circumstances, for example, during the Norse and Norman invasions of England. (Barber 128–134).

In contemporary uses of language, generally the storage of these lower levels of reuse is widespread. Letters may be stored in font files on our computers and thus reused directly from that single source each time we press the letter key on a keyboard. The physical representations of words are, of course, also "stored" in separate dictionaries or perhaps as terminology lists on company web sites. For those writers who use terminology software, words may also be stored in a database and copied from that source.

Standard Phrase Reuse

Beyond this basic reuse of language components, there is a fourth level of reuse: standard phrases. Such phrases have long been a mainstay of writing and publications. Take, for example, such phrases as "Copyright © 2009 ABC Company. All rights reserved." For years, publishers have employed these or similar phrases in order to copyright their materials. A publisher may reuse such a phrase thousands or millions of times in each copy, each edition, and each book that the publisher prints.

As far as granularity, the phrases often are short and have a strictly limited meaning.

With the advent of word-processing tools in the latter half of the 20th century, it became possible for writers to employ such capabilities as "Autotext" functions whereby boilerplate phrases like the copyright phrase above could be stored, sometimes in a central location, and inserted with a few keystrokes. Another method for reusing boilerplate phrases includes placement of the phrases within a template.

Purposeful collaboration among writers on the development of such phrases has taken place much more rapidly than that of the letter, the morpheme, and the word. Typically, when boilerplate phrases are developed, a team of SMEs is involved in the crafting and review of those phrases. The standard phrases are then disseminated in some fashion, perhaps in a style guide, throughout an organization along with instructions on their use. Using the example of the copyright statement, a legal team may write and review the text, and a standards or documentation team might notify writers or publishers of the precise text to include and where to include it. Thus, collaboration is necessary to arrive at common boilerplate phrases, agree on their use, and ensure their consistent implementation. For more information on standardizing content, see Chapter 13.

The Next Level of Reuse: The Content Unit

It is important to pay greater attention to the four aspects of reuse—granularity, meaning, collaboration, and storage—when the writer considers the content unit, the next higher level of content reuse. Here, an additional factor—that of *structure*—comes into play for successful reuse at the content unit level.

While, it is possible to reuse any type of content unit across documents or other outputs, if the structure of the content unit has not been clearly defined at the outset, chances are that the writer will not be able to reuse the content in different documents. For this reason, the reuse of a content unit is best accomplished by developing the unit according to a pre-defined structure. Once the structure is defined, writers use *containers* to hold all of the necessary units that compose a structured information product. A container may take various forms. For example, it may represent a chapter in a document, a help file, or a complete document.

Finally, a dynamic pointer is set to the unit from within the container, typically through the use of a CMS as indicated in Chapter 9. By using dynamic pointers to reference the content units, rather than embedding the units within the container, authors can modify or maintain content units independently of any containers that reference the unit. In this way, as the information in the content unit changes, the containers may be automatically updated as the content changes. For example, suppose a writer needs to provide customers with the conformance statements for a piece of equipment in three different documents: a brochure, a user guide, and a product label. Figure 2 illustrates the concept of using a content unit, dynamic pointers, and containers to achieve this result.

Writers should be alert to writing environments, however, that do not employ true reuse. A critical point to consider when writing content in a reuse environment is that the term *reuse* must be distinguished from *copy-and-paste*, which is the process of copying text developed in one context and pasting into another context. In a CMS environment or with the help of other CMC tools, true reuse specifically does not involve such copying and pasting because the CMS enables dynamic updating of all information products in which the original text appears, which is an inherent benefit of a pure reuse strategy. (See "Benefits of Reuse" later in this chapter). Reliance on the copy-and-paste feature increases maintenance costs because it creates multiple copies of information, each of which would need to be updated in a coordinated manner should the information need to be modified. Further, copy-and-paste of content obviates the benefit of translation and distributed development processing at the unit level. Nonetheless, in collaborative writing settings that do not have the benefit of a CMS, writers should still follow the basic principles involved in true reuse when using copy and paste. In addition, it seems useful to note that a CMS is not needed to do true reuse; it can be done successfully, for example, in a flat file directory structure with Adobe® Framemaker® software.

Figure 2. Reuse of content units in multiple documents

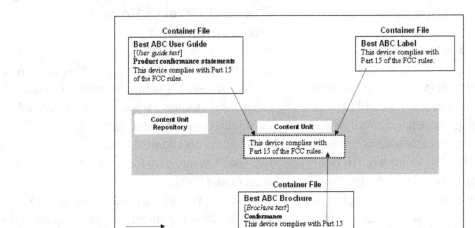

Basic Principles of Reuse

A project that implements content reuse includes several essential components:

- Close collaboration between content writers
- A well-defined information product architecture
- A well-defined content unit architecture
- A way to describe and identify each content unit (in other words, metadata)
- Standard authoring and formatting guidelines
- A CMS (ideally)

As these components suggest, collaborating writers will find that in order to reuse content units, those units should be developed and stored in common source formats using authoring standards and formatting guidelines, topics considered in more detail in Chapter 13. To this end, a CMS is exceptionally helpful; however, writers without access to a CMS will be able to adjust some of their processes to reuse content without it.

In addition to adhering to these basic principles, a reuse project is based primarily on a two-phased approach. The first phase of implementation of the reuse concept is accomplished by developing a standard information product architecture. In other words, standard deliverables such as a user guide or a training course and their structure must be defined. In addition, any invariable components that populate certain parts of the information product structure, such as a legal notice or a standard technical support section, are also identified in this architecture. As a result, all information products are developed starting with a certain amount of content that is already available. Regarding the example washer and dryer combination, described later, the installation and user guides for both appliances may include the same standard Warranty text as well as the same standard Technical Support paragraph containing the telephone numbers to call for repairs.

The second phase applies to the development of content. Instead of writing content per product or project or document, writers who work with content reuse collaborate to assess the design specifications—the outline—for each information product and identify any content that may have been already developed for another related project. If such content exists, it can be reused potentially to further populate the information product structures. Where new content is needed, the writers develop the appropriate content units in conformance with the prescribed content architecture. Those content units then become candidates for subsequent reuse by other projects. Again, in the case of the example washer and dryer combination, a procedure that explains how to attach a dryer vent hose may have been previously written for another dryer model and could be reused or adapted for the new dryer model.

To aid in locating appropriate existing content for reuse, standard metadata values are applied at the content unit and information product structure level. That is, all content units, when stored in a CMS, will have associated with them values for various attributes, such as product line name, audience, related standards, and relevant keywords. These metadata values also can be used to help writers identify content units that can be delivered independent of an information product. An example of this type of alternative information delivery strategy is the presentation of procedure topics through a knowledge management system designed to address proficiency gaps and fulfill just-in-time customer information needs. Where a CMS is not available and content units are stored within a directory structure, authoring teams may use alternative methods, such as entering metadata as comments directly into content units. To locate such content units based on metadata values, authors may use the search capabilities of the operating system to find relevant content units.

SINGLE-SOURCING AND STRUCTURE

An essential tenet of content reuse is single-sourcing. Single-sourcing assumes that a given instance of a content unit of a particular type is the only location for that content. Thus the unit becomes the "single-source" for the desired information. For example, a writing team might decide that the height, width, and depth of any product manufactured by their organization—say, a washer or a dryer—always appears in a "Specifications" content unit and in no other content unit. Single-sourcing enables information developers to modify fewer content units to update their information products. Perhaps more important, as the facts change, single-sourcing helps to ensure that all information products are accurate; that is, the facts are consistent wherever they appear.

One important enabling factor to implementing single-sourcing is the common definition of structures for various types of content units. Figure 2 illustrates how these principles can be applied on a small scale. In this example, the product manager, the writers of each document, and the conformance engineer will collaborate to define the appropriate conformance statements and their structure. They determine that the level of granularity most efficient for all documents is a content unit that contains only the FCC statement. The writers also collaborate to define the filename of the content unit in which the statement is to be stored, "OBJ_FCC_BestABC," and the structure of the unit to maximize the reuse potential of the unit.

While this unit is relatively small, a structure that fosters reuse still can be discerned. For example, the collaborating writers may determine that only the text, and not a heading, should be included in the unit "OBJ_FCC_BestABC." By doing so, they allow for other possible headings to appear in the resulting document in which the unit is used. For this example company, all such conformance statement units could be structured

as sentences to maximize their reuse potential. In some cases, it may be advisable to include a standard heading within the unit if the desired information product should include the same heading every time the content appears.

A more complex example of a content unit structure is shown in Table 1. In this example, authors for a software firm have collaborated to determine the type of information they will provide for each window that appears in their software applications. Through collaborative discussions with subject matter experts (SMEs), results of client surveys, industry standards research, competitive analysis, and their own expertise, the writers have determined that the best way to meet user needs is to provide the field characteristics shown. To define content unit structures, industry standards can be particularly useful. For example, the ISO/IEC 26514, Systems and Software Engineering—Requirements for Designers and Developers of User Documentation Requirements standard defines minimum requirements for parameter descriptions:

"11.7.2, Procedural steps shall include or provide references to documentation of the acceptable range, maximum length and applicable format, and unit of measurement of data fields for user-supplied data." (ISO/IEC 142).

Even in writing teams where content reuse is not a stated goal, definition and use of such standard structures helps to ensure a consistent look-and-feel in customer documents. But in situations where a company produces various software applications that reuse the same graphical user interface (GUI) windows, the benefits of such standard structures becomes clear. In this example, one writer can develop the content for the field description table of a given GUI window as a reusable content unit. Once the author has ensured that the content unit has been fully tested, reviewed, edited, and indexed, the unit can be made available to other writers for reuse in their documents.

Table 1. Example content unit structure: field description table

Field name	Type	Length	Range/Values	Units	Description
[Name of field 1]	[C, N, B,]	[maximum length of field]	[range of possible values or predefined values]	[unit of measurement. Refer to terminology standards for standard abbreviations]	[Provide a complete description of the field. Include relationships to other fields. If the field offers pre-defined values, describe the result of selecting each value.]
[Name of field 2]	[C, N, B,]	[maximum length of field]	[range of possible values or predefined values]	[unit of measurement. Refer to terminology standards for standard abbreviations]	[Provide a complete description of the field. Include relationships to other fields. If the field offers pre-defined values, describe the result of selecting each value.]

Terminology Standards in a Reuse Environment

Another aspect of reuse illustrated in Table 1 is the requirement to adhere to terminology standards. Note that the writers have agreed that, for the Unit column, they will each use the standard abbreviations for units of measurement. Such requirements should be made clear in any content unit structure. As indicated in Chapter 13, these requirements can be included, for example, within the content unit template or as a separate set of instructions that accompany each pre-defined structure.

Identifying and adhering to terminology standards has benefits for the collaborative writing team. Among these benefits are the ability to develop standard index markers, present a consistent writing style, and provide unambiguous meaning to readers.

Ideally, standard terms to be used both across an organization and for specific projects are developed and stored centrally. As with other aspects of reuse, various team members should be involved in the establishment of standard terminology. For organizations fortunate enough to have a terminologist on board, the terminologist will be the primary person involved in setting such standards with input from SMEs, writers, and editors. As writers develop new content and encounter situations in which new terms are needed, some level of collaboration is required with the corporate terminologist, if available, and with the other members of the writing team. As soon as new terms and their spellings are defined and codified, this information should be made available in real time to all team members.

Related to the development of standard terminology is the creation of standard index markers for reuse. Just as writing, editing, and translation are reusable skills, so too is indexing. Involving indexers in the development of standard terminology early in the writing process helps to ensure consistency of indexes when content units are reused in multiple information products and helps to avoid situations where similar but not identical index markers appear in the same document.

A General Example of Reuse

As indicated throughout this chapter, content reuse can take many forms, from the most simple reuse of boilerplate text to complex projects that involve extensive collaboration and planning within the writing team. The following example of a moderately complex reuse project is one that involves three writers, who will produce documents about a matching washer and dryer combination. The four documents that these writers will produce include an installation and user guide and a two-page data sheet for each appliance. Through this example,

I examine how these writers can structure their content to render it reusable by their colleagues, to produce consistent and accurate documents, and to increase efficiency.

Documentation to support a washer and dryer combination has specific aspects that make it a potential candidate for content reuse:

- The appliances are a matching set, so some characteristics, such as dimensions, are similar.
- The manufacturer used similar or identical parts in the appliances.
- The same types of documents are to be produced for each appliance.
- The same structure is to be used for each document type.

Collaboration in a Reuse Environment

As described in Chapters 10 and 12, collaborative writing environments require some strategy for assigning writing tasks, a strategy that must be established for the washer/dryer product information. Various factors should be taken into account in defining assignments, including:

- Subject matter expertise at the content unit level
- Subject matter expertise at the information product level
- Knowledge of the audience
- Experience in writing for specific types of information products
- Availability to interact with SMEs
- Efficient use of resources

For this example of a collaborative writing strategy, the collaborative writing team is tasked with writing installation and user guides for the matching washer and dryer: "The Best-Ever Washer" and "The Best-Ever Dryer." Both guides must be translated from the English language into French and Spanish. Each guide is expected to be 40 pages in length and to contain the following major sections:

1. Safety instructions
2. Parts list
3. Feature descriptions
4. Installation instructions
5. Use instructions
6. Maintenance
7. Troubleshooting
8. Specifications
9. Optional accessories
10. Warranty

For each appliance, the Marketing group also will create a two-page data sheet, also to be translated into French and Spanish, that includes:

1. A product description
2. Feature descriptions
3. A description of the benefits
4. The product specifications

Various reuse writing scenarios could be defined for this project. Two primary scenarios are the "one book, one writer" approach, which typically employs serial and parallel collaboration, and the "reusable content unit writing" approach, which adds collective collaboration to these other two. In practical application, some variation of the two approaches may be used.

Approach 1: One Book, One Author

In the "one book, one writer" approach, author Smith writes the complete installation and user guide for the washer. Writer Kumar writes the complete installation and user guide for the dryer. Writer Tempe writes the data sheet for each appliance. This approach is illustrated in Figure 3,

Throughout the process, each writer collaborates with the appropriate SMEs to write content for each section of their respective documents,

Figure 3. One book, one author approach

Smith writes the installation and user guide for the washer.

Kumar writes the installation and user guide for the dryer.

Tempe writes the data sheet for each appliance.

meeting occasionally and sending content back and forth. For example, Kumar works with a safety engineer to write the safety precautions for the dryer, while Smith works with the same or a different safety engineer to write the safety precautions for the washer. While writing their documents, Smith and Kumar may compare notes on the content they have written for each section of their documents. Using such communication vehicles as e-mail or face-to-face meetings, the writers exchange ideas and collaborate to help ensure consistency across their documents. At various points in the writing process, the writers may determine that they need to include a very similar or an identical content unit in their guides. Smith and Kumar may then agree to create a content unit for the Warranty Period for each appliance. They decide that Smith will create that content unit and both Smith and Kumar will set dynamic pointers to the unit from their guides.

At the same time, Smith and Tempe collaborate on writing the feature descriptions and specifications for the washer. Kumar and Tempe may also hold separate discussions on the same type of content for the dryer. At review time, Smith, Kumar, and Tempe work with their document reviewers to ensure the technical accuracy of their respective documents. If, after the review is completed,

information that appears in one document must be modified, the writer for that document must inform the writers for the other documents in case the changes affect their documents. For example, suppose the engineer for the washer determines that the specifications table needs to include an additional piece of information: the capacity of the appliance. Smith will need to contact both of the other writers to make appropriate changes in their documents. Kumar may need to add the capacity information to the dryer guide. Tempe will need to update the washer data sheet to include the capacity information and may also need to work with Kumar to update the data sheet for the dryer.

The complete development cycle for the English versions of each guide, based on industry standard estimates of seven hours per page, is seven calendar weeks (Hackos 169). Each data sheet is expected to take approximately two weeks to write and lay out.

Approach 2: Reusable Content Unit Authoring

In the "reusable content unit authoring" approach, Writer Smith serves as the primary *facilitator* for the installation and user guide for the washer, while Writer Kumar serves in the same role for the dryer guide, and Tempe facilitates development of the data sheets. Content writers contribute to developing the documents by writing content units based on such factors as their areas of expertise or their access to the appropriate SMEs. Based on these factors, content units for each area to be used in the final documents are assigned to the appropriate writers.

Table 2 shows a possible plan, using "reusable content unit writing" for developing the content units for each document. In this example, Kumar has more experience in researching technical specifications, developing parts lists, and working on legal content. Smith has greater expertise in writing procedural content. Tempe has particular skills in writing product and feature descriptions and describing product benefits. Assigning each writer according to their particular skills addresses this volume's virtual collaborative writing principle of tapping into the team's talents for their

Table 2. Example plan: reusable content unit writing

Content unit	Installation and use guide, washer	Installation and use guide, dryer	Data sheet, washer	Data sheet, dryer	Writer
Safety instructions (common)	X	X			Kumar
Safety instructions (washer)	X				Kumar
Safety instructions (dryer)		X			Kumar
Parts list (washer)	X				Kumar
Parts list (dryer)		X			Kumar
Installation instructions (washer)	X				Smith
Installation instructions (dryer)		X			Smith
Use instructions (washer)	X				Smith
Use instructions (dryer)		X			Smith
Maintenance instructions (common)	X	X			Smith
Maintenance instructions (washer)	X				Smith
Maintenance instructions (dryer)		X			Smith
Troubleshooting (common)	X	X			Smith
Troubleshooting (washer)	X				Smith
Troubleshooting (dryer)		X			Smith
Specifications (washer)	X		X		Kumar
Specifications (dryer)		X		X	Kumar
Optional accessories (washer)	X		X		Kumar
Optional accessories (dryer)		X		X	Kumar
Warranty (common)	X	X			Kumar
Product description (washer)	X		X		Tempe
Product description (dryer)		X		X	Tempe
Feature descriptions (washer)	X		X		Tempe
Feature descriptions (dryer)		X		X	Tempe
Benefits list (washer)			X		Tempe
Benefits list (dryer)				X	Tempe
Graphics (washer)	X		X		Graphics artist
Graphics (dryer)		X		X	Graphics artist

leadership work. Leadership is needed when implementing this approach to help all the writers understand how to coordinate their activities and assemble the content into coherent information products (see Principle 2, Chapter 1). Accordingly, this approach also requires adapting Principle 5 regarding structure to synchronize the proper hand-off of tasks.

As Table 2 shows, some of the content units, such as the common safety instructions, are planned for reuse across the four documents.

Advantages and Disadvantages of Each Approach

Each of the reuse writing approaches described has advantages and challenges, some of which follow.

Advantages of Approach 1

In the "one book, one author" approach, all of the authors are comfortable with "ownership" of all of the content for their guides. Some opportunities exist for collaboration, but in general each author works more independently of the others, which facilitates coherence within each book. Additionally, all of the authors become thoroughly familiar with each content unit in their respective guides.

Challenges of Approach 1

One of the challenges of the "one book, one author" strategy is that the translation of the guides cannot take place until all content is final because changes made to one guide may affect the content of another guide in the set. After all the guides in the set have been deemed final, all writers can index their documents and submit them for translations. Delivery of the guides in French and Spanish cannot begin until the English content is complete, however. The number of calendar days required to develop and publish all of the documents may be greater than for Approach 2. Finally, the review often will not take place until a complete draft of the document is ready, and because the SMEs must work with multiple writers, they likely will spend more time in reviewing the content. While this book-based model of writing includes elements of collective collaboration, such that the writers confer with each other synchronously to ensure consistency, working collectively within the book paradigm can be difficult to accomplish, as the case study in Chapter 6 makes clear. Despite efforts to collaborate on similar content between the two guides, some inconsistencies in the level and type of content, the standard text, and the structure of similar content may appear in the final documents. Especially when deadlines are tight, some writers who are not in the habit can forget to coordinate with colleagues. This can occur when the modifications in question affect many different products and projects, and writers become overwhelmed trying to finish their own books and staying synchronized with so many other writers.

Advantages of Approach 2

In the "reusable content unit authoring" strategy, writers work in their specific areas of expertise on the same types of content units. This approach often results in greater accuracy and consistency across documents. Additionally, the translation and indexing of the guides can begin as soon as a content unit or, preferably, a group of content units, has been deemed final. Writers can submit their content units for translations before the final documents are ready, which means that the delivery of the guides in French and Spanish can begin before all English content is complete. If the deadline for completing the documents is shortened, additional writing resources can be applied more easily, allowing for a greater number of content units to be developed concurrently. This approach also positions a company to reduce more easily the number of calendar days required to complete the documentation project. Finally, the review of document content can occur as soon as content units are ready. SMEs can work with a single writer and likely will spend less time in reviewing the content. The review of common units to be used in all documents is centralized and reviewers need not review common units more than once for all documents.

Challenges of Approach 2

On the other hand, in the "reusable content unit authoring" strategy, authors are not as familiar with all of the content in their guides. This challenge can be mitigated by using "rotating" assignments. In other words, each author spends time becoming familiar with different subject matter and takes turns with other writers in developing content units of a given type. For example, when the documents are next updated, Smith can train Kumar in aspects of writing troubleshooting content, and Kumar can train Smith in writing safety instructions. The benefits to this content unit reuse approach seem to outweigh its challenges, making it a powerful tool for virtual collaborative writing. Again, leadership and structure are essential to help guide writers through the processes, rotating roles and coordinating tasks.

ORGANIZATIONAL ISSUES

For reuse to succeed in an organization, writers involved with each function must work collaboratively and supportively with those in other functions, understanding both the benefits and the requirements of the reuse strategy and infrastructure. In other words, they must create a culture of collaboration. Such elements as planning, management, writing, information architecture, tools, and review are crucial to developing such a culture.

Planning

Two particular axioms emerge when planning for content reuse in a culture of collaboration:

- Planning for reuse must take place at the outset of new projects and for subsequent releases of existing projects.
- Frequent interaction and communication between planning functions is necessary.

For example, assume that Product A and Product B are both new products being introduced by the Greatest Furniture company. The products use similar components and offer the same basic functionality with some feature variations. Product A is a four-shelf bookcase made of pine, while Product B is a five-shelf bookcase, made of oak. Both are manufactured in a similar fashion. The consumer must follow the same basic instructions to assemble and maintain each bookcase. If, at the outset, product managers plan for reuse of the information products for Product A and Product B—just as they planned to reuse aspects of the manufacture of the bookshelves—they are more likely to deliver to customers consistent and accurate information about both products.

Management

Similarly, two axioms emerge when considering the responsibilities of management in a culture of collaboration:

- Throughout the design of information products and the information architecture, management support of the reuse approach is required for long-term efficiency.
- Management must understand and be able to communicate the benefits of the approach.

While additional time in up-front planning of the structure of content units and deliverables typcially is required, managers also must understand the benefits, including consistency for the customer and cost savings, that will be achieved in the long-run as documents are maintained. For example, assume that a salesperson is anxious to sell hundreds of units of the Product A bookshelf to a retail outlet. The salesperson may learn that the documentation writers are taking more time than usual to plan the structure of the documents and brings concerns to management. Managers must be able to communicate that the additional planning will yield such benefits as concurrent translation and simultaneous roll-out of the product in multiple countries.

Writing

Not surprisingly, writing itself requires developing a culture of collaboration:

- No function in the reuse approach requires greater collaboration than that of the writers involved in developing and reusing content.
- As writers envision the end deliverables they will produce and the content units needed for those deliverables, they must assume that the content they write may be reused in other documents and be proactive in promoting reuse.

Discussions among writers can take the form of tabletop reviews of proposed reusable content units, consistent e-mail exchanges between the writers on changes planned for a given content unit, and automatic notifications through a CMS whenever a content unit used in multiple contexts is modified by a given writer. (See Chapter 9 for more information on CMS features.) Indeed, foremost in the writer's mind must be the understanding that all content units being shared across the writing team are candidates for reuse by another writer of a different document.

Information Architecture

Working closely with the writing team are the information architects who design the common structure of information products and the content units that will be used to populate those documents.

The information architecture function must also take on a major role in developing the organizational culture of collaboration:

- Information architects must define the information products and content structures that are most useful for the audience based on audience analysis, customer feedback, and industry and competitive research.
- Information architects must work closely with the writers and be prepared to modify standard structures as a compelling need arises.

For some writing teams, the writers will serve in the role of information architects. Regardless of who carries out this function, the more up front planning that can be done in the structure of standard documents and the level and type of content needed to populate the documents, the greater the likelihood of success in implementing a reuse methodology. Once the content unit and information product structures are defined, writers will put them to use. As SMEs review written content, they may make suggestions for restructuring content units or information products. To maintain a consistent reuse architecture, writers need to provide feedback to those who maintain the information architecture so that improvements can be captured in future writing projects.

Tools

Three axioms emerge when considering the tools necessary for creating a culture of collaboration in a content reuse setting:

- The choice and maintenance of the authoring and production tools to implement reuse significantly affect the extent to which writers can reuse content and the ways in which the writers will create content.
- Templates must be developed for the various types of content units as well as for the overall information product structures.

- A content unit repository (for example, a CMS) accessible by geographically dispersed writing teams is necessary for reuse.

Using one authoring toolset for textual information and defining standard formats for graphics and multimedia elements helps to ensure that files are technically interchangeable. True reuse of content cannot be achieved by converting various file formats. For example, if one of the writers involved in a reuse project writes and maintains textual content in Microsoft® Word, while another writes in XML, the content units will need to be converted to a common file format each time a writer makes changes. To use dynamic pointers to content units, the whole team must write using the same tool. If options for using conditional text will be employed in the reuse methodology, careful planning and collaboration between writers, information architects, and tools experts must take place so that the tools fully support the project goals. Finally, a common repository for storing and managing content units is required. Particularly within virtual teams, each writer must have real-time access to the content units. Downloading and revising content units outside of a common repository, for example, on the writer's local hard drive can lead to multiple versions of a content unit and loss of data. The use of one CMS (that is, one that employs one defined set of metadata, one standard architecture, and defined workflow and handoff procedures) ensures that reusable content units can be identified, administered, and tracked. Especially when content units are reused across various projects, it is of critical importance to track writer, review status, reuse links, and other metadata.

Review

Finally, in developing a culture of collaboration in the content reuse setting, content review must become part of the entire process. Editors, proofreaders, SMEs, indexers, testers, and transla-tors must be made part of the collaboration and be informed of the end-to-end process. Chapter 16 provides more information about reviewing content.

In the ideal reuse environment, review takes place to some degree first at the unit level and later at the full document level. But writing in a reuse environment can represent a significant change in the way editors, proofreaders, SMEs, testers, and translators have worked in the past. For example, an editor may be accustomed to editing an entire document. As the writing team shifts to a reuse approach, the expectations for the editor to review and edit content must be made clear. In some cases, the editor may request that content units be assembled into less granular groups of topics so that the context may be taken into account. Writers should consider that editing individual content units is particularly challenging if one of the editor's primary responsibilities is to review the content for consistent terminology. While reviewers must understand the benefits of reuse, writers should be prepared to make accommodations so that these contributors can provide the most effective support possible to the project in their respective roles.

CUSTOMIZATION OF INFORMATION PRODUCTS THROUGH REUSE

In complex reuse strategies, collaborating writers employ techniques that render content units in slightly different forms—more or less content—depending on the requirements of specific information products. In addition to using smaller levels of granularity to achieve this end, writers can employ tagging techniques and use variables within the content unit. Such techniques increase the reusability potential of content units, but also place greater demands on the level of collaboration needed among the writers who will reuse the units.

Tagging Schemes

Tagging may be implemented through such software features as conditional text tagging when Adobe® FrameMaker® software is the authoring platform or profiling for XML-based authoring platforms.

Because multiple information products have certain content precisely in common, it is possible to design content units so that they can be used in multiple information products without modification. Such units may be considered "boilerplate" units and are not considered candidates for a conditional tagging scheme.

When content units cannot be used as is across multiple information products, writing teams should consider the use of tagging schemes that will enable a content unit to be reused, with variations, in multiple contexts. If tagging is to be used, tagging schemes must be well-defined and implemented to render content into its desired end states, depending on the specific needs, when the information product that houses that content is referenced by different containers. In this way, only certain portions of the information will appear in the destination information products. Such tagging schemes may be multi-dimensional. For example, tagging may be based upon audience or information product type. However, writing teams also should try to envision other tagging schemes that meet the needs of their environment. A tagging paradigm that considers diverse presentation environments (such as paper, web sites, user assistance, and computer-based training) or that is based on the subject matter may prove to be the most useful for a given project.

Returning to the feature descriptions assigned to writer Tempe for the washer and dryer, recall that the feature descriptions are to be reused in the installation and user guides and in the data sheet for each appliance. Here, Tempe must consider the audience for each document. The data sheet is a pre-sales document, intended to induce readers to purchase the product. The installation and user guides are a post-sales document that product owners can refer to for information on the features of the appliances they have purchased. Since the goals for these information products are different, all three writers may agree that some customization of the feature descriptions is warranted to address the needs of each audience. The authors may decide first that each feature description should be developed, stored, and used as an individual content unit. In addition, they may agree that subtle differences in language and style may be necessary to render the feature description useful in each information product.

Because Tempe is more familiar with writing marketing-related content, and Kumar and Smith know the needs of their users, each writer must bring to the discussion their unique perspectives based on their expertise. Assume that one feature of the washer is a load-sensing mechanism. For the data sheet, Tempe may decide that the description of this feature should read as follows:

The Best-Ever Washer includes a unique load-sensing mechanism that automatically detects the weight and size of washer loads. Using this sophisticated feature, you can more accurately gauge the amount of detergent to use for each load and save significant costs over time. You can access this user-friendly option with just the touch of a button by selecting "Auto-load" sensor on the washer's sleek digital control panel.

On the other hand, Kumar and Smith believe that their users will need more basic information:

The Best-Ever Washer includes a load-sensing mechanism that automatically detects the weight and size of washer loads. Using this feature, you can more accurately gauge the amount of detergent to use for each load. You can access this option by selecting "Auto-load" on the washer's digital control panel.

Tagging scheme 1 shows a possible approach to structuring and tagging the content unit for this feature description:

The Best-Ever Washer includes a *unique* load-sensing mechanism that automatically detects the weight and size of washer loads. Using this *sophisticated* feature, you can more accurately gauge the amount of detergent to use for each load *and save significant costs over time.* You can access this *user-friendly* option *with just the touch of a button* by selecting *the* "Auto-load" *sensor* on the washer's *sleek* digital control panel.

In the earlier example, all of the content is tagged with a conditional text setting defined as "Marketing." All of the text, *excluding* the text shown in italics is tagged with a conditional text setting called "Installation_User."

Tagging scheme 2 shows another possible approach.

[Comment: Marketing-related content.]

The Best-Ever Washer includes a unique load-sensing mechanism that automatically detects the weight and size of washer loads. Using this sophisticated feature, you can more accurately gauge the amount of detergent to use for each load and save significant costs over time. You can access this user-friendly option with just the touch of a button by selecting "Auto-load" sensor on the washer's sleek digital control panel.

[Comment: Installation and user guide content.]

The Best-Ever Washer includes a load-sensing mechanism that automatically detects the weight and size of washer loads. Using this feature, you can more accurately gauge the amount of detergent to use for each load. You can access this option by selecting "Auto-load" on the washer's digital control panel.

In this example, all of the content shown in italics is tagged with a conditional text setting defined as "Marketing." All of the text that does not appear in italics is tagged with a conditional text setting defined as "Installation_User."

The advantage to using Tagging Scheme 2 is that the writer can clearly identify which content will appear in each guide and avoids use of conditional text tagging at the word level. Both paragraphs are included in the same content unit to remind the author that if a change is made to one paragraph, a similar change might be needed to the other paragraph. For example, suppose that the product engineers change the option name on the control panel from "Auto-load" to "Sensor." Because both paragraphs appear in the same unit, the writer responsible for maintaining the feature descriptions can more easily update all references to the option name.

Tagging Scheme 3: Content unit chaining.

Another possibility for structuring such content is to create separate units for the marketing-related feature description and the feature description to be used in the installation and user guide. The units can then be "chained" through either a comment within each unit, directing the writer to update the related content unit, or through a mechanism in the CMS. The following example shows how chaining could be implemented for the two units:

Marketing-related content unit, feature description, load sensing (Filename: FD_Load_Sense_Marketing)

[Comment: Writers, if you update this content unit, review FD_Load_Sense_Installation_User and update as needed.]

The Best-Ever Washer includes a unique load-sensing mechanism that automatically detects the weight and size of washer loads. Using this sophisticated feature, you can more accurately gauge the amount of detergent to use for each load and save significant costs over time. You can access this user-friendly option with just the touch of a button by selecting "Auto-load" sensor on the washer's sleek digital control panel.

Installation and User guide-related content unit, feature description, load sensing (filename: FD_Load_Sense_Installation_User)
[Comment: Writers, if you update this content unit, review FD_Load_Sense_Marketing and update as needed.]

The Best-Ever Washer includes a load-sensing mechanism that automatically detects the weight and size of washer loads. Using this feature, you can more accurately gauge the amount of detergent to use for each load. You can access this option by selecting "Auto-load" on the washer's digital control panel.

Definition and implementation of tagging schemes have significant implications for the amount and type of collaboration that must take place among all participants in the documentation project. As a starting point, information architects must be thoroughly familiar with the advantages and disadvantages of each approach outlined earlier. In close consultation with writers, the information architects must be able to see the larger picture of how content might be reused in multiple contexts and be prepared to propose corporate-wide, standard tagging schemes. For example, information architects must consult with project managers across the company to identify the level of commitment each organization—from corporate communications and marketing, manufacturing, and human resources to the technical documentation team—to determine which groups will participate in the reuse methodology. Just a few of the considerations for these in-depth interviews include:

- Does the company plan to reuse content across all of the types of documents?
- Will the tagging schemes be based on audience, on subject matter, on delivery media, or on some other factor?

- What similarities in design, manufacturing, and development of the company's products should be reflected in the tagging scheme?

Using the input gathered from these discussions, information architects then develop proposals as a foundation for subsequent collaboration with authors, testers, editors, indexers, and SMEs to define the best implementation approach. At this level of collaboration, writers must fully understand the implications of the proposed content structuring and markup. For example, if the tagging scheme is to be based primarily on product lines, writers must work with the other roles to determine how that decision will affect the way content units are structured for both a pre-sales and a post-sales audience. In such a case, the team may determine that Tagging Scheme 1 imposes too much complexity on the editors and SMEs tasked with reviewing the content. A modified version of Tagging Scheme 3 might be the best approach. In this case, the team may conclude that writers will develop a content unit that describes for a post-sales audience the load-sensing feature of two different washer models, Washer A and Washer B. They may decide to use conditional tagging to indicate variations in the load-sensing capabilities of the two washer models. In addition, the team may also decide that chaining of that content unit to a separate content unit for the marketing-related descriptions of the features will render the units easier to review and to maintain.

Use of Variables

Within a content unit, variables may also be inserted for eventual definition in the container file. Like the tagging scheme to be used, the universe of variables available to the writers must be predefined so that the context in which the variables are used is consistently understood and employed by the information developers.

For example, a content unit may be planned that describes the purpose of the destination information product. Within such a content unit, a variable defined as "IP_Title" may be inserted. When the unit is referenced by the container file, the "IP_Title" variable is defined from within the container file, such that the following content unit:

The purpose of the <InformationProductTitle> is to explain how to design reusable content units.

Appears as:

The purpose of the *ABC Guide to Reuse* is to explain how to design reusable content units.

As with the tagging schemes, close collaboration with all roles that will interact with the content is necessary for the definition and use of variables. Information architects will need to take into account not only the current needs of the organization, but also allow for future expansion. As writers develop content, they may identify circumstances under which additional variables could be introduced and must be prepared to work closely with the information architects and other writers to test their proposals. The tools representatives, in particular, play a vital role in any collaborative effort to define and implement the variable names across the content unit and container templates.

ARCHITECTURE OF CONTENT UNITS

In a sound reuse methodology, a predetermined functional paradigm, or architecture must regulate content units, defining the scope of information to be stored in each content unit. Content units must first be known as being of a given unit type to ensure consistency across information products. Collaboration among writers is necessary at every level to achieve the desired consistency.

Granularity

A major aspect of the content unit architecture is the level of granularity anticipated for each unit type; that is, the size and scope of each content unit type. Units must be defined at a level of granularity sufficiently concise to maximize the unit's reuse potential while minimizing the conditional tagging or profiling placed on their content. In general, the smaller a content unit's granularity, the greater its potential for reuse without the need for conditional tagging or profiling of the content. However, with greater granularity comes increasing management overhead to store, maintain, and retrieve a larger number of units. When indicated, the notion of chained units should be employed where the threshold of conditional tagging or profiling of a given unit instance rises to 50% of the unit's content. With chained units, authors have the opportunity to state—through the use of metadata—explicit linkages to related units that should be analyzed for changes when the "chained from" unit is modified.

Classification of Content Unit Types

In order to define the standard content unit types that compose a content architecture, a classification system must be defined and established that will provide a framework into which units may be organized. This classification system helps to guide the architect's definition of the scope and intent of each content unit type. It is this classification system that ensures that consistent levels of content can be provided across multiple projects and products. Ideally, the classification system is based upon the subject matter itself, and is not constrained by formatting decisions of the output. Thus, while one can envision a classification system that includes such categories as "Procedure" or "Warning," such categories serve no purpose in satisfying expectations about the actual scope and type of information we may expect to find in those units.

A more useful classification system embodies more refined characteristics of the actual content. For example, by establishing the highest-level domains into which content units may be classified within a given universe, writers begin to add definition around the type of content contained in a given unit. As the universe of content development needs expands, additional domains may emerge and be defined. A fundamental requirement of the classification system is that teams employ thorough planning and sound instructional design techniques. These design techniques must take into account audience needs and consider the learning goals of the end users as well as the proficiency gaps that must be closed to provide users with useful content. The classification system also must consider the media choices that will best address the user's needs depending on their work environment, their skill sets and education, and the tasks they perform.

Metadata

In a reuse development environment, the classification scheme is implemented through a clearly defined metadata strategy. Metadata is, literally, data about data, and consists of a set of attributes whose values provide such details as clarity around what is contained in the unit, what skills have been applied and when to the unit, and what is the current state of the unit in the workflow. Metadata is applied both at the unit level and at the information product structure level in the development process to aid in developing and constructing content, but it can and should become available to end users, who can locate content that will fill in knowledge gaps.

A music DVD provides a real-world example of how metadata is applied at the unit and information product structure levels for both information development and delivery. The exterior cover in this metaphor represents the information prod-

uct structure, or the assembled product. On the cover is the title of the product, as well the date of publication, the producer, and the artist. Each of these descriptive elements are in fact metadata about the structure. Within and imprinted on the DVD, there are metadata elements about the units, which in this case are the songs that comprise the structure. Such metadata elements often include the title of the song, the order in which the song appears on the DVD, and the length in minutes of each of these songs. Depending on the delivery strategy, one also may expect to find the writer of the piece of content. The metadata needs of the audience must, therefore, be taken into account in determining how much of the information will be provided to end users to meet their needs and must be considered as part of the overall delivery or deployment strategy.

Without strong collaboration between the information architects and the writing team, the metadata associated with a content unit or a container probably will be inconsistent and lack usefulness. For this reason, writing teams should collaborate initially on both the metadata fields that will yield the most benefit in finding and retrieving reusable content units, but also on the values that authors will use to populate the metadata fields. As part of the metadata collaboration, all users who need access to the content—information architects, authors, SMEs, indexers, testers, editors, and tools experts—must provide input to the metadata scheme. This initial level of collaboration is best done as a tabletop or brainstorming session with subsequent followup sessions. A key point that all contributors must keep in mind during this collaboration is the amount of time involved in maintaining the metadata fields while addressing the minimum needs of each user.

As an example, suppose a writing team has determined that they will develop, among others types, four basic content unit types: field descriptions, specifications, procedures, and alarm descriptions. The team has also elected to use a tagging scheme based in part on product model.

Among other fields, the team may determine that three metadata fields they will use are content type, product model, and audience. For these metadata fields to be useful in retrieving content, standard values for certain fields should be pre-defined. For example, the content type metadata field may have the possible values: FD (field description), SP (specification), PR (procedure), and AD (alarm description). The product model field may have the values: Washer A, Washer B, Dryer A, Dryer B. The audience field values may be: user, installer, buyer. To the extent possible, the tools expert should code the standard values into the CMS if a CMS is used. But where a CMS is not available, metadata can be carried as comments within the content unit. In such cases, all users must agree on the format they will use to express the metadata. The resulting comment in a procedure content unit for Washer A to be used in an installation guide, would include:

- Content Type: PR
- Product Model: Washer A
- Audience: Installer

Once the first round of collaboration on metadata has taken place and the initial fields and values have been established, additional fields or values may need to be added. For example:

- A writer may need to develop content for a new audience.
- An information architect may define another content unit type.
- A tester may request a field that indicates the specific level of testing required.
- A product manager and manufacturing may introduce a new product model.

Before any such metadata fields are added, all team members should be consulted both for the field name and the possible values. This round of collaboration need not be as formal as the initial metadata development sessions, but can take place,

for example, through e-mail exchanges. In any case, team members must agree both on the need for the new metadata field and on the metadata standards that they will use and implement in the architecture. See Chapter 11 for more information about decision making.

STANDARD WRITING IN A REUSE ENVIRONMENT

Another requirement for success when developing content collaboratively in a reuse environment is the development of and adherence to clear guidelines for writing style and in particular terminology. Clearly, information developers engaged in writing content units must employ terms consistently. Such terms may be reused in multiple contexts in which the meaning of terms as they are understood by readers of the final information products may differ greatly from the intent of the writer of the original content unit. To this end, information developers also must be highly attuned to the potential reuses of a given unit and build such content on the assumption that they will be used in multiple contexts. This skill is not easily attained, and it is one that is aided by a sound underlying information architecture and classification system.

RETRIEVAL AND MANAGEMENT OF CONTENT UNITS

Once developed, content units can be classified to form a database of units that can later be organized and combined into information products or made available through another structured delivery mechanism. As the potential number of units can be significant, two tools for helping to track the state of units and retrieve them for reuse are the CMS and metadata. With the large number of content units that can and will ensue from development in a reuse environment—and because content units can and should be reused—implementation of a CMS is strongly recommended for developing an efficient reuse environment. The CMS provides the functionality that enables writers to apply metadata to each content unit stored in the system. It also enables writers to track the workflow of a content unit and record the state of the content unit along with the information product structure.

For example, the CMS enables writers to maintain and track information on whether the content unit is currently in development, review, test, or editing, and whether it has been approved by designated SMEs authorized to confirm its accuracy. In a reuse development environment, of primary importance is the ability of the CMS to report on all information product structures in which a given unit currently is being used. This capability is particularly important so that those structures can be re-evaluated as a content unit changes to ensure that the changes are appropriate in all delivery contexts. Such notifications of content unit changes can also trigger appropriate scheduling of review of all affected information product structures as warranted. Additionally, the CMS is vital for planning to identify existing content units that are candidates for reuse in planned projects.

BENEFITS OF REUSE

The cost efficiencies realized through reuse of skill, distributed development, concurrent translations, and dynamic updating of information products are among the most significant benefits for collaborative writing teams. These benefits are described in the following sections.

Reuse of Skills

Skills other than writing often and routinely are applied to content before it is rendered suitable for readers. Such skills include—but are not limited to—instructional design, audience analysis,

editing, indexing, review for translatability, SME review, testing, quality assurance, and translation. Clearly, if a content unit can be reused to suit multiple purposes, all information products that use that content unit (for example, online help systems, user guides, and brochures) benefit from the technical skills that were applied to the source content unit. Thus projects that employ content reuse make more cost-efficient use of these various skills, which can free writing teams for new and different tasks or jobs.

Distributed Development

By developing content as discrete units, multiple writers can contribute to the body of a given information product concurrently and up to the point where the finished product is considered final. In situations where ambitious deadlines are imposed, this benefit has clear advantages; where appropriate, multiple writing resources can be applied to the project. Such distributed development is the essence of virtual collaborative writing in many contemporary settings.

While traditional writing methodologies also can employ this technique by, for example, assigning chapters or sections of a book to various authors, the assembly in draft or final form of such books becomes problematic. Once the information product is assembled, if changes are needed to any portion of the text, authors are compelled to lock other authors out of the assembled information product structure while changes are being made. Such limitations slow the progress of the project. In a reuse environment, distributed development and review can take place in a more structured way. Multiple writers can access the units to which they are assigned, and incorporate revisions, up until the time that the information product is finalized.

Concurrent Translations

As with the distributed development benefit, the work of translations also can occur in a distributed fashion and can be performed concurrently with the development of the content in the source language. With the long lead times often required to translate documents, developing reusable content units facilitates faster translation as units may be sent for translation even while the remaining content for a given information product is still being developed in the source language. Additionally, language-specific container files may be established for the various language versions, and the information products may be re-assembled in their native format using the translated instances of each unit. As individual units are developed and once they achieve a given threshold of confidence (roughly 70%), they can be passed off to the translations team to begin their work. This benefit significantly decreases the time between content being available in the source language and when it can be delivered in all target languages.

Dynamic Updating of Information Products

True reuse, coupled with adherence to the principle of single-sourcing, is critical to realizing the benefit of dynamic updating of information products in a reuse environment. As true reuse implies the use of dynamic pointers to content units from the structures, or containers that need those units, it is clear that as the units change, all information product structures that reference those units can be automatically updated, or made current and true, as the units change.

In a writing environment where content simply is copied and pasted into information product structures, inconsistency may arise and technical accuracy suffers. For example, assume that a reviewer identifies an inaccuracy in the content of a guide or that engineering has changed the way a feature operates. Suppose, too, that the feature is described in two different guides, but that the material was cut and pasted between guides. The writer who learns of the necessary changes makes the modifications to his or her guide. Yet, the other

guides that use the same material will also need to be updated and the writer may not be aware of all of the guides in which the description has been pasted. Unless strong collaboration among writers and tracking of pasted content is used, documents that describe the feature will become out of sync.

To avoid this problem, designate one content unit to contain the feature description. In addition, use of a CMS that provides a "where-used" capability is highly useful. With such an approach, when a writer makes a change to the feature description, all writers whose documents include dynamic pointers to that content unit are notified of the change. Those writers must update their documents to capture the changes. Alternatively, depending on the authoring platform and CMS in use, all documents may be updated automatically. In any case, the writers will be made aware of the changes and they will need to plan on republishing their documents at the appropriate time.

Another consideration for reuse is that the same group of facts may reside in multiple content units rather than being single sourced. In the ideal reuse environment, a given fact on a particular subject resides in a specific content unit. Wrtiers then need to identify all information products in which that particular fact or set of facts appears. When a given fact changes, writers must verify that all relevant content units have been updated. In such cases, implementation of a CMS or a process for chaining units is recommended.

By combining the principles of reuse and single sourcing, the task of updating content can be centralized and automated, resulting in significant cost savings to all projects. As suggested in the opening vignette, users also benefit from these strategies because they receive consistent and accurate messages about functionality and features—indeed about how to use their products. Writers can ensure uniformity in a far more cost-efficient and timely manner. Finally, and not incidentally, the actual job of the collaborating team of writers is made more straightforward and effective through these strategies.

SUPPORTING REUSE ACROSS THE ORGANIZATION

Introducing the reuse concept and its consequent re-engineering will lead to organizational changes to support essential process requirements. These organizational changes might include:

- The introduction of a planning function that assesses all information product design specifications and identifies content that is either already developed or contained in design specifications of parallel projects
- The evolution of project/product focused teams to larger teams functioning as "resource pools" for content creation
- The possible centralization of supporting content development functions like editing, indexing, graphics, assembly/information product master generation, and so on
- Possible changes in the way the handoff of masters to deployment is organized
- Changes in the way resource teams develop content (following the defined process)

What follows are checklists that contain the basic steps that a writing team could complete for any information development project. These checklists, presented in Tables 3 and 4, employ the reuse principles outlined in this chapter to guide virtual collaborative writing teams in up-front planning and implementation tasks. Table 3 addresses planning tasks, and Table 4 addresses implementation tasks. Collaboration is central to this process among individuals responsible for information architecture, standards, and writing. Initial analysis, classification, and structuring of information results in long-term efficiency throughout the life cycle of the writing process.

FUTURE RESEARCH DIRECTIONS

Increasingly, writing teams working in large-scale global environments need to gain proficiency in managing standard approaches to information architecture, including methods for standardizing information products and strategies for reusing content. The information product architecture is based on customer-focused user and task analysis as well as product analysis and requires continuous verification and enhancements. Required changes need to be considered for architecture standards rather than just to individual information products. The information product architecture must be supplemented by a policy for additional and customized deliverables.

Table 3. Checklist for teams preparing for content reuse

Step #	Role or team	Action
A1	Information architecture	Define a list of standard information products based on initial user needs analysis. The architecture requires regular verification and update.
A2		Define the content structure for all standard information products based on initial user and task analysis.
A3		Define the content units that are needed for each of these information products.
A4		Define the model for the categorization of content units through standard metadata.
A5		Define the structure of content units.
A6		Define the tagging and variable-use schemes.
A7	Standards	Develop appropriate guidelines, including writing, graphics, and terminology standards.
A8	Indexing	Develop, to the extent possible, standard index markers that can be inserted into content units as appropriate.

Table 4. Checklist for teams implementing reuse within a project

Step #	Role or team	Action
B1	Writing	Use the "skeleton" documents prepared by Steps A1 to A3 as a starting point.
B2		Develop an Information Development Specification (IDS) based on skeleton documents and the information product architecture, following guidelines and specific content needs of the reader. The writing team identifies the content units that are required to complete the document as defined in the IDS.
B4		Identify content units that already exist, and revise the IDS. Whenever a new project is evaluated, any new IDS is checked against all planned units that are already in the CMS.
B5		Develop content units from the revised IDS. Content units also can be provided by SMEs, such as engineers or other professionals in the given discipline. Implement the tagging and variable scheme in the content units, as appropriate. The writing team completes all required metadata fields. Content units are edited, reviewed, indexed, and, if necessary, tested and translated.
B6		Assemble all documents for the content units in the CMS, following the information product architecture.
B7	Various	Complete and review the documents (test if needed), then, edit, revise, index, and translate.

As described more fully in Chapters 12 and 13, organizations need to support workplace writing teams in the process of developing and implementing information modules and standards. At a minimum, teams need to agree upon:

- A list of standard deliverables, such as documents and training courses
- The standard titles of deliverables (for example, books, documents, courses, online products)
- The standard content structure per deliverable (for example, the document outline or the topic structure)
- A standard tools set for authoring (for example, graphics, text, and multimedia elements) and content management
- A standard set of components, or content units, that create the structure of information products
- How content is structured in content units
- The definition of a content unit
- A classification of the content units to store and retrieve them
- A strategy for labeling content units (for example, metadata)

- How the content units are organized internally
- The granularity of the content units
- A tagging and variable-use scheme to be used by the organization
- Standards for creating and using graphics

One result of information product architecture standardization is that a new project could build on a set of predefined structure and content units. For example, a writing team may already have 10% of its content in place as generic, pre-defined modules before they begin their development project.

Standardized information architecture enables teams to implement content reuse. Implementation of standards requires a well-defined process, as described in Chapter 10. The process should include workflows for design and developing content. Well-defined processes help to ensure that content units are developed consistently so that they can be reused, that content is accurate and user-centered, and that development teams build consistent and complete information products from the content. Writing teams need formal guidance on how to work effectively in this type of virtual environment.

CONCLUSION

Given the underlying principles for reuse, collaborating writing groups will need to plan carefully and develop an implementation approach that works for their organization. Such reuse approaches are built on three pillars:

- The information product and content architecture
- The tools, standards, and guidelines for implementation
- An organizational structure that supports the reuse concept

In closing, this chapter describes the components of an initial information product architecture defined for the organization, and describes some recommended strategies for writing collaboratively in virtual environments. The first two principles of collaboration that ground this book are especially pertinent to developing reusable content, creating a culture of collaboration and providing effective leadership to help writers adapt to this different approach to developing content.

REFERENCES

Barber, C. (2000). *The English language: A historical introduction.* Cambridge, UK: Cambridge University Press.

Hackos, J. (1994). *Managing your documentation projects.* New York: John Wiley & Sons, Inc.

ISO/IEC. (2008). *ISO/IEC 26514, Systems and software engineering—requirements for designers and developers of user documentation requirements.* Switzerland: International Standards Organization Copyright Office.

Section 6
Supporting Quality Writing through Virtual Collaboration

Chapter 15
Case Study:
Managing Content Quality and Consistency in a Collaborative Virtual World

Kent Taylor
acrolinx® North America, Inc., USA

ABSTRACT

The application of quality management tools in the content development process provides a range of benefits to writing, production, and program teams. This case study of a Natural Language Processing (NLP)-based information quality management solution developed by acrolinx® GmbH describes the results that real-world virtual collaborative writing practitioners have realized, and provides a roadmap for applying quality management strategies within writing organizations. When information products have consistent style, voice, terminology, and brand identification no matter where, when, or by whom the materials written, they are easier to read, understand, translate, and use. Quality management tools support collaboration within writing teams by centralizing access to the standards as writers are creating content, and providing objective quality metrics and reports at handoff points in the information supply chain. This process ensures consistency and clarity across information products, which makes them easier for writers to develop and for customers to use.

INTRODUCTION

First, a bit of personal background will set the stage for this chapter and offer some perspective. An engineer by birth defect, a manager by accident, and quality zealot by choice, I am currently a recovering Tech Pubs manager, with 20 years of experience at a large equipment manufacturing company, and six

years consulting in enterprises with large publishing operations. I have experienced just about every conceivable way to do everything associated with information development and delivery—the good, the bad, and the ugly. I have instigated and lived through a number of traumatic transitions, starting with the shift from pencils and blue-line pads to green-screen input terminals, up through large scale, all electronic multimedia, multi-language simultaneous shipment (sim-ship) operations. In

DOI: 10.4018/978-1-60566-996-4.ch015

the context of these transitions, I have deployed generic code (GenCode), Standard Generalized Markup Language (SGML), Extensible Markup Language (XML), machine translation, and International Standard, Quality Management and Quality Assurance Standards (ISO 9000) processes along with those related to content management systems (CMSs) and single sourcing. While the transitions to some of these technologies were more difficult than others, nearly all of them eventually resulted in improvements in terms of productivity and throughput.

The deployment of ISO 9000 in the information development arena was an exception, however. After months of planning and startup activity, we had a general feeling that quality was improving, but could not demonstrate any significant productivity improvements. This surprised me, as I had seen stunning results in a previous assignment managing a large, complex manufacturing operation. In the manufacturing environment, we were able to establish strict quality standards, measure conformance to standards objectively at every work station, provide feedback to the operators (quality assurance, or QA), and employ an independent quality department to test a statistical sample of our output against the standards (quality control, or QC). Quality, productivity, cycle time, and yield all improved shortly after we started providing feedback to the operators; scrap and unit cost both plummeted.

This positive outcome did not occur when implementing ISO 9000 in the information development environment because, in my opinion, the writers lacked real-time objective, actionable metrics and feedback. In the manufacturing environment, employees got real-time feedback about how their work conformed to standards—generally automated dimensional and electrical measurements. And managers got summary reports indicating the types and numbers of defects encountered each day; if a specific type of error peaked on any given day, the cause could be

identified, and corrective action taken to resolve the issue.

This level of monitoring and tracking was not feasible in the information development environment of the early 1990s. While our editing team provided feedback to the writers in terms of marked up documents, it generally came weeks after the writing activity, and it was subjective and actionable only to the extent that editors' comments, additions, changes, and deletions had to be inserted in the documents. Summary reports to managers consisted only of the number of documents and pages processed, time spent, and associated costs. Such activities are examples of serial and parallel collaboration as described in Chapter 1 of this book.

It appeared that the triad of cost, timeliness, and quality was impossible to achieve. Given real-world constraints, writing managers invariably focus on cost and timeliness and sacrifice quality, making uneven quality a fact of life in the world of information development. That is, the cost of manually collecting actionable metrics at the individual document and writer levels was prohibitive. However, that reality was 15 years ago, and breakthroughs in Internet-based (sometimes called *cloud*) computing and the field of Natural Language Processing (NLP) have changed the game. NLP employs sophisticated algorithms to analyze language at the word- and sentence-level. Software systems based on NLP technology can analyze text the same way that a human copy editor does, by checking for conformance to established standards for spelling, grammar, style, and terminology. Thus, real-time feedback on language rules can be provided to writers via spell-check-like highlighting and guidance in their native authoring environment, and managers can get aggregated summary reports on demand.

This case study examines how NLP-based technology improves the ability for virtual collaborative writing teams to manage quality and consistency. Currently, this technology is deployed as the core component in the information quality management system considered in this chapter. The software under discussion, acrolinx® IQ, helps information development organizations achieve the same type of results realized in manufacturing and software development environments. The application of proven quality management principles and practices in the information development process enables virtual writing teams to achieve substantial cost, timeliness, *and* quality improvements.

BACKGROUND

In a one-document, one-writer environment, quality and consistency are controlled entirely by one person, or perhaps by one person with help from an editor. Left to their own creative devices, individual writers develop content according to their own internalized standards, which likely were established in school and modified over time through feedback from teachers, readers, editors, and supervisors, among others. The quality of their content may be good or bad, but at least it generally will be consistent in terms of spelling, grammar, terminology, vocabulary, and style. In other words, it will look like it was written by the same writer. Most readers generally can cope with all but the poorest quality content; as long as it is consistent, the quality may not prevent them from using a product or service.

However, single-writer documents are becoming rarer in commercial, corporate, and even academic publishing environments around the world. Increasingly, collaborative teams of writers, subject matter experts (SMEs), editors, and other support staff create content for documents, Web pages, knowledge bases, or other forms of published information. As Chapter 10 explains, the obstacles involved in getting writers to coordinate their activities can proliferate. Accordingly, the need to standardize information is becoming increasingly critical as noted in Chapters 13, 14,

and 17. Yet the ability to implement standards is difficult, especially if the writing teams are:

- Geographically distributed, which makes it harder to coordinate work across time zones
- Culturally diverse
- Composed of individuals with varied backgrounds and experience, including education or field of specialization
- Constrained by tight deadlines

The results of inconsistent information quality are even less desirable than consistently poor quality. Inconsistencies can have substantial consequences in terms of an organization's or product's image and reputation, as well as both top- and bottom-line financial performance. For example, inconsistent style, grammar, spelling, terminology, and voice within or across documents, Web pages, knowledge bases, training material, and even packaging can lead to a number of problems:

- Reader confusion and dissatisfaction
- Unnecessary calls to support desks
- Increased translation/localization costs
- Incorrect/improper and potentially dangerous product operation
- Equipment damage, injury to personnel, and litigation

Given these circumstances and the difficulties inherent in writing collaboratively, it should be apparent that some degree of management and control is required to ensure quality and consistency across most collaborative writing activities. It is possible to achieve desired results solely with intensive manual effort, but results can best be achieved with the help of virtual tools that support and encourage conformance to corporate standards for style, terminology, grammar, and spelling. Such a tool becomes valuable because that teams can collaborate about preferred terms and required standards for good writing, which then can be encapsulated in the tool for writers to access each time they review a document. This process represents a type of collective collaboration as described in Chapter 1.

The tool considered in this case study is acrolinx® IQ, based on NLP technology developed at the German Centre for Artificial Intelligence Research (DFKI in Saarbrucken, Germany), and brought to market and further developed by acrolinx® GmbH. The acrolinx® IQ linguistic analysis engine resides on a central server that houses the NLP-based linguistic engine, style and grammar rules, dictionaries, terminology banks, reuse repository, and customer-specific customizations. Writers and editors access the server via a simple toolbar plug-in to their editing environment (for example, Adobe® FrameMaker®, Microsoft Word®, XMetaL®, Arbortext Editor™, and Author-IT®). When they click the "Check" button, they can get information about their use of spelling, grammar, style, or terminology. Writers can then click a highlighted term, opening a window that identifies the issue (for example, passive voice, future tense, or unapproved terminology). The interface provides either drop-in suggestions for spelling and terminology issues or a direct link to relevant information from an organization's style guide for grammar and style issues.

Formal quality management processes and tools can help to influence organizational culture, which is the first principle of collaboration, and build trust among collaborators, which is the third principle of collaboration that grounds this book as described in Chapter 1. Insofar as it is practically impossible to implement quality management processes in the information development environment without the effective use of tools, there is a clear connection to the fourth principle—using tools and collaborative modes effectively. Effective quality management also addresses the fifth principle of collaboration—creating structure, which requires a joint management and staff governance to direct activities related to standards, metrics, monitoring,

and reporting. Quality management depends not only on a formal approach to developing standards but also on measuring compliance to them at every step in the process—the operational embodiment of the sixth principle, measuring and tracking performance. Quality management also contributes to some degree to the second principle—finding and promoting leadership; a joint quality governance team consists of individuals who are champions of quality. If the organization is serious about quality, these individuals will be empowered to promote the use of tools and processes that will improve quality.

INFORMATION QUALITY AND COLLABORATIVE WRITING

Quality management approaches like six-sigma, total quality management (TQM), Kaizen (the Japanese word for improvement), and ISO 9000 have been deployed successfully in manufacturing and software development environments for decades, and they share common high-level principles at their core, including:

- Formal, documented standards and processes
- Reliance on objective metrics for quality monitoring
- Real-time, objective feedback to process participants (quality assurance)
- Formal metrics and reports at process gates (quality control)
- A strong focus on building in quality from the very beginning of the process
- Role understanding by everyone in the supply chain
- Knowledge of the quality output by everyone in the supply chain (how well it conforms to standards)

The process of managing information quality involves applying well-known quality management principles to the tasks and activities found in a corporate or commercial information supply chain. Managing "quality" in the context of content development can evoke a range of interpretations related to degrees of compliance with standards, which can vary. Information quality standards for different organizations can vary greatly.

This case study draws on a straightforward definition of information quality developed by the acrolinx® GmbH and acrolinx® North America staff. While it may not apply in all contexts, this definition seems relevant to various institutional perspectives, including corporate, commercial, and academic settings. The German Research Center for Artificial Intelligence (DFKI) first developed this definition, which we then refined based on real-world experiences. From this standpoint, information quality is observable if it conforms to standards, including:

- Style guidelines
- Grammar and spelling rules
- Terminology and phraseology selections
- Minimalist principles for readability and usability
- Translatability guidelines

Information quality management is a good practice that organizations can employ to save substantial time and money. The experience of acrolinx® analysts and associated linguists is that translation cost is a good indicator of source content quality. Ask a translator why translation costs so much, and the answer generally will be that the source content was poorly written, difficult to read, and hard to understand. Historically, the effort to achieve quality has been subjective and based on individual internal standards and preferences. Even when assessing quality on a simple 5-point scale (from poor to excellent), the scores are imprecise and can result in 2- to 3-point differences among individuals evaluating the same information. In addition to being subjective, human scoring of document quality has been time consuming and expensive. It also has been

difficult to deploy due to the subjective nature of the written word and the difficulty associated with collecting and tracking objective quality metrics.

Most professional writing organizations have taken the first step toward quality management by developing and publishing standards—usually in the form of printed or online style guides for grammar and style. Some organizations also maintain terminology lists, or glossaries of approved or suggested words and phrases, and custom dictionaries for spelling. Few organizations, however, document information quality goals or monitor conformance to standards via formal, objective metrics.

Because monitoring conformance with published standards has been expensive and time consuming, this activity usually is sporadic and subjective. Quality assurance in terms of real-time, objective feedback falls primarily on the individual writers, who have differing knowledge and interpretations of the standards. Quality control in terms of formal metrics and reports, if it exists at all, has become the purview of the editing staff, which in large corporate environments is becoming an endangered species. Ideally, a single editor modifies each writer's work to conform to the editor's interpretation of the standards, which is a form of serial collaboration. This approach results in relatively consistent quality across individual documents. Consistency across document collections—written by different writers, and edited by different editors at different times, in different places—has been difficult to achieve, especially in a deadline-driven environment where editing is something to be done if there is spare time.

Evolving technology has helped teams manage quality on three levels: (1) structure (for example, SGML, XML, and DITA), (2) presentation (for example, CMS, single-sourcing, and automated assembly and publishing processes), and (3) workflow. These technologies have enabled many aspects of distributed collaborative writing and have both encouraged and forced the shift from single-author, single-book writing paradigm to that of writing and reusing content, as described in Chapters 1 and 14. Economic forces have spurred the rapid growth of global collaboration, along with cultural and translation issues to be addressed in the distributed writing environment. All of these influences combine to increase the need for formal quality management practices while the degree of difficulty associated with any manual procedures or processes also increases.

Various technological tools such as spelling and grammar checkers, terminology management systems, and controlled language (most notably Simplified Technical English) checkers, provide some aspects of quality management, principally in the area of quality assurance (spell-check-like functionality). While most tools address various aspects of information quality to a greater or lesser degree, they fall short in terms of generating objective, actionable metrics for quality control. Most of the systems also are limited as to the number and types of rules that they can process, the languages supported, and integration with other information management systems. In contrast, NLP technology supports deep text analysis and greater precision. The acrolinx® IQ tools, which employ this technology, provide repeatable, objective, actionable metrics that can be used to drive cost, quality, and time-to-market improvement. Moreover, because writers access the tools through a central location over a corporate network or the Internet, writers benefit virtually from the collaboration that produced the standards, terminology lists, and rules.

Such tools integrate within the authoring environment (for example, Word®, FrameMaker®, Arbortext Editor®, and XMetaL®) and access the standards stored on a server. The most frequently used functions are the "check" and the "report" buttons. The check button initiates a quality check of the whole document or selected content, much like a common spellchecker. The client sends the selected text to the server for analysis, and the server responds with a summary of issues found, followed by spellchecker-like highlighting of suspect text Figures 1 and 2 are screenshots of summary and detailed highlighting, respectively. The different colors indicate different issues: red for spelling, blue for grammar, magenta for terminology, and green for style and translatability.

As with spelling and grammar checkers, writers click highlighted text to open a dialog box that identifies the issue, and offers drop-in suggestions where appropriate. Most style and grammar issues

Figure 1. Quality assurance summary

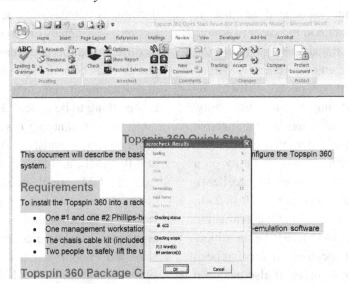

Figure 2. Quality assurance detailed feedback

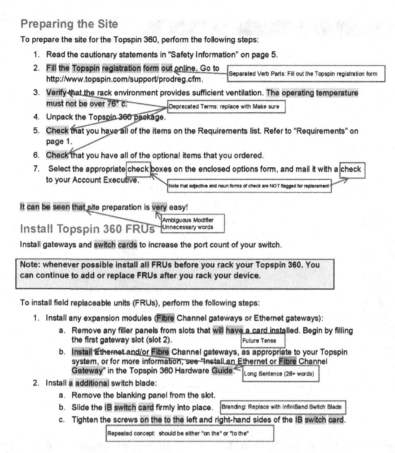

can be resolved in more than one way and depend on the writers' discretion.

Writers can adapt quickly to the feedback, and they can see how use of these tools can improve the quality of their work. Initially, addressing the issues identified by a full quality check takes somewhat longer than working with an ordinary spellchecker, because generally there are more corrections to consider, especially in the areas of style, translatability, and. On the other hand, there are fewer false alarms to dismiss. Additionally, the real-time feedback provides an on-the-job learning experience that helps the writers to avoid common errors in the future.

Editors also can adapt quickly to the information provided in available quality control reports that highlight spelling, grammar, style, terminology, and reuse issues. After a few weeks of continuing to look for (without finding) copy edit issues, they generally stop proofreading and look at the report to determine whether there are any substantive copy-edit issues remaining. If the quality score is within an acceptable range, they can focus on developmental editing.

Every time a writer runs a quality check, the system similarly stores a quality control report on the server. The report button on the writers' toolbar retrieves a copy of the most recently run check results; these reports provide the writers and editors with both a high-level and detail-level view of the quality status of their work. Reports include an overall summary of errors found by category

Figure 3. acrolinx® IQ aggregated report

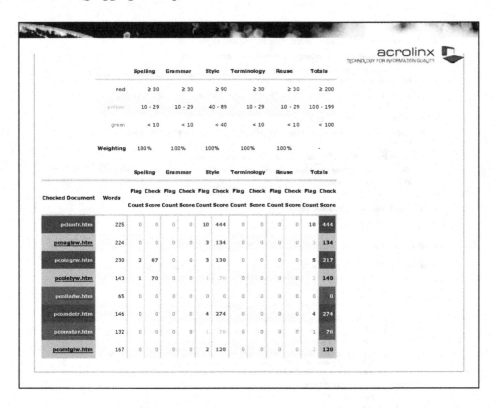

(that is, spelling, grammar, style, and terminology), administrative information (that is, the file name and file type, who ran the check, date, and so on), the quality score, and summary and detail-level results for each error category—including the individual issues in context. Optional settings allow checking for reuse opportunities at phrase- and sentence-level, and harvesting of new terms in the checked file. Terminology management is an ongoing activity; automatic identification of potential new terminology greatly simplifies this task.

All quality control reports also are available to other members of the organization, either as separate reports or in aggregated reports and charts. Since all checking information is stored in an internal database, it is possible to generate custom reports and charts via an appropriate database connecter and report generator. Figures 3 and 4 provide examples of typical reports.

In my experience, editors typically use the aggregated reports to prioritize their work. They know that green highlighted files meet or exceed copy-editing quality standards, so they do not have to proofread these files at all. For the red- and yellow-highlighted files, they can look at the individual files' quality reports to plan their work, again without having to open the actual files.

Generally, virtual writing teams have indicated that they use custom reports and charts to monitor quality at project and departmental levels, to identify opportunities for process improvement, and to identify areas where remedial action or training might be needed. The ability to monitor and track quality along with cost and time metrics can also provide valuable input to the budget planning process.

Figure 4. acrolinx® IQ style and grammar issue frequency

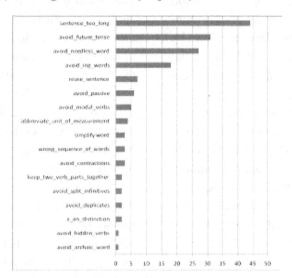

ACHIEVING QUALITY RESULTS

The acrolinx® staff members have been involved with NLP-based quality initiatives at large global enterprises over the past seven years. Thousands of writers, editors, and managers who have integrated information quality management processes and tools worldwide have realized the benefits described—improved quality and reduced cost and time-to-global market. In this section, I consider the steps organizations need to take to achieve these results.

Strategic information quality management implementation generally follows a straightforward process. This process, while not unique to NLP-based technologies, is well-suited to managing quality in organizations with distributed collaborative writing teams. The five elements include:

- Developing a sound business case
- Establishing a project plan, which includes a process definition and metric strategy
- Deploying a pilot
- Defining a rollout strategy
- Overseeing continuous quality tracking and process improvement

My experience is that the deployment of any virtual quality management tool will go more smoothly if everyone understands why information quality management is important and how the new processes and tools, including those that derive from NLP research, can help ensure organizational efficiency in terms of developing, processing, translating, and distributing their information products. Because writers run the quality management tool on their desktop, their daily work processes do not change greatly. The biggest changes to collaborative writing processes will be for the individuals chosen for governance of the overall quality management system. Specifically, the individuals that will manage style, grammar, and terminology standards will have to adapt to processes that may not have existed before.

Step 1: Developing a Business Case

The first step in deploying any new tool or process entails building a business case or gaining support for an improvement plan. This step thus involves collaboration between information development teams and managers to secure the resources needed to employ a strategic approach to quality. Teams need a budget to plan and execute the migration from a manual process to a formal quality management practice. Teams, therefore, must start by developing a business case to justify the initial time and expense associated with the deployment of new tools and processes.

In its simplest form, a business case compares the cost of doing something new with the anticipated benefits in terms of reduced costs and/or increased revenue. If the benefits are substantially greater than the costs, implementation might be a good idea. Whether a given business case moves forward depends on how well it contributes to corporate objectives (compared to other initiatives) and how much the company has to invest in new projects.

In terms of information quality initiatives, most global organizations build their business cases around anticipated translation cost savings. Teams, for example, can build a case estimating that automated quality management can reduce translation costs by 15%. Table 1, which assumes a 15% savings in translation costs, reveals a corresponding increase in savings as translation volume increases. Specifically, the annual savings estimate will increase with increases in word count, translation cost/word, number of languages supported, and estimated cost reduction.

As the volume grows from 5,000 – 100,000 pages, the absolute dollar savings increases accordingly. But regardless of volume, the dollar savings across seven languages is greater than the translation cost for an individual language. Put another way, the savings are sufficient to fund the translation of an additional language at any volume. Organizations can customize this spreadsheet to estimate the potential savings that can result from automating the management of standards and terminology. Teams can also add to this table estimated savings related to developing content in English, including savings in the editing and review processes.

While this business case alone often promotes the business case to the corporate short list, translation savings come with a corresponding reduction in translation time. That is, improved information quality reduces the amount of time needed to translate content, which in turn accelerates time to market. In most industries, the sales resulting from the first-to-market advantage dwarfs the cost savings.

Once approved, share the business case with the organization to underscore the value of automating standards to improve quality. The main message should convey that quality at the source streamlines the development, reuse, review, and translation of content. Managers also can provide an overview of how the use of a tool to manage quality will affect certain roles.

Step 2: Establishing a Project Plan

Following the approval of the business case, teams must focus on planning activities that will prepare

Table 1. Annual translation cost savings as volume increases

pages	5,000	10,000	20,000	50,000	100,000
words/page	200	200	200	200	200
words	1,000,000	2,000,000	4,000,000	10,000,000	20,000,000
translation cost/word	$0.25	$0.25	$0.25	$0.25	$0.25
translation cost/language	$250,000	$500,000	$1,000,000	$2,500,000	$5,000,000
languages	7	7	7	7	7
total translation cost	$1,750,000	$3,500,000	$7,000,000	$17,500,000	$35,000,000
translation cost reduction	15%	15%	15%	15%	15%
annual savings	**$262,500**	**$525,000**	**$1,050,000**	**$2,625,000**	**$5,250,000**

the organization to use a quality management tool effectively. Implementation of a new tool is most successful when organizations assign key people to evaluate standards and define processes, metrics, governance, and change management strategies. The team members should include project leaders, writers, and editors with an ample knowledge of products and standards. Also, involve an individual who has expertise with tools to help with tool configuration.

Together these individuals, who form a quality review board, can determine governance, an infrastructure for tool implementation, and a pilot rollout of the system. Specific responsibilities include the following:

- **Establishing or refining and maintaining standards**. Teams just starting out should ensure that rules support clarity, accuracy, and readability. When standards are already in place, take steps to refine the rules and ensure content optimization. Managing consistency also entails defining terminology lists that contain preferred words and phrasing. Once defined, the technical expert on the team can help to configure the tool with the standards established.

- **Defining initial and ongoing processes and tool specifications**. Without defined processes that guide repeatable behaviors, the implementation of a tool that drives quality is of little value. The quality review board should establish protocols for using the tool—when to run checks, how to leverage the reports during the review process, how to gather feedback for refining the standards and terminology lists, and when to update the tool to accommodate changes in the organization.

- **Identifying metrics and a framework for tracking and reporting**. Organizations readily set goals for error-free information products, but without documented targets that define high quality, teams will struggle to produce documents without errors. Figure 4 illustrates a handful of metrics that might be monitored: sentence length, terminology, verb structure, superfluous words, passive voice, and units of measure. The key is setting targets or expectations related to these categories, which the tool will track and report on, providing immediate feedback and alerting authors of missed targets that will affect quality.

- **Determining pilot requirements**. Finding a sponsor and articulating requirements is essential for implementing an effective pilot project. Teams should consider baseline quality issues, the scope of the project, the life cycle of the product (avoiding end-of-life products), the experience and size of the team, the workload of pilot testers, aspects of quality that the pilot should target, training components, and evaluation criteria.

- **Establishing a production rollout strategy**. For the rollout, teams can focus on some of the same considerations addressed in the pilot. In addition, they should assess how to work around product launch schedules for determining what projects to consider in a particular order. A phased implementation facilitates continual learning with one team benefiting from what others have discovered.

- **Two-way communications with process participants**. Learning occurs throughout the rollout process, which highlights the importance of communication throughout implementation. Teams need an effective method for handling questions, requests, and troubleshooting. Establishing a centralized communication system using Web technology, such as workspaces and discussion boards that incorporate workflow, enables all team members to collaborate virtually and adapt the tool as products change and standards are updated.

Throughout the planning phase, team members can begin to see how a well-designed quality management system can simplify the content development process. As more teams begin using the tool, writers will see firsthand that their peers will get the same feedback to ensure the consistent and reliable application of standards. Knowing that the content will meet the established standards goes far in helping teams establish trust when sharing content, which in turn supports collaboration.

Step 3: Deploying a Pilot

Pilot implementation of quality management technologies should proceed according to decisions made when determining pilot requirements. During deployment, the quality review board helps guide members chosen for the pilot. Pilot testers quickly identify the features they like and those needing adjustment. Pilot testers provide valuable input for improving and refining to tool, including occasionally removing some rules altogether. As writers use the tool and see how the feedback helps them control the quality of their content, they often become excited about how the tool will enable them to achieve results and save time. The excitement can infect the rest of the organization. By the time the pilot ends, the quality review board can determine if another pilot is necessary to test the changes required by the initial testers. Once all testing is complete, the review board should evaluate the success of the pilot (or pilots), document the results, and present them to the organization.

While word spreads quickly about the benefits of a quality management tool, organizations should target effective ways communicate positive outcomes across the organization. Teams should balance informal conversations with frequent formal communication of the decisions made, expected outcomes, and anticipated impact on individual writers. Formal presentations are best delivered by the management sponsor along with input from the quality review board.

Step 4: Defining a Rollout Strategy

If the preceding phases are carried out effectively, the production rollout of the selected technology should be the easiest step in the process. Adhering to the rollout schedule defined in the planning and preparation step is essential for smooth implementation. Organizations need to be strategic so that the quality review board can provide adequate training and startup support. Kickoff meetings for implementation should include:

- **A management overview**. This summary should focus on *why* quality management processes are being implemented, emphasizing the need for consistent quality in terms of style, terminology, corporate identity, and messaging. Part of the message also should address how important the tool will be for collaborating virtually and for managing overall costs across the organization.
- **An overview of the process**. The person who leads the quality review board should describe the value of a governance structure and *how* quality management processes will work going forward, emphasizing the need for close cooperation and collaboration between the governance body and the writing teams. This discussion also should describe the metrics, monitoring, and tracking strategies.
- **A thorough description and demonstration of the tool**. The quality review board should provide a detailed description and demonstration of how the tool is implemented to support the quality management

initiative. The demonstration is the team's first exposure to the tool and it functions to shape perceptions and prepare teams for training by the member of the quality review board that will be responsible for training and support of the attendees.

- **An interactive Q&A discussion**. It is important to schedule interactive sessions for members of the organization to understand the potential impact of the quality management initiative on writers, editors, support, and management staff.

Step 5: Overseeing Continuous Quality Tracking and Process Improvement

The quality management board is responsible for monitoring the implementation of the tool, tracking and monitoring quality metrics, and communicating results to the organization. Throughout the implementation and maintenance periods, the board supports the organization by assembling key players to implement improvements or address problems. As results are gathered, the review board should create opportunities for communicating formally with the organization to track trends revealed in quality reports and charts. This information enables teams to modify processes as needed, to drive ongoing improvement, and to facilitate the management of quality at the various organizational levels.

With acrolinx® IQ, for example, most writers and editors will find implanting the quality management tool to be straightforward. They would begin with the acrolinx® IQ check button instead of the spell checker. And if teams "forget" to run a check, a quality control report will indicate the need to run the tool. For managers, the change entails access to useful data to manage quality throughout the organization, generally, a welcome change.

A Look into the Future

The application of NLP technology to real-world information development processes has come a long way since the turn of the century, but commercial application of the technology is still in its infancy. Ongoing academic research and commercial research and development continue to improve basic accuracy and precision of NLP analysis, and real-world deployments continue to identify new uses for the technology, including:

- **Machine Translation (MT) pre-editing:** A growing number of companies are investing heavily in machine translation processes for large volumes of time-sensitive or other critical information. Machine translation is fast, but typically requires 50% or more post-editing for most languages. Many believe that pre-editing content for machine translation can improve quality of the output and reduce post-editing activities, but manual pre-editing adds more cost and time. Instead, with the help of information quality tools and by applying slightly more restrictive rules and limiting approved terminology, some companies have reported that writers can create content that flows easily through MT processes, requiring only 15% or less post-editing. This outcome will only improve as MT technology advances.
- **Automated Markup Guidance:** The use of linguistic pattern matching to identify text strings that should be tagged in certain ways (for example, UI strings, Commands, Product Names, Part Numbers, and Telephone Numbers).
- **Reuse at phrase and sentence level:** The use of linguistic, meaning-based matching algorithms can suggest approved text for "creative" variations of common sentences and phrases. For example, in the UI strings of a single large software system, we found

over 30 different variants of the simple sentence "*Contact technical support.*" We found 50 variants of "*The end date must be later than the start date.*" All of these variants were translated to over 30 languages.

- **Translation quality assurance:** Checking translated documents for conformance to spelling, grammar, style, and terminology requirements currently is available for English, German, French and Japanese. Enhancements will include translation accuracy assessments and extension of checking capability to additional languages.

- **Non-native speaker guidance:** As global collaboration continues to grow, we increasingly find teams that include writers fluent in different native languages. These individuals are expected to write in the approved corporate language. While quality tools can help teams normalize language differences, more work is needed to identify linguistic traits and patterns associated with specific language pairs and to develop linguistic rules to address them.

- **Quality management software for additional languages:** English is, of course, the language of choice for most North American companies, and it generally is preferred as the source for translation to other languages. Yet because much content is generated in other languages, quality management tools and practices are needed for additional languages.

CONCLUSION

Modern NLP-based information quality tools have enabled the effective deployment of well-known and proven quality management principles and practices in today's global virtual collaborative writing operations. The deployment of quality management processes while writers develop information has resulted in quality, cost, and time-to-market improvements.

The Benefits of Quality Management

The reasons why an enterprise might want to invest in quality management tools for information development teams include the following: improved customer experience, improved process efficiencies, reduced time-to-market, reduced information supply chain costs, and increased revenue and profitability.

Improved Customer Experience

Clear, concise, consistent, and correct content is easier to read, especially by poor readers and non-native speakers—both large and growing segments of the North American population. It also is easier, hence quicker and less costly, to translate. Consistent use of approved terminology also leads to improved indexing, which leads to better retrieval performance for online content, better self-help, and reduced reliance on support centers.

Improved Process Efficiencies

Documented processes with clear quality expectations at every handoff point result in smoother handoffs, substantially less rework, and reduced review and editing times. Customers have reported that editing time reductions have ranged from 65% to 75%. Additionally, they have reduced the cost of fixing errors significantly by addressing or avoiding them early in the process. The cost of correcting errors at various points in a production process can be illustrated graphically as a "quality pyramid." In the context of collaborative virtual writing, the pyramid might look like Figure 5.

As demonstrated here, if an SME introduces an error into a specification that a writer will use to develop content, the costs will cascade as the content moves through the process. To fix the error immediately might cost $1. But what hap-

Figure 5. Quality pyramid

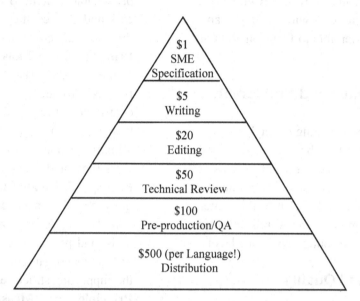

pens if the SME does not identify and fix the problem?

- If the writer thinks the specification is in error, he or she will likely do some research, and check with colleagues before going back to the SME, who agrees to check it out "next week." Two or more interactions may ensue before the issue is resolved, and the error now costs $5 to resolve.
- What if the error is caught during editing? The editor now has to deal with both the writer and the SME, and perhaps an impartial "referee." Net cost $20.
- What about during a technical review? Writer, editor, multiple SMEs, project manager, scribe and others go through an agonizing process of arguments, opinions, justification, finger-pointing, escalation to engineering and writing management. Net cost $50.
- During pre-production? At this stage, three independent organizations may be involved, and more ruffled feathers. Net cost $100.

- What if the error gets distributed to print, Web, and CD-ROM/DVD? And gets translated to 20 or 30 languages? *Priceless!*

Reduced Time-to-Market

Deployment of quality management processes and tools in the information supply chain can lead to significant reductions in time-to-market, not only because of editing efficiencies but also because of those involving translation. That is, helping writers manage translation issues at the source has resulted for some in 10% to 25% reductions in downstream translation times.

Reduced Supply Chain Costs

As mentioned earlier, the largest cost reductions are in the area of editing (up to 75%). Customers have also reported translation cost reductions of up to 25%. In large, global enterprises, the cost of translation often exceeds the cost of writing, and small percentage improvements in source language translatability can lead to large cost savings. While more difficult to quantify, reduced technical review time and effort also are important benefits. After a few reviews without finding any typos, SMEs are better able to focus on content accuracy.

Increased Revenue and Profitability

The money saved by managing quality can open new markets if organizations begin translating into additional languages. They can also reduce translation time, which can provide a significant competitive advantage in global markets. Ultimately, better information quality improves the overall customer experience and raises customer satisfaction levels.

Collaboration and Quality Management

The practices for quality management outlined in this chapter directly reflect five of the six principles of effective collaboration that ground this book, and at least indirectly reflect the sixth principle as follows:

- **Principle 1, Develop a Culture of Collaboration:** Formal quality management processes and tools can help to influence organizational culture, by establishing quality as a shared value, and by providing tools and processes that emphasize this value.
- **Principle 2, Identify and Promote Leaders:** The establishment of a joint management/staff quality review board provides an opportunity for informal leaders to interact regularly with several levels of the organization.
- **Principle 3, Establish Trust:** It is easier to build and maintain trust in any organization, whether local or global, physical or virtual, if everyone plays by the same rules, which includes objective assessments. Making information quality equally accessible will lead to more uniform and

predictable content. If writers trust the process and the results, it will be easier for them to share content.

- **Principle 4, Use Tools and Collaborative Modes Effectively:** Tools like acrolinx® IQ, that provide common guidance to all contributors from a single, central source help to improve quality and consistency, minimize handoff issues, and help to reduce cycle times and stress.
- **Principle 5, Create Structure:** A commitment to quality management practices, supported by effective governance structures, tools, and processes can provide the overarching macro-structure within which all of the supporting structures function.
- **Principle 6, Measure and Track Performance**: Quality is not the only performance metric to be monitored and tracked. In the information development and delivery environment, however, quality has been the most difficult to measure and, undoubtedly, the most contentious. By measuring roughly 100± attributes objectively and automatically, the playing field is leveled for everyone. Real-time feedback for all participants gives everyone an equal opportunity to succeed.

For these principles and benefits to work in the real world, it is important to emphasize that humans will always be required in the process. While NLP-based tools are very powerful and sophisticated, they are still *tools*. And like all tools their effective use depends on appropriately skilled artisans for their effective use. Technical accuracy, relevance, context, effectiveness, and other developmental editing assessments still require manual processes. In other words, such virtual technology carries the potential to improve a collaborative writing team's performance rather than to replace the team, as some may fear. To this end, innovative quality management technologies can benefit the organization, its customers, and its writers alike.

NOTE

For more information about quality management tools and processes, www.acrolinx®.com offers a starting place. Additional reference material is available at www.acrolinx®.com/presentatinos_en.html and at www.acrolinx®.com/media_en.html.

REFERENCES

International Organization, Information processing—text and office systems—Standard Generalized Markup Language (SGML) ISO 8879, 1986/Amd 1:1988.

International Standard, Quality management and quality assurance standards. International Organization for Standardization ISO 9000, 1987/Amd 1:1994.

The Chicago Manual of Style. (2003). *The essential guide for writers, editors, and publishers* (15th ed.). Chicago: The University of Chicago Press.

Chapter 16
Caution! Empowered Reviewers Ahead:
The Challenges of the Review Process in Collaboration

Robbin Zeff Warner
Independent Scholar, Belgium

Beth L. Hewett
University of Maryland University College, USA

Charlotte Robidoux
Hewlett-Packard Company, USA

ABSTRACT

One aspect of writing in government, business, and academia that always has been collaborative is the document review process. In this process, all persons with a stake in the final writing product are invited to help shape the piece in terms of content, style, or structure. Their review work has primarily been both serial and parallel. However, problems and perils of document review can strike at any stage in the review process: from the reviewer not knowing how to give useful comments to the writer not knowing how to interpret and use comments constructively. In today's Web 2.0 world, what once was a more closed and controlled collaboration review process becomes open and organic because digital and online information is accessible to intended and unintended audiences alike for commenting, ranking, and reviewing. Response to this new openness in review has been mixed among and within institutions. And yet, the momentum for open and even unsolicited reviews is not only impossible to stop but also difficult to manage. While computer-mediated communication (CMC) and content management system (CMS) tools have automated the writing process, the review process has lagged in terms of being efficiently collaborative. This chapter explores collaborative review in a user-empowered Web 2.0 world, including how CMC tools can facilitate the review process. Finally, this chapter exemplifies Principles 1, 2, and 4 that ground this book.

DOI: 10.4018/978-1-60566-994-6.ch016

INTRODUCTION

In a wired world of nearly instantaneous access and communication, consumers no longer suffer in silence; they post their frustrations online for everyone from the company to current and potential customers to read. On May 18, 2009, for example, a customer of American Airlines was frustrated with his poor online experience at AA.com and decided to redesign the website to be more user-friendly and efficient. This dissatisfied customer, Dustin Curtis, was a user interface designer by trade and kept a weblog, or blog. He posted his revised design and commentary about his frustration with the AA.com website on his blog as an open letter to American Airlines with a link to his redesign. Figure 1 features his blog with portions of the redesign (Curtis, May 18, 2009).

His post led to an e-mail exchange between a UX architect from the AA.com official design team and himself, which he then posted in part to the blog (Curtis, May 22, 2009). Curtis wrote that he was shocked to learn that AA.com not only had a UX architect, but that judging from the UX architect's other work, he was good. The UX architect's response expressed his own frustration with the design and provided an explanation of how a collaborative writing project can go bad.

Curtis posted Mr. "X"'s full e-mail on his blog with permission from the writer provided that the writer's name and some other information were withheld. Mr. X explained that the problem with the design of AA.com "lies less in our competency (or lack thereof, as you pointed out in your post) and more with the culture and processes employed here at American Airlines" (Curtis, May 22, 2009).

Figure 1. Screenshot of Dustin Curtis's May 18, 2009 blog post with the open letter to American Airlines showing his redesign next to the current AA.com web site

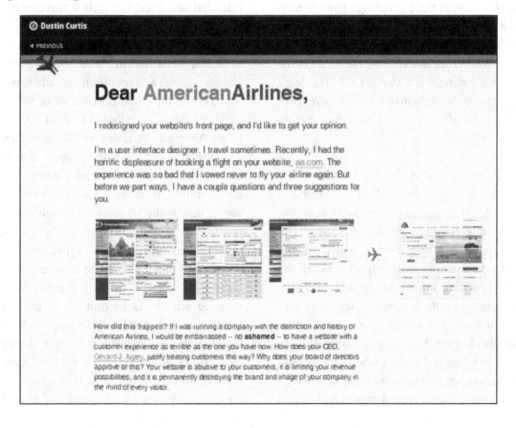

He then describes the many people and departments involved in the website that resulted in a product lacking cohesion and focus:

The group running AA.com consists of at least 200 people spread out amongst many different groups, including, for example, QA, product planning, business analysis, code development, site operations, project planning, and user experience. We have a lot of people touching the site, and a lot more with their own vested interests in how the site presents its content and functionality. Fortunately, much of the public-facing functionality is funneled through UX, so any new features you see on the site should have been vetted through and designed by us before going public.

However, there are large exceptions. For example, our Interactive Marketing group designs and implements fare sales and specials (and doesn't go through us to do it), and the Publishing group pushes content without much interaction with us… Oh, and don't forget the AAdvantage team (which for some reason, runs its own little corner of the site) or the international sites (which have a lot of autonomy in how their domains are run)… Anyway, I guess what I'm saying is that AA.com is a huge corporate undertaking with a lot of tentacles that reach into a lot of interests. It's not small, by any means. (Curtis, May 22, 2009)

Mr. X's main point is that while redesigning a Web page is easy, "those of us who work in enterprise-level situations realize the momentum even a simple redesign must overcome." The momentum he is referencing is fueled by the many outside voices that can impact or derail the success of a writing project. Momentum becomes negative when the outside voices hijack the project rather than work in a coordinated or collective collaborative fashion. Collective collaboration, as explained in Chapter 1 occurs when each person contributes to a project in coordination with everyone else. Such collaboration assumes both serial (each person contributes to a project in sequence) and parallel (each person contributes to a project concurrently) collaboration. The unfortunate result of an uncoordinated review process is the implementation of all stakeholder requests such that the project loses a unified focus. For the consumer, who is the forgotten audience in a review gone wild, the result can be an incomprehensible document, website, or other information product.

The dialogue between Curtis and Mr. X was covered in the online press, which produced a lively debate on the perils of corporate culture's impact on design and collaboration (Kuang, 2009). As one author said, "The biggest challenge to better design isn't getting better designers. The problem is organizational" (Kuang, 2009). Indeed, when uncoordinated input from empowered stakeholders occurs, what was done in the spirit of inclusive collaboration becomes a disjointed patchwork of pieces that do not form a solid whole for its intended purpose. With AA.com, all the internal voices were served rather than the intended audience, the airline traveler trying to book a ticket online.

Today's Web 2.0 tools—from wikis to blogs to social bookmarking and social networking clients—invite and encourage people to post their opinions online whether solicited or not. Having outside voices—like that of Curtis (2009) talking to an American Airlines employee—engage in a dialogue about a written project is indeed an important step in the writing process wherever collaboration is understood and valued. What seems new is the voracity and popularity of this practice from voices that reside both inside and outside the organization and that may be either solicited or unsolicited. The issue is not whether such open access reviewing is good or bad; the practice already is ubiquitous in the Web 2.0 world, and it is not likely to stop. Indeed, from the customer's perspective at least, the fact that (sometimes uninvited) reviewers are expressing their opinions so strenuously suggests that the customers as reviewers need these reviewing opportunities. It seems important, therefore, to figure out what can be learned from such reviews. Chapter 17 addresses how to solicit and make the best use of customer collaborations in online settings.

Undoubtedly, organizations themselves benefit from internal and external reviews of their information products. Reviews run amuck, however, can make an already challenging writing project much more difficult. Rather than eliminate the review process, it is possible to identify steps for a virtual collaborative review process based on the writers' needs; doing so may provide writers with greater opportunities to keep the deliverable focused on the audience's needs overall. If tools or the technology is not sufficiently transparent, information overload can cripple the ability to shape, influence, or publish the text in any useable form (Geisler, et al., p. 285). To manage information overload, content needs to be the basis of "reciprocal activity in which technologies adapt to users and users adapt to technologies" (p. 285). It seems possible to apply more effective review practices to today's new virtual openness and inclusiveness in commenting, ranking, and reviewing. Developing such review practices are the main subject of this chapter.

THE BENEFITS AND CHALLENGES OF REVIEWS

Information products regularly receive reviews in most workplace settings. For example, the academic paper submitted to a journal is reviewed by three to five outside subject matter experts (SMEs), who provide independent (parallel) feedback about the content and the writing. Internal editors also vet the documents; there may be several levels of review before publication if the text is accepted at all. Government documents, for another example, receive reviews that may take months and involve multiple reviews from stakeholders at various levels. One book-length

document on emergency planning that was published in 2009, for instance, was more than a year in the writing. It received internal review of 40 people in the writing group, external review of more than 20 people in the Federal interagency, and then a nationwide review of as many as 1,000 readers (P. Hewett, 2009). The writers then had the job of sorting and compiling the reviews to make sense of which stakeholders had particular needs and how to meet those needs in revision. The many voices involved in the contemporary collaborative review process can put reviewers at odds with one another, and can make the writers' job in sorting through and integrating those reviews a veritable nightmare.

Collaborative review also brings personal agendas to the surface. Perhaps nowhere is the political nature of collaborative writing and review more apparent than when collaborative writing is done collectively. A blog post by Eugene E. Warner, a diplomatic attaché with the U.S. Mission to NATO, provides a glimpse of what this review process is like at NATO where documents are drafted in real time with representatives of all 28 nations sitting around the same table (Warner, 2009). NATO works by consensus. In other words, nothing is agreed until all is agreed. In document development, this process can be difficult and unwieldy because not only does NATO have two official languages—English and French—with most documents drafted in English, but only a few who sit around the table are native speakers of English. Equally important, NATO is a political and diplomatic body where every word in a document is taken politically. Warner's blog post is a fictitious account of what drafting sessions for a NATO committee document might be like if the topic was recommending dessert for a ministerial dinner. The topic of discussion is fake and the names have been removed, but the author states, "the pacing and flow are very representative."

Chair: *"Can we agree on the statement 'ice cream is the preferred choice?'"*

Country A: *"Thank-you Mr. Chairman. My capitol wishes to see '...a preferred choice' as opposed to 'the'"*

Chair: *"Thank-you very much...comments? Country B?"*

Country B: *"Thank-you Mr. Chairman. And I'd like to thank my colleague from 'A' for an insightful addition. But I'd like to point out that we have already identified ice cream as the preferred choice in our communiqué language from the 1998 summit."*

Chair: *"Thank-you very much. Comments from colleagues? Country C?"*

Country C: *"Thank-you Mr. Chairman. And thanks to my colleagues from A and B for this fruitful discussion. But I would like to strike mention of ice cream from this document completely, as it pre-supposes a solution to the ministerial dessert dilemma."*

Chair: *"And you have some proposed language?"*

Country C: *"Thank-you Mr. Chairman. Yes, my capitol has recommended substituting the phrase 'near frozen sweet cow juice with some chocolate bits' as appropriate language."*

Chair: *"Thank-you very much...comments?... Country D?"*

Country D: *"Thank-you Mr. Chairman. But what about sorbets? Are we not excluding another class of appropriate desserts for the ministers? We would like to see it amended to 'near frozen sweet cow juice with some chocolate bits, but not excluding, to the maximum extent practicable, other appropriate near frozen dessert solutions which most likely could, in all reasonable possibilities, serve as the basis for post-dining ministerial excursions.'"*

Chair: *"Thank-you very much...no more comments? This statement has grown very long, and I wonder if we could ask any of our native English speakers if there's some way we could clean it up a bit...United States?"*

US: *"Thank-you Mr. Chairman. Just from a readability standpoint, it certainly looks like English, but I'd like to note the sentence does run on for seven or eight lines with a lot of what may be unnecessary language...I think the original term 'ice cream' might have been the best."*

Chair: *"Thank-you, thank-you very much. Well, going back to the original language...this is a very different kettle of shoes...comments? (Warner 2009)*

From this example, one might wonder how any writing can get done collaboratively. However, when many stakeholders are involved, the collaborative writing process builds the necessary consensus; Chapters 3 and 6 address such consensus building.

What happens when the writing's review occurs online outside of a controlled corporate or government environment? This online input may be uncontrollable and unsolicited, but when the intended audience becomes empowered as now occurs online through Web 2.0 tools such as blogs, rankings, and ratings, the impact can be beneficial to a project in better reflecting the needs and desires of its intended audience. One well-documented example is the 2006 movie *Snakes on a Plane* (Brown, 2006; Waldon, 2006). It all started with a 2005 blog post by screenwriter Josh Friedman, who had been approached by the studio to revise the screenplay (Friedman, 2005). Friedman's post lamented the studio's decision to change the title of the movie from *Snakes on a Plane,* which Friedman thought was a brilliant title, to *Pacific Air Flight 121.*

Friedman's post innocently launched an online frenzy of interest in the yet to be released movie that resulted in hundreds of blog posts, parodies, and mock movie trailers. The studio quickly learned of the movie's exploding online fan base and not only changed the movie title back to *Snakes on a Plane* but even solicited direct input from the online fans. Friedman liked the title so much that he posted on his blog that he thought the title had the potential to become a catch phrase for those small annoyances in life, as Friedman demonstrated:

WIFE: "Honey you stepped in dog poop again."

ME: "Snakes on a Plane…"

DOCTOR: "Your cholesterol is 290. Perhaps you want to mix in a walk once in a while"

ME: "Snakes on a Plane…"(Friedman, 2005)

By the time the movie was released in 2006, not only was it a cult classic, but the phrase "snakes on a plane" was appearing in slang dictionaries as a synonym for *ç'est la vie* (Brown, 2006).

The *Snakes on a Plane* example is presented here tongue-in-cheek, but it provides a view of how important the review process is to getting a document or information product "right" for its audience. How reviews take place—or how we think they should occur—is the subject of the next section.

WORKING WITH REVIEWS

The problems that occurred for AA.com because of multiple reviewers with individual agendas are not unique. They can happen in any review process. Whenever a document is reviewed, if a writer tries to address each reviewer's agenda, the purpose and flow of the document can get lost. The audience's needs, in particular, likely will not be met.

For example, co-author of this chapter Robbin Zeff Warner worked as a writing consultant with accident investigators at the National Transportation Safety Board (NTSB) from 2006 to 2008. The NTSB is an independent Federal agency that investigates civil aviation and other modes of transportation (that is, railroad, highway, marine, and pipeline) accidents. The NTSB investigators are on-call 24 hours a day, 365 days a year and travel to accident sites in the United States and throughout the world. Since it was founded in 1967, the NTSB has investigated 124,000 aviation accidents and 20,000 surface transportation accidents (NTSB, 2004). For each accident, the NTSB produces a report, making it one of the most prolific government publishers for an organization of its size. All accidents investigated by the NTSB culminate with a public report that explains the causes of the accidents and makes related safety recommendation. What this means for the investigators is that they spend more of their time writing about accidents than investigating them in the field. Moreover, these investigators were trained at investigating transportation accidents, not as technical writers.

The writing process at NTSB begins when an NTSB investigator launches an accident investigation at a crash site. The on-site crash investigator can be anywhere in the country while writing the preliminary draft of the accident report. The document then is sent through an initial review process that includes supervisors and technical experts who can be in multiple locations. By the time the document goes to the NTSB editors in Washington, DC, the document already has been molded by many writers to get the technical elements just right. The editing stage can put the crash investigators at odds with the editors, however, whose changes in the name of coherence and conciseness sometimes can affect the accuracy and precision of the initial statement. The tension results in trying to find the balance between technical precision and readability for its primary audience, the lay public. Moreover, as with any government document, all writing at NTSB is political. And yet, even with having to walk a political tightrope in producing their reports, the investigators wholeheartedly believed in their work. For them, discovering why an accident occurred was a job with a higher purpose, no matter how politically charged a finding might be. Conveying that finding was a different matter altogether—in large part because of the review process.

For another example, from 2006 to 2007, Warner worked as a technical writing consultant with engineers at the National Highway Transportation Safety Administration (NHTSA), a division within the Department of Transportation (DOT). The head of the department wanted to provide his engineers with writing assistance and initiated the training program. These were seasoned engineers who spent the majority of their time writing up results of automobile crash tests. Her task was to provide weekly one-on-one technical writing consultation to help them develop stronger written communication skills. After speaking with the supervisor, she discovered that he had a healthy and realistic understanding of writing and what it takes to write well. He described himself as a not naturally good writer, but rather one who became a good writer through hard work and determination. He was initiating this internal writing-mentoring program because he wanted his engineers to develop stronger writing skills, a necessity for them to move up the administrative and professional ladder in government.

Over a two-year period, Warner worked with engineers of different levels on various technical writing tasks. The one consistent challenge voiced by all the engineers was traversing the document review process. They expressed that they could never meet the needs of all the reviewers, which led them to doubt their abilities as writers. Although each had aspects of their writing that was benefiting from the mentoring program, none were poor writers at the outset. Instead, they were

highly trained engineers whose formal education had paid little attention to the writing demands of an engineer. Interestingly, it used to be that some people would choose engineering and the sciences to get away from positions where writing was necessary; no one told them that people write quite a lot in all fields. This oversight fortunately is being addressed in undergraduate education with formal and informal writing across the curriculum (WAC) programs that teach strong writing skills in all majors from the humanities to the sciences.

After hearing repeated stories from the engineers about their frustrations with the document review process, Warner asked them to draw a map of each step in the process: who reviewed the document first, then second, and so on. One of these mapped processes is shown in Figure 2. The review maps demonstrated that a document could be reviewed by up to eight people, each inserting an agenda and his or her preferred stylistics. For example, an engineer would produce a report and it would be shuttled back and forth between the writer and his/her supervisor. Then the report would go to the supervisor's manager. From there, it would go to the supervisor's manager's boss. Once that part of the review was complete, the document would start its travels through a slate of external reviewers with a stake in the project. Then the document would return to the original writer or writers who might make such significant changes that the document would have to travel through the review chain again. The engineers did not begrudge the reviewers; the reviewers were stakeholders and responsible parties whose concerns needed to be addressed. At the same time, the writers all expressed frustration at not being able to meet the needs of all the audiences reviewing the document. The result was that the writers would lose confidence in their writing, even though these audiences contradicted each other so that a change requested by one could be reversed by another.

The supervisor and engineers saw this disagreement among reviewers and the ensuring revision it necessitated as a failure in their writing skills. On closer inspection, Warner saw the problem as a failure in collaboration coordination. Each reviewer looked at the document through his or her own agenda lens. When a document did not meet a reviewer's agenda needs, the reviewer was quick to criticize the engineer's writing ability—despite the fact that even the most skilled writer would have difficulty meeting all the needs of such a diverse constituency. Successful collaborative review requires clear instructions about the role and responsibilities of each reviewer. Otherwise, a reviewer might take on the easy and comfortable role of proofreader unintentionally molding the writing into something he or she would produce rather than acting in the intended role as SME and providing a content review.

Learning to Conduct a Review

It is possible to extrapolate from what student writers learn about peer review and revision to learn about what might work well in business settings.

The Student Writer's Peer Review Process

An example of the basic skill set required to write and use comments constructively can be found with young writers in a college composition course. In many cases, an instructor returns a student's paper with comments inserted in the margins. Such comments usually pertain both to content and style issues in the current draft. In trying to please the instructor, the student may make each revision that the instructor suggested or requested without considering or evaluating how each revision decision impacts the other revision needs and the document as a whole. Although skilled writers realize that each revision change can (and often should) engender further changes, novice writers tend not to understand that reality. What often results from their "revision" is a paper that addresses each marginal comment by adding or deleting material or by "fixing" errors, but it no longer works as a unified document.

There is an abundance of scholarship on the benefits of peer review in the teaching of writing (Howard, 2009). These benefits include improving the skills of the writer, improving the quality

Figure 2. Map drawn by an NHTSA engineer of the internal document review process

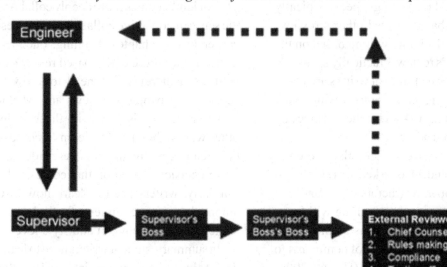

of the writing, as well as improving the reading and writing skills of the reviewer. When instructor review moves to peer review, which is the model most like the one under discussion in this chapter, student writers find themselves in a new dilemma. Whereas they often assume wrongly that all of the instructor's comments must be addressed, with their peers they realize they have choices and must figure out whether to take such feedback into consideration in revision. Without guidance as to how to use the feedback—when to accept it and when to reject it and when to use it as a spur to new or different thinking—student writers risk missing the point of the review and they lose an opportunity for developing a stronger piece of writing.

Students also need to learn, therefore, about whether and how to choose among the many comments they may receive about their writing When student writers have more than one peer reader in addition to an experienced reader (the instructor), the comments they receive in traditional face-to-face settings typically happen in a serial and/or parallel collaboration process, as noted earlier in this chapter. In this sense, they are collaborating particularly in a parallel manner to provide a set of reviews for the writer—not one single review that collects or incorporates many voices. In traditional face-to-face settings, peers typically do not have the chance to read other's reviews or to comment on the initial writing based on the context of another's review. Practically speaking, this scenario means that student writers are likely to receive conflicting advice among which they must choose—or they risk an incoherent piece by using all the offered advice.

For the peer reviewers, there also are challenges. When a student is asked to review another student's paper, instructors often find that students without peer-review training will focus on the surface level errors such as grammar and punctuation. These are the kinds of comments to which students most often respond (Hewett, 2004-2005) in their own revisions. To do otherwise and

provide more substantive comments, students need to be trained to give feedback on content that will improve the quality of the writing and not just try to fix grammar and spelling errors (which we are simply calling "style" in this chapter although we recognize the many sophisticated levels of style that need consideration in any writing project). For this reason, scholarship also recognizes that one needs to learn how to review writing. Ideally, in learning to give constructive feedback, students learn about themselves as writers improving their own writing. Strategies that help them learn this skill include question prompts and rubrics that specify what kinds of content and stylistic issues to read for. Peer review in traditional settings may use such prompts and rubrics, but likely will do so in parallel with each student reviewer handing the writer a separate review sheet for the writer to compile or consider separately.

The nature of the peer review changes for student writers with virtual technology. Add CMC tools to the mix and the potential arises for virtual collaboration beyond serial and parallel collaboration among peer reviewers. Once a shared desktop or other document sharing tool is used for circulating both the writing and the peers' comments, then the reviewers can develop their comments within the context of the other reviews. The review becomes more deeply collaborative in the sense of collective collaboration, as described earlier in this chapter. Training, once again, is necessary for these CMC-based reviews to work well. Student reviewers need to know how to access other people's reviews and whether and how to agree or disagree with those reviews. In other words, they need to learn to contextualize their reading within that of other readers and then make decisions based on that contextualization. Similarly, writers need to learn how to choose among the review comments for the best revision strategies at both content and style levels.

In summary, student writers need to learn—and do not always have appropriate guidance for—the following skills:

- How much emphasis to place on review comments that come from their instructors,
- How much emphasis to place on review comments that come from their other reviewers (peers),
- How to compile the various reviews efficiently, and
- How to develop a coherent, unified document based on such reviews.

Student reviewers need to learn:

- How to give feedback that is responsive to content, as well as to style issues;
- How to apply prompts, rubrics, or other standards to their reading of another's writing (serial and/or parallel collaboration);
- How to provide feedback that contextualizes other's feedback (collective collaboration); and
- In virtual settings particularly, how to use the technology to provide feedback in the collaborative model used by the course.

Collaborative Peer Review in the Virtual Workplace

Students eventually graduate and become the novice writers in business settings, which mean that they need preparation for writing beyond school, as Chapter 18 discusses. Interestingly, the serial and parallel kinds of review process described above may be the ones that most novice writers in business and other professional settings know best because they are what writers and reviewers most often practiced in college. Such practices may be what many writers bring to their workplace settings, even though student writing does not carry the responsibility and importance that a workplace project does. One important result of this skill transfer is that both writers and reviewers need to learn new rules for the process. For example, whereas the student writer typically is free to accept or reject peer reviews as feedback

that may or may not influence the writing, the workplace writer has many stakeholders to whom he or she is obliged to listen. Choosing among conflicting feedback becomes more challenging as the stakes move beyond the writer's grade and into the sphere of the writer's job security and the audience's practical needs.

To this end, it is possible to extrapolate that writers in business settings also need to distinguish among their supervisors' and peers' reviews to determine which revision changes need to be made. Some of this work is accomplished through appropriate and clearly written standards, as Chapter 13 considers. Standards enable writers to make decisions quickly (see Chapter 11) about what needs to change to comply with organizational guidelines. Handling other comments can be unwieldy because of the political implications. Each workplace culture is different; as such writers need to be politically astute in addressing conflicting comments as well as arguing why some changes, which could confuse the reader, should be dismissed. Part of building writers' skills also involves a range of learning related to (1) serial and parallel collaboration, which tends to be asynchronous, and (2) collective collaboration, which tends to be synchronous.

In reference to asynchronous work, writers need to learn how to respond to the review comments with speed and precision, even though the process is mostly manual. While the days of rifling through countless changes scribbled or pasted on many versions of hardcopy manuscript pages may be a thing of the past, writers still are required to compare, reconcile, consolidate, and incorporate disparate comments from different reviewers. Managing the review process using serial and parallel modes can be extremely labor intensive, time consuming, and difficult to manage. Whether this process occurs electronically and whether the work occurs in colocated or remote settings, the experience of assimilating comments asynchronously is fraught with complexity as shown in Figure 3, which illustrate a serial and parallel review processes related to a particular government writing process within a national laboratory (P. Hewett, personal communication, 2009).

The task is grueling because the writer or teams of writers efficiently must catalogue, track, and resolve all comments at least twice. As indicated in this flowchart, review comment information not only is gathered in the documents being reviewed, but also online in discussion boards and Web conferences, through instant messaging, in face-to-face meeting, and in a spreadsheet that tracks all the comments provided. Accordingly, teams must find a way to ensure that all comments recorded within documents are reconciled with other decisions agreed upon outside of the documents themselves—in meetings, online, or through other media. The ability for one or more writers assigned to the project to create accurate snapshots

of the required revisions, which can change almost daily, is nearly impossible. Even with the help of commenting spreadsheets that list each reviewer's comment and on what page it can be found, it is challenging for writers to keep the spreadsheet up to date when, for example, hallway conversation (even virtual ones) lead to changing someone's mind, reversing an earlier decision about what change should be made in the document. That all changes actually make it into a document as they were intended by all reviewers is unlikely. And the scenarios presented earlier in this chapter reveal, having all the changes incorporated by reviews is not necessarily beneficial to readers. Often, the review process demands more organizational skill, record keeping, and ego protection than in actually writing meaningful documents that benefit an audience. Despite these circum-

Figure 3. Optimized asynchronous review process (serial and parallel collaboration)

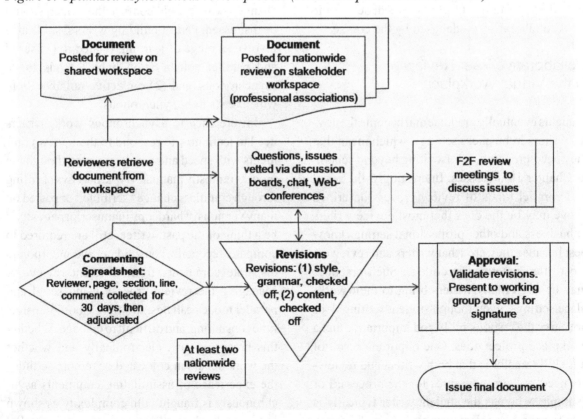

stances, writers quickly must learn how to develop a coherent, unified document based on such reviews, one that does not alienate the reviewers in the process. Geisler, et al. (2001) indicated the importance of tools that support "participatory design practices" that enable writers to develop more coherent and meaningful texts for their audiences (p. 286).

As CMC tools have become more sophisticated, workplace writing practices also have evolved to accommodate what the tools have made possible. Within the past decade, the very concept of what is considered a manual process has changed dramatically. At first, the idea of faxing changes to a writer seemed novel. But this technology was eclipsed by the advent of PDF files, which made it possible for reviewers to enter comments directly into an electronic file. Editors and reviewers struggled at first to learn how to manipulate drawing tools that enabled them to insert comments into PDF files. But even with electronic assistance, the use of PDF still has entailed serial and parallel collaboration as writers have to wait for reviewers, working in parallel, to submit their comments. And despite improvements made possible with electronic files, writers have continued to struggle through the process of reconciling the changes of various reviewers and editors, who have marked up different versions of a PDF document. Especially when confronted with a deadline, the shifting back and forth from one electronic file to another introduces errors because it can be easy to mix up comments and enter them into a document incorrectly.

While word-processing systems offer another way of managing comments electronically through the use of track changes, this option for large organization can be frustrating for writers to employ for these reasons: (1) when many review copies of the file have track change revisions, it is difficult to find a way to consolidate or merge numerous files with the desired set of comments; (2) if only one file is sent out for review (an option writers dislike because they lose control of the source

file), the process is slower because it is serial; (3) word-processing files have been known to become corrupt, which adds unnecessary risk to the review project; and (4) writers can lose efficiency when spending inordinate amounts of time formatting and reformatting their own or someone else's text. When the virtual tools are asynchronous in the case of word-processing tools or wikis or commonly shared spreadsheets, the serial nature of the process creates a push-pull operation. To see what the other writers have done, each reviewer must go through a deliberate process of pulling up the former reviews, integrating his or her thoughts with the feedback, and then pushing his or her own reviews back to the writer. The writers, then, have to prompt reviewers to deliberate over conflicting comments. If they do not reach some resolution, writers have to make a unilateral decision or find some workaround to meet a given deadline.

Strengthening writers' skills also is important for writers trying to conduct reviews more synchronously. While some CMC tools have added more synchronicity into the process of developing content, such as wikis and Google Docs, the tools generally speaking have lagged behind in providing equivalent real-time functionality for reviewing content. For example, a writer and review can occupy the same writing workspace on a Web conference whiteboard or in a file posted on Google Docs; however neither of these technologies provide enough sophistication to enable efficient complex reviews. In content management system (CMS) environments, while writers typically are able to add, modify, and delete the components that make up a document, allowing them to work on one document simultaneously, the reviewers often do not have system access for providing comments on the content, nor would they want to in many cases because of the complexity involved in learning how to use the system.

Some single sourcing tools are now providing features that enable near simultaneous reviews. For instance, one XML authoring tool, XMetaL reviewer, runs on a server and allows reviewers to access and review documents concurrently. Such a tool allows the writer to launch a review cycle that automatically notifies individuals that documents are available for online review. Once notified, reviewers can view and provide comments about documents without the inconvenience of seeing XML markup tags. As comments are added, each reviewer can see each others' comments in near real time, which facilitates the process of vetting comments that are in conflict. At the same time, a writer can monitor the comments and invite online discussion as disagreements arise. Moreover, the writer is able to track and retain a history of all comments provided and why some were incorporated and others omitted. This type of functionality is greatly needed to advance the review process, to promote parity for both reviewers and authors. Similarly, CMS technology also has begun incorporating features that enable an automated review process. For example, as indicated in Chapter 9, Vasont Systems offers a collaborative review module that facilitates the process of managing reviewer comments, expediting review cycles, and tracking the history of completed review projects (Mescan, 2009). Figure 4 illustrates the features related to content reviewing in a CMS that can be carried out more synchronously within a networked environment.

A flowchart of this process begins with a member of a writing team, a review coordinator,

launching a review process through a CMS. This feature allows the review coordinator to choose the appropriate people who need to provide feedback, send automatic notifications to reviewers and editors that content is ready for review, determine what actions must be taken (such as adding new information, clarifying points, and so on), and decide when the review needs to be completed. Once notified, the reviewers can access the CMS and provide responses in near real time. Reviewers can see comments made both by other reviewers and editors, which allows them to carry on an exchange of ideas and resolve issues immediately. As a result of such synchronous features, writing teams are more likely to conduct a more efficient review process. Similar to the XML authoring environment, the system tracks the input of each reviewer and the status of their review comments so that writers can stay on top of lagging reviewer, and notify them and the team as to why a review process still is incomplete. Once the review process is closed, writers can compile the comments efficiently without disrupting the source material, a problem when using track change functionality in a word-processing tool. That is, they can accept (or accept with changes) and reject all feedback and then upload the changes into the CMS without putting the original content at risk. Moreover, the writing team can output a report that verifies all the deci-

Figure 4. Synchronous review process (collective collaboration) through CMS automation

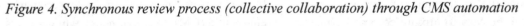

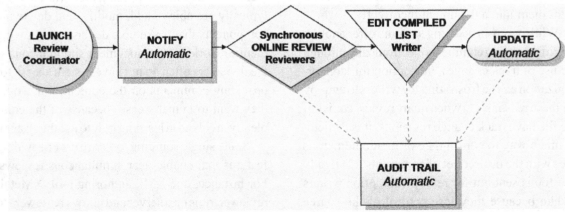

sions made about what feedback to include or exclude. This feature is valuable in large organizations that have document retention requirements.

Another example of an automated review process comes from Aquent Studios, which addressed the need for simultaneous reviews by building its Online Review Tool. The tool is based on a Microsoft Access database and uses Web pages to create an intuitive user interface. When a review period begins, notification is sent via e-mail directing the reviewer to a secure website to download the review files. Any file that will support hyperlinks can be reviewed using the tool. All comments related to a heading or page appear in a table format. As comments are added to the database, they are published for all other reviewers to read. Team members can sort and filter all of the comments for a document. If reviewers want to add to a comment submitted during the review, they can do so by entering text into a field called "Additional Remarks." By checking the "Add/Edit" box and clicking the "Edit Selected Items" button, review coordinators can assign an owner, note an action to be taken, note a resolution to a comment, or select a status, as indicated in Figure 5.

This centralized review process promotes an online dialog and often results in the resolution of questions during the review period. Writers are not faced with review downtime because they are able to continue development and even implement comments throughout the review period. As the writers resolve comments, the status of the com-

ments are updated and notes regarding the resolution of the comments are added to the database for reference by the reviewers, the writers, and managers, The interaction and feedback offered to the reviewer can promote increased collaboration over time.

The tool itself is the fruit of collaborative development. As a homegrown application, it has evolved organically to meet users' needs. Searching, sorting, tracking status, and replying to and verifying comments are all features of the application implemented in response to input by review team members.

When tools integrate features in the review process that enable tasks to be carried out synchronously, writers working collaboratively are likely to manage reviews more effectively, potentially creating information products that are more useful to an audience. However, in large-scale settings, if a more sophisticated, synchronous review processes is not available, the benefits of automation information development can be undermined. That is, while authors can benefit from the tools that automated authoring, not only will productivity wane if editors and subject matter experts cannot review the content efficiently but also document quality will be degraded as some of the examples provided in this chapter reveal. While some CMC technologies are beginning to integrate more synchronous functionality for reviewing content, especially in XML-related environments, writers working collaboratively need richer features in the

Figure 5. Synchronous review process (collective collaboration) through access database

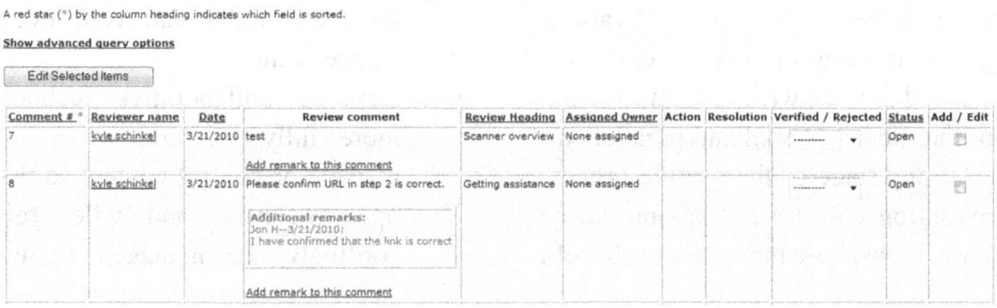

To add/edit fields, select the checkbox(es) for the comment(s) in the table below, then click **Edit Selected Items**.

A red star (*) by the column heading indicates which field is sorted.

Show advanced query options

> Edit Selected Items

Comment # *	Reviewer name	Date	Review comment	Review Heading	Assigned Owner	Action	Resolution	Verified / Rejected	Status	Add / Edit
7	kyle schinkel	3/21/2010	test Add remark to this comment	Scanner overview	None assigned			-------- ▼	Open	☐
8	kyle schinkel	3/21/2010	Please confirm URL in step 2 is correct. Additional remarks: Jon H--3/21/2010: I have confirmed that the link is correct Add remark to this comment	Getting assistance	None assigned			-------- ▼	Open	☐

tools to ensure efficiency, usability, and quality throughout the life cycle of document production. Does the tool, for example, allow reviews to view both the individual components that make up a document and the documents itself? That is, the tools can incorporate even more opportunities for synchronicity so that comments are not overlooked, ignored, or unresolved and so that the learning curve is not exceedingly onerous.

The review process in large, multi-channel authoring environments is one of the most critical aspects of information development, yet CMC technology has been slow in developing tools that equally support writing and reviewing. For instance, while wikis have played a central role in allowing collaborative development and review of content, the technology does not function effectively to enable teams to manage and secure versions of content. Rather, as indicated earlier in this chapter, wiki-like technology can spawn endless reviews of content, which can make the document life cycle interminable and, as a result, of little use to any audience. Indeed, content must at some point be stabilized—or published—and shared or it never will have use to either the writers or its audience. Such stabilization, as Geisler, et al. (2001) noted, is a function of workplace text: "texts provide shared visions around which joint work can be organized" (p. 279). To this end, we add that not only the joint work, but the potential for joint understanding and use for the text, can be organized by such shared visions.

In a virtual setting, as this book has considered, there are various kinds of virtual tools and processes that assist writers in developing and reviewing their work collaboratively. Ultimately, the lag apparent in the review aspects of various tools is significant enough to impede collective collaboration and to force writing teams to work only in familiar modes—serial and parallel collaboration. Of any stage of the writing process that can benefit from collective collaboration, the review process is the phase that can most benefit

from the affordances inherent in CMC tools that enable synchronous work.

NEXT STEPS TOWARD NEW PRACTICES

Some advice for developing changes in common review processes emerges in this chapter:

- Focus on synchronicity in the review process on the presumption that bringing collective collaboration to the review can benefit both the processes and the writers/reviewers. Because synchronicity is a measure of time—the closeness of virtual communicators to each other in terms of information and response, the greater the synchronicity, the stronger the potential communication among writers and reviewers. Therefore, both technology and review processes would benefit from enabling and finding ways to use synchronicity.

- Enable transparency in the virtual interactivity between or among reviewers and authors. If transparency is the nature of creating clarity through communication (aided, not incidentally, by the immediacy of synchronous virtual tools), increased transparency may help prevent both the content and the review process becoming so mired in the technology that no one can penetrate the content.

- Promote transparency in the author-to-reviewer discussion regarding the focus of the review so that it emphasizes the content more than individual word-level or stylistic preferences.

- Develop collaborative technology that more fully supports writers' efforts to manage or control content so that it is not open to constant and endless revision; accordingly, the management and control should be considered both in terms of the virtual tools under development and the review processes developed for use with such tools. One way to achieve this end might be to include customizable features that allow writing teams to direct reviewer feedback through pointed questioning or rubrics that identify key issues to consider. Implementing such standards within tools can help teams streamline stakeholder agendas and get reviewers and writers on the same page regarding both content and style issues.

- Establish mental prompt or process scripts (see Chapter 10) to give a voice to the end reader, who is the audience for a document or information product. Such prompts and process scripts would help writers and reviewers to remember the audience, providing them with ways to interact with the usually invisible audience during the writing and review processes. Writers and reviewers need to have language for interacting with reviewers that would keep them focused on the end-reader rather than themselves as writers/reviewers.

CONCLUSION

This chapter has considered the nature of the virtual collaborative review process, which is crucial to writing documents in various workplace settings. In doing so, it has stressed that there is much to learn about collaborative review in a Web 2.0 environment. As Tapscott and Williams (2008) discussed, people are collaborating in official and unofficial capacity through online openness, peering, sharing, and acting globally (p. 3). This collaboration is forcing a rethinking of how open access, for example, impacts business, government, education, and the arts. Tapscott and Williams offered no road map for success other than demonstrating key moments in virtual col-

laboration history. While this chapter does not pretend to have developed such a road map, it has provided various ways to rethink the virtual collaborative review.

Three of the core principles that ground this book stand out as providing valuable guidance regarding virtual collaborative review. First, both writers and reviewers are learning how to conduct reviews and how to work with the products of those reviews. Yet, with a cultural change, as noted in Principle 1 (see Chapter 1), both writers and reviewers can engage actively in developing and learning about new technologies and/or processes that would streamline and improve the work's efficiency. Second, Principle 2 involves finding and promoting leaders who can prompt the necessary cultural changes for stronger, more efficient reviews and review incorporation. Such leaders may be able to push for increasingly better virtual technology regarding virtual collaborative reviews, which lags behind such technology for virtual collaborative writing, and to encourage the organization's writers and reviewers (internal and external) to deepen their approaches to collaboration beyond serial and parallel modes. Indeed, Principle 4 encourages writing teams to use tools and collaborative modes more efficiently, which includes determining when serial and parallel collaborative review are better or less beneficial than collective collaboration.

In the Internet boom days of the late 1990s, tools and technologies were often criticized for being a solution looking for a problem. The media crowned these Web tools "hip and cool," but the underlying question was whether anyone would need or use them. In looking back at those early days of unrelenting Internet hype, it was all about promise and potential. And yet, 10 years later, what was once merely promise and potential is now daily online practice. We are seeing the same hype and proliferation of early tools with Web 2.0. But online history may repeat itself such that today's hype will be tomorrow's accepted reality. Without doubt, technology is having an unavoidable impact on the review process. For some it may seem like a time for caution, while for others it is a time for experimentation and innovation. But when it comes to document reviews in a Web 2.0 world, as the fictitious chairperson on the NATO committee was quoted as saying; it is a different kettle of shoes.

REFERENCES

Brown, M. (2006, August 18). *Snakes on a Plane* leaves critics flying blind [Electronic Version]. *The Guardian*. Retrieved August 1, 2009 from http://www.guardian.co.uk/uk/2006/aug/18/film.filmnews

Curtis, D. (2009, May 18). *Dear American Airlines*. Retrieved July 24, 2009, from http://www.dustincurtis.com/dear_american_airlines.html

Curtis, D. (2009, May 22). *The Response*. Retrieved July 24, 2009, from http://www.dustincurtis.com/dear_dustin_curtis.html

Friedman, J. (2005, August 17). I find your lack of faith disturbing: Snakes on a motherfucking plane. *Another screenwriter blog*. Retrieved August 1, 2009 from http://hucksblog.blogspot.com/2005/08/snakes-on-motherfucking-plane.html.

Geisler, C. (2001, July). IText: Future directions for research on the relationship between information technology and writing. *Journal of Business and Technical Communication, 15*(3), 269–308. doi:10.1177/105065190101500302

Hewett, B. (2004-2005). Asynchronous online instructional commentary: A study of student revision." *Readerly/Writerly Texts: Essays in Literary, Composition, and Pedagogical Theory. 11 & 12*(1 & 2)L, 47-67.

Howard, R. M. (2009). *Collaborative learning and writing: A bibliography for composition and rhetoric*. Retrieved on August 5, 2009 from http://wrt-howard.syr.edu/Bibs/Collab.htm

Kuang, C. (2009, June 1). American Airlines Web site: The product of a self-defeating design process. *Fast Company.com*. Retrieved June 6, 2009 from http://www.fastcompany.com/blog/cliff-kuang/design-innovation/how-self-defeating-corporate-design-process-one-designer-finds-ou?page=1

Mescan, S. (2009). *Collaborative Review in Vasont*. Emigsville, PA: Vasont Systems.

NTSB. (September 2004). About the NTSB. Retrieve August 1, 2009 http://www.ntsb.gov/Abt_NTSB/history.htm

Schinkel, K. (2009, November 13). Senior Project Manager, Aquent Studios. Interview.

Tapscott, D., & Williams, A. D. (2008). *Wikinomics: How mass collaboration changes everything*. New York: Portfolio.

Warner, E. E. (May 24, 2009). *A different kettle of shoes*. Retrieved July 30, 2009 from http://web.me.com/gene.warner/Site/Innocents_Abroad/Entries/2009/5/24_%E2%80%9C...A_Different_Kettle_of_Shoes%E2%80%9D.html

Chapter 17
Collaborating with Customers Virtually to Improve Content

Mirhonda Studevant
Ceridian Corporation, USA

ABSTRACT

Writers often are challenged to measure the effectiveness of their deliverables. Measurement is frequently difficult because the writer is expected to act as a reader advocate without direct customer or audience input. Fortunately, this trend is changing. Today, technical writers have a wealth of opportunities to seek input directly from the internal or external consumers of their deliverables. In today's globally competitive marketplace, organizations constantly strive to deliver high-quality goods and services. Many companies are recognizing customers as a critical strategic partner in their product development and quality improvement programs. This recognition of customers as development and quality partners extends to documentation resources such as training materials, web-based help, support knowledge bases, user manuals, quick-reference guides and virtual tours and tutorials. More and more, the voice of the customer is becoming the most important consideration in product and process decisions, including the delivery of documentation. Collaborating with customers goes beyond fostering goodwill. Employing various methods to invite customer collaboration accelerates documentation development and significantly improves documentation quality. By considering strategic partner values, organizational culture, cost and complexity, and availability of resources, technical writers can develop customer feedback programs that increase customer retention and positively impact revenue. This chapter explores methods and processes that help to ensure successful virtual collaboration with customers.

DOI: 10.4018/978-1-60566-994-6.ch017

INTRODUCTION

The following scenarios each reflect a company's attempt to solicit feedback directly from the customer. Throughout this chapter, the terms "organization" or "company" are used interchangeably to indicate an information product provider. Similarly, references to "reader," "user" or "customer" indicate information consumers:

One by one, a short chime announced each person and a small icon appeared online, next to each attendee's name. After a brief round of introductions, Beth, the meeting facilitator, welcomed all the customers. For the next 45 minutes, Beth walked customers through several exercises that allowed them to highlight their current product likes and dislikes as well as future features for which they were willing to make an additional investment. By the following week, Beth translated her meeting notes into a prized list of findings, including organized lists of product, documentation, and training recommendations as well as a prioritized future feature list.

Kris was desperately trying to run a report that his manager needed by noon. While attempting to generate the report, Kris saw an error message he had never seen before. Desperate to find a solution, Kris searched the online help and found a topic that contained wording similar to, but not exactly like, the error message he had encountered. He followed the procedure and, thankfully, it worked! He wondered whether other users had ever had a similar situation and, if so, had they tried the advice in the help topic or had they assumed that it did not apply because of the slightly different wording of the error message? Just as he was about to close the online help topic, he saw a suggestion link. He sent a quick e-mail, explaining that the documented topic applied to multiple situations.

Julian absolutely loved the MindFrazzle gaming series. After joining their online gaming club, Julian was delighted to receive an invitation to try the unreleased Beta version of their latest game for free. An e-mail invitation stated that he would have 45 days of unlimited access to the game in exchange for completing a brief survey after the trial period.

Computer giant, Dell, uses councils and regional forums to stay in touch with customer needs. Dell's largest customers in their U.S., European and Asian-Pacific markets share their views about Dell's latest developments and product direction. Dell found that information gleaned from customers during these meetings greatly assist the company in forecasting product demand. (Thompson, Strickland & Gamble, C-124-C-125)

These scenarios indicate that technical writers often are challenged to measure the effectiveness of their deliverables. Measurement can be difficult because the technical writer may be expected to act as a reader advocate without direct customer or audience input. This lack of input can result in pseudo-collaboration with customers to improve the quality of writing. Fortunately, this trend is changing. Today, technical writers have a wealth of opportunities to seek input directly from their internal or external customers. In many cases, documents serve a dual purpose of being designed for external customers, but referenced by internal customers. For example, if a customer experiences an issue and contacts a support center, the support personnel may refer to a training or user guide to assist that customer. Another common example occurs when customers use a knowledge base that contains online diagnostic or troubleshooting information as an initial research step prior to contacting customer support. When customer feedback is sought and welcomed, customers do not have to resort to personal weblogs (blogs) or other potentially inefficient methods for complaining about a product or discussing its merits, as they do in the scenarios presented in Chapter 16.

By providing access to the same resources both internally and externally, support personnel can help customers learn about the resources available to address issues. This increased learning effort—understanding where to find what information—helps the customer to be more confident and self-sufficient about product use. This effort represents one way to measure and track writers' performance, which is the sixth principle that grounds this book (see Chapter 1). To that end, this chapter particularly explores the methods and processes of customer feedback programs that can help to ensure successful virtual collaboration with customers.

BACKGROUND

Customer feedback programs are an important facet of product improvement, including documentation deliverables. Such programs may be classified as a form of intelligence analysis, which is the process of taking known information about situations and entities of strategic, operational, or tactical importance; characterizing the known; and, with appropriate statements of probability, assessing the future actions in those situations and by those entities. Computer-Mediated Communication (CMC) tools, such as Web-based conferencing, expand customer feedback and collaboration opportunities. Web cameras and headsets are common collaboration tools. Software applications such as Cisco Web-Ex ® and Microsoft Live Meeting ® allow companies to share presentations, demonstrate products, and even take polls among online attendees. Even teleconferencing has gone online with applications like Skype® that allow people to make voice calls over the Internet. Organizations using CMC must have some understanding about the level of technology and related security that their customers use.

Some customers are considered Pioneers—early technology adopters who often are among the first to attempt to upgrade to new platforms, applications, or methods. Early adopters are individuals who implement new technology before a group does. They usually provide feedback regarding their experience, which, in turn, helps developers improve a product, technology, or service before it is made available to a general population of users, both internal and external. External early adopters are also called lighthouse customers. Early adopters are the customers that companies most often may target for feedback because the company culture more readily supports trying new products. Furthermore, such companies usually have tools and security protocols necessary for ongoing collaboration.

Successful implementation of customer feedback programs requires several considerations to maintain effective customer relationships. Within the company, goals and strategies for seeking customer input must be established. Appropriate roles and processes must be defined not only to gather feedback, but to incorporate it into various aspects of the product development cycle, including documentation. Once strategy is established, customer relationships must continue to be cultivated to promote customers as strategic partners who are essential to the company's success. This chapter explores various considerations and methods to incorporate customer feedback programs to improve documentation offerings.

ESTABLISHING VIRTUAL RELATIONSHIPS: THE IMPORTANCE OF COLLABORATION

Technical writers understand that virtual relationships are just as important as the readers' relationships in traditional face-to-face settings. Contacts, teams, and norms are the key components of virtual relationships. Relationships, or interpersonal ties as they are called in sociology, may be described as connections that carry information among people. Virtual relationships may be strong, weak, or absent in terms of these interpersonal connections. Teams in the sense of virtual collaborative writing are based on shared interests or experiences rather than personal affection given that these are transactional relationships. The team norms itself by making general team-based decisions about what is good or bad in their business and interpersonal interactions. Collaboration is an approach for working together towards a known goal, and it can occur successfully, as this book attests, both in face-to-face and distributed settings (Wodtke & Govella, 2009, pp. 237-240; see also Chapter 1).

Collaboration with their customers allows writers to know empirically, rather than to guess, what their readers need. Indeed, customer retention is higher when customers are actively invited (but not harassed) to participate. In addition, retention is higher when customers observe their feedback translated to action—changes in the documentation, product, or process that makes their lives easier. For example, BizRate.com found that 59% of their users considered customer reviews to be more valuable than expert reviews. (Einsenberg, 2007) It was important for managers to be able to measure how well they solved customer problems and to gauge their ability to provide customer value (Robbins & Coulter, 2001, p. 556).Organizations that foster customer or reader communities appear to increase the level of trust and value with their customers. Naturally, providing value to customers is important to organizations because if customers are not receiving something of value from their interactions with organizations, they will look elsewhere. Managers should monitor how well they are providing customer value, and they can do so when they measure performance.

Creating a Customer Feedback Program Strategy

The potential for virtual collaboration relies heavily upon the organizational culture of the reader and writer. In both cases, management must support and allocate resources toward activities like customer feedback programs. From the customer's organizational perspective, managers should view customer feedback program activities as valuable because the organization as a whole can benefit from them. Such programs can be conducted in a variety of ways. On a small scale, for example, customers may be invited to participate in brief online surveys or other types of evaluations, such as discussion groups. On a large scale, companies may invite customers to attend conferences where customer feedback events such as focus groups or usability labs are part of the agenda. Before initiating any sort of customer feedback program, however, the management must define the goals and expectations clearly for the effort, as well as the types and volumes of resources they are willing to invest. Traditionally, customer feedback programs have been managed as a marketing activity because marketing groups often facilitate data and requirements gathering. However, additional groups, including product management, training, and documentation groups also have contributed their diverse skill sets to understand the needs of the customer better. Keeping in mind the customer's preferences and priorities is a key factor in ensuring customer satisfaction and retention, future product development, and documentation improvement.

Considering Culture

Before initiating a customer feedback program, it is important to consider company culture and whether such programming would be supported. One of the six principles that ground this book, understanding an organization with respect to its culture is fundamental to developing virtual collaborative writing (see Principle 1, Chapter 1). Corporate cultures that are more adaptive tend to be more successful in both implementing customer feedback programs as well as in integrating what they learn from such programs into the product development cycle to promote continuous improvement. Adaptive organizations identify and respond to challenges within an environment of rapid change and increased customer demands. In addition, corporate cultures that promote an alliance approach—where the customer is viewed as a strategic partner—tends to be a more fertile environment in which a customer feedback program can effectively grow. Such a culture is one where collaboration between the organization and its customers develop.

Additionally, companies that incorporate strategic alliances—not just with customers, but with other companies that offer complementary products or services—tend to become stronger. According to Gordon (2002), strategic alliances "strengthen companies by bringing additional resources to solving problems and competing in the marketplace. Strategic alliances can create opportunities for learning from a partner" (p. 412) Successful alliances rely heavily on several aspects of collaboration including ongoing and honest communication, stakeholder commitment, and a desire to work toward shared goals and benefits. When implemented successfully, a strong trust develops between the company and the customer. When a company is more heavily invested in the customer through collaborative efforts, the partnership is far less likely to dissolve.

Considering Resources

Understanding an organization's internal strengths, weaknesses, opportunities, and threats (SWOT) is essential to developing an effective customer feedback program. An organization's resources, abilities and opportunities are factors that contribute to a comprehensive SWOT analysis (Robbins &Coulter, 2002, p. 204). Elements to consider include the organization's size, length of time in business, any strategic alliances or acquisitions, geographical dispersion of employees, product distribution range (e.g., local, regional, national, or global), attrition rates, the length of time that the company and customer have had a business relationship, and leadership or policy changes that may affect the relationship. Any of these elements may be viewed positively or negatively, depending on the history and culture of the company.

Companies and their customers need to determine the amount of resources—including time, travel, and equipment—they willing to invest to support a program. For example, at a company's request, a customer may identify two employees to serve as respondents or liaisons for a customer feedback program. Depending on their employer's guidelines and the company's customer feedback program, those employees may participate in activities ranging from a post-implementation survey to a focus group meeting or a remote usability study. While some activities can be conducted face-to-face, there are a variety of events that can be managed via a virtual interface. Teleconferences, Web-based seminars, online surveys, telephone interviews and designated e-mail addresses for customer comments are some of the virtual methods that companies may employ to better understand the voice of the customer. The adaptation of virtual collaboration methods eliminates restrictions that traditionally may occur across geographically restrictive elements, such as various time zones.

Companies must identify appropriate resources to facilitate the customer feedback program. An inventory of available resources—such as existing teleconferencing or Web-conferencing accounts, online surveys, e-marketing or usability software, as well as personnel to serve as facilitators and managers of the program—should be considered. Depending on the complexity of the program, other roles such as note taker/recorder, coordinators (for events and administration) and analysts (to compile results) also should be considered. The actual collaboration method depends on several factors including program goals, available resources, current phase of production, and the desired timeframe for gathering data.

Customer feedback program leaders must be realistic about constraints—especially in terms of time, support, and human resources. In many instances, customer feedback program responsibilities are conducted in addition to an employee's primary job, which makes it important to have a realistic understanding about how much time employees will be permitted to spend on such activities. When approaching managers to request an employee's time to work on a customer feedback program, leaders should present a plan that outlines clear expectations about the number of resources needed as well as the duration that they will be needed. The more time that a customer feedback program leader requests, the more specific he or she will need to be to help managers justify time away from an employee's primary duties.

Establishing Goals

Companies must establish realistic goals for their customer feedback programs. A variety of data can be used to drive and support such goals. For example, companies may review their call center or support data to identify issues where customers need the most assistance. Companies may also ask those who have direct interaction with customers, such as trainers, about areas where customers appear to have difficulty. Goals need to be as specific as possible. Such specificity includes setting an explicit intent for a program; for example, goals could be "identify tasks that are most frustrating to customers" or "identify areas within the product interface that are confusing to customers" or "evaluate effectiveness of the search engine." Goals should be defined within the context of overall product development goals to ensure that feedback can be readily incorporated into the product improvement cycle.

In establishing goals, it is important to remember that a successful customer feedback program must be supported at every level within the company. It is not beneficial for operational-level employees to create and execute a program of which executive management is unaware or unsupportive. Conversely, executive level employees cannot fully administer a program without the support of operational-level employees. For example, when consumers contact a customer support center, they often are invited to participate in a survey at the conclusion of the call. Although the survey program may have originated as an executive-level directive, the operational-level call center staff may be responsible for its proper execution. If the call center staff does not follow through as expected, then the program itself is useless. Indeed, the implementation of a customer feedback program requires sufficient appropriation of resources and support at various levels within the organization. The collaboration begins with intradepartmental planning and then extends to the customer. Internal support, training, and product management staff may identify focus areas for the post-call survey; writers within a training or documentation team may design the survey questions; and marketing personnel may be involved wording the invitation and analyzing the results of the survey. A collaborative internal effort is critical to successful customer feedback program implementation.

Identifying Metrics

Customer feedback program leaders must identify which metrics are needed to accomplish goals best, as well as a limited target. It is best to pilot the virtual collaboration initiative on a relatively smaller scale rather than trying to implement a large-scale, wide-range collaboration initiative without feedback from a more limited initial approach. Companies must consider what customer experience data already is automated and readily available, such reports that reflect Web or call center activity. In addition, companies also must identify what information is needed based on direct customer feedback. Typically, a combination of automated and direct feedback methods is necessary to establish a comprehensive view of the customer's experience. The same automated and direct concepts also apply to documentation feedback. Web reports reflecting hit and search engine data automatically gather information. Other methods such as documentation feedback links, Web-based training evaluations and surveys permit writers to ask more specific questions that gauge documentation effectiveness.

For direct feedback, it is useful to determine an approach that is realistic and manageable given the available virtual collaboration resources. Steps include:

- Identify which segment of the customer population is needed to respond to the program goal and focus.
- Identify a target sample size of participants once the customer segment is determined.
- Identify the extent of the program.
- Be mindful about the number of requests any given customer would receive within a year although it is most beneficial to establish an ongoing relationship with customers.
- Carefully coordinate the process internally to ensure that the company is not constantly bombarding customers with feedback or collaboration requests. Understanding the customer is essential in understanding their tolerance to respond to such invitations.
- Plan the virtual collaboration approach as a series of shorter sessions or a single extended session depending on the documentation focus.

Exploring Collaboration Methods

Next, it is important to consider which collaboration method would generate maximum feedback given the available resources and anticipated level of effort. In developing an approach, leaders need to consider cost and complexity in terms of which methods maximize participation from the audience and meet resource needs. It is critical to understand the costs associated with virtual collaboration, both for the requestor and the participant. Some CMC tools, such as a licensing for a Web-based, desktop-sharing application, are priced at an enterprise-level and flat rate. Other CMC methods involve a cost per usage or user. In addition, the virtual collaboration initiative development cycle usually requires additional internal support and resources at inception. Network, telephony, and information security support services are vital to ensure a successful program.

Assigning Collaboration Roles

Once leaders determine an approach, they need to develop and refine the collaboration method. A useful first step is to identify and assign the roles that are needed; in other words, they should consider who will construct questions, facilitate discussions, and compile or analyze the results. Common roles include:

Sponsor

A sponsor is an executive-level supporter who provides primary directive for the customer feedback program. The sponsor provides upper-level support and reports program results to other executives. The sponsor also serves as a coach and primary contact for the program manager – assisting him or her with securing internal resources to execute the program.

Program Manager

The program manager is the designated leader of the customer feedback program. As such, this person coordinates by translating the sponsor directive into specific goals. In addition, the program manager acts as a project manager, identifying timeframes, milestones, and needed resources for the program's execution. The program manager also often serves as the key point of contact for customers.

Coordinator

The coordinator synchronizes the logistics and ensures that all components are in place for the event to run smoothly. If additional internal resources or setup is needed at any point in the process, the coordinator ensures that all required components are in place. The coordinator also may be responsible for advising customers of any prerequisite steps, such as the installation or testing of Web conferencing software, that are needed for customer feedback program participation.

Facilitator

The facilitator serves as the primary feedback recipient and point of contact for a customer feedback program. If the program involves real-time, synchronous discussion, the facilitator asks initial and follow-up questions, conducts exercises, presents various scenarios, and strives to keep all customer participants engaged in the discussion. If the program is asynchronous, the facilitator usually is the first person to receive or retrieve customer feedback. He or she is responsible for keeping careful records regarding who has responded and how their comments align with program goals. The facilitator must coordinate closely with the analyst to ensure that the collected data is evaluated and applied in the most efficient manner.

Recorder

The recorder may be a machine or a person. Either via automated or manual means, information must be captured from the customer. In some cases, the method is automatic, such as with online surveys. In other instances, like user group meetings, a per-

son may be designated to take notes or to compile session results. As much as possible, the capture of data should be automated to maintain data integrity and to facilitate analysis. Increased manual effort often results in increased manual error.

Analyst

An analyst reviews recorded data and translates it to metrics that are useful to the company. The analyst may compare captured results against other collected customer information and historical data. The analyst interprets results of a customer feedback program and identifies primary areas for improvement.

Analytical Considerations

In some cases, leaders may need to assign multiple roles to a single person. Collecting feedback is worthless without analysis. The more the leaders or facilitators understand the reader and identify patterns in feedback results, the better they can identify strategies to enhance and improve future iterations of documentation. Analysts should look for commonalities among customer comments and consider what customers like or dislike most about the company's current deliverables. It is important to retain the elements that the customer appreciates about the product while making improvements in other areas that are current sources of confusion or frustration.

Customer feedback programs allow companies to gain perspective about customer's needs, priorities, and expectations. Analysts should compare customer expectations against the current documentation offering to identify the differential that exists. Exploring the differential between the current state and expected state is known as gap analysis. The degree of emphasis about certain improvements also helps the company to prioritize. Items that companies consider important may not necessarily be at the top of particular customer's lists of needs. In such instances, the company should be flexible enough to adapt at least some of their goals to be in stronger alignment with customer demands, and the company should convey the results of that flexibility to customers. Finally, the customer feedback program team must identify ways to apply the virtual collaboration results for the benefit of the customer.

COLLABORATION METHODS

There are a variety of ways to collaborate with customers. Generally, collaboration is a matter of finding the most effective method for one's environment and audience. As with any other type of product or deliverable, customer impressions and ideas about the effectiveness of documentation deliverables or information products have far-reaching implications. In identifying a collaboration method, it is good to consider the audience as well as needs for setup, execution, and analysis or compilation. The following methods will help writers in various settings. Making a decision among them will require considering both Principles 4 regarding choosing and using tools effectively and 5 regarding creating a virtual structure for a collaborating team, which in this case includes the customer (see Chapter 1).

Asynchronous Methods

In some instances, it is feasible to invite feedback whenever the audience is available to provide it. The advantage of asynchronous methods is that they usually are low cost, relatively easy to implement, and typically allow content consumers to provide feedback during times of high usage or exposure. In addition, many asynchronous methods may be built directly into or closely associated with the product interface. For example, a survey that appears as a user is leaving a Web page can invites the user to share impressions of an experience that occurred only moments ago. Another

example is a brief question like "Did this answer your question?" that has a simple radio button rating option that is listed at the bottom of many help or knowledge base topics. Other commonly used asynchronous virtual collaboration practices complete this section.

Rating Question Directly Within the Interface

This practice is good for a single, general question. Readers often select a rating from an established option listing. From a setup standpoint, the cost is low because it is integrated into an existing interface. However, the complexity is medium because it often relies upon expertise of people outside of a documentation function to get the question added. A single rating question is a more automated solution and allows focus on a single metric. Such programs usually are accompanied by automated feature to compile the results.

The downside of a rating question is infrequent responses. For every reader who answers the question, there may be hundreds who choose not to respond. Such limited responses may make it difficult to consider how heavily such feedback should measure into improvement efforts. There also may be a built-in type of user bias in that those who do not respond are not invested customers or have had satisfactory interactions with the product. Without the specific feedback, it is difficult to predict the relative weight of what has not been offered or said. These rating question programs usually have to become a permanent product fixture to capture any sort of extensive trend or other analysis. Unfortunately, the necessary longevity of this program reduces its flexibility. The company cannot significantly change the question without possibly confusing the reader. Also, the rating question needs to identify a way to capture the product and document version associated with the comment or risk misinterpretation.

Online Surveys (Multiple Questions)

Online surveys often allow the company to leverage software it already owns. They are flexible and relatively easy to generate. Online surveys may be Web-based, using a tool such as SurveyMonkey or PollDaddy, or it may involve electronic documents that users can complete and send online or print, complete, and e-mail or mail through the post office. Since there is no facilitator to answer questions, surveys must be worded carefully to ensure clarity. The most successful surveys are brief with a very narrow focus. Occasionally, companies add incentives such as prize drawings or product discounts in exchange for online survey participation.

However, online surveys usually exist outside of the product, forcing users to provide impressions after their interaction with the content instead of in real time. Also, careful consideration must be given about the importance of demographics for each survey. How important is it to understand the reader's knowledge and experience of the company and product? Is it important to understand their role within the company? Is permission and contact information needed to follow up with a user? Is the intention to conclude the customer feedback program with the survey or is the plan to invite the user to participate in other, more extended programs? Depending on the mechanism, survey-takers may be anonymous, and such anonymity may enable them to express their likes and dislikes more freely. There are technology-based and other ways to obtain customer demographic data, but capturing such data should be incorporated into the overall feedback strategy to be successful.

Feedback Links Directly Within Online Documentation

Feedback links are flexible and make it easy for the reader to respond. However, it is important to be clear about the purpose and destination of the feedback as well as expectations about responses. The organization or company must allocate a resource to ensure that the feedback is given the appropriate amount of attention in a reasonable timeframe. A rating question is one type of feedback link. Others may be free-form text fields where the user can submit a comment or request.

Drawbacks of feedback links resemble those of online surveys. Depending on the mechanism, it may be difficult to determine the area within the product from which the feedback was sent. Such information can be incorporated into the feedback form, but advanced development efforts may be needed.

Providing an E-Mail Address for Users to Forward Comments

Providing an e-mail address or link is a flexible and inexpensive strategy because it leverages existing resources. As with the feedback link, one must be clear about the purpose, destination, and response expectations. Best practices dictate establishing a functional, rather than personal, mailbox for such correspondence. Leaders must make a process determination about how the e-mail and associated mailbox will function. Will e-mails be sent to a separate, designated mailbox that multiple customer feedback program members could access if needed? Should the e-mail simply be an alias for a designated owner's company e-mail address? Could an automated response be established to acknowledge receipt of the e-mail? What is the process for managing e-mails that are unrelated to the focus of the customer feedback program? Establishing the associated response and data collection process is critical to successful implementation of an e-mail collaboration method.

Synchronous (Real-Time) Methods

Remotely-Run Usability Studies

Remotely-run usability studies are flexible, allowing the organization to conduct and observe a usability study without being physically close to customers. Initial setups and permissions are required to install the appropriate usability software in the customer's environment. However, customers complete the study in their regular working environment, rather than a formal lab. Remote usability studies provide extensive data capture capability but often are less intimidating for users than formal labs. Usability studies also require a lot of planning and setup to run smoothly. Additionally, remotely-run usability studies often are more expensive than other methods, but they also can be highly effective. Such studies allow one to capture multiple streams of data including audio, video, and click-streams as a user completes a designated exercise. Usability software also excellent analysis features.

One limitation to usability studies is that they require a lot of resources with planning, setup, and analysis. Remotely-run usability studies may be more time-consuming for the requestor and the user than some other strategies.

Virtual User Forums/Groups

Virtual user forums and groups also may leverage existing resources for Web or teleconferencing. However, since it is a virtual situation, a strong facilitator is necessary to ensure collective, representative participation. A target audience with certain levels of product exposure and experiences also need to be established. It is helpful to seek recommendations about good candidates to participate in this forum from others in the organization. Virtual user groups may occur as Web-based meetings, chat rooms, or teleconference calls. With careful collaboration, virtual user forums also may be held in conjunction with face-to-face forums to maximize participation. For example, a company may add virtual meeting components to a physical customer conference. Such a forum would allow customers, who otherwise might not participate, an opportunity to provide feedback. Adding an interactive, remote component

promotes more participation. However, there are potential compromises to the team dynamic when everyone is not in the same room. Careful attention must be paid to technical aspects—audio and video—to ensure that virtual attendees have equal opportunities for participation. Facilitators must be careful not to ignore the concerns or feedback of virtual participants. A balance must be established that promotes participation without making onsite or virtual participants feel that they are at a disadvantage.

Feedback Number or Teleconference

This type is a good forum for open comments regarding effectiveness or appeal. Depending on the existing telephony system, a feedback number or teleconference usually is cheap and easy to implement. However, this option is highly manual because the organization or company needs to allocate resources to manage this process and capture feedback. Nonetheless, this option permits a lot of flexibility with frequency and nature of questions. This method actually may be asynchronous or synchronous, depending on whether there is a designated phone line where the user leaves comments in a voice mailbox or real-time designated resources to answer the phone and speak with customers. Planners must carefully consider resource limitations and effectively manage expectations when feedback numbers or teleconference tools are implemented. In the instance of voicemail, if customers should not expect a return phone call, that needs to be explicitly stated in the greeting or invitation literature. Similarly, customers should have solid communication regarding during frequency of teleconferences prior to an initial meeting. Expectations must be carefully managed to ensure that customers meet often enough to encourage and understand the impact of their participation without such meetings becoming a time-consuming burden.

USING COMBINATIONS OF METHODS

To maximize effectiveness, the company may employ a combination of virtual collaboration methods. For example, leaders may initiate an online survey, then arrange a teleconference to present results and request further comments. It is important to be considerate of the customer's time. It is challenging but vital to find a balance where the organization can offer opportunities for collaboration and maintain strong relationships without overwhelming the customer or making unrealistic demands on his or her time. Understanding the customer is the key to selecting an appropriate collaboration method or combination of methods.

Inviting the Customer to Participate

Another critical component of a successful customer feedback program is the initial invitation to participate. Customers are just like everyone else—busy, multitasking, and trying to complete various important tasks as efficiently as possible. Therefore, it is critical to foster a welcoming invitation in a succinct and professional way. It is important to know the customer well enough to understand the limits of his or her patience. How much time and energy is the customer willing to invest to provide feedback regarding the product, including the documentation? Whether it is an afternoon of formal usability lab, a one-hour teleconference call or a series of virtual forums, facilitators must extend an invitation that helps the customer to make a decision about whether to participate. Effective invitations should always convey the following:

Purpose

The purpose is the nature and intent of the specific feedback program in which the organization would like the customer to participate. This statement of purpose should align closely with the established customer feedback program goal.

Resource Expectation

The resource expectation is an expectation regarding the amount of resource (i.e., time, equipment, and number of participants) necessary for participation. The customer/user should understand whether participation is a one-time event or part of an ongoing effort.

Process Explanation

The process explanation is a brief explanation outlining the feedback process, including any incentives for participation. The collaboration method should be introduced and provide the user with enough information to understand what will happen once feedback is submitted.

Follow-up Expectation

The follow-up expectation is a direct statement or statements regarding the level of anonymity associated with the feedback. If customers are asked to provide information, specific statements must be made regarding whether customer contact information will be shared with others within the company or whether participation assumes agreement to possibly be contacted regarding their responses. These are both courtesy and legal matters.

Application

Application is an overview of when and how customer feedback would be used. The application component helps the customer to understand whether the feedback is being used to improve an existing product or initiate requirements for future offerings.

Contact Information

Contact information connects the customer/user with a specific company contact to address technical issues with the feedback mechanism or to address related questions.

Sample Invitation for Customers to Participate in a Remote Usability Test

To: A CUSTOMER
From: Jonathan Rogers, HR/Payroll Product Manager (use@HRurray.com) [CONTACT INFORMATION]
Subject: Coming Soon - Evaluate Online Support Tool
You're invited to participate in the evaluation of online support documentation from HRurray! [PURPOSE]
As a valued HRurray client, beginning March 10, 2008, you are invited to access the HRurray Knowledge Base (KB), our comprehensive online repository for all product support information. This is the same tool that Client Service Analysts (CSAs) use to research your support questions. HRurray is testing the feasibility of making this resource permanently available to customers. [APPLICATION]
Imagine having procedures that link to forms, help pages, government agency Websites and other helpful resources, right at your fingertips! When contacting HRurray Customer Care, you'll be able to view and discuss the same articles as your CSA.
During the 2 week trial period, you may access the support site as many times as you would like. [RESOURCE EXPECTATION] Each time you visit this site, your session will be recorded so that the HRurray team can evaluate your user experience. [PROCESS EXPLANATION] If you are interested in being among the first to use this tool by participating in our pilot study please reply to this e-mail by February 13, 2009 so that we

can send you software installation instructions. [FOLLOW UP EXPECTATION]

Applying Customer Feedback

In collaborating with customers, it is helpful to start with a pilot or trial effort that leverages existing resources, such as Web-based meeting tools or existing teleconference services. Next, maximizing automated features for data collection or compilation allows the organization to complete the study efficiently and to apply the results to improving the product. In promoting the benefit of the virtual collaboration initiative, it helps to justify increased attention and resources for more advanced methods. Figure 1 reflects this ongoing quality cycle.

In reaching these conclusions, it is important to share and promote the findings, emphasizing the benefits of the customer feedback program to both the organization and the customer. Those findings also provide a baseline for future comparisons. In evaluating these findings, it is helpful to remember the need to evaluate the effectiveness of the collaboration itself. The good thing is that those who are involved in the customer feedback program can control the scope and change the scale of the program as necessary.

Barriers to Customer Collaboration

Several factors may adversely affect the customer's ability or willingness to participate in a customer feedback program. Time is a primary consideration. If a feedback program takes too much time away from the customer's primary activities, he or she is far less willing to participate. Technical difficulty is another potential barrier. If the virtual collaboration tools cost the customer money, are time-consuming or difficult to implement, or otherwise require extensive set-up, then the customer will not see the benefit as worth the effort. Personnel resources are another barrier to collaboration. If the customer does not have a clear

Figure 1. Customer feedback cycle

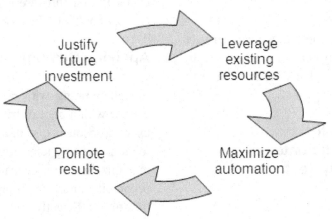

understanding about the type of person needed to participate, then the effort will not be fruitful. For example, if support documentation is being evaluated, then the customer needs to identify the representative within their organization who has the most experience with that function. Customers must have a clear understanding about the goal and intent of the virtual collaboration effort. Feedback about user interface changes places the customer in a difference mindset than providing feedback about a quick reference checklist. Setting clear expectations enables customers to make a solid commitment about collaboration. Finally, customers need to be reassured that their feedback is actually making a difference in terms of improving the documentation. Customers will not continue to support a feedback program if they are unable to have tangible proof that their feedback directly affects the product or service they evaluate.

Benefits of Customer Collaboration

There are several extensive benefits to customer collaboration. Perhaps the most important benefit is establishing and reinforcing customer goodwill. Virtual collaboration makes customers feel that they are not simply a purchaser of goods or services and the company is not simply a vendor, but the two are partners, forming an alliance to deliver

the best possible product or service. Once that partnership relationship is established, customers are much less likely to sever ties. Companies benefit from collaboration because it provides a clear and direct link to the voice of the customer. Although customer feedback programs have a specific focus, collaboration activities often provide insight beyond the initial scope of the program. Companies learn a more about situations and ways in which customers use their product or service, including related documentation. Understanding the customer's perspective and usage—to what extent and under what conditions the customer uses the product—helps the company to develop systems that align closely and better satisfy the needs of the customer. From a marketing perspective, collaboration programs provide even more detailed customer profile and demographic information. Collaboration programs help companies to understand customer's priorities.

Cultivating Customer Relationships

Customer feedback programs can be considered as part of a business process improvement act for the customer and thereby an act that increases customer satisfaction. Efforts to improve quality begin by working with customers to identify their needs, preferences, and expectations. Teams of employees collect this information, asking questions then translating information into better products and services (Gordon, 2002, p. 478).

Keys to Successful Virtual Collaboration

As an initiator, facilitator, or other contributor to a virtual collaboration program, the following factors should be considered:

- *Acknowledgement:* Let the customer know his or her feedback is valuable as well as the plan for applying the results of the feedback.
- *Awareness:* Have a strong knowledge and understanding of the strengths and capacity of team group to support a virtual collaboration initiative.
- *Alertness:* Stay on the lookout for other efforts that provide opportunities for interacting with the primary audience using existing programs or meetings.
- *Budget:* Know how much money is available for implementing an appropriate plan.
- *Time:* Have a realistic expectation of how much time can be spent with the customer feedback program—both from the design and execution as well as the analysis phases.
- *Promotion:* Be sure that others in the organization are aware of these efforts and, most importantly, the results.
- *Accountability:* Follow through in translating the feedback findings into action and documentation and, whenever possible, into product improvements.

Both promotion and accountability are ways of implementing Principle 6 of the principles that ground this book (see Chapter 1). Measuring and tracking an individual or team's efforts in such collaboration with customers are essential both to having a repeatable workplan and in receiving the credit necessary for continued financing of the plan and individual or team recognition and rewards.

FUTURE TRENDS

Opportunities for virtual collaboration will increase as technology advances. Just a few years ago, mail-in surveys or telephone interviews were the primary means of gathering customer feedback. Pervasive adoption of the Internet has reduced the cost and increased the convenience of virtual collaboration, thereby increasing the volume of customers who are able to participate in such programs. Currently, in addition to company-generated documentation, customers are forming communities (with or without the company and many of them Web-based) and generating their own documentation to discuss common issues, provide reviews of newer products, and discuss their overall experiences. Many companies, including Microsoft ® have established user communities, such as developer networks, on external Web sites. In the future, customer-generated documentation may become the newest form of source content. Customer or user discussions can be closely monitored and reviewed, then promoted as trusted material and incorporated into the company's official documentation.

CONCLUSION

Organizations are constantly building and disseminating knowledge. Collaboration represents ongoing relationship development and should be considered part of any successful continuous improvement program. Most organizations already employ various collaboration methods, either synchronously or asynchronously. It is critical for the collaboration initiator to consider technologies and resources that are already available that may be applied to the external customer audience. Virtual collaboration implies a level of trust; indeed, inviting customers to a common place such as a teleconference line or web-based meeting site reassures the customer that he or she is part of a team where their questions and comments are welcomed.

REFERENCES

Aberdeen Group. (December 2007). *The role of real time virtual collaboration in product development*. (2007). Retrieved August 16, 2009 from http://www.tandberg.com/collateral/The_Role_of_Real_Time_Virtual_Collaboration_in_Product_Development.pdf

Crow, K. (n.d.). *Voice of the customer.* Retrieved from http://www.npd-solutions.com/voc.html

Eisenberg, B. (2007). *How to use customer reviews to increase conversion.* Retrieved from http://www.clickz.com/3627269#

Gordon, J. R. (2002). *Structuring high-performance organizations. Organizational behavior: A diagnostic approach* (7th ed.). Upper Saddle River, NJ: Prentice-Hall.

Robbins, S. R., & Coulter, M. K. (2001). *Management* (7th ed.). Upper Saddle River, NJ: Prentice-Hall.

Thompson, A. A., Jr., Strickland, A. J., III, & Gamble, J. E. (2005). Case 8: "Dell computer in 2003: Driving for industry leadership" (C-124-C125). In Crafting and executing strategy, The quest for competitive advantage: Concepts and cases (14th ed.). Boston: McGraw-Hill Irwin

Wodtke, C., & Govella, A. (2009). *Information architecture: Blueprints for the Web* (2nd ed.). Berkeley, CA: New Riders.

Chapter 18
Preparing Writers for Virtual Environments

Pavel Zemliansky
James Madison University, USA

ABSTRACT

This chapter offers practical strategies for instructors, trainers, and managers to use while preparing writers for virtual collaboration. It first considers various existing barriers to successful virtual collaboration, both in the writers' individual preparation and in organizational structures within which they work. Next, the chapter offers a set of specific guidelines designed to prepare writers for virtual writing collaboration and to facilitate their work. In order to prepare writers for virtual collaboration, instructors and trainers must develop trust among members of virtual teams, carefully structure writing assignments, and design learning spaces that promote collaboration and interaction.

INTRODUCTION

The purpose of this chapter is to outline practical strategies that instructors, trainers, and managers could use to prepare writers for virtual collaboration. First, it considers various barriers to successful virtual collaboration. Then, it offers a set of specific guidelines designed to prepare writers for virtual writing collaboration and to facilitate their work.

A word about the scope of this chapter is in order. Most chapters in this volume offer methodology and advice from an industry perspective of virtual collaborative writing. No doubt, any instructor or trainer of writers will find such perspective useful and interesting. Clearly, understanding ways in which professional writers see and use writing on the job is important for any meaningful training of writers to occur. However, the opposite is true as well. Employers and on-the-job trainers of writers need to be aware of current teaching theories and practices in places where their future employees are being taught to write and to collaborate. Such places are writing and technical communication programs and departments in universities and colleges.

Much of the advice that this chapter provides is grounded in rhetorical and composition theory and

DOI: 10.4018/978-1-60566-994-6.ch018

practice (see Chapter 2). Some of the content of this chapter stems from my training and experience as an instructor in a university technical communication program. Therefore, the primary audience for this chapter is instructors of writing and technical communication who work at the college level, both in undergraduate and graduate programs. Such instructors are charged with instilling attitudes towards writing collaboration in their students, which then will transfer into the workplace. Managers and workplace trainers of writers comprise a secondary audience for this chapter. While they certainly will find foundational value in this chapter's approach and guidance, they may have to adjust and supplement it depending on the realities of their particular organization and their training situation.

BARRIERS TO EFFECTIVE COLLABORATION

Readers need to be aware of barriers to effective collaboration before beginning the design and implementation of their virtual collaboration training programs. For a more extensive discussion of barriers to virtual collaboration, see Chapter 7.

Preparing writers for virtual writing collaboration begins with preparing them for writing collaboration in general. While there are strategies and techniques specific to virtual collaboration, the foundational competencies required of collaborating writers, whether face to face or virtually, overlap significantly. Removing ideological, organizational, and disciplinary barriers to collaboration is essential for training effective writing collaborators.

These barriers fall into three general categories:

- Writers' resistance to ceding control of the text they perceive as "their own" to others;
- Organizational failure to recognize collaboratively produced works as valid and to reward collaborating writers; and

- Dominance in the workplace of software tools that make collaboration difficult, as well as writers' unfamiliarity with the collaboration and productivity tools and methods available to them.

Writers' Resistance to Ceding Control

Text ownership is a fundamental issue which may prevent writers from collaborating effectively. Writers who are accustomed to working alone or even in groups in which members split writing tasks into manageable and defined portions for which individuals take responsibility (we call these *serial* and *parallel* collaboration; see Chapters 1 and 6) likely will find it difficult to accept the notion of a mutually owned text. The idea of individual ownership can be difficult to release—at least in the beginning of writers' collaboration experiences and until they are taught to see the process of collaboration differently. Many writers, especially beginning writers, may find it easier to cooperate (take responsibility serially or in parallel for parts of writing project which are then combined into a larger text) than to truly collectively collaborate, or write a text together in a recursive manner as described in Chapters 1 and 6. The reasons for writers' unwillingness to cede control of a text and of the writing process are complex. They involve commonly held perceptions of writers and writing, the current reward and intellectual property system, and cultural and organizational norms, including assumptions of how writers work on the part of software companies that design electronic tools for writing.

The Notion of the Solitary Writer

Perhaps the most fundamental reason that resistance to successful collaborative writing should be examined and reconsidered is the notion that many writers hold that writing is a solitary and individualistic activity and the notion of the writer as a solitary and insulated figure. Traditionally in Western culture, the single writer has been responsible for the production of the text, and it is that single writer who is judged and rewarded for the quality of the text that he or she produces. College students of writing and even professionals who write on the job have undergone many years of schooling that emphasizes the solitary nature of writing. Those school years have valued individual writing products and rewarded or punished them with grades. As a result, this attitude is deeply seeded in most people's minds and in their work habits.

In addition, despite the seemingly firm entrenchment of the *process* approach in writing courses at many educational levels, many writing programs that train writers still fail to emphasize the writing process enough and to teach beginning writers not to be afraid of changing a text in progress. The process approach to writing encourages writers to see their writing skills and activities as part of a recursive and generative process of brainstorming, drafting, redrafting, editing, revising, and proofreading—with new idea development encouraged at every stage. Nonetheless, students of writing continue to fear revising a hard-won draft, sometimes holding onto sometimes incoherent early writing with a clenched fist that does not consider the need for change. The failure to emphasize the need for change in a written piece may be connected partially, at least at the college level in the United States, to the fact that outside of general education-type writing courses, one rarely sees a concerted effort by professors to teach revision as part of writing's process. Consequently, when students are given writing assignments, they often opt for the most efficient way of completing those assignments—individually—and with as little reconsideration and revision as possible.

The published literature about this issue seems to confirm this assertion. Writing in the journal *College Composition and Communication*, Hawisher and Selfe (1991) stated: "In many English composition classes, computer use simply reinforces those traditional notions of education that permeate our culture at its basic level: instructors talk, students listen; instructors' contributions are privileged; students respond in predictable, instructor-pleasing ways (p. 55). They further said that in many writing classes where computers are used, "students labor at isolated workstations on drill-and-practice grammar software or in word-processing facilities where computers are arranged, rank and file, so that instructors can examine each computer screen at a moment's notice to check on what students are writing" (p. 56). Hawisher and Selfe's argument, while dated, remains important for issues of collaboration because, according to them, the classroom culture does not encourage the kinds of lateral exchanges and interactions among students that are necessary for successful collaboration. In discussing the review process and what postsecondary students need to learn to both review and use feedback wisely, Chapter 16 asserts a similar perspective.

Certainly, significant changes have occurred in educators' understanding of how to configure collaborative computer-mediated spaces for leaning. In many places, instructors now use such collaborative writing tools as wikis and content managements systems (CMSs). In addition, advances both in pedagogy and in software have moved many instructors from the kind of "drill and kill" use of computers for instruction mentioned by Hawisher and Selfe (1991). Moxley (2008) argued that writing instruction, especially online writing instruction, has been influenced by what he calls "the Community of Power" for too long (p. 186). Central to my argument here is Moxley's idea that the members of the "Community of Power" who are interested in "claiming academic territory and copyright" tend to design learning spaces that promote a vertical or top-down teaching and learning experience. According to Moxley, such spaces aim to limit the power of the writer and to record everything that goes on in a class. Moxley specifically critiqued such popular e-learning platforms as Blackboard™ and WebCT® for these qualities (p. 187), calling those interfaces "surveillance tools." (p.188).

Although the ideologies behind learning space design are interesting in themselves, my purpose in discussing Moxley's article is to demonstrate that the kinds of interfaces and environments that writers who are learning to collaborate often face in the classroom (either brick-and-mortar or virtual) may, in fact, deter them from the kinds of behaviors and skills that are useful for collaboration. Designing learning spaces that actually encourage collaborative activities and behaviors remains at the forefront of many educators' agendas, both in composition studies, professional writing, and other disciplines. Stringer (2009) noted, for example, that during the design of a new Stanford Medical School building that contains multiple spaces for collaborative learners, instructors and designers who favored the inclusion of such spaces encountered significant opposition from some faculty members. According to Springer, one faculty member indicated that having too many classrooms where students are not sitting in rows listening to lectures would make the Stanford Medical School look a lot like a kindergarten classroom (2009).

My own experience as an instructor and administrator seems to confirm that some educators still express such views. At my institution, as recently as 2007, our department had considerable trouble convincing the people responsible for remodeling our building that the arrangement of computers in computer labs should privilege collaboration and lateral exchange over the Foucauldian "panopticon" set up that allows the instructor to observe the students' activities but makes working together difficult. In the end, we were unsuccessful in our efforts. It is therefore not uncommon to see computer labs that organize workstations by rows, those that are equipped with desktop monitors that prevent writers from seeing each other's work or faces, and those in settings where no common meeting table exists apart from the computers. Despite intranets and the Internet and despite collabora-

tive software and discussion-based assignments, ultimately, the typical student is a solitary writer. Fortunately, educators now understand better how computer-mediated teaching and learning can shape students' attitudes towards writing collaboration. With the advances in computer technologies and in accessibility of those technologies to most North American postsecondary students, we also understand better how to use those technologies to create learning spaces that promote collaboration. At the same time, we still have much work to do in learning to take full advantage of such technologies and spaces.

Current Concepts of Authorship Reward the Individual Writer

Related to this issue of the solitary writer are the Western legal and cultural frameworks of receiving credit for one's work, which are tied to the idea of writer as a "solitary writer." These frameworks see work produced by an individual as more valuable and more original than those developed in collaboration with others. Fanderclai (2004) confirmed this idea: "our research traditions and reward systems can be barriers to collaboration. Humanists tend to value individual projects and great minds; the greatest rewards are for individual works." (p. 314) According to Fanderclai, an example of such favoring of individual writing is the academic dissertation whose purpose is to "prove that [a student] is capable of producing a large-scale work alone" (p. 314).

Perhaps with the exception of natural sciences and some professional fields where research and writing collaboration have been the norm for a long time, educational institutions and professional organizations often discourage writers from fully collaborating with others. For example, in the humanities, collaborative writing projects only recently have begun to be recognized as equal in status to those written and published by individual writers. This change is significant because many writers who end up working in private, for-profit, and government organizations graduate from programs that may be classified broadly as "humanities," or "humanities-related" (that is, English, Professional Writing, and Communication) and they bring their cultural baggage and expectations to the organization. Often, colleagues see such people as experts on writing, which propagates the culture of individual authorship in an organization. To overcome this barrier and promote collaboration, instructors, workplace trainers, and managers need to dispel the notion of the "solitary writer" and introduce writers to the culture of collaboration through training and exposure to the appropriate tools and processes, which are Principles 1 and 4 of the principles grounding this book (see Chapter 1).

Popular Software Tools Can Make Collaboration Difficult

Until recently, there has been a powerful assumption that writers should compose in isolation on their desktops both in school and workplace settings. A change has occurred with the recent advent of cloud computing where services are available over the Internet through virtual servers. With that change has come the advent of collaborative online writing tools such as online word processors, wikis, and desktop sharing software. The kinds of tools described in Chapter 15 are an example of cloud computing. According to this new approach, some sharing among different members of a writing team may occur, but that usually happens after a document draft has been prepared; the sharing tends to happen via e-mail for others to comment upon. Leading manufacturers of software for writing and document creation, while not excluding collaborative functions from their products, often make the prospect of collaboration tools inconvenient and cumbersome. For example, Microsoft® Office allows multiple users to add comments and to track change to a document. However, in order for all the users to see and accept or reject those changes, a document

must first be sent around via e-mail or uploaded to an online space. Similarly, Adobe® Professional® lets users collect comments from readers, but it is then the original writer's responsibility to integrate those comments into the document. While these popular writing software products technically do not preclude writers from collaborating on a single document, they assume that text in a document is created by one individual who may or may not gather feedback from others.

The dominance of the software market by Microsoft® and Adobe® has led to the expectation that most writers will use these manufacturers' tools in their work. For example, a typical incoming university student would be expected to have access to Microsoft® Office and to use Word™ when writing papers for classes. The mutual influence between software design and cultural norms is well-researched and documented. See, for example, the critiques of computer interfaces by Johnson-Eilola (2005) or recent works by Nelson (2008), among others. Commercial software developers claim that their products respond to users' needs. Microsoft's® advertising slogan, for example, claims to design software that matches "the way people really work." Because of their dominance, these tools perpetuate writing practices that may prevent effective collaboration even though virtual collaboration is the way that many writers *need* to work. For a more detailed discussion of overcoming barriers to collaboration with respect what people need to learn about working together when using specific tools and software applications, see Chapters 6 and 7.

TEACHING WRITERS TO COLLABORATE: PRACTICAL STEPS

Teaching writers to collaborate successfully and comfortably requires time and a carefully designed instructional environment. Writing instructors at colleges and universities will have an easier time setting up such an environment because they are unlikely to face the pressures of real workplace deadlines and other constraints. Managers, on-the-job trainers, and others responsible for the success of collaborative workplace writing projects need to understand the challenges and constraints of collaborative writing within their particular business cultures, and they need to create, within reason, conditions that would enable them and their trainee writers to overcome those difficulties.

Treat and Teach Writing as a Social Process

Fundamental philosophical obstacles to collaboration need to be mediated first. As discussed earlier, writers' unwillingness to cede control of their texts is one such fundamental obstacle. A significant reason for this unwillingness to share control over texts with others may be that inexperienced writers place too much emphasis on the product of writing rather than the process. In order to overcome this obstacle, writing instructors and trainers need to teach writers to see writing in general and collaborative writing in particular as a process. Students need to learn to see writing as a recursive and often messy process of negotiation, renegotiation, rethinking, and change. Some may find that the need to teach writing as a process can run contrary to the need to complete writing tasks quickly and efficiently, especially in large organizations. However, the writer's ability to see the composition of a text as a recursive process rather than a "one shot" activity is crucial if that writer wants to learn how to collaborate—indeed, if that writer wants to write well at all. Here are some practical steps that writing instructors and trainers can take in order to teach writing as a process:

- Give clear guidelines for writing projects, based on sound rhetorical and communication principles (that is, attending to the purpose, audience, and occasion for the writing; see Chapter 2).

- Give writing teams sufficient time to complete writing projects. Adequate time allows them to break projects into stages, thus enabling them to discover their ideas, revise, and discuss the project with their teammates before having to produce the final version of a document.

- Build benchmarks into the project management flow that note and evaluate the completion of a writing project's stages. In other words, develop an assessment system that recognizes not only the final information product but also the process by which it was developed. Doing so enacts the sixth principle that grounds this book, which is to measure, track, and ultimately reward the collaboration's success.

- Teach writers effective ways to review and comment on each other's work in progress and encourage frequent conversations among writers in the course of a collaborative writing project. If the organization teaches collaborative writing in a structured environment, have writers read and discuss a common text on peer review (see also Chapter 16).

- Get writers used to the idea that composing is a social rather than a solitary process and that creating a rhetorically effective text without readers' feedback along the way is nearly impossible. Once they understand that fact through the practices encouraged in their classrooms and training, they will be more likely to see their collaborative text as one that needs input from multiple team members. As a result, they may be more willing to cede a part of their authority over that text, thus making collaboration easier for themselves and others. This suggestion speaks to Principle 1 in this book, which is to develop a culture of collaboration.

On the other side of this equation is the need to get writers acquainted with the idea of contributing to a text that was started by someone else. Inexperienced collaborators likely will have reservations about changing or adding to someone else's written language, which they may see as a violation of the other writers' intentions, message, or style. Following the suggestions outlined earlier, especially those that deal with effective feedback on works in progress, will help writers to become accustomed collaborative writing as, essentially, a conversation among colleagues and will encourage them to provide more input to a work in progress.

The steps listed earlier suggest that overcoming reluctance and fear of collaborative writing is an organizational and cultural issue as much as an individual one. Because collaboration, by definition, involves many people, training one or two writers within a group or organization to collaborate will do them or the organization little good if the rest of the group does not subscribe to the same philosophy.

Obviously, in some situations, writers in the workplace may not have time for extensive collaborative commenting on drafts and revising. While these types of situations definitely will make writers adjust their behaviors compared to the ones outlined above, the core habit of seeing any text as a social and evolving entity will remain in their minds. Nonetheless, even when the current culture does not value or teach collaboration, many workplace writing situations demand at least some degree of collaboration among writers, even when those writers do not have structured time for drafting, feedback, and revising. As such, following the steps outlined earlier will condition writers to approach writing as a social process that, by necessity, involves others. This approach is especially crucial for technical writers who are used to working in tandem with engineers and other non-writers, essentially creating collaborative works in many aspects of their jobs.

Example Lesson for Preparing Collaborative Writers

To illustrate how a training project of this kind might work, here is an example of a writing assignment I prepared for students in a class entitled "Digital Rhetoric." The class consisted of seniors and graduate students, most of whom majored in Technical and Scientific Communication and were preparing themselves for technical communication careers in industry, government, or business. There were 17 students in the class, and we met twice a week in a computer lab to help simulate the business setting.

The assignment was to create a "beginner's guide" to digital rhetoric as a field of study and practice. Rhetorically, this was a real activity—not simply created for grading purposes—since, to the best of our knowledge at the time, there was no single published text defining digital rhetoric and covering its key concepts and issues. As we regarded the need for such a text to be strong, the students had good reason to work together to produce a strong information product. They worked in a wiki, and the results of their work can be seen online at http://en.wikibooks.org/wiki/Digital_Rhetoric.

The purpose of this project was two-fold. On the one hand, it was to be a "writing-to-learn" experience, during which the students would reconsider and reinforce the key topics and issues we had been discussing during the semester. On the other hand, knowing that the majority of the class members would soon begin careers as technical communicators, I wanted to give them practice in collaborative project management.

After I explained the assignment, the students were asked to develop the rhetorical situation for the project, defining its basic elements in terms of its purpose, audience, and occasion. We brainstormed together as a class. At the end of the session, two of the students volunteered to post the results of the brainstorming activity on the wiki.

Next, during another class brainstorming session, we created a list of possible topics that needed to be covered in this online guide. Naturally, as the instructor of the class, I gave the students feedback and guidance on their ideas, but I wanted them to be guided primarily by the parameters of the rhetorical situation that we had developed collaboratively. After the topic brainstorming was completed, two more students volunteered to write up its results on the wiki. During the following class meeting, some of the topics we had originally listed were voted down and replaced with others or combined.

As the project progressed, it became clear to me that most of the students were quite comfortable with the kind of self-pacing and self-governance that this assignment afforded them. When asked to volunteer for various tasks, they did so willingly based on their interests and areas of expertise with technology.

The next step was to form writing teams of two or three students and to assign topics to those teams. Instead of assigning students to topics and teams, I asked them to discuss their interests with their colleagues and then to put their names next to any potential topic of interest to them on the project's wiki. This approach worked well and, by the next class meeting, the teams were formed and topics assigned.

Next, a project schedule was devised and posted on a separate page in the wiki, as well as a to-do list, where team members were encouraged to record their plans, tasks in need of completion, and so on. The whole project cycle took about three weeks, which provided the students with a realistically short time line. The resulting project was published online, which again provided them with a realistic situation that required them to perfect the writing for an outside audience.

As an instructor, I learned several important lessons during the project. The first lesson was that instructors and trainers can ease even novice collaborators into an environment of discussion, negotiation, and compromise—all necessary elements

in a successful collaborative venture—through a carefully structured guided project management sequence that attempts to imitate workplace collaborative writing. Such a structure is advocated in Principle 5 of the principles that ground this book (Chapter 1). Second, such a project presents students with a life-like writing and collaborative situation—one that they are likely to encounter on the job—because such a collaborative project avoids the traditional lock-step method in which the instructor sets all the parameters for the students and tracks all the benchmarks. Finally, such a project simulates the structure of a professional virtual collaborative project, during which various team members might be responsible for the success of its various tasks, by designating some students as "tech experts" who were able and willing to help their colleagues with, for example, wiki formatting and use

CREATE ORGANIZATIONAL AND ASSESSMENT STRUCTURES THAT ENCOURAGE COLLABORATIVE WRITING

The organizational and formal structures necessary for encouraging collaboration among writers will be different among educational institutions (that is, colleges, universities, and technical schools) and on-the-job training sites. The learners are different; the context of instruction is different; and the desired outcomes of collaborative writing projects may be different. Whereas in the case of college or university education, the primary goal of collaborative writing is learning (although there may be other goals as well, such as producing documents for clients in professional writing or service learning courses), in workplace settings, the primary goal of every writing project is the production of high-quality documents for an external client or for in-company use by staff. Despite that, if managers and workplace trainers want to improve collaborative writing skills of their staff members, they need to make a concerted effort for structured on-the-job training. Regardless of the setting, instructors and workplace trainers need to develop learning and project management structures that encourage and reward collaboration. Below are some directions in which this activity could proceed.

Teaching Collaboration: General Strategies

As with any instructional design project, when designing a course or program to teach virtual collaboration, it is important to consider students' current knowledge and skill-set and whether they may be ready to embrace the notion of virtual collaboration from the start or whether they may need first to be taught some basics of collaboration in a face-to-face environment. Instructors know their students best, of course, and individual instructors should follow that knowledge to design programs and courses that suit their needs and their students' level. However, I believe that even those learners who do not have much experience with collaboration, let alone virtual collaboration, should be taught strategies for both face-to-face and virtual collaboration simultaneously by alternating face-to-face and virtual activities, assignments, and projects. Later in this chapter, I propose several sequenced activities and projects that can help students and other novice writers to become comfortable not only with the idea of collaboration but also with the idea of virtual collaboration.

First, collaborating writers, especially those just learning to collaborate, need sufficient time and resources to develop collaborative relationships among prospective teammates as well as techniques for being collaborative. Effective writing teams require time to cohere and collaborative relationships take time to develop; the third principle that grounds this book speaks to the need to develop trust among collaborating writers (see also Chapters 4 and 5). It is impor-

tant that writers who are learning to collaborate should have enough time and resources to develop those relationships with one another. In academic settings, where outside pressure from clients and co-workers is not strong or does not exist at all, writing instructions need to give novice writers time to work on collaborative projects in bite-sized steps. To do this, instructors need to give writers clear project guidelines, including appropriate guidelines on idea development (or invention), revision, peer feedback, project management, and so on. Specific advice on organizing invention, revision, and peer response activities are outside of the scope of this chapter and are available in literature on rhetoric and composition and teaching writing methodology.

The obvious—and valid—argument against this advice is that writers in workplace situations frequently face a lack of time for this kind of group cohesion. Nonetheless, team building and cohesion strategies are necessary. Even when it is impossible to designate much time for groups to gel and prepare for collaboration, writers who have undergone such training as students will be more likely to have the skills and mental attitudes to adjust to and welcome their new colleagues than those who have never been taught how to enter a new collaborative venture. Some practical training steps to achieve this goal during training might include informal meetings, brainstorming sessions, and opportunities to develop associations (see the section on training in Chapter 1).

In a workplace setting where deadline and other pressures are higher, managers and other trainers of collaborating writers need to give more experienced team members more responsibility for project structuring and management and for mentoring of less experienced project participants. This advice echoes the fourth principle that grounds this book. Again, in the overall structure of the company, some type of an assessment and reward structure should be instituted to recognize the contributions of everyone to the training of collaborating writers as well as of the writers themselves.

Published research demonstrates that it is beneficial for companies to involve professional writers in the early stages of the design and product development processes. Doheny-Farina (1991) supported this argument through assembled case studies that clearly demonstrated that the process of technology transfer is a rhetorical one and, consequently, that the people responsible for communication during this process need to be included into the collaborative decision making process of the design and production teams. Involving technical communicators into the design and production process early on will help those writers position themselves as members of the production team, thus increasing their effectiveness as collaborators. One current theory of technical and scientific communication suggests that professional writers need to position themselves as more than mere transmitters of technical knowledge. Instead, they should see themselves as "symbolic-analytic workers" (Reich, 1991; Johnson-Eilola, 2005), and "rearticulators" (Johnson Eilola, 2005; see also Chapter 2). Through responsible and ethical use of language and other means of communication, professional writers can and should help shape the collaborative processes of product design and development and of knowledge transfer. Ultimately, the responsibility for creating the appropriate conditions for such positioning of professional writers will reside with their workplace managers, but the college-level instructors of those writers should make sure that their students receive an appropriate introduction to these concepts before entering the workplace.

The second direction towards more effective collaboration training is achieving appropriate balance between providing clear and manageable writing project guidelines and teaching writing teams how to manage themselves. An important skill that all successful collaborators share is their ability to self-manage and self-regulate. This ability allows them to understand and fulfill not only the overall purpose of a collaborative writing project, but also to understand their own strengths and weaknesses and objectively see how they can contribute to the overall success of the project. To teach writers self-regulation and project management skills, instructors need to know when to stop managing the novice writers while still giving them sufficiently specific instructions and directions for a particular project. Collaborating writers certainly need some initial parameters on which they can act in the beginning of the project. Such initial parameters can be framed in terms of the basic components of the rhetorical situation—purpose, audience, and occasion (see Chapter 2). However, a part of the project's process and assessment system should be encouraging and even allowing writers to set their own parameters and benchmarks. Taking initiative in project planning and management should be rewarded alongside actual contributions that collaborating writers make to the document that is being created, which is the sixth grounding principle of this book. As the example of the wiki writing project earlier in the chapter shows, many students will adjust to such an arrangement rather easily.

Teaching self-regulation and project management skills may be an area in which managers and workplace trainers of collaborating writers have an advantage over their counterparts in educational institutions. Workplace writing situations are dictated by parameters set by clients. These parameters often are vague and general, and it is up to the writers to "fill in the blanks." In effect, professional writers may be seen as creating the project for their clients because they are the ones who have the expertise to understand the rhetorical situation and to respond to the rhetorical challenges appropriately. In conditions like these, with proper mentoring, writers who are learning to collaborate can acquire important self- and project-management skills.

In the sometimes more structured environment of a writing class, on the other hand, students often are given too many details about a writing assignment, which make it less necessary for them to learn how to take initiative in the management of a writing project. At least in part, the instructors' desire to give students as many parameters for a project as possible can be explained by existing institutional assessment systems that highly value "clarity of instructions" for a classroom project. Often, the perception by students and administrators regarding the quality of writing instruction is tied directly to amount of detail and instructions an instructor gives to the class. While I do not deny the importance of clear and manageable writing assignments, giving students too much information about what they are supposed to do and how the finished document is supposed to look actually may discourage learners from taking initiative and learning valuable project management techniques.

Explaining to learners the need for developing self and project management skills is tied to teaching them that writing is a social, not solitary practice. In real-life situations, especially including workplace situations, writing projects' parameters and criteria for success typically are negotiated by all stakeholders and not dispatched from above. These stakeholders include, but are not limited to, clients who are also the audience, the writers themselves, and any external players, such as supervisors who can influence the writing situation. Additionally, there are budgetary, time, and other constraints. This process of negotiation is sometimes much more complex than the task of producing the target document after the parameters and criteria of the project have been agreed upon, and novice writers need to learn to deal with them.

Self-regulation need not be seen as a "solitary" skill either. That would contradict the vision of collaborative writing as a social and recursive process that this chapter advocates. Instead, collaborating writers need to be shown how what they do as members of a writing team affects the decisions and actions of others and how those decisions and actions in turn affect their own behaviors. Self-regulation thus is best learned and practiced within the parameters of the collaborative group.

Writers can be taught to collaborate in these situations through case and project-based learning. In creating cases and projects, instructors should emulate workplace-like collaborative writing situations. This emulation, especially in professional writing classes, should include not only such traditionally-taught constraints of the rhetorical situation as purpose, audience, and occasion, but also other types of constraints described above. In a separate section later, I outline several possible types of writing projects through which these collaborative outcomes can be taught.

Overall, the degree of success in creating organizational structures that promote collaboration will depend on the degree to which writing instructors and workplace trainers of writers succeed in creating an atmosphere in which writers are not afraid to share their work with one another and to contribute to the same project. That will happen only if writers learn to cede individual ownership of a given text and begin to see writing as a social and collaborative endeavor.

Most of the strategies for teaching collaborative writing discussed thus far are relevant to teaching and learning both face-to-face and virtual collaboration. But what about the unique facets and challenges that are introduced with the collaboration dynamic when writers work with one another virtually and without regular face-to-face contact?

When training writers to be effective collaborators in virtual environments, educators need to understand that face-to-face and virtual teams are similar in some respects and different in others. McDaniel (2008) noted that face-to-face teams are similar to virtual teams in that members of both must have shared goals, trust, and leaders able to move the project forward (p. 15). However, McDaniel also mentioned "tremendous" differences between the two types of teams (p. 15). McDaniel attributed the main difficulties for participating in and managing a virtual team to the absence of "tone of voice and body language" in virtual collaborative spaces. (pp. 19-22). Lack of face-to-face contact means that participants of a virtual team must rely on communication-mediating technologies, such as computers or telephone, in order to interact. That, McDaniel wrote, poses significant challenges for virtual team managers, or, to extend that term to the context of this chapter, for educators teaching virtual collaborators. (p. 22). McDaniel suggested having at least one face-to-face meeting of all the team members in the beginning of a project as well as having "small deliverables" due soon after the project begins. (p. 20). This strategy, according to McDaniel, should help team members to build trust, which is a necessary condition for success of any team project. (McDaniel 2008, p. 22; see also Chapters 4 and 5).

Writing Projects That Promote Virtual Collaboration

To restate, practical steps in helping writers become better collaborators—particularly in virtual environments, the main subject of this book—must be preceded by addressing some fundamental philosophical and epistemological issues. The most important of these issues is helping writers see themselves as participants in a collaborative process and getting them accustomed to the idea of partial or shared ownership of a text. One example of how such a training process might work is the wiki writing project described earlier in this chapter. In addition, Doheny-Farina's (1991) collection of case studies contains a classroom-applicable case that asks technical or business communication students to participate in a decision-making process within a company. Supplementary cases for classroom use will not be hard to find, either in print or online. In the paragraphs that follow, I suggest several more writing projects that promote collaborative attitudes among writers. These projects need to be adjusted to specific contexts in which virtual collaborative writing is taught and the specific needs of specific courses, educational programs,

or enterprises and organizations. In addition, the specific ways in which these and other collaborative projects are assigned to students depend on whether the collaborating group of writers meets exclusively online or whether there is time and space for face-to-face meetings.

The kinds of collaborative writing projects outlined later attempt to teach both the process of virtual collaborative writing and strategies for a strong information product. As I hope has been made clear earlier in the chapter, it is impossible to teach collaborative writing if writers do not buy into the idea that a collaboratively written document is a fluid and ever-changing artifact. Therefore, it would behoove writing instructors to give learners projects that lead to the creation of effective products (document) through meticulously planned and executed development stages. The assignments below range from smaller collaborative tasks, in which writers work on various pre-writing and planning activities, to project and term, or even academic-year length virtual collaborations.

Collaboratively Created Dictionaries, Glossaries, and Encyclopedia Entries

Group size may vary, but relatively small teams of three to five writers may work best for this assignment, especially when the writers involved are not experienced in virtual collaboration. The project can be accomplished using wiki or an online word-processing program, such as Google Docs™.

It is likely that beginning collaborators will split the task, each taking care of some portion of the project. Thus, technically speaking, they would be cooperating, not collaborating, particularly in the sense of collective collaboration as defined in Chapter 1 and discussed in Chapter 6. Instructors may want to take students from cooperation to various levels of collaboration by requiring them to revise and edit texts created by their teammates as well as to do such tasks *with* their teammates.

Structured Peer Review Sessions

While not directly asking writers to create texts collaboratively, structured sessions during which writers are required to comment on their colleagues' work in progress may help them see the process of writing as one of interaction and collaboration (see Chapter 16). Providing comments on the drafts created by other writers helps students become better and more active readers. This, in turn, leads to better writing later on. One way to help writers with this review process is to have them collaboratively develop a rubric for the document's required benchmarks. Doing so enables them to buy into the review process more completely and, as a bonus, encourages writers who might not otherwise have invested themselves in their writing to try to meet those benchmarks prior to and after peer review. Regular and structured peer review sessions also are useful to keep members of a team on track and to continue developing a sense of belonging to a team and trust among the team's members.

Collaboratively-Written Essays, Reports, and White Papers

In order to develop students' ability to participate in sustained and complex virtual collaborative projects, instructors would do well to build up to assignments that require higher levels of collaborative interactions among students as well as result in longer, more complex documents. Once student writers become more comfortable with the idea of virtual collaboration, they may be asked to create full-scale documents working together online. As with other types of projects, it is important that writers be given adequate time, project management structures, and support and mentoring during the writing process. To bring the classroom as close as possible to many real-life workplace collaboration and writing situations, students should be given projects and assignments that treat collaboration and collaborative writing

not only as exercises in consensus among group members (where governance models suggest that consensus is necessary; see Chapter 1), but also as sites of disagreement, dissent, and productive contradiction. For an example of such a collaborative writing project, readers may refer to Doheny-Farina (1991). But, in order for these more complex projects to succeed, student need a high degree of trust for one another and a strong "buy" into the value of collaborative project. These attitudes can be developed through smaller assignments with lower stakes, as mentioned earlier.

Specific Web-Based Writing Projects

In courses that emphasize Web design and Web writing, one underexplored and underused area is creating collaborative websites and webtexts using open source CMSs. By this I do not mean the kinds of CMSs used by technical writers for single-sourcing documents, but rather Web design systems like Drupal™, Moodle™, Joomla™, and others that allow students to design Web sites and intranets that then can be used as online writing platforms. Organizations in the business, academic, government, and non-profit sectors use these platforms to design collaborative Web spaces and webtexts, whose users collaboratively contribute content. By becoming proficient with these systems, learners will understand better what it takes to collaborate virtually on a project and to be a part of a professional community. An added benefit to working in these platforms is that because they are open-source, the study of their communities of developers and contributors is a good lesson in virtual collaboration.

CONCLUSION

Preparing writers for virtual writing collaboration, either face-to-face or virtual, is a long and challenging process. There are many obstacles that both the instructors and the writers need to overcome in order for this teaching and learning process to be successful. As demonstrated in this chapter, perhaps the most significant of these challenges may be the ones related to the culture of solitary writing. Overcoming the view of writing as a solitary activity may be difficult for college students particularly. After all, in the majority of their courses, they still are being assigned and assessed on individual writing projects and, in many cases, writing collaboration is discouraged, if not prohibited because of fears that students will not learn the material on their own or that they may plagiarize others. In a recent online writing class that I taught in which students were asked to collaborate on writing assignments, one student e-mailed me asking for a special dispensation from having to collaborate with others. Her argument against collaboration was that she was much better at working alone when she does not have to depend on others. Although her argument might have been valid, it also demonstrated her unfortunate lack of successful collaborative experiences—and it suggests a strong need for implementing the kinds of steps suggested in this chapter and throughout this book.

In North American postsecondary institutions, perhaps with the exception of the natural sciences and business schools, the default mode of training remains individual writing and other assignments. It is no wonder that many students retain negative attitudes toward collaboration. To overcome such attitudes and to prepare such students for workplace collaboration in writing, instructors and trainers must show students what successful collaboration looks like, provide them with useful strategies and opportunities to learn it, and teach them how to overcome the inevitable obstacles and pitfalls they will encounter as collaborative writers. The advice provided in this chapter takes a step in that direction.

REFERENCES

Doheny-Farina, S. (1991). *Rhetoric, innovation, technology: Case study of technical communication in technology transfers*. Canbridge, MA: The MIT Press.

Fanderclai, T. (2004). Collaborative research, collaborative thinking: Lessons from the Linux community. In Inman, B. J., Reed, C., & Sands, P. (Eds.), *Electronic collaboration in the humanities: Issues and options* (pp. 311–320). Mahwah, NJ: Lawrence Erlbaum Asociates.

Hawisher, G., & Selfe, C. (1991). The rhetoric of technology and the electronic writing class. *College Composition and Communication, 42*(1), 55–65. doi:10.2307/357539

Johnson-Eilola, J. (2005). *Datacloud: Toward a new theory of online work*. Cresskill, NJ: Hampton Press.

McDaniel, C. (2008). Removing space and time: Tips for managing the virtual workplace. In Zemliansky, P., & St.Amant, K. (Eds.), *The handbook of research on virtual workplaces and the new nature of business practices* (pp. 530–543). Hershey, PA: IGI-Global.

Moxley, J. (2008). Datagogies, writing spaces, and the age pr peer production. *Computers and Composition, 25*(2), 182–202. doi:10.1016/j.compcom.2007.12.003

Nelson, T. (2008). Ted Nelson on software. *Youtube*. Retrieved from http://www.youtube.com/watch?v=zumdnI4EG14

Reich, R. (1991). *The work of nations: Preparing ourselves for 21st century capitalism*. New York: A.A. Knopf.

Stringer, J. (2009). *Designing the new Stanford school of medicine*. Paper presented at the EDUCAUSE Learning Initiative 2009 Online Fall Focus Session. Retrieved October 7, 2009, from http://net.educause.edu/content.asp?SECTION_ID=443

Youngblood, N. E. (2008). Collaborative writing tools in the virtual workplace. In Zemliansky, P., & St.Amant, K. (Eds.), *The handbook of research on virtual workplaces and the new nature of business practices* (pp. 530–543). Hershey, PA: IGI-Global.

Section 7
Using New Media in Virtual Collaborative Writing

Chapter 19
Case Study: Writing, Rhetoric, and Design:
A Virtual Collaboration Case Study

Douglas Eyman
George Mason University, USA

ABSTRACT

This chapter presents a case study of virtual collaboration that focuses on a research and production team's approach to making choices about the most appropriate technologies to support the team's interactions. The study highlights the importance of establishing clear, well-defined roles for collaborators as well as the importance of explicitly acknowledging the institutional context within which the work was undertaken. The chapter concludes with a series of recommendations based upon the experience of this virtual collaboration.

INTRODUCTION

Because of the nature of the project, we needed a media-rich communication infrastructure. This chapter, therefore, frames "writing" within the context of multimedia/new media production. The design team also worked within a rhetorically derived heuristic, following a research process that is driven explicitly by our training and work as rhetoricians. This digital rhetoric approach informed both design decisions and the choices made with regard to implementing the underlying technological

infrastructure of the new interface. In essence, the team both worked within and produced a collaborative writing space that existed at the intersections of rhetoric, design, and code.

As a case study of virtual collaboration, this chapter addresses the choices we made about the technologies we used to support our interactions. It highlights the importance of establishing clear, well-defined roles for collaborators. Additionally, the chapter considers the importance of explicitly acknowledging the institutional context within which the work was undertaken as both the collaborative practices of the team and the final product of the collaborative work needed to connect to the goals

DOI: 10.4018/978-1-60566-994-6.ch019

and expectations of the journal's editors and readers. Finally, this chapter points to the first, fourth, and fifth principles of virtual collaborative writing that ground this book. The kinds of collaboration necessary in distance-based website design can only be accomplished in a culture that values collaboration as a primary value. To be successful, it is necessary to use tools and collaborative modes effectively in the context of ongoing and ever changing goals. Thus, creating structure for each working member of the writing team is essential.

BACKGROUND

Kairos: **Virtual Collaboration by Design**

In 1993, the National Center for Supercomputing Applications (NCSA) released Mosaic, a simple graphical interface to the World Wide Web (WWW) and the first cross-platform Web browser (Andreessen, 1993). Mosaic provided access to the Web in ways that made it available to non-specialist computer users, but it also provided a mechanism through which theories of hypertext and hypermedia could be engaged on a much wider scale than earlier stand-alone systems such as Hypercard. In the late 1980s and early 1990s, the field of composition studies was exploring how notions of hypertext might complicate the view of the rhetorical functions of writing (Bolter, 1991; Landow, 1992) as well as how writing technologies more generally might change the way we teach composition and rhetoric (Hawisher & Selfe, 1991; Hawisher & LeBlanc, 1992; Selfe & Hilligoss, 1994). It is at this historical convergence of theory and application that a group of graduate students decided to launch an online journal that would take on the questions of technology-mediated writing as both its content and its delivery platform. The journal's founding editors were rhetoricians who wanted to use the faculties of rhetoric for both analysis and produc-

tion; to provide scholars with a venue not only for examining how "born-digital" texts worked within digital networks but also for producing scholarly work that could itself be composed of multiple media and could take advantage of the network and the link.

From the outset, *Kairos* required virtual collaboration: the first editorial staff members resided at five different universities[1]. Michael Salvo (Doherty & Salvo, 2002), one of the founding editors, recalled that "With *Kairos*, a handful of graduate students in half a dozen states, with no budget and no sense of what was and was not possible (or acceptable), created something that caught (and continues to catch) peoples' attention." With that lack of a budget came a volunteer-based business setting that necessarily required high levels of collaboration and cooperation among a disparate team whose binding quality was their mutual interest in developing a quality online journal about the intersections of rhetoric, technology, and pedagogy.

The original editorial staff primarily used e-mail to communicate, but they also used synchronous online communication via the Massachusetts Institute of Technology's (MIT) MediaMOO. A MOO is a multi-user object oriented communication domain, similar to the more currently ubiquitous IM client; it was used primarily for earlier computer gamers until the academic community picked it up as a networked classroom venue and a communication vehicle. According to Doherty and Salvo (2002): "We spent so much time online together that [Greg] Siering built an office in MediaMOO where we would hold and log weekly 'staff meetings.' The topics ranged from what our editorial process would be to... well, what should we call this thing?"[2]

Unlike most academic journals, the *Kairos* editorial staff is not housed at a single institution. Although it is common to have distributed editorial boards (advisors and peer-reviewers), it is uncommon also to distribute both the editorial staff and production processes (the latter, however, are more and more often being outsourced to commercial publishing enterprises such as Sage and Elsevier). This state of affairs has required *Kairos* to be fairly innovative in its communication and production processes.

Like most journals, *Kairos* publishes a range of genres and organizes the content it publishes into sections. We currently have sections for our "features" (the *Topoi* section), features that are oriented more toward pedagogy than toward theory (the *Praxis* section), reviews, interviews, letters to the editor and other response pieces (the *Disputatio* section), and a special section that highlights the process of developing scholarly work that uses both text and design to promote an argument (the *Inventio* section). Each section has one or two primary editors who work with a crew of assistant editors in order to produce each issue of the journal, which publishes in the spring and fall, and occasionally in the summer. The operating principle of the journal has been that each section should function autonomously—that is, the section editors have a great deal of responsibility for defining, promoting, and producing each individual section without having to ask the main journal editors for permission to make changes, institute innovation, or approve production processes. The overall hierarchy is still in place, and the journal's senior and principal editors still do set standards, attend to personnel changes, and provide the overall vision for the journal, but the responsibility for the production is, like the production labor itself, distributed.

Over time, the number of editors and assistant editors has grown[3], and this growth has necessarily led to a more complex organizational structure. This increased complexity has put pressures on the informal systems we have used in the past—a combination of direct person-to-person e-mails and e-mail discussion lists. In addition, the individual sections have implemented a variety of disparate strategies to assist with the production work (for example, using wikis, content management systems, separate e-mail lists); these approaches work well for each section, but they do not al-

low for the establishment of organization-wide communication archives or the sustainability of institutional memory (which is a high priority for the journal because we have a relatively high rate of turnover on the editorial staff). To help restructure our production processes, the editors decided to create a technology-based infrastructure that could help support the distributed and autonomous nature of the production (for each section). But before implementing this infrastructure, the same team would develop a re-design of the journal's interface and information architecture as a necessary precursor to developing back-end systems.

CASE STUDY

Virtual Collaboration in Action: The Redesign Project

When *Kairos* launched its first issue in January of 1996, it was clear that the design reflected the possibilities and Web affordances available at that time. The original editors wanted to be certain that readers immediately would see that the journal published webtexts rather than traditional print articles and that the journal explicitly valued Web design as an integral element of argumentation for digital rhetoric. In terms of content, design, and function, *Kairos* was cutting-edge. The initial design was color-rich, with a darker series of elements framing the brighter table of contents or content area, and it used frames (a mechanism for displaying the content of multiple files in a single screen; frames have since been discarded as a viable design tool for Web pages).

In 1999, the first major redesign of the journal (beginning with issue 4.1) eliminated frames from the top-level navigation and reduced the frames to just two for the content pages and established a cleaner, brighter look.

However, the design still used code that could not be considered standards-compliant, and also used a JavaScript-based design feature that added

Figure 1. First design (issues 1.1 – 3.2)

Figure 2. Second design (issues 4.1 – 12.2)

a vertical "binder" to the journal content, providing a link back to the journal's home page, the table of contents for the issue in which the webtext appeared, and a visual marker that the webtext was part of the journal. The drawback to this approach was that information (and metadata) about the individual webtexts was not easily accessible, thus making it difficult to cite or link to the journal's content accurately. Over the past few years, as the editorial expertise on questions of circulation, archiving, and preservation of webtexts has matured, it also has become clear that the journal needed to develop a standards-based architecture that could contain and expose metadata to other systems if we wanted to have access to some of the more powerful systems for circulation and dissemination.

In 1995 (the year the journal was designed and implemented), we did not have a good sense of what was accessible or inaccessible. Cascading style sheets (CSS)—now the standard for separating structure and design—was available but not supported by the available browsers at the time, and the question of standards had not yet become a pressing issue for Web designers and users. So our previous approaches to interface and infrastructure were lacking in important aspects: standards-compliance, accessibility, and content metadata. Beginning in 2006, the editors began a long-term project designed to update the public interface of the journal and to correct these shortcomings. Tied to this effort was a concurrent project (headed up by the same project team) to build editorial systems that would help to improve upon communications and establish archives of decision-making processes and journal activities that would be accessible to the full editorial staff rather than sequestered in section-based e-mail accounts.

In order to maintain flexibility and also to reduce the amount of time that normally would have been spent on decision-making and approval processes, we decided that a small development team would lead the project and would have the authority to make design and infrastructure decisions without going to the full editorial staff or editorial board for approval. As part of the process, we were careful to build in opportunities for all of the editors to contribute to both the research and the review process, but the ultimate decisions were in the hands of the team. The team had three members: Senior Editor Douglas Eyman provided both institutional memory and journal history and provided the authority for implementing the design

team's decision; Associate Editor Kathie Gossett was selected to serve as program manager and to guide the several research projects that would inform the work of developing the new design; and *Inventio* Editor Karl Stolley provided the technical and design expertise.

Although we planned to both re-design the journal interface and develop a systematic editorial infrastructure, it was agreed that we would focus on the way the journal connects to and is accessed by readers as our first priority; we would work on the external features before tackling the more complex task of building the editorial system. Thus, during this phase of our work we were known as the "redesign team."

Communication Infrastructure

The first task of the redesign team was to figure out how we would work together. We planned to move beyond the asynchronous virtual tools (that is, e-mail and e-mail-based listservs) that the journal currently was using for nearly all internal communications. Our experience in this project agrees with Idoura's premise that "a good decision-making process contributes to better decisions and, overall, more successful virtual teams" (see Chapter 11). Our team needed to address many of the technical, administrative, and managerial decisions outlined in Tables 2 and 3 of that chapter.

Like all of the journal's activities, we would be working together at a distance: I was in Northern Virginia, Kathie was in Southern Virginia, and Karl was in Chicago. Luckily, we only had to contend with two time zones—and those were only an hour apart. We began with the assumption that regular meetings would help us to keep the project on track and visible, which is particularly important for collaborating academics, which often have to work on a wide range of projects and activities simultaneously. We opted for synchronous IM for our weekly meetings and e-mail for questions, follow-up, and scheduling of other online meetings. Although we could have used an audio/video conferencing system (such as Skype) for our meetings, we selected IM because we were familiar with the features and functions of IM communication, and (more importantly) we could archive our written conversations and keep them as reference resources throughout the project. While it certainly is possible to record audio/video conference sessions, we knew we would be generating a lot of information, which meant that we would need to consider virtual storage space (working with very large media files versus very small text files) and the available tools for searching our conversations and decisions.

We decided that we would use a wiki as a repository of our research findings, prototypes, and IM conversations because we could quickly organize and build a wiki-based knowledge repository. We knew that we also could use the wiki as a collaborative workspace, both for organizing the data we collected and drafting initial specifications (and, later, academic articles about the project). We had all used wikis in other projects and for our teaching, so we were familiar with the environment and its conventions, which was an important consideration, given the relatively short time frame in which we would have to produce the main deliverable (the new journal interface). We simply did not have time to learn how to navigate and use any systems that were not familiar to all of the team members. Time as a factor, by the way, should be considered whenever teams are assigned to or develop such a project. If one does not have time to learn new systems, then the ability to choose the best tools for the situations—to develop culturally, so to speak—certainly is influenced and sometimes negatively so (see Chapter 1).

The wiki also worked well for us because it could accommodate multiple functional needs. A wiki is essentially a simple database, so we could add records and files related to the research we were conducting (including interview transcripts and survey results), but it also allowed us to work

in and through each others' texts as we produced specification documents based on our research materials and as we wrote up progress reports and reader guides for the rest of the journal's staff. Unlike shared word processed documents, wikis provide a robust interface for both collective collaborative writing (where multiple writers are writing, rewriting, and editing each other's words) and cooperative writing (where writers write different sections of a single document that are later edited for consistency of style and usage) (see Chapter 1 for more about these kinds of collaboration). We had tried using systems such as GoogleDocs™ in the past but found that wikis provide a better mechanism for comparing versions and also, by design, privilege collaboration in ways that word-processing oriented systems do not. The other benefit of using the wiki is that it forces the users to co-develop an organizational schema—on individual PCs or online word-processing systems, there is a built-in structure that allows individual files to be placed into directories; however, with a wiki, this structure is not present and links to the items in the database have to be established by the users (rather than by the system). Our team worked together to make decisions about how to organize our materials and what kinds of links we could make between and among the various data sets and textual artifacts we compiled during our research process.

Because we made a conscious decision to utilize the wiki as the common workspace and repository, we found it easy to retrieve the information we needed for each aspect of the project and to keep all of the team members updated when changes or additions were made (the wiki itself notified everyone on the distribution list of a change). Although each team member did some individual work outside of the project workspace, the wiki provided a central clearinghouse of information (including research data, project management tools, and records of our progress) in a way that offered both context and coherence for the project team. As with the other decisions we made during the project, explicitly working together to develop our collaboration infrastructure both in terms of the tools we would use and the manner in which each would support specific goals contributed to the success of the venture.

Design Workspace

Much like the project described in Chapter 21, ours included both collaborative writing in the sense of textual production and collaborative design of the journal interface. As rhetoricians, we see a deep connection between writing and design—content and form—both of which are rhetorical processes[4]. Indeed, we often use the term "writing" to describe both traditional texts and multimodal/multimedia texts and interfaces, or, as both discursive and non-discursive forms of writing (see Chapter 20).

In addition to our synchronous discussions via IM and our collection of resources and collaborative writing space in the project wiki, we also set up server space that all team members could access and upon which we could both build and test the new site design and the interface elements we wanted to develop. While we did post wireframes, design mock-ups, and examples of color schemes (and several iterations of the logo) on the wiki, to collaborate on the design and implementation of the site our team needed to work with writing, design, *and* code.

CHALLENGES AND PROBLEMS

Contextual Inquiry at a Distance

At the outset of the project, the team decided that our initial activity would be to research the needs of our readers as well as to identify both technical and procedural requirements for the redesign and the development of the editorial system. As technical writers, we understand that writing and research are intertwined—so we knew that we

needed to be able to transform our data collections into forms that we could share and utilize (in other words, we had to both produce and disseminate what Latour (1990) called "inscriptions"—in this case, the records of our research and observations).

Our first challenge was to carry out the data collection and research phase of the project. While there are ways to collect data remotely (via server logs, e-mail, IM, or virtual-world interviews), the lack of immediacy in terms of feedback impacts both the researcher's ability to pursue follow-up lines of inquiry and the responsiveness of the research participants (that is, a participant is unlikely to put off a scheduled face-to-face interview, but an asynchronous e-mail interview or survey often will be perceived as a low-priority task). We ended up collecting data via phone interview as well as e-mail, even though that added to the overhead labor costs. We also culled information from interviews and surveys undertaken for previous projects and ultimately collected quite a bit of information. Still, one of the challenges of virtual research mirrors that of virtual collaboration—we do not yet have tools that are designed specifically to support data collection in multiple media (but see Chapter 21 for more on the development of collaborative virtual technologies).

Communicating with External Audiences and Stakeholders

Although the project team itself worked well together (due in large part to the time and effort expended in making decisions about our communication strategies and making sure we agreed on our roles, goals, and priorities), we found that we were less adept at communicating with external stakeholders and other interested parties such as the journal's communications staff and the editorial board. We had taken into account our needs as collaborators, and we had focused our research on the needs of the staff and the journal's readers, but we had overlooked one crucial opportunity—providing transparent access to stakeholders throughout the process. We had a situation where certain staff members believed their input was not being heard or accounted for. If we had been more careful about making some of our work more accessible, we could have mitigated some of the interpersonal conflicts that arose from our lack of foresight and transparency. While there are many cases where institutional hierarchies are clear, sometimes these structures actually make it easier to understand one's audience in a limited and limiting way. We ultimately were able to make our process more transparent, but this is a challenge that could well have been avoided by planning with more stakeholders in mind.

Time Constraints and Academic Collaboration

With regular IM meetings and just-in-time e-mail communication, we were able to keep the project on task and on time, but there were times when our disparate schedules and competing interests threatened to derail the smooth operation of the process. This is one of the challenges that we met simply by developing and keeping to our milestone deadlines and also by being flexible about meeting times. However, the regular IM meetings did keep us in touch and apprised of each other's progress. We scheduled and held meetings even when no issues or milestones were apparent, just to make sure that we were still in agreement about our roles and goals. We also set aside some time at each of these meetings to discuss other projects or issues related to our teaching or research; this kind of social interaction helped to keep us functioning as a collectively collaborative team rather than as separate individuals with distinct tasks and mandates.

RECOMMENDATIONS

One of the reasons that our virtual collaboration was successful is that we drew upon our own expertise in composition and rhetoric when making decisions about the tools and systems we would use and as a foundation for a shared vision for the project itself. The art of rhetoric in many ways relies upon the rhetor to examine a series of assumptions about audience, style, and effective means of presenting an argument, but it also provides a heuristic for thinking through the process of production. Our team used our understanding of this process as way—a template or flowchart of sorts—to think about planning and establishing agreed-upon goals for the overall project. In terms of recommendations for virtual collaboration, three primary elements of rhetoric—audience, *praxis*, and *kairos*—may contribute to the success of projects like the one described here.

Audience

In the context of teaching writing, I am sometimes asked whether it is more important first to formulate a clear statement of the argument or to articulate a clear understanding of the audience. As a rhetorician, the clear answer is that understanding the audience is the most important consideration (but that the audience is part of the larger rhetorical situation and cannot be separated from the context). With virtual collaboration, it is important to consider the multiple audiences engaged by each individual project. These audiences include the collaborators and team members, as well as the audience or readers of the text or project and the institutional audiences who may serve as evaluators. Identifying these audiences and articulating the various needs and positions they have will help the team to establish more effectively the two key elements of the process for which they are the primary audience members: goals and roles.

Goals

Each team member should clearly understand and be able to explain in concrete detail what his or her goals are for the project. But the team members should also view their collaborators as audience members who have their own needs, desires, goals, and contexts. In order to be an effective team, each individual needs to align his or her goals with the goals of the other members and the stated goals of the overall project. Establishing a shared understanding of both personal and institutional goals provides the framework that will support the work of collaboration.

Roles

Each team member's individual goals also should connect to the specific roles that are established among collaborators. If roles match goals, then the team members are more likely to be satisfied with the overall process. Clearly establishing the roles also helps to delineate lines of communication and responsibility for project tasks.

Considering both goals and roles in light of the multiple audiences and readers who have an interest in the project is, in many ways, similar to the notion of alignment presented in Chapter 21. Alignment is an important issue because colocation means that team members do not have to keep in mind the need for creating a common workspace. I would suggest that the notion of alignment is one of the key principles of effective rhetorical planning and communication.

Praxis

Taking the time to define roles and goals at the outset of a project (and taking into account the multiple audiences in play) is important, but an additional element for successful collaboration is the practice of continual reflection on the success of the process as it is happening. Rhetoricians call this type of active reflection *praxis*. Praxis is also the concrete application of theory to practice; in the case of the *Kairos* redesign project, our team consciously drew on our knowledge of rhetorical theory to help inform the work that we did, and we made sure to reflect (collaboratively) on the

success of each element of the project as we developed it. Additionally, post-project evaluations can contribute to the success of future collaborations and making such reflective assessment a commonplace activity should be a goal of any collaboration.

Kairos

Finally, our team recognized the need for flexibility as we worked on a complex problem. Aside from being the title of our journal, kairos is also a rhetorical term. As White (1987) defined it, "kairos stands for a radical principle of occasionality which implies a conception of the production of meaning in language as a process of continuous adjustment to and creation of the present occasion" (p. 14). In other words, much like praxis, kairos requires openness to changes in timing or venue. (Roughly speaking, a shorthand definition of kairos might be the "right time/right place," indicating that both time and location are in play when considering whether an activity or decision is "right.")

Engaging both praxis and kairos clearly is a simpler task for smaller teams, and, indeed, many of the recommendations here echo those made by other contributors to this book (see, in particular, Table 1 in Chapter 5).

CONCLUSION

Through the case study of the *Kairos* journal redesign process, this chapter has demonstrated some of the ways in which rhetorical theory—as both analytical tool and heuristic for production—can be applied to the practice of collaboration in ways that strengthen and sustain the likelihood of success for any given virtual writing project. Rhetoric is a powerful tool, but many of the points here reflect the same practices and principles—particularly Principles 1, 4, and 5—identified in other chapters in this volume. Rhetoric is, in this case, more of a communicative and productive framework and a way of thinking through process in terms of action and reflection. While knowledge of rhetoric is not necessarily required for successful collaboration, however, we found that in our case at least, it was extremely valuable as a shared foundation for both the work of the project per se and the work of collaboration as well.

REFERENCES

Andreessen, M. (1993). *NCSA Mosaic technical summary*. National Center for Supercomputing Applications.

Bolter, J. D. (1991). *Writing space: The computer, hypertext, and the history of writing*. Hillsdale, NJ: Lawrence Erlbaum.

Bridgeford, T. (2006). "Kairotically speaking": *Kairos* and the power of identity. *Kairos 11*(1). Retrieved from http://kairos.technorhetoric. net/11.1/ binder.html?topoi/bridgeford/

Doherty, M., & Salvo, M. (2002). Kairos: Past, present and future(s). *Kairos, 7*(x). Retrieved from http://www.technorhetoric.net/7.x/kairos/ title.htm

Eyman, D. (2006). The arrow and the loom: A decade of *Kairos*. *Kairos 11*(1). Retrieved from http://kairos.technorhetoric.net/11.1/ binder. html?topoi/eyman/

Eyman, D. (2008). Learning from *Kairos*: Value, visibility, and virtual teamwork. In Zemliansky, P., & St. Amant, K. (Eds.), *Handbook of research on virtual workplaces and the new nature of business practices* (pp. 590–598). Hershey, PA: IGI Publishing.

Hawisher, G., & LeBlanc, P. (Eds.). (1992). *Reimagining computers and composition: Teaching and research in the virtual age*. Portsmouth, NH: Boyton/Cook Heinemman.

Hawisher, G., & Selfe, C. (Eds.). (1991). *Evolving perspectives on computers and composition studies: Questions for the 1990s*. Urbana, IL: NCTE.

Kalmbach, J. (2006). Reading the archives: Ten years of nonlinear (*Kairos*) history. *Kairos 11*(1). Retrieved from http://kairos.technorhetoric. net/11.1/binder.html?topoi/kalmbach/index.html

Landow, G. (1992). *Hypertext: The convergence of contemporary critical theory and technology*. Baltimore: The Johns Hopkins University Press.

Latour, B. (1990). Drawing things together. In Lynch, M., & Woolgar, S. (Eds.), *Representations in scientific practice* (pp. 19–68). Cambridge, MA: MIT Press.

Selfe, C., & Hilligoss, S. (Eds.). (1994). *Literacy and computers: The complications of teaching and learning with technology*. New York: MLA.

Tirrell, J. (2009). *Mapping digital technology in rhetoric and composition history*. Retrieved from http://www.digitalparlor.org/mappingrc/

White, E. C. (1987). *Kaironomia: On the will to invent*. Ithaca, NY: Cornell University Press.

ENDNOTES

1. RPI, NDSU, TTU, SUNY-Binghamton and Ball State
2. For more on the history of the journal, see Bridgeford (2006), Eyman (2006), and Kalmbach (2006).
3. For a visualization of both the distributed nature of the journal and the increased distribution resulting from the growth of the editorial staff, see Tirrell (2009).
4. See Richard Buchanan's "Declaration by design: Rhetoric, argument, and demonstration in design practice" (*Design Issues* 2.1 (Spring, 1985), pp. 4-22) for an example of the way that rhetoric functions as a foundation for design.

Chapter 20
Inventing Non–Discursive Text in Virtual Collaboration Environments

Joddy Murray
Texas Christian University, USA

ABSTRACT

Virtual collaborative writing must acknowledge and encourage a range of symbolization practices because textual products simply are likely to be hybrids of words (discursive) and visual images, aural images, haptic images, olfactory images, and even gustatory images (all non-discursive). Though digital technologies are still limited to aural and visual technologies, the authors must theorize collaboration for and within media that are as yet not widely developed or possible. Today's collaborative environments require more from interfaces if we are to invent texts that become edited images, Web pages, films, and/or animations. This chapter argues that virtual collaborative environments must accommodate the invention of non-traditional, multimodal texts.

INTRODUCTION

Much is written already about the importance of creating virtual environments for effective collaboration. In fact, most of the research about collaboration is about identifying and assessing technologies primarily through the perspective of how well they afford collaboration itself: how well the technology allows for "media richness," how well the technology allows for social structures and "information-processing schemas," or

how well these two may interact together as part of a "biological evolutionary theory as a lens for understanding e-communication behavior" (Kock & Garza, 2008). The efforts to date seem to focus on how well we collaborate in virtual environments without sufficient attention being paid to what *products* collaborators are striving to consume, produce, and distribute. This chapter starts with the question, "How have changes in writing products (textual artifacts) complicated virtual collaboration?" Or, asked differently, "In the era in which both industry and academia are creating products that are necessarily multimodal—constructed with varying degrees of

DOI: 10.4018/978-1-60566-994-6.ch020

multiple modes such as printed text, audio text, video text, etc.—and requiring multiliteracies, how must collaborative technologies for virtual environments also change to keep up with this rich array of multimedia?" In particular, this chapter considers these questions by focusing primarily on video collaboratively constructed for the Web because this type of text significantly changes the nature of writing and collaborative production overall. In doing so, it implicitly underscores the importance of developing a culture of collaboration whereby that culture reconsiders collaborative writing as beyond text alone, which is the first principle of virtual collaborative writing that grounds this book.

Even if the question about what virtual collaborative writers are producing through collaboration is set aside for a moment, a question remains regarding how various new media products construct themselves rhetorically. Subsequently, a question emerges regarding how they create a view of collaboration that is may be more fluid, continuous, and recursive than before. In other words, if a collaborative interface does not afford the invention of non-traditional texts (such as hypertext, audio, or video), then it actually may be reproducing a bias towards discursive, or word-based texts strung along in sentences. Such a writing environment also must consider how multimedia texts challenge traditional notions of the single writer producing a static text. Given that there has been a paradigm shift from the single-writer constructing monomodal, or typically text-based, documents that remain fixed through time, that shift can be considered seismic in the composing of writing. It necessitates, as well, a new paradigm of the product and process of writing (see Chapter 1). Key to the point of this chapter, writing cannot be considered monomodal anymore. At the least, much writing is visually oriented with both discursive text and non-discursive text (such as visual images). Further, web-based writing engages aural modalities, and eventually may engage haptic (touch-based), olfactory, and even gustatory images.

These changes about the way writers are viewed also changes the way collaboration is done, virtually or not. Add to this point the dissolution of time and space in today's collaborative environments, and the result is a remediation of both the way writing happens virtually and the way it continues to happen as the texts mutate, get absorbed, become viral, disappear, and even reappear in a new form. In other words, just because a team of collaborators build a website (as one example) from geographically and temporally dispersed physical conditions does not change the fact that the multimodal product produced is dynamic, constantly rewritten, redistributed, mashed into other digital constructions, and perhaps remediated into an older or newer technology. That website, in other words, must have had as its context a rhetorical situation that assumed an already dynamic, multimodal, fractured, and vastly distributed life cycle.

With this complexity in mind, it is important to imagine which affordances are needed from virtual collaboration environments to create texts biased towards non-discursive symbology and distribution patterns rather than the traditional, text-based symbology and distribution patterns. Indeed, there are few virtual environments that have the type of tools needed to collaboratively compose multimodal textual hybrids—hybrids that include still, moving, or holographic images, hypertexts, textures, sounds, tastes, or aromas, through synchronous and asynchronous interfaces. In short, virtual environments that allow for virtual collaboration of Non-discursive, multisensory texts simply do not yet exist.

Clabby (2002) indicated that "the next big step in human communications will be to make our electronic communications multimodal—in other words, it will be the use of electronic media to provide three-dimensional visuals and audio as well as scent, touch, and taste sensations" (3); that is, communication technologies are moving toward a type of convergence of sensory input and output. We have overly relied upon (and, consequently, biased our technologies upon) printed, word-based discourse, as well as interfaces that favored the visual (the book, the Web, the banner, the traffic light). Perhaps a necessary, even obvious, reason is that technological interfaces moved rather quickly to interfaces that privileged textual (or keyboard) communications, and it could be argued that we have remained in that realm—relying on graphical interfaces as shorthand for routines, subroutines, interface manipulation, and, on occasion, basic signals of expression (emoticons). But other than creating these graphic interfaces, how has collaborative technology afforded the opportunity to interface multimodally to create multimodal texts? Clabby noted:

Today, we can communicate in two modes simultaneously—audio and video—using videophone or videoconferencing technologies. And the technologies needed to produce touch and scent sensations already exist today—commercially available touch and scent devices can be used to provide haptic and olfactory experiences over the Internet. With the imminence of new multimodal peripherals and the broader availability of high-speed networks, we are now poised to enter new, sensory-rich electronic worlds where we can meet and collaborate without having to be physically present. (p. 4)

Clearly, these "multimodal peripherals" experiments have come and gone, and though there are new attempts at a forced-feedback mouse or sound effects that mimic the result of touch (that is, typewriter clicks and the scratch of pen on paper), and though there is ongoing research regarding new haptic interfaces (for example, touchscreen pop-up buttons, pre-interaction feedback, and tactile reconfigurability), these interfaces still are regarded merely as experiments and writers' primary sensory interaction in virtual collaboration still is auditory/visual. The sensory-rich environment that Clabby suggested remains elusive.

And when it comes to textual production and commonplace workflows, the promise of an immersive sensory engagement with symbols is even further from everyday practice. It is the case that the Internet has allowed more face-to-face, audio/video interfaces for collaboration, but it also remains the case that multimodal texts themselves, and the space needed for collaborators to invent such multimedia-rich texts within virtual environments, are biased toward discursive—or word-based—texts, rather than the multisensory, non-discursive texts (whether digital or not).

NON-DISCURSIVE TEXT, MULTIMODALITY, AND DISTRIBUTED AUTHORSHIP

What is non-discursive text? Put simply, texts that are image-based texts rather than word-based texts are considered non-discursive. As Langer (1942), who coined the phrase "non-discursive symbolization," remarked in her influential text *Philosophy in a New Key*: "[T]he symbolism furnished by our purely sensory appreciation of forms is a *non-discursive symbolism*, peculiarly well suited to the expression of ideas that defy linguistic projection" (93). Discursive text, as the etymology of the word implies, relies on the ordered, sequential running-along of text for there to be meaning, but non-discursive text is perceived all at once (at least at first), relying less on ordered symbols to build meaning and more on the "*presentation* of the individual object" (96). Although there is some overlap between discursive and non-discursive text, what Langer created is two categories of textual symbols: one that relies more on grammars and words strung out in a particular order; the other that relies primarily on images in the mind, whether those images are visual, aural, haptic, gustatory, or olfactory. Indeed, as Chapter 21 considers, texts aligned in "materiality, practice, and expertise" directly affect how they are "comprehended, interpreted, and put to use." Non-discursive text, then, works as image, constructing its meanings from associations present both internal and external to the immediate rhetorical situation, providing the rhetor with an ability to affect, or shade, multiple meanings and connotations in order to make an appeal. In the end, composing images through non-discursive symbology allows elements such as color, line, juxtaposition, scale, tempo, textual simultaneity (layers), counterpoint, and even the timber of a narrator's voice to imbue a text affectively and to create a kind of communication that is otherwise ineffable and unutterable. This ambiguous, affect-derived language also is important during collaboration and is pervasive when text is multimodal.

The field of composition and rhetoric has accomplished extensive work that is designed to move the definition of writing to include both discursive and non-discursive symbolic composition (Murray, 2009; Wysocki, et al., 2004; Selber, 2004; Fleckenstein, Calendrillo, & Worley, 2002; Kress & Van Leeuwen, 2001; Self, 1999; Lanham, 1993). Writing and composition programs in colleges all over the country are in the process of creating curricula that prepare contemporary students for workplaces that already are about creating well-designed, rhetorically appropriate textual products ranging from print-image hybrids to print-audio-video hybrids. Indeed, some schools include these kinds of curricula in their graphic design programs; at times, the lines between the two are no longer clear and may require some cross disciplinary collaboration. The overwhelming presence of the Internet has made it a necessity that textual products have the "ability to display information in appealing graphical interfaces, rather than text format," and that instructors and trainers must be able to understand online discourse to teach it (Austin, 2005; St. Amant & Zemliansky, 2005). Not only do students have to learn to write multimodal texts (and faculty are learning how to teach them to do this), but writers in the professional workplace often are offered only a very short time to address what can be a steep learning curve so that they also can compose in multiple modes.

Other scholars in fields as diverse as communications studies, cultural studies, and neuroscience agree that the cultural environment of today demands both a concerted effort to invent and understand the texts of tomorrow, but also to observe how older technologies are being remediated by newer ones. Bolter (2001) underscored this point as he emphasized how remediation throughout the history of writing often is mutual:

Print and prose have undergone remediations in the past, but the task may be more difficult today in the face of the cultural success of analog and now digital visual media. What is happening is a readjustment of the ratio between text and image in the various forms of print (books, magazines, newspapers, billboards), and the refashioning of prose itself in an attempt both to rival and to incorporate the visual image. Remediation can be, perhaps always is, mutual: older technologies remediate newer ones out of both enthusiasm and apprehension. (p. 48)

I would take Bolter's statement even further by saying that not only is the ratio between traditional printed text (that is, alpha centric texts) to visual image (for example, photos and graphics) changing, but the demand and rhetoricity of discursive text as a ratio to non-discursive text is reversing from the prevalence of the former to the prevalence of the latter. Although both types of symbolic language always have co-existed, the bias towards discursive text is lessening. Texts, and the composing of these texts, must include non-discursive modes.

Added to this focus on the non-discursive is a reminder that the texts that are produced are not fixed or static, and many new media texts become repurposed, rewritten, and even reinvented. Collaboration methods change when the texts being produced are assumed to be dynamic and interactive. As one collaborator interacts with another, another rhetorical dimension emerges as those collaborators realize the text itself will interact with other texts, other people, and even other cultures. The collaboration, on one hand, is an interaction between collaborators, but it must also take into account (to the degree possible) future interactions between the audience and the text because "electronic communication is increasingly the medium through which we form and maintain our affiliations" (Bolter, 2001). Collaborative interaction and textual interaction are both distributed, not centralized, and, as Chapter 19, emphasizes, so is the "responsibility for defining, promoting, and producing... without having to ask... permission." The distribution of authorship means, in turn, a distribution of power, and a distribution of power discourages singular authority, authenticity, or authorization. Today's virtual collaborative environments need to be ready to handle these complexities—complexities involving multiple writers using multiple modes of text—in order to aid both the process of collaboration itself as well as aid the invention of those texts in the first place. For example, if a collaborative environment does not allow for multiple writers to interact at the same time as they edit a video or produce an audio track, or if that environment does not help the writers anticipate how that product may be used, reconstructed, or rhetorically appropriated in the future, then that environment is not providing a rich enough tool set for the collaboration *by design*.

A concrete example of this may be found in the current fascination that some people have with the mash-up, especially video mash-ups created from movie trailers distributed online. Created (collaboratively, no doubt) to motivate viewers to buy a ticket at a movie theater, these video trailers are being rewritten most commonly through precise editing, changing the soundtrack, and modifying or altering completely the narration. Such rewriting is done as a way to revitalize text that normally has a very short life cycle while reversing (even conscripting) the typical marketing power dynamic between large corporations and small, savvy multimedia writers. Some are merely funny, some satirical, and some comment directly on current cultural issues and hierarchies. The genre-bending result of these mash-ups is found in texts that turn *Sleepless in Seattle* into a horror movie, or Steven King's *The Shining* into a romantic comedy, as found on the Web blog www.thetrailermash.com (and hosted on youtube.com). Figures 1 and 2 provide scenes from these mash-ups.

Even the header image for this blog is a remediation: the plush, deep red curtains of a movie theater or stage highlighted with spotlights are identified with the tagline "movie trailers, recut." This form is pervasive on the Web—on YouTube as well as personal pages such as The Trailer Mash—but there also are sponsored contests by gaming companies (Machinima for Ironman) and production houses (Lionsgate recently sponsored a mash-up contest for *Saw VI* as a way of promoting the film). My point is that the writers of these movie trailers must consider not only what content to put up on the Web to promote the films, but also what content may lend itself (or not) to being rewritten as a mash-up, either officially sanctioned or not. This type of text simply has different discursive and non-discursive demands placed on it during collaboration, and it is assumed the text will become appropriated and changed over time. Specifically, this type of collaboration requires the ability to strip audio from a video file, edit the order and duration of scenes, audition and edit new audio tracks (including, often, a new narrative track)—all while considering standard rhetorical concerns such as audience, style, and delivery (these files tend to stay small, allowing for wider distribution). Changing a horror film into a romantic comedy may be seen by some as a perversion of the original and a waste of talent, but it is also clear that such a change demonstrates the flexibility of symbols and the ability of images (in both sight and sound) to create meaning—in this case, meaning that is vastly different from what was intended by the original.

Figure 1. Mash-up of Sleepless in Seattle

Figure 2. Mash-up of The Shining

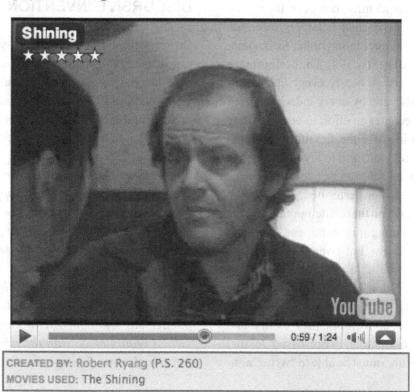

Figure 3. The Trailer Mash blog (www.thetrailermash.com) (header image)

Delivery, as one of the five canons of rhetoric, has always influenced the way a particular text ultimately appeals to an audience. In the case where delivery and performance are especially linked, the non-discursive elements of the text are especially crucial to its overall persuasiveness. According to Brooke, (2009): "Although we understand at some level the idea of performing a role or particular identity, however, the notion that discourse is performed is largely foreign... seeing discourse as circulating rather than some-*thing* that we circulate" (p. 192). The performance of the text differs with nearly every link, every click of the mouse, and by every individual user. Collaboration becomes an effort to open up these possibilities, to increase the flexibility of a text in both degree and kind, and to invent new ways to experience, persuade, and be persuaded by the text as it is delivered or performed.

There is no question that contemporary writers must know everything nineteenth and twentieth century writers knew, but twenty-first-century writers must also be able to compose non-discursive texts; indeed, many will find themselves primarily writing multimodal texts. Although collaborators must concern themselves first and foremost with discursive, word-based textual production, they also must be able to "write" non-

discursive texts in virtual environments, allowing them to collaborate and invent visual and aural texts as well (for example, photos, hypertexts, and film).

VIRTUAL COLLABORATION ENVIRONMENTS AND NON-DISCURSIVE INVENTION

In primarily addressing the quality of the collaboration itself (and not how the nature of the textual products may dictate a change in the collaboration), Clabby (2002) indicated that the problem of most virtual collaboration environments has to do with the amount and quality of sensory feedback:

The problem with collaborative applications in the past has been that collaborative applications have been one or two-dimensional. Real collaborative exercises had to be conducted in person in order to get all the sensory information needed to make decisions.... The new Sensory Virtual Internet is all about using additional technologies to provide collaborators with the ability to conduct joint intellectual and commercial engagements in a virtual reality mode with the added luxury of a full complement of sensory feedback.... The whole point of the Sensory Virtual Internet is to make it possible for us to use our computers to capture, relay, or present sensory data. We no longer have to be on site to gather this rich sensory information. (p. 286-7)

A virtual collaborative environment would need to improve the ability of collaborators to "conduct joint intellectual and commercial engagements in virtual reality" to be able to handle non-discursive as well as discursive collaboration. Collaborators who may be working on an image for the initial page of website that provides an interface with the public must be able to change key compositional components of that image, in near-real-time, while the system records the session and provides helpful cues based on past interactions, access to galleries of non-discursive content that is context sensitive, and various viewing and distribution options depending on the collaborative community working on the project. Each decision—the color of the background, the point-of-view of the image, what is blurred and what is in sharp focus, the composition of the main elements based on the rule-of-thirds (or not), and so on—has a rhetorical effect on the audience. Each decision must exist within a virtual environment that can "capture, relay, or present sensory data" beyond words.

Granted, most wikis and blogs allow for users to post graphics and photos for a team of collaborators to consider. But a truly rich, immersive virtual environment also would allow for the simultaneous, synchronous revisions and edits of these images, along with all the tools and resources possible. It is not enough for collaborators to do much of this work on their own, only to "collaborate" later by showing a finalized product for a thumbs-up or down vote by the others in the group. In this book, such collaboration would be termed "serial" in nature—if it is collaborative at all; I argue for the possibility of collective collaboration that engages virtual writing teams in the mutual construction of webtexts and other multimodal products. Levy (1998) anticipated this condition, noting that:

The text will always exist, but the page has been stripped of its significance. The page, the Latin pagus, blank field, territory enclosed by white margins, intersected by lines and sown with characters, is still weighed down by the Mesopotamian clay and clings to the Neolithic soil. This ancient page is slowly disappearing beneath the informational flood, its untethered signs carried away by the digital ocean. It is as if digitization were establishing a kind of immense semantic plane, accessible from anywhere, which each of us can help produce, manipulate, or modify. And yet—as if the point needed to be emphasized—the economic and legal forms inherited from previous centuries prevent the movement of deterritorialization from reaching its fulfillment.... The same analysis could be applied to images, which virtually constitute a single hypericon, boundless, kaleidoscopic, growing, subject to a multitude of chimeras. (p. 54)

The print-based page is being replaced by the computer screen, and what writers create may create best on a screen. The images and sound in a film are pieced together through thousands of edits, each a subjective (if not aesthetic) decision, each with rhetorical ramifications. If such a product must be composed collaboratively through a virtual environment, how would it be done? What software or website would you use to co-edit a film with a colleague located hundreds of miles away?

Virtual editing of such a complex multimodal product requires much from a virtual environment. Not only is the environment dispersed in dimensions such as time, geography, and culture (Zigurs & Khazanchi, 2008), but the discursive and non-discursive textual elements are also dispersed across modes and modalities. Such editing across time and space must account not only for the compositional possibilities and complexities of words, but equally the compositional possibilities of image. This kind of computer supported collaborative work (CSCW) not only requires a huge disparity between people and places, but also between discursive and non-discursive texts, perhaps even necessitating the creation of new genres and cultural objects (Oravec, 1996). The video and audio mash-ups are new cross-genre products that apparently were not predicted although music remixes have existed for years; interestingly millions of people now experience them every hour. What new filmic or hypertextual products and genres are not being invented or produced right now because collaboration of non-discursive texts in virtual environments is discouraged or made difficult simply because the interfaces are slow to adopt multimodal, multi-sensory affordances into their designs?

One virtual environment that seems to be addressing some of these issues comes from the open-source software movement, specifically Google Docs™ and SketchUp™. Although the Google's SketchUp™ platform is not synchronous, and even though it does not have a stocked library of non-discursive invention aides, this platform allows for the virtual collaboration of non-traditional text: in particular, drawings. As part of the Google Docs™ suite of software, SketchUp™ allows for some basic 2-D and 3-D renderings that are fairly intuitive and allow for some basic animation (slide shows and fly-throughs). Collaborators incrementally can invent basic animations (such as dynamic logos or animated "rooms" or libraries of information) and then export the final ideas as sketches to be

presented to decision-makers before the allocation of any significant resources. According to Jongh (2006), the Pro version of SketchUp™ allows for more advanced features, including exporting files into more sophisticated software formats such as virtual reality markup language (VRML). The advantages to collaborating using something like this over advanced software like Photoshop® is that (1) it is available at no cost to all collaborators via Google™ and (2) the files can be stored via Google Docs™ and shared with online collaborators. Unfortunately, such a system would not help collaborators who wish to work together on more complex, hybridized non-discursive products that use animation beyond the fly-over or slideshow or for film/video because the software is not built for that level of time line editing. But this product does allow for several users to make choices and communicate those choices simultaneously over time and space.

Another class of products that allow for some virtual collaboration of non-discursive texts is that which enables users to share their entire desktop in near-real time, such as Apple's iChat™, Hewlett Packard's Remote Graphics Software™ (RGS), and Elluminate Live™ from Elluminate, Inc. (among others that increasingly are becoming available). These online collaboration platforms allow users to share the same space at the same time, see each other's desktops, and even share applications on various desktops being viewed

Figure 4. Three online collaboration platforms for synchronous collaboration: Apple's iChat™, HP's RGS™, and Elluminate Live™

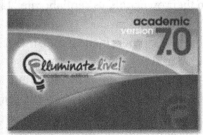

by the team. Some of these platforms enable multiple users to share keyboard control, which, in essence, allows one person to try out ideas that another person may have started. They enable idea development collaboration by sharing the desktop with the entire writing team in the manner of a virtual blackboard, which allows participants to interact and alter the idea in whatever way the group agrees to allow. Sessions can be recorded and then played back whenever collaborators want, allowing not only for the possibility of perusing several possible design ideas at once, but also for reflective practice on collaboration efficacy.

Specifically, it is possible to use software like Elluminate Live to have several people work and edit a storyboard for a film, an image for the background of a website, some music being used during an opening sequence of a documentary, or even various possible editing choices of images and/or video being used in hybrid multimedia products. Although such a service is not free, some institutions and organizations already subscribe to these systems and allow for a certain number of hours of pre-paid collaboration for set time periods. Even when a site or individual license for such a system has to be purchased, it is possible that the final cost will be more manageable than what face-to-face collaboration may cost a geographically dispersed team. As Levy (1998) stated: "Just as the virtualization of text implies the growing confusion between the roles of reader and author, the virtualization of the market highlights the convergence of consumption and production" (p. 81). As with movie trailers, there is no way of telling how recorded sessions of collaboration that occurred in the act of production may itself become consumable, possibly to be mashed-up in various alternate compositions long after the immediate purpose of the collaboration is itself complete.

As hybridized multimodal texts become more and more the norm, what will be different from our print-dominated history is that the ef-

fort that went into producing texts is no longer as ephemeral, or transient, as it once was. Such efforts could themselves be consumed—either as a way to facilitate future collaboration or as a type of "mash-up" product themselves (as might be evidenced in "extras" like behind-the-scenes video, outtakes, and interviews included in the way DVDs currently are marketed). In addition, the transparency taken for granted (and even promoted) by most software interfaces and collaborative environments necessarily may need to be reassessed because what this transparency may be assuming is the continual production of monomodal, discursive text by a single writer for a static product. The cultural and technical assumptions these interfaces include directly affect how those artifacts are viewed and used during the textual invention. For example, if a collaborative interface allows for 100 options to edit or manipulate words, but only five to ten options are available to manipulate images or sound, then that interface is both assuming word-based textual invention as well as production. If, on the other hand, an interface allows for the editing of dynamic images and sounds as well, then that interface may be taking into account the way textual production and collaboration is changing. As writers struggle with questions across spaces and across past, present, and future timeframes, how are the current interfaces necessarily limiting what gets produced? Bolter and Gromala (2003) indirectly answered this question:

Designers must also bear in mind that the strategy of transparency, although popular, is not the only one available to them.... This is the most important lesson, perhaps, that digital art has to offer digital design: an interface can not only be a window but also a mirror, reflecting its user. (p. 56)

As interfaces such as iChat™, Elluminate Live™, and RPS™ are used in virtual collaboration, they reflect as well as reveal. Like any cultural artifact, software systems reveal assumptions by designers, by an industry, and by the technologies employed or available. A quick reflection of consumer software from the 1980s to present day may illustrate how composition in part has been dictated by what the tools allowed people to invent in the first place—an observation that can carry itself back to the adoption of the printing press, the alphabet, and papyrus (Bolter, 1999). Even within a single software platform like Microsoft® Word, it is clear that the modes of text that users would be inventing has changed from nearly exclusively discursive texts with the occasional pie chart or bar graph to a much richer, more multimodal, non-discursive texts with new tools for collaboration, layouts, and the editing/embedding of images and video.

INVENTING COLLABORATION: SOME RECOMMENDATIONS

Clearly, the problem is not just about how writers will collaborate in virtual environments; the problem also is how people will create multimodal, multimedia texts in these environments, from invention to distribution. Collaborating writers must acknowledge the importance of consciously developing a culture of collaboration (Principle 1, Chapter 1) to accomplish the myriad of tasks needed for non-discursive texts: everything from choosing suitable graphics, colors, and photos (McKay, 2008), to enhancing the quality of the explanatory power of illustrations and animations through CAD data (Meloni, 2008), to 3D visualization using remote personal interfaces (Aspin, 2007). Writers also must acknowledge the complex and computing-reliant nature of e-communication in schools, in public, and in workplaces.

Every day, writers employ software and hardware systems to work on these types of text, but few of these systems have collaboration features that offer immediate, real-time, multisensory experiences. Choosing and using tools effectively, therefore, becomes vital to the process (see Principle 4, Chapter 1). Interfaces, as they are developed, tested in the marketplace, and used in virtual collaboration environments benefit from rigorous investigation of the assumptions within the choices that are or are not present—from the modality of texts being assumed, to the nature of the temporal environment within which texts are being invented, to the limitations and possibilities of collaboration being directly or indirectly encouraged.

In order to invent non-discursive texts in collaborative environments—either through their interfaces or through what interfaces those environments allow—I recommend maximizing the following values:

Non-Discursive Affordances

The environment not only allows for, but also encourages, the invention of multimodal texts of a multi-sensory nature. To the degree technologically possible, writers may invent not only words through the keyboard, but visual images, sounds, tastes, and other modes of text at least as easily as words. Interfaces constructed without a built-in discursive bias will allow for the free invention of non-traditional texts without penalty of speed, ease of use, or number of options available.

Non-Discursive Resources

Just as modern discursive collaborative tools may help users organize, view, and record separate versions of the same text, so too must non-discursive collaborative tools. Historical (or tracked) versions of the invented non-discursive text would be a valuable collaborative tool as writers negotiate among various versions of the same image, same track of audio, or same edited version of film. In addition, to the extent possible, non-discursive resources also may contain various libraries of images, sounds, videos, for example, for writers to use as blanks, or sketches, for storyboard ideas, rough drafts, or models.

Aids in Post-Production Elements

As shown in the mash-up examples, collaborators of digital texts with multiple writers must assume alternate uses of the material they invent and construct. Like movie trailers, whatever gets posted online or made available digitally one day may become another cultural artifact, and rather than resisting or insisting on a static final product, composers need resources that will help them compose how elements may be rewritten or re-appropriated. For example, if the collaborative environment helps the writers offer elements for rewriting, then the product itself could mark or isolate those elements as a secondary feature of the multimedia product.

Aids for Multiple Writers Working Simultaneously

As writers collaborate, they need tools to help them work with multiple modes simultaneously. This means not only being able to edit, say, an image at the same time, but to allow more than one writer to edit an image at the same time. The aids also might allow for various options for simultaneity, allowing one writer to work on a certain area while other work on another, or a certain time-frame, such as the first five minutes of a video while other team members work on the next five minutes. Not only will writers need to invent from different places at different times, but they need to invent from the same place at the same time.

CONCLUSION

Traditional textual collaboration has moved toward a more synchronous, virtual engagement, and as such, its primary emphasis has been on the collaborator's experience within the collaboration: how well the collaborators can interact and how often. What is needed now is a similar movement towards a more synchronous, media rich collaboration of non-traditional texts. Collaborating writers seem not to be much further into immersive virtual collaboration of non-discursive text than where Clabby (2002) observed:

At this stage in the development of the Sensory Virtual Internet, collaborative applications are largely text-based workflow type applications, videoconferencing, or e-learning-related.... However, the big changes that need to take place to enable collaborative collocation applications that include rich, sensory-enabled sight, sound, touch, scent, and taste are still a few years away. (p. 69)

Even at the time of this writing, fully immersive collaboration for multisensory invention in virtual collaboration seems fantastical. But if the technology is limiting what texts are produced and how, the attitudes and perspectives that virtual collaborative writers have about the distributed and dynamic nature of image-based, affective text in the digital realm need not be limiting; together we can invent what it means to collaborate virtually in the twenty-first century.

REFERENCES

Apple, Inc. (2009). *"iChat"* [Photo]. Retrieved August 3, 2009, from http://www.apple.com/macosx/what-is-macosx/ichat.html

Aspin, R. (2007). Supporting collaboration, in colocated 3D visualization, through the use of remote personal interfaces. *Journal of Computing in Civil Engineering, 21*(6), 393–401. doi:10.1061/(ASCE)0887-3801(2007)21:6(393)

Austin, W. W. (2005). *Hypertext theory and Web writing assignments in the writing and professional communication classroom. Internet-based workplace communications: Industry & academic applications* (pp. 24–39). Hershey, PA: Information Science.

Bolter, J. (2001). *Writing space: Computers, hypertext, and the remediation of print* (2nd ed.). Mahwah, NJ: Lawrence Erlbaum Associates, Publishers.

Bolter, J., & Gromala, D. (2003). *Windows and mirrors: Interaction design, digital art, and the myth of transparency.* Cambridge, MA: MIT Press.

Brooke, C. (2009). *Lingua fracta: Toward a rhetoric of new media.* Mahwah, NJ: Hampton Press, Inc.

Clabby, J. (2002). *Visualize this: Collaboration, communication & commerce in the 21st century.* Upper Saddle River, NJ: Prentice Hall PTR.

Elluminate, Inc. (n.d.). *Elluminate Live* [Photo]. Retrieved August 3, 2009, from www.elluminate. com/ products/els/v95/index.jsp

Fleckenstein, K., Calenrillo, L. T., & Worley, D. A. (2002). *Language and image in the reading-writing classroom.* Mahwah, NJ: Lawrence Erlbaum Associates.

Hewlett-Packard Development Company. L.P. (2009). *HP remote graphics software* [Photo]. Retrieved August 3, 2009, from http://h20331.www2. hp.com/hpsub/cache/286504-0-0-225-121.html

Jongh, R. de (2006, Oct 26). Sketching software captures AEC ideas fast. *Machine Design*, 102-105.

Kock, N., & Garza, V. (2008). The ape that used email: An evolutionary perspective on e-communication behavior. In Kock, N. (Ed.), *E-collaboration in modern organizations: Initiating and managing distributed projects* (pp. 242–254). Hershey, PA: IGI Global.

Kress, G., & Leeuwen, T. (2001). *Multimodal discourse: The modes and media of contemporary communication.* London: Oxford UP.

Langer, S. K. (1942). Philosophy in a new key: A study in the symbolism of reason, rite, and art, (pp. 3rd ed.). Cambridge, MA: Harvard University Press.

Lanham, R. (1993). *The electronic word: Democracy, technology, and the arts.* Chicago: U of Chicago P.

Levy, P. (1998). *Becoming virtual: Reality in the digital age* (Bononno, R., Trans.). New York: Plenum Trade.

Lyall-Wilson, D. (2006). "Sleepless in Seattle (horror)" [Film]. *The Trailer Mash.* Retrieved August 3, 2009, from http://www.thetrailermash. com/sleepless-in-seattle-horror/

McKay, E. (2008). *The human-dimensions of human-computer interaction: Balancing the HCI equation.* Washington, DC: IOS Press.

Meloni, W. (2008). Maximizing the design process. *Computer Graphics World*, *31*(1), 32–36.

Murray, J. (2209). *Non-discursive rhetoric: Image and affect in multimodal composition.* Albany: SUNY P.

Oravec, J. A. (1996). *Virtual individuals, virtual groups: Human dimensions of groupware and computer networking.* New York: Cambridge UP.

Ryang, R. (2006). "Shining Romantic Comedy" [Film]. *The Trailer Mash.* Retrieved August 3, 2009, from http://www.thetrailermash.com/ shining-romantic-comedy/

Selber, S. (2004). *Multiliteracies for a digital age.* Carbondale, IL: Southern Illinois P.

Selfe, C. L. (1999). *Technology and literacy in the 21st century: The importance of paying attention.* Carbondale, IL: Southern Illinois P.

St.Amant, K., & Zemliansky, P. (2005). *Internet-based workplace communications: Industry & academic applications.* Hershey, PA: Information Science Reference.

Wysocki, A. F., Johnson-Eilola, J., Selfe, C. L., & Sirc, G. *Writing new media: Theory and applications for expanding the teaching of composition.* Logan, UT: Utah State UP.

Zigurs, I., & Khazanchi, D. (2008). Applying pattern theory in the effective management of virtual projects. In Kock, N. (Ed.), *E-collaboration in modern organizations: Initiating and managing distributed projects* (pp. 315–334). Hershey, PA: IGI Global.

Chapter 21
The Mutual Presence of RP–7 and the Future of Virtual Collaborative Writing

David W. Overbey
Bellarmine University, USA

ABSTRACT

This chapter examines virtual collaboration, including the production and use of writing, between doctors at different hospitals mediated by RP-7, a robot that enables a specialist at one hospital to evaluate the vital signs of and provide diagnosis for a patient at another hospital. Analysis of RP-7 is situated in a theoretical deliberation about the shift from print to digital texts and technologies. I argue that a consequence of this shift is the loss of mutual presence—the alignment of materiality, practice, and expertise—in the production and use of texts. This alignment is transparent and intrinsic to print texts but is lost in digital environments precisely because they afford access to texts irrespective of a user's background, location, or access to and familiarity with other tools, technologies, or workplaces. Study of the writing used and generated during the collaboration between doctors mediated by RP-7 is grounds for the claim that the future of virtual collaborative writing in professional contexts will involve the re-alignment of mutual presence. In other words, the success of digital writing technologies in social practice will depend on the extent to which they bare similarity to, rather than differ from, print texts and technologies. The chapter concludes by emphasizing the value of this research to both academia and industry.

INTRODUCTION

A recent front page article in the Sunday *New York Times* (Lewin, 2009) captured a prevailing perspective on digital communication technologies. Lewin's

DOI: 10.4018/978-1-60566-994-6.ch021

article depicted the future as one that is exclusively digital, a departure from the materially-bound, print-based texts common to workplace and educational settings for centuries. A simple contrast represents digital texts literally as the "future," while print texts are "history." There are at least two important oversights that this binary perspective perpetuates.

One is that print texts—like the "textbook"—are soon to be a thing of the past. The second is that the complexity and dynamic quality of print texts are greatly oversimplified.

Lewin quoted Sheryl R. Abshire, the chief technology officer for the Calcasieu Parrish school system in Lake Charles, LA: "Kids are wired differently these days. They're digitally nimble. They multitask, transpose, and extrapolate. And they think of knowledge as infinite." She then drew a simple contrast to the print qualities of textbooks, saying that students "don't engage with textbooks that are finite, linear, and rote," adding that teachers need to get "beyond the plain vanilla curriculum in the textbooks." Later, Lewin cited California Gov. Arnold Schwarzenegger as describing textbooks as "antiquated."

This contrast between digital and print texts, one apparently entrenched not only in popular culture but also education and government, paints digital texts as superior to print ones. Digital texts open up knowledge as "infinite" and interactive, while print texts are "plain," and outdated. Never mind, for the moment, that the discoveries and inventions of Galileo were mediated and constructed by print texts, or that Newton formulated the principles of calculus without the aid of computers, software, or Wikipedia. And one has to wonder how Abshire would respond to the fact that three-hundred years ago, while making engravings of art and poetry, Blake wrote, "when the doors of perception are cleansed, all appears as it is, infinite" (Blake, 1997).

The assumptions about the relationship between digital and print texts articulated in the Lewin (2009) article are a microcosm of widespread beliefs in both scholarly and popular circles. The crux of these assumptions is that digital texts are both "new" and that print texts are archaic and replaceable. Crystal (2006), for example argued that Internet users have developed an entirely new language called "Netspeak." This perception of digital communication is one that sees it as a break from print-mediated communication, rather than an extension on a larger continuum of mediated communication. Again, the notion that digital media are a clear break from print media and the past is the basis for the belief that print media are replaceable. In popular literature, similar claims are made: "The Net is controlled by no one; no is in charge... The users of this media are creating an entirely new writing space, far different from that carved out by the printed book," wrote Kelly. He continued, "Net writing is of a conversational, peer-to-peer style, frank and communicative, rather than precise and self-consciously literary." The rigid contrast Kelly depicted of digital and print media exemplifies a popular and growing mentality that digital media are "entirely new," and that writing which occurs in this space is altogether different from that which occurs in print media, which are implicitly associated with the caveman days, as that kind of writing is "carved out of the printed book," in the manner a Neanderthal might carve out of drawing on a cave wall.

The primary argument of this chapter is a challenge to these prevailing views on the relationship between digital and print texts: the future success of digital texts and technologies in industry and academia will depend on how well they make up for what has been lost in the transition from print to digital media, not how different or "revolutionary" digital media may be in comparison to print. The critical variable that has been lost in this transition is *mutual presence*, which I define as the alignment of materiality, practice, and expertise in the production and use of texts. In what follows, I demonstrate through the example of the RP-7 robot how medical practice makes up for this loss through the robot's physical presence in a hospital room, which aligns a digital network with the medical expertise of doctors.

My argument is especially important for the future of virtual collaborative writing because it challenges practitioners to question prevailing views on the relationships between digital and print texts, such as the one Lewin (2009) reported. Assumptions that practitioners of virtual collaborative writing have about the relationship between print and digital texts will determine how they design and implement technologies for virtual collaborative writing in the future. This focus on the RP-7 robot also encourages practitioners of virtual collaborative writing to realize there is a different between how digital environments work in casual social networks versus professional workplace settings like hospitals where expertise and timely performance is critical.

Preliminary Remarks

I wish to make it clear to the reader here at the beginning what my positions are on print and digital media to avoid possible misunderstanding. First, I do not intend to argue that either medium is better than the other. However, fundamental differences between print and digital texts exist, which means that the latter cannot be a wholesale replacement of the former, as popular opinions often express. The overriding concern that motivates the research and argument in this chapter is the widespread assumption that digital media can replace print media, and by extension, that print media are old fashioned and on the way to obsolescence. A likely outcome of such an assumption is the unfortunate tendency to ignore or dismiss print media as the world and workplace become increasingly digital rather to study and learn about how print media work from the standpoint that digital media exist in a continuum of media in general as opposed to representing a break from an "older" or out-dated type of media. That print and digital media are different does not mean that digital media are better than print media. On the contrary, as I explain in this chapter, digital media lack certain qualities endemic to print media that are rhetorically vital to how all media convey meaning. Thus, the future success of digital media—particularly in professional workplace settings—will require adapting qualities inherent to print media to the design and implementation of digital media.

There are at least two fundamental differences between print and digital media. One is that print media always are situated in a precise location, and that location plays a critical rhetorical role in how print media are interpreted and in turn figure into organized human behavior. Standing at a street corner illustrates this point. Signs that communicate the location and type of businesses in the area and traffic signs that demarcate street names and rules of the road mean what they do because of where they are and for whom and at what moment they are present. Digital media—and the digital texts they transmit—are not anchored to a specific location. I can access the wiki used in the production of this book from Edinburgh, Scotland or my office in Louisville, Kentucky, and my location or the location of the wiki makes no difference as to how I interpret it or put it to use. Advocates of digital media regularly draw attention to the "speed and ease of use" (Haas and Wearden, 2004) technologies like the Web afford users who do not have to mobilize to a certain location in order to access information. But expert performance in the professions requires more than just access to information, and this point underscores the pitfall of assuming digital media can integrated into the workplace without attention to how they differ from print media and what has been lost in the transition from print to digital media.

The second main difference between print and digital media is the range and amount of content that the texts transmit. Print texts inherently communicate a limited amount of content, and that content always corresponds to the materiality of the print media that transmits it. This is not the case with digital media. The kindle, for example, does not correspond to any particular text, and the range and amount of text it potentially could transmit is endless. The danger, again, is to assume that digital media are superior because they can transmit any conceivable type and range of texts, whereas print media are constrained to a limited type and range of content. But as I assert in this chapter, professionals do not need an endless array of content when confronting workplace problem-solving situations. They need a narrow range of content that precisely addresses the task that is their focus. The challenge is to harness the capabilities of digital technology and at the same time adapt the constraining qualities of print media and the boundaries print texts place around a range of content. My position is that the RP-7 serves as a model for future VCW technologies because it meets this challenge.

Mutual Presence and the Production and Use of Print Texts

What is at stake here is the perception of the relationship between digital and print texts, as well as the implications this perception has for the future of virtual collaborative writing and the digital technologies that mediate it. The ways in which print texts have operated for centuries—both in terms of their production and use—are fundamental to how humans use and interact with any kind of text, whether print or digital, and these fundamentals cannot be by-passed simply because texts now exist in a digital, non-material form. The text as a human construct is super-ordinate to the forms in which it comes and operates.

The oversimplified contrast reported in Lewin's article and countless other publications ignores this proposition, insisting that digital texts can offer a clear break from print texts and, by extension, the artifact "text" as a general classification. Hence, the digital text versus print text binary fails to realize that (1) print texts, which have been vital to human performance in social practice for centuries, no sooner will disappear than the physical, material world in which humans live and work, and (2) far from being "plain" and "finite," print texts are highly complex and varied in how they communicate and mediate the "generative" and inter-textual meaning-making processes (Witte, 1992) that have been a funda-

mental component of human cognition in modern times. The problem is that the complexity and variation of print texts and how they operate in human performance are transparent—and it is only through studying their differences to digital texts that these qualities of print texts become apparent and their value understood. Mutual presence explains how these transparent qualities become operational in the production and use of texts, specifically the constraining effects they have on how texts are comprehended, interpreted, and put to use in everyday life. The stop sign illustrates mutual presence. Its materiality—the octagonal shape, red color, and physical location determine what that sign means and for whom it means what it does as much as the word *stop*. The sign really means for cars to stop parallel to where the sign is, not just when drivers see the word. And it also means that cars should stop—not pedestrians. It also means that drivers should stop their cars rather than for people in general to stop whatever it is they might be doing at the moment—talking, listening to music, reading a book. As this chapter explains, stop signs—because they are print texts—can create meaning in ways that are highly specific to a certain situation that people could not understand unless they were participants in that situation, even if it is hard to think of a text more simple than "STOP."

A Reconsideration of Prevailing Perspectives on Digital Texts

The discussion of the RP-7 robot presented in this chapter looks at a specific question critical to workplace literacy in digital environments: what happens when communication technologies change from print to digital, and by extension, what are the potential rhetorical consequences of a shift from print to digital texts? These questions and their potential answers are important to virtual collaborative writers because through examination of digital technologies like RP-7, they can identify how such technologies operate successfully in professional situations where the stakes are high, and thus have some theoretical perspective on how the future of virtual collaborative writing could or should develop. Without attention to specific digital technologies like RP-7, the future of virtual collaborative writing risks setbacks due to unexamined assumptions about and oversimplifications concerning the qualities of digital texts in comparison to print. To reiterate the earlier point, contrary to the assertions made in the *Times* article, I believe that the success and effectiveness of digital texts will not rest on how different they are from print texts but on their capacity to adapt the intrinsic qualities of print texts to digital environments. In other words, they will have to make up for the loss of mutual presence in the transition from print to digital texts. This position is an opposing perspective to the notion that the value and promise of digital texts derive from the ways in which they are *not* like print texts. Instead, I argue that digital environments will have to bridge the gap between digital and print texts rather than increase the distance between them. To illustrate this point, this chapter will focus on the practice of medicine and the RP-7, a robot that mediates interaction between a specialist doctor at one hospital and a patient and doctors at another hospital. My argument is that the success and effectiveness of the RP-7 robot (hereafter called *RP-7*) and the future of virtual collaborative technologies involves making up for what has been lost in the shift from print to digital texts.

Key Terms

Before turning to RP-7, the terms *materiality*, *practice*, and *expertise* must be defined in relation to one another in order to reinforce how their alignment affects mutual presence.

Materiality

Materiality is defined here as the physical presence of a text in a certain location as well as the physical features that distinguish different kinds of texts from one another (for example, an eye chart in an optometrist's office, road sign on the highway, license plate on a vehicle, tape measure at a construction site, case law book in a court room, menu at a restaurant, business marquee in proximity to that respective business, the number and color or stripe of a billiard ball on a billiard table, a tag with a button on it attached to a shirt, a travel map folded up to fit in the pocket of a mountain hiker). The size and shape of these texts makes them compatible with the activity in which they are situated and for which they have been designed.

The materiality of print texts gives them an inherent nondiscursive quality, a quality that digital texts, being non-material, cannot replicate (see Chapter 20). A common, everyday example of the nondiscursive quality of print texts would be the signs on buildings and vehicles that identify them. One does not identify buildings or vehicles exclusively through the linguistic content that announces what they are but also through recognition of their material size, shape, and location. For example, a sign on a building that reads, "Dave's Seafood" really means "Dave's seafood is here in this building"—it is not merely communicating the two words that comprise the sign. The same can be said for signs one sees on trucks along the interstate. These signs communicate that the truck itself is associated with a certain business or service. In both cases, the building that houses a restaurant and the truck that transports products and materials provide a transparent nondiscursive context for interpreting and comprehending the words they display.

Practice

The physical features of these texts play a vital role in constraining how they are interpreted because they immediately cue readers as to the *practice* in which they are situated, such as medicine, optometry, engineering, law, athletics, and business. Print texts convey their meaning not just through their linguistic content but also through the workplace corresponding with the practice in which they are situated, such as the optometrist's office, court room, hospital, restaurant, construction site, or other workplace.

Expertise

This physical location of print texts in workplaces that correspond with a specific practice aligns them with individuals who are co-present who bring *expertise* to the reading and interpretation of these texts. This alignment plays a generative and constraining role in how individuals comprehend these texts (for example, a doctor reading vital signs, a bartender receiving drink orders, basketball players huddled around a coach who is drawing up a play). Expertise is not limited to the specialized knowledge of professionals in social practice but extends to anyone participating in a specific event at a precise location, such as fans at a sporting event, mountain hikers reading signs along the trail, travelers negotiating their way through airports or train stations. Expertise is a vital component of context—what makes sense to whom, where, and when.

RP-7 AND THE RE-ALIGNMENT OF MUTUAL PRESENCE IN DIGITAL WORKPLACE ENVIRONMENTS

RP-7 is a robot in a medical setting that uses a "secured wireless, broadband, internet connection" to connect a specialist doctor from one hospital to patients and doctors at another hospital. The University of Louisville hospital explained that the RP-7 provides "remote physician presence" that makes the "expertise of our medical faculty" accessible to patients at other hospitals in the Commonwealth of Kentucky (www.uoflhealthcare. org). The use of the terms *presence* and *expertise* strongly support the idea that digital environments need to re-create mutual presence to be adapted

Figure 1. Dr. Kerri Remmel making rounds

successfully to social practice: materiality (RP-7), practice (medicine), and expertise (medical faculty). The RP-7 demonstrates that digital environments cannot bypass expertise and the workplace setting that corresponds with that expertise (for example, medical specialists and the facilities those specialists use to treat patients). Not only is the RP-7 vital to sustaining expertise in patient care, but its physical characteristics also mimic the embodied presence of a doctor. Figures 1, 2, and 3 provide a way to imagine this simulated presence.

Beginning with Figure 1, Dr. Kerri Remmel is the face in the monitor of the RP-7. Most obvious in this image is the monitor at the top of the robot through which the doctor can see and talk to the patient; it is a monitor in proportion to the

Figure 2. Dr. Remmel collaborates with doctors at another hospital

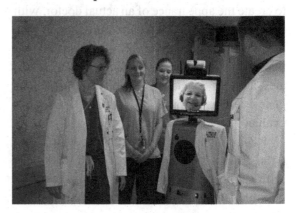

Figure 3. RP-7 mediates another specialist collaborating in emergency care

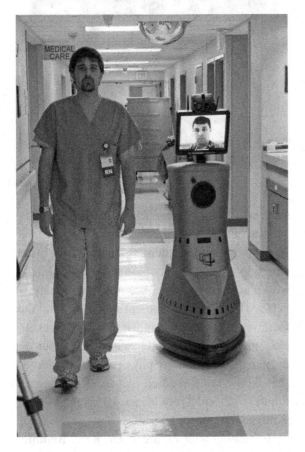

size of her head. In Figure 2, Dr. Remmel interacts and collaborates with doctors at another hospital. In Figure 3, the robot's 5'6" approximates the average height of a human body. Dressed in a clinician's trademark white jacket and with a stethoscope draped around its neck; RP-7 attempts to create the appearance of an actual doctor, with the hope of making the patient's interaction with the mediated doctor a familiar experience, rather than an alienating one. In this image, RP-7 mediates another specialist collaborating in emergency care as it travels to a patient's room for evaluation and treatment.

RP-7 connects a digital environment to a material artifact located in a specialized workplace setting. The digital environment that makes RP-7 possible facilitates the presence, rather than by-passing, of the medical expertise of a physician. RP-7 gives a materiality to a digital environment that in turn provides a structure and modality (Chartier, 1994) to what the doctor reads and the patient hears. In so doing, RP-7 re-creates, or re-aligns the mutual presence that typically is missing in a virtual or computer-mediated setting. The result is the optimum probability that the specialist doctor at University of Louisville hospital and the patient and doctors at the other hospital will achieve an "adherence of minds" (Perelman, 1969) concerning diagnosis and treatment for the patient.

RP-7 and the Future of Virtual Collaborative Writing

A study of RP-7 provides numerous valuable observations about the role that virtual collaborative writing plays in workplace environments and implications concerning how digital technologies are adapted to social practice. While the writing that is used and produced in conjunction with RP-7 is nothing out of the ordinary in medical practice—follow-up reports on patient treatment, and the reading of diagnostic information and vital signs—the contexts of use and production in which this writing is situated reveal how digital environments are successfully adapted to social practice. In turn, these contexts provide cues as to how the dynamics of virtual collaborative writing will operate in the future. RP-7 is a valuable unit of analysis (Haas and Witte, 2005; see also Chapter 2) for the study of virtual collaborative writing.

First, RP-7 plays a potentially life-saving role in the timing of when writing is used and produced. By putting a stroke victim in direct (though mediated) contact with a stroke specialist at another hospital, the patient's diagnostic chart and vital signs are read and interpreted by an expert more quickly than if the patient had to be flown from one hospital to another, or if the specialist doctor had to rely on the reading and interpretation of these texts by another doctor who did not have the same level of expertise. As the specialist doctor explains, when it comes to the treatment of stroke victims "time saved is brain saved" (www. uoflhealthcare.org). The crucial rhetorical variable here is *kairos*, the role of timing and proportion in human performance. RP-7 expedites the use and production of writing with potentially life-saving consequences. This same principal applies to the writing the specialist doctor produces in collaboration with the doctors at the patient's hospital to document the patient's condition and update diagnosis and treatment.

In addition, RP-7 demonstrates that virtual collaborative writing comes out of oral contexts of production that also are virtual and collaborative. The conversations that the specialist doctor has with the patient and other doctors at the other hospital are inseparable from the reading and writing that doctors perform over the course of patient treatment mediated by RP-7. Figure 4, for example, shows a version of the screen that the stroke specialist at University of Louisville

hospital uses while operating RP-7. Note that at the bottom left there is a mini-screen where the doctor with her headset on is shown. This headset mediates oral communication with the patient and doctor at another hospital. The rest of the content on the screen consists of visual displays of information concerning the patient's vital signs, including the monitor at the patient's room at the top center. This monitor demonstrates how the virtual collaborative writing generated by the interface of monitors at two different hospitals integrates simultaneously with virtual collaborative speech.

In pre-technological or pre-digital collaborative writing, the oral contexts of production out of which the writing was generated likely were face-to-face. Because the technologies that mediate virtual collaborative writing are multi-modal, they also mediate oral discourse. Thus, the production and use of virtual collaborative writing likely will be tied increasingly to virtual collaborative oral communication involving the same participants. Before the digital era, communication

Figure 4. The multi-modal screen of RP-7. Note that the doctor operating RP-7 is in the bottom left screen

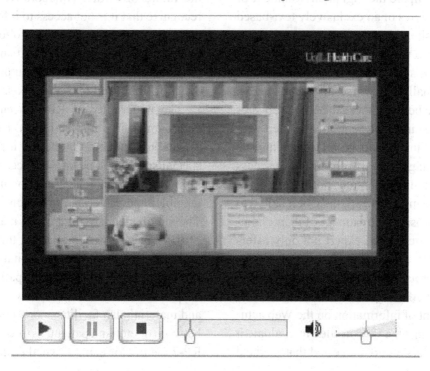

technologies were confined to either speech (that is, tape recorder, telephone, radio) or writing (that is, typewriter, word processor, pencil and paper). With the convergence of these modes of communication in multi-modal technologies, virtual collaborative speech and writing increasingly will become interdependent, both because of the necessity to bring together collaborators from increasingly distant locales and the affordance of the multi-modal technologies to mediate their collaboration as both interlocutors and writers.

Based on these observations, I would predict that in both virtual collaborative speech and writing, alignment of specialized texts with experts situated in workplaces that correspond to the experts' practice will involve a physical, material technology akin to RP-7 that will re-embody the experts. Such grounding of digital collaboration reinforces the position that access to digitally mediated writing is insufficient for coherent, effective communication—especially in highly complex and specialized workplace contexts. The point is that one needs access to more than the text to have access to the text. To illustrate this point, I compare the digital environment of RP-7 to the failures of an exclusively text-based medical Web site.

According to Gupta (2004), individuals who sought diagnosis and treatment from medical Web sites actually got worse instead of better. The difference between these medical Web sites and RP-7 is the mutual presence of an expert with the person seeking diagnosis and treatment. The people consulting medical Web sites have access only to texts and information, not expertise, or the appropriate medical workplace best suited to facilitate diagnosis and treatment of their condition. The presence of the expert not only offers specialized knowledge but a way to constrain the information through which the user of a medical Web site must sift. Burbules (2001) argued that the vast amount of information on the Web actually works against the time needed to evaluate it carefully. Gupta's report suggested that medical

Web sites fail to help patients get better because of this paradox. The absence of medical expertise probably explains the difference between "well-developed knowledge on a medical issue and just having load of information" (Gupta, 2004, p. 48).

This report on medical Web sites that are exclusively text and information based illustrates a stark contrast to RP-7, which situates texts and information in a context of expertise mediated by medical specialists in a setting optimally designed for a specific kind of medical treatment. Thus, the future of virtual collaborative writing will not only involve multi-modal contexts of use and production of writing, they also will provide vital constraints to what would otherwise be an unwieldy mass of information accessed by people who lack both expert guidance and the attendant technologies necessary for successful practice, medical or otherwise. The future of virtual collaborative writing will move away from the popular appeal of easy access to a great deal of information to exclusive access to limited information that is relevant to the problem-solving contexts that make expertise vital to social practice. In other words, the future of virtual collaborative writing will recognize that it is not access to information, but expertise that counts most. The following section reinforces the major points that demonstrate how RP-7 makes up for the loss of mutual presence in the shift from print to digital texts.

The materiality of RP-7 grounds a digital environment in a material form. RP-7 creates a digital environment that makes it possible for a specialist doctor to be in two places at once; at the same time, it makes that environment physical, tangible, and material—not exclusively digital. The simultaneously digital and material quality of RP-7 is essential to aligning the expertise of the specialist doctor at one hospital with the vital signs and diagnostic chart of the patient at another hospital. This hybridized quality of the digital and material also facilitates oral communication between doctor and patient, as through the lens of RP-7 the doctor can see whether the patient can move limbs or is experiencing numbness or other abnormalities symptomatic of stroke—rather than rely exclusively on written or spoken language to make such a determination. Again, these points reinforce that virtual collaborative writing (in terms of vital signs, diagnostic chart, visual and symbolic representations on the computer screen) is integrated with both oral communication (the dialogue between doctor and patient) as well as gestural communication (the capacity and ease with which the patient can demonstrate voluntary bodily movement so the doctor can discern the extent to which the patient has been debilitated).

The materiality of RP-7 indicates a digital environment in a highly specialized practice. Both materiality and practice require that the production and use of collaborative writing as well as oral communication are situated by practitioners in a specific setting—in this case, hospitals—which are the workplace setting fundamental to the practice of medicine. Here is another example of how RP-7 makes up for what has been lost in the transition from print to digital technologies. Popular literature, like the Lewin (2009) article, is notorious for praising the quick and easy access digital technologies afford people to texts and information. Such affordances result from the fact that the reader does not have to go to a specific location—such as a hospital or other workplace setting—in order to access a particular text. But as the RP-7 aptly demonstrates, in real world situations, access to texts and information of itself often is not enough; the specialist doctor needs to interact with the patient, not just the texts that provide her with information about the patient. She also has to interact with the doctors on location with that patient, whose own expertise is vital to comprehending and applying the diagnosis and recommendation of the specialist doctor operating RP-7.

To this end, RP-7 aligns the production and use of collaborative writing with the appropriate expertise, expertise that is also collaborative. The mutual presence of RP-7 with doctors at another hospital demonstrates that the specialist doctor cannot do this work alone. She depends on both the aid and expertise of the other doctors to communicate effectively with the patient, to interpret patient's vital signs and diagnostic chart, and, in the end, to get the patient well again.

Finally, RP-7 demonstrates an example of virtual collaborative writing. The texts relevant to the patient's condition and diagnosis are virtually—or digitally—mediated by RP-7. Since the production and use of these texts occurs in a collaborative context, that is, during real-time interaction between doctors at two different hospitals collaborating on the treatment of a patient, these texts are products of virtual collaborative writing. Furthermore, RP-7 reminds us that writing is important because in real world settings it is part of something larger than itself. Virtual collaborative writing is but one of many crucial variables involved in the use of RP-7 and the treatment of patients—but this point underscores how important virtual collaborative writing is in this context.

RP-7, Digital Media, and the Web Cam

One popular digital technology that bares similarity to RP-7 is the web cam, which, like a movie or television camera, transmits video footage from one location to another. The video component of RP-7 is vital to its performance and effectiveness. No doubt it helps the patient to build trust with the doctor and robot to see the doctor's face in real time, and it is equally vital, of course, that the doctor can see the patient in order to observe the patient's condition and respond to prompts to move different body parts.

But there are important ways in which RP-7's use of video differs significantly from the typical web cam. A web cam affords the viewer access to video footage regardless of the viewer's location, just like web-based information affords the reader access to texts irrespective of the reader's location. The use of RP-7, however, is not so simple. The alignment of materiality, practice, and expertise that mutual presence generates involves more than aligning textual information with expertise;

it requires that such an alignment take place in specific workplace settings that correspond with the expert's practice. Successful professional performance depends on more than information. The information must be accessed in the same location where the other tools vital to that profession also is located, and that is what makes a workplace what it is: an assembly of tools and information that correspond to a specific practice. What good would it do for a medical specialist to view a patient if the specialist were not situated in a hospital, and what good would RP-7 be in the treatment of patients if the specialist doctor was not also simultaneously interacting with other doctors located in the same hospital room as the patient?

Another important difference between the video component of RP-7 and the web cam is that, like print media, the video component of RP-7 is highly constrained in terms of the type and range of content that it transmits. This type and range of content is transmitted to experts who need the content to be so constrained. What these doctors need is not easy access to unlimited information but timely access to a narrow range of visual, oral, and written content about the particular patient under treatment at the moment. Web cams, by contrast, transmit a range of content determined not by the needs of professionals working on a specific task but by the scope of the lens and screen used in the transmission and whatever happens to within the lens' range. Furthermore, access to the content of a web cam only requires access to web cam technology, in drastic contrast to the doctors working with RP-7, who need access to a variety of medical workplace technologies as well as the collaborative input of one another.

MUTUAL PRESENCE AND LITERACY

This latter portion of the chapter builds upon my observations and arguments about RP-7 as a platform for a more theoretical discussion of mutual presence and the differences between print and digital texts. The construct of mutual presence builds on Perelman's (1969) discussion of presence as a persuasive factor in argumentation[1]. Although the immediate context of Perelman's discussion of presence concerns speech, his introduction makes clear that contemporary study of rhetoric and communication must consider argumentation through writing as well as speech (pp. 6-7). In addition, while presence explicitly is connected by Perelman with argumentation and not literacy, certainly a significant part of the production and use of writing in educational and workplace settings is the construction and interpretation of arguments in written form.

For the future of virtual collaborative writing, the concept and reality of presence should figure prominently in practitioners' concerns over how to align certain texts with certain readers; additionally, practitioners should address the need for that alignment to occur in settings where readers can put these texts to use with best results. Because digital texts are not constrained in their location and circulation the way print texts are, the creation of digital texts by themselves will not be enough. The future of virtual collaborative writing will require more than the traditional priorities of industry writing in terms of clarity, organization, and accuracy of information. Instead, virtual collaborative writing will need to address the reality that the professionals who interpret and put such information to use do not just need information—they need certain specific information that corresponds to the task at hand; they need that information to be present in the same location with the other tools and technologies attendant to that profession; and they need connection to other professionals with whom they are collaborating all at the same time. RP-7, I would argue, achieves these needs. By being physically located next to a particular patient and other doctors in a hospital room, RP-7 transmits information to a specialist doctor at another hospital that is directly relevant to the condition and treatment needs of that patient; it provides such information in a workplace setting equipped with the other tools and technologies necessary to successful patient treatment; and it simultaneously puts all the collaborating doctors in touch with the same information and with one another at the time of treatment and diagnosis.

Thus, the digital environment of RP-7 achieves an alignment between materiality, practice, and expertise in the production and use of texts that is vital to and compatible with the readers' rhetorical comprehension of these texts because the texts match up with both the readers' needs at the moment and their expertise. The connection between mutual presence and literacy, then, concerns the co-presence of texts, practitioners, and various workplace settings and technologies that ensure the texts will be comprehended and put to use in a way that meets the expectations of all involved. That is, how individuals read and write depends on the shared expectations of those whose expertise aligns with a certain practice and specific settings.

Amidst popular views such as the one Lewin (2009) reported, practitioners of virtual collaborative writing should understand that the digital network of RP-7 is worlds away from popular, commonplace uses of digital networks, where the need for a complex and narrow range of information is far less of a priority than access to unlimited information, and where one's physical location and the physical location of others is irrelevant precisely because of the affordance digital texts offer users in terms of access irrespective of location.

Mutual presence is essential to fostering these shared expectations, which is necessary to restricting the range of interpretation of print texts so that their meaning coheres and corresponds with the practice in which they are situated, and the individuals participating in that practice.

Some studies in literacy have focused on how texts have been aligned with individuals situated in certain practices and settings fundamental to those practices. Chartier (1994) considered both historical developments and perspectives on the production and use of writing, drawing on de Cer-

teau's (1992) idea that reading, unlike the durable and unchanging qualities of writing, is fluid and dynamic, comprised of a connection of many different acts that are difficult to trace. Of particular interest to Chartier (1994) was how de Certeau's (1992) insight about the practice of reading, what Chartier (1994) identified as a "silent production," impacted changes in the technological, formal, and cultural factors behind increased production and use of writing in France from the sixteenth to eighteenth centuries.

Chartier's historical perspective is relevant because one common concern about digital texts is their rapid and explosive proliferation among countless, often difficult-to-trace, groups and individuals (Flanigan & Metzger, 2000; Gilster, 1997; Kapoun, 1997). Hence, consideration of how the historical proliferation of print texts, one some scholars such as Chartier (1994) argue delineates print-based literacy from scribal-based literacy, may shed light on problems with digital literacy and the current day proliferation of a digital texts in workplace and educational settings.

Chartier made two critical points about reading. First, reading is a creative and inventive act that cannot be extrapolated from the texts used by readers; and second, readers' strategies follow writers' conventions, rules, logical systems, and models. These qualities of reading and writing adhere to the principle that for any activity to be generative—creative and inventive—it must also be restrictive in that it must follow conventions and rules. For Chartier, one key factor of how reading's creativity is restricted was through the material form of the text. RP-7, by situating a digital environment in a highly specialized medical setting, affects this restrictive quality by aligning the texts vital to patient treatment with doctors who follow the conventions and rules appropriate to medical practice, including the reading and interpretation of texts used during patient treatment.

Materiality, Practice, and Expertise

Chartier explained that the materiality of texts delivers a controlling influence on how readers read texts and make meaning of them. This point would seem consistent with the argument that material conditions and the interplay between certain kinds of texts and specific individual readers that are mutually present influence how individuals produce and use texts. As Chartier articulated: "readers and hearers... are never confronted with abstract or ideal texts detached from all materiality; they manipulate or perceive objects and forms whose structures and modalities govern their reading (or the hearing), thus the possible comprehension of the text read" (p. 3). A major challenge for the future of virtual collaborative writing will be the creation of an effective materiality for digital environments that provides the necessary structure and modality to govern the reading and hearing of practitioners, since such structures and modalities are not intrinsic to the digital environments of virtual collaborative writing, as they are to print texts. Designers of virtual collaborative technologies must avoid the mistake of assuming that just because a text is digital that it can be abstract—that is, that digital texts can be put to use effectively in professional settings without attention to issues of materiality, structure, and modality. The re-creation of structure and modality in digital environments must "govern the reading" and use of texts in professional contexts such that texts will be comprehended and put to use in order to meet the shared expectations of that profession. The materiality of RP-7 has been designed to govern the reading and hearing of medical professionals such that they interpret a highly specific range of information in the treatment of an individual patient. Since professions correspond to certain workplaces like hospitals, the future of virtual collaborative writing will have to meet the traditional challenges of writing for industry in addition to the new challenges of creating "objects and forms" that physically locate digital texts in those workplaces. RP-7 would appear to do so effectively.

Popular depictions of digital texts, such as those recounted in Lewin's (2009) article, regard them as "ideal texts" because they are "detached from all materiality" rather than expressing the curiosity or concern about this detachment that practitioners of virtual collaborative writing should harbor. While Chartier (1994) did not refer explicitly to rhetoric in this passage, textual materiality plays a rhetorical role in determining what range of comprehension is possible when readers read texts, which is essential to ensuring that texts are comprehended in ways that meet professional expectations. The difference between print texts and digital texts derives from the absence of the constraints that Chartier claimed "govern their reading" since digital texts do not require or involve the alignment of texts with certain individuals in specific settings (p. 7). On the contrary, digital texts often are praised because they permit individuals to access texts irrespective an individual's location and the other individuals with whom they are interacting as they access these texts.

The problem with the loss of such "governing constraints" on how readers read print-based texts is that it promotes an "autonomous" view of texts, which Haas (1994) claimed impairs a rhetorical understanding of texts because they are seen as isolated from a larger discourse involving specific authors driven by particular motives. A rhetorical understanding of texts would also seem, based on her longitudinal study of a biology major, to be situated in a particular practice and knowledge of that practice and the settings fundamental to it (for example, laboratories and biology departments). That is, texts are produced and used in the context of some activity that exists beyond that text, and knowledge of this activity is a necessary prerequisite for comprehending texts related to that activity with a rhetorical awareness of authors, motives, and other texts that have prompted and constrained the ways in which a given text is produced and the meaning its author wishes to impart.

The act of constraining how texts are read is rhetorical because it sets boundaries around what interpretations are legitimate or credible and thus acceptable and admissible in professional problem-solving situations. In other words, these constraints ensure common understanding between the writers of texts and their audiences. Practitioners of virtual collaborative writing must be mindful of how important it is that such boundaries are in place in the design and implementation of the digital environments in which virtual collaborative writing occurs. Such control is necessary, of course, since effective application of texts in professional practice depends on how practitioners interpret those texts. The loss of these "governing constraints" in digital texts that orient readers' rhetorical comprehension of print texts leads to a mode of reading that assumes *the content* of texts alone can provide the necessary constraints readers need to comprehend texts in ways that lead to favorable results in practice. This perspective overlooks the importance of *the materiality* of texts in constraining readers' comprehension of them: their distinctive physical characteristics that set them apart from other texts, the professions that correspond to those texts, and their physical location in proximity to corresponding workplaces and other professionals. A perspective on reading that places unquestioning value on access to textual content fails to consider the alignment of materiality, practice, and expertise that provides important rhetorical cues for comprehending those texts. As a result, digital texts are now accessible to readers absent those things with which print-based texts are intrinsically aligned: a context of practice (for example, biology) and expertise (for example, other biologists interpreting and debating the meaning of a text) by way of a physical location common to both practice and expertise (for example, laboratories, natural habitats, libraries of science, and so on).

While in contexts of popular usage the loss of this alignment may not have measurable consequences, the failure to attend to this loss and consider its implications could have disastrous results in professional settings. Absent constraints on how readers comprehend texts or which texts will be aligned with which readers and in what location, the expertise vital to successful practice can be missing, or the narrow range of content that an expert needs at a given moment may become awash in an unmanageable volume of information. Since the materiality of print texts enacts such constraints, digital texts used in virtual collaborative writing will require some equivalent materiality, which the RP-7 exemplifies.

These points also should remind practitioners of virtual collaborative writing that there is cause for concern that readers of digital texts may be unaware of limitations of their comprehension of these texts that are not correctable through better access to texts or better digital technology. This problem goes beyond texts and points to the rhetorical contexts that surround the vital role of expertise in their production and use. Knowledge of these rhetorical contexts requires more than access to texts because it depends on such expertise and digital technologies cannot provide readers with access to expertise just because they provide access to texts. In fact, those who praise digital texts because of the access they provide to texts are praising that it does so precisely because it affords readers the convenience of by-passing expertise: the rhetorical contexts and the settings in which those contexts come to be understood that always surround and influence the ways in which texts are put to use in industry. Such is the mindset that privileges the "autonomous text" and "access" thereto. Digital technologies fail to put constraints on the range of texts available to a given reader at a given time and place, meaning the texts to which it gives access are not intrinsically tied to particular types of settings because digital texts cannot restrict a reader's comprehension through the quality of materiality.

The problems with reading absent the rhetorical contexts that align the materiality, practice, and expertise of texts have much to do with why educators and practitioners of virtual collaborative writing should be cautious about a wholesale shift from print to digital texts, a caution that the Lewin (2009) article is missing. To say again, one needs access to more than "the text" to have access to a text. The construct mutual presence attempts to explain the process human beings have engaged in over the centuries to make sure certain kinds of texts interface with certain kinds of individuals, and vice versa. To whatever degree such an understanding has been explicitly recognized, I would argue that the interface between texts, individuals, and the subject matter or common interest that mediates this interface is something to which readers also need access in order to use texts in ways that are educational or meet the needs of industry.

For this reason, practitioners of virtual collaborative writing should not fall into the "autonomous text" mode of reading that can be seen as a lost memory of the importance that materiality plays in readers' comprehension of texts. As Chartier (1994) noted, the materiality of texts and the space texts occupy are fundamental elements of reading that literacy scholars have "too often forgotten" (p. 10). The result, he claimed, is that these scholars either assume texts are abstract and their forms unimportant or valorize the history of readers as one where reading is postulated as an unmediated experience, meaning the "effect produced" by the text is independent of the "material forms that operate as vehicle for the text" (p. 10). Such forgetfulness may explain why the public as well as scholars assume digital texts can replace or by-pass the intrinsic constraints of print texts, as the Lewin (2009) article shows. These assumptions about texts that Chartier (1994) criticized would seem consistent with the notion of the autonomous text, since one could argue reasonably that the "material forms that operate as vehicle for the text" would include the settings in which those texts are accessed and shared, and the embodied presence of the individuals who gather and interact in such settings. In the case of RP-7, it

is crucial to remember that it allows the specialist doctor access not only to the texts relevant to the patient's condition, but to the patient as well as the doctors at the patient's hospital, all at the same time and all in a timely manner. Thus, the use of RP-7 demonstrates that texts are not autonomous, and require a context that includes other texts as well as people to be comprehended and applied successfully to social practice. As the vehicle for the texts used during patient treatment, RP-7 is far from unimportant to how and by whom those texts are comprehended and put to use.

For Chartier, the materiality of texts plays a crucial role in how readers generate meaning from those texts. This materiality is even more important when one considers Chartier's point that European societies long have been organized around the presence of written material, a position similar to that of Goody (1977), who argued that the development of Eurasian cultures bares a similar thread that distinguishes them from those who have not had as long a history of the spread and prominence of writing. The presence of writing and the material forms that print texts take, then, are critical in restricting the generative creation of meaning endemic to the practice of reading and, thus, to social organization. This point certainly should not escape the way practitioners envision the future of virtual collaborative writing, because the loss of these "material forms" that transmit texts and constrain the meaning making they mediate would, therefore, have considerable implications for how humans identify, perceive and comprehend texts and how organized behavior revolves around a shared or collective rhetorical comprehension of them.

Another scholar who argues materiality figures prominently in understandings of literacy is Haas (1996), whose comparison of how readers process print and computer-based texts is one of the earliest to consider how changes in materiality affect the practice of literacy. Her work is foundational for the argument I present here, both because of her precedent for comparing print and digital texts in reading practices, and her emphasis, similar to Chartier's (1994), in understanding the importance of materiality in those practices.

Haas and Weardon (2003) considered how reliance on digital texts alone as a technology contributes to problems in evaluating the credibility of Web-based information. They argued that Clark's (1983) notion of common ground is valuable for understanding problems with how Web users evaluate the credibility of Web-based information. Their main argument, that problems with e-credibility are more than matters of information, has a common theoretical thread with Chartier's (1994) claim that reading cannot be understood by texts alone; both points seem to emphasize that the point of view and background of the reader are major factors in how meaning is generated from readers' encounters with texts. The implications of this research for the future of virtual collaborative writing, again, are to reinforce the importance of materiality in the production and use of texts and the need for expertise that goes beyond access to texts to ensure successful problem-solving performance

To illustrate the connection between mutual presence and literacy more extensively, I posit that one way the restrictive meaning-making came to be established in print literacy during the time period Chartier studies was an alignment between materiality, practice, and expertise. As I will proceed to demonstrate, this relationship, for which no equivalent exists in digital literacy, has molded literate practice with print texts over time. A closer look at this relationship can illuminate what has been lost in digital-based literacy, and how it differs from print-based literacy.

Digital Texts and the Absence of Mutual Presence

To demonstrate how digital texts lack mutual presence, in this section I turn to what is the most common and familiar digital communication technology: the Web. The Web is at once a delivery tool and a composite of inter-linked texts that are unlike print texts, which become physically separated from their delivery tool, as a newspaper is separated from its printing press. As a result, Web users do not have the kind of material cues that distinguish one kind of text from another—typically all must fit on a computer screen or projection screen, as is the case with PowerPoint. Because it exists in cyber space rather than physical space, the Web does not provide a cue for understanding what kind of activity for which a Web text is to be put to use the way a phone book, restaurant menu, or case law journal immediately cue a reader as to which one will help them find the number for the local fire department, which one will tell them tonight's dinner special, and which one will tell them what precedent has been established for a particular legal issue.

One result has been the peculiar need to designate certain Web terminals for certain practices. A library research area, for example, posts a sign next to certain Web terminals specifically designating them to be used for educational research. It is difficult to imagine the need for such instructions with print texts, whose materiality already designates them for a certain kind of practice; one would find it odd to see a sign next to a set of encyclopedias or reference books telling potential users that they were to be used only for educational research and not for writing letters or playing games.

The relationship between materiality and practice is important because many educators, most notably Scribner and Cole (1981), widely agree that literacy is best understood as something situated in practice. Scriber and Cole explained that their study of the Vai, a non-school based literacy, led them to conclude that acts of writing and reading take place within certain types of tasks, and the capacity for individuals to write and read is constrained as much by their familiarity with and capacity for performing these tasks as it is by what one might call *literacy* per se (pp. 234-250). What they do find, however, is a "practice account of literacy" in which the production and use of scripts and signs takes place within some kind of practice, where certain kinds of skills, knowledge, and tools are aimed at completing certain kinds of goals. Because literacy is practice-bound, one can also see it as embodied, as something performed by certain individuals in certain settings where the materiality of texts, their material forms and physical existence in a certain place and time, are crucial to understanding how the production and use of writing takes place in different contexts of organized behavior.

Mutual Presence in Action: How Print Texts Differ from Digital Texts

In this section, I illustrate mutual presence as it unfolds in various settings and organizational contexts. The goal is to emphasize the material qualities of particular print texts, as well as the alignment of these texts with individuals whose backgrounds suit them to comprehend their rhetorical context by way of the specific location of the text and the practice or activity out of which it has emerged.

One type of site for studying mutual presence is the construction or renovation project often found in municipal settings. These sites present a cornucopia of signs, both linguistic and non-linguistic, positioned at particular locations that provide essential rhetorical contexts for those who interact with them. Consider the following:

* Example 1: CUT 6" FROM WALL
* Example 2: RNC
      F/Q
      DUCT

While simple to decode, it is impossible to comprehend these linguistic signs rhetorically by only looking at them as "information" to which one has access. These signs mean what they mean because of where they are. For the signs to be anywhere else would change the way they are read and comprehended because their rhetorical context would change. This change would involve primarily their dislocation from the individuals who are expert in the practice from which the signs come and the material setting in which they are oriented and to which they make reference.

The ridiculousness of thinking there could be a digital equivalent for these signs becomes evident when one asks, "What wall?" regarding Example 1. There is, of course, no wall or any other kind of tangible, three-dimensional object behind a computer screen. And while the image of a city worker cutting into the concrete six inches from the wall next to which the sign has been made in order to widen the sidewalk is easily imaginable, it seems farcical to visualize someone taking a saw to a computer screen. One also becomes puzzled over the usefulness of such a sign being accessible to people who have no connection to the time and place where it is present and the project to which it is relevant. The same can be said for Example 2. The message is intended for someone who knows what that organized set of symbols means in relation to the downtown renovation project. And the existence of this sign goes beyond the accessibility of information. For whom are the sign accessible, where such individuals need to be to access that sign, and why he or she needs to be there instead of somewhere else are vital rhetorical factors for understanding the production and use of this sign. While brief, this sign reveals a rather intricate alignment between its material presence and specific individuals who are expert in the practice to which the sign is relevant—an alignment that is essential to affecting the constraints necessary for its comprehension by these experts. This alignment, I might note, also helps to reinforce the credibility of these signs. Without it, how could they be distinguishable from graffiti?

Other linguistic signs in municipalities reveal the same dynamic of mutual presence in action. The presence of an actual antique rail reinforces the meaning and credibility of the sign attached to it that says "Antique rail; do not lean." The rail itself that is co-present with the sign serves as a non-linguistic sign that is part of the rhetorical context of the linguistic sign telling passers-by not to lean on it. And the readers for whom this message has been produced are the ones who, because of their proximity to the rail, are experts on the significance and meaning of the print text that advises them not lean against the rail. The tendency for pedestrians on occasion to lean on rails or other available objects along their path also is fundamental to understanding the presence of the sign and its rhetorical influence on certain individuals mutually present with the rail and the sign that accompanies it.

To show the contrast of what happens when such mutual presence is lost, imagine how ridiculous it would be to consider how the same sign could have the same meaning and rhetorical effectiveness if it were on a Web site and viewed on a computer screen. Just as one can ask "What wall?" in reference to the sign posted under Example 1, one can ask "What rail?" in response to a digital text telling one not to lean on a rail that cannot possibly be within reach behind a computer screen. Mutual presence explains the meaning this sign has precisely because of where it is located in terms of its connection to a specific object, the rail, and the people who approach it. Just as is the case with Examples 1 and 2, the antique rail sign means what it does because of where it is. For that sign to be accessible to anyone in the world who goes online would alter its materiality, location, and co-presence in relation to other individuals, which, in turn would change how it is comprehended. For one thing, the linguistic imperative not to lean on the rail would have no relevance online since the rail is not really there and the readers of the sign could not lean on it even if they wanted to. It is difficult to see how such a sign could have any meaning or usefulness online.

These examples of municipal signs also underscore the point I made earlier concerning what it means to be an expert as a reader of print texts. The passers-by who come within reaching distance of the antique rail may not be experts in risk communication or antique preservation but they are experts of what it means to be in the time and place where they find themselves close to that rail and the sign telling them not to lean on it. To be absent from the setting in which both the rail and sign exist would, again, alter the way a reader would comprehend the sign. This point leads to another important principle concerning mutual presence; expertise requires physical existence in a specific time and place as well as access to texts. The material qualities of the rail, not just its physical presence at a certain location, but its "antique" condition, reinforce and elaborate the meaning of the linguistic sign attached to it. For this sign to be digital and detached from its own materiality as a print sign integrated with the antique rail would make it nonsensical; why instruct someone not to lean on a rail that is not there? The expertise of the reader of this sign, then, derives from that reader's embodied presence in the mutual setting that puts them within close range of the sign and the rail.

As one broadens perspective on public settings, the alignment of materiality, practice, and expertise becomes evident in all kinds of contexts. Here are some examples of mutual presence in action that extend beyond how it operates in municipal projects. Consider the following:

- Example 1: STOP
- Example 2: 7:32
- Example 3: "You've been Pittsnoggled."
- Example 4: "Good hand washing is the best way to prevent the spread of germs."
- Example 5: "Must be as tall as Jackie to enter pool."

As with the previous examples, on the surface these messages appear simple and straightforward. But a closer look at how and where these messages exist reveals alignments of materiality, practice, and expertise that are essential to how they are comprehended by the particular individuals who become mutually present with them. Consider the context of Example 1. A volunteer traffic cop, stationed at an intersection near a school, holds up a manual stop sign whenever school children prepare to cross. On this afternoon, however, he deviates from his routine. As a runner approaches the path perpendicular to where the traffic cop stands, the cop moves over to that path, and holds the stop sign so that the runner can proceed without automobile interference. As the runner passes by and offers a thankful wave, the cop says, "The pedestrian always has the right of way!"

It is impossible to understand what is happening in this example by merely having access to the message "stop," partly because, as is the case with any stop sign, what it really means is "stop here," and where "here" is depends on one's location in proximity to the point at which one is supposed to stop, since one is not supposed to stop as soon as one sees the sign but rather at the place parallel to the sign. In this case, however, the meaning of the sign and its transfer from its usual spot where it serves to protect schoolchildren to the runner's path cannot be understood without a temporal context that explains the history behind this particular event.

Three days before, the same runner had approached the same intersection at the same time of day with the same volunteer traffic cop present. As the runner began to cross the intersection where the light was green, an oncoming car made a left turn into his path, cutting him off, and prompting him to yell at the driver, "The pedestrian always has the right of way!" Hence, the cop's act of moving from his usual spot to the perpendicular route, which changes the meaning of the stop sign since it tells drivers coming from a different direction to stop, stems, in part, from the familiarity between the cop and the runner and the event three days prior. How someone could understand all of this just by accessing the word *stop* online seems baffling. What the sign means at the moment the cop moves to the perpendicular path from where

he normally is stationed is inseparable from what is happening at that time and place as well as the shared knowledge between the cop and runner concerning the rude driver who had gone through that exact spot seventy-two hours earlier. This shared knowledge between the cop and runner is what makes them experts concerning the use and meaning of the hand-held stop sign. While this episode lasts only seconds, to understand what is happening with the stop sign and how it is comprehended by the cop, runner, and any potential approaching driver requires far more than "access" to the "information" on the sign.

Example 2 reinforces an understanding of the role that time and place play in the use and comprehension of a sign. In this case, "7:32" is the clock on a cell phone that has just changed from "8:32" as the driver crosses from the Eastern to Central time zone. The mutual presence of the driver, the cell phone, and the exact location where the time zones change provide a context for understanding why suddenly it is an hour earlier. Imagine the confusion if someone saw a clock change with no awareness of passing to another time zone. In this case, the driver is an expert for understanding the change in time, because that person is mutually present with both the clock and the location where the time zone changes. The car is both literally and figuratively a "vehicle," to reference Chartier (1994), for transmitting the meaning of the text.

Expertise and mutual presence with a specific time and place also explain the meaning of the sign, "You've been Pittsnoggled" in Example 3. Here, the word "Pittsnoggled" refers to a basketball player named Pittsnoggle, and the sign is held up to face fans of the opposing team whenever Pittsnoggle hits a shot—and in this particular game he hit many (although his team lost in overtime). The fans at the game are experts at understanding what this sign means because they are mutually present with the sign and the practice of basketball being played at that moment. This particular sign, and how it is to be comprehended depends on such a precise alignment of materiality, practice, and expertise that not only does the sign not make sense absent the game, the player named Pittsnoggle, and the opposing fans in front of whom the sign is held, it also makes no sense unless Pittsnoggle has just scored. How someone could understand this sign in the same way looking at a digital text, absent from the gym where the game is being played, and further, being absent from the seating section across from where the sign is displayed, makes no sense, and highlights how mutual presence is essential to the comprehension of print texts.

The timing of the display of the sign "You've been Pittsnoggled" also demonstrates the importance of materiality in the use and comprehension of print texts. For one, the sign only appears at the moment the player has scored; its material presence is synchronized with this event in order to mean what it does. The sign would be absurd if displayed after the player had missed a shot, committed a foul, or gone to the bench with foul trouble. The sign becomes present because the fans who made and display the sign and the audience for whom the sign is displayed are not only experts of basketball, they are experts of that particular basketball game, they know who Pittsnoggle is, when he scores, who the teams are, and what the game situation is. The materiality of the sign means what it does because of the precise time and place in which it becomes present and for whom it does so.

Another important characteristic of this sign's materiality are its size, shape, and ink lettering, all of which tell anyone remotely familiar with sports culture that this is a sign made for this particular basketball game. Its meaning, then, is immediately restricted by its materiality; one will not confuse it with a stop sign, a treatise on religion, a dinner menu, phone book, or a journal of case law. Thus, the materiality of this sign—and I would argue print-based texts in general—performs two crucial restrictive functions concerning how it is to be comprehended: (1) its material characteristics initially make clear what general type of sign it is

and (2) its presence within a precise time and place explains specifically what it means. These restrictive functions are rhetorical because of how they persuade audiences to comprehend them. Digital texts, by contrast, have no equivalent material characteristics that restrict how audiences initially identify them in relation to a particular practice, e.g. sports watching, and a specific event whose participants, in this case, fans of the two basketball teams, are experts for understanding the sign that becomes mutually present with the fans and the game at precise moments when its meaning becomes relevant to the event itself and the fans' participation in the event. The same things that garner praise for the Web—its instant access to information from any place on the globe by way of a computer screen—come at the expense of an alignment of materiality, practice, and expertise vital to how print texts effect an "adherence of minds" (Perelman, 1969) or adherence of meaning and comprehension, between those who produce and display them and the audiences for whom they are produced and displayed.

The drawback, again, of digital texts is that there are no material constraints—beyond access to the necessary technology—for how and where these texts are to be accessed and, in turn, interpreted and applied to a problem-solving context. Print texts accomplish much of their rhetorical purpose precisely because their accessibility requires mutual presence on the part of audiences in specific settings, at specific times, whereas digital texts are praised precisely because audiences can access texts irrespective of where either text or reader may be. Example 4, "Good hand washing is the best way to prevent the spread of germs" demonstrates this point. This particular sign is located, not surprisingly, in a bathroom, but not just any bathroom. Who really needs to be reminded of washing one's hands? Children. And this particular bathroom is located in the downstairs children's section of a municipal library, the sign posted right above the toilet. Again, time and place are essential to understanding the restrictive influences of its materiality on how and by whom it is to be comprehended. The mnemonic impact of this sign serves to remind children to wash their hands at the exact moment when doing so is most important for sanitation and public health reasons: after using the toilet.

As is the case with this bathroom sign and all the others I have discussed, the mutual presence of texts with specific places and individuals in those places serves a vital rhetorical function since no text can be persuasive without an awareness of audience; in each of the examples I have examined, texts are situated purposefully to be in view of particular audiences at a specific time and place where their messages offer optimum persuasive influence. Digital texts cannot impart such rhetorical influence because they are not situated in a particular time and place; their value is that they can be accessed by anyone anywhere with a computer and Web access. Regardless of the possibilities digital technology may offer, the absence of a precise alignment of texts with particular individuals in particular settings means digital texts can be, and I would argue often are, as rhetorically useless as a poster on how to perform the Heimlich maneuver on a choking victim would be above the toilet in a children's library bathroom rather than in a restaurant, or the print outs for drink orders going to someone washing dishes rather than to the bartender.

Example 5—"Must be as tall as Jackie to enter pool"—demonstrates how the rhetorical effectiveness of print texts depends in part on their materiality. In this example, the materiality has an additional rhetorical dimension beyond its presence in a specific time and place. The size and shape of the sign play a crucial role to persuading small children, or more accurately the parents of small children, not to go into the swimming pool. "Jackie" is really a life-size caricature of a child on a painted piece of wood approximating the size and shape of a child old enough or big enough to be allowed in the pool. Thus, the words "Must be as tall as Jackie to enter pool" obviously make no

sense if there is no "Jackie," nor if "Jackie" is the size and shape of a bee, dog, elephant—or to draw a parallel to the Web, a computer screen—rather than a child of roughly five or six years of age. This sign means what it does because of where it is (at the entrance of a municipal swimming pool), who is standing next to it (small children who may or may not be allowed in the pool), and its size and shape. The materiality of the sign and the co-presence of children at the pool are essential to how the sign is comprehended by readers—the linguistic sign cannot be comprehended without evaluation of whether or not a given child is as tall as the caricature next to the swimming pool entrance. For all of the hype given to the capacity for digital texts to be multi-modal and interactive, they cannot match the malleability and flexibility of print texts, which can be made out of any kind of material, take any shape or size, and perhaps most importantly, can be located at precise and specific places that complement and enhance their meaning by restricting who reads them, where, and for what purpose. How could there be a digital equivalent of "Jackie"? Perhaps a better question is, why would there need to be one?

This example and the others preceding it reinforce that representations of print texts as "finite," "plain," and "antiquated" are misguided and cavalier. The scope, variety, and situated contexts of production and use of these texts illustrate how mutual presence acts as an essential constraint to how audiences comprehend them and demonstrate how complex—albeit subtle—the production and use of those texts is. Regardless of the extent to which mutual presence is explicitly understood by those who produce and use print texts, the alignment of texts with certain places and people operates as a vital component of the meaning-making processes that go into their comprehension and interpretation. As a construct, mutual presence explains how the settings, objects, and individuals co-present with print texts provide a rhetorical context for how they are read, by whom, when, where, and for what reasons. Absent this rhetorical context, meaning-making becomes random, idiosyncratic, and isolated, results detrimental to social practice and an obvious impediment to effective collaboration mediated by digital technologies.

If mutual presence is vital to restricting the comprehension of these rather basic print texts in order to affect shared meanings and interpretations of them, imagine how important mutual presence becomes when the focus turns toward opaque and complex texts situated in professional workplaces that involve extremely challenging tasks and highly specialized technologies such as RP-7.

The Value of RP-7 Research to Academia and Industry

A major goal of the research and theory I have presented here is to draw attention to the proposition that print texts function rhetorically in a different manner than digital texts, and that digital texts cannot simply replace print texts without consideration of the intricate, complex, and transparent ways print texts function rhetorically. Digital texts are not unqualified or absolute improvements over print texts. As I stated at the opening of this chapter, digital texts cannot transcend the inherent qualities of print texts or defy the ways in which they are produced and used. Their popularity notwithstanding, digital texts, the array of technologies that mediate them, and the formal and personal ways in which they are put to use must be scrutinized by the scholarly community rather than blindly endorsed wholesale.

I would argue awareness of the differences between digital and print texts should provoke hesitation toward endorsing sensationalist perspectives on digital texts precisely because digital texts are not rhetorically constrained in the manner print-based texts are. The loss of these constraints, and the mutual presence such constraints effect, is cause for concern and doubt about the educational promise of digital texts as well as their practical value in the workplace. Unfortunately, the Lewin (2009) article reflects the opposite mentality: the loss of the constraints inherent to print texts makes digital texts "free" and "open sources" that spare students from the expense, nuisance, and strain of transporting print texts. The implications of the differences in the rhetorical contexts of print texts and digital texts are grounds for dissuading scholars and educators from emphasizing facility with digital technology and access to multi-modal texts that mediate the circulation of information at the expense of the skills, tools, and knowledge essential to participating in different kinds of social practice, building relationships and credibility among people expert in those practices.

To this end, my hope is that research on RP-7 serves as a fruitful reminder of "the importance of paying attention" to the attitudes toward and applications of digital technologies. Here I make reference to Selfe's (1999) pivotal book at the end of the 20th century that pleaded with scholars not to get swept up in the frenzy of the digital technological revolution, and instead to look closely and thoughtfully at what these technologies actually can and cannot do with an earnest concern for an honest appraisal of their educational value. Scholars also have an obligation both to the academy and the public to assess the merit of prevailing attitudes toward digital technologies, how they compare to print media, and the credibility of claims made about the comparative educational value of digital and print media.

For industry, research on RP-7 hopefully provides a model of a highly specialized and collaborative digital technology put to use in a real world workplace environment where lives and large sums of money are at stake. The degree of success RP-7 has had should be valuable to members of industry as they contemplate the design and implementation of future digital technologies that will mediate, among other things, virtual collaborative writing in contexts where problems must be solved, goals met, and customers satisfied. And while industry certainly has good reasons to be more concerned with the practical rather than the theoretical, RP-7 does provide a means for testing theories—including my theory based on the construct of mutual presence—that attempt to explain how and why digital technologies succeed or fail in workplace settings. Perhaps the greatest value that academia has to offer industry is theories based on what industry itself does. To this end, research on RP-7, and the theory I have extrapolated from its operation, provides members of industry a possible insight as to how digital environments best can be put to use tests the proposition that one key to this endeavor is to make up for what has been lost in the transition from print to digital texts and technologies.

Principles of Collaboration

Virtual collaborative writing mediated by RP-7 demonstrates three principles of collaboration that ground this book: Principle 1, Developing a Culture of Collaboration; Principle 3, Establishing Trust; and Principle 4, Using Tools and Collaborative Modes Effectively.

Principle 1: Specifically, RP-7 demonstrates the need to develop a *local* culture of collaboration. The group of doctors operating at hospitals in different regions shares goals and expectations that are highly specific to that group. RP-7 illustrates a topic-based paradigm, but practitioners of virtual collaborative writing should recognize that this topic is highly specialized and requires a precise medical expertise. The value of efficiency demands a digital technology like RP-7 that is suited to the local culture of collaboration among doctors dealing with a specific medical problem. This local culture of medical collaboration can only come into existence and be sustained by a technology like RP-7 that is specially designed for that particular local culture. In the future, a culture of collaboration will be the product of many and varied local cultures of collaboration, each with a corresponding technology like RP-7 that is designed to meet the needs of that local culture.

Principle 3: In the case of RP-7, there is a different kind of trust established than in examples from other chapters. Here, the need is to establish trust with the technology, with RP-7 itself. The collaborating doctors already have established trust with one another; that trust is the foundation of the RP-7 project. Their challenge is to get comfortable using the robot to mediate their collaboration and to trust themselves and one another in working through the robot to facilitate patient treatment. The patient also has to build trust with RP-7 for without that trust, confidence in the medical team erodes, hindering the effectiveness of the treatment and the collaboration not just between doctors but also between the doctors and patient.

Principle 4: Here, there is significant overlap with the points made in reference to Principle 1. To use collaborative tools and modes effectively requires that practitioners of virtual collaborative writing identify the goals and expectations of the local cultures of collaboration in which tools and modes are put to use. The more designers of these tools and modes can anticipate how the needs of a given local culture of collaboration are distinct from other cultures, the greater the likelihood for success in virtual collaborative writing. As a tool, RP-7 appears to provide the modes of communication that the collaborating doctors need in order to interact with each other and the patient to reach the goal of successful diagnosis and treatment. RP-7 adheres to the demand for efficiency because it puts the patient in contact with a specialist doctor more quickly than if the patient had to be transported to another hospital. But RP-7 also upholds the medical expertise necessary to successful treatment, and does not compromise the expertise vital to the local culture of collaboration it sustains in the name of efficiency. Thus, effective use of tools and modes in virtual collaborative writing in the future will demand increasing efficiency and maintaining the expertise that characterizes the local culture of collaboration for which those tools and modes have been designed.

Recommendations

RP-7 challenges practitioners to think about the fundamentals of virtual collaborative writing. In a future that will see an inevitable exponential rise in the number and variation of digital tools and modes for communication, practitioners will have to keep a firm grasp on the basics. What are the basics of virtual collaborative writing? In this chapter, I have made an argument that to answer that question practitioners of virtual collaborative writing should recall the fundamentals intrinsic to the production and use of print texts, rather than depart entirely from the past. The risk practitioners of virtual collaborative writing take if they forget the world of print in their design and implementation of digital environments in virtual collaborative writing is that they will be operating without any shared understanding of the basics or fundamentals that are guiding pillars to their work. A shared understanding of the basics of effective collaboration will also need to include the collaborators themselves, and the fundamentals of the local culture of collaboration in which they are working.

Given the complexity of virtual collaborative writing in terms of the constantly increasing variety of digital tools and modes of communication as well as the expertise and goals of different local cultures of collaboration, the need for practitioners of virtual collaborative writing to observe a set of basics that consistently apply to different contexts of collaboration will be essential. The more complex an operation becomes, the more valuable memory of the fundamentals to that operation are. Otherwise, chaos is unavoidable, and digital technologies continue to change and become increasingly sophisticated at a rate that overwhelms designers, practitioners, and collaborators. Everyone becomes so consumed with the technologies themselves that they forget how to harness and focus these technologies to meet the human needs that ultimately determine the success or failure of virtual collaborative writing. Given

the prevailing attitudes toward the relationship between digital and print tools and modes of communication, there will be a temptation for practitioners of virtual collaborative writing only to look forward, put blind trust in the next innovation in the digital world, and harbor a false hope that it will be a breakthrough that will get the job done. While the future of virtual collaborative writing certainly promises fascinating developments in digital technologies, when practitioners find themselves scratching their heads and uncertain of what to do next, they should also look to the past and remember the basics of communication and writing that have sustained effective collaboration in the professions for centuries.

REFERENCES

Blake, W. (1997). *The complete poetry and prose of William Blake* (Erdman, D. V., Ed.). Port Moody, Canada: Anchor Publishing.

Caruso, C. (1997). Before you cite a site. *Educational Leadership, 55*, 24–25.

Chartier, R. (1994). *The order of books*. Stanford, CA: Stanford University Press.

Clark, H. H., Schreuder, P., & Buttrick, S. (1983). Common ground and the understanding of demonstrative reference. *Journal of Verbal Learning and Verbal Behavior, 22*, 245–258. doi:10.1016/S0022-5371(83)90189-5

Crystal, D. (2006). *Language and the Internet*. Cambridge, UK: Cambridge University Press. doi:10.1017/CBO9780511487002

De Certeau, M. (1992). *The writing of history*. New York: Columbia University Press.

Flanigan, A. J., & Metzger, M. (2000). Perceptions of Internet information credibility. *Journalism & Mass Communication Quarterly, 63*, 515–540.

Goody, J. (1977). *Domestication of the savage mind*. Cambridge, UK: Cambridge University Press.

Haas, C. (1994). Learning to read biology: One undergraduates' rhetorical development. *Written Communication, 8*(3), 43–83. doi:10.1177/0741088394011001004

Haas, C. (1996). Text sense and writers' materially based representations of text. In *Writing technology: Studies in the materiality of literacy* (pp. 116–133). Mahwah, NJ: Lawrence Erlbaum.

Haas, C., & Wearden, S. T. (2003). E-credibility: Building common ground in Web environments. *Educational Studies in Language and Literature, 3*, 169–184. doi:10.1023/A:1024557422109

Kapoun, J. (1997). *Teaching undergrads WEB evaluation: A guide for library instruction*. Retrieved June 28, 2002 from www.ala.org/acr;/undwebev.html

Kelly, K. (2009, November/December). The virtual world. *Adbusters. Journal of the Mental Health Environment, 6*(17).

Lewin, T. (2009, August 9). In a digital future, textbooks are history. *New York Times*, A1.

Perelman, C. & Olbrechts-Tyteca. (1969). *The new rhetoric: A treatise on argumentation*. South Bend. IN: Notre Dame Press.

Schultz, K. (1997). Discourses of workplace education: A challenge to the new orthodoxy. In Hull, G. (Ed.), *Changing work, changing workers: Critical perspectives on language, literacy, and skills* (pp. 43–83). Albany, NY: State University of New York Press.

Scribner, S., & Cole, M. (1981). *The psychology of literacy*. Cambridge, MA: Harvard University Press.

Selfe, C. (1999). *Technology and literacy in the 21st century: The importance of paying attention*. Carbondale, IL: Southern Illinois University Press.

Witte, S. P. (1992). Context, text, and intertext: Toward a constructivist semiotic. *Written Communication, 2*(9), 237–308. doi:10.1177/0741088392009002003

ENDNOTE

[1] See pp. 115-120: "By the very fact of selecting certain elements and presenting them to the audience, their importance and pertinence to the discussion are implied. Indeed, such a choice endows these elements with a presence, which is an essential factor in argumentation, and one thing that is far too much neglected in rationalistic conceptions of reasoning. Presence acts directly on our sensibility. As Piaget shows, it is a psychological datum operative already at the level of perception: when two things are set side-by-side, say a fixed standard and things of variable dimensions with which it is compared, the thing on which the eye dwells, that which is best or most often seen, is, by that very circumstance, overestimated. The thing that is present to the consciousness thus assumes an importance that the theory and practice of argumentation must take into consideration."

Section 8
Collaborating Virtually to Develop This Book:
A Discussion

Chapter 22
Collaborating Virtually to Develop This Book

Charlotte Robidoux
Hewlett-Packard Company, USA

Beth L. Hewett
University of Maryland University College, USA

ABSTRACT

The focus of this chapter is to describe how the writers and editors of this book attempted to employ virtual collaborative writing strategies, including those described throughout this text, in the process of developing and writing this book. This discussion reflects on the processes the writers of this book used to write collaboratively in a virtual environment, as well as strategies and tools that facilitated or hindered their efforts. The discussion draws on the six principles underlying virtual collaborative writing to evaluate the experience of using technology to develop content collaboratively. In so doing, the writers present recommendations that workplace teams can use to manage virtual collaborative writing more effectively. This chapter provides practical examples of success and failure that can guide professionals committed to improving virtual collaborative writing in range of workplace environments. These experiences point to lessons for improving overall performance— whether teams are just forming, looking for ways to manage or plan collaborative writing projects, confused about making decisions virtually, or in search of standards and processes that enable virtual collaborative writing.

INTRODUCTION

A Vignette Continued

In August of 2008, IGI Global contacted Beth about writing a book about CMC technology and online communication, building on work that she and her son conducted for another IGI Global book. Because her son was working on his Ph.D. and could not participate, Beth asked Charlotte if she would be interested in such a project. Charlotte indicated that she could take on such a large project only if the topic were related to her full-time work at HP—virtual collaborative writing. Independently, Charlotte was researching the strategies needed for teams of writers to collaborate effectively in virtual

DOI: 10.4018/978-1-60566-994-6.ch022

work environments. Beth was open to the idea and we wrote a proposal describing a project that would engage individuals from both industry and academia to help increase understanding among professionals interested in teaching and/or doing technical writing.

Once the proposal was accepted, we sent out requests for chapters and eventually had over 35 writers interested in the project. By December, it was clear that some individuals who expressed interest were less eager to take on the tasks of writing collaboratively because of other research interests or commitments. After we had phone conferences with all interested writers, close to 30 participants committed to the project. We also included our publisher's editorial communications coordinator in the virtual experience to observe the process. She was given wiki access, which meant that she was notified automatically whenever writers posted something to the wiki and that she could read the drafted writing at any time. She also was included as an observer to the listserv. These open communications provided her with a clearer sense of our experiences and may have enabled IGI Global to be more flexible if we needed to adjust the timetable. In sum, over a roughly nine-month period, our writing team collaborated in one form or another and carried out discussions on a wiki both to advance our ideas and to reflect on our experiences.

Our primary goal for writing a book on the subject of virtual collaborative writing was not only to draw on the experiences and research of the book's writers, but also to learn by doing—to gather practical experience within our own team about various approaches and technologies that support writing in this way. Even though it was apparent to us that our experience would not encapsulate the experiences of all virtual collaborative writing teams, we believed that any hands-on information that we collected would enable us to comment authentically on the challenges that emerge when writers collaborate virtually in the workplace.

As we prepared for our work on this book and established a writing team that would collaborate virtually, we wondered about others who may have undertaken such an experiment, though we were not aware of any. We did not presuppose that our pilot model of virtual collaborative writing would be unique or scientific in nature in terms of our findings. Rather, in undertaking such a pilot—trying to practice what we were studying and describing—we sought to deepen our understanding of what it means to create an integrated, distributed writing team, to share ownership of content, and to depend on others for contributions to an overall product. Being able to appreciate the experience of writing collaboratively in virtual environments has enabled us to cull important observations from our team's feedback; thus, recommendations for virtual collaborative writing have emerged from our hard-earned experiences.

The Value in Reflecting on Our Work

The primary purpose of providing descriptive information about how we were able to collaborate successfully and unsuccessfully is to enable professionals in research and industry to draw on and extend the ideas presented here. In the information age, which emphasizes the global distribution and consumption of modular content, practitioners and researchers alike can uncover new ways of writing collaboratively in distributed workplace environments. Additionally, in keeping with the premise established in Chapter 1, writing teams need to investigate their own collaborative processes and uses of online technologies to understand more about improving their performance. Accordingly, we employ the training principles of investigation and reflection (Hewett and Ehmann, 2004; Ehmann Powers and Hewett, 2008) outlined in Chapter 1 to probe more fully about our own strengths and weaknesses as a collaborative writing team. This chapter also represents our enactment of the sixth principle of collaboration that grounds this book, measuring and tracking our success.

In this final chapter, we evaluate our work using the principles of collaboration presented in this book as well as the measures established by Lowry, Numamaker, Curtis, and Lowry (2005). This chapter provides an evaluation of our accomplishments, lost opportunities, and lessons learned. We draw on observations documented in the wiki; expressed in group phone conferences, e-mails, and instant messages (IMs); articulated in one-on-one phone calls; and culled from online surveys. Using the daily work of our writing team, we evaluate the collected information about what we have learned and what we would recommend to other teams undertaking virtual collaborative writing projects in industry or academic settings. Finally, we draw on the six principles of collaboration established in the Introduction and Chapter 1 to organize and evaluate our experiences.

ABOUT EDITED COLLECTIONS, COLLABORATION, AND TECHNOLOGY

This volume represents an attempt at developing an edited collection that encouraged and employed collaboration among writers and editors. Further, it used available virtual technology to simulate the virtual conditions under which many collaborating writers operate. The result, as this chapter shows, is what we think is a strong book in terms of content—what one would expect from an edited collection that that includes a range of views on a subject—but it is one that succeeded only moderately in promoting collaboration among participants and in using virtual technology. Although this chapter discusses various reasons for arriving at unimpressive results, perhaps the most significant one is the fact that we had too many unknown or understudied variables and not enough stable structures in place. Therefore, it is useful to understand something of the nature of each variable with regard to our book's goals.

Generally speaking, edited collections consist of a range of writers, each of whom contributes a distinct chapter focused on the main subject of the book. Typically, there is minimal contact among all contributors. That is, the edited collection achieves continuity or integration through the guidance of an editor or set of editors who work with each contributor; editors help to shape the whole of the text so that an underlying coherence permeates to create some degree of uniformity for audiences interested in the collection's primary subject. As such, more often than not, this book genre entails serial and parallel collaborative interactions. The work is serial in that the writers tend to work on first a proposal, which an editor reads and helps to shape, and then on an early draft, which the editors also shape, and then a final draft, which the editors edit. The collaboration is parallel in that the writers work on different parts of the project (different chapters) simultaneously with the editors also addressing different sections like, for example, the introduction or editorial housekeeping chores. In the meantime, external reviewers often provide guidance, first, to editors as to what is publishable and, second, to writers as to how to make their work publishable.

This standard approach to edited collections serves many valuable purposes, such as gathering research on a similar subject from different perspectives, quickly publishing the most current ideas on a subject since a team of writers can accomplish this task faster than one writer working alone, and republishing seminal materials that have been published in different media at various times. This format allows readers to gain access to a one or more perspectives on the subject considered in a collection. Edited collections also can be used as comprehensive references in the classroom to expose students to a range of viewpoints.

How then can a different approach to edited collections be of value if the standard approach to the genre is already useful? Generally speaking, what edited collections do not provide is a fully integrated view of a subject such that all writers have a shared vision, unified sense of goals for the text, agreement on the contributions and commitments of each writer, and a commitment to interactivity among the writers that will make the text cohesive and organic. Those in favor of the standard approach to edited collections might counter this view with the reasonable statement that if readers are looking for integration, then perhaps they should consult singly or doubly authored book on a particular subject. Texts developed by one or two writers do have enormous value. Nonetheless, such texts do not always benefit from a range of perspectives, which is something we sought in our volume.

We argue that a cohesive edited collection can benefit those looking for integrated points of view on a subject. While a traditional edited collection has enough implicit consistency in some of the basic premises to provide readers with traction when reading the material, more explicit consistency is better. Edited collections also benefit from both internal *and* external review. That is, while the editors gain a full view of the whole text, the writers typically do not comment on specific parts or the overall text. Thus, the text loses the benefit of deeper readings by the experts who are writing it. Another benefit of a more cohesively edited collection is that such texts can provide a more holistic approach to terminology since all contributors can make agreements about what terms to use for key concepts. In addition, this approach provides more opportunities for invention—or idea development—about a subject given a wider range of writer interactivity and potential synergy.

While rare, collaborative texts are available. One example of such a collaboratively written text with extensive cohesion is an article written by 11 authors in *Journal of Business and Technical Communication*, "IText: Future Directions for Research on the Relationship between Information Technology and Writing" (Geisler, et al., 2001). That article reads much like one with a singular voice, yet it covers a wider range of material than

most experts in an area have. Another example is *Writing and Online Education: Global Questions, Local Answers* (Cargile-Cook & Grant Davie, 2005), a co-edited book with over 20 contributors. In this case, the editors had planned explicit cross-referencing from the outset. The editors were colocated and shared copies of the proposals and drafts with each other. When they found potential connections between or among chapters, they marked the connections and informed the writers. They did the same with the first drafts. Then, they posted the drafts to a website and encouraged writers to familiarize themselves with them. They assigned two to three chapters to each writer, asked each to read those chapters, and requested that each writer mark inside the texts where they saw inter-chapter connections. The editors followed the same process. This reading led to a number of parenthetical internal connections; however, writers did not comment on others' content or drafts (Cargile-Cook, November 4, 2009, personal communication). The result was, in our opinion, a strong edited collection with some cohesion created through a conscious use of serial and parallel collaboration.

Our goal was to develop similar integration among chapters, but to do so collectively. We asked writers to sign on to the project with explicit collaboration in mind. We explained that the proposals and early drafts would be posted in a shared digital space so that everyone could become familiar as quickly as possible with all of the book's major themes and writing. We encouraged connections among chapters in terms of references to other chapters, but we wanted writers to influence and challenge each other's thinking. And we wanted them to comment on *and* revise each other's writing much as educators might encourage deep level comments from their students who read in peer responses groups (see Chapter 16). In short, we wanted them to become collectively responsible for the content and quality of the book through such internal review. While we also planned external reviews, we believed that the strongest interaction and feedback would come internally.

As defined in Chapter 1, collective collaboration occurs when writers contribute concurrently to a project through topic assignments based on a writer's knowledge of the product or tools (specialty areas) and on activities related to project tracking. Based on this work, specific predefined roles are delineated. All team members provide equally important contributions to the project and have shared ownership of the overall project success.

However, despite our desire to increase the intensity of collaboration beyond that of serial or parallel forms, we made another deliberate choice to keep individual names on chapters. If essentially singly authored, the chapter would bear a single writer's name; if multiply authored, every writer with substantive "touch" on the chapter was to be named. While this model does not engage collective collaboration fully in that writers did not share chapter ownership equally, we did not think it fair to ask writers who were volunteering for an intense project to give up chapter ownership. For many, the best reason to participate involved the need to demonstrate their continuing value to their employers, which included showing their grasp of technical communication content or their ability to publish in a peer-edited volume. In retrospect, we think that a collectively collaborative book ideally would have equal representation of all writers, but we realize that the North American work culture and our own technological and practical collaborative processes were not ready for that outcome.

As this book addresses throughout, virtually developed and shared writing is becoming more typical in our globalized, digitized world. So, it is not unusual to find all kinds of publications that have been developed virtually and collaboratively—from the online academic journal discussed in Chapter 19, to magazines (or *zines*), to books written by authors who are destined never to meet, to government documents that will be distributed nationwide as described in Chapter 16, to product-specific documents in industry that increasingly rely on co-written content to serve global consumer-based audiences, as described in Chapters 9, 10, and 12. What makes our venture different is its attempt to conduct our collaborative work using virtual tools self-consciously and experimentally in this genre. Hence, combined with this goal of internal cohesion, we planned to use virtual tools to enable collaborative activities. First, we wanted to provide geographically distributed writers with an effective means for communicating beyond the telephone (that is, a single synchronous modality) and e-mail (that is, a single asynchronous modality), which we suspect are the two most commonly used virtual tools. Second, we wanted to study our writers' and our own processes qualitatively while the book work developed. All the writers who signed onto the project agreed to this goal and method in an initial phone conference. We researched available technologies and chose several synchronous (that is, one-to-one and group-based conference phone calls, IM, and where possible, desktop sharing) and asynchronous (that is, e-mail, listserv, a wiki, and Google Docs) tools. Our belief that we were ready was only true in theory.

In practice, as the rest of this chapter details, we were underprepared for the venture. The central challenge that we faced was insufficient practice using the tools selected for complex writing projects, even though both Beth and Charlotte had ample experience as managers using virtual tools. Somehow the newness of the tools caused us to forget our experience; in short, although we had in mind some principles for leading virtual teams with technology, we lost sight of those principles quickly and found ourselves acting as through we were just learning our skills instead of calling consciously upon known *and* transferable skills. Add to that self-created dilemma, we were working with a model of collaborative writing and editing that made sense theoretically but that was new to us in practicality. Ultimately, we had set up the situation with too many unknown variables and failed to provide enough recognizable structure—hence, stability—to the process. In retrospect we would have handled things differently, given the research conducted by Lowry, et al. (2005, p. 348), which demonstrated that virtual collaborative writing efficiency depends upon training and practice on a tool set that is tested to support the project requirements. In the end, we did indeed learn a lot, but it was from the position of scrambling to catch up rather than from the preferred position of managing the project proactively.

SUMMARY OF PROCESSES AND RESULTS

With a strategy for working virtually underway, we prepared guidelines for collaborating and selected tools for interacting. The goal was to avoid proprietary tools, choosing cost-free options that anyone could use, so as not to create an "unfair" advantage that could be considered a reason for success if indeed we were successful. The technology included most of the virtual tools described in Chapter 1 as indicated in Table 1.

Our experience writing this book while using some of the virtual collaborative strategies under discussion was challenging. We had our share of setbacks from setting up the virtual tools just described to finding the time to engage in collaboration as comprehensively as we had envisioned. Far beyond the cliché that "my dog ate my homework," we had a writer with a hard drive crash and another who moved cross country. Still others experienced sudden and significant illnesses; some were hit with job loss concerns in a dicey economy; and still others just never made lift off. We had to find every creative way possible to make our book organization logical as writers left, joined, and became available. We never lost sight of the idea that our team of writers volunteered to take on this work as an extracurricular activity. No one was paid or had any idea of the real-time commitment necessary beyond the fact that on some levels this work seemed like an interesting idea—at first, anyway. The same can be said for us. As editors, we were engaged in full-time work and completing of other projects; we had remarkably unrealistic visions of the time commitment we needed to complete the project on time and in excellent condition within such a short period.

Table 1. Options for working virtually

Technology	Requirements	Tool selected
Wiki	Manage discussions and brainstorming	PBworks wiki recommended by team
Repository	Enable synchronous writing and secure storage of files on a restricted domain	Google Docs, selected based on research
Web conferencing	Hybrid technology to link audio and visual communications for 2 or more individuals, interactive work sessions	HP Virtual Rooms
Telephone	Address individual and group concerns synchronously	Any telephone device
Instant messaging	Synchronous interactivity to resolve issues immediately	Various client types
E-mail	Individual questions and answers to one or a few writers	Various work and personal mail accounts
Quality management	Tool for ensuring consistent terminology and language throughout the book	acrolinx® IQ
Online survey	Gather feedback from writers on their experience	Zoomerang

Our 1-year time frame for completing a book based on an atypical process seemed ludicrous to the two of us, but that did not stop us from moving forward. We really did not fully understand how many of the principles of collaborative writing we were in danger of violating as we moved forward. At times, we made the wrong decisions, second guessed ourselves, and we repeated mistakes in making decisions about the use of virtual tools, whether to establish certain processes, and how best to communicate with our team. While the academic contributors were accustomed to publishing, they seemed disenchanted with our schedule especially during the school year. Although practitioners were accustomed to deadlines, they seemed ill at ease articulating their ideas in front of academic contributors. Indeed the culture clash we observed—the gap between theory and practice—became apparent at every turn. Virtually, we spilled too much ink discussing the nature of teams, what it means to collaborate, and whether and how much theoretical material to include. Repeatedly, we considered different ways to impel certain action, realizing yet again that as a pilot, our team was made up of volunteers, which is not the typical virtual writing team experience. To our credit, both editors are active rhetoricians, which helped us to find interesting ways to spin the situation and lead our writing team forward on our virtual collaborative journey.

With every mistake, apparent failure, and unexpected turn of events, we reminded ourselves that we were learning something valuable—and that our setbacks would become useful information for the book's final chapter reflecting on our experiences. "Our readers will benefit from what we learn," we reminded ourselves.

We highlight our experience in terms of the six principles we identify in the Introduction and Chapter 1. Table 2 is a summary of the points related to these principles, which we discuss later in greater detail.

At the end of the project, we implemented a survey modeled on the one that Lowry et al. (2005, p. 344) used to measure virtual collaborative writing team performance. In that study, the researchers identified five areas of virtual collaboration to measure: productivity, document quality, process satisfaction, relationship quality, and communication quality. We created a brief survey on Zoomerang and asked different questions based on these five categories. Out of the 22 writers that made up our virtual team, 14 (64%) responded to the survey: We asked respondents to rate their experiences as low, average, or high. Figures 1, 2, 3, 4 and 5 illustrate the results for each of the five categories.

Figure 1 indicates that 46% of respondents found their productivity in the book-writing process largely to be average, while 33% rated it high

Table 2. Summary of results related to principles

Principle	Strength	Weakness
Cultural	Editors spanned both cultures	Cultural divide, differing values deeper than anticipated
Leadership	Reactive, able to correct problems before they became insurmountable	Fragmented because of competing demands; influence limited, voluntary team
Trust	Ability to establish rapport quickly	Insufficient team building given culture clash, and size of team too large
Tools/Modes	Implemented a solid plan for use of tools and modes despite team size,	Understood concepts but made some wrong decisions, ad hoc learning; should have tested tools more thoroughly
Structure	Implemented explicit processes initially and for critical tasks	Limited formal procedures, no scripted processes to guide coordination, sporadic follow-up
Measures	Discussion board for reflections; post-book survey	No set expectations, interspersed tracking, limited follow through

Figure 1. Productivity results

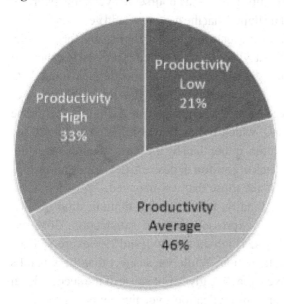

Figure 2. Document quality results

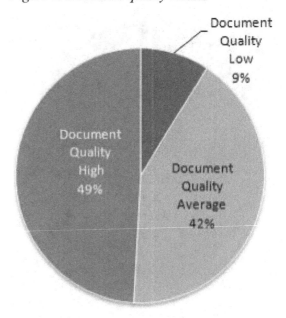

Figure 3. Process satisfaction results

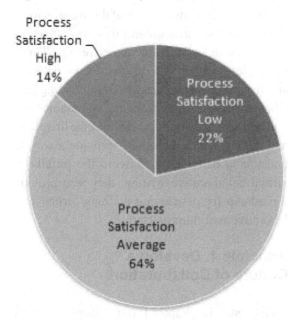

Figure 4. Relationship quality results

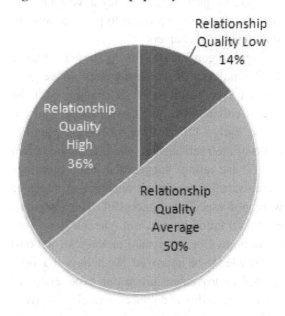

and 21% rated it low. These results suggest that team members may have experienced some dissatisfaction with their own or others' productivity. Indeed, in an open-ended response at the end of the survey, some stated that they blamed themselves for not being more interactive or for not producing more text in a timely manner. We sus-

pect both that our processes (seen in Figure 3) and everyone's busy status, as employed individuals working on other projects, are at least partly responsible for such comments.

Figure 2 indicates that 49% of the respondents found the document quality to be high, while 42% rated it average and 9% rated it low. We do not

Figure 5. Communication quality results

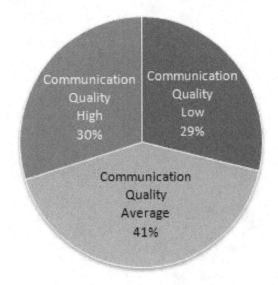

know whether participants were thinking of their own chapters or the book as a whole; however, the response suggests that they may have found the virtual collaborative process to produce reasonably developed chapters.

Figure 3 confirms the results shown in Figure 1. The majority of the participants—64%—expressed average levels of satisfaction with the virtual collaborative processes that we had engaged. Only 14% rated the processes as high in terms of their satisfaction, while 22% rated them low. These ratings suggest that team members were aware that our virtual collaborative processes were not especially successful. The questions we asked failed to tease out whether it was the collaborative or the virtual processes (or both) that needed to be improved. We believe that both needed improvement given our experiences of "forgetting" what to do once we decided to work with some unfamiliar technology to encourage the large-scale collaboration.

Figure 4 shows that 50% of the respondents were moderately satisfied with the quality of relationships that they developed during the 1-year project. While 36% expressed high satisfaction, 14% admitted to low satisfaction with relationship

quality. During the course of a year, however, we had hoped that the writers would get to know each other better through IM or the listserv, for example. Most with whom we spoke expressed that they did not get to know anyone outside their immediate team. Some did indicate that they felt a sense of comradery when there was a small group phone call, which typically was initiated by one of the editors rather than by the participants, suggesting a lack of comfort or desire to develop relationships outside those that we managed.

Finally, in terms of communication quality, 41% expressed average satisfaction, 30% expressed high satisfaction, and 29% expressed low satisfaction. While we suspect that these results were realistic given our sense of the success level for communication over the course of the year, they are far below our anticipated goals at the outset of the project.

The following discussion of the six principles of collaboration that ground this book helps to explain these satisfaction survey results. These principles—which we discovered inductively and from an iterative process of interacting collaboratively, reading chapters, communicating with individual authors, researching the literature, and talking with each other—provide a way to understand better how to avoid the pitfalls of virtual collaborative writing; they also provide a roadmap for developing a strong virtual collaborative writing project.

Principle 1. Develop a Culture of Collaboration

As indicated in Chapter 1, our highly networked global economy promotes the quest for multimedia information anywhere and anytime. This emphasis creates a shift away from lengthy, linear texts toward topic-based writing and content that often must stand alone, requiring collective input to ensure completeness and accuracy. Writing in the digital age necessitates a culture that supports virtual collaborative interactions. And changing a culture takes time. In this project, we not only had precious little time to address cultural issues, but also we never fully imagined the power of cultural differences to create rifts within our team. We often dismissed the idea that cultural norms—underlying values and tacit assumptions—would take us off course. Our goal in this section is to investigate the concept of culture so that we can provide overarching recommendations for virtual collaborative writing teams to consider.

The statements that follow from team members about inherent differences in basic beliefs underscore the importance of understanding the cultural underpinnings within a team as well as devising a strategy both for assessing cultural norms at the local level and in terms of what it means for writers to share their writing and ownership with others. Indeed, the comments provided here reflect cultural differences on two levels: (1) in reference to the issue of *ownership* or owning a text and (2) in terms of local allegiances.

We're welcomed/invited/encouraged even to add text to others' chapter wikis, but it's still "their" chapter.

I've mentioned before that I've avoided adding a comment/suggestion to a particular chapter wiki area out of deference to that chapter's designated "author"... I hesitate to affect any author's content before seeing a draft-text. I might offer suggestions once more text is present.

We write comments to each other or comment within the text, but even given the affordances of the wiki, no one (?) has gone in and actually changed or added to the words originally authored by another. We're delicately stepping around that possibility by making oblique suggestions.

Initially I was reluctant to even comment on the wiki in the presence of others—especially the academicians—who, I assumed, must know more than I do. I got over this, but it was reminiscent of

the reluctance we see in my department by some writers who are afraid to speak up in front of more senior writers, or others whom they perceive as "the experts" in some domain.

One thing this project has brought home to me is that there are different motivators in industry and academe, and that affects how we collaborate, and what we value in it.

In industry—especially in today's agile projects—deadlines and efficiencies have at least equal weight with achieving quality. Not that we don't value and strive for quality—of course we do—but in our collaborations, often the primary drivers are efficiency and the ability to meet deadlines, while still achieving "good enough" quality.

Culture of Ownership

Apparent in these statements is what we call a "culture of ownership"; that is, creating a culture of collaboration requires "seeing" evidence of how and where writers own texts. The comments reveal that writers are afraid of touching text written, hence "owned," by others. Ownership of work, in this case written products, gave owners rights about how to manage the text. In our team, although we encouraged cross-pollination, the idea that someone's name was associated with a chapter suggested ownership and thus limited discussion within and around someone else's content. While commenting about the text may have been reasonable to the writers, the idea of revising or modifying the text itself seemed to be off limits. Given time constraints and missing content in some chapters, as editors we eventually seized control of the texts and became ghostwriters, adding, modifying, and removing information. Beth was bolder in this regard at first, but out of necessity, Charlotte soon became more comfortable with the process.

In terms of workplace writing, without the concept of ownership, it is easy for someone to drop out of action, thinking that it is someone else's responsibility to carry out certain tasks. We experienced the problem in our own team. For example, academic contributors were seen as having special ownership of theoretical material, which made it easier for practitioners to remain uninvolved with that content. While it makes sense that theory would be less familiar to industry contributors and thus difficult to work on, in workplace settings not everyone gets to work on what they know, are good at, or like to do. If virtual collaborative writing means that texts are co-authored to some degree, then creating a culture of collaboration means changing the "culture of ownership" so that writers work cooperatively, even with material that may seem foreign. This change implies finding ways to share ownership of special areas of knowledge (theory, for example), administrative tasks, project tracking activities, planning work, tools management, and so on. A collaborative model means that ownership is shared in terms of who writes what and who carries out other nonwriting-related tasks.

Changing the culture of ownership thus implies the assignment of roles for coordinating a range of tasks that had been carried out by one person. The concept of roles can help to instill a different kind of ownership that hopefully will ensure accountability if implemented effectively. In our project, the strategy for distributing ownership was minimal. For instance, although we created an outline and structure for the book, which grouped writers in terms areas of interest (planning chapters, for example) or sections of the book, we did not establish expectations related to shared ownership for a given section. We might have been more effective if we had redefined ownership and guided writers on how best to oversee and take responsibility for different sections of the book as well as how to collaborate with the writers assigned to that section. A comment from our survey indicates that assigning responsibility may have helped: "Perhaps if I'd been assigned to give response to one or two other chapters, the

task would have seemed more doable." While the idea of "assigning" work seems more pertinent to the principle of structure, it also entails ownership, which goes beyond delegating a task to owning the role and responsibility. Even so, because our team was made up of volunteers, as one writer described it, "a temporary team," we must assume that recreating ownership would have shaped the culture differently. One writer pointed to a recurring conflict between what we were writing about and what that content indicated that we should be doing: "We had an interesting disconnect between the theories and advice we were addressing in our chapter and our own processes. However, this would be a totally different situation if we were doing this project as part of our jobs rather than as an add-on."

Local Allegiances

The comments related to culture from our writing team also point to the issue of closely held beliefs and ingrained behavioral norms. Our cultural divide was between the industry and academia, between talking about and teaching writing and being immersed in that very practice. A list of oppositions described by Miller (1989) epitomizes the cultural divide that was ever present in our project: "theory versus practice," "academy versus industry," "ivory tower versus marketplace," "inquiry versus action," and "knowing-that versus knowing-how" (p. 21). The local allegiances on our team reflected these incompatibilities; that is, contributors either valued ideas for their own sake or because they had to complete a deliverable. Miller recognized that the best case scenario for these dichotomous viewpoints is the notion of "creative tension," a concept that may have been a helpful starting point for addressing our cultural divide (p. 21). Ultimately, all workplace writing teams will have local allegiances, biases, and social norms that guide their interactions or their inaction.

Once discussions began to emerge on the wiki, the tension became apparent. As suggested in the comments provided earlier, the academic contributors started the discussion and largely began looking at theories of collaboration and the nature of the writing team. The reticence about responding due to feeling intimidated by a scholarly presence was very real for practitioners, who sometimes grew weary of the hair splitting nature of some discussions. Indeed, the very idea of the academic persona diminished any opportunities for felt social presence on the part of practitioners. That is, presuppositions about formality and distance actually became enacted on the wiki through words about theory that seemed foreign to writers from industry.

And while trying out ideas may have been easier to accomplish for academics, some practitioners who got past feeling intimidated became anxious about saying anything for another reason—for fear of violating their company's intellectual property rights. Although the industry writers were quite capable of delivering written products, some of them were unable to share their ideas until they received permission from their companies. Thus, the cultural norm in business related to intellectual property was another dimension that impeded collaboration. Even if business writers wanted to share, they had either corporate restrictions or tight production deadlines. Some industry writers, overcome by deadlines, remained on the virtual fringes: "The lack of time was an outside factor that limited my contribution to the team."

Recommendations for Creating a Culture of Collaboration

Creating a culture of collaboration would be easy if the process was quick, but instead the process evolves over time (Schein, 2009, p. 189) with the help of a carefully considered plan. Changes initiated by the plan build on each other. One change that enables writers to survive and thrive in a new setting—like virtual collaborative writing—can then engender another change in time. Through such changes, the subculture within the culture

at large develops and takes new paths. Cultural change should be guided organizationally in ways that both promote the task and support the writers. As Schein advised, the starting point is not the cultural change itself but the issues that the organization faces. Clarity from leaders is crucial to ensure incremental changes.

From our experiences, we suggest that cultural change is best accomplished after leaders or managers determine what the cultural shift/s should be. In our case, all of our writers expressed familiarity and comfort with collaborative writing and excitement about writing a book with the deliberate use of CMC tools that enable collaboration virtually. We expected that we had a pre-made culture of collaboration. Therefore, the first signs of culture problems should have alerted us about what needed to be shifted. Top-down actions connected to cultural concerns include:

- *Determine if the project's goals are out of synch with the writing culture.* Our own discomfort with removing names from chapters should have been a signal to us that we needed to address a cultural shift. As soon as we decided to use writer's names in each chapter, we should have been alerted to the disjuncture of our goals (a collaboratively written book) and the cultural expectations (authorship of chapters). While our decision to keep chapter authorship may have remained the same, the need to make that decision was a clear signal that cultural change was essential.
- *Consider the makeup of the writers and anyone with whom they are to collaborate directly or indirectly.* In some cases, writers are familiar with collaborating with SMEs, technology specialists, and engineers. However, as the case study of Chapter 6 points out, working with people from different backgrounds may entail a need to acculturate one group or another to new tools or processes. Our own decision

to draw deliberately from both academic and industry writers for the strengths they could bring to the book should have suggested that with their strengths also come differences. The goal should have been to help them write within a culture that recognized their strengths and differences while it encouraged their willingness to stretch and adopt a new cultural perspective.

- *Describe the culture shift that needs to occur for the project or organization to succeed.* In our case, we needed academic writers to write in more inclusive and accessible language for a broader audience. Although we described the intended audience and its needs early in the recruitment process, we did not succeed in moving most academic writers to use this different level of formality or accessibility, or as they would call it, *register*. Similarly, we needed industry writers to disregard the potential intimidation of theory, letters behind the name (for example, *Ph.D.*), and inaccessible language so that they would not be intimidated into silence but instead be vocal about what they found to be useful or unclear in others' writing and content. We also needed industry writers to change jargon usage and adopt more accessibly language. A single attempt to describe that culture shift to them was insufficient; we needed to address it forthrightly, often, and with specific guidance regarding how to change.

- *Determine and enact specific activities that can enable the desired culture shift.* Recognizing where change needs to occur is one step; providing clear and doable activities that will engender the change is the next step, and it is crucial. If writers do not know what to do or how to do it to meet the project's cultural needs, they are set up to fail. In our case, doable steps would have included:

1. Asking writers to identify themselves with the academic world, industry, or as straddling both in virtual discussions to raise the level of consciousness about the importance of a primary culture;
2. Asking writers to clarify in a second or third discussion post (if written) what they mean when their language is too "academic" or "jargon-filled" depending on their primary culture;
3. Pairing academic and industry writers in subteams for necessary activities like reading and commenting on each other's chapters;
4. Providing all writers with a language accessibility target or model for their writing; and
5. Requiring writers to revise their writing until it meets the audience's needs rather than that of their primary culture.

Principle 2. Find and Promote Leadership

The process of creating a collaborative culture is allied closely with effective leadership. Strong guidance is essential for establishing a collaborative culture. To the extent that leaders understand, value, and advance collaboration, they are more informed about how to support their writers in finding effective ways of collaborating. As one contributor explained, "Everyone knew how and what to write; not everyone knew how to collaborate, especially for a loose collaborative such as this one." Leaders as advocates, therefore, must avail themselves of effective strategies to help writers integrate new practices and norms for collaborating and for identifying team leaders, who can pinpoint opportunities for evolving a mindset of collaboration. Our aim in this section is to explore our own lapses in leadership to recommend ideas for leading effectively.

In comparison to other statements from our team that relate to the principles of collaboration, the comments regarding leadership were less obvious. While there was a reference to good leadership on our team, we maintain from observing our reactive approach to some issues that we should have defined an explicit leadership strategy to ensure that writers understood how to collaborate collectively across the team. The few comments that follow reflect insufficient leadership.

The one thing that might have improved collaboration: project leaders setting clearer expectations and doing more regular follow up for the collaborative aspects of this project.

When I had time set aside to work on the project I would often waste a lot of time trying to figure out *how* I was supposed to do something (write!) rather than actually doing it.

I did try to engage others, but it didn't seem that other authors wanted to collaborate much.

I ignored the many opportunities that were provided for communicating with authors of other chapters and editors

In many ways, these comments get to the heart of the matter—that leaders need to create shared vision, set clear expectations, follow up regularly, and intervene when there are breakdowns.

How did our attempt to lead fail? The fact that we published this book is an indication that we achieved some degree of success. And, in terms of our survey, we were rated 46% average productivity and 33% high productivity. For us, these percentages seem high because while we produced a deliverable, our process was not efficient with the editors working exhaustingly to fill in the gaps and compensate for collaboration that did not happen. In Table 3, we measure our leadership ability in terms of collaboration and elements that Schein (2009) identified as necessary for cultural change, as explained in Chapter 1.

Recommendations for Finding and Promoting Leadership

Everyone knows that management is essential to any project involving more than one person. As co-editors, we certainly recognized ourselves as the book's managers just as we recognized our contact at the publisher as a manager over our plans and activities. As managers, we took specific roles. Beth was the book's program manager and Charlotte was the project manager. But management is not the same as leadership.

While management is a static and rote position from which to engage workers, leadership is a dynamic and driving force. Management moves the organization, while leadership moves the people who work for the organization. According to Bennis and Goldsmith (2003), "Managers are people who do things right and leaders are people who do the right thing. The difference may be summarized as activities of vision and judgment—*effectiveness*—versus activities of mastering routines—*efficiency*" (pp. 7-8).

With these distinctions in mind, good leadership in the virtual collaborative writing setting requires understanding the values that individual writers hold and how those values emerge in team activities. It requires a "learning-oriented, feedback seeking climate" and a "collaborative relationship…between those who are running the ongoing business and those who are changing it" (Anderson & Anderson, 2001, p. 79). In terms of seeking effectiveness and a learning-oriented, collaborative climate, we were fairly successful. Yet, significant elements of leadership were, indeed, lacking in this book project. To that end, we recommend an action-based approach that appreciates values, the need for feedback, and the importance of moving writers into a position where they can feel led and not managed.

- *Remain people-focused rather than overly goal or product-focused.* Leaders guide people while mangers guide projects.

Table 3. Elements for leading cultural change

Element	Use of Elements to Guide Virtual Collaborative Writing Team
A compelling positive vision	• We had a vision that we conveyed in one-on-one interviews, but the vision was not defined clearly enough in the context of the team. • While everyone supported the concept of collaboration by virtue of being on the team, we did not have a shared vision for tool selection. For example, we tried to set up a secure domain on Google Docs for storing files; this approached required special e-mail accounts, a decision that frustrated a number of writers. Almost 25% of our team was affected, which disrupted of efforts to collaborate. • We suspect also that some of team members did not really understand the value of bridging the gap between theory and practice or what it entailed in terms of working together.
Formal training	• If training helps team members adopt new values, ways of thinking, and behaviors for conducting their work, we did not provide training that would influence underlying assumptions. • Training was needed to address attitudes about tools. Early on we did provide an orientation of acrolinx® IQ to ensure the consistent use of terminology and quality. In one session, however, the dialogue about the tool was less about using it and more about how this kind of tool limits the development of ideas, the use of complex verb structures, and the length of sentences—concerns that are related particularly to academic discourse. • Because our team struggled to follow procedures generally, we decided not to ask writers to use acrolinx® IQ; instead, just the editors used it. Because standard tools implementation is required for collaborative teams, we view this outcome as a failure to lead and guide our team.
Involvement of the learner	• We did not set up synchronous interactions often enough to make sure that new ideas were taking root to ensure progress. • We tried to engage the whole team in developing terminology and definitions on the wiki, but discussions about terms were largely unresolved. • At the last minute, we used the listserv to ask people to vote on terms related to information, content, modules, and objects. Collaborating on a standard terminology is essential for collaborative teams. But we never agreed formally, as one writer indicated: "I am still struggling with applying correctly in my chapter some of the common terms we agreed on."
Informal training of teams	• This element entails meeting with the whole team. We were never able to convene the whole team at one time to discuss the project, issues, or progress.
Practice sessions and feedback	• We did not set up synchronous interactions of offer one-on-one "how to" sessions often enough to give or get feedback.
Positive role models	• We set up some meetings with small teams or with individuals who were struggling with issues related to theory versus practice and audience. In these sessions, we modeled collaborative dialogue. The success of these meetings indicates that we should have scheduled small meetings with all the writers. • We asked one especially responsive team member to become a leader in a theory chapter. The amount of theoretical text that different writers provided in response to his requests and his interactive discussion model suggests that assigning more such roles would have helped the team to cohere and be more productive overall.
Support groups	• We did not have a forum for writers to talk about problems with tools or modes of collaborating. Random questions came mainly through personal e-mail accounts. • When the debates over theory and practice reached a fever pitch, Charlotte ran Web conferences to discuss options for incorporating theory and to get feedback on the idea of adding "real-world" vignettes at the front of each chapter to make them more practical. These sessions gave writers direction and modeled synchronous collaboration.
Consistent systems and structures	• Strong leadership means that the teams within organizations have a definite framework (processes and technology) that guides activities. • While we tried to establish a virtual technical framework for collaborating, our strategy for using a wiki and Google Doc created confusion and frustration for many (including the editors!). We documented and issued instructions about accessing the tools at the outset of the project, but did not review the material frequently enough. • We had few formal processes to guide interactions, which we now know was a mistake and a factor that impeded collaboration. That said, without different conditions (for example, more than a year to produce, structured processes, and reliable technology), our makeshift/imitation team would be hard pressed to function optimally as a "real" team.

Being people-focused suggests that when individuals express concern, such feedback is taken very seriously and considered in the context of the whole team. Being people-focused also suggests that managers or editors need to keep a finger on their own pulses. When discomfort or a sense of dissatisfaction with the project arises, leaders will consider how they also need to change. Leaders thus need to be a barometer for the group at large—as we should have recognized at different junctures.

- *Develop a vision for the organization or project and implement it.* Doing so might mean making requests for particular activities or methods; we needed to get permission from the publisher to deviate somewhat from the typical external chapter review process when we promised writers that we would remain a stable team even if early drafts were in need of significant revision. This vision should be shared, articulated, and reiterated as needed so that everyone understands the work at hand in relation to project as a whole.

- *Provide development opportunities for the team.* Opportunities to grow can reward good work and promote leadership across the project. Although on-going development opportunities were hard to find in our short 1-year book project, we found at least one in which we provided a promising writer with sub-leadership opportunities. Because we did not provide such close guidance and equal opportunities for others in the team, however, we all lost a chance for others to grow; indeed one writer expressed dissatisfaction that only one sub-leader had been chosen.

- *Be respectful of those who trust you with their hard work.* Trust is difficult and risky for writers to provide, as Principle 3 later discusses. Therefore, it is critical for leaders to address everyone respectfully and with special care when all communications occur virtually. Doing so means providing everyone with the information needed, opposing gossip about other writers or project difficulties for which they cannot offer solutions, and having the utmost of honesty and integrity about the written products under development and review.

- *Inculcate a sense of purpose in the team so that they understand why and how the project has value.* To that end, leaders should include the writers in decision-making wherever possible, should elicit their feedback about processes and products, and should inform them of major changes and developments. For example, we used the writers' listserv to discuss the nuanced meanings of "virtual collaborative writing" and "collaborative virtual writing" to ask the publisher to let us change the title of the book to reflect how it actually developed as opposed to how it originally was conceived to develop. Writers expressed a sense of inclusion and of having done something important for the project after we informed them of the publisher's agreement.

Principle 3. Establish Trust

Collaborative writing teams need to be confident in the abilities, competencies, and intentions of fellow team members. They depend on strong relationships, which entail predictability about how their other writers operate and how they communicate. Teams need to agree that they will "pull their own weight" and that they will follow procedures and produce high-quality content so that the whole team can be task focused and not distracted by competition. Teams with these qualities have trust, which is difficult to achieve on any deep level. It is unlikely that every writing team will reach "dream team," a status that is not necessary. We were not a dream writing team, and this book, while not perfect, is complete and we believe it will be useful to readers. Sufficient trust is crucial to complete work of good quality and to make it reader-centered. In this section, we assess how well our team formed trust in order to provide practical recommendations.

In terms of our strategy for developing trust, we were convinced that the winning personalities of the editors would be sufficient! In truth, both of us have track records with establishing rapport in virtual work settings, but charisma is not enough <grin>. Teams need to be systematic about addressing the issue of trust based on a number of factors as indicated Chapter 5. Admittedly, we did not explicitly look for ways to build trust; rather, we presented our plan, provided our schedule, and carried out activities based on prior successful experiences. As the comments that follow indicate, we fell short at establishing trust across the whole team.

As has been discussed in various chapters of this book, in any collaboration, it's important to establish trust, and ground rules for working together. These can be difficult to achieve under any circumstances, but they present an even greater challenge in a virtual environment. This was especially so in our collaboration, where it was a temporary team, not colocated, with almost no opportunities to actually speak with each other and thus to establish the personal ties that help people work collaboratively, and work through disagreements that inevitably arise—especially with such intelligent, thoughtful participants from widely varying backgrounds. Some direct communications with Charlotte and Beth and a few others helped me develop trust in them early in the project; however, for most others, the exchange of ideas on the wiki was the first place I got to know them. This exchange was intellectually invigorating, but often served to

highlight differences rather than commonalities, and in particular, exposed some gaping chasms between academic and industry participants. It was not until several of us met by phone to resolve some questions on the organization of book, and a similar conversation among authors of some related chapters, that trust grew—at least for me.

I agree with the writer above...that trusting other members of this collaborative was a challenge. [We] wrote about virtual social presence in our case study. To achieve social presence requires developing and maintaining the social-relational mechanisms of commonality, safety, respect, rapport, and interdependence. While I would not say that we lacked these traits within our group (for example, I never felt disrespected or unsafe), because the group is so large and so diverse and temporary, these traits/relations were not developed among us...Even on the phone conversations, I felt like it was 8 or so writers trying to interact with Beth and Charlotte rather than with each other.

I still haven't touched others' chapters; though. Collaboration involves consensus-building; and stepping on toes, no matter how gently, can negatively affect that effort.

I felt completely detached from the extended team. I would say that is more my fault than the editors because work responsibilities prevented me from dedicating the time that this project deserved. The problem was that the process for communicating and collaborating was complicated and confusing. The lack of a connection with the entire team made me somewhat shy.

In Table 4 we evaluate our sense of the team's trust based on the checklist of elements provided in Chapter 5 on forming trust in teams. Refer to Chapters 1 and 5 for more information about these elements.

Table 4. Assessment of trust elements

Trust Element	Components	Low	Medium	High
Team Traits	• Team size	✓		
	• Diverse team membership		✓	
	• Interdependent relationships	✓		
	• Shared team vision	✓		
	• Articulated team processes	✓		
	• Performance oriented		✓	
	• Social presence		✓	
Team actions	• Get started right away	✓		
	• Communicate frequently		✓	
	• Multitask getting organized and doing substantive work simultaneously	✓		
	• Overtly acknowledge that you have read another's messages		✓	
	• Be explicit about what you are thinking and doing		✓	
	• Set deadlines and stick to them	✓		
Individual Traits	• High tolerance for ambiguity			✓
	• Self-reliance		✓	
	• Excellent communication sills		✓	
	• Self-motivation		✓	
	• Unique skills within the team			✓
	• Strong goal-orientation		✓	
	• Collaborative spirit			✓
	• Strong propensity to trust		✓	
	• Experience with virtual collaboration that leads to forming trusting opinions of others from the outset			✓
	• Ability to launch into action immediately without prior knowledge of others		✓	
	• Persistence in the face of stress		✓	
Environment Traits (Virtual)	• Lean media used for routine or mundane tasks			✓
	• Richer media used for complex tasks		✓	
	• Same suite of technologies available to all team members	✓		
	• Synchronous technologies used to create social presence		✓	
Totals		8 (29%)	15 (53%)	5 (18%)

While this survey reflects the perceptions only of the editors, it provides us with a way to quantify our experience, so that we do not rate ourselves simply on an impression, especially since our initial sense was that trust on our team was low.

Yet, when we consider trust in terms of specific research-based elements, we can see beyond just a hunch. In the end, we did have enough trust to complete the work. That said, likely our performance would have been better if the score for average and high had been better. This survey also gives us insight into what areas would need improvement.

Without question, we believe that at 22 our team size was too large. As described in Chapter 5, some studies indicated that teams of 20-25 individuals were ineffective. Given the complexities of writing, Chapter 5 suggests a team size of three to five members. (The study of virtual collaborative writing teams conducted by Lowry, et al. (2005) evaluated teams consisting of three members.) Although writing teams comprised of 20-25 individuals can be and are successful (for example, edited collections that rely primarily on serial and parallel collaboration), teams that also are trying to employ collective collaboration should be contained, especially for novice teams. At a minimum, if we needed such a large team to complete the book, we needed to distribute writers into subteams of a more reasonable size where they could achieve doable goals.

Another dimension to consider pertains to the degree of trust in our team. In keeping the stages of trust laid out in Chapter 5—Stage 1: deterrence-based trust, Stage 2: knowledge-based trust, and Stage 3: identity-based trust—most of interactions reflect that our team was at Stage 2. The first comment provided at the outset of the section can be understood as Stage 2. That is, while it was not easy to achieve, we realized this degree of trust through recurring interactions, coordinating tasks, and by communicating frequently and with predictability.

Interestingly, the ratings for individual traits are almost uniformly high, which suggests how much we recognized and valued the individual members of the team for what they brought to the effort. Had we, as leaders, harnessed these individual traits for the benefit of the project and the team, we would have developed a more cohesive group—doing so would have used the individual traits to enhance the collaboration." Hence, providing people with roles that are suited

to their personal strengths would have enhanced the project and, we suspect, improved the book.

Recommendations for Building Trust

For teams to function effectively in environments that require serial, parallel, and collective collaboration they need to know they can count on all the members of the team. While writing teams may have successful experiences writing collaboratively when employing serial and parallel forms of collaboration, they may have difficulty performing with the same level of efficiency when integrating collective modes of collaboration. When a writer develops a document from beginning to end, there is little need to depend on other members of the team. However, when writing collectively, writers must share content and depend on each other to carry out tasks. This change in approach requires a strong sense of trust.

If trust is formed naturally within teams familiar with serial and parallel collaboration, then leaders cannot assume that the levels of trust will remain constant when their ability to control and own documents becomes altered. Without a systematic way of understanding the underlying concerns of the team, teams will have difficulty establishing trust. Without a strategy for managing team interactions so that writers believe that the work will get done and get it done well, trust will unravel. What makes the issue of trust so complex to address is that trust entails complex emotions that underlie individual performance, pride of ownership, and the motivation for writing. Understanding the nature of this complexity enabled us to formulate the following recommendations.

- *Determine the right team size, roles needed, and the goals of your project.* As indicated in Chapter 5, team size makes a big difference in terms of the psychology and sociology of interacting effectively. Although depending on the kind of work, teams of 20-25 can function effectively, our experience revealed that coordinating the activities of up to 20 people is extremely challenging without a high degree of structure. When collaborating on writing tasks in virtual environments, teams of up to five members have a greater chance of being effective. For this reason, larger teams need to be divided into smaller subteams to ensure the implementation of all modes of collaboration. Along with team size is the need to establish roles that both enable interactivity and support team goals. Rotating roles also helps teams build trust because team members have a better understanding each other's work.

- *Implement team building activities and mentoring strategies for less skilled members.* In global, virtual settings, writing teams can change frequently with members being added, reassigned, and removed. Organizations restructure themselves, departments merge, and groups realign with changing products and services. Leaders have to find ways to help teams form and reform, engaging them in activities that help individuals build rapport and become comfortable with each other quickly. This process entails finding ways for teams to interact informally in order to establish trusting relationships, as indicated in Chapter 4. The use of "virtual outings"—creative ways of having fun online—enable teams to discover common interests. And when inexperienced writers join the team, leaders should assign senior staff to mentor these people so that skill levels and trust remain intact.

- *Identify what values drive members of the team.* In the context of forming teams, leaders need to find ways for the team to understand each other's commitments or values, such as speed, quality, innovation, or technology. In our project, assumptions

flourished that the academic interest in theory was at cross-purposes with the need in industry to be productive. It was easy for us to fall into a set of stereotypes. In truth, academics recognize the need for productivity and practitioners realize that there is a role for research. But getting beyond a dichotomy like this would not occur without virtual interactions that emulate face-to-face interactions. When individuals understand how their teammates operate, what motivates them, and how they communicate, they have more of context for resolving differences, managing moments of stress, and thus preserving trust.

- *Establish rules around the use of tools that will develop and preserve trust.* The characteristics of virtual technology, described in Chapter 1, can help teams understand what technologies to use for interacting effectively. For example, because e-mail is an asynchronous technology that does not centralize communication, it should not be used for complex questions or issues that require immediate attention. Rather, complicated issues require the telephone or IM to get someone's immediate attention. Issues that are less urgent but just as intricate can be posted to a discussion board, a central location where the complete history of the communication related to particular topics can be found by everyone on the team. When tools are used consistently and effectively, team members can communicate more effectively, which helps to strengthen trust within a team.

- *Address issues that emerge both within the group and also with individuals.* When problems become apparent, disagreements arise, and misunderstandings occur, leaders need to find ways of addressing concerns immediately within the team and, as needed, individually. When issues are addressed within the whole team, everyone can hear the leader's suggestions and the different views of team players. Team discussions help individuals feel heard and facilitate finding solutions to problems with input from everyone. More sensitive issues should be handled in individual meetings so that leaders can revisit expectations and goals, helping each person understand his or her contribution to the team. Addressing issues at both levels helps to preserve trust across the team.

Principle 4. Use Tools and Collaborative Modes Effectively

While tools alone are not the answer for getting teams to collaborate effectively on writing projects, insufficient training or proficiency can create frustrations, disrupt or delay the completion of tasks, and undermine team satisfaction, all of which can have a negative influence on trust. This outcome also is likely if teams are not comfortable coordinating complex tasks with each other or if they lack an understanding of different types of collaboration, specifically how to maximize the use of all three types. In our team, all the writers had some proficiency in the use of many tools and multiple modes of collaboration. Yet, even though we chose tools that almost everyone had some experience using, we did not share the same level of expertise on all of the tools. Also, Beth and Charlotte decided on what tools to use without input from the rest of the team. Our decision-making process was not collaborative, as discussed in Chapter 11; that is, we did not take the time to gather enough input from the team to make the best decisions. We also did not provide enough guidance on what processes to follow, which caused confusion when we started to have problems with the tools and found ourselves needing to create processes on the spot. In this section, we provide suggestions for the effective use of tools and collaborative modes.

The comments that follow provide a unique look at the range of tools and types of collaboration—how important even simple tools were in advancing the project.

For me, the phone was most productive for this project. The best text that my collaborators & I produced occurred over the phone in conversations across 3 time zones & often outside work hours. The most connected I felt to the many collaborators of the VCW book occurred as a result of our phone conference w/ editors & a phone conference on protocols & aims. It was nice to hear voices. It helped bond the experience. The next most useful tool for communicating for me was e-mail. E-mail is embedded into my daily life (sometimes hourly). I was much more likely to attend to notes from the book participants when they were provided via email. I believe that if the usability of the other tools we used to interact (wiki and google docs) were improved, I would have spent more of my hours on this project in them.

Working on this project also affirmed my position on the future success of these technologies, because the relationship I built with the editors via the old-fashioned telephone was the single most important aspect of this process for me. After a while, it became impossible to communicate exclusively through emails, the wiki, and googledocs. Thus, a blend of the old and new--which I advocate for practitioners and designers of VCW—made me feel I was actively involved in the project rather than floating in and out of virtual margins.

As is, I'm still getting lost on the wiki, & I believe that despite our intentions, we did not fully participate or take collective advantage of the wiki and google docs. Yet when I found what I wanted on them, I was glad they were there. Much frustration occurred for me not as I worked on the project but when I wasn't/couldn't.

I do feel that use of the good old telephone—in conferring with the editors—made a key difference. I don't think it's possible to do all collaborative work mediated by computer, although I was pleasantly surprised as to how effectively computer-mediated collaboration was executed during the project.

The many means of communication made it challenging to figure out what was where, especially after we switched from one tool to another. The wiki was better than Google Docs because we could see the delta (where changes were made) as opposed to just knowing that some document was updated, but not knowing if there were major changes or if a typo was corrected.

I found the use of both the wiki and google docs somewhat superfluous since both tools seem to be able to accomplish the target goal.

To understand the context behind these comments as well as our tools and collaborative modes, we provide an overview of our strategy. Table 5 builds on the information in Table 1, adding information about our results in terms of usability.

Of all of the tools we used, the one that was the most stable for one-to-one or group synchronous virtual interactions was the telephone. The Web tools selected had some synchronous capabilities, but they did not function as anticipated; therefore, this old technology was one of the most effective for the purpose of establishing rapport, explaining complex ideas and processes, managing problems or concerns, making intellectual connections, and moving tasks forward. Along with the telephone, the use of virtual desktop sharing enriched discussions that needed visual dimensions, for example, to show team members how semantic tags are used to describe content and to demonstrate acrolinx® IQ functionality. Because these tools support synchronous interactions, they were the ones that most enabled the team's collective collaboration. The editors were the team members who relied most extensively on these tools (including IM) for collective collaboration, which makes sense given their long-term relationship, established trust, and mutual access to the tools. Even so, phone and virtual desktop sharing were effective for other team members in the process of developing ideas synchronously, but we had thought that more tools, like Google Docs, would have enabled collective collaboration for writers working on related chapters. In the end, because the features of this tool were so inconsistent for our project (that is, login problems, access issues, and missing files), we had to defer to the wiki. One synchronous feature that was helpful on the wiki was the automatic notification, which tracked all added and uploaded content and alerted team members that a change had occurred.

In terms of asynchronous technology, the most effective tools the team used were e-mail, the listserv, and the wiki. These forms of technology, which supported serial and parallel collaboration, enabled team members to post announcements, ask questions, provide updates, share information, issue deadline reminders, and provide simple instructions. A little more than midway through the project, a writer who is experienced and comfortable with Google Docs could not locate a file he had posted, and nothing we tried helped. At this point, we considered abandoning Google Docs completely (and we should have), but decided not to in order to avoid confusing everyone. Unfortunately, by second-guessing our intuitions, we created more confusion for the team toward the end of the project when people had the least time and patience for disruption. Two weeks before the end of the project, we had to move all of our work back to the wiki to ensure that no complete files would be lost. Ultimately, and as indicated in the comments from writers, we confused the writers by using two separate workspaces.

Table 5. Tool strategy and results

Tool selected	Strategy and Goal	Result
PBworks wiki	We intended to use this free tool to have discussions, discover overlapping interests, and build rapport. Google wiki was too complex. Once ideas formed, we planned to move content into .doc files and onto Google Docs so that writers could collaborate more synchronously on the texts themselves.	• Easy to manage • Enabled discussions • Automatic notification of any usage • Contact information collection area not always complete • Loaded research material • Could not edit documents online from the wiki or synchronously • File and folder structure confusing • Somewhat effective for intended purpose
Google Docs	We intended to use this free tool as a workspace that provided secure file storage, synchronous online editing support, and a restricted domain for security (given intellectual property concerns). We did not have time to test it fully with many people, so the use of Google Docs was a risk.	• Not easy to manage a restricted domain: • Access issues, password management, forgotten passwords, locked out users • Confusing documentation • Glitches viewing uploaded files. Had to "reshare" (hide and seek or lost files) • Required dedicated e-mails accounts for write access • No automatic notification • No integrated wiki feature • Ineffective for intended purpose
HP Virtual Rooms	We intended to use this tool for complicated interactions because of richer media and ability to view and communicate about a single document with everyone literally on the same page.	• Enabled shared desktop to display information • Used to implement classroom interaction to collect data about beginning chapters with vignettes • Facilitated data sharing in small groups • Access problems for some users behind firewalls • Used by editors weekly to support collaboration • Not accessible to team at large without Charlotte's presence • Somewhat effective for intended purpose
Telephone	Intended for individual calls, group calls.	• Enabled editors to communicate vision and strategy to writers, speak with publisher • Used to develop and clarify ideas • Used to discuss complex questions and problems, acrolinx IQ® functionality • Used by editors to work collectively • Very effective for intended purpose
computersand-writing.com mailing lists	We wanted a dedicated listserv for communicating announcements to all: procedural changes, updates, polling.	• Easy to manage • Messages processed quickly • Did not support attachments or html • Effective for intended purpose
Individual e-mail accounts	Intended for individual questions and answers to one or a few writers.	• Used by editors to document feedback for the writers, to communicate with publisher • Used to answer simple questions • Occasional mix-up of multi-e-mail accounts, especially with the e-mail accounts required for Google Docs • Effective for intended purpose
Instant messaging (various clients)	Encouraged use for synchronous interactivity to resolve issues immediately.	• Used daily by editors • Editors occasionally used to communicate with two writers • Few writers seemed interested in this tool • Effective/essential for editors primarily
acrolinx® IQ	Promoted use for maintaining consistent terminology and language throughout the book.	• Required assistance from acrolinx® IQ to install and configure (term harvesting), testing, training • Decided to restrict use of tool to editors to avoid overloading writers with new technology at the end of the process • Effective for editors only because of the aggressive production schedule

continued on the following page

Table 5. continued

Tool selected	Strategy and Goal	Result
Zoomerang	We sought a free online survey tool to gather feed-back from writers about their experience working on this project.	• Easy to use • Enabled writers to access without having an account • Allowed us to quantify information about our process for future improvement

Recommendations for Using Tools and Collaborative Modes Effectively

It makes sense that technologies for supporting virtual collaborative writing should be chosen for their true affordances—for what value they add to the project rather than for their bells and whistles. In our case, we tried to select tools with the greatest capability for supporting collective collaboration. We believe we succeeded in selecting the right categories of tools in terms of synchronous and asynchronous modalities and their characteristics. Nonetheless, the specific tools we chose were untested and had numerous bugs, which led to team confusion, frustration, and heavy reliance on known technology—on the phone and e-mail and thus on more traditional serial and parallel collaborative modes.

Being thoughtful about the tools is not enough. It is critical, we learned, to factor in how much time it will take to become proficient in the use of specific technologies. In terms of modality—synchronicity and asynchronicity—we made good decisions. We grossly underestimated our own learning curves and those of our team. For that reason, the choice of both PBworks wiki and Google Docs was premature and ill-advised. We needed to build far more time than we did into the front end of the project—before we contacted and negotiated topics with proposal writers. With adequate time, we would have discovered the challenges of working with Google Docs and would have found another alternative or worked to develop protocols for PBworks wiki to meet our collective collaborative goals better. To be sure, time was a major factor in our difficulties with all of the principles of collaboration. The

decision to enter a contract for a 1-year project that had basically a 9-month writing and editing was ill considered and irresponsible to the project, the writers, and ourselves. Our recommendations for choosing and using tools effectively with regard to collaborative models, therefore, begin with estimating and planning the best use of time.

- *Front load the project with sufficient time to choose and test the tools selected.* Given the numerous unforeseen problems that can occur, spend adequate time selecting and testing technology. Define your requirements and goals for the use of specific tools, find ones that closely align with your needs, survey users of the tools, and test them adequately for potential difficulties and desired actions.

- *Choose tools with the specific types of collaboration in mind.* Plan the types of collaboration you will use for different dimensions of your project. First determine if the tools support the types of collaboration anticipated and then establish norms for using the tools. For example, consider what tools are available to help writers interact synchronously with each other and the content. Do not underestimate "old technology," such as the telephone, which our writers preferred. If possible, require everyone to use IM technology to strengthen synchronous interactions.

- *Provide writers with activities that introduce them to the tools through immersion.* It is critical to introduce people to new technologies through project-related activities that immerse them in the technology.

For example, we asked all writers to place a biography and their contact information in different folders on the wiki, which made them use the technology right away. Similarly, we asked them to create a Gmail account and to log into our restricted Google Docs site immediately upon signing on. Their feedback about the challenges of entering this site should have alerted us right away to the need (1) for additional immersive activities in Google Docs or (2) to eliminate this tool from the toolbox.

- *Engage other principles of training in virtual environments as outlined in Chapter 1.* The training principles that the authors have found to be useful for virtual settings include investigation, immersion, individualization, association, and reflection (Hewett and Ehmann, 2004; Ehmann Powers and Hewett, 2009). The need for adequate preparation for tool users cannot be overstated. To that end, we recommend that readers adopt and adapt these training principles at every necessary step of their virtual collaborative writing projects.

- *Re-evaluate the use of technologies regarding their support of desired collaborative models, but do not change tools mid-project unless necessary.* Stability is important especially if substantial learning curves are required. Be open to feedback, but work with—not around—stated or found challenges whenever possible. Changing tools can be a good decision; it was for us. But doing so late in the process can increase the potential for confusion and frustration right when the content and the writing needs should take precedence over any technology considerations.

Principle 5. Create Structure

We learned both through our research, especially Lowry, et al. (2005), and through our experiences that writing teams need structure to collaborate virtually—to engage team members in immediate action, to carry out tasks individually, to use virtual tools, and to coordinate interdependent work processes. Creating structure is not easy for many reasons, not the least of which is that all of the other principles are involved in the process. That is, adding, modifying, and implementing structure influences culture, leadership, trust, the use of tools and ways of collaborating, and the process of measuring and tracking performance. Thus, the integration of structure ricochets off the other principles. But without adequate structure, interactive methods of writing cannot grow, trust will unravel, and collaborative work will be held responsible. Structure requires explicit work patterns, communication, discipline, and accountability. Our aim in this section is to examine how our lack of structure on different levels undermined our efforts to collaborate effectively so that teams can assess how best to integrate structure.

A key sticking point about structure is that some individuals who prefer to rely on their own work patterns—not an uncommon expectation for writers trained to write books on their own—can generate a range of reactions. In our team, some writers strongly objected to the use of acrolinx® IQ, the style management tool used in Chapter 15's case study, claiming that it would inhibit their creativity. Other statements from the writers, however, indicate that they wanted more structure, as shown in the following comments.

Everyone knew how and what to write; not everyone knew how to collaborate, especially for a loose collaborative such as this one.

When I had time set aside to work on the project I would often waste a lot of time trying to figure out *how* I was supposed to do something (write!) rather than actually doing it.

The problem was that the process for communicating and collaborating was complicated and confusing.

I found it hard to make time to write and revise, let alone follow discussion threads & respond to others' drafts. Perhaps if I'd been assigned to give response to one or two other chapters, the task would have seemed more doable.

As has been discussed in various chapters of this book, in any collaboration, it's important to establish trust, and ground rules for working together. These can be difficult to achieve under any circumstances, but they present an even greater challenge in a virtual environment.

Once the decision was made to "team" me with (writer X) and (writer Y), the collaboration process came easier

Perhaps the most difficult part of the project aside from working with an array of digital programs was the gaps in time between my interactions with the editors. While such gaps are probably unavoidable given a project of this scope and the number of contributors, they did cause me some tension and concern. What's going on with the VCW project? What do they think of my latest revision? Is there something I'm supposed to be doing that I'm not doing?

That some of these comments were articulated earlier underscores how the principle of structure is comingled with the other principles. The first four statements, for example, reflect the lack of guidance that led to confusion over how to approach the task of collaborative writing when typically the practice is solitary. Guidelines represent authenticated leadership; teams need leaders to help set up ground rules, formalize structured processes, oversee their implementation, and guide their interactions. If the work required is too open ended, as one our writer stated, and has too many competing demands, writers need explicit steps on how to proceed—procedures that team leaders need to provide. As such, process scripts, which we discovered late in the game, would seem to be

helpful. If the approach and steps are new to the team, they can experience cultural disorientation. If a newly structured process pairs up writers who do not have matched virtual skills, issues of trust can surface. If leaders are not tracking the work, writers can feel lost as expressed in the last comment: "What's going on with the VCW project?… Is there something I'm supposed to be doing that I'm not doing?" As the comments from our writers suggest, the principle of structure can give way to one or more of the other six principles.

At some points during the project, confusion over how to collaborate became more apparent. In these cases, we helped smaller groups of people make connections, as the second to the last comment indicates; once the task at hand out was clear, the process was easier. Lowry, et al. (2005) reported that process structure especially for novice teams is more likely to "to decrease confusion and increase production" (p. 344). While this advice seems so obvious (worthy of the response, "Even I could have told you that!"), apparently something this obvious often is overlooked, as evidenced by the lack of structure on our team. Although occasionally we helped guide collective collaboration, more often we disregarded the need for explicitly defined procedures because, after all, we thought were working with scholars and practitioners who study this material and who know all about what to do. In actuality, this statement might be true, but what is also true is that these professionals had no prior experience or practice working together and had no repeatable processes at hand to draw on for working together as a team. Just like sports players that practice consistently, collaborating writers need structure and practice interacting.

In our project, we lacked structure in terms of:

- Presuming the culture clash within our team would resolve itself; we should have set up synchronous Web conferences to help the scholars and practitioners understand each other better

- Issuing, publishing, and following up on ground rules beyond the editorial guide for the book provided by the publisher
- Testing tools that would be scalable; writing procedures for using them, and providing immersive training
- Setting expectations and measures for team success—giving people a target at which they could aim
- Establishing small teams and providing specific assignments for reviewing chapters
- Providing scripted processes for interacting within teams
- Providing structured assignments for individuals to follow in their writing
- Defining explicit procedures for building rapport
- Sending out regular team messages to keep the project on track and to keep everyone feeling connected to the book's progress
- Setting up regular meetings with subteams to assess progress and keeping writers on course
- Testing acrolinx® IQ our own files to find a more agreeable approach for implementation
- Scheduling Web conferences for defining terminology and making decisions
- Establishing roles within the subteams and across the whole team

Recommendations for Creating Structure

Through our research and based on our experiences throughout this project, we learned that lack of structure affected efficiency in terms of managing cultural differences, overcoming those differences to begin establishing trust, using tools effectively, and implementing measures to track performance. Indeed, as this section has shown, often the principle of structure simultaneously reflects other principles of collaborative writing.

For this reason, collaborative teams need to think about the ways that the integration of structure can influence the other principles.

Writing teams with experience employing serial and parallel modes of collaborating will recognize how they already employ structure within their teams and throughout their projects. Understanding what structured processes have worked and building on existing structures can be a useful starting point. At the same time, existing structures can be insufficient for learning how to implement collective collaboration. Teams must learn to rethink the idea of structure and how it will enable efficiency across a project. Rethinking new ways of carrying out familiar tasks is not easy, especially when writers have many years of experience writing and performing on teams effectively. Without a strategic approach to defining and implementing new structures, teams are likely to slip into prior methods that may undermine performance. Thus, we recommend a holistic approach to creating structure.

- *Identify the structures underlying existing cultural norms that need to change.* Before new structures can be implemented, leaders must understand existing cultural norms that guide behavior. Teams accustomed to serial and parallel collaboration are more accustomed to independent activities and the processes that support them. Examining current processes and how these do *not* support interactivity can help teams determine the gaps or weak areas that require processes that are more highly structured, ones that can support various modes of collaboration. It also is essential that leaders understand how process changes will create upheaval and concern. Before new structures can take root, leaders must help teams unlearn patterns and feel as though it is safe to learn new ones.
- *Establish structures for creating value and building trust.* Single-author writing is not

only a way of doing something; it is also a way of being. Writers are accustomed to seeing themselves as having value because of their independent work, which they can point to as an indicator of their success. Without owning a whole document, writers can begin to feel as though their value is more limited or compromised. Leaders, therefore, must help team members find new ways of appreciating their own value. One way to make this happen is by having writers develop expertise in the areas of content development, tools expertise, or project management and planning. Recognizing the importance of various proficiencies can help the team members appreciate their specific contributions. Just as an athlete contributes incredible value on a sports team even when performing a specific role, so can a writer add value when not owning a whole document. Leaders, then, must establish structures for representing the value of each role, such as posting descriptions of every role with explanations of why each is important.

- *Create a reliable set of rules for using virtual tools.* As indicated earlier in the recommendations for establishing trust, using tools effectively is a way to support successful interactions and thus help to preserve trust. Because collaborative writing teams depend upon each person performing a role correctly and at the right time, leaders must establish rules that support the coordination of activities. Understanding the features of the tools will help leaders make the best decisions about what tools can support specific processes. Input from each individual helps teams make better decisions, as described in Chapter 11, and makes it easier for the team to endorse the rules put into place.

- *Delineate an inventory of tasks that will require complex interaction and coordination and develop scripted processes that will guide effective team performance.* Most writing organizations document procedures for guiding individuals in what processes to follow and how to use various tools. These procedures serve as a useful starting place for outlining individual activities, but more coordinated activities are needed to ensure efficient collective collaboration. Once the procedures are identified, teams can develop more structured processes, as described in Chapter 10, that account for the different social dimensions of writing. Teams also might consider what tasks cause writers the most problems. Likely, problem areas will benefit from more structure to support collaboration.

- *Establish a training strategy for supporting the use of tools and modes of collaboration.* Teams need to understand how to collaborate using virtual tools. Without training or a learning strategy, teams can become overwhelmed with many new processes. They also can become frustrated if they no longer have the skills that once made them feel successful. Negative experiences can cause teams to conclude that topic-based and collaborative writing strategies do not work, that solitary writing is more efficient. To prevent this kind of outcome, leaders need to find ways to integrate training. As discussed in Chapter 1, the training principles of investigation, immersion, individualization, association, and reflection can help with learning (Hewett and Ehmann, 2004; Ehmann Powers and Hewett, 2009). In addition, process scripts can facilitate training needs, as described in Chapter 10.

Principle 6. Measure and Track Performance

When one writer is assigned to carry out all the tasks on a single document, the measurements relate to on-time delivery and attaining a certain level of quality. If three writers own a document on a project, the measurements entail having all of them delivering high-quality documents on time. When writers share work on the same documents, measuring their work in terms of productivity and quality alone do not help the team learn how to interact effectively. Thus, writers need to understand what is expected of them when employing collective collaboration. Without clear expectations about how to write collaboratively in virtual environments, writers will continue to think in terms of their prior experiences and have difficulty envisioning new behaviors. Teams need targets to guide their work and opportunities for gauging how effectively they are performing. The focus of this section is to provide suggestions for measuring and tracking team performance.

The writers' comments that follow reveal the importance of feedback in helping team members assess and modify their behaviors.

I wasn't sure how my chapter fit into the whole.

The one thing that might have improved collaboration: project leaders setting clearer expectations and doing more regular follow up for the collaborative aspects of this project.

Perhaps the most difficult part of the project aside from working with an array of digital programs was the gaps in time between my interactions with the editors. While such gaps are probably unavoidable given a project of this scope and the number of contributors, they did cause me some tension and concern...In the end, however, the direct communication I had with the editors alleviated these concerns and helped me feel for the most part that I was in the loop.

In my real world, Beth or Charlotte would have required me to participate in peer reviews, topic reviews, and provide a status weekly.

The editors were accessible, helpful, and supportive. I feel working on this book made the ideas I had been working with more articulate and lucid.

I was delighted to participate & honored to work amidst to the other authors & editors who have shared amazing insights & ideas

These statements from the writers both reveal our inconsistency in providing feedback to guide collaboration and highlight the importance of feedback to help teams gauge their performance. To understand more about how we employed measures within our project, we examine our own performance relative to the factors mentioned in Chapter 1. Table 6 provides a summary of informal attempts to manage expectations, measures, and tracking based on a "Guidelines for Collaborative Work" document, which we issued at the outset of the project for all book contributors.

While we did document a set of expectations for our team, our strategy for setting forth expectations and using them to measure and track performance was relatively weak, reactive, and inconsistent. What follows is a list of missed opportunities.

- Did not establish a shared vision that addressed our collective interests.
- Failed formally or informally to measure performance as a team until end of the project.
- Did not articulate or schedule regular meetings; that is, they were only ad hoc. Since the telephone was effective to a number of writers, we should have scheduled regular meetings.
- Failed to create and measure subteams.
- Did not provide ongoing feedback to whole team and or to subteams to keep the writers

engaged and interested. As the earlier quoted writer said, *"What's going on with the VCW project?"*

- Failed to set up a terminology team as described in Chapter 13.

- Did not promote the importance of the telephone in setting expectations.
- Failed to repurpose terminology list as a style sheet for copy editors who were not using acxrolinx®IQ.

Table 6.

Expectations	Measure	Tracking
Program/project manager roles (Beth & Charlotte)		
• Book's scope, schedule, processes, and tools	Posted to workspace, content review	Periodic e-mail and listserv requests for improvements to processes
• Publisher's requirements	Compliance with template, images	Periodic e-mail and listserv requests for improved adherence to requirements
• Provide quality assurance system, technical standards	acrolinx®IQ	Conducted by book editors at end stages
• Define structure of book parts, chapters, assignments	Posted to workspace, few assignments	Minimal as questions came up
• Monitor the schedule and time frame, keeping the writing team alerted to any concerns	Assess content submissions	Periodic e-mail and listserv reminders
• Assess quality	acrolinx IQ®, copy editing	Conducted by book editors, copy editors
• Manage and troubleshoot tools	Monitor login status, number of queries	Regular e-mail and listserv to address tools problems
• Report on progress	Monitor and review content	Often reactive, comments on wiki, detailed reviews in e-mail, track changes
• Supervise copy editing process	Assess edits, ad hoc style sheet creation	Regular e-mails to copy editors
Writer responsibilities		
• Brainstorm, write, and revise initial drafts using the wiki and Google Docs	Assess content submissions	Provided feedback via comments, track changes
• Read others' drafts and offer supportive, constructive feedback that helps to keep the project coherent and practical in nature	Observed on wiki, not in actual drafts except if team and subteams were convened	Periodic on wiki, minimal in files
• Share ideas for improving our collaborative efforts	Wiki comments, Zoomerang survey	Minimal, listserv request at end, survey at end
• Use the designated technology/tools for communicating and working with the team	Observe on wiki, automatic notification, e-mails	Regular e-mail and listserv to address tools problems
• Report and discuss the advantages and disadvantages of using these technologies either on the listserv or through the wiki	Review of comments, discuss as needed	Periodic in e-mail and listserv
• Meet deadlines	Assess content submitted	Periodic e-mail and listserv reminders, missed deadline reminders
• Contact the editors with any problems, concerns, or questions	Review e-mail, listserv	Responded to e-mail, listserv to troubleshoot
Publisher responsibilities		
• Assess progress on PBworks wiki, listserv, e-mail	Monitor progress via notification of posted content	Automatic wiki notices for new or changed content, all listserv messages, e-mail as needed

In retrospect, as editors, we see that we did only the bare minimum to keep the project alive although such laxity was never our intention or goal. If structure is central to virtual collaborative writing, we were remiss in not developing our own process scripts for interacting with each other as editors and for interacting with and guiding the team. Creating more structure for ourselves as leaders would have enabled us to provide structured processes for our team, which in turn would have enabled us to measure and track performance throughout the life cycle of the project. As one writer who dropped out of the book project midway said, we were working with too many unknown variables, giving the project the appearance of a pilot than of a fully conceived project that was ready for prime time.

Recommendations for Measuring and Tracking

In general, writers are most comfortable with the words *measure* and *track* when they are using them as words in a text. Typically, individuals become interested in workplace writing because they want to write and not to spend time measuring and tracking, particularly because the terms often are used in the context of budgeting. A number of managers also resist the idea of performing measuring types of activities, as revealed in our own project. But the importance of these activities cannot be underestimated. Because we did not have a formal strategy for tracking and measuring performance, our ability to manage the project effectively—to advance collective collaboration—was impeded significantly. If we had developed a strategy at the outset of the project, we might have been able to pinpoint problem areas, correct them, and then find ways of improving collaborative opportunities.

Because measuring and tracking are less inspiring to writing teams, it is important to help them understand how to connect these activities to the shared vision and stated goals. Teams also need to appreciate why this work is central to effective

collaboration and that it is essential to improving performance. Our recommendations for measuring and tracking are intended to improve virtual collaboration.

- *Define expectations and measures, align with shared vision, and review regularly.* Virtual collaborative writing teams need precise explanations of the expectations that will enable the team to work effectively. Relate expectations to the team vision and each role for all members on the team. As we demonstrated with our own project, expectations that are not alive in the organization have little value. Leaders must keep the expectations present in the minds of the team itself and in individual conference sessions. Everyone must understand how team performance will be measured. When teams know the rules of the game, it is easier for them to be successful.

- *Create a simple, consistent, and visible method for tracking and measuring performance throughout the project.* Without a way to measure performance, teams will have a difficult time knowing what types of changes to make. Leaders need to decide what they are going to measure. If the method for measuring performance is too complicated, few will comply. As indicated in Chapter 10, Lowry et al. (2005) identified key measures that can be adapted to particular writing organizations: productivity, document quality, process satisfaction, relationship quality, and communication quality. What gets measured will get done.

- *Define strategies for working individually with team members who need to improve performance.* When team members are struggling because they lack of experience with the tools or with different ways of collaborating, they need help getting up to speed. Leaders need to consider how individuals needing extra help can get it, though the help of mentors, for example. Otherwise, these people will be singled out as a cause for lower team performance, which will lead to mistrust. With a strategic approach to learning, team members should be able to access materials used for training, such as self-paced learning sessions on particular skills and subjects.

- *Assess team performance and discuss improvement strategies regularly.* In our team, we implemented an online survey at the end of our project. Gathering feedback and measuring at this point only is insufficient to help the team make improvements throughout the process and project. If we were to start over, we would set expectations at the start of the project and provide opportunities for the team to measure itself half-way through the project and at the end. We also recommend that teams write out their experiences in terms of the six principles of collaboration. We had an impression of our results, but it was not until we evaluated our performance relative to the six objective points that we began to understand how we could improve our uses of CMC technologies and processes in the virtual collaborative writing workplace.

- *Establish a system for recognizing team contributions and how individuals have supported the goals of the team.* All writers want to feel good about their work. When changes in a culture are intensely difficult, teams have to feel safe and confident about working differently. A formal program for recognizing team performance and for recognizing how individuals contribute to the team's overall success is crucial. Without formal recognition, it is hard for writers to establish new behavior patterns and to see value in their work.

CONCLUSION

At various points in this volume, we have employed the sports analogy to help readers more fully appreciate the degree of interactivity required to write collaboratively in virtual environments. Players on a team practice tirelessly to become experts and to be of value to their team. As indicated by Gladwell (2008), it takes roughly 10,000 hours of hard work—over the course of 10 years, for many people—to become expert: "Ten thousand hours is the magic number of greatness" (p.41). Indeed, Gladwell used sports figures, musicians, business moguls, and chess players as hard-working hallmarks of greatness. Many great writers have spent at least this much time refining their skills and expertise. Workplace writers may not be looking for a Pulitzer Prize in writing, but certainly they want to do a great job. Fortunately, because writers have devoted a large amount of that time already perfecting their writing skills, the task at hand in contemporary distributed settings is to practice collaborating virtually.

Understanding collaborative writing in terms of other types activities is useful because the comparisons help illuminate characteristics that we might not see otherwise. In addition to viewing collaborative writing in terms of sports teams or musical groups, another interesting comparison is the game of chess. In many ways, virtual collaborative writing is like playing chess. Although chess is a competitive two-person game, players must be mindful of the vision and strategy for a game in the context the next move. The game entails a set of rules for setup, movement, and time. Specifically, chess masters or leaders must manage a complex set of rules for moving pieces of a certain type over the course of a game or "project" life cycle—the opening, midgame, and endgame. At the opening, players must take into account numerous factors or variables, such as the value of the pieces on board, control of the center, and the structure of the pieces. Writers collaborating must anticipate how their actions distributed across different roles along the way will affect the overall project or endgame. Virtual collaborative writing, like chess, is highly strategic. No longer is one writer in change of the complex set of tasks related to one piece of writing. Rather the whole team must consider their work in the context of the whole team.

Our intention in writing a book collaboratively was to learn more about how a cohesive text could be woven together with a team's contributions. We were trying to synthesize many ideas into an integrated whole. While we did not succeed in all the ways we would have liked, we believe that we—the entire writing team, editors, and publisher—have helped to establish a foundation for effective virtual collaborative writing upon which others can draw. We leave you with a comment from one of our writers, whose words to some extent reflect the team integration we hoped to find:

I have not felt part of any other book project, and it's a good feeling to be involved to the extent that was possible. In particular, I think that our editors allowed us to create a collection of people, not just text and words. A good thing, that.

REFERENCES

Anderson, D., & Anderson, L. A. (2001). *The change leader's roadmap: How to navigate your organization's transformation*. San Francisco: Jossey-Bass/Pfeiffer.

Bennis, W., & Goldsmith, J. (2003). *Learning to lead: A workbook on becoming a leader*. New York: Basic Books.

Cargile-Cook, K., & Davie, G. (2005). *Writing and online education: Global questions*. Local Answers.

Ehmann Powers, C., & Hewett, B. L. (2008). Building online training for virtual workplaces. In St. Amant, K., & Zemliansky, P. (Eds.), *Handbook of research on virtual workplaces and the new nature of business practices* (pp. 257–271). Hershey, PA: Information Science Reference.

Geisler, (2001). IText: Future directions for research on the relationship between information technology and writing. *Journal of Business and Technical Communication, 15*(3), 269–308. doi:10.1177/105065190101500302

Gladwell, M. (2008). *Outliers: The story of success*. London: Allen Lane.

Hewett, B. L., & Ehmann, C. (2004). *Preparing educators for online writing instruction: Principles and processes*. Urbana, IL: NCTE.

Lowry, P. B., Nunamaker, J. F. Jr, Curtis, A., & Lowry, M. (2005). The impact of process structure on novice, virtual collaborative writing teams. *IEEE Transactions on Professional Communication, 48*, 341–364. doi:10.1109/TPC.2005.859728

Miller, C. R. (1989). What's practical about technical writing? In Fearing, B. E., & Keats Sparrow, W. (Eds.), *Technical writing: Theory and practice* (pp. 14–24). New York: Modern Language Association.

Schein, E. (2009). *The corporate culture survival guide* (2nd ed.). San Francisco: Jossey-Bass.

Virtual Collaborative Writing Glossary of Common Terms

Content management-related terminology is also available at: http://www.cmsglossary.com/.

Audience: The audience for a virtual collaborative project includes both the collaborators and the end users. Additional audiences include stakeholders, enforcers of regulations, and other interested parties. The key is to understand that there are multiple audiences and to identify (as much as feasible) who those audiences are and what their needs and desires will be with regard to the project outcomes.

Author: See writer.

Asynchronous: A communication modality in which the message is persistent, and author and recipient are not required to be present simultaneously for communication to take place. The communication is extended over time as well as distance. It includes text-based, audio-visual, and graphical markup tools.

Blog: See weblog.

Business Process Improvement (BPI): A systematic approach to help any organization optimize its underlying processes to achieve more efficient results.

Collaboration: Collaboration is an interactive process in which two or more individuals contribute to creating a deliverable document or information product. It includes three types:

- **Serial**: Occurs when writers work on an information product one after another. Each person works separately on a piece of the writing or the whole document, each performing a distinct function in the creation of the finished work. Each person in the chain to finish before another person can continue working. An example of serial collaboration is a one-writer project, where Writer 1 drafts book A, Editor 1 reviews book A, Engineer 1 reviews book A, and Writer 1 reviews and updates the final copy.
- **Parallel**: Occurs when writers work on different pieces of the same project simultaneously. Each person works on one piece of the whole, usually based on a set of negotiated standards or requirements, and engages in coordinated communication with other collaborators as required from time to time. Parallel collaboration also entails

serial collaboration. An example of parallel collaboration is a project with more than one writer: Writer 1 drafts book A for the project, Writer 2 drafts book B for the project, Writer 3 drafts book C for the project, Engineer 1 provides input for one or more books of the project, and Engineer 2 also provides input for one or more books of the project.

- **Collective**: Occurs when writers contribute concurrently to a project through topic assignments based on a writer's knowledge of the product or tools (specialty areas) and on activities related to project tracking. Based on this work, specific predefined roles are delineated. All team members provide equally important contributions to the project and have shared ownership of the overall project success. An example of collective collaboration shows how tasks are differentiated by projects with more than one writer: Writer 1 drafts content A, B, C to for three books; Writer 2 drafts content D, E, F to for two books; Writer 3 manages book assembly; Writer 4 updates content in all books; Writer 4 oversees project planning, graphics, and inventory; Engineer 1 provides input for the project; Engineer 2 provides input for the project; and so on.

Collaborative writing (also termed writing collaboratively): An opportunity whereby a writing team has the intention, need, and ability to provide input, offer feedback, and/or receive feedback, as well as to respond to and/or use that feedback while a text is in-process. It involves strategic and generative interactivity among individuals seeking to achieve a common goal like problem solving, knowledge sharing, and advancing discovery. Collaborative writing includes a wide variety of writing strategies, pre- and post-writing activities, team roles, and work modes necessary for collaborating in contemporary colocated and distributed work settings.

Computer-mediated communication (CMC): Any form of information or intrapersonal exchange across two or more networked computers and other digital tools, such as instant messaging (IM), e-mail, wikis, graphical user interfaces, workspaces, Web conferences, and other interactive modalities.

Container: An outer layer of an information product, such as a chapter, a book, a training module, a help project, from which content units are dynamically referenced.

Content: Information with a scope, structure, and context that can be used for a particular purpose.

Content model, type: See Information model, type.

Content management system (CMS): A software package that consolidates, organizes, and manages content efficiently and accurately as a single source in a repository so it can be reused and repurposed in multiple publications and media channels; content management software is best suited for content that is repeatedly revised and published.

Content unit: A building block that is structured according to a set of standards, ideally in keeping with a specific information type. Examples of the form content units may take include text, graphics, or other digitally-stored information, such as audio, video, and animation. Content units can be combined with other each other to form standalone topics that address customer issues or questions.

Customer feedback program (CFP): An exercise or series of activities designed to gather information about product usage, impressions, issues and experiences from the customer. The gathered information is analyzed and used to advance various aspects of product development, including documentation.

Data: Raw material without a specific context, purpose, or meaning.

Desktop sharing: Refers to a relatively synchronous virtual technology that enables individuals to collaborate through software, graphical user interfaces, and the Internet, combining hybrid features, both visual and oral. The software allows individuals to join a Web conference for the purpose of having one or more attendees share desktop activities with other attendees. The technology allows geographically distributed team members to engage in collaborative tasks because individuals share what they are working on with each other. In virtual collaborative writing environments, while desktop sharing occurs in real time, it does not allow writers to employ collective collaboration entirely because while one writer types, another (or others) watch. However, writers still can use the technology to share ideas and advance content development. Teams also use the technology to carry out tools-related troubleshooting activities.

Digital rhetoric: A collection of various ideas and rhetorical schools of thought attempting to organize the impacts of digital media on the process of persuasion. According to many theorists, the main interest of digital rhetoricians lies in the examination of the shift away from persuasion through finite products (texts) to expressions through a range of electronic media.

Digital technology: With regard to virtual collaborative writing, any technology that enables communication and/or collaboration through the Internet, Intranet, user interfaces, and telephone technologies.

Darwin Information Typing Architecture (DITA): A topic-based DTD that provides specifications for authoring in XML and for producing a range of information outputs. The base topic types known as concept, task, and reference not only facilitate the production of modular documents but also enable topics to be specialized to accommodate specific domains of knowledge.

Designed for the reuse of content, DITA allows users to store source content units in a CMS and to organize them using a DITA map, which defines the topic hierarchy and interrelationships. DITA is an open source technology that that can be implemented through the Open Toolkit, which a technical committee oversees.

Document: Traditionally a static artifact or work product that consists of an organized unit of information within well-defined boundaries, and it is simply a sequence of text and graphics without any dynamic properties or behavior. Increasingly, documents also include automated properties in collections or webs that are constantly growing, changing, being added to, and being culled. In increasingly technological environments, writing requires collaboration to support the use of the shared content that makes up documents or information products.

Document Type Definition (DTD): A formal specification for creating various kinds of XML-based information products, one that defines what markup elements are permitted and the structural rules they must follow.

Domain: An overarching subject area that can be used as an organizing structure for categorizing content units.

Early adopters: Individuals who implement new technology before others do. Early adopters usually provide feedback regarding their experience, which, in turn, helps developers improve a product, technology, or service before it is made available to a general population of users, both internal and external. External early adopters are also called lighthouse customers.

Eclipse: Originally created by IBM, Eclipse is an open-source multi-language software development community now supported by a range of organizations and individuals. Eclipse is organized to maintain the numerous open-source projects that rely on extensible tools for developing and managing software solutions. Some XML-based authoring environments incorporate Eclipse software into their overall development solution.

Element: XML markup tags, which function semantically to describe the meaning of the content contained inside the tags. For example, the tags <procedure> <step> <para></para></step> </procedure> refer to some task a user would have to perform.

File sharing: Refers to various ways that individuals can share their work with one another. In virtual environments, rather than handing off files folders literally, individuals share digital files of many types (for example, text-, image-, and video-based files). Writers use numerous CMC technologies to share digital files, including e-mail, Internet workspaces (for example, wikis), virtual conference rooms, and content management systems, to name a few.

GenCode (generic coding): Refers to a movement established in the 1960s to establish a system of generic coding to mark up electronic documents. The goal of a project termed "the generic coding project" was to use descriptive coding that would separate form and content. Eventually, the project gave rise to the GenCode Committee, which influenced the development of the SGML standard. See SGML.

Hybridity: Functional characteristics of communication that involve the degree to which communication combines elements of spoken and written language. Virtual collaboration tools that are more like face-to-face interactions will involve (1) spoken language (e.g., telephone/video conferences) or (2) written language with a sense of dialogue and open-endedness (e.g., instant messaging or IM). Unless oral conversation or IM is involved in the communication, e-mail messages that send edits back and forth are not considered hybrid. In some cases, greater hybridity might be more useful for developing and completing a writing project.

Impression management: The process of taking control of how others will build perspectives and images of oneself.

Information: Knowledge about a particular subject, product, or service that is shaped and communicated to a particular audience.

Information architect: An individual who develops and manages the structural design of information that is shared in digital environments. They work both with writers and system administrators to ensure that the development, publishing, and delivery of information operate effectively in the context of a content management environment. Single-sourced projects require information architects to design and implement reuse technologies and metadata strategies that enable writers to collaborate and share content in a CMS.

Information architecture: Refers to the underlying structure that directs the classification, arrangement, development, flow, and management of information in digital environments. Well-designed information architecture supports the consistent creation of modular content that can be combined, linked, and reused to form various outputs. It is designed to enable users to navigate and find information within information products and across Web sites.

Information model: Also known as a content model, an information model refers to an organization's strategy for developing and managing information products. It often consists of an array of output or information products, the building blocks (such as a procedure, concept, or example) used to create these products. It also refers to metadata or naming conventions assigned to describe and locate the building blocks stored in a database. The aim of developing standard categories of information is to maximize its efficient reuse and to ensure content consistency and usability. Creating an information model requires collaboration among writing teams, who must agree that the model describes all aspects of organization's information products.

Information product: Refers to artifacts that follow specific standards about what contents various kinds of products should contain and how the contents should be organized. Through information modeling, an organization must determine how many kinds of information products are needed to describe its goods and services. With XML and style sheets, an organization can create a range of dynamic information products, including HTML, online help systems, and electronic files. Finished products can be distributed within software applications, on CDs, on the Web as electronic files, or as printed material for end users.

Information type: Also known as a content type, an information type refers to the standards that define the attributes of specific kinds of content, such as a procedure, concept, or glossary item, and the required building blocks that constitute it.

Infrastructure: Includes both the material support systems that make virtual work possible (such as computers and computer networks) and the embedded practices of communication that have been established within a particular community of workers.

Intelligence analysis: The process of taking known information about situations and entities of strategic, operational, or tactical importance; characterizing the known; and, with appropriate statements of probability, assessing the future actions in those situations and by those entities.

Interactivity: Concerns whether participants can cross the interpersonal distance that virtual collaboration creates. It occurs on a spectrum from (1) a dynamic face-to-face setting to (2) a static text or other setting that disallows interaction with others. Both spatial and interpersonal distances must be overcome for virtual collaborative writing. The more interactivity allowed by the technology, the more feedback among participants is enabled and traditionally face-to-face purposes can be accomplished virtually.

Interdependence: The reliance of collaborating writers upon each other to develop and share ideas, complete projects, and when necessary to reach consensus in decision making.

ISO 9000: Refers to a family of quality management standards—pertaining to quality management and quality assurance—that the International Organization for Standardization (ISO) maintains. ISO-certified organizations have been independently audited and to be compliant with a particular set of ISO standards. Certifications are particularly important for organizations that that conduct business globally.

Kairos: A rhetorical term that expresses the context in which conditions are right for the accomplishment of a crucial action. This context includes both time and location, and an understanding of the most appropriate time and place for an action can also help determine the proper amount of force that is necessary to propel that action.

Learning spaces design: The creation of learning spaces (both face-to-face and virtual) that would enable learners and teachers to fulfill the goals and objectives of instruction.

Localization: The process of adapting information and software to meet the needs of a specific region or language by adding locale-specific components and translating text.

Materiality: The physical and nondiscursive qualities of print texts that serve as a vehicle for transmitting their linguistic content, as well as the physical features that distinguish different kinds of texts from one another. Materiality also includes the physical location of a text, which impacts its rhetorical influence on readers, and serves as a rhetorical act by those who produce and display print texts.

Metadata: Naming conventions assigned to document and information types so that writers and users can conduct searches that will help them locate, use, and reuse content. Writing teams must work collaboratively to determine what metadata components and list of values are needed to enable them to categorize, describe, and locate the content stored in a CMS effectively. For example, metadata can include a component called keyword, which may contain a list of terms or values that writers can select to label information.

Multi-channel publishing: Publishing the same content to multiple formats, including printed material (books, journals, etc.), electronic files (on CD, for mobile devices, etc.), online help systems, and HTML files.

Mutual presence: A construct that attempts to explain the alignment of materiality, practice, and expertise in the production and use of writing. This term is an adaptation of the construct "presence" from Perelman and Olbrechts-Tyteca.

NLP (natural language processing): A field of computer science related to linguistics, which pertains to the use of computers to process human language. NLP entails the use of meaning-based matching algorithms that allow computers to process and understand languages. This technology facilitates machine translation and is used in tools that can help writers analyze their text in real time to ensure compliance with standard grammar rules style guides.

OEM (original equipment manufacturer): Refers to companies that manufacture products without and sell them to other companies that will put their own brand on them and may customize the products in other ways.

Practice: The particular profession in which texts are produced and used that corresponds with their materiality. Practice is understood here as a human organized activity comprising a specific set of tools, knowledge, and skills directed toward the accomplishment of particular goals.

Praxis: A rhetorical term that represents action that is predicated upon and mediated by reflection. Praxis is also the application of theory to real-world, practical, problems.

Presence awareness: Concerns whether participants in a virtual interaction know who is present or available to communicate. Tools may provide the status of participants' names and activity levels. Presence awareness gives team members a sense of immediacy regarding the relative availability of others with whom they may need to collaborate.

Process scripts: Highly structured, documented processes that relate to a set of complex tasks, combining process information that not only sets forth procedures about what individuals should do but also about how they should carry out tasks with others. What makes a process script different from a documented process is that a script adds to the process instructions for interactivity across and throughout time and space and. Scripted processes may include many of the following elements: rules, resources (people and objects), organizational standards, corporate culture, and group norms and experiences. In virtual collaborative settings, writers beneft from knowledge provided in process scripts that can coordinate complex series of tasks and flow of work within and across writing teams.

Repurpose: Modifying text developed for use in one context so that it can be used in another context.

Reuse: The systematic practice of developing content for use in more than one context to reduce the overall development effort, improve consistency, and facilitate translation into multiple target languages.

Semantic markup: Refers to the use of markup to define the type of content rather than its appearance. For example, the markup <prereq> identifies certain text within a procedure as a prerequisite to a task. Style sheets can then be designed to apply specific formatting to all text tagged with <prereq> and to vary that format depending on the type of output.

SGML (Standard Generalized Markup Language): An international standard (ISO 8879 1986/AMD 1988) for defining markup conventions, a metalanguage that describes document components. A markup language must specify what markup is allowed, what markup is required, how markup is to be distinguished from text, and what the markup means. SGML also defines document types along with its components. Documents coded with markup have "intelligence" and thus can be processed automatically for publication. A derivative of SGML, XML is considered by some to be an easier to learn and implement. See XML.

sim-ship (simultaneous shipment): A shorthand term for translating products into all designated languages simultaneously to accelerate the introduction of products into a global economy.

Single sourcing: The process of applying specific writing standards to the development of information so that information can be stored one time in a content management system and reused in various contexts and across many types of media. The goal of single sourcing is to improve the efficiency of information development and the quality of information products.

Specialization: In DITA, adapting basic topic types to create new ones that meet the needs of an organization and remain compatible with the complete toolset. The new topics inherit the structural characteristics of their parent type. Examples of specialized DITA topic types include tutorial, troubleshooting, and user interface help.

Synchronous: Communication modality in which the message is delivered in real time, enabling the author and recipient to have a sense of immediate contact and to interact almost as if they were physically present to each other. May include communication that is delivered instantaneously

(real-time) as well as communication that is delivered with a brief lag required by instructing the computer to "send" the message (near-real-time). Synchronous communication may or may not be persistent and is extended over distance but not time. It includes text-based, audio-visual, and graphical markup tools.

Tagging scheme: A customized use of tags or labels that define the conditions of reusing content. For example, content units that will function in user and installation guides would require the definition of a set of tags such as "user_guide" and "installation_guide" and so on.

Team: A group of two or more people who are assembled (with or without explicitly defined roles) with the specific, shared goal of a material outcome. A virtual team may or may not be assembled in a face-to-face setting, but it is coordinated via digital technology. A writing team is a group with the shared goal of producing a written product.

Team formation: The process of convening a group of individuals into a purposeful unit.

Team norming: The process of establishing shared expectations and common practices among a group of individuals working on a shared product.

Topic: Refers to the modular approach to creating information products, hence the term modules. Because topics are intended to address a specific issue or question posed by users, they should function as standalone entities. Writers draw on basic building blocks or content units and information types to form self-contained modules that can be reused. Creating topics effectively requires collaboration among writers.

Virtual acquaintances: Online colleagues with whom interactions tend to be direct and formal, with few interpersonal elements.

Virtual cohorts: Online colleagues with whom one has frequent contact, some informal conversations, and few breaches of professionalism.

Virtual intimates: Online colleagues with whom one can, while working and interacting, feel comfortable expressing feelings or attitudes beyond what would be considered primarily professional discourse, to include frustrations, personal information, and humor.

Virtual meeting room: Refers to a relatively synchronous virtual technology that enables individuals to collaborate through software, graphical user interfaces, and the Internet. This CMC technology facilitates hybrid interactions, using both visuals and oral features to enable geographically distributed individuals to attend meetings, conferences, presentations, seminars, and learning sessions. Virtual writing teams can collaborate using this technology so that teams can participate in meetings and see the same digital files or other writing-related materials.

Virtual collaborative writing: Work by a team of writers using means and tools other than face-to-face contact. Virtual writing collaboration can occur over the Internet, over the phone, or over other communication technologies.

Virtual communication: Any interaction that decouples time/space attributes even if several dynamics of face-to-face communication are maintained (e.g.; as in videoconferencing). That is, "virtual communication" can be any communicative act that is mediated digitally through Internet, intranet, or telephone technologies.

Virtual doughnuts: A relevant piece of information or other contribution that is shared and appreciated among team, often leading to two-way appreciation and goodwill that helps a team maintain as a unit.

Virtual writing team: A team of writers whose processes may be distributed across geographic locations, but also within the colocated space of an office or institutional setting. Unlike traditional document sharing and face-to-face or telephone interactions, virtual writing requires participants to communicate using computer-mediated communication (CMC) technologies.

Voice of the customer (VOC): The stated and unstated customer needs or requirements. The voice of the customer can be captured in a variety of ways, such as direct discussion or interviews, surveys, focus groups, customer specifications, observation, warranty data, and field reports.

Weblog: An online Web site or journal on which the writer published a regular commentary about various ideas, which can be themed for particular audiences. To "blog" can be used as a verb.

Webtexts: Texts that reside on the Web. These texts are distinguished both from hypertext (because their structures may be linear rather than hypertextual) and from print texts that have been placed on the Web (such as PDF copies of journal articles).

Wiki: Collaborative Web site that relies one of many types of wiki software. Wiki sites are designed to be easy for technically unsophisticated users to add to and edit, making it a useful venue for multiple authors to develop, revise, and edit collaborative documents.

Workflow: A feature within a content management system that allows users to define the flow of a process and automates the assignment of tasks, users, and due dates to ensure a consistent process is implemented by all users.

Writer: In a topic-oriented writing environment, the person who researches and writes the topics that an end user accesses to gain understanding or carry out tasks.

Writing bounce: The practice of moving between open screens and tasks displayed on one's monitor.

Writing project management: Design and implementation of a series of steps and procedures allowing members of a writing project team to complete their work and a final product to be created.

XML (Extensible Markup Language): A machine-readable markup language that defines how to create markup tags to create structured documents. XML is made up of elements or tags that describe the function of the text contained within the tags, such as <title> </title>. The purpose of semantic tags is to separate content from form so that writers can focus more on writing content and less on how content is displayed.

XSL (Extensible Style sheet Language): Refers to a family of style sheet languages used for rendering XML documents.

Compilation of References

Aberdeen Group. (December 2007). *The role of real time virtual collaboration in product development.* (2007). Retrieved August 16, 2009 from http://www.tandberg. com/collateral/The_Role_of_Real_Time_Virtual_Collaboration_in_Product_Development.pdf

Alexander, P. A., Schallert, D. L., & Hare, V. C. (1991). Coming to terms: How researchers in learning and literacy talk about knowledge. *Review of Educational Research, 61*, 315-343.

Alred, G. J., Brusaw, C. T., & Oliu, W. E. (2003). *The handbook of technical writing* (7th Ed.). New York: St. Martin's.

Anderson, D. & Anderson, L.A. (2001). *The Change leader's roadmap: How to navigate your organization's transformation.* San Francisco: Jossey-Bass/Pfeiffer.

Andreessen, M. (1993). *NCSA Mosaic technical summary.* National Center for Supercomputing Applications.

Andres, H. P. (2002). A comparison of face-to-face and virtual software development teams. *Team Performance Management: An International Journal, 8*(1), 39-48.

AP Stylebook. (2009). The Associated Press. Accessed October 1, 2009. http://www.apstylebook.com/

Apple, Inc. (2009). *"iChat"* [Photo]. Retrieved August 3, 2009, from http://www.apple.com/macosx/what-is-macosx/ichat.html

Apps, J. W. (1991). *Mastering the teaching of adults.* Malabar, FL: Krieger.

Aristotle. (1975). *The art of rhetoric.* (Trans. John Henry Freese). The Loeb Classical Library. Cambridge, MA: Harvard University Press.

ASD Simplified Technical English. (2004-2005). ASD Simplified Technical English Maintenance Group. Accessed October 1, 2009, http://www.asd-ste100.org/INDEX.HTM

Ashton-Jones, E. & Thomas, D. K. (1995). Composition, collaboration, and women's ways of knowing: A conversation with Mary Belenky. In G. A. Olson &E. D. Hirsh (Eds.) *Women writing culture,* (pp. 81-101). Albany, NY: State University of New York Press.

Aspin, R. (2007). Supporting collaboration, in colocated 3D visualization, through the use of remote personal interfaces. *Journal of Computing in Civil Engineering, 21*(6), 393-401.

AT & T (2008). *Building a framework for 21st century literacies.* Retrieved April 15, 2009 from http://www.kn.pacbell.com/wired/21stcent/framework.html

Austin, W. W. (2005). Hypertext theory and Web writing assignments in the writing and professional communication classroom. *Internet-based workplace communications: Industry & academic applications,* (pp. 24-39). Hershey, PA: Information Science.

Baker, G. (2004). A study of virtual teams. In M. Khosrow-Pour (Ed.), *Advanced Topics in Information Resources Management,* (pp.333-352). Hershey, PA: Idea Publishing Group.

Baker, Gary. (2002). The effects of synchronous collaborative technologies on decision making: A study of virtual teams. *Information Resources Management Journal, 15*(4), 79-93.

Barber, C. (2000). *The English language: A historical introduction.* Cambridge, UK: Cambridge University Press.

Barton, M. (2008). New media and the virtual workplace. In P. Zemliansky & K. St. Amant, (Eds.), *Handbook of research on virtual workplaces and the new nature of business practices* (pp. 382-394). Hershey, PA: IGI Global.

Baumard, P. (1999). *Tacit knowledge in organizations.* London (UK): Sage.

Beautfort, A. (1999). *Writing in the real world: Making the transition from school to work.* New York: Teachers College Press.

Beck, E. (1995). Changing documents/documenting changes: using computers for collaborative writing over distance. In S. Star (Ed.), *The cultures of computing,* (pp. 53-68).). Oxford, UK: Blackwell.

Bennis, W. & Goldsmith, J. (2003). *Learning to lead: A workbook on becoming a leader.* New York: Basic Books.

Billings, M., & Watts, L. (2006). The model of relational communication: Explaining difficulties encountered through the use of technology in alternative dispute resolution. In *Proceedings from the 8th Australian Mediation Conference.*

Blake, W. (1997). *The complete poetry and prose of William Blake.* Erdman, D. V. (Ed.). Port Moody, Canada: Anchor Publishing.

Bleich, D. (1983). Discerning motives in language use. In W. B. Horner (Ed.), *Composition and literature: Bridging the gap,* (pp. 91-95). Chicago: The University of Chicago Press.

Blickensderfer, E., Salas, E., & Cannon-Bowers, J. (2000) When the teams came marching home. In M. Beyerlein (Ed.) *Work teams: Past, present and future* (Social Indicators Research Series), (pp. 255-274). Amsterdam: Kluwer Academic Publishers.

Boczkowski, P. (1999). Mutual shaping of users and technologies in a national virtual community. *Journal of Communication, 49,* 86-108.

Bolter, J. & Gromala, D. (2003). *Windows and mirrors: Interaction design, digital art, and the myth of transparency.* Cambridge, MA: MIT Press.

Bolter, J. (2001). *Writing space: Computers, hypertext, and the remediation of print,* (2nd ed.). Mahwah, NJ: Lawrence Erlbaum Associates, Publishers.

Bolter, J. D. (1991). *Writing space: The computer, hypertext, and the history of writing.* Hillsdale, NJ: Lawrence Erlbaum.

Bond, A.H., & Gasser, L. (Eds.) (1988). *Readings in Distributed Artificial Intelligence.* San Mateo, CA: Morgan Kaufmann.

Bos, S. et al. (2004). In-group/out-group effects in distributed teams: An experimental simulation. In *Proceedings Computer Supported Cooperative Work,* (pp. 429-436). doi: 10.1145/1031607.1031679

Bottitta, J., Idoura, A. P., & Pappas, L. (2003). Moving to single sourcing: Managing the effects of organization change. *Technical Communication, 50* (3), 355-370.

Bouldin, T., & Odell, L. (1993). Surveying the field and looking ahead: A systems theory perspective on research on writing in the workplace. In R. Spilka (Ed.), *Writing in the workplace: New Research perspectives* (pp. 268-281). Carbondale, IL: Southern Illinois University Press.

Bouwman, H., van den Hoof, B., van de Wijngaert, L., & van Dijk, J. (2005). *Information and communication technology in organizations. Adaption, implementation, use and effects.* London: Sage.

Bracewell, R. J. & Witte, S. P. (2003). Tasks, ensembles, and activity: Linkages between text production and situation of use in the workplace. *Written Communication, 20*(4) (October), 511-559.

Brewer, P. E. (2008). Gaines and losses in the rhetoric of virtual workplace. In P. Zemliansky & K. St. Amant, (Eds.), *Handbook of research on virtual workplaces and the new nature of business practices,* (pp. 1-14). Hershey, PA: IGI Global.

Bridgeford, T. (2006). "Kairotically speaking": *Kairos* and the power of identity. *Kairos 11*(1). Retrieved from http://kairos.technorhetoric.net/11.1/ binder.html?topoi/ bridgeford/

Britton, J., Burgess, T., Martin, N., McLeod, A., & Rosen, H. (1975). *The development of writing abilities* (pp. 11-18). London: Macmillan Education.

Bronack, S. C., Cheney, A. L., Riedl, R. E., & Tashner, J. H. (2008). Designing virtual worlds to facilitate meaningful communication. *Technical Communication*, 261-69.

Brooke, C. (2009). *Lingua fracta: Toward a rhetoric of new media.* Mahwah, NJ: Hampton Press, Inc.

Brown, H.G., Poole, M. & Rodgers, T. (2004). Interpersonal traits, complementarity, and trust in virtual collaboration. *Journal of Management Information Systems, 20,* 115-138.

Brown, M. (2006, August 18). *Snakes on a Plane* leaves critics flying blind [Electronic Version]. *The Guardian.* Retrieved August 1, 2009 from http://www.guardian.co.uk/uk/2006/aug/18/film.filmnews

Brufee, K. A. (1993). *Collaborative learning: Higher education, interdependence, and the authority of knowledge.* Baltimore: The Johns Hopkins University Press.

Bruffee, K. A. (1984). Collaborative Learning and the 'Conversation of Mankind.' *College English, 46,* 635-652

Brumberger, E.R. (2003a). The rhetoric of typography: The awareness and impact of typeface appropriateness. *Technical Communication, 50*(2), 224-231.

Brumberger, E.R. (2003b). The rhetoric of typography: The persona of typeface and text. *Technical Communication, 50*(2), 206-223.

Brumberger, E.R. (2004). The rhetoric of typography: Effects on reading time, reading comprehension, and perceptions of ethos. *Technical Communication, 51*(1), 13-24.

Burkhardt, V. (2009. Virtual teams. *Idea Connection.* Retrieved from http://www.ideaconnection.com/articles/00117-Virtual-Teams.html

Cargile-Cook, K. & Davie, G., (2005). *Writing* and *online education: Global questions, local answers.*

Carlstedt, L.G. (1998). Prediction of fitness for service in UN military units. *Storming Media.* Retrieved 19 May 2009 from http://www.stormingmedia.us/31/3122/A312263.html

Caruso, C. (1997). Before you cite a site. *Educational Leadership, 55,* 24-25.

Cerrato, T. & Rodriguez, H. (2002). Studies of computer supported collaborative writing: Implications for system design. In M. Blay-Fornarino, A. Pinna-Derry, K. Schmidt & P. Zarate (Eds.), *Cooperative systems design,* (pp. 139-154). Amsterdam: IOS Press.

Chapman, A. (1995). *Tannenbaum and Schmidt—Model of delegation and team development.* Retrieved from http://www.businessballs.com/tannenbaum.htm

Chartier, R. (1994). *The order of books.* Stanford, CA: Stanford University Press.

Chidambaram, L. (1996). Relational development in computer-supported groups. *MIS Quarterly,* June 143-165.

Chrislip, D. D. & Larson, C. E. (1994). *Collaborative Leadership.* San Francisco: Jossey-Bass.

Church, A.H., & Waclawski, J. (2001) Hold the line: An examination of line vs. staff differences. *Human Resource Management, 40,* 21-34.

Clabby, J. (2002). *Visualize this: Collaboration, communication & commerce in the 21st century.* Upper Saddle River, NJ: Prentice Hall PTR.

Clark, H.H., & Brennan, S.E. (1991). Grounding in communication. In L.B. Resnick, R.M. Levine, & S.D. Teasley (Eds.), *Perspectives on socially shared cognition,* (pp. 127-149). Washington, DC: American Psychological Association.

Clark, H.H., Schreuder, P., and Buttrick, S. (1983). Common ground and the understanding of demonstrative reference. *Journal of Verbal Learning and Verbal Behavior,* (22) 245-258.

Coen, N. (August 13, 2009). Care to write Army doctrine? With ID, log on. *The New York Times.* Accessed October 28, 2009. http://www.nytimes.com/2009/08/14/business/14army.html?_r=1&em

Cohen, S.G., & Bailey, D.E. (1997). What makes teams work: Group effectiveness research from the shop floor to the executive suite. *Journal of Management, 23,* 239-290.

Coppola, N. W., Hiltz, S. R, & Rotter, N. G. (2004). Building trust in virtual teams. *IEEE Transactions on Professional Communication, 47*(2), 95-104.

Coutu, D. L. (1998). Trust in virtual teams. *Harvard Business Review, 76*(3), 20.

Crow, K. (n.d.). *Voice of the customer.* Retrieved from http://www.npd-solutions.com/voc.html

Crowley, S. (1989). *A teacher's introduction to deconstruction.* Urbana, IL: NCTE.

Crystal, D. (2006). *Language and the Internet.* Cambridge, UK: Cambridge University Press.

Cummings, J.N. (2004). Work groups, structural diversity, and knowledge sharing in a global organization. *Management Science, 50*(3), 352–364

Curtis, D. (2009, May 18). *Dear American Airlines.* Retrieved July 24, 2009, from http://www.dustincurtis.com/dear_american_airlines.html

Curtis, D. (2009, May 22). *The response.* Retrieved July 24, 2009, from http://www.dustincurtis.com/dear_dustin_curtis.html

D'Ambra, J.G. (1995). *A field study of information technology, task equivocality, media richness and media preference.* Dissertation. The University of New South Wales, School of Information Systems.

Dabbish, L., & Kraut, R. E. (2006). Email overload at work: An analysis of factors associated with email strain. In *Proceedings of the 2006 ACM conference on computer supported cooperative work* (pp. 431 - 440). New York: ACM Press.

Dabbish, L., Kraut, R., Fussell, S., & Kiesler, S. (2005). Understanding email use: Predicting action on a message. In *CHI 2005, Proceedings of the ACM conference on human factors in computing systems* (pp. 691 - 700). New York: ACM Press.

Daugherty, M., & Funke, B. L. (1998). University faculty and student perceptions of web-based instruction. *Journal of Distance Education, 13*(1), 21-39.

De Certeau, M. (1992). *The writing of history.* New York: Columbia University Press.

Dede, C. (*1995*). The evolution of constructivist learning *environments*: Immersion in distributed, *Virtual* worlds. *Educational Technology, 35*(5), 46-52.

DeMarco, T. & Lister, T. (1986). *Peopleware: Productive projects and teams.* New York: Dorset House.

Dennis, A. (1996). Information exchange and use in small group decision making. *Small Group Research, 27*(4), 532-549.

Dennis, A. R. & Kinney, S.T. (1998).Testing media richness theory in the New Media: The effects of cues, feedback, and task equivocality. *Information Systems Research, 9,* 256-274.

DeRosa, D. (2008). *Collaborating from a distance: Success factors of top performing virtual teams.* OnPoint-Consulting. [white paper].

DeSanctis, G., & Monge, M. (1998). Communication processes for virtual organizations. *Journal of Computer-Mediated Communication, 3*(4). Retrieved from http://jcmc.indiana.edu/vol3/issue4/desanctis.html

Doheny-Farina, S. (1991). *Rhetoric, innovation, technology: Case study of technical communication in technology transfers.* Cambridge, MA: The MIT Press.

Doherty, M., & Salvo, M. (2002). Kairos: Past, present and future(s). *Kairos, 7*(x). Retrieved from http://www.technorhetoric.net/7.x/kairos/title.htm

Doner, S. & Hood, L. (2008) A democratic approach to overcoming DITA and CMS issues. *Proceedings of CMS Strategies/DITA North America 2008.* Santa Clara, CA: Center for Information-Development Management.

Dressman, M., Wilder, P., & Connor, J. (2005). Theories of failure and the failure of theories: A cognitive/sociocultural/macrostructural study of eight struggling students. *Research in the Teaching of English, 40,* 8-61.

Eble, M. F. (2009). Digital delivery and communication technologies: Understanding content management systems through rhetorical theory. In G. Pullman & B. Gu, (Eds.), *Content management: Bridging the gap between theory and practice* (pp. 94-95). Amityville, NY: Baywood Publishing Company, Inc.

Ede, L. & Lunsford, A. (1990). *Singular texts, plural authors: Perspectives on collaborative writing* Carbondale, IL: Southern Illinois U P.

Ehmann Powers, C. & Hewett, B.L.(2008). Building online training for virtual workplaces. In K. St. Amant & P. Zemliansky, (Eds.), *Handbook of research on virtual workplaces and the new nature of business practices,* (pp. 257-271). Hershey, PA: Information Science Reference.

Eisenberg, B. (2007). *How to use customer reviews to increase conversion.* Retrieved from http://www.clickz.com/3627269#

Elluminate, Inc. (n.d.). *Elluminate Live* [Photo]. Retrieved August 3, 2009, from www.elluminate.com/ products/els/v95/index.jsp

Engeström, Y. (1987). *Learning by expanding.* Helsinki: Orienta-Konsultit. In Tasks, ensembles, and activity: linkages between text production and situation of use in the workplace. By Robert J. Bracewell and Stephen P. Witte. *Written Communication 20*(4) (October), 511-559.

Erickson, F. (1987). Transformation and school success: The politics and culture of educational achievement. *Anthropology and Education Quarterly, 18,* 335-56.

Erkins, G. et al. (2005). Coordination process in computer supported collaborative writing. *Computers in Human Behavior, 21,* 463-486.

Ewald, H. R., & Burnett, R. E. (1996). *Business communication.* New York: Prentice Hall.

Eyman, D. (2006). The arrow and the loom: A decade of *Kairos. Kairos 11*(1). Retrieved from http://kairos.technorhetoric.net/11.1/ binder.html?topoi/eyman/

Eyman, D. (2008). Learning from *Kairos*: Value, visibility, and virtual teamwork. In P. Zemliansky & K. St. Amant (Eds.), *Handbook of research on virtual workplaces and the new nature of business practices,* (pp. 590-598). Hershey, PA: IGI Publishing.

Fanderclai, T. (2004). Collaborative research, collaborative thinking: Lessons from the Linux community. In B J. Inman, C. Reed, & P. Sands, (Eds.), *Electronic collaboration in the humanities: Issues and options* (pp. 311-320). Mahwah, NJ: Lawrence Erlbaum Asociates.

Fish, R.S., Kraut, R.E., Root, R.W., & Rice, R. (1993). Evaluating video as a technology for information communication. *Communications of the ACM, 36*(1), 48-61.

Fisher, K, & Fisher, M. D. (1998). *The distributed mind: Achieving high performance through the collective intelligence of knowledge work teams.* New York: AMACOM.

Fisher, K. & Fisher, M. D. (2001). *The distance manager: A hands-on guide to managing off-site employees and virtual teams.* New York: McGraw Hill.

Fisher, L. (2008) Staffing information architects for a world of topic-based information. *Best Practices, 10* (5), 105.

Fisher, R. & Ury, W. (1983). *Getting to yes: Negotiating without giving in.* New York: Penguin Books.

Fjermestad, J. (2004). An analysis of communication mode in group support systems research. *Decision Support Systems, 37*(2), 239-263.

Flanigan, A. J. & Metzger, M. (2000). Perceptions of Internet information credibility. *Journalism and Mass Communication Quarterly, 63,* 515-540.

Fleckenstein, K., Calenrillo, L. T. & Worley, D. A. (2002). *Language and image in the reading-writing classroom.* Mahwah, NJ: Lawrence Erlbaum Associates.

Fleming, D., Kaufer, D.S., Werner, M., & Sinsheimer-Weeks, A. (1993). Collaborative argument across the visual/verbal interface. *Technical Communication Quarterly 2*(1), 37-49.

Flower, L. (1988). The construction of purpose in writing and reading. *College English, 50* (5), 528-550.

Forman, J. (1990). Leadership dynamics of computer-supported writing groups. *Computers and Composition, 7,* 35-46.

Friedman, A.A. (2004). The relationship between personality traits and reflective judgment among female students. *Journal of Adult Development, 11,* 297-304.

Friedman, J. (2005, August 17). I find your lack of faith disturbing: Snakes on a Motherfucking Plane. *Another Screenwriter Blog.* Retrieved August 1, 2009 from http://hucksblog.blogspot.com/2005/08/snakes-on-motherfucking-plane.html.

Fuller, R.M., Vician, C., & Brown, S.A. (2006). E-learning and individual characteristics: The role of computer anxiety and communication apprehension. *Journal of Computer Information Systems, 46*, 103-115.

Galbraith, M. W. (1991). The adult learning transactional process. In M. W. Galbraith (Ed.), *Facilitating adult learning: A transactional process* (pp. 1-32). Malabar, FL: Krieger.

Galbraith, M. W., & Zelenak, B. S. (1991). Adult learning methods and techniques. In M. W. Galbraith (Ed.), *Facilitating adult learning: A transactional process* (pp. 103-133). Malabar, FL: Krieger.

Garbuio, Massimo, et al. (2009). How companies make good decisions: McKinsey Global Survey Results. *McKinsey Quarterly*. Retrieved from https://www.mckinseyquarterly.com/Strategy/Strategic_Thinking/How_companies_make_good_decisions_McKinsey_Global_Survey_Results_2282

Garrison D.R., Anderson, T. & Archer, W. (2000). Critical inquiry in a text-based environment: Computer conferencing in higher education *The Internet and Higher Education, 2*(2-3), 87-105.

Gee, J. P. (2004). *Situated language and learning: A critique of traditional schooling.* New York: Routledge.

Gee, J. P. (2008). *Social linguistics and literacies: Ideology in Discourses* (3rd Ed.). New York: Routledge. (Original work published 1990).

Geisler, et al. (2001). IText: Future directions for research on the relationship between information technology. *Journal of Business and Technical Communication, 15*(3), 269–308.

Gergle, D., Millen, D. R., Kraut, R. E., & Fussell, S. R. (2004). Persistence matters: Making the most of chat in tightly-coupled work. In *CHI'04: Proceedings of the Conference on Human Factors in Computing Systems,* (pp. 431-438). New York: ACM.

Gersick, C.J.G. (1988). Time and transition in work teams: Toward a new model of group development. *Academy of Management Journal, 31*(1), 9-41.

Gibson, Cristina B., & Cohen, Susan G., (eds.), (2003). *Virtual Teams that Work: Creating Conditions for Virtual Team Effectiveness.* San Francisco: Jossey-Bass.

Gladwell, M. (2008). *Outliers: The story of success.* London: Allen Lane.

Golde, C.M. (2005). The role of department and discipline in doctoral student attrition: Lessons from four departments. *Journal of Higher Education, 76*, 669-700.

Goody, J. (1977). *Domestication of the savage mind.* Cambridge, UK: Cambridge University Press.

Goody, J., & Watt, I. (1963). The consequences of literacy. *Comparative Studies in Society and History, 5*, 304-345.

Gordon, J.R. (2002). Structuring high-performance organizations. *Organizational behavior: A diagnostic approach,* (7th ed.). Upper Saddle River, NJ: Prentice-Hall.

Grudin, J. (1988). Why CSCW applications fail: Problems in the design and evaluation of organizational interfaces. In *Proceedings of the ACM 1988 conference on Computer-supported cooperative work.* (pp. 85-93). New York: ACM.

Gurak, L. J. (1997). *Persuasion and privacy in cyberspace: The online protests over Lotus MarketPlace and the clipper chip.* New Haven, CT: Yale University Press.

Gurak, L. J. (2001). *Cyberliteracy: Navigating the Internet with awareness.* New Haven, CT: Yale University Press.

Gustafson, K. & Kleiner, B. H (1994). New developments in team building. *Work Study, 43*(8), 16-19.

Haas, C. & Wearden, S. T. (2003). E-credibility: Building common ground in web environments. *Educational Studies in Language and Literature, 3*, 169-184.

Haas, C. (1994). Learning to read biology: One undergraduates' rhetorical development. *Written Communication 8*(3), 43-83.

Haas, C. (1996). Text sense and writers' materially based representations of text. In *Writing Technology: Studies in the materiality of literacy.* (pp. 116-133). Mahwah, NJ: Lawrence Erlbaum.

Haas, C. (1996). *Writing technologies: Studies on the materiality of literacy.* Mahwah, NJ: Lawrence Erlbaum Associates.

Haas, C. (1999). On the relationship between old and new technologies. *Computers and Composition 16*, 209-228.

Hackos, J. (1994). *Managing your documentation projects*. New York: John Wiley & Sons, Inc.

Hackos, J. (2004, August). *Pursuing a minimalist agenda*. Web seminar, Comtech Services & Vasont Systems.

Hackos, J. (2007a). *Information development: Managing your documentation projects, portfolio, and people*. New York: John Wiley & Sons.

Hackos, J. (2007b). *Information modeling*. Comtech Services, Inc. Workshop at CMS Strategies/DITA North America, April 2007 (pp. 1-48). Boston: Center for Information-Development Management.

Hackos, J. T. (1999). An application of the principles of minimalism to the design of human-computer interfaces. *Common Ground, 9*, 17–22.

Hackos, J. T. (2007). *Information development: Managing tour documentation projects, portfolio, and people* (3rd ed.). Indianapolis: Wiley.

Hackos, J., & Priestley, M. (Eds.). (2007, August 1). *DITA Version 1.1 Architectural Specification OASIS® Standard, OASIS Darwin Information Typing Architecture (DITA) TC*. Retrieved from http://docs.oasis-open.org/dita/v1.1/OS/archspec/archspec.html

Hahn, M. (2004, August). *Vasont and the minimalist agenda*. Web seminar, Comtech Services & Vasont Systems

Havelock, E. (1980). The coming of literate communication to Western culture. *Journal of Communication, 30*, 90-98.

Hawisher, G. & Selfe, C. (1991). The rhetoric of technology and the electronic writing class. *College Composition and Communication, 42*(1), 55-65.

Hawisher, G., & LeBlanc, P., Eds. (1992). *Re-imagining computers and composition: Teaching and research in the virtual age*. Portsmouth, NH: Boyton/Cook Heinemman.

Hawisher, G., & Selfe, C., (Eds.). (1991). *Evolving perspectives on computers and composition studies: Questions for the 1990s*. Urbana, IL: NCTE.

Heath, S. B. (1983). *Ways with words: Language, life, and work in communities and classrooms*. New York: Cambridge University Press.

Henderson, P. & De Silva N. (2006). A narrative approach to collaborative writing: A business process model. In *8th International Conference on Enterprise Information Systems (ICEIS)*, Cyprus.

Henry, C. (2007). Ensuring quality coding in your data source. *Best Practices, 9*(2), 40-43.

Henson, J. (2006). *Muppets magic* (video). (Available from Pegasus Entertainment, Unit 5 Brook Trading Estate, Deadbrook Lane, Aldershot, Hampshire, GU12 4XB, United Kingdom.) (Original "Computer Dinner" sketch 1971).

Hertel, G., Geister, S., & Konradt, U. (2005). Managing virtual teams: A review of current empirical research. *Human Resource Management Review, 15*, 69-95.

Hewett, B. (2004-2005). Asynchronous online instructional commentary: A study of student revision." *Readerly/Writerly Texts: Essays in Literary, Composition, and Pedagogical Theory. 11 & 12*(1 & 2)L, 47-67.

Hewett, B. L. & Ehmann, C. (2004). *Preparing educators for online writing instruction: Principles and processes*. Urbana, IL: NCTE.

Hewett, B.L. & Hewett, R.J. (2008). *Instant messaging (IM) literacy in the workplace,* (pp. 455-472). Hershey, PA: IGI Global.

Hewlett-Packard Development Company, L.P. (2009). *HP remote graphics software* [Photo]. Retrieved August 3, 2009, from http://h20331.www2.hp.com/hpsub/cache/286504-0-0-225-121.html

Hill, C., Yates, R., Jones, C. & Kogan, S. L. (2006). Beyond predictable workflows: Enhancing productivity in artful business processes. *IBM Systems Journal, 45*(4), 663-682.

Hirokawa, R.Y. & Salazar, A.J. (1999). Task-group communication and decision-making performance. In L.R. Frey, D.S. Gouran, & M.S. Poole (Eds.), *The handbook of group communication theory and research,* (pp. 167-191). Thousand Oaks, CA: Sage.

Hofstede, G. & Hofstede, G. J. (2005). *Cultures and organizations: Software of the mind. Intercultural cooperation and its importance for survival.* New York: McGraw Hill.

Holton, J. (2001). Building trust and collaboration in a virtual team. *Team Performance Management, 7,* 36-47.

Howard, R. M. (2009). *Collaborative learning and writing: A bibliography for composition and rhetoric.* Retrieved on August 5, 2009 from http://wrt-howard.syr.edu/Bibs/Collab.htm

http://www.thetraits.org/index.php

Hull, G. (2000). Critical literacy at work. *Journal of Adolescent & Adult Literacy, 43,* 648-652.

Hurley, J., & Eberharter, S. (1995). CMF 12 advanced Noncommissioned Officer Course program of instruction. *Engineer, 25,* 1-17.

Huszczo, G.E. (1990). Training for team building. *Training and Development Journal, 44. 2, 37*(7). Academic OneFile. Gale. Clemson University Libraries. 16 Sept. 2009.

Huws, U. (2005). Fixed, footloose, or fractured: Work, identity, and the spatial division of labor. *Monthly Review, 57,* 23-39.

Iaccono, C. Z. & Weisband, S. (1997). Developing trust in virtual teams. In *Proceedings of the 30th Annual Hawaii International Conference on System Sciences.* Retrieved from http://uainfo.arizona.edu/~wiesband/Hiccss-97

IBM. (2008). *The new collaboration: Enabling innovation, changing the workplace* (white paper). Accessed August 9, 2009 at http://www-935.ibm.com/services/us/cio/pdf/new-collaboration-white-paper.pdf

IJesselsteign, W., Harper, B., & Group P. W. (2002). *Virtually there? A vision of presence research,* (pp. 2000-31014). Brussels: Presence—Information Society and Technology, European Community Public Deliverable.

Inkster, C. & Rouiller, S. (2008). Improving code quality with DITA code reviews. In *Proceedings of CMS Strategies/DITA North America 2008.* Santa Clara, CA: Center for Information-Development Management.

International Organization, Information processing—text and office systems—Standard Generalized Markup Language (SGML) ISO 8879, 1986/Amd 1:1988. (n.d.).

International Standard, Quality management and quality assurance standards. International Organization for Standardization ISO 9000, 1987/Amd 1:1994. (n.d.)

ISO/IEC. (2008). *ISO/IEC 26514, Systems and software engineering—Requirements for designers and developers of user documentation requirements.* Switzerland: International Standards Organization Copyright Office.

Jarvenpaa, S. L. & Leidner, D. E. (1999). Communication and trust in global virtual teams. *Organization Science, 10*(6), 791-815.

Jarvenpaa, S. L., & Leidner, D. E. (1998). Communication and trust in global virtual teams. *Journal of Computer-Mediated Communication, 3*(4). Retrieved from http://jcmc.indiana.edu/vol3/issue4/jarvenpaa.html

Johnson, T. S., Smagorinsky, P., Thompson, L., & Fry, P. G. (2003). Learning to teach the five-paragraph theme. *Research in the Teaching of English, 38,* 136-176.

Johnson-Eilola, J. (1999). Negative Spaces: From Production to Connection in Composition. In T. Taylor & I. Ward (Eds.), *Dialogic Spaces,* (pp. 17-33). Urbana, IL: NCTE.

Johnson-Eilola, J. (2005). *Datacloud: Toward a new theory of online work.* Creeskill, NY: Hampton Press.

John-Steiner, V., R. J. Weber, & Minnis, M. (1998). The challenge of studying collaboration. *American Educational Research Journal, 35*(4), 773–83.

Jones, E. & Schell, D. (2007). Delivering the right content to the right person at the right time: defining the total information experience. In *Proceedings of CMS strategies/DITA North America conference,* Boston.

Jones, E., & Peterson, D. (2007). Total information experience: Defining an IBM-integrated approach to developing information in a flat world via effective global collaboration. *Best Practices, 9*(2), 29-34.

Jongh, R. de (2006, Oct 26). Sketching software captures AEC ideas fast. *Machine Design,* 102-105.

Kalmbach, J. (2006). Reading the archives: Ten years of nonlinear (*Kairos*) history. *Kairos 11*(1). Retrieved from http://kairos.technorhetoric.net/11.1/binder.html?topoi/kalmbach/index.html

Kapoun, J. (1997). *Teaching undergrads WEB evaluation: A guide for library instruction.* Retrieved June 28, 2002 from www.ala.org/acr;/undwebev.html

Kaptelinin, V. & Nardi, B. (2006). *Acting with technology: Activity theory and interaction design.* Cambridge, MA: MIT Press.

Kasemvilas, S. & Olfman, L. (2009). Designing alternatives for a mediawiki to support collaborative writing. *Journal of Information, Information Technology and Organizations, 4*, 87-105.

Katzenbach, J. R. & Smith, D. K. (1993). *The wisdom of teams: Creating the high performance organization.* Boston, MA: Harvard Business School Press.

Kehrwald, B. (2007). The ties that bind: Social presence, relations, and productive collaboration in online learning environments. In *ICT: Providing choices for learners and learning, Proceedings Ascilite Singapore 2007*, (pp. 502-511). Retrieved from http://www.ascilite.org.au/conferences/singapore07/procs/kehrwald.pdf

Kelly, K. (2009, November/December). The virtual world. *Adbusters: Journal of the Mental Health Environment, 6*(17).

Kezim, B., Pariseau, S.E., & Quinn, F. (2005). Is grade inflation related to faculty status? *Journal of Education for Business, 80*, 358-363.

Klein, C., DiazGranados, D., Salas, E., Le, H., Burke, C.S., Lyons, R., & Goodwin, G.F. (2009). *Small Group Research, 40*(2), 181-222.

Knowles, M. (1990). *The adult learner: A neglected species,* (4th ed.). Houston, TX: Gulf.

Kock, N. & Garza, V. (2008). The ape that used email: An evolutionary perspective on e-communication behavior. In N. Kock, (ed.), *E-collaboration in modern organizations: Initiating and managing distributed projects,* (pp. 242-254). Hershey, PA: IGI Global.

Kraut, R. & Streeter, L. (1995). Coordination in large scale software development. *Communications of the ACM, 38*(3), 69-81.

Kraut, R. E., Fussell, S. R., & Brennan, E., Siegel J. (2002) Understanding Effects of Proximity on Collaboration: Implications for technologies to support remote collaborative work. In P. Hinds & S. Kiesler (Eds.) *Distributed Work* (pp. 137-162). Cambridge, MA: The MIT Press.

Kraut, R. E., Galegher, J., Fish, R. S., & Chalfonte, B. (1993). Task requirements and media choice in collaborative writing. *Human-Computer Interaction, 7*(4), 375-408.

Kraut, R., Galegher, J., & Egido, C. (1988). Tasks and relationships in scientific research collaborations. *Human-Computer Interaction, 3*, 31-58.

Kraut, R.E. (2002). Applying social psychological theory to the problems of group work. In J.Carroll (Ed.), *Theories in Human-Computer Interaction,* (pp. 325-356). New York: Morgan-Kaufmann Publishers.

Kraut, R.E., Egido, C., & Galegher, J. (1990). Patterns of communication and contact in scientific collaboration. In J. Galegher, R.E. Kraut, & C. Egido (Eds.). *Intellectual teamwork: The social and technological bases of cooperative work* (pp. 149-171). Hillsdale, NJ: Lawrence Erlbaum Associates.

Kress, G., & Leeuwen, T. (2001). *Multimodal discourse: The modes and media of contemporary communication.* London: Oxford UP.

Kuang, C. (2009, June 1). American Airlines Web site: The product of a self-defeating design process. *Fast Company.com.* Retrieved June 6, 2009 from http://www.fastcompany.com/blog/cliff-kuang/design-innovation/how-self-defeating-corporate-design-process-one-designer-finds-ou?page=1

Lam, E. (2006). Culture and learning in the context of globalization: Research directions. *Review of Research in Education, 30*, 213-237.

Lampel, J., and Bhalla, A. (2007). The role of status seeking in online communities: Giving the gift of experience. *Journal of Computer-Mediated Communica-*

tion, *12*(2), article 5. Retrieved from http://jcmc.indiana. edu/vol12/issue2/lampel.html

Landow, G. (1992). *Hypertext: The convergence of contemporary critical theory and technology.* Baltimore: The Johns Hopkins University Press.

Langer, S. K. (1942). *Philosophy in a new key: A study in the symbolism of reason, rite, and art,* (pp. 3rd ed.). Cambridge, MA: Harvard University Press.

Lanham, R. (1993). *The electronic word: Democracy, technology, and the arts.* Chicago: U of Chicago P.

Laru, J., & Jarvela, S. (2008). Social patterns in mobile technology mediated collaboration among members of the professional distance education community. *Educational Media International, 45*, 17-32.

Latour, B. (1990). Drawing things together. In M. Lynch & S. Woolgar, (eds.), *Representations in scientific practice,* (pp. 19-68). Cambridge, MA: MIT Press.

Lee, C. (1990). Beyond teamwork. *Training: The Magazine of Human Resources Development, 27*(6), 25-33.

Leont'ev, A.N. (1978). *Activity, consciousness and personality.* (Translated from original Russian by Marie J. Hall). Englewood Cliffs: Prentice-Hall.

Levi, D. (2007). *Group Dynamics for Teams.* Los Angeles: SAGE Publications.

Levy, P. (1998). *Becoming virtual: Reality in the digital age,* (R. Bononno, trans.). New York: Plenum Trade.

Lewicki, R.J. & Bunker, B.B. (1996). Developing and maintaining trust in work relationships. In R.M. Kramer & T.R Tyler, (Eds.), *Trust in organizations: Frontiers of theory and research,* (pp. 114-139). Thousand Oaks, CA: Sage.

Lewin, T. (2009, August 9). In a digital future, textbooks are history. *New York Times,* A1.

Lindholm, K. (2004). Pathways to the professoriate: The role of self, others, and environment in shaping academic career aspirations. *Journal of Higher Education, 75*, 603-635.

Lipnack, J. & Stamps, J. (2000). *Virtual teams people working across boundaries with technology,* (2nd ed.). New York: John Wiley & Sons.

Lipnack, J. & Stamps, J. (2000). *Virtual teams: Reaching across space, time, and organization with technology.* New York: John Wiley.

Lowry, P. B., Curtis, A. & Lowry, M. (2004) Building a taxonomy and nomenclature of collaborative writing to improve interdisciplinary research and practice. *Journal of Business Communication, 41*, 66-99.

Lowry, P. B., Nunamaker, Jr., J. F., Curtis, A. & Lowry, M. (2005). The impact of process structure on novice, virtual collaborative writing teams. *IEEE Transactions on Professional Communication, 48*, 341-364.

Lowry, P.B. & Nunamaker, J.F. (2002). Synchronous, distributed collaborative writing for policy agenda setting using Collaboratus. In *Hawaii International Conference on System Sciences (HICSS),* (10), (pp. 4051-4060).

Lowry, P.B., Albrecht, C.C., Nunamaker, J.F., & Lee, J.D. (2002). Evolutionary development and research on Internet-based collaborative writing tools and processes to enhance eWriting in an eGovernment setting. *Decision Support Systems, 34*, 229-252.

Lyall-Wilson, D. (2006). "Sleepless in Seattle (horror)" [Film]. *The Trailer Mash.* Retrieved August 3, 2009, from http://www.thetrailermash.com/sleepless-in-seattle-horror/

Macbeth, D. (2002). From research to practice via consultancy and back again: A 14 year case study of applied research. *European Management Journal, 20*(4), 393-400.

Majchrzak, A., Malhotra, A., Stamps, J. & Lipnack, J. (2004). Can absence make a team grow stronger? *Harvard Business Review, 82*(5), 131- 147.

Majchzak, A., et al. (2004). Radical innovation without Collocation: A case Study at Boeing Rocketdyne. *MIS Quarterly, 25*(2), 229-249.

Manafy, M. (2008, December). Welcome to the eight annual EContent 100—Our list of companies that matter most in the digital content industry. *EContent, 31*(10), 26-57.

Manovich, L. (2007). *Understanding hybrid media.* Accessed October 28, 2009 from http://www.manovich.net/DOCS/hybrid_media_pictures.doc

Martin, J. (2004). *Organizational behavior and management,* (3ʳᵈ ed.). London: Thomson Learning.

Mayer, R.C., Davis, J. H., &Schoorman, F.D., (1995). An integrative model of organizational trust. *Academy of Management Review, 20*(3), 709-734.

McDaniel, C. (2008). Removing space and time: Tips for managing the virtual workplace. In P. Zemliansky, & K. St.Amant, (eds.), *The handbook of research on virtual workplaces and the new nature of business practices* (pp. 530-543). Hershey, PA: IGI-Global.

McGrath, J. E. & Hollingshead, A. B. (1994). *Groups Interacting with Technology: Ideas, Evidence, Issues and an Agenda.* Thousand Oaks, CA: Sage Publications.

McGrath, J.E. (1991). Time, interaction, and performance (TIP): A theory of groups. *Small Group Research, 22* (2), 147-174.

McGrath, J.E. (1984). *Groups: Interaction and performance.* Englewood Cliffs, NJ: Prentice-Hall.

McKay, E. (2008). *The human-dimensions of human-computer interaction: Balancing the HCI equation.* Washington, DC: IOS Press.

McKenzie, J. & Potter, R. (2004). Five keys to better virtual collaboration. *Knowledge Management Review, 7,* 8-9.

McShane, B.J. (2009). Why we should teach XML: An argument for technical acuity. In G. Pullman & B. Gu (Eds.), *Content management: Bridging the gap between theory and practice* (pp. 73-85). Amityville, NY: Baywood Publishing Company.

Meloni, W. (2008). Maximizing the design process. *Computer Graphics World, 31*(1), 32-36.

Merry, P. (2002). *Effective online decision making.* Retrieved from www.genderdiversity.cgiar.org/EffectiveOnlineDecisionMakingMerry2.doc

Mescan, S. (2009). *Collaborative review in Vasont.* Emigsville, PA: Vasont Systems.

Mescan, S., & Robidoux, C. (2008). All I really need to know about successful content management I learned in kindergarten. In *Proceedings of CMS Strategies/DITA North America 2008.* Santa Clara, CA: Center for Information-Development Management.

Miller, C. R. (1979). A humanistic rationale for technical writing. *College English, 40,* 610–617.

Miller, C. R. (2004). Expertise and agency: Transformations of ethos in human-computer interaction. In M. Hyde (Ed.), *The ethos of rhetoric* (pp. 197–218). Columbia, SC: University of South Carolina Press.

Miller, C.R. (1989). What's practical about technical writing? In B. E. Fearing, & W. Keats Sparrow, (Eds.), *Technical writing: Theory and practice,* (pp. 14–24). New York: Modern Language Association.

Moore, M., & Trahan, R. (1998). Tenure status and grading practices. *Sociological Perspectives, 41,* 775-782.

Moxley, J. (2008). Datagogies, writing spaces, and the age pr peer production. *Computers and Composition, 25*(2), 182-202.

Murray, J. (2209). *Non-discursive rhetoric: Image and affect in multimodal composition.* Albany: SUNY P.

Myerson, D., Weick, K.E., & Kramer, R.M. (1996). Swift trust and temporary groups. In R.M. Kramer & T.R Tyler (Eds.) *Trust in organizations: Frontiers of theory and research* (pp. 166-195). Thousand Oaks, CA: Sage.

Nardi, B. (1996). Studying context: comparison of activity theory, situated action and distributed cognition. In B. Nardi (Ed.), *Context and consciousness: Activity theory and human-computer interaction* (pp. 69-102). Cambridge, MA: MIT Press.

National Center on Education and the Economy. (2006). *Tough choices or tough times: The report of the New Commission on the Skills of the American Workforce.* San Francisco: Jossey-Bass.

National Council of Teachers of English. (2009). *21ˢᵗ century literacies.* Retrieved April 15, 2009 from http://www.ncte.org/positions/21stcenturyliteracy

National Writing Project, & Nagin, C. (2003). *Because writing matters*. San Francisco: Jossey-Bass.

National Writing Project. (2008). *Research brief: Writing project professional development for teachers yields gains in student writing achievement*. Retrieved July 23, 2009 from http://www.nwp.org/cs/public/download/nwp_file/10683/NWP_Research_Brief_2008.pdf?x-r=pcfile_d

National Writing Project. (2009). *National Writing Project receives MacArthur grant: Grant will support new "Digital Is" technology program*. Retrieved April 15, 2009 from http://www.nwp.org/cs/public/print/resource/280

Neck, C., Manz, C., & Anand, V., (2000) Self-managing teams in a crystal ball: Future directions for research and practice. In M. Beyerlein (Ed.), *Work Teams: past, present, and future*, (pp. 311-322). Amsterdam: Kluwer Academic Publishers.

Nelson, T. (2008). Ted Nelson on software. *Youtube*. Retrieved from http://www.youtube.com/watch?v=zumdnI4EG14

Neuwirth, C.M., Kaufer, D.S., Chandhok, R., & Morris, J.H. (1990). Issues in the design of computer support for co-authoring and commenting. In *Conference on Computer Supported Cooperative Work* (CSCW '90) (pp. 183-195). New York: Association for Computing Machinery.

Nilsson, T. (2000). A history of teams. In M. Beyerlein (Ed.), *Work Teams: Past, Present and Future* (Social Indicators Research Series), (pp 275-288). Amsterdam: Kluwer Academic Publishers.

Norman, D.A. (2002). *The design of everyday things*. New York: Basic Books.

Northwest Regional Educational Laboratory (2009). *6+1 trait writing*. Retrieved July 23, 2009 from

NTSB. (September 2004). About the NTSB. Retrieve August 1, 2009 http://www.ntsb.gov/Abt_NTSB/history.htm

OASIS Darwin information typing architecture (DITA) Technical Committee FAQ. (n.d.). Retrieved August 17, 2009 from http://www.oasis-open.org/committees/dita/faq.php

OASIS DITA (2007). *Version 1.1 Language Specification, OASIS Standard*, August 1, 2007. Retrieved from http://docs.oasis-open.org/dita/v1.1/langspec/ditaref-type.html

O'Keefe, S. S., & Pringle, A. S. (2000) *Technical writing 101: A real-world guide to planning and writing technical documentation*. Cary, NC: Scriptorium.

Olson, D. R. (1977). From utterance to text: The bias of language in speech and writing. *Harvard Educational Review, 47*, 257-281.

Olson, D. R., Bloome, D., Dyson, A. H., Gee, J. P., Nystrand, M., Purcell-Gates, V., & Wells, G. (2006). Orality and literacy: A symposium in honor of David Olson. *Research in the Teaching of English, 41*, 136-179.

OMNI Institute. (n.d.). *Working together: A profile of collaboration, an assessment tool*. Retrieved October 11, 2009, from http://www.omni.org/instruments.aspx

OMNI Institute. (n.d.). *Working together: A profile of collaboration, a companion to the assessment tool*. Retrieved October 11, 2009, from http://www.omni.org/instruments.aspx

Onwuegbuzie, A. (1997). Writing a research proposal: The role of library anxiety, statistics anxiety, and composition anxiety. *Library and Information Science Research, 19*, 5-33.

Oravec, J. A. (1996). *Virtual individuals, virtual groups: Human dimensions of groupware and computer networking*. New York: Cambridge UP.

O'Reilly, T. (2005). *What is Web 2.0? Design patterns and business models for the next generation of software*. Retrieved from http://www.oreillynet.com/pub/a/oreilly/tim/news/2005/09/30/what-is-web-20.html

Orvis, K., Wisher, R., Bonk, C.J., & Olson, T. (2002). Communication patterns during synchronous web-based military training in problem solving. *Computers in Human Behavior, 18*, 783-795.

Pargman, T.C. (2003). Collaborating with writing tools. Retrieved March 9, 2007 from http://journals.ohiolink.edu/ejc/xml_ft.cgi/Cerratto_Pargman_Teresa.html

Parker, R. (1997). *Looking good in print*. Research Triangle, NC: Ventana Communications Group, Inc.

Partnership for 21st Century Schools. (2006). *Are they really ready to work?: Employers' perspectives on the basic knowledge and applied skills of new entrants to the 21st century U.S. workforce*. Retrieved August 9, 2009 from http://www.21stcenturyskills.org/documents/FINAL_REPORT_PDF09-29-06.pdf

Partnership for 21st century skills. (2004). Retrieved April 15, 2009 from http://www.21stcenturyskills.org/index.php

Pauleen, D. J. (2004). An inductively derived model of leader-initiated relationship building with virtual team members. *Journal of Management Information Systems, 20*(3).

Perelman, C. & Olbrechts-Tyteca, L. (1969). *The new rhetoric: A treatise on argumentation*. Notre Dame: University of Notre Dame Press.

Perlow, L. (1999): The time famine: Towards a sociology of work time. *Administrative Science Quarterly, 44*(1), 57-81.

Pisano, G. & Verganti, R. (2008, December). Which kind of collaboration is right for you? *Harvard Business Review, 10*, 78-86.

Porter, G. & Beyerlein, M. (2000). Historic roots of team theory and practice. In Michael Beyerlein (Ed.) *Work Teams: Past, Present and Future* (Social Indicators Research Series), (pp. 3-24). Amsterdam: Kluwer Academic Publishers.

Priestley, M. & Swope, A. (2008). *DITA maturity model: A JustSystems white paper*. JustSystems, Inc. and IBM Corporation. Retrieved from www.na.justsystems.com/files/Whitepaper-DITA_MM.pdf

Pullman, G. & Gu, B. (2009). *Content management: Bridging the gap between theory and practice*. Amityville, NY: Baywood Publishing Company.

Purdum, T. (2005). Teaming take 2. *Industry Week/WI, 254* (5), 41-43.

Qiu, Y. F., Chui, Y. P., & Helander, M. G. (2004). *Knowledge-based Decision Making in Virtual Team Environment*. In *Proceedings IEEE International Engineering Management Conference,* (Vol. 2, pp. 556-560). doi: 10.1109/IEMC.2004.1407440

Rainie, L. (2006). *New workers, new workplaces*. Retrieved August 5, 2009 from http://www.pewinternet.org/Presentations/2006/New-Workers-New-Workplaces.aspx

Reich, R. (1991). *The work of nations: Preparing ourselves for 21st century capitalism*. New York: A.A. Knopf.

Rice, R. E. (1993). Media appropriateness: Using social presence theory to compare traditional and new organizational media. *Human Communication Research, 19*(4), 451-484.

Rickly, R. (2006). Distributed teaching, distributed learning: Integrating technology and criteria-driven assessment into the delivery of first-year composition. In K. B. Yancey (Ed.) *Delivering college composition: The fifth canon* (pp. 183-198). Portsmouth, NH: Boynton/Cook.

Robbins, S.R. & Coulter, M.K. (2001). *Management,* (7th ed.). Upper Saddle River, NJ: Prentice-Hall.

Robey, D., Khoo, H. M. & Powers, C. (2000). Situated learning in cross-functional virtual teams. *Technical Communication 47*(1), 51-66.

Robidoux, C. & Hewett, B. L. (2009). Is there a write way to collaborate? *Intercom. 56*(2), 4-9.

Robidoux, C. (2008). Rhetorically structured content: Developing a collaborative single-sourcing curriculum. *Technical Communication Quarterly, 17*, 110-135.

Roch, S., & Ayman, R. (2005). Group decision making and perceived decision support: The role of communication medium. *Group Dynamics, 9*(1), 15-31.

Rockley, A. (2003). *Managing enterprise content: A unified content strategy*. Indianapolis: New Riders Press.

Rorschach, E. (2004). The five-paragraph theme redux. *Quarterly of the National Writing Project, 26*(1), 16-25.

Rosen, E. (2007). *The culture of collaboration*. San Francisco: Red Ape.

Rovai, A., & Jordan, H. (2004). Blended learning and sense of community: A comparative analysis with traditional and fully online graduate courses. *The International Review of Research in Open and Distance Learning, 5*(2). Retrieved October 27, 2009 from http://www.irrodl.org/index.php/irrodl/article/view/192/274

Rumelhart, D. E. (1980). Schemata: The building blocks of cognition. In R. J. Spiro, B. C. Bruce, & W. F. Brewer (Eds.), *Theoretical issues in reading comprehension,* (pp. 33-58). Hillsdale, NJ: Erlbaum.

Rushton, P. (1982). Moral cognition, behaviorism, and social learning theory. *Ethics, 92,* 459-467.

Ryang, Robert (2006). "Shining Romantic Comedy" [Film]. *The Trailer Mash.* Retrieved August 3, 2009, from http://www.thetrailermash.com/shining-romantic-comedy/

Saarinen E., Lainema T., Lahteenmaki S., (2008). Experiencing virtual team membership decentralized decision-making processes leading to meaningful learning. In *Proceedings of the Seventh IASTED International Conference Web-based Education*, Innsbruck, Austria, March 17-19, (pp. 328-332).

Sakellariadis, A., Chromy, S. Martin, V., Speedy, J., Trahar, S. Williams, S. & Wilson, S. (2008). Friend or foe? Technology in a collaborative writing group. *Qualitative Inquiry, 14,* 1205-1222.

Salas, E. & Cannon-Bowers, J.A. (2000). Teams in organizations. In M. Beyerlein (Ed.), *Work Teams: Past, Present and Future* (Social Indicators Research Series), (pp. 323-332). Amsterdam: Kluwer Academic Publishers.

Salas, E., Priest, H.A., Stagl, K.C., Sims, D.E., & Burke, S. (2006). Work teams in organizations: A historical reflection and lessons learned. In L.L. Koppes (ed.), *Historical perspectives in industrial and organizational psychology,* (pp. 407-438). Mahwah, NJ: Lawrence Erlbaum Associates.

Schein, E. (2009). *The corporate culture survival guide,* (2nd ed.). San Francisco: Jossey-Bass.

Schendel, E. et al (2004). Toward a theory of online collaboration. In B. Huot, B. Stroble & C. Bazerman (Eds.), *Multiple literacies for the 21st Century* (pp. 195-209). Cresskill, NY: Hampton.

Schmidt, J. et al. (2001). New product development decision-making effectiveness: Comparing individuals, face-to-face teams, and virtual teams. *Decision Sciences, 32*(4), 575-600.

Schneider, T.J. & Stepp, J. R. (1998). The evolution of U.S. labor-management relations. In J. A. Auerbach, (Ed.), *Through a glass darkly: building the new workplace for the 21st century* (148). Retrieved from http://www.restructassoc.com/case/06.pdf

Schrage, M. (1990). *Shared minds: The new technologies of collaboration*. New York: Random House.

Schultz, K. (1997). Discourses of workplace education: A challenge to the new orthodoxy. In G. Hull (Ed.) *Changing work, changing workers: Critical perspectives on language, literacy, and skills* (pp. 43-83). Albany, NY: State University of New York Press.

Schuman, S.P. (2001). ed. "Editor's note," Special issue on group development. *Group Facilitation: A Research and Applications Journal, 3,* 66.

Scribner, S & M. Cole. (1981). *The psychology of literacy.* Cambridge, MA: Harvard University Press.

Selber, S. (2004). *Multiliteracies for a digital age.* Carbondale, IL: Southern Illinois P.

Selfe, C. (1992). Computer-based conversations and the changing nature of collaboration. In J. Forman (Ed.), *New visions of collaborative writing* (pp. 147-169). Portsmouth, NH: Boynton-Cook.

Selfe, C. L. (1999). *Technology and literacy in the 21st century: The importance of paying attention.* Carbondale, IL: Southern Illinois P.

Selfe, C., & Hilligoss, S., (Eds.), (1994). *Literacy and computers: The complications of teaching and learning with technology.* New York: MLA.

Sharples, M. et al. (1993). Research issues in the study of computer supported collaborative writing. In M. Sharples (Ed.), *Computer supported collaborative writing* (pp. 9-28). London: Springer-Verlag.

Shrage, M. (1990). *Shared minds.* New York: Random House.

Siegel, J., Dubrovsky, V., Kiesler, S., & McGuire, T. (1986). Group processes in computer-mediated communication. *Organizational Behavior & Human Decision Processes, 37*(2), 157-187.

Sperling, M., & Freedman, S.W. (2001). Research on writing. In V. Richardson (Ed.), *Handbook of research on teaching* (4th Ed.), (pp. 370-389). Washington, DC: American Educational Research Association.

Spitzer, D. (2007). *Transforming performance measurement: Rethinking the way we measure and drive organizational success.* New York: Amacon.

Sproull, L. & Kiesler, S. (1991). *Connections: New ways of working in the networked organization.* Cambridge, MA: The MIT Press.

Sproull, L. (1984). The nature of managerial attention. *Advances in Information Processing in Organizations, 1,* 9-27. Greenwich, CT: JAI Press.

Sproull, L. S., & Kiesler, S. (1986). Reducing social context cues: The case of electronic mail. *Management Science, 32,* 1492-1512.

St.Amant, K. & Zemliansky, P. (2005). *Internet-based workplace communications: Industry & academic applications.* Hershey, PA: Information Science Reference.

Stasser, G. & Titus, W. (1985). Pooling of unshared information in group decision making: Biased information sampling during discussion. *Journal of Personality and Social Psychology, 48*(6), 1467-1478.

Steeples, C., Unsworth, C., Bryson, M., Goodyear, P., Riding, P., Fowell, S. et al. (1996). Technological support for teaching and learning: computer-mediated communications in higher education. *Computers and Education, 26,* 71-80.

Street, B. (1995). *Social literacies: Critical approaches to literacy development, ethnography, and education.* Reading, MA: Addison Wesley.

Stringer, J. (2009). *Designing the new Stanford school of medicine.* Paper presented at the EDUCAUSE Learning Initiative 2009 Online Fall Focus Session. Retrieved October 7, 2009, from http://net.educause.edu/content.asp?SECTION_ID=443

Suchan, J. & Hayzak, G. (2001). The communication characteristics of virtual teams: a case study. *IEEE Transactions on Professional Communication, 44*(3), 174-186.

Tapscott, D. & Williams, A. (2006). *Wikinomics: How mass collaboration changes everything.* New York: Portfolio.

Taylor, S.K. (2005). *Preparing technical communicators for the software industry: Teaching technology or teaching theory?* Paper presented at the Association for Teachers of Technical Writing. San Francisco, CA.

The Chicago Manual of Style Online. (2009). (15th ed.). Accessed October 1, 2009 http://www.chicagomanualofstyle.org/home.html

The Chicago Manual of Style: The Essential Guide for Writers, Editors, and Publishers, 15th edition. (2003). Chicago: The University of Chicago Press.

The HP Specialist. (2009, March 26). *8 rules for recognizing and rewarding employees.* Retrieved on 6/24/2009, http://www.thehrspecialist.com/26695/8_rules_for_recognizing_and_rewarding_employees.hr?cat=tools&sub_cat=memos_to_managers

The Rockley Group, Inc. (2005, February 15). *The role of standards in content management.*

Thompson, A.A., Jr., Strickland III, A.J. & Gamble, J.E. (2005). Case 8: "Dell computer in 2003: Driving for industry leadership" (C-124-C125). In *Crafting and executing strategy, The quest for competitive advantage: Concepts and cases* (14th ed.). Boston: McGraw-Hill Irwin

Thomson, A.M., Perry, J.L. & Miller, T.K. (2007). Conceptualizing and measuring collaboration. *Journal of Public Administration Research and Theory, 36.* Retrieved April 3, 2009 from http://jpart.oxfordjournals.org/cgi/reprint/mum036v1

Tierney, R., & Pearson, P.D. (1983). Towards a composing model of reading. *Language Arts, 60,* 568-580.

Tierney, R., & Shanahan, T. (1991). Research on the reading-writing relationship: Interaction, transaction, and outcomes. In R. Barr, M.L. Kamil, P. Mosenthal, & P.D. Pearson (Eds.), *Handbook of reading research: Volume II* (pp. 246-280). White Plains, NY: Longman.

Timmerman, C.E., & Scott, C.R. (2006). Virtually working: Communicative and structural predictors of media use and key outcomes in virtual work teams. *Communication Monographs, 73*(1), 108-136.

Tirrell, J. (2009). *Mapping digital technology in rhetoric and composition history.* Retrieved from http://www.digitalparlor.org/mappingrc/

Tjosvold, D. & Johnson, D. (2000). Deutsch's theory of cooperation and competition. In M. Beyerlein (Ed.), *Work teams: Past, present and future* (Social Indicators Research Series), (pp. 131-156). Amsterdam: Kluwer Academic Publishers.

Tuckman, B.W. (1965). Developmental sequence in small groups. *Psychological Bulletin, 63*(6), 384-399.

Tuckman, B.W., & Jensen, M.A. (1977). Stages of small-group development revisited. *Group Organizational Studies, 2,* 419-427.

Tullar, W. L., Kaiser, P. R., & Balthazard, P.A. (1998). Group work and electronic meeting systems: from board-room to classroom. *Business Communication Quarterly, 61*(4), 63-65.

Van de Ven, A.H., Delbecq, A.L., & Koenig, R. Jr. (1976). Determinants of coordination modes within organizations. *American Sociological Review, 41,* 322-338.

Van Laan, K., Julian, C., & Hackos, J. (2001). *The complete idiot's guide to technical writing.* New York: Alpha Books.

Van Raaphorst, A. & Johnson, D. (2007, April 18). *DITA open toolkit user guide,*(3rd ed.). Retrieved on June 22, 2009 from http://dita-ot.sourceforge.net/doc/ot-userguide131/xhtml/index.html. All files are copyright 2006-2007 by VR Communications, unless otherwise indicated. Licensing and usage of this document and related materials is regulated by a Common Public License (CPL) granted by OASIS (Organization for the Advancement of Structured Information Standards).

Vasont Systems. (2009). *Software: Vasont CMS.* Retrieved July 26, 2009 from http://www.vasont.com

Vathanophas, V. & Liang, S. (2007). Enhancing information sharing in group support systems (GSS). *Source*

Computers in Human Behavior, 23(3), 1675-1691. doi: 10.1016/j.chb.2005.10.001

Vygotsky, L.S. (1978). *Mind in society: The development of higher psychological processes.* (M. Cole, V. John-Steiner, S. Scribner, & E. Souberman, Eds). Cambridge, MA: Harvard UP (Russian original work published in 1930). In Tasks, ensembles, and activity: Linkages between text production and situation of use in the workplace. *Written Communication 20 (*4) (October) 511-559.

Wallis, C., & Steptoe, S. (2006, December 6). How to bring our schools out of the 20ᵗʰ century. *Time magazine, 51-56.*

Walsh, J. P., and Maloney, N. G. (2007). Collaboration structure, communication media, and problems in scientific work teams. *Journal of Computer-Mediated Communication, 12*(2), article 19. Retrieved from http://jcmc.indiana.edu/vol12/issue2/walsh.html

Walther, J.B. & Bunz, U. (2005). The rules of virtual groups: Trust, liking, and performance in computer-mediated communication. *Journal of Communication, 55*(4), 828-846

Wang, A., & Newlin, M. (2000). Characteristics of students who enroll and succeed in web-based psychology classes. *Journal of Educational Psychology, 92,* 137-143.

Warner, E. E. (May 24, 2009). *A different kettle of shoes.* Retrieved July 30, 2009 from http://web.me.com/gene.warner/Site/Innocents_Abroad/Entries/2009/5/24_%E2%80%9C...A_Different_Kettle_of_Shoes%E2%80%9D.html

Warschauer, M. (1997). Computer-mediated collaborative learning: Theory and practice. *The Modern Language Journal, 81,* 470-481.

Weaver, R., & Qi, J. (2005). Classroom organization and participation: College students' perceptions. *Journal of Higher Education, 76,* 570-601.

Weisbord, M. R. (1987). *Productive workplaces: Organizing and managing for dignity, meaning, and community.* San Francisco: Jossey-Bass.

Weiss, E. (2002). Egoless writing: Improving quality by replacing artistic impulse with engineering discipline. *Journal of Computer Documentation, 26,* 3-10.

Weng, C. & Gennari, J.H. (2004). Asynchronous collaborative writing through annotations. In *Proc of ACM Conference on Computer Supported Cooperative Work (CSCW'04)*, Chicago, (pp. 578-581).

Wesley, K. (2000). The ill effects of the five paragraph theme. *English Journal, 90*, 57–60.

White, E. C. (1987). *Kaironomia: On the will to invent.* Ithaca, NY: Cornell University Press

Witte, S. P. (1992). Context, text, and intertext: Toward a constructivist semiotic. *Written Communication, 2*(9), 237-308.

Witte, S.P. & Haas, C. (2005). Research in activity: An analysis of speed bumps as mediational means. *Written Communication, 22*, 127-165.

Wodtke, C. & Govella, A. (2009). *Information architecture: Blueprints for the Web* (2nd ed.). Berkeley, CA: New Riders.

Wolfe, J. (2009). *Team writing: A guide to working in groups.* Boston: Bedford.

World Clock Meeting Planner. (2008). Retrieved from http://www.timeanddate.com/worldclock/meeting.html

Wysocki, A. F., Johnson-Eilola, J., Selfe, C. L., & Sirc, G. *Writing new media: Theory and applications for expanding the teaching of composition.* Logan, UT: Utah State UP.

Young, M. (2002). *Technical writer's handbook: Writing with style and clarity.* Sausalito, CA: University Science Books.

Youngblood, N. E. (2008). Collaborative writing tools in the virtual workplace. In P. Zemliansky & K. St.Amant, (eds.), *The handbook of research on virtual workplaces and the new nature of business practices* (pp. 530-543). Hershey, PA: IGI-Global.

Zappen, J.P. (2005). Digital rhetoric: Toward an integrated theory. *Technical Communication Quarterly, 14*, 319-325.

Zigurs, I. & Khazanchi, D. (2008). Applying pattern theory in the effective management of virtual projects. In N. Kock, (ed.), *E-collaboration in modern organizations: Initiating and managing distributed projects,* (pp. 315-334). Hershey, PA: IGI Global.

About the Contributors

Beth L. Hewett holds a Ph.D. from The Catholic University of America and is a consultant in on-line communication in educational settings. She is an adjunct Associate Professor with the University of Maryland University College. Beth was an editor for *Kairos: Journal of Rhetoric, Technology, and Pedagogy* for seven years; all of this web-based journal's interactions are conducted virtually. She also developed an online writing program for Smarthinking, Inc., the country's leading Web-based learning support service. Beth is the author of *The Online Writing Conference: A Guide for Teachers and Tutors* (Heinemann Boynton-Cook, 2010), co-author of *Preparing Educator's for Online Writing Instruction: Principles and Processes* (NCTE, 2004), co-editor of *Technology and English Studies: Innovative Professional Paths* (Erlbaum, 2005), and author of various journal articles about writing, technology, and rhetoric. She is the national committee chair for the CCCCs Committee for Best Practices in On-line Writing Instruction Also a professional writing coach, Beth's webpage can be accessed at www.defendandpublish.com and she can be emailed at beth.hewett@comcast.net. She is the author of *Good Words: Memorializing Through a Eulogy* (Grief Illustrated Press, 2009) and is a grief facilitator trainer with the National Catholic Ministry for the Bereaved; she has developed numerous grief-healing work-shops, seminars, and retreats.

Charlotte Robidoux holds a Ph.D. from The Catholic University of America and specializes in rheto-ric, technical communication, and science. Charlotte's doctoral work focused on the role of rhetoric in genetics research. She is a content strategy manager for the Enterprise Storage & Servers division at HP and leads the organization's single-sourcing initiative, overseeing content reuse and the team's content management system. Her interest in collaboration stems from the development of processes for reusing content effectively across products. Because typically writers have been accustomed to working inde-pendently, they need best practices for writing collaboratively in virtual settings. Charlotte joined HP in 2000 and has worked in technical communication for over 17 years as an author, editor, and manager. She is a recipient of the Center for Information Development (CIDM) "Rare Bird" award for her work on an HP document tracking database. She began her career in technical communications as a consultant for Washington, DC. firms holding contracts with the Department of Defense, Department of the Navy, Environmental Protection Agency, and others. In addition to writing numerous articles of the CIDM Best Practices newsletter, she is the author of "Rhetorically Structured Content: Developing a Collaborative Single-Sourcing Curriculum" published in *Technical Communication Quarterly*, co-author of "Is There a Write Way to Collaborate?" published in STC's *Intercom*, and co-author of "Streamline Your Path to Metadata" published in *The Information Management & Architecture Framework*.

* * *

France Baril has a B.A. in Communication from the University of Ottawa and a B.Sc. in Computer Science from Université de Sherbrooke. This unique background along with the fact that she is fluent in more than one language serves her well in a Tech Pub industry that embraces evolving content models, new technologies, localization and process automation. France has been able to wear many hats in this field of practice: computer programmer, analyst, technical writer, technical localization/translation specialist, documentation architect, and product manager of a Content Management System (CMS) designed for DITA. Today, she owns Architextus through which she offers her services to organizations that want to profit from her 360° view of the documentation processes and life cycle. Whether clients need her to acts on one or many levels, she always keeps an eye on systemic coherence and often acts as interpreter between managers, writers and developers.

Kristin Blicharz is a technical writer at IBM in Littleton, MA. She has been working as an information developer with virtual teams all around the world for the past three years. Her work involves creating online support documentation, authoring core documentation in DITA, and facilitating knowledge sharing between customer service teams and writing teams. Kristin works on Windows based data analysis software and database software on the mainframe. Prior to joining IBM, she enjoyed teaching business writing, science writing, and technical writing courses at New Mexico State University. In her spare time she participates in a range of sports leagues and enjoys cooking dinners for friends. She also enjoys weekend trips exploring all the unique areas of New England and taking trips all around the world. Her best trip so far was visiting the Jokulsarlon glacial lagoon in Iceland.

Beth Brunk-Chavez is an Associate Professor of Rhetoric and Writing Studies at the University of Texas at El Paso. She is a 2009 recipient of the University of Texas System Regents' Outstanding Teaching Award and is the Director of First-Year Composition. Beth teaches graduate and undergraduate courses in Rhetoric and Writing Studies and serves on several national committees. Her research interests are in teaching with technology, writing with technology, composition pedagogy, and writing program administration. Her work has appeared in *Kairos, Writing Program Administrator, Teaching English in the Two-Year College,* various edited collections, and a forthcoming textbook for first-year composition. Beth is also participating on a number of grants intended to revise instruction and improve the quality of education at the college-level. She and her husband, Eddie, have two inquisitive boys: Jackson and Carter.

William Carney is an Assistant Professor of English and Director of Composition at Cameron University in Lawton OK. He holds a PhD in English from Texas Tech University and MA degrees in English from the University of Texas at San Antonio and in Applied Psychology from Stevens Institute of Technology. His research interests include social and psychological factors in the dissemination of tacit knowledge, the training of composition instructors, and the writing behaviors of international university students. In his rapidly dwindling spare time, he enjoys jazz and "classic" country music, baseball, and cooking. These days, he and his wife spend much time on their new home in a truly scenic part of Southwestern Oklahoma with a wonderful view of Mt. Scott.

Anne DiPardo is a Professor in the School of Education at the University of Colorado at Boulder, where she works with literacy-studies graduate students and prepares secondary-level language arts teachers. Her published work has focused on the nature of English education as a field, the role of collaboration in teaching and learning, and the development of writing competence. She collaborated with Mike on a previous piece, "Toward the Metapersonal Essay," which was published in *Computers and Composition* and reprinted in *Literacy: Major themes in education* (Routledge, 2004).

Mike DiPardo is a director of applications development with a global software company that designs products for use in the healthcare industry. A telecommuter since 1991, he and his geographically dispersed coworkers have witnessed the evolution of technologies that mediate and support collaboration, enriching their work and relationships as tools such as e-mail, instant-messaging, and live Web meetings have become commonplace. When he's not developing software, he enjoys snowshoeing and cycling in the Rockies.

Norma Emery holds a BA in English from Hood College, Frederick, Maryland, and is currently completing a graduate-level certificate program in French proficiency. She has more than 30 years of experience in content and document development with an emphasis on content reuse and quality assurance. Prior to joining Alcatel-Lucent in 1998, Norma worked as a senior technical writer and project manager for GE Information Services and for a computer systems contractor to the U.S. Department of Energy. In her career, Norma has authored numerous technical manuals and guides, primarily for telecommunications products and computer applications. As a senior technical editor for Alcatel-Lucent, Norma is involved in technical writing and editing, research, analysis, and project management. Norma's primary professional focus is the development of writing, content, terminology, and information architecture standards for Alcatel-Lucent. She currently serves on the Localization and Industry Standards Association (LISA) Terminology Special Interest Group. Her personal interests include spending time with her three sons, studying French, painting, needlework, and contributing her time to community and environmental issues in Washington County, Maryland. She currently serves as Chair of the county's Solid Waste Advisory Committee and on the board of directors of Camp Joy, a volunteer mission project that assists low-income families by making home repairs and improvements. She is also a member of the Hancock Arts Council.

Douglas Eyman, Senior Editor of *Kairos: A Journal of Rhetoric, Technology, and Pedagogy,* is an assistant professor of English at George Mason University, where he teaches in the professional writing and rhetoric program. He coordinates the Computer Connection at the annual Conference on College Composition and Communication, serves as list and reviews editor for H-DigiRhet, and recently has joined the editorial staff of *Enculturation: A Journal of Rhetoric, Writing, and Culture.* His PhD dissertation, Digital Rhetoric: Ecologies and Economies of Digital Circulation (Michigan State University), received the 2007 Computers and Composition Hugh Burns Best Dissertation Award.

Alexia P. Idoura has been in the information development business for almost twenty years. She has managed and supported global teams of writers for large software companies for over eleven years. As an internal consultant and trusted advisor, collaboration and communication have been a key part of her involvement with teams. At one of the companies, she received the Chairman's award for teamwork, analysis, and execution. Her current team of information architects both collaborates on content creation as well as supports other teams in the technical aspects and process aspects of collaborative writing. Previously, she worked for eight years as a manager, information developer, and trainer for the software and steel industries. Alexia has a Professional Writing degree from Carnegie Mellon University, a Masters certificate in Business Management from Tulane University, a certificate in Supply Chain Management through Stanford University, and Lean Six Sigma Black Belt course completion through the University of Notre Dame (certification pending). She also has participated in a number of other collaborative writing efforts, including commercial books and a technical journal article; has been an instructor for an STC Content Management certification course; and has traveled to China as a citizen ambassador for the Technical Communication profession.

Judy Kessler has worked in technical communication in the software industry for more than 30 years. She has worked as an author, editor, and manager in the U.S. and internationally. Currently she serves as an information architect and DITA transition leader for Sybase, Inc., helping Sybase's 60+ member Tech Pubs organization move to DITA and content management, by providing guidelines, training, information models, and user support. Judy also oversees the Sybase Tech Pubs Initiative councils, a collaborative approach to developing policies and processes, and educating writers and managers in new roles. She has presented at conferences and published articles for technical writing audiences. Judy received her B.A. in English and teaching certificate from the University of Michigan, where she also managed classified advertising for The Michigan Daily. When time and inspiration allow she enjoys writing fiction. Judy and her husband live in the Boston area, and are extremely proud of their two adult children. r.

Catherine Colalillo Lyman is the director of the Information Engineering team at NetApp, Inc. The NetApp IE team of about 80 staff members creates the product documentation and is also a 'center of writing excellence' with which other teams in NetApp partner. It is spread across five sites (in addition to home-based staff) in the U.S. and India. Ever since she was a writer at Informix Software in the 1980s, she has been imagining how database technology could be used to deliver targeted information to end users. Catherine received her BS in Mechancal Engineering from Princeton University and holds advanced degrees in management and communication from the schools of Parenting and Silicon Valley. She has lead information development teams at Informix Software, Compaq, Hewlett-Packard, and NetApp. When not working, Catherine enjoys meeting people from around the world and many outdoor activities including backpacking and trail running, and is proud of recently making it to the top of Mount Whitney (with her husband and two college-age children) via the Mountaineer's route. She deeply appreciates all of the writing and management teams on whom she has tried new techniques and from whom she has learned more than she could ever have taught to them.

Suzanne Mescan learned through part-time jobs in high school to never work in a food business if you ever intend to eat it again (she no longer eats donuts or peppermint patties). After college, she briefly marketed financial services, and then joined the information publishing and content management industry in 1987, currently serving as the Vice President of Marketing for Vasont Systems. Prior to this role, she spent 12 years creating and managing Progressive Publishing Alternatives, a full-service division of the Company offering editorial, design, and project management services. She earned a BS in Marketing from The Pennsylvania State University, where she also marched with the Penn State Blue Band for four years. Suzanne and husband Chris have two feline "kids" who love to shred furniture in their spare time. They put lots of blood and sweat into their 1803 log home that they spent six years gutting and remodeling.

Joddy Murray teaches rhetoric and new media as an Associate Professor at Texas Christian University in Fort Worth, Texas. He recently published *Non-Discursive Rhetoric: Image and Affect in Multimodal Composition* from SUNY Press (2009), and he continues to research the intersections between rhetoric, language, and image. In addition, Joddy writes and teaches poetry, publishing in journals such as *River Oak Review, Cider Press Review,* and *Hubbub.*

David W. Overbey is an Assistant Professor of English at Bellarmine University, USA, where he teaches writing and rhetoric in convergent media. His current scholarship and research focuses on how digital environments are adapted to social practice. He has presented at numerous international conferences on literacy and technology. David has published *Verifying web-based information: Detailed accounts of web use in real time,* based on a quantitative and qualitative study of how adult professionals make credibility judgments of online information in real time.

Sunay Palsole is the Director of Instructional Support at the University of Texas at El Paso. A geophysicist by academic training, he began to design multimedia applications for teaching and learning in the mid 1990's. Since then, he has helped faculty from varied disciplines integrate technology in teaching, learning and research. He has also taught and designed various blended learning and online courses, most of which use Web 2.0 technologies integrated into the curriculum. Sunay also co-developed the Digital Academy, a training program that was a finalist for the Innovation Award by the Professional and Organizational Development Network. This Academy has been taught in diverse locations as El Paso, New Jersey, India, and Chile. Sunay has collaborated on and has been PI and co-PI on a number of grants related to education, educational technology, and online course development. He has also served on review committees for a variety of national conferences. Sunay has presented at numerous national and international conferences including Educause, E-Learn, ED-Media, CSCL and First Year Experience.

Dirk Remley is a Lecturer at Kent State University, where he teaches professional writing and technical writing courses. His research into collaborative writing practices has focused on how students use collaborative technologies and activity theory perspectives on the collaborative writing process. He is also interested in how technology shapes writing activity. Dirk has presented at numerous conferences nationally and regionally, and he has published work in *Across the Disciplines, Computers and Composition Online,* and the *Community Literacy Journal.*

Mirhonda Studevant works as a Lead Knowledge Base Content Developer within Ceridian's Training and Information Development group. Mirhonda was awarded the first-ever undergraduate degree in Technical and Professional Communication from Southern Polytechnic State University (www.spsu.edu). She also earned an MBA, with a Knowledge and Learning Management concentration, from Walden University (www.waldenu.edu). Mirhonda's key areas of interest include information design, usability, search engine optimization, decision sciences and knowledge management. Mirhonda is Senior Member of the Society for Technical Communication. She has contributed articles to the STCAtlanta (www.stcatlanta.com) newsletter as well as *Intercom.* Her favorite saying is "Vision without execution is hallucination."

Kent M. Taylor is a 30-year industry veteran, and recovering Pubs Director. An engineer by birth defect, a manager by accident, confirmed technology junkie and Quality zealot, with 18 years of Tech

Pubs management experience at a very large equipment manufacturer, 5 years of SGML/XML/Content Management consulting, and 5 years working with industry start-ups, he has experienced the good, the bad, and the ugly. He arrived on the scene just in time to help drive the transition from pencils and blue-lined pads to green-screen terminals, and has driven deployments of everything from gen-code to large-scale multi-language multi-media production systems and ISO-9000 certified publication processes. Currently VP & GM of acrolinx® North America, Kent continues to work with leading-edge technology in the industry he knows and loves, while satisfying his passion for Quality. (The acrolinx® IQ tools enable Departmental and Enterprise-level Information Quality Management, employing sophisticated Natural Language Processing and Linguistic Analysis Engines that analyze text for spelling, grammar, style/readability/translatability, and terminology issues, and enable automated, objective Quality Management processes in the Information Development environment.)

Stephanie Taylor has been a technical writer at IBM for six years. She lives in San Jose, California, but works with a team based in North Carolina and Paris. She has never met any of her current teammates face to face, which she consider lucky because many of them have expressed a strong desire to throw office supplies at her. Her work involves creating online support documentation for software development tools. Prior to joining IBM, she taught technical writing courses at New Mexico State University while she attended graduate school. Prior to graduate school, she worked at museums and newspapers in a variety of writing, editing, and marketing positions. When she's not working, you can find her watching St. Louis Cardinals and San Francisco Giants baseball games with her partner and son. If you're a Cubs, Dodgers, or Yankees fan, you just might not want to talk to her.

Robbin Zeff Warner holds a Ph.D. in Folklore and American Studies from Indiana University and a B.A. in Anthropology from Berkeley. She has a long background with technology and writing. Her interest in the teaching of writing started through her involvement with the National Writing Project in 1993. Her interest in online technology was launched when she wrote the landmark book *The Nonprofit Guide to the Internet* in 1996 when there were so few nonprofits online one could actually count them. This book initiated a series of books on Internet use for the nonprofit community by John Wiley & Sons. She then moved into Internet advertising and not only wrote the first book on online advertising back in 1997 (*Advertising on the Internet*), which eventually was translated into 6 languages, but she also managed the 10-city "Advertising & Marketing on the Internet" training conference. In addition to being a professional writer and researcher, Zeff has taught business, technical, and academic writing since the early 1990s. In 2009 Robbin and her husband Gene moved to Brussels, Belgium. Her current research interest is Belgium chocolate: milk and dark, praline and ganache. You can find her chocolate-related work at writingwithchocolate.com

Sean D. Williams, Professor of Professional Communication at Clemson University, has published in information architecture, industry/academy relationships, visual communication, and most recently 3-D virtual worlds. His most recent project, *Technical writing for teams: Tools and techniques*, (co-authored with Alex Mamishev) will be published by Wiley (IEEE imprint) late in 2010. In all, Sean has published more than 30 articles and book chapters, and presented more than 40 different conference papers. Sean has also received significant funding for his work, totaling nearly $2M, most recently serving as the co-Principal Investigator on an NSF award of $1.4M to study 3-D virtual worlds. This award forms part of the work of the Carolinas Virtual Worlds Consortium, a multi-university research group that interacts with both private companies and K-12 school districts to investigate the role of 3-D virtual worlds in educational settings.

Patti Wojahn is an Associate Professor in Rhetoric and Professional Communication at New Mexico State University. She has worked with and studied how computers and other technologies support communications, particularly during collaboration. She prefers writing collaboratively and has done so in a range of face-to-face as well as virtual contexts. She enjoys teaching courses that are supplemented by digital spaces while considering new strategies for online teaching and learning. While pursuing her PhD at Carnegie Mellon University, she worked with a team that researched and developed software for reviewers and writers. Because her main research interest is in communication in collaborative work, she welcomed the opportunity to contribute to this volume by working with two former graduate students who continue to teach her about life as well as the needs of writers in the world. When she gets the chance, she enjoys hiking in the mountains with her dog, cooking something new each week, as well as taking pictures of old things in New Mexico.

Pavel Zemliansky holds a Ph.D. and is an Associate Professor in the School of Writing, Rhetoric, and Technical Communication, where he also coordinates the graduate program. Pavel teaches courses in writing, rhetoric, and technical communication. He has published books, book chapters, and journal articles in the fields of rhetoric and composition as well as technical communication. His latest book is *The Handbook of Research on Virtual Workplaces and the New Nature of Business Practices*, which he co-edited with Kirk St. Amant (IGI-Global, 2008). He has a book on the design and implementation of educational computer and video game, which he co-edited with Diane Wilcox, forthcoming from IGI-Global in early 2010.

Index